Yalla Feminists

Yalla Feminists

Arab Rights and Resistance

Lina AbiRafeh *and*
Rebecca O'Keeffe

Foreword by Joumana Haddad
Afterword by Aya Chebbi

McFarland & Company, Inc., Publishers
Jefferson, North Carolina

Library of Congress Cataloguing-in-Publication Data

Names: AbiRafeh, Lina, 1974– author. | O'Keeffe, Rebecca, 1992– author. |
Ḥaddād, Jumānah Sallūm, writer of foreword. | Chebbi, Aya, writer of afterword.
Title: Yalla feminists : Arab rights and resistance / Lina AbiRafeh and Rebecca O'Keeffe ;
foreword by Joumana Haddad ; afterword by Aya Chebbi.
Description: Jefferson, North Carolina : McFarland & Company, Inc.,
Publishers, 2023 | Includes bibliographical references and index.
Identifiers: LCCN 2023030420 | ISBN 9781476691152 (paperback : acid free paper) ∞
ISBN 9781476650746 (ebook)
Subjects: LCSH: Feminists—Arab countries. | Feminism—Arab countries. |
Women—Civil rights—Arab countries.
Classification: LCC HQ1729.5 .A63 2023 | DDC 305.42097/4927—dc23/eng/20230724
LC record available at https://lccn.loc.gov/2023030420

British Library cataloguing data are available

ISBN (print) 978-1-4766-9115-2
ISBN (ebook) 978-1-4766-5074-6

Front cover image: mural titled "Women Make Peace"
by artist Haifa Subay (used with permission)

Printed in the United States of America

*McFarland & Company, Inc., Publishers
Box 611, Jefferson, North Carolina 28640
www.mcfarlandpub.com*

For feminists resisting—everywhere.
We are with you.
Fight on.

Table of Contents

Abbreviations	ix
Acknowledgments	xi
Foreword: Hear Them Roar by Joumana Haddad	1
Preface	5
1. Feminist Foundations	19
2. Feminist Phases	48
3. Feminisms on the Frontlines of Crisis	84
4. Feminisms on the Frontlines of Creativity	114
5. Fragmented Feminisms	134
6. Feminist Futures	173
Conclusion: So What? Now What?!	210
Afterword by Aya Chebbi	218
Glossary	221
Chapter Notes	223
Bibliography	258
Index	283

Abbreviations

AiW	Arab Institute for Women
AMEWS	Association for Middle East Women's Studies
ATFD	Association Tunisienne des Femmes Démocrates
CAWTAR	The Center of Arab Women for Training and Research
CEDAW	Convention on the Elimination of All Forms of Discrimination Against Women
CRSV	Conflict-Related Sexual Violence
ESCWA	UN Economic and Social Commission for Western Asia
FGM	Female Genital Mutilation
FSI	Fragile States Index
GBV	Gender-Based Violence
GCC	Gulf Cooperation Council
GDP	Gross Domestic Product
ICPD	International Conference on Population and Development
IDP	Internally Displaced Persons
IMF	International Monetary Fund
ISIL	Islamic State of Iraq and the Levant
ISIS	Islamic State of Iraq and Syria
LGBTQ+	Lesbian, Gay, Bisexual, Transgender, Queer, and Others
MP	Member of Parliament
NAP	National Action Plan
NCLW	National Commission of Lebanese Women
NGO	Non-Government Organization
PLO	Palestinian Liberation Organization
PTSD	Post-Traumatic Stress Disorder
RAP	Regional Action Plan
SCW	Supreme Council for Women
SDG	Sustainable Development Goals
SRHR	Sexual and Reproductive Health Rights
UAE	United Arab Emirates
UK	United Kingdom
UN	United Nations
UNESCO	United Nations Educational, Scientific, and Cultural Organization
UNICEF	United Nations Children's Emergency Fund
UNSC	United Nations Security Council
UNSCR	United Nations Security Council Resolution

Abbreviations

U.S.	United States
VAW	Violence Against Women
WCSS	Women's Cultural and Social Society
WPS	Women, Peace and Security

Acknowledgments

We believe, as academic and author Dr. Mervat Hatem rightly stated, that "We have come a long way, but our journey is far from over. There is a lot of work that still needs to be done, but [we are] more than confident in our collective ability to do it."[1]

This book is a collective effort, a years-long journey, and a labor of love. We would not have undertaken this monster endeavor if we did not believe it to be worth it. And, we have so many who joined us on this journey, believing both in us and in this book being "worth it." We thank you.

We are indebted to all of you—and hope that you know who you are, and you receive our gratitude. We cannot even mention you all—it would fill another book.

There are a few extraordinary people we would like to thank—in no particular order:

Tom Abraham—This book would not have been possible without Cedar Rock Entertainment, a foundation that supports research, development, and programs in Lebanon and the Arab region. We are grateful for the support, and also the vision for this to grow beyond a book to reach wider audiences.

Myriam Sfeir and the entire AiW team, past and present—This book is released in time for the Institute's 50th birthday, so we have 50 years of feminist and activist energy to draw from—starting with the Institute's legendary founder, Julinda Abu Nasr, on whose shoulders we stand.

Gabriella Nassif—Dr. Googs of vast wisdom and wit. You step in, step up, and save the day. Again and again. Every book needs your blessing to be born.

Stephanie Chaban—you helped us understand the history of Arab feminisms. We are in awe of your knowledge.

Moufeeda Haidar—You joined Lina on this journey from the beginning, and initiated Rebecca (with help and hummus) when she took this on. You are wonderful in many ways.

Karma Ekmekji—You waved a magic wand and made things happen, including bringing the talented Nour Daboussi to us.

Joumana Haddad and Aya Chebbi—You agreed to lend your words to this work. You are the bookends, telling us where to start, and how to finish. Thank you for lighting the fire—and for showing us the way forward.

Lucy Gaffney-Maguire (our origin story)—Without you, there would be no Lina-and-Rebecca, and therefore no book(s)! We owe you a drink!

Interns, research assistants, friends, supporters: AJ Pruitt, Ashley Merly, Carly Paul, Caroline Mendoza, Ellie Strong, Josie Hale, Lynn Mounzer, Madison White, Mathilde Krähenbühl, Mira Kadapurath, Reema Saleh, Stephanie Nasr, Vanessa Zammar, Vani Bhardwaj. And any others who supported in any way—we appreciate you.

Lina also wishes to thank....

The incredible fierce relentless feminist army that is just a phone call away. In addition to the list of brilliant bulldozers named above—Xena Amro, Tarek Zeidan, Tala Harb, Rita Stephan, Rana Alamuddin, Mariam Jalabi, Mehrinaz El Awady, Hayat Mirshad, Chérine Kurdi, Charlotte Karam, Carmen Geha, Alexander Nehme. Your words light fires!

My feisty fabulous fireball next door, Lee—You're the best thing on the 4th floor, and any floor.

The Chicken, C—You saw this through from day one, cheering for me until the last page.

The ever-patient parents, Salwa and Souhail—For never quite knowing what I'm doing, but supporting it anyway.

The two Salmas—Teta, my first feminist, and Koosa, my most important feminist.

The best thing ever to come out of Ireland—Rebecca. In the last book, I wrote: "Without you, there's no book." I'm just gonna put that line on repeat—for this book, and the next book(s)! Us two, we've got lots to do!

And in the words of Mona Eltahawy: "To the girls of the Middle East: Be immodest, rebel, disobey, and know you deserve to be free."

Rebecca also wishes to thank....

Mam, Dad, Dave—Thanks doesn't even cover it.

Jules, Louise, Chris, Gina, Alanna—Your care and kindness (and voice notes) have not gone unnoticed, grma.

My basketball and GAA community—Thank you for (trying) to keep me sane throughout, the healthy dose of humor helped.

Lina—Without whom none of this would have been possible. Thank you for your support and your trust. You are magic and it's a privilege to know you and work with you. I look forward to meeting you!

Le grá.

About the Cover Art

Haifa Subay is a Yemeni visual artist and recent recipient of the Prince Claus Seed Award. Her work engages with social and political issues in Yemen with a particular thematic focus on women, children, the human cost of war, and the continuous quest for peace. The art chosen for this book is aptly titled "Women Make Peace," symbolizing women, peace, and power. The mural first appeared in the Singapore Art Museum as part of the 2019 Singapore Biennale. Subay was happy to lend her work to this book because she says, "As a woman who believes in the great power of women to make change and bring peace wherever they are, I consider women to be the force of peace in this world."

Foreword

Hear Them Roar

by Joumana Haddad

I am not a feminist by family teachings. I am not a feminist by cultural influences. I am not a feminist by societal trends.

You could say I am a feminist by inborn *rage*.

Like many fellow feminists, I was one before I even knew there was a word for it, and that the notion even existed. It was an initiation by raw indignation, by innate mutiny, by sheer instinctive pride. How else could I describe the angry eight-year-old me who snubbed her Christmas gift because it consisted of a set of miniature household items? I'll never forget that tiny washing machine, nor the pink ironing board, and let's not even mention the flowery tea set. They had my gender's predetermined destiny written all over them, sneering me, repressing my greediness, murdering the endless realm of prospects in my future… "Aren't they cute?," my aunt asked me that day. "No they are not!" I heatedly replied, deserving a severe stare from my mother for my impoliteness. Well, maybe they were cute. But I didn't want "cute." I didn't want pans and plates and mops and brooms. I didn't want dolls and baby carriages and feeding bottles. I simply wanted challenges. Open-ended ones.

And books. And dreams. And ambitions. And accomplishments.

(And almost anything that didn't come in the color pink.)

Why? I still don't have an answer for that, and I probably never will. There were even earlier incidents of "insurrection" that were described to me by my bewildered parents, like slow magma outpours announcing the upcoming burst of the volcano. Premonitions, they call them, that raise some of my most haunting questions on the subject: Is being a feminist a mere reaction, or a state of being? Does one "become" a feminist or is it the natural condition of each and every female, which many/most "un-become" because of circumstances or lack thereof? I like to believe it is the latter. I like to think that this primal anger of mine was, and still is, an intrinsic survival reflex, as it should be for every single female on earth, should she have the disposition, or the opportunity, or the willingness to explore it, dig it out and use it. I repeat, I was merely eight then: I hadn't read Simone de Beauvoir, I hadn't heard about the principle of equality, nor knew anything about the history of the fight for women's rights. Moreover, I didn't have evident reasons to be angry. My parents were conservative indeed (thus my rebellious "equal and opposite response," invigorated by the absurd restrictions of the Catholic school they sent me to), but rather empowering, each in his/her own way: My dad with his obsessive focus on my education, and my mom with her inspiring iron will and indomitable determination. But the anger was there, as if I had read and heard and known. As if I had seen it all. As if I had already figured out that a life with a boxed future, with a bowed head, with broken wings and a trodden dignity and stolen freedom, that a life like that was just another form of death, I dare say crueler than the actual one, because you incur it while allegedly conscious.

I had, nevertheless, witnessed first-hand the existence of discrimination, as well as its surreptitious little brother, condescendence, whether in the wider family circle, or at school, or in my community and society. I grew up in a country torn by war and violence, but not only. Soon I was to discover it was *as* torn, if not more, by hypocrisy, double standards, sexism, and various forms of injustice and abuse. Women in my family (my mother included) cooked and cleaned and took care of the kids, while men went to work and made money and achieved things. In schoolbooks, the stories we were told and taught tragically echoed the same stereotypes I was seeing around me in real life. "Men this and women that." Even the fairytales we'd read at bedtime were all infected with the damsel-in-distress versus the savior-chap frustrating truism. Also, a good number of my mom's friends were victims of abuse, whether verbal or physical: Renée, whose swollen left eye and bruised cheek I shall never forget; Mariam the divorcee deprived of her three children by a religious court; Garinée, nicknamed the slut spinster at a mere 33 because she wore miniskirts and went on multiple dates with multiple men. Last but not least, in the neighborhood's shelters where we had to hide every other day because of the bombings, women sat together and talked about "women stuff," while men gathered to discuss politics, history and economy. The cut was painfully clear.

And painfully infuriating.

Every time a girl/woman I knew was being denied a dream or judged because of who/what she was, I used to think: "this is how it must feel to be buried alive," and an overwhelming feeling of suffocation would make me want to roar with anger. And oh, how I roared. If I had to choose a soundtrack for my childhood and adolescence, this would be it. Later on, in my teens and early twenties, I was to discover that this fury of mine meant I was a "feminist." But the word, the label, terrorized me. Everyone was saying that being a feminist meant hating men altogether. I most certainly did not. It also meant, apparently, that I shouldn't act too feminine, for it was a sign of weakness, a submission to the patriarchal gaze and male standards. But I loved my red lipstick and my sexy outfits and my high-heeled shoes. I found power in them. Not the kind of patriarchy-generated, illusionary power that being drooled at gives; rather the self-emanating power of proudly owning and displaying and celebrating my womanhood. Was I "programmed" to love those things? Was I automated to believe that these "superficial" signs were expressions of womanhood and its celebration? Why couldn't I be both feminine and a feminist, I constantly wondered? Too many ambiguous questionings. But one thing was certain: I suffered, for I used to feel like a phony. It didn't matter that I had a larger-than-life personality, a big (impertinent) mouth, dreams that I was achieving with my hard work: I still didn't feel I was "enough." It didn't matter that I strived to become financially independent; that I never shied away from confrontation, nor allowed anyone, be it man or woman, to step on my painted toes and leave unscathed; that I did whatever I wanted to do and said whatever I wanted to say and "to hell with what they thought": still I judged and flagellated myself whenever I shaved my legs, or went to the hairdresser, or enjoyed being submissive in sex. I was not strong enough, I thought. Not determined enough. Not feminist enough. And it all confined me back into the vicious circle of shame and shaming, of typecasts and tags, that I was initially so angry about and rebelling against. Shame here and shame there: Was there no way out? Was I to be a pariah in both camps? Was I, in fact, a "real feminist"?

Then I read more, I educated myself more, and most importantly, I reflected more. And I came to the conclusion that being a feminist cannot, and should not, be just another reductive stereotype. It cannot entail submitting to a set of physical and behavioral criteria or expectations, beyond the basic universal conviction that every human being is equal to each and every other human being, and thus deserves equal rights and opportunities. It cannot have different ceiling heights depending on culture or geography or race or religion, etc. I started rejecting anything that came after sentences like "real feminism is" or "real feminism means." I also started challenging any adjective that came before the word feminism. Not to cancel it, or deny that it mattered to some people, but because there was, in my view at least, a fundamental truth called Equality that transcended all notions of cultural relativism and religious, socio-political and economical particularities, and that using such attributes can undermine its absoluteness.

Subsequently, do I believe there is something called Arab Feminism? Yes and no. Yes in the sense of the movement itself, its specific struggles, tools and voices, as well as the various phases of its development in different parts of the Arab world. No in the sense that it aspires to goals different than those of, let's say, Greek Feminism or Mexican Feminism, etc. At the risk of sounding redundant, to me the goal is and will always be one: Equality. That is, justice. That is, dignity. That is, freedom. That is, choice. And in the word "choice" lies the real dilemma of feminism today. Forgive me if I try to express this dilemma with a banal, worn-out duality: Did the woman wearing a head-scarf really "choose" to wear it, or was it the result of a socio-cultural imposition and/or religious brainwashing, or, even trickier, a mere reaction covertly induced by a hostile action against what she considers to be the symbol of her faith and culture? The same applies to a woman over-exposing her body. So where do we draw the line between unconscious influence and conscious choice? It demands a high level of awareness and daring, unapologetic self-exploration, which outcomes cannot even guarantee a clear answer.

The universality that applies to the significance of feminism and its objectives doesn't, however, apply to its challenges. Some of the challenges we feminists face are common all over the world (machismo and feminicide, to cite but two plagues), while others can be indeed different from one region or culture to another. In the case of the Arab world, among many (too many) challenges, I'd like to highlight the biggest one in my opinion: religion, or rather its level of implication in people's personal and public lives. Personally, I am convinced that feminism is *a priori* and inherently secular, without the need to state it even, due to the level of complicity between patriarchal systems and religions, or rather due to the fact that religion *is* a major player in patriarchy. Bigotry, double standards, misogyny, hypocrisy, compliance, sexual repression, you name it: all the ingredients of the perfect patriarchal recipe are in those so-called sacred books and their deriving institutions and "representatives." Thus, if you do not have the tools, or the will, or—let's say it at the risk of offending some people, the *courage*—to emancipate yourself from the sexist religious dogmas, and to turn your faith, should you need it in your life, into a mere spiritual support system without allowing it to poison your self-worth or self-image, then you are stuck.

… And it is high time for us in the Arab world to become un-stuck.

Then there is our second biggest challenge, much related to the first: Sex, or rather, women's sexuality, or rather, the long awaited, long overdue, much feared (and for a good reason) sexual liberation of Arab women. Behold the greatest, scariest scarecrow of Arab patriarchy: it starts with a V, and it is the birthplace, not of life—not only at least—but of a great deal of stress and trauma and terror in so many Arab men (and women, unfortunately). To turn the table on the heads of the male oppressors, the female self-victimizers and vice versa, let me share the following basic reasoning, which is a crucial exercise in seeing the half full part of the glass and changing one's perspective of things: if we think about the level of angst our vaginas cause, proven beyond any reasonable doubt by the level of repression and constraints and harassment and control that these vaginas are subjected to, we cannot, and should not, as women, NOT feel empowered, and most importantly, NOT act on that power that we undeniably and irrevocably possess. We cannot, and should not, as women, merely complain and point fingers and squeeze our thighs shut and blame the system. We cannot, and should not, wait for this aberrant system to "allow" us to own our bodies, live our sexualities, and make our decisions regarding what we wish to do with our bodies and how and when and where and with whom. We hold the power, you see; the decision is ours. So, what are we waiting for? What is stopping us from telling those terrified chastity crusaders—all the machos and the priests and the Mullahs and the Sheikhs and their likes out there—to go fuck themselves while we actually, exaltingly, simply, fuck? Sex in such a context, in our context, is not "just sex." It is an allegory of freedom, of self-affirmation and of life. It is a political statement, a vital act of rebellion, a big fat NO in the faces of those who have subjugated us, or tried to, and who will keep on doing so if we let them instead of finally standing up for ourselves.

Again: We hold the power. We *are* the power. So, what are we waiting for?

This necessary and brilliant book between your hands is my story; it is our story, as well as our history—"herstory." But it is also and mainly our future, our roadmap, a guiding light that takes root in our past challenges and victories, to show us the way ahead towards more solidarity and better forms of collaboration and synergy between the younger generations of feminists. It is a magnificent, hopeful and compelling call to action that speaks to our collective and individual rage. And it is one of the reasons why we should never give up. True, the road is still long and arduous, but we shall get to where we must go. Struggling, defying, resisting, pushing: we shall get there.

Yes, I dare be confident, because then I see little angry Arab girls everywhere. I see them wherever I turn, around every corner, inside every household. In Lebanon, in Egypt, in Saudi Arabia and beyond. They are breaking molds, defying limitations and snubbing those dangerous, nicely wrapped, pink-poisoned time bombs. Most importantly, they are *growing*, and so is their anger. And I know for a fact that they will not wait much longer.

… And I, for one, cannot wait to hear them roar: Yalla Feminists!

Joumana Haddad is an award-winning Lebanese author, journalist and human rights activist. She was named one of the world's 100 most powerful Arab women by Arabian Business *magazine. Haddad has published sixteen books in different genres, including* I Killed Scheherazade *(Saqi Books, 2010) and* Superman Is an Arab *(Westbourne Press, 2012). Her most recent novel is titled* The Book of Queens *(Interlink Publishing, 2022).*

Preface

Overview

The most subversive thing a woman can do is talk about her life as if it really matters.

—Mona Eltahawy[1]

Arab Feminisms. *What are they? Why are they? How are they?!* These are the questions we set out to explore in this book.

This book offers a snapshot of feminisms in the region, highlighting nuances in movements to better understand the ways they manifest, and the impact they have on people's lives.

This book looks back and looks forward. We explore milestones in feminist movements against the backdrop of significant regional events over the past decades. Examining feminisms in the Arab region over the last 50 years enables us to understand what the next 50 years might hold. In doing so, we might understand what is holding the region back, what is holding it together, and what is driving it forward.

Why feminisms—in plural? This is a feminist book, written by feminist authors, informed by a feminist analysis. We assert that there is no greater struggle in our lifetime, and no more critical time to be a feminist than now. With equality centuries away and major backlashes against once-solidified gains, the world is not moving in the right direction. At least not for women. In response to these challenges, we recognize that there are many different feminisms. We continue to refer to this term in the plural in recognition of that diversity. Our feminism is intersectional and includes minorities and other vulnerable groups. However, given the research and data (both conducted and available) we leaned more heavily on women and we believe that advancing women's rights also advances rights for all. Furthermore, study participants frequently conflated women and feminism, and so we let their voices speak for themselves in what is an evolving discussion.

We believe in the power of women. And we believe in equality. And we believe that equality is better for everyone—individuals, communities, countries. Feminism is a global movement—and a global imperative. Feminism is our calling, and this book speaks to that calling. This is the conscious unapologetic bias that we bring.

Why focus on Arab feminisms? Firstly, we do not know enough about Arab feminisms—what they are, where they exist, how they manifest, and more. We believe that the history of Arab feminisms merits greater research and wider dissemination. Feminist movements are not limited to documented evidence. In fact, too many movements remain unrecorded and unrepresented. Their stories should be told.

Understanding Arab feminist movements is a growing field, surely, but more needs to be said, more needs to be understood, and much more needs to be done. There is a need for greater data—qualitative and quantitative—but an even greater need to look beyond the numbers. The voices in this book are a starting point to speaking "beyond the numbers."

We do not critique women's movements, but instead allow the voices of the individuals behind the movements to speak for themselves, telling us how they view their efforts, and what they hope for the future. A conversation about hopes also raises concerns about challenges, fissures, disconnects—and how we can constructively channel the hope (and anger) to tackle these challenges.

While not enough is said about feminist movements in the Arab region—there is certainly not enough about *young* feminists. We hope to fill this gap in our understanding, and our action. Young women are on the rise, leading feminist movements around the world. In the Arab region, young feminists are a galvanizing force, championing the charge for change. They are a transformative force. Here we give them a platform to tell their story, and to chart the future direction of women's rights and gender equality in the Arab region.

Why 50 years? We take a long view looking back so we might benefit from a long view looking forward. This battle will be a long one! A comprehensive history is beyond the purview of this book, so instead we zoom out to examine trends and patterns in women's rights across the region with the hope that this sheds light on the future change to paths.

Why all Arab countries—and is that even possible, or necessary? The Arab region is not a monolith. We recognize that there is vast diversity in this grouping of 22 states, including some of the world's wealthiest and poorest countries side by side. We have endeavored to include all 22 Arab states as best we can, despite the challenges and limitations this presents. A thorough analysis is both beyond our scope and impossible to fit in the pages of a book. Instead, we set out to be as inclusive as possible.

This story is not meant to be exhaustive. There is other research out there, and we hope there will be more. In fact, we hope *this book* will inspire more. Such research is part of an ongoing conversation.

This book is both academic and activist in that it speaks to both worlds—and allows them to be in conversation with each other rather than relegating them to their respective silos. Theory is only paper until it is applied in practice. This book marries theory, practical knowledge, research, lived realities, and ideologies. Here we strive to bring youth in conversation with the old, academia in conversation with activists, policymakers in conversation with practitioners, and so on. Is it chaotic? Surely. But not any more so than the region itself. It is authentic. We elected to deliberately cross boundaries rather than to reinforce them.

And so this book looks back over 50 years, and across a region that is just as diverse as its inhabitants, to understand Arab feminist movements. Without a critical reflection of *what happened then*, we might not be able to understand *what is happening now*.

This book is animated by interviews, surveys, conversations with people from the region, particularly feminists—and particularly *young* feminists. Their voices form our analysis, setting the tone for the present and laying the hopes for the future.

We believe this book will be valuable as it draws together movements and actors across the region, bringing them into conversation about what feminism is, and where it is going.

Positionality

*They said, "You are a savage and dangerous woman." I am speaking
the truth. And the truth is savage and dangerous.*
—Dr. Nawal El Saadawi[2]

Our position reveals our perspective.

We explain who we are because we recognize that our experiences and perspectives—who we are—cannot be divorced from what we see and what we say. We are both actors and observers, activists and academics.

Who we are matters. It determines both what we see and what people say to us. We share stories and highlight voices of those on the frontlines of feminist movements, while also recognizing that there are things we are *not* told and things we do *not* hear—because of who we are and how we might be perceived. There are findings in the silence, too.

We endeavor to be observers and amplifiers in sharing the stories and perspectives of others throughout this book. At the same time, we are *active* observers, inserting ourselves in places throughout the book—where necessary—with the use of "we." We intend this to indicate our analysis, our thoughts, our reflections, and our positions. This book is very much a product of these positions—of us as a collective and also as individuals.

Rebecca

I have always been outraged by injustice. Without sounding sanctimonious, I thought how, as someone with more privilege than most by virtue of birth, do I use this most effectively? I felt the best way was through education. Teaching a little mind to read is one thing, seeing what they do with that power is another thing entirely. And it is inspiring. Inside the classroom you see children dream and you encourage it because it is pure and it is magic. Education as a tool can open endless possibilities—give someone the gift of education and it can be the great equalizer.

Or so you think.

My teaching career in the region brought me to a school in Saudi Arabia where I was teaching six- and seven-year-old girls. I saw how, no matter what, sometimes education is just not enough and will never be enough. There will always be barriers and obstacles in the way of these girls' dreams, not insurmountable, but definitely making life more difficult than it ever should be. Outside the classroom you know reality is lurking, poised to determine a different path for their futures.

I first came to the region in 2015, aged 23—curious, observant. I was drawn to the history and culture and set out to experience it. Experiencing it as a woman on my own, however, was eye-opening. It stirred in me the activist, the advocate. I have always been motivated by younger generations and continue to be a youth leader volunteer in Ireland. I am also a mediator, researcher, and writer. I have numerous publications specifically on the topics of feminism, women's rights, and violence against women. Safe to say, it is no accident I have ended up in this area.

While I left the field of education, it never left me. I returned to learning, constantly grappling with the question: do we seek to effect change from inside these systems or externally tear them down to rebuild new, better ones? After completing a Master's in

International Peace Studies and working in the field of women's rights specifically for some time now, I found myself drawn back to the region once more—but this time in a different capacity. With this book I blend my passions of activism, academia, and youth engagement.

At the same time, I am acutely aware of my positionality in this endeavor as someone who is not from the Arab region. I am, however, a woman. So while this is not my story, this is still personal. I fully believe every woman everywhere knows violence in some form. Every woman has experienced discrimination, inequality, unfairness, injustice. Every woman everywhere has felt fear. I am in no way comparing like-for-like, but this fear is universal.

I am also a feminist. I truly believe no one is free unless all women are free—everywhere. So, in researching and writing this book, centering voices and experiences from the region was the top priority.

In fact, it was the only priority. There is no greater authority and this is their story.

Yet, at the same time, these stories are far more than words on paper. The lived realities, the trauma, the experiences—all so graciously shared with me, but all so heavy.

I feel it.

And still I feel the hope too, the determination, the spirit, and most importantly, the fight.

My intention with this book is to further the conversations that need to happen, to highlight the incredible work being done—and all the work still to be done, to create dialogue, to show solidarity, and most of all, to open up space for curiosity. When we lead with curiosity, we leave less room for criticism and more room for learning, growing.

More room for hope.

Lina

I start with this: I am a feminist. The rest, to me, is far less important.

But, for clarity, here is the rest. I am Lebanese-Palestinian: a child of two countries, two religions—and two wars. I am Arab-American: an insider-outsider to the Arab world. I exist on both sides—as a native, and as part of the diaspora. My positions are multiple. My loyalty is singular. I am a feminist. Feminism is my country.

I am also a *majority world* feminist. I am Arab, and I am "of color" in America. All of this explains the perspective I bring and the biases I own. I either belong nowhere—or everywhere. Most of the time it's both.

My feminist consciousness was born out of my origins and experience, my perspectives and biases. It was built out of a reality that denies women and girls equality everywhere. My academic and professional work has always been focused on efforts to remedy that inequality.

And so I became an activist, fighting for women's rights and equality and fundamental freedoms. And then I became an aid worker, covering over twenty countries in over two decades, focusing on ending violence against women—the greatest manifestation of that inequality. And during that time, I also became an academic—an "accidental academic" specifically—with research and publications and other academic things behind my name, giving me a stronger platform on which to stand. Today I am still those things, and I am also an advisor, author, and speaker—still screaming about the same things, day after decade.

While my experience has been global, I zoomed in on the Arab region for seven years. From 2015 to 2022, I served as the Executive Director of The Arab Institute for Women at the Lebanese American University, working at the intersection of academia and activism to advance change for women in the Arab region. It was in this context that my curiosities for this book were born.

There is history here, too. I am the third generation of women in my family to work at this university. My Palestinian grandmother graduated from this same university in 1938—her diploma hangs on my wall as a reminder of what determined women can do. She went on to work at the university for 20 years. My aunt, her eldest daughter, also worked at the university, publishing *The Status of the Arab Woman: A Select Bibliography* on behalf of the Institute in 1980, 35 years before I would be its director.[3]

So, just like the story of many Arab feminists, my feminist activism started generations ago.

I am an advisor for the Institute, a supporter, a fan. The Institute turns 50 as this book comes to life. This is not a coincidence. Here, too, we celebrate 50 years—of progress and regress, of setbacks and advances. Most of all, we celebrate 50 years of survival. And look to the next 50.

I am an advocate for young feminists. I do not "give them a voice." No. They *have* a voice. What they need is a microphone. For me, this book is one such microphone. Their words are powerful, and my role here is to share them with you.

I am a social scientist—nosy-by-nature—and determined to bring this book to life. And so this book endeavors to do "too much," but I have always been accused of doing "too much"—and being "too much."

"It is my superpower," I now say. Better than being "not enough."

Every activist is "too much," setting out to accomplish a seemingly-impossible task. *Equality! Freedom!* This takes courage and imagination. And perhaps a little madness.

And so, yes, we took on a colossal task—22 countries, 50 years, 200+ voices. They are bursting out of this book! I struggled with those we could not include, could not reach. There are millions—I see you! Let's hope there is room for many more books, filled with many more voices of courage—and rage.

Methods Used

> *Just remember what Satan says: "I teach men what I learn from women!"*
> —Dr. Hanan Al-Shaykh[4]

This book began with curiosity, with an urge to better understand *what is going on* with feminism(s) across the Arab region. All books are born from critical inquiry—a desire to examine circumstances and form some conclusions. This book is built from nearly a decade of such inquiry.

Our initial points of entry to this inquiry were conversations with other feminists. We built this book firstly from their perspectives. We then examined the existing research to learn what has been documented, recognizing that what is on paper does not do justice to what actually exists in practice. Meaning, feminisms exist, even as they are not always recorded. This book hopes to add to that record.

With a theoretical framework in mind, we then returned to the voices of those on the frontlines through participant observation and action research. We adopted a mixed methods approach to reach people where they are—using surveys, interviews, conversations, emails, voice notes, and whatever other means of communication were open to us, and accessible to those we were trying to reach.

This feedback was rich. We could have written several books.

With their words, themes, patterns, and trends emerged. Their words fueled our understanding of where we have been, where we are, where we are going—and what we need to do to get there.

In writing, we adopted a conversational tone that might be viewed as "informal." This is deliberate. Academic writing has its value, but it can also be obscure, alienating, and elitist. We wanted to be understood, accessible, and actionable.

The book triangulates academic research, feedback from our survey, and excerpts from interviews conducted. Analysis is bolstered and supported by theoretical frameworks including feminism, intersectionality, and non-violent civil resistance theory, amongst others.

We used qualitative methods because quantitative data on all things "women" remains incomplete, inaccurate, or an underestimate of reality. This is more true for "feminism," and even more so for "Arab feminism." While there are some quantitative measures throughout the book, qualitative methods were given priority in order to elevate people's voices and stories. It is through these voices and stories that we can understand lived realities.

The book is part of a longer inquiry that started with Lina in her capacity as Executive Director of The Arab Institute for Women (AiW). We would like to acknowledge that some data has been used with permission from research carried out by AiW. For this, and for the inspiration that AiW and its team provides, we are grateful.

Segments of this investigation build on previously published analyses that have appeared in a variety of articles and reports. All of these are cited where relevant.

The survey we conducted in English and Arabic was anonymous, meaning names were not asked and are not included. Study participants are referred to as "young feminist" or "young activist," with country of nationality specified—where participants have chosen to do so. Online surveys have limitations in that, for the most part, we are unable to control or describe the population(s) the survey is able to reach. Additionally, there are biases in terms of participants who select themselves into—or out of—the sample. Our wording also has an impact. For instance, use of the word "feminist" in the title may have had a bearing on who might respond—and how. Surveys are a useful starting point, but we recognize that further investigation would be needed in order for analyses to be conclusive.

Interviews were conducted either in person or online with verbal agreement in line with ethical procedures. We spoke to a wide range of stakeholders and experts on the topic whose experiences and opinions further informed our analysis. At times, these people took exceptional risks to their personal safety in order to share their views—we do not take this lightly. In this regard, voices, words, and sentiments behind the words are prioritized—not the names. Safety is a key concern, hence our right to change names, to exercise care, to be deliberately vague (for instance: "a young feminist said..."), and to protect people as much as possible from the risks of potential backlash. We encouraged study participants to self-select a title that best fits them and their identity, rather than a title they have been given. This is not only about safety but also about a desire to allow participants to claim their own identity by naming themselves. This is in line with ethical research protocols, our knowledge of the dangers that activism can present, and our own conscience and convictions.

Challenges

There is no turning back for Arab feminists.
—Dr. Sahar Khamis[5]

This was an ambitious project, as all research should be. Still, a number of challenges presented themselves. Our points of access were somewhat restricted. Temporal, financial, and geographical constraints were a major factor and had multiple attendant effects.

While the authors have both lived and worked in the region and traveled extensively throughout, neither of us currently live in the region. During the project, therefore, we had limited time in the region and onsite data collection could only be conducted in Lebanon. This likely accounts for lower levels of engagement in the Gulf and North and sub–Saharan Africa. We made every effort, however, to rectify this imbalance and reach across the region. We also effectively utilized online space by carrying out the bulk of interviews through various online platforms to ensure wider representation.

We are functional in the language but by no means fluent. We also do not read Arabic, meaning research and literature in Arabic was either unavailable to us or we had to rely on translations. This is not ideal. At the same time, there is significant research available in English. This, however, highlights a different problem in that more research actually *should* be in Arabic. We hope to translate the book into Arabic in order to do our part to close this gap.

The survey we created was completely online and this was also limited insofar as we were reliant on engaging our contacts to share amongst their networks—with no guarantee it would be completed. Even though the survey was available in English and Arabic, we received more responses in English, which is indicative of accessibility. We also found there were lower levels of engagement in some parts of the region than others. Participation covered 16 of the 22 countries from the region, plus 2 from the diaspora. We received 113 responses but unfortunately did not receive any from Algeria, Comoros, Djibouti, Mauritania, Oman, and Somalia.

Through the interview process, we were deliberate in our efforts to be as representative as possible both in terms of country and stakeholder. Over 60 formal interviews—and countless conversations—were conducted involving a range of different actors including activists, students, academics, journalists, politicians, lawyers, aid workers, government representatives, artists, musicians, and more.

The deadline for this book also presented a challenge. There is never enough time for research such as this. We sought to coordinate the release of this book with several important feminist conferences and events. We had six months from start to finish to collect data, conduct research, analyze our findings, and write the book. Although it was a short timeframe, we did not compromise on quality. In any case, no matter how much time is given, there is always a need for more.

Ultimately, this book is a contribution to a critically understudied area—

thematically and geographically. We hope that this book will pique curiosities, that more research will be born, and that more conversations will be created. We can never have enough. For those who see gaps, we see them too. And we encourage you to fill them, as we will continue to endeavor to do in our work and in our lives.

Definition of Terms

If your idea disturbs a conservative man, hang onto it, I said to myself. It will probably lead to important discoveries.

—Dr. Fatima Mernissi[6]

There are several terminologies at the heart of this study. To understand these terms, we need to clearly define them. Definitions are not static—they require ongoing dialogue and examination. And they evolve, just as language does—often for the better.

For the purposes of this book we chose certain definitions in the interest of clarity and consistency but acknowledge many definitions are subject to interpretation. We posit these as questions rather than statements and, in the end, we trust that readers will make their own decisions about these terms.

What Is Arab?

Arab generally refers to Arabic-speaking populations. Arab is both a cultural and a linguistic term, not a race. Arabs are of varying religions—while many are Muslim, there are also Christian and Jewish Arabs. For these purposes, our usage of the term Arab entails a more inclusive definition, as will be elaborated below.

What Is the Arab Region?

The region is not a monolith. Rather, it is a collection of diverse national, political, religious, economic, cultural, and social conditions. While the Middle East and North Africa (MENA) is often used, this includes or excludes certain states and is therefore not interchangeable with the Arab region. The Arab region is comprised of 22 states that are members of the Arab League, namely, Algeria, Bahrain, Comoros, Djibouti, Egypt, Iraq, Jordan, Kuwait, Lebanon, Libya, Mauritania, Morocco, Oman, Palestine, Qatar, Saudi Arabia, Somalia, Sudan, Syria, Tunisia, United Arab Emirates, and Yemen. These countries are diverse in terms of their ethnicities, as well as their linguistic and religious communities.

Often, regional groupings such as MENA, for example, do not include or capture all Arab states, highlighting some and sometimes marginalizing others. Moreover, we believe that representation beyond the acronym is vitally important. Important nuances fall through the cracks. It is also worth reiterating that the "Arab world" and the "Muslim world" are not synonymous.

We also acknowledge the decolonial project to use the term S.W.A.N.A. to mean South West Asia and North Africa instead of Middle East, Near East, Arab World, Islamic World, and other geographic demarcations that have colonial origins.[7]

Where relevant—throughout the book—we use the following subregions:

- The Gulf: Bahrain, Kuwait, Oman, Qatar, Saudi Arabia, United Arab Emirates, Yemen.
- North and sub–Saharan Africa: Algeria, Comoros, Djibouti, Egypt, Libya, Morocco, Sudan, Tunisia, Somalia, Mauritania.
- The Levant: Iraq, Jordan, Lebanon, Palestine, Syria.

It must be noted that although "North Africa" is more commonly used as a category, we choose "North and sub–Saharan Africa" in order to be as inclusive as possible for countries not geographically located in Northern Africa.

Who Are Women from the Arab Region?

We recognize that not everyone from, or in, the Arab region is Arab, and not everyone who is Arab is in the region. As such, we have chosen to refer to "women from the Arab region" rather than "Arab women." Where we refer to "Arab feminists," we specifically mean "feminists in—or from—the Arab region." Our shorthand is not meant to be exclusive or based on racial or ethnic identities but rather built from origins from or existence in "Arab countries."

In the spirit of S.W.A.N.A. as defined above, communities include but are not limited to Arabs, Armenians, Afghans, Assyrians, Azeris, Chaldeans, Circassians, Copts, Druze, Imazighen, Iranians, Kurds, Nubians, Sudanese, Turks, Turkmen, Yazidis, and other identities and their intersections. The region is also home to a diverse population of migrant workers from countries such as Bangladesh, India, Nepal, Kenya, Indonesia, and the Philippines, among others. Their rights also hang in the balance. While we feel that much more needs to be said and done for these communities, it is beyond the scope of this particular book. At the same time, we hope that you will read our words and understand our terms in the spirit of inclusion through which they are intended.

Our perspective on inclusion stems from Yassine Temlali's definition of Pan-Arabism that is not racial or ethnic but formed by a more inclusive political stance.[8] Building from this, Maria Najjar defines Pan-Arab-Feminism as a grouping that is in/on/from the region who "seek to collectively, collaboratively dismantle patriarchy."[9] This is the understanding we share.

It is important not to essentialize a group that is not homogenous, and we feel this term captures the diversity of women across ethnic, religious, diasporic, and national lines. While we aimed to be as inclusive as possible, we did not specifically concentrate on ethnic minority groups present in the region as demographic categories and recognize there may be other issues exclusive to these groups that merit investigation.

What Is the Arab League?

The Arab League, formally the League of Arab States, established in 1945, is a coalition of Arab states with the intention of cooperating in areas of common interest within the region. Initially consisting of six members, the alliance has since grown to 22 members—listed above. The Arab League is an example of a Pan-Arab entity based on a shared language and culture, despite having some of the poorest and richest countries in the world side by side. The Arab League issues recommendations but states are not obligated to comply with, or legally, implement resolutions.

What Is an Activist?

An activist is a person who advocates, promotes, and campaigns for social or political justice. Methods of activism differ, but the role of activists in agitating for change or reform in society is hugely important. From spreading awareness to highlighting injustices, challenging oppressive structures, or amplifying critical voices—no effort is too small. Anyone can, and arguably should, be an activist and an agent for positive change.

What Is Empowerment?

We take empowerment to mean women's agency, power, and autonomy over the full range of their rights. It is also the *process* by which women gain power over their lives and choices.

What Is Equality and Equity?

Equality refers to everyone having the same opportunities and resources. Equity, on the other hand, is understanding that not everyone has the access to these opportunities and resources. Equity is providing everyone with the specific opportunities and resources needed to achieve equality. Within the context of social systems, while equality refers to providing the same level of support to each individual or group, equity means providing varying levels of support depending on the need to achieve greater fairness of outcomes. When used throughout this book, equality and equity are chosen intentionally, given the important nuances of each term.

What Is Feminism?

We define feminism as a movement, belief system, and way of living that seeks equality and equity in rights, opportunities, and freedoms for women and other vulnerable and minority groups. There are multiple feminisms—therefore we refer to this word in the plural.

While the word feminism has many interpretations, our feminism aligns with Lebanese feminist academic and activist Zeina Zaatari as "an ideology of change" that "seeks to overthrow the entire patriarchal or paternal system by overturning the balance of power that prioritizes men as a social group and those who benefit from the patriarchal system."[10]

We recognize, however, that people can be feminists and not identify as such. The importance lies in the action. We acknowledge the misconceptions of this term and the weight it carries. The book constantly scrutinizes the term, its interpretations, and its manifestations. In short, we use a feminist lens to understand everything. Even the word "feminism."

And this is the basis of the entire book.

What Is Intersectionality?

Intersectionality, first coined by Kimberlé Crenshaw in 1989, recognizes that inequality and discrimination have many interconnected and intersecting factors such as gender, race, sexual orientation, disability, and class, amongst others. Intersectionality is a critical component of feminism in order to be as inclusive and representative of as many experiences as possible. Without intersectionality, oppressive structures are at risk of perpetuation.

Who Are Members of the LGBTQ+ Community?

We recognize there are multiple acronyms and no universally agreed acronym to refer to the full range of sexual orientations, gender identities, and expressions. We do not wish to restrict labels and aim to be as inclusive as possible. For the purposes of this book, we use LGBTQ+ which stands for lesbian, gay, bisexual, transgender, queer, and others. In this way, we cover a range of identities with the understanding that this is an evolving conversation.

What Is Patriarchy?

The patriarchy refers to systems, structures, and beliefs that favor men and men's dominance over women and marginalized groups. Societies within the Arab region are highly patriarchal and women's position is determined by discriminatory patriarchal structures legally, socially, educationally, politically, economically, and so on. We assert that the feminist fight everywhere is, first and foremost, against the patriarchy.

What Are Western and Non–Western?

The West usually refers to the regions of North America and Europe. Therefore, Western relates to ideologies and processes specific to those contexts. We also acknowledge the usage of different terminologies such as Global North or "Developed Nations" in reference to Western. Conversely, non–Western refers to regions outside of North America and Europe. And, by the same logic, we acknowledge the terms Global South and "Developing World," but recognize these are not all synonymous. For the latter, we prefer to use "Majority World" rather than "Developing World." Our choice here is deliberate, as we do not accept the belief that Western countries are "developed" while all others are beneath them. Dr. Salmah Eva-Lina Lawrence and others have underscored the hierarchical and demeaning implications of terms like "first" or "third" world. They advocate instead for use of Majority World to cover all countries in the Global South, particularly given that the populations in this region constitute the planet's demographic majority.[11] These terms are political and hold weight.

What Are Women's Movements?
What Are Feminist Movements?

We refer to women's movements both in terms of organizations and instances of activism. Women's movements began as a response to the social inequalities that exist in society, especially between men and women. Women have sought to address social injustices through organizing, agitating, and resisting. Women's movements are not all homogeneous, and great differences exist in terms of ideologies, methods, and aims.

We note that "women's movements" are not always the same as "feminist movements" and vice versa. Not all women's movements are feminist, and feminist movements are not comprised solely of women. There are diversities within these movements as well as between them. And there are various interpretations and, understandably, no universal agreement. The terms are often conflated, including in the responses we received from those we consulted.

Mazur and McBride define women's movements as having two elements: the discourse and the actors.[12] We understand these movements to also include a third element: the actions. They assert that women's movement discourses focus on women as a category, using language that is gendered, and promoting ideas as women representing women. Feminist movement discourse is a sub-category that includes the above as well as the goal to challenge gender-based hierarchies and to dismantle structures of subordination of women and other vulnerable groups.

That being said, we use feminist movements and women's movements interchangeably throughout the book—in an aspirational sense. This was the case with our study participants as well. We believe that feminist movements are the power that will put an end to patriarchy. And, by extension, we *hope* that women's movements are feminist in their intent.

What Is State Feminism?
What Is State Co-opted Feminism?

State feminism refers to state efforts to institutionalize feminism, creating spaces within government institutions for women in politics and for agendas that promote women's causes. The term itself was coined by Norwegian politician Helga Hernes in the mid–1980s to connect questions of welfare with questions of power, based on the Scandinavian welfare state.[13] Hernes argued that women's lives are dependent on—and determined by—state policies. At the same time, women were mobilizing against patriarchy and in favor of their rights. The two work together, Hernes asserted, combining state feminism from above and feminization from below in order to foster an alliance between women and the state. Ideally.

Australian researchers advanced this understanding by examining the avenues through which feminist activists within government entities might promote a feminist agenda in their work.[14] The assumption of government-created or sanctioned feminist action can be controversial because it suggests that the state can be "feminist" in its promotion of women's rights.

In the mid–1990s, the term was used to define the *actions* of women's policy agencies— state-based mechanisms that we more commonly call "national women's machineries."[15] The United Nations also championed the creation of such women's machineries as critical vehicles for women's advancement and the promotion of the Beijing Declaration and the Platform for Action in 1995. Also in 1995, the Research Network on Gender Politics and the State was formed. They put forward the following definition of state feminism: "The effectiveness and impact of women's policy agencies as allies of advocates for women and equality."[16] The Research Network has conducted extensive studies on state feminism in Western post-industrial democracies. At the same time, a rigorous comparison of the effectiveness of state feminisms across the Arab region has yet to be fully conducted.

What followed was conversation around the effectiveness of such agencies. Indeed, there is a difference between the *structures* and the *processes*—neither of which are being assessed here. Further conversations are held around the effectiveness of women themselves inside these agencies, government bureaucrats, and whether or not they are victims or tools of the patriarchy. For our purposes, we are interested in the *perceptions* of those we consulted rather than assessing the effectiveness of the agencies, their policies, and their staff.

As such, we distinguish between state feminism—which may or may not be successful—and state *co-opted* feminism—which entails the hijacking of feminist causes by the state. While many cited throughout this book *perceive* state feminism to be negative, we operate with the assumption, in line with Kantola and Squires, that "state feminist practices (as a form of representation) have been both enabling and constraining."[17] State *co-opted* feminism often entails actions that are hollow, perpetrated by actors—state *co-opted* feminists—who are not actually feminists.

In the Arab region—and likely elsewhere in the world—"state feminism" implies government-sanctioned action that is unlikely to disrupt the patriarchal status quo.[18] Many governments co-opt feminist demands, thereby limiting the potential for radical reform. This is the definition we use here. And, by extension, state feminists are those who subscribe to and support so-called state feminism. Additionally, women in politics are not, by default, feminists. As such, we distinguish between women who enter politics and those who actively support feminist principles and legislation.

The term state feminism is assumed to be negative because the state is an inherently patriarchal institution. The state is not often likely to take a feminist stance in its quest to end the power imbalance perpetrated by patriarchy. As such, the term is often used to refer to action that is top-down, bureaucratic, elitist. These actions do not set out to tackle questions of power and politics, and they are often not representative of the full range of women. Throughout this book, when study participants refer to state feminism, it is likely that they mean state *co-opted* feminism. We have left quotes in their original wording, although we understand the nuance. We also believe that the use and evolution of this term is an interesting finding in and of itself that merits further research.

Structure of the Book

Arab women are the true measure of change in the region.
—Dr. Alanoud Alsharekh[19]

All our choices in this book are deliberate, starting with the title. *Yalla* is a colloquial Arabic word that encompasses a range of meanings—come on, let's go, hurry up, okay, and more—depending on the context. It is widely used and understood by all nationalities across the Arab region and in non–Arabic speaking countries. In fact, it is often the first—or only—Arabic word that non–Arabic speakers learn. We use this in the title—*Yalla Feminists*—as a call to action, to continue to galvanize feminist movements in the region so they may rise, resist, and (re)claim their long-overdue rights. Yalla!

Firstly, we are honored to have the **Foreword** written by the extraordinary feminist activist, author, speaker, and journalist Joumana Haddad. Her words start the fire and set the tone for this book.

Chapter 1 builds our Feminist Foundations, starting with a snapshot of women's rights in the region, built from the latest data and statics. Data only presents a partial picture, and the next section tells us where we are today in greater detail—examining the status of women's health and education, political and economic representation, legal rights, and violence against women. We then ask how we reached this particular socio-political place, and what might be holding the region back. The following section examines the questions worth exploring—the inquiries upon which we built this research. It begins with the question "What is Arab feminism?"—a question we will turn to throughout this book.

Chapter 2 is our (re)organization of Arab feminist history, covering phases of feminisms in the Arab region. These Feminist Phases orient us and pave the way for discussions that bring in the voices of feminists and activists from the Arab region in later chapters. In recognizing that our history is not linear, we nonetheless identify five phases of feminist history: Reawakening, Galvanizing, Agitating, Regressing, Collaborating. Analysis takes into account regional and national landscapes alongside international events, with a feminist lens.

Chapter 3 documents Feminisms on the Frontlines of Crisis—because we cannot speak of feminisms in the region without also speaking of conflict. In this chapter, we cover the different forms of revolution, protest, and uprising beginning with the so-called Arab Spring and moving on to specific country examples of activism. Women's role—and resistance—in conflict was clearly present prior to the Arab Spring. The chapter makes a case for exploring resistance in multiple forms, and argues that the frontlines for women are many and one—the patriarchy.

Chapter 4 presents alternative forms of activism—particularly art-activism—in addressing Feminisms on the Frontlines of Creativity. This chapter covers a range of artist-activists in their efforts to creatively push boundaries as political actors—even at great risk. We cover stories of musicians, street artists, filmmakers, and others to illustrate the range of artist-activists in the region.

Chapter 5 examines the fissures and challenges within women's movements locally, nationally, regionally. This chapter on Fragmented Feminisms is also built from the voices and experiences of over 200 people who were consulted as part of this research. Challenges to feminisms are arranged thematically and include categories such as misconceptions of feminism and gender, patriarchal structures, intergenerational disconnects, lack of collaboration, elite entities, superficial gains, Western agendas, religion, conflict, and more.

Chapter 6 covers our Feminist Future, centering youth voices and their hopes for the future of feminisms in the region. Here too, we highlight key areas for advancing women's rights in the region including listening to young people, reclaiming the core tenets of feminism, learning and education, abolishing discrimination, making sure efforts are intersectional and interconnected, engaging men, reaching the diaspora, protecting our bodies, mobilizing online, collaborating amongst ourselves, and preparing for the long fight ahead. It is in these voices that the future of feminism in the Arab region is (re)imagined.

The **Conclusion** ties together the key elements of the book and asks the recurring question: *So what? Now what?!* Here, we provide a brief summary of our findings, along with our perspectives as authors. Just as you read our personal positions and motivations in the Preface, the conclusion will also allow us to bring back our own voices to close this book.

Finally, we are honored to have the **Afterword** written by the unstoppable, award-winning, pan–African feminist Aya Chebbi. Her words seal this book and set us forth on our mission to further our feminist future.

1

Feminist Foundations

All over history and all over the world, you always have women without voice or without image. But you know that she exists here and there.
—Dr. Hatoon Al Fassi[1]

Let us start with this: feminisms exist everywhere, and feminisms are essential everywhere.

But with that, we should also add that patriarchy exists everywhere, which is why feminisms must fight even harder to exist.

It is no secret that *no* country in the world has achieved full gender equality. In fact, no country is even close to achieving it. Empowering women is not just a human rights principle, it is a precondition to sustainable development and the strongest vehicle for peace, prosperity, and progress. Without women's rights and equality, we will *all* lose. The stakes are high. It is, quite literally, a fight for our lives.

Women's rights remain highly contested, and the progression of feminisms has not been linear. In fact, it has been characterized by massive setbacks. This is not unique to the Arab region, but there, feminist progress is too often met with patriarchal push-back. Ultimately, it would seem that patriarchal power remains firmly entrenched in the region.

The Arab region's diverse collection of 22 countries has one thing in common: women continue to experience a backlash against their own long-overdue rights and fundamental freedoms. So that is the bad news.

This book takes a strong view. It is animated by the voices of feminist activists in all their diversity. In this book, we will share their own views of feminisms in the region—what they look like, where they come from, and where they are going. This book has been organized entirely around the themes raised in the more than 200 conversations with people from all demographics, backgrounds, and contexts from the Arab region. Most of these conversations are with young people. This book also addresses a gap in the literature as not enough studies center young people's voices, especially young people from the Arab region.

This book takes a long view. We will examine the many manifestations of feminisms in the Arab region by first exploring our feminist foundations to give us an understanding of where we are today, how we got here, and why we are not further along. Throughout, we will question what "Arab feminisms" actually are, and how they manifest. We will explore the disconnects—and the possible synergies.

This book takes a broad view, looking at feminisms across the 22 Arab states and over a period spanning 50 years. Ultimately, the point is to understand the feminist trajectories in the region in order to gain clarity on where we are going—and where we *must* go. While there are risks to this approach, we seek not to generalize but rather to bring the varied representations of the region together in one place. It is about opening the conversation and giving it space to evolve.

Above all, this book takes a feminist view. We firmly believe that women's rights and gender equality in the Arab region are non-negotiable imperatives. In the spirit of legendary Arab feminist Dr. Nawal El Saadawi, we assert that:

> Women are half the society. You cannot have a revolution without women. You cannot have democracy without women. You cannot have equality without women. You can't have anything without women.[2]

This is urgent, necessary, and *now*.

Women are the face—and the force—of revolutions. From the revolution in Beirut to more violent conflicts in Gaza, Sana'a, and Baghdad, women continue to demand rights, equality, and justice. Women are the best hope the region has. In fact, they are its only hope. Without full women's rights, we cannot hope to achieve an Arab region that treats everyone with dignity.

This is a historic moment because it pushes us slightly closer to ending the centuries of inequalities that have characterized women's lives in the region. At some points, we can almost see an end in sight! And yet, it continues to elude us.

Where Are We Today?[3]

> *Women have to mutually support each other and demand their rights.*
> —Dr. Hoda Badran[4]

The Arab region has long been plagued by challenges. Traditional patriarchal culture, protracted crises, lack of religious freedom, discriminatory legal frameworks, and chronic insecurity have all contributed to pushing women further from equality.

The feminist story of the Arab region cannot be divorced from the story of the Arab region itself insofar as it is fraught with conflicts, instabilities, and insecurities. From Yemen to Syria, Palestine to Iraq, the region's multiple protracted crises have destroyed systems of social protection, reduced access to safe services and support, displaced communities, and increased vulnerabilities. Humanitarian needs show no signs of abating.

As a result of the region's multiple crises, the region is experiencing "one of its most profound transformations in its modern history."[5] Conflict often brings opportunity for social change, but this has yet to fully manifest in the region. In fact, the record is patchy, as we will explore in Chapter 3. Protracted cross-border crises, civil wars, refugee and migrant movements, climate-related effects, and COVID-19 have together pushed countries in the region to near-breaking point.

Arab states are, in a word, fragile.[6]

With the Arab region at the eternal center of geopolitical struggles, the "crisis of the Arab nation-state" has been brought to the fore—and women's rights are a prominent feature.[7] In fact, women's rights are the cornerstone. We will keep saying this because we believe it to be true. Feminism really is the answer.

And yet, how can feminisms exist in crisis? In contexts of conflict, insecurity, or emergency, feminist issues are sidelined in favor of urgent, immediate needs. As one activist puts it, "…women who are struggling to feed their families and keep them alive often feel that gender issues are secondary to the issues of economic, political and health security."[8] This order of priorities is not unique to the Arab region, but given the region's likelihood of upheaval, this provides a permanent impediment to feminisms.

Conflicts and insecurities intensify pre-existing vulnerabilities, and women are the hardest hit. Women's rights are the first to be stripped away, and take the longest to recover. In this context of systemic crises, women's movements—and social justice overall—wrestle against entrenched socio-economic, cultural, and political powers (aka the patriarchy) who readily bargain away their rights. These challenges are overlapping, meaning progress—or regress—in any of these areas has an impact on all aspects of women's lives. Insecurities do not stay neatly confined within their borders.

Meanwhile, the question remains: *Why have we not progressed? And, what are we waiting for?*

In the Arab region, women's rights are characterized by non-linear progress—and great regress. Changes are few and far between. And the likelihood of positive changes tends to be viewed with a hearty dose of pessimism. Advances such as inching towards greater political representation and economic opportunity, and reducing the many discriminatory provisions embedded in national laws are still not enough. The path to equality remains long—too long.

As Khamis and Mili contend, these challenges include:

> The difficulty of organizing effective sociopolitical reform movements in the midst of a highly turbulent political environment; the need to fight reactionary social forces and stagnant cultural mindsets and traditions, which are still alive and well in many parts of the Arab world; the rise of political Islam, as witnessed in the success of some religious groups and their rise to power, which could be an impediment to further gender equity; the continued imposition of a top-down, cosmetic feminism, which only serves the elites and those in power and does not take into account the best interests of the sweeping majority of women; and an unsafe public space, which poses the risk of rape, humiliation, and harassment, which are all shamefully exploited to deter women from full participation in the public sphere and to discourage them from continuing their activism and moving forward with their struggles.[9]

Inequalities and discriminations present constant hurdles that are playing out in real time across the region. Between patriarchal societies, increased conservative movements, and lack of political will to move toward equality, the Arab world today is seeing a backlash against women's rights and freedoms. Arab manifestations of patriarchy are "promoted and sustained by religion, culture, tradition, laws, and governance" produced and reinforced by society as a whole, meaning women are also complicit in perpetuating patriarchal practices.[10] This will be explored further in Chapter 5.

To put it in a global context, the region has made scant progress when compared to the rest of the world. International indices that measure gender gaps reveal a painful picture: we have a long way to go. At present, the Arab region faces great social challenges and ranks the lowest—or near enough the lowest—in terms of social indicators across multiple indices like the Women, Peace and Security Index, Sustainable Development Goals, the Global Gender Gap, and the Gender Inequality Index. These barometers are not the sole measure of progress, and can mask significant disparities and realities. They are, however, useful overall indicators and provide necessary data to understand "the big picture" in terms of gender parity—or lack thereof.

The low rankings expose a range of inadequacies such as discriminatory policies, lack of support and services, and damaging social norms, amongst other challenges. But these indices also signal the missing efforts that need to be undertaken to address the problem, fueled by generations of entrenched patriarchy. These measures are a combination of data points, any one of which can tell us where the inequalities exist, and what might need to be remedied. At the same time, in the words of one United Nations report, the situation of women and girls in the Arab region remains "unresolved."[11] And yet, according to the 2022 Arab Region Sustainable Development Goals Index and Dashboard Report, gender equality is the most crucial challenge in the Arab region.

We argue that both of these are understatements.

Let us start with the World Economic Forum's Global Gender Gap Report 2022, an annual report that measures the gaps separating women from achieving equality in education, health, politics, and the economy. Despite the urgency to reach gender equality, the Arab region ranks second to lowest in the world, only after South Asia, for having the largest gender gaps. The report estimates that it will take the Arab region 115 years to close the gender gap—a milestone none of us will likely be around to witness.[12] This also means that multiple generations of women in the Arab region will have to wait to see equality.

Only one Arab country—the United Arab Emirates—is in the top 100 countries included in the Index. Most Arab countries are towards the bottom, meaning they are among the worst countries in the world in which to be a woman. Comoros, Bahrain, Kuwait, Egypt, and Saudi Arabia are among the bottom 20 countries. At the very bottom of the Index, four of the worst ten countries are Arab, namely Algeria, Oman, Qatar, and Morocco.[13]

Other global indices, like the 2022 Gender Development Index and the Gender Inequality Index report similar findings.[14] Out of 191 countries, both indices find more Arab states occupying the lower end of the scale, with the worst countries being Djibouti ranking at 171, Sudan at 172, and Yemen at 183.[15]

And then there is the Women, Peace and Security (WPS) Index, measuring women's well-being through "women's inclusion (economic, social, political), justice (formal laws and informal discrimination), and security (at individual, community, and societal levels)."[16] The index is centered around the notion that countries are more prosperous and peaceful when women have equal rights. Put simply, "peace is synonymous with women's rights" and the biggest indicator of peace in a country is how the country treats its women.[17] It should come as no surprise, therefore, that some of the world's widest gender gaps and worst records in terms of women's rights are from the region.

The 2021/22 WPS report covers 170 countries and finds disparities have widened and progress in women's status has slowed globally. Regionally, eight of the bottom 20 states are Arab, namely, Djibouti, Mauritania, Somalia, Palestine, Sudan, Iraq, Yemen, and Syria.[18] Yemen and Syria have consistently been in the bottom three countries since the report's inception in 2017.

In terms of fragile, insecure, and near-disastrous states, the region houses Somalia, Syria, and Yemen on one end of the spectrum. According to the 2022 Fragile States Index (FSI), Yemen ranks first on the list as the most fragile state in the world, followed closely by Somalia and Syria in second and third.[19] Yemen, Somalia, and Syria have been among the top 20 most fragile states since the FSI began in 2005. Meaning, these protracted crises have become generational.

Sudan ranks seventh and is classified as "high alert." Iraq fared *slightly be*tter. Libya made some progress thanks to an economic uptick and gains in their peace process, but these variables are volatile and the country remains highly fragile.[20] Lebanon is among the "most worsened" countries on the index, due to an escalating financial and political crisis, and increase in violence and unrest. Mauritania, Palestine, Egypt, Comoros, and Djibouti are classified as "high warning," possibly on the brink of full-blown insecurity.

The region's propensity for conflict and insecurity has resulted in a huge population of internally displaced persons (IDPs), migrants, and refugees. Some 10.3 million IDPs and 2.7 million refugees reside in the region, mostly stemming from conflicts in Syria, Iraq, Yemen, and Libya.[21] The Gulf states are particularly resistant to granting refugee status to those fleeing conflicts in the region. On the other hand, Jordan and Lebanon, sharing borders with Syria and Palestine, host the most refugees per capita in the world, subjecting their infrastructure to severe pressure.[22]

Intra-national conflicts are evident too, with divisions presenting across rural-urban lines, socio-economic backgrounds, and other points of contention. Religious discrimination and sectarian divisions in the region such as tensions between Sunni and Shi'a Muslims in Bahrain; power sharing instability between Lebanese religious sects; and Muslim-Christian divisions in Egypt, to name but a few, have also disproportionately affected women.

Ultimately, these measures emphasize the fact that the region is not doing well at all. "The underlying message is this: unless we're addressing inequalities everywhere, we will achieve equality nowhere."[23]

We now focus on the specific aspects of our lives that are not progressing. We have divided them into categories—marginalized healthcare, incomplete education, economic disempowerment, political disengagement, codified discrimination, egregious violence—to give names to these obstacles to equality in the region.

One step forward, but…

Marginalized Healthcare

Levels of women's health and wellbeing are uneven across the region. For the majority, women's health is not viewed as a priority. While this is true globally, the Arab region is obstructed by lack of awareness, information, or interest. In addition, stigma around women's health needs, as well as insufficient investment and research, collectively impede women's access to health services and support.

To be sure, there has been some progress in terms of general health indicators. UNICEF's decade-long (2010–2020) situational analysis report of the Arab region found a reduction in maternal mortality rates, an increase in female life expectancy, and a decrease in disease burden.[24] Out of 21 countries in the study, 14 countries reduced maternal deaths to less than 70 per 100,000, and every country increased female life expectancy from an average of 68 years in 1995 to 71 years in 2019.[25]

There are, however, dramatic downsides, the most dramatic being women's lack of control over their sexual and reproductive health. The majority of women in the region do not control their own bodies and choices. It is difficult, if not impossible, for women—and men—to access family planning tools. The prevalence of contraception for women aged 15–49 varies across the region. On the high end, contraceptive use is 71 percent in Morocco, 63 percent in Tunisia, and 59 percent in Egypt. On the other end, contraceptive use is only 34 percent in Yemen and 28 percent in Libya.[26] Contraception is critical, and can be lifesaving. In the region, two in five pregnancies are unplanned, with half of those ending in abortion.[27] Abortions are not readily available and are too often unsafe, financially out of reach, or illegal. Moreover, health impacts of unsafe abortions are not well known or understood due to insufficient research and lack of information.[28] Some states allow abortion in the case of danger to the mother's life, but legislation varies across the region.

Stigma and social taboos persist around understanding and addressing menstrual health needs resulting in period poverty, meaning a lack of menstrual products, sanitation facilities, and education. Lack of access to sanitation facilities—especially in schools—prevents proper, safe, and hygienic management of menstruation. According to a 2021 study, one in five schools do not have access to hygiene services, leading to increased drop-out rates for girls.[29] As a result, girls are not reaching their full potential.

There is a lack of comprehensive sex education in the region. A 2020 report found that many Arab countries oppose sex education on religious grounds, or according to traditional and conservative societal norms.[30] There are also widespread misunderstandings of sexual health terminologies which can result in the perception that sex education promotes promiscuity. Where available, sex education is often incomplete or inaccurate, and built from shame and taboos. The result is erroneous—and potentially dangerous—information that is particularly harmful to women. Too many young people learn about sex through pornography, an area that disadvantages women and promotes violence. There is little to no information on sexual risks, and stigma and discrimination continue to exist regarding HIV and other sexually-transmitted infections. Sexual health services are scant, and access to those services even more so.

Other health indicators are just as worrisome. Women in the region also face specific health risks from smoking, obesity, osteoporosis, and breast and cervical cancer, amongst other health issues.[31] The persistence of violence against women gravely affects women's physical and mental wellbeing, as will be elaborated in the following section.

In countries such as Saudi Arabia, women's health care is severely impeded by gender segregation induced by the guardianship system, as male guardians demand only female health workers and physicians treat women patients. This delays health service delivery and endangers women's lives.[32]

On top of all this, conflict and insecurity bring new—and deadly—health risks, and impede access to health services. This is especially pronounced in the Arab region, with insecurities that disproportionately and persistently affect civilians—and women in particular. Moreover, COVID-19 continues to have deleterious effects on women in the region. The Arab region initially performed well compared to global averages with regards to low mortality rates and low transmission of the virus. But this did not last due to inadequate health infrastructures, economic deterioration, lack of resources and pandemic preparedness, and very low social and political cohesion, all of which negatively affected resilience.[33]

Women are the majority of carers, and also the majority of frontline and healthcare workers, meaning they are more exposed to risk of infection. In the context of the pandemic, women are more likely to be unemployed, more likely to be poor and food-insecure, and more likely to experience domestic violence from which they can neither escape nor report. And, in conflict settings, women are disproportionately affected by the increased risk of COVID-19 infection in refugee and displacement camps.[34]

Food security is an increasing concern, due to conflicts and economic insecurities. In 2020, there were 69 million undernourished people in the region—a 91 percent increase in the last two decades.[35] The same year, approximately 32 percent of the Arab region—141 million people—did not have adequate access to food, while 49 million people experienced severe food insecurity.[36] Food insecurity is most visible in countries affected by protracted crises such as Somalia, Syria, Palestine, Iraq, and Yemen. It is also becoming a greater concern in Lebanon, as economic insecurities and poverty levels continue to increase. There is a gendered element to food security and nutrition. The majority of the malnourished are women and girls, with more girls dying of malnutrition than boys.[37] Furthermore, food insecurity often results in women resorting to risky measures in order to provide food for themselves and their families.

On the other side, obesity also presents more frequently among women and girls in the region. The region is the second most obese in the world, with 24 percent of women affected, compared to 15 percent of men.[38]

Physical health already presents great challenges, but women also face barriers in accessing mental health information, services, and support. There is a great deal of stigma attached to mental health, and diagnoses are characterized by misunderstanding. The region has the highest rate of mental disorders, particularly for women.[39] One study found that depression ranks higher in women from this region than any other. In fact, in 2013, seven of ten countries with the highest rates of women's depression were from the region.[40] Another study estimates that one half of teenagers living in Gaza have Post-Traumatic Stress Disorder (PTSD) symptoms as a result of the crisis.[41] There is also a distinct lack of attention given to improving mental health services and legislation through national policies.

Incomplete Education

Education appears to be an outlier because it is the strongest indicator with significant progress made and gaps reduced. But numbers only present a partial picture. In other words, women and girls have made advances on paper but they continue to lag behind because, too often, education fails to translate into actual opportunities, and opportunities fail to translate into actual freedom, choices, and resources. Here, too, we grapple with disconnects.

Women and girls from the Arab region are highly educated, performing as well as—and often better than—men. School enrolment and literacy rates in the region have increased and specifically, more girls are able to pursue an education. Advances mask striking disparities, however, and inequalities persist. For instance, in 2020, the adult literacy rate for the region was 73 percent, compared with a global average of 87 percent. Breaking this down, 66 percent of women and 80 percent of men in the region are literate.[42] The disparity means women have less access to information, resulting in fewer opportunities.

Female students outnumber male students enrolled in universities degrees.[43] However, despite the region's high rate of graduation and education attainment for women, this has not converted into labor force participation.[44] In many Arab states, "highly educated women are actually more likely to be unemployed than women with less education."[45] Further, *rates* of education also say nothing about the *substance* of education.

Unequal access to education severely affects women and girls in rural, impoverished, nomadic, and displaced communities. Rates are even more stark for women and girls living with disabilities—too many are denied any education at all. A study conducted by UNICEF found between 63 percent and 92 percent of females with disabilities report having no schooling at all.[46]

COVID-19 continues to have a detrimental impact on access to education. Remote learning disproportionately affected girls and women because they have less access to computers and the internet, meaning their education was disrupted or discontinued. For example, during isolation in Iraq, 98 percent of men had access to the internet compared to 51 percent of women.[47] Even online learning discriminates against women.

Economic Disempowerment

Women in Arab countries are an underutilized economic force. The Arab region has the world's highest unemployment rate for women.[48] In fact, female unemployment in the region is nearly three times the world average.[49] Arab youth too, face the highest unemployment levels in the world. Palestine is one dramatic example, where 63 percent of young women and 40 percent of young men are unemployed.[50]

Only 19 percent of women in the Arab region are in the workforce—significantly lower than the world average of 46 percent.[51] In these cases where women are employed, and when they are able to access male-dominated fields, traditional gender dynamics remain firmly entrenched. So women are promoted less and have less access to decision-making positions. The gender gap is most evident in senior positions. Women from the Arab region are less likely to be in managerial positions compared to their global counterparts—11 percent versus 27 percent, respectively.[52] Here too, they experience workplace discriminations and are not likely to be supported, prioritized, promoted, or retained. Real progress is when women are fully integrated across all levels of decision-making and leadership in line with their needs, experiences, and choices.[53]

Low wages for women plus the absence of adequate childcare provision often means women must give up their professional aspirations in order to raise their families. Women in Arab states disproportionately shoulder the burden of unpaid care, performing nearly five times as much unpaid care work than men—the highest disparity in the world.[54] This is one critically visible manifestation of the patriarchy at work.

Unsurprisingly, most female employment in the region is relegated to traditionally feminized sectors. Deeply entrenched patriarchal and traditional attitudes determine "suitable" roles for women. And, ultimately, the patriarchy prefers that women remain neatly confined within these prescribed roles. Many women leave the workforce once married or with children. Being married works against women, making them *less* employable. So, while men's employment is a prerequisite to marriage, women's employment often ends with marriage.

Increased levels of unemployment among youth and women force them to settle for insecure and irregular jobs in the informal economy. Women make up 62 percent of the informal labor force in the region.[55] Informal employment brings its own risks and insecurities such as low salaries, inadequate working conditions, and very few protections. To compensate for the poor income, many women are forced into exploitative situations in order to survive. Too often, women in the informal economy are at risk of sexual harassment and other forms of sexual violence. Female migrant domestic workers are often the most at risk, with high rates of sexual violence and nearly no ability to report or seek support.[56]

The COVID-19 pandemic significantly impacted the Arab region's economy. Prolonged duration of lockdowns jeopardized women's already-precarious role in the economy. Sectors with a majority of women—such as manufacturing, services, and the informal sector—were hardest hit. The most recent estimates from 2020 projected that as many as 1.7 million jobs in the Arab region will be lost—700,000 of them held by women.[57]

Gender equality is not just better for women, or better for societies—it is better for countries. There is worldwide evidence of this. Greater equality brings significant economic gains. At present, women in the region's labor force contribute only 18 percent to the region's overall Gross Domestic Product (GDP) but full participation could increase regional GDP by $2 trillion.[58] With women's full labor force participation, this would translate into a dramatically transformed region—for everyone.

Political Disengagement

Women in the Arab region lag behind significantly in terms of participation and representation in politics. Even when women are present in politics, they are still kept from exerting power to influence change. This lack of political participation is largely due to cultural barriers, little access to economic and financial resources, and the absence of female role models in political and public life. If women continue to be left out of leadership and activism, the patriarchal consolidation of power will have even more devastating effects on women's rights, equality, and autonomy.

Historically, political empowerment has been extremely uneven throughout the region. Suffrage is a good illustration of this. At the earliest, women in Djibouti were granted suffrage in 1946 while women in Syria were allowed to vote in 1949, although restrictions were not lifted until 1953.[59] Countries such as Comoros, Somalia, Lebanon, Egypt, Tunisia, Mauritania, Libya, Sudan, Morocco, and Algeria then granted this right throughout the 1950s and 1960s.[60] The Gulf states were significantly later, with Qatar and Bahrain following in 1998 and 2002 respectively. In 2005, Kuwait amended an election law which allowed women to vote and run for office.[61] The United Arab Emirates granted suffrage in 2006, and Saudi Arabia in 2011, although Saudi Arabian women did not vote until municipal elections in 2015.[62]

It is shocking—but perhaps unsurprising—to learn that politics is still viewed as men's domain, and women's roles as political actors are not only shunned but also mocked in the region. Research from as recently as 2019 showed that the majority of citizens surveyed believe men are more capable than women as political leaders.[63]

There is a long way to go.

The political gender gap remains the widest around the world, and the Arab region is no exception. According to the 2022 Global Gender Gap Report, the region has only closed 15 percent of its political empowerment gap, ranking third lowest globally.[64] While there are marginal improvements, for instance in terms of the share of seats women occupy in national parliaments, an increase in women's *presence* does not necessarily mean an increase in women's *power*.

In some states, quotas have been utilized to facilitate greater participation of women in politics. Although quotas are a solid start to leveling a significantly skewed playing field, they continue to be met with resistance. At the same time, there is no way these gaps will close on their own. More than half of the Arab states introduced quota systems to ensure women's representation, yet women in the Arab region still lag significantly behind in political space.[65] Quotas are also no guarantee of progress, and sizeable barriers remain. Furthermore, quotas do little to change the *perception* of women in politics.

In some cases, weakly-designed quotas have actually served to inhibit women from remaining in political structures.[66] Take Algeria as an example. In 2011, the country introduced a quota reserving one-third of its parliamentary and local government seats for women.[67] In 2021, the quota was replaced with a law mandating parity among candidates.[68] Parties that did not reach parity were required to inform the election authorities and continue, as if it was simply a matter of making a feeble attempt, confessing failure, and carrying on. Additionally, this law replaced closed with open lists, meaning voters could see—and select—the individual candidates. At the same time, a patriarchal campaign was launched to erase women's photos from campaign materials, blurring their images and placing blank avatars on ballot papers. Women were rendered invisible—again.

Too many Arab countries have too few women representatives. As of 2022, women held 16 percent of parliamentary seats in the region.[69] Even with legal provisions and quota mechanisms, few women present as candidates and even fewer are elected or appointed. For instance, when Lebanon held its long-awaited parliamentary elections in 2022, only eight female representatives out of 120 members of parliament were elected—a mere six percent of the parliamentary body.[70]

Iraq has the highest number of women elected to their parliament to date, with 95 women in the Council of Representatives, comprising 29 percent of members.[71] This was aided by a 25 percent quota, established in 2005.[72] The quota helped women not only achieve, but also exceed, presence in political space. While this says little about the quality of that presence, the point remains that when administered correctly, quotas are critical vehicles to help us reach parity—a crucial first step.

The picture is less positive in Qatar. The country's 2021 elections had 26 female candidates out of 233 total candidates, yet none were elected. There, the Emir appointed women to two of the 15 reserved seats for the Consultative Assembly. While it is a micro-move in the right direction, this number only translates to four percent of the Assembly.

Female political representation in Algeria decreased in 2021. Out of 407 seats in the National People's Assembly, only 33 of those elected were women. This marks a 17 percent decline from 2017, and was the most severe decline for women's representation in parliaments worldwide.[73] The aforementioned change to the quota system contributed to this decline.

Libya appointed Najla El Mangoush as the first female head of foreign ministry in 2021. Also in 2021, Tunisia appointed Najla Bouden Romdhane as its Prime Minister, making her not only the first woman in the country to reach that position, but also the first to do so in the Arab world.[74] The appointment has been touted as a major milestone. At the same time, we repeat that women's presence in politics does not necessarily bring power in politics. In other words, patriarchal structures still exist which hinder the impact of women in government. Moreover, a woman in office does not mean a *feminist* woman in office. Still, there is more work to be done.

And when women are elected to serve, they take great risks in doing so. Among others, these include risks to family, safety, and reputation, but also personal risks in the form of additional harassment and violence. Women politicians are routinely attacked in parliament. For example, Tunisian Member of Parliament Abir Moussi was slapped and attacked by male colleagues during a parliamentary debate in 2021—and that's not the first time she has been verbally and physically assaulted.[75] In Algeria, there have been several incidents of women Members of Parliament being physically attacked, even during parliamentary sessions. None of this is unique to those countries, or to the region.

Codified Discrimination

The law—also a patriarchal institution—does nothing to help. Inequality in legislation is not unique to the Arab region. In fact, nearly 2.4 billion women live in countries with discriminatory economic laws, and women still have only three quarters of the legal rights afforded to men.[76] Women do not have financial decision-making power at home which negatively impacts their position in society, the community, and the economy. Real power is placed even farther out of reach as a result. Specifically in the region, however, discriminatory laws abound.

"Gentlemen, this is justice," said Dr. Huda Shaarawi, legendary Egyptian feminist and foremother of Arab feminism, in her speech at the 1944 Arab Feminist Conference, "and I do not believe that the Arab man who demands that the others give him back his usurped rights would be avaricious and not give the woman back her own lawful rights, all the more so since he himself has tasted the bitterness of deprivation and usurped rights."[77]

At the same time, men and women are equal in rights and obligations according to the 1994 Arab Charter on Human Rights.[78] However, the Charter indicates respect of these rights "within the framework of the positive discrimination established in favour of women by the Islamic *Shari'a*, other divine laws and by applicable laws and legal instruments."[79] Meaning, religion trumps universal human rights, and women's rights are once again at the mercy of religion.

Moreover, while most Arab states have ratified the Convention on the Elimination of Discrimination Against Women (CEDAW), many still hold reservations that render the Convention futile. This will be explored in more detail in Chapter 2.

Discriminatory laws are deeply embedded and have wide-ranging consequences—a legacy of the patriarchy. In the region, the boundaries that define women's lives begin with the family—the first place women and girls experience discrimination. And this discrimination permeates every aspect of their lives. For instance, laws still exist that restrict the type of work a woman can do, requiring that she obtain her husband's permission before pursuing a job.[80] Citizenship and nationality laws continue to be governed by the strong patrilineal nature of Arab families and societies. A father may pass his nationality on to his children but the same right is not afforded to mothers in many Arab states.

Discrimination is justified by the patriarchy since the laws in the region often fall under religious jurisdiction—and religion presents itself as untouchable, beyond reproach. Interpretation of religion is often used as the basis of restriction, and while it is not the only site of repression and control, it is a major element. Many religious laws and social mores dictate women's roles in the family, but the absence of a secular family code leaves women subject to outdated religious edicts. Religion, and by extension, culture, wields extraordinary power over women.

As a result, many women's lives are still dictated by personal status laws which are based on varying (and invariably misogynistic) and often outdated interpretations of religious law across all faiths.[81] Personal status laws are legal procedures that govern women's bodies and lives. As a result of these laws, women are disadvantaged in areas such as marriage, divorce, child custody, inheritance, citizenship, property ownership, guardianship, and freedom of movement.

In short, the most important aspects of our lives are decided based on interpretations by old men of religion, none of which favor women. Attempts at reform further expose the gap between the law and social reality.[82] As a result, women's legal lives are schizophrenic—and openly discriminatory.[83] Personal status laws uphold gender inequality and actively reduce women to mere puppets of male decision-makers.

For instance, marriage presents one area of control. Many women must receive the approval of a male guardian to marry, completely denying their ability to decide their own lives and futures. In many countries in the region, women are not granted child custody—or only up to a certain age—in the event of divorce. Often, women cannot even initiate a divorce. The absence of equal divorce rights is reflective of women's lack of agency. It is a prevalent problem in countries such as Bahrain, Iraq, Egypt, Oman, Morocco, Lebanon, Syria, Qatar, and Yemen. In states where women can seek a divorce, it is often expensive and also considered socially unacceptable to do so. In instances of a Muslim *khul'* divorce, a woman can initiate a divorce but must rescind all her financial rights and at times even pay compensation to the husband.[84]

Inheritance laws do not side with women as, in some countries, they are only entitled to half of what a man is set to inherit. Meaning, women are literally seen as half the value of a man. Freedom of movement is also restricted according to personal status laws, and often women must seek permission from their male guardian—a father, brother, or son in some cases—to travel or work.

To illustrate the severity of these codes, it is worth understanding how they manifest at the country level. While these laws differ across the region, they agree on one thing: they continue to obstruct gender equality by defining the status of women in society in overly narrow—and overwhelmingly patriarchal—terms. Women are, in a word, property.

For example, Lebanon has 18 religious sects with 15 related personal status codes. This means every woman is treated differently based on her religion. This also results in a schizophrenic and dramatically unequal existence, particularly in the most personal—and most important—aspects of women's lives. For instance, civil marriage, or a marriage recorded and recognized by a government official instead of a religious cleric, is still not recognized within the country.[85] Meaning, women are not entirely free to choose whom to marry. They cannot pass their Lebanese citizenship onto their non–Lebanese spouses or children, depriving their families of critical citizenship rights.[86] And, Lebanese women are subjected to unfair rulings in child custody cases, which are determined exclusively in religious courts with little to no government oversight.[87] In short, a woman's life choices remain subjected to religious interpretations.

The Algerian Family Code continues to discriminate against women and girls. Reform has been long overdue—despite amendments in 2005.[88] Algerian women and girls are still second class citizens when it comes to marriage, custody, divorce, and inheritance. For example, women still require permission from their *wali* (male guardian) for certain decisions, like marriage.[89]

Predominantly in the Gulf states, women must abide by harsh male guardian systems, meaning women's autonomy is restricted when it comes to making decisions on marriage, travel, education, employment, and even reproductive health. In 2019, Saudi Arabia relaxed certain elements, allowing unmarried women to travel without the permission of their *mahram* (male guardian in Saudi Arabia) but Qatar still requires unmarried women under 25 to travel with their guardian's consent.[90]

Essentially, "family law is the best example of state sanctioned violence."[91] The bottom line is this: personal status codes do not protect women and girls. Without equality in the family, we have no hope for equality in society. Full freedom will never be possible until there is full reform. In fact, reform probably does not go far enough. Personal status codes should be abolished in favor of universal secular law. This is a major battleground for women in the region.

Meanwhile, legal discriminations continue. As of 2019, only six Arab countries—Tunisia, Jordan, Bahrain, Saudi Arabia, Lebanon, and Morocco—have introduced legislation to protect women against domestic or intimate partner violence[92] Even at that, these provisions have been largely insufficient.

No state explicitly criminalizes martial rape. Egypt, Lebanon, and Syria have rape laws that circumvent the inclusion of marital rape. The understanding is that, once married, a woman's body belongs to her husband. There is no greater denial of bodily autonomy than this, the actual loss of control of our own bodies upon marriage. As such, many (men) will argue that there is simply no such thing as "marital rape," because to them, that *is* marriage. As one example, in Lebanon, a domestic violence law was passed in 2014 but in the discussions during the drafting of the legislation in 2010, one religious leader went so far as to say that marital rape must *not* be included in the domestic violence legislation because including marital rape as a form of violence would destroy the social fabric of the family. In fact, not only did the draft legislation fail to criminalize marital rape due to pressure from these religious authorities, it introduced the concept of a "marital right to intercourse" as a form of compromise.[93] Here, the underlying assumption is that the so-called "social fabric of the family" is built on men's control of women's bodies.

Also repulsive, several Arab states—Algeria, Bahrain, Iraq, Kuwait, Libya, Syria, and Gaza—still have so-called "marry your rapist" laws that allow perpetrators to avoid punishment if they marry the victim.[94] The fear of "dishonor" influences governments to carry out such repressive laws.[95] This means that the rapist's crime is absolved if he "agrees" to marry the woman or girl he has violated, further condemning her to a life of violence and abuse.

Some countries are working towards positive changes.

Morocco's family code, the *Moudawana*, underwent reform in the 1990s thanks to pressure from women's movements. Reforms included raising the legal age of marriage to 18 and putting an end to male guardianship over adult women.[96] In 2014, Morocco also removed their "marry your rapist" law.

Tunisia, often the leader in the region, repealed a decree in 2017 that prohibited Muslim women from marrying non–Muslim men, the first action of this kind in the region.[97] Tunisia also enacted a Law on the Elimination of Violence Against Women in 2017 to address physical, political, economic, sexual, and moral violence against women. Here too, the "marry your rapist" law was rescinded. And, both women and men can file for divorce in Tunisia.

Yet, there is more to be done.

Even when discriminatory laws are removed and protections are in place, information asymmetry ensures that women and girls remain unaware of the legal provisions and protections to which they are entitled. So, if there are laws in place, they are unapplied, incomplete, or ignored. Government officials are also not trained in handling cases, or not interested in doing so. And, there are more men than women in legal and security fields, meaning that women are not likely to report, or the cases are not likely to be acted upon.

Countries fail to amend laws, authorities do not take adequate action, and perpetrators continue to enjoy impunity. Political bodies in the region are often unwilling to pass laws that may be controversial to religious leaders in order to retain the power of their political support. Support from religious leaders is often necessary to appease and maintain control over populations, and as such, it is viewed as indispensable. Additionally, legislative changes are not possible as long as old men of politics remain in power. Without a total overhaul of the patriarchal system, women will continue to be victimized in the name of "culture" and "tradition." This is nothing short of legalized misogyny. In the words of Lebanese feminist academic and activist Dr. Zeina Zaatari:

> When laws are written according to the prevalent social customs, the fate of those who dare defy them is often alienation from family and society, harassment and humiliation, and at worst violence, murder or imprisonment.[98]

Egregious Violence

Universal rights, freedoms, and opportunities cannot be named and claimed as long as women are unsafe in public and private space. Globally, one in three women worldwide has experienced some form of violence in their lifetime.[99] This drastically underestimates reality. The Arab region is no exception. It is estimated that 37 percent of women in the region have experienced some form of violence, but the real figure is probably far higher.[100] Definitions, rates, and reporting also vary from country to country.

Across the region, violence against women takes many forms. Intimate partner violence is the most common, and the least reported. In fact, women often fail to label intimate partner violence as violence. But when it is recognized as such, social stigma and family and community pressures keep women from reporting it. This is further hampered by lack of knowledge of—or access to—support, services, and safe spaces. And in the unlikely event that women seek access to justice, it is often not served.

More than one-third of women are affected, likely much more. The Arab region has the second-highest rate of prevalence worldwide.[101] Egypt recorded the highest numbers in the region, with approximately 86 percent of married women experiencing abuse. In Palestine, one study found 61 percent of those who have experienced such violence preferred to stay silent or not report.[102]

Intimate partner violence increased as a result of the pandemic. Lockdowns boosted violence across the region, trapping women with their abusers, making it more difficult to access help—or to escape. Crucial resources, services, and spaces were rerouted to COVID-19 responses meaning services for intimate partner violence—or non–COVID-19 related health services—were disrupted, and women suffered as a result. In Egypt, almost half of young women surveyed faced violence from their brothers and fathers.[103] Generally, across the region, male guardianship fuels this violence, granting men—as alleged "guardians"—authority to perpetuate violence against women.

Conflicts are breeding grounds for gendered inequalities, manifesting most dangerously in increased violence against women. Sexual violence is rampant in these settings. Sexual exploitation and abuse perpetrated by men in power is extremely common. Women experience assaults, abductions, virginity tests, and all forms of sexual violence at the hands of police, armed groups, militias, and soldiers. And as insecurities increase across the region, so too does trafficking and forced prostitution, along with other egregious abuses. Men continue to find ways to take advantage of and benefit from women's vulnerabilities—particularly in times of desperate need. And this violence does not end when the conflict ends. In fact, new forms are created, and longer-term violence and discrimination begin. In the aftermath, women experience increased intimate partner violence along with continued sexual violence.

So-called "honor killings" remain prevalent in the region. It has been said by many that there is nothing "honorable" about this. In the words of Sophie Bessis, Tunisian-French historian and feminist, "…the fact that women's bodies are the source of men's honor is the tragedy of women in this part of the world."[104] At the same time, Kuwaiti women's rights activist Dr. Alanoud Alsharekh rightly states, "In the West it's called a 'murder.' Not naming the problem is also the problem."[105]

No country in the Arab region publishes official figures of these murders, but the practice is common, well known, and silently condoned.[106] Figures from 2016 suggest Jordan registers between 15 and 20 reports each year.[107] Many more likely remain unregistered. Iraq, Jordan, Kuwait, Egypt, Palestine, and Lebanon all have had cases that garner media attention for a moment, but little action is taken. In 2022, several of these murders took place: both Naira Ashraf in Egypt and Iman Irshaid in Jordan were killed at their universities.[108] There are too many more whose names we do not know. In the case of Ashraf, at the time of writing, local media reported that the court was considering annulling the death sentence handed down to the murderer.[109]

In Libya and elsewhere in the region, even rape survivors face "honor killings" since rape is perceived to be more dishonorable than death, especially when it results in the loss of virginity. Even the use of social media for women becomes part of the narrative of dishonor: a woman can be punished or arrested simply for liking a photo that allegedly violates the "honor" of families.[110] According to a 2019 study conducted by Arab Barometer, "honor killing" is more acceptable than homosexuality in all the countries surveyed, namely, Algeria, Morocco, Sudan, Jordan, Tunisia, Lebanon, and Palestine.[111]

Female genital mutilation (FGM) also continues in the region, and beyond. The Arab region accounts for one quarter of all FGM cases globally.[112] Roughly 50 million girls and women have undergone the harmful practice in the region including Egypt, Djibouti, Sudan, and parts of Yemen and Iraq.[113] Egypt alone has the second highest percentage globally—86 percent of Egyptian women and girls aged 15–49 have undergone this form of abuse.[114] At the same time, while rates of FGM are high in those countries, the practice is all but absent in Morocco, Algeria, Libya, Saudi Arabia, and Tunisia.[115]

There are 700,000 girl-child brides in the region every year, and this figure is increasing alongside increased insecurities.[116] One in five girls in the region is married before the age of 18, and one in 25 is married before the age of 15.[117] Nine Arab states legally allow girls to marry before the age of 18.[118] This varies across the region where instances of girl-child marriage are high in Somalia, Yemen, and Iraq but very low in Algeria, Tunisia, and Qatar.[119]

Being a girl-child bride means a lifetime of lost opportunities, and a lifetime of abuses. These girls are denied their childhood, their education, and rights to their own health and safety. The damage done continues for generations. Girl-child marriage often entails marriage to an older man. And this often entails a sexual relationship—which amounts to rape of a girl-child. A 2018 study revealed that the sexual slavery of girls and women is directly correlated to increased instances of girl-child marriage in the Arab region.[120]

In Iraq and Syria, the Islamic State of Iraq and the Levant (ISIL) codified girl-child and forced marriages, while the armed militants of Al-Shabaab in Somalia have normalized girl-child marriage as an acceptable practice.[121] In too many cases, girl-child marriage becomes a culturally justified coping mechanism in times of conflicts in the Arab region. Families are often forced to sell their girls in order to have one less mouth to feed. And, as insecurities and conflicts continue, girl-child marriages increase as a response to ongoing crises. In short, this crime shows no sign of stopping.

The situation is worse for women and girls who are already vulnerable or marginalized. For instance, refugee and migrant women, women with disabilities, domestic workers, and women from ethnic or religious minorities are doubly discriminated against and more vulnerable to violence. They do not report for fear of arrest or deportation—or worse. For example, in Lebanon, two-thirds of female migrant domestic workers experience sexual harassment.[122] The *kafala* (sponsorship) system, common across the region but particularly prevalent in the Gulf countries, is a form of modern-day slavery.[123] Not only is the worker's status dependent on employer's sponsorship, but workers must seek permission from their employer to travel or transfer jobs. As the majority of female domestic labor is under the *kafala* system, many women are subject to exploitative working conditions and abusive treatment.

Even those on the frontlines of human rights advocacy experience abuse. Women human rights defenders face harassment, intimidation, and imprisonment across the region. Some are forced to live in exile or remain under travel bans. From the imprisonment of women's rights activists in Saudi Arabia who attempted to drive, to brutal crackdowns in Libya, even those who defend others cannot keep themselves safe.

Women and girls in the region continue to face violence and threats of violence. At the same time, women and girls lack bodily autonomy and integrity because, in the Arab region, "a woman's body belongs to the entire family."[124]

Despite legal reforms, cultural norms remain unchallenged—and unchanged. Even where laws exist, violence persists. There are gaps in legislation, implementation, accountability—and women's rights to bodily autonomy fall through these cracks. As long as violence against women and girls continues unabated, all other gains are moot. This is the greatest impediment to women's rights, and the greatest manifestation of misogyny.

How Did We Get Here?

> *The question of women is truly the question that enables us to really understand what liberty is. In the notion of liberty, there is freedom and equality. And if we don't have both at the same time, then we have nothing.*

Feminism is a political idea. We cannot think of feminism without political freedom, freedom of opinion.

—Wassyla Tamzali[125]

"We are celebrating the many achievements of Arab women ... but primarily in the art of survival." So said ESCWA Executive Secretary Rima Khalaf to commemorate International Women's Day in 2016.[126]

Years later, this still rings true.

In her chapter in the book *Arab Feminism—Obstacles and Possibilities: An Analytical Study of the Women's Movement in the Arab World*, Dr. Suad Zayed al-Oraimi explains:

> Though Arab feminism may indeed exist, it has not yet won social recognition. No intellectual change-seeking movement can rise and prosper without first going through a long struggle with those who wield influence in society, and on the decision-making process. It is also impossible for such a movement to form deep historical roots without a strong supportive and seasoned popular base. Feminist movements all over the world are born after much effort and a long struggle with the authorities and laws in effect; they are also the result of a bitter struggle by women who paid a heavy personal and social price, and the brainchild of women who suffered different forms of injustice.[127]

Given this somewhat bleak overview, we are prompted to ask: *How did the region get here? Why is it not further along? And, what is holding the region back?*

These questions cannot be answered by facts and figures. Chapter 5 will explore the challenges in depth from the perspectives of those who formed the crux of this book. The below serves as an orientation and starting point.

Women in the Arab region face a complex web of barriers across every aspect of their lives. But above all else, the problem is patriarchy. This is the greatest crime of our time. In the words of feminist journalist Mona Eltahawy: "The biggest challenge in the world and the biggest form of oppression across the world, regardless of where you live, is patriarchy. It's the form of oppression that straddles the world."[128] The deep-seated nature of patriarchy allows for these abuses to continue, actively holding women back from any semblance of progress.

Arab governments govern through patriarchy. They prevent, restrict, suffocate movements for equality and often reinforce structural inequalities and negative socio-cultural norms and practices that are found within the law.[129] Too many Arab states condone, and implement, restrictive policies that limit the choice, voice, and potential of women and girls.

Along with patriarchy, conflict is a character in the story. In fact, it has a leading role. National, regional, and global insecurities fuel—and are fueled by—socio-political and economic insecurities. Conflict and occupation are inescapable realities that cross borders. We know from global experience that conflict brings greater gender inequalities and greater human rights violations, specifically women's rights violations. And the Arab region has more than its share of political and economic instability, as we have mentioned. In times of crisis, resources are scant, services are few, rule of law is absent, and society is fragmented—not the best conditions for women's rights to flourish. And of course, the pandemic has impacted everything—for the worse. The region has a heightened susceptibility to crises, but the pandemic further amplified the long term challenges that already plague the region. Those most affected were women who were already "living on the periph-ery."[130] The cycle of crisis continues, and the region—and its women—remains on shaky ground.

While many of these challenges lie within the region, global geopolitics has a role to play. Feminist researcher Dr. Gabriella Nassif argues that it is not sim-ply about "interference from the West" but rather about those in power who play puppet-politics, bolstering leaders that they claim to hate—but still support—in order for the West to benefit. Even as they claim that these leaders "aren't good for wom-en's rights or for gender and sexual minorities," Dr. Nassif explains, Western nations "still support these dictators, and they still support these regimes because financially they're good for the West."[131]

Reinforcing this view, academic Dr. Najla Hamadeh adds:

> The dominant currents that support world feminism today still oppose the objectives of Arab feminism. The international order is only interested in hybridizing the reality of Arab women, while it continues to support the very authorities that insist on discriminating against them.[132]

And, anyway, as Palestinian-American anthropologist Dr. Lila Abu-Lughod famously asked: "Do Muslim Women Really Need Saving?"[133] While her question focuses specif-ically on the "rhetoric of rescue," the moral crusade to save Muslim women from their own cultures following September 11, 2001, her analysis can be extended to the region as a whole and continues to be relevant today.[134]

As we addressed in the previous section, inequality is embedded in the law. "There's just no legal equality," explains Dr. Nassif. She continues, "so even when you're living in a state that might have a law that, supposedly, protects your rights, it's very rare that the state is actually going to implement or enforce that law."

We might argue that even when laws are improving, and even when support for women is increasing, such changes are microscopic when compared with women's realities. Gender inequalities and denial of women's rights persist—and in some cases increase. Women in the region continue to live with great risk and are not safe in their lives, in their homes, in school, in public places, in public office. Without safety in our bodies and our lives, all other rights are futile.

In these contexts, feminisms become all the more important—and all the more challenging.

What Are the Questions Worth Exploring?

> *The Arab mind is in crisis. And because of this it wants everyone to be in crisis with it…. The Arab mind cannot handle questions, because questions can hurt and upset the murky calm of the swamp.*
>
> —Joumana Haddad[135]

The questions below come from our review of existing literature and our expe-rience in the region. Building from these, we expected certain themes to emerge that might present resistance to feminisms in the region. These obvious obstacles are not meant to be an exhaustive list, and there are surely many other reasons feminisms in the region remain obstructed. However, these are a starting point, an invitation to explore where the synergies and disconnects might be. More important are the themes that emerge from the voices of people from the region, as explored throughout this book.

What Is "Arab Feminism"?

Academic and author Mervat Hatem tells us that "there is a need for a critical retrospective assessment of the history of the feminist projects in the region that reflects and privileges the voices of women instead of the dominant views of men."[136]

In undertaking this critical assessment, we might ask: *What is Arab feminism? Or—Arab feminisms?*

While feminism has many interpretations, we feel Lebanese feminist academic Dr. Zeina Zaatari captures the spirit of our feminism in describing it as an ideology that aims to overthrow the patriarchy. This notion is built on the practice of prioritizing men, therefore power is imbalanced, asymmetrical, and needs to be adjusted.[137]

Is there an Arab feminism? This book sets out to explore this question, but we begin with some reflections.

When it comes to understandings of Arab feminisms, we do not assume an Arab homogeneity, nor the idea that there exists a "single Arab feminist perspective." Feminisms have evolved as a result of socio-political and ideological shifts in the Arab region. Saudi Arabian novelist Dr. Badriah al-Beshr notes that "there are different versions of [feminism] and these can vary depending on the political and social circumstances of a place."[138] This idea of feminism implying the existence of numerous forms is further explained by Dr. Sahar Khamis, as "...never a 'one size fits all' type of feminism," emphasizing the various cultural, political, and socio-economic situations that exist in the region and thus require different definitions of feminism.[139]

In Dr. Maya Mikdashi's article on *How to Study Gender in the Middle East*, she reminds us that we cannot "...assume that gender politics or feminist concerns come in neat and familiar packages."[140] While this is true globally, she explains that the region in fact has a "long history of considering questions of gender rights."

Feminist activist scholar Dr. Charlotte Karam articulates that "there is absolutely such a thing as Arab feminism," animated by different forms and "tied to different paradigms of knowledge and different grounding assumptions about the world."[141] "What ties them all together," she continues, "is a genuine commitment to creating more opportunities for women and girls to live more dignified lives." This comes in many forms: "having greater access to learning, a livable dignified wage, more freedoms in terms of body rights and basic human rights." Dr. Karam concludes that "there are some shared ways of seeing the world, but also a lot of complexities, ways of defining what dignity is or defining what a dignified life would look like, basic differences that cause conflict between different Arab feminisms."

While there is a burgeoning literature on Arab feminisms, research is still insufficient. In other words, whatever evidence we have does *not* give us the full picture. Anyway, feminisms are not limited to documented evidence. Many movements existed but remain unrecorded and unrepresented. In short, our history is incomplete. Ultimately, the voices in these pages will tell us if Arab feminisms exist, what shape they take, and where they are going.

Is It the Word or the Deed?

In the Arab region, there is no universal acceptance of the concept of "feminism," nor what it means or how it translates. *What does feminism mean to those in the region? And do they even want to claim it?*

The terms "Arab feminism" or "feminist" alone spark negative reactions from conservative societies throughout the region, frequently causing activists to lose energy defending the actual term rather than what it represents.[142] In a 2003 study interviewing women in the Arab region about their thoughts on the term, a few expressed that "feminism" is useful, with one study participant noting that it "denotes women's struggle for their rights and the defense of their interests."[143] Others took issue with the term but recognized its relative necessity, stating that "language cannot perfectly reflect our understanding of the world."

Gender, and its related terms—gender equality, gender mainstreaming—are even more complicated. In Arabic, there is no straightforward translation of the word "gender." Although Arabic is itself a gendered language, the word gender remains a challenge to translate, and even harder to understand and apply. According to Egyptian literary professor, Dr. Samia Mehrez:

> There is a whole array of translations that range from *al-bu'd al-junūsi* (the gender dimension) to *dirāsat al-nau'* (studies of kind), to *al-tashakkul al-thaqāfi wa'l-ijtimā'i li'l-jins* (the cultural and social construction of sex), to an outright refusal to translate the concept of "gender" since it is perceived as a Western introduction for which there is no Arabic translation.[144]

Language matters. It offers expression, and as a result, opportunity for representation and empowerment. As a reflection of society and identity, language is constantly evolving. Evolutions of our understanding enable language to be more inclusive—and words to represent the diversities of sex and gender are a case in point. For instance, there has been significant progress in the region in developing LGBTQ+ terminologies. As one example, activists in Lebanon and Palestine have been instrumental in (re)appropriating language to be inclusive of sexual identities. Shifting vocabulary, mixing Arabic and English words, coining new terms, and playing with words has allowed them to create positive expressions of LGBTQ+ terms in Arabic.[145] As these words evolve, so too will the understanding of the meanings behind them.

Many who demonstrate feminist actions and principles still eschew the term, preferring other terminology such as activist or advocate of gender equality. In the end, the words matter less as long as there are commitments and actions. As long as there is a movement.

Is There a Movement?

Dr. Zaatari tells us that while "we may not be able to say for sure that there exists today a solid freestanding Arab women's movement," there are many regional and class-based movements.[146] She continues to explain that until these distinct movements find synergies and forge alliances, Arab feminisms will remain fragmented.

Palestinian scholar Jean Said Makdisi adds that "the cautious strategies of the women's movements" can claim certain successes, but "have not achieved the kind of wide support—especially from the mass of women—that is required for truly radical change."[147] In other words, mild reforms are insufficient, particularly when a radical restructure is required. Makdisi posits that campaigns centered on singular issues are part of the problem. Not only does this highlight a lack of synergy, it also highlights women's lack of power as they pursue issues or change that is most likely to be effected in the limited space they have. This ad hoc or "step by step" approach reaches for realistic goals and avoids making larger claims or challenging the oppressive structures. In effect, this is not a direct feminist stance and "many of them unambiguously denounce feminism." As a result, successes have been scant Makdisi explains, because "they have not been backed by a sufficiently active or widespread feminism."[148] *How, then, to lay the foundation for widespread feminism? And, in such a diverse region, is that even possible?*

Young academic and activist Maria Najjar reminds us that Arab feminists have attempted to foster regional alliances in the past.[149] Egypt is widely regarded as having the region's oldest organized feminist movement. And the first feminist union, the Egyptian Feminist Union, was established in 1923.[150] The Union convened the Arab Feminist Congress in Cairo in 1944, leading to the formation of the Arab Feminist Union. This Union was in response to calls for Arab nationalism and independence, and also a reflection of the disconnect with international feminist movements. The Union survived for over a decade, but no longer exists.

Feminist academic Dr. Hoda Elsadda believes a possible reason for the disconnect in Arab feminisms is due to the existence of "several Arab feminist languages" that are often in operation in isolation of each other. The lack of intersection is a challenge and, as such, Dr. Elsadda explains, "for historical and political reasons, Arab feminism is in a highly volatile inbetween space that impacts directly and indirectly on how matters develop, including questions on language, identity, strategies of confrontation, and resistance."[151]

Myriam Sfeir, Director of The Arab Institute for Women, the region's first academic and activist institute focused on women, reminds us that:

> There is no "one woman" in the region. There are so many women, and the conditions that are deemed desirable vary from country to country and sometimes even within the same country from area to area. The region is very diverse. Even though we speak the same language, we don't look at things from the same perspective.[152]

Feminisms across the region—religious and secular, modern and conservative—exist in their plurality. Our diversities and divisions are not insignificant.

Najjar asserts that a Pan-Arab Feminism "has less to do with an imagined collectivity based on a shared identity as Arab women, and more to do with an alliance constructed on the basis of an active struggle against the various manifestations of patriarchy."[153] In other words, perhaps we have more in common across the region than we think.

This time, we might argue that Pan-Arab Feminism has a better chance of success because it could channel the momentum, agency, and anger of the so-called Arab Spring. The voices in this book will tell us.

At the same time, we know the challenges are massive, and resistance to feminisms can be strong.

Is Feminism "Western"?

Feminisms exist all around the world. And, feminisms are resisted all around the world. And yet, the need for feminism was born out of resistance. In non–Western countries, one of the most common ways to counter feminism is to label it as "Western." In the Arab region, opponents of women's rights usually argue that feminism is not relevant to Arab culture, but rather is seen to be "the adoption and adaptation of Western ideals, values and ways of life."[154] Many argue that feminism is a Western import and imposition, a new manifestation of an old colonialist agenda, an attempt to corrupt and control "our women" by turning them against men. And on and on it goes. We have heard it all before.

Such posturing ignores the social contexts which have influenced the ideological evolution of feminisms in the region. This view is essentially invalidating an indigenous Arab feminist movement—a feminism that was born out of the social, political, and economic contexts specific to the region. In the words of one writer, it is:

> …impossible to reduce the Arab feminist experience to just an imported or quoted idea, rather, it is an authentic experience that not only confronted the conservative Arab patriarchal society but also the Western Orientalist view that assumes that women in Muslim-majority societies are always marginalized, and the means of Western media portraying Arab women as victims, oppressed and submissive, in general.[155]

In societies with elements of opposition to the West, labeling feminism as Western fortifies "views that Arabness and feminism are necessarily opposed," making it more difficult for feminisms to gain traction.[156] As a result, culture and tradition are weaponized to counter these "foreign" ideologies, denying the indigenous manifestations of feminism that have long existed in the region. In her book *Embodying Geopolitics: Generations of Women's Activism in Egypt, Jordan, and Lebanon*, Dr. Nicola Pratt, academic at the University of Warwick, argues that we need to challenge these "Western frameworks" and the "binary thinking that associates women's participation and women's rights with Western/secular culture and, conversely, views Arab-Muslim culture as the cause of women's oppression."[157] Reinforcing this, Dr. Alanoud Alsharekh adds:

> I believe that feminist progression is an organic act. These first attempts were very "Arab," and I don't like when people say that feminists were influenced by the West! The desire to be treated like a human being is universal.[158]

Further, the binary distinction between public and private space, assumed to be a core component of "Western" feminism, is problematic when applied to the life of women in the Arab region. Women exert influence in the public sphere through family structures as the primary unit in Arab society.[159] Avoiding this binary reveals the multidimensionality of women in the region, along with their resistance to social injustices—*their* feminisms.

As well as accusations of being Western, feminist movements in the Arab region must simultaneously overcome Western assumptions. Western misrepresentation of women in the Arab region has always been repackaged colonialism and Orientalism.[160] In fact, as feminist activist and scholar Dr. Therese Saliba posits:

> …the West has imposed on the region … conceptions of time, history, geography but also transnational economic structures, globalized/US culture, and even its own brand of liberal feminism.[161]

Inaccurate and essentializing depictions of women from the region abound. Feminists from the region, and worldwide, therefore must work to deconstruct—and remake these images, in line with their *own* feminisms.

Arab feminisms have evolved. Chapter 2 will explore these phases, each of which is a reflection of its social, cultural, political environment. And each of which has been met with resistance for allegedly being a Western import. Some iterations of Arab feminisms were influenced by international presence and geopolitical events, while others took on resistance to imperialism in national struggles.

Do Feminisms and Nationalisms Coexist?

Feminisms cannot be separated from their socio-political contexts. Women's movements in the Arab region have, in some instances, developed alongside national movements struggling for independence. This is particularly pertinent in colonized countries, where "legacies of colonialism [have shaped] the relationships between gender, state building, and national sovereignty."[162] Dr. Mounira Charrad's work on Tunisia, Algeria, and Morocco, as well as Dr. Nadje Al-Ali's documentation of Egypt and Palestine, add to the discourse on women's rights in the Arab world by anchoring analysis in national struggles and in the "political and historical contexts surrounding independence from colonial rule."[163] Still, according to gender and women's studies professor Dr. Nawar Al-Hassan Golley, some feminisms were "born out of the struggle between the dying, traditional, religious, feudal Ottoman way of life and the rising, modern, secular, capitalist European ways of life."[164] Ultimately, inequality is not simply just a consequence of cultural or religious problems, and women's activism in the region can be linked to regional and international geopolitics as well as national political contexts. Dr. Pratt reminds us to look at:

> How dominant gender norms have been historically produced in relation to colonialism and neocolonialism, how these gender norms have both enabled and constrained women's activism and women's rights, and how women's activism and women's rights have served to reproduce and to disrupt dominant geopolitical power, depending upon the historical context.[165]

National struggles can both support and sideline women. On the one hand, they can provide women with a platform to claim greater roles and, ultimately, rights. Contemporary movements led by young women in Palestine, Syria, Egypt, Yemen, and Sudan are a case in point. However, too often, the national struggle supersedes the feminist struggle. There is no national liberation—and no nation at all, in fact—without women's involvement.

In her article *From Women's Rights to Feminism: The Urgent Need for an Arab Feminist Renaissance*, feminist academic and activist Dr. Zeina Zaatari writes that "women were used by the national movements for the purpose of expanding their bases of support, without proposing any comprehensive programme to change the patriarchal criteria of society."

Building on this, in their book on Arab Feminisms, Jean Said Makdisi, Noha Bayoumi, and Rafif Rida Sidawi write:

> The place of feminism in this context is extremely problematic, as nationalist, sectarian, religious and class interests, not to mention the interests of occupation authorities and the resistance movements that oppose them, override feminism as a public concern, even among

many women. Feminists are either co-opted by these interests or find themselves in the frustrating position of negotiating their way through a minefield of contradictory imperatives and loyalties.[166]

At the same time, while women are on the frontlines, they end up excluded from decision-making. They are often on the streets, but hardly ever at the table. Even when independence is achieved, women remain marginalized. There is irony in detaching national independence from women's independence. In the words of Dr. Al-Hassan Golley:

> The call for women's freedom, for example, is instantly challenged by men, who might very well believe in equality between the sexes, arguing that, in the light of the oppressive regimes that prevail in most Arab countries, women cannot be free because men are not free either.[167]

Women fight two patriarchal fronts at once: against foreign men who occupy their nation, and against their own men who occupy their lives. As a result, women are further oppressed on both fronts—occupier or occupied.

Palestine is a clear example of the interconnectedness of nationalism and feminism on the one hand, and conservatism and exclusion on the other. The struggle for Palestinian sovereignty continues to be at the center of feminist debates, with feminists viewing this as an opportunity to advocate for women's rights in nation-building. Despite their strong roles in defending the nation, women remain excluded. Palestinian nationalist rhetoric can, in some instances, be linked to Hamas, the Islamic resistance movement, which has aided the "resurgence of traditional thought" and therefore is no friend to women.[168] How, then, might women embrace both feminism *and* nationalism?

Post-independence Egypt, Jordan, and Yemen also saw the marginalization of women and the repression of feminist movements. And as with Palestine, this is often accompanied by a call to return to traditional roles. This is not unique to the Arab region, clearly, but the expectations of "traditional female submission" are particularly acute.[169]

The case of Algeria is similar, with the anti-colonial nationalist struggle heavily dominated by men. Here, too, women recognized their own dual oppression. In the words of Algerian female activists:

> You make a revolution, you fight colonialist oppression but you maintain the oppression of women; beware, another revolution will certainly occur after Algeria's independence: a women's revolution![170]

Both the colonizers and the colonized seem to agree on the oppression of women, with disregard for the role women play in anti-colonial struggles. This dual patriarchy has, in many cases, galvanized women into action, even as it is harder for them to do so.

In this colonial and post-colonial landscape, women's bodies are the battleground. And occupation is both of countries and women's bodies. These are the dual sites of colonization. Women, women's bodies, and women's rights continue to be pawns in the struggle between western, capitalist forces, and old, traditional ones.[171]

Resisting colonialisms and fighting patriarchy are one and the same—whether the patriarch is foreign or national.

What About Religion, Culture, and Tradition?

And then, there's religion. In particular, Islam. Too often, there are new edicts and proclamations about whether or not Islam and feminism can co-exist. Islam plays a role, yes, but not all Arab populations are Muslim. And not all Muslims are feminists, or anti-feminists, or whatever political project is at play.

While this is an ongoing discussion, many prominent feminist thinkers have offered theories on this subject. Dr. Huda Shaarawi, considered the founder of the women's movement in Egypt, sought women's rights within an Islamic framework. She is well known for organizing the "March of Veiled Women" in Cairo and she also famously removed her face veil in a train station, as an act of protest, on her way back from the International Women Suffrage Alliance conference.[172] The early Egyptian feminist movement was able to advance the nationalist cause while also working within the parameters of Islam. Dr. Hoda Badran also dismantles the belief that feminism and Islam are not compatible and instead links the feminist agenda to national activism as part of women's efforts to claim voice and space in society.

The region is home to a Muslim-majority population, however other religions exist. Arab Christians—and their various factions—are present across the region. Other faiths exist to a lesser extent. Regardless of the faith, religion continues to play a major role in understanding and accepting—or rejecting—feminism. Religious women from the region prefer to see their rights within the frameworks of their own religions, and are more likely to be accepting of those rights if they align with their religious views.

Religion cannot be divorced from the socio-economic and political context in which it exists.[173] There are a range of religions, with myriad—often conflicting—views on just about everything. However, they all restrict women in different ways, even those with supposedly more liberal views. At the same time, faith has a strong hold, and the region is perpetually balancing religion and rights.

And then, there is the veil. Much has been said about the veil and all aspects of covering, the denial of agency, the perception of oppression—and the subsequent need for "liberation." There remains a divided stance among women regarding the social practice of veiling but ultimately, as Dr. Al-Hassan Golley remarked, "both wearing the veil and discarding it in different situations should be seen as symbolizing political struggle and women's political agency."[174]

At their inaugural conference, Dr. Nawal El Saadawi's Arab Women's Solidarity Association (AWSA), even used the slogan "Removing the veil from the mind."[175] El Saadawi, a socialist feminist anti-imperialist, rejected the oppressive use of Islam and fundamentalism but simultaneously countered Western misunderstandings and critiques of Islam.[176] As she writes in *The Hidden Face of Eve,* "it is important that Arab women should not feel inferior to Western women, or think that the Arabic tradition and culture are more oppressive of women than Western culture."[177]

Studies have shown that framing gender equality in the context of religion can be a powerful strategy for greater uptake, particularly in more conservative Muslim communities.[178] The (in)compatibility of feminism and religion remains an evolving conversation, as the voices from Chapter 5 reveal.

Are We Intersectional and Inclusive?

Men can—and should—be feminists. Men from the Arab region too. Regional and global evidence reveals that engaging men and understanding (read: reforming) masculinities can advance feminist gains. The fight against patriarchy is collective, and equality benefits everyone. Men and boys need to be engaged in undoing patriarchal hierarchies of power.[179] The 2017 International Men and Gender Equality MENA Survey, focusing on Palestine, Egypt, Morocco, and Lebanon, was the first to examine men's concepts of masculinity and attitudes towards equality. The study revealed that most men support "a wide array of inequitable, traditional attitudes."[180] At the same time, a "sizable minority" supports women's rights and equality. This was unsurprising, and is likely true throughout the rest of the region.

In terms of inclusion, stronger alliances can also be formed between LGBTQ+ and feminist activists. Current relations between feminist and LGBTQ+ organizations vary. Some argue that there is a need to focus on "women only," while others assert that true feminism means being fully intersectional. While we advocate for the latter, this continues to be a subject of debate.

What is not up for debate is treatment of LGBTQ+ populations across the Arab region. These communities continue to experience "severe and pervasive human rights violations" including "extrajudicial killings, to mass arrests to censorship of pro–LGBT speech."[181] Same-sex relations and non-conforming gender expressions are criminalized, with sentences ranging from arrest to death. Yet, activists and ally organizations in the region continue to fight against criminalization and discrimination. Protests across the region have brought small successes for the movement—but also significant backlash. Despite this, LGBTQ+ activism "survives under severe constraints, in repressive states and conflict zones, in places where activists risk social exclusion, prison sentences, and violence by security forces, armed groups, and even their own families."[182]

While human rights causes are often aligned, there is much more room to ally with LGBTQ+ populations in the feminist quest for rights and justice. Ultimately, research shows that there is more work to be done in engaging men to promote women's rights and in forging solidarities with LGBTQ+ activists.

Are We Collaborating and Coordinating—or Competing?

Evidence and experience revealed that feminisms are scattered, further hampered by the lack of willingness to collaborate, whether due to differences in priorities, ideologies, or tactics. Feminist groups are too few, too small, and too underfunded. The dire need of funding impedes collaboration, instead fueling competition between women's organizations as donors (sometimes inadvertently) pit organizations against each other in a fight for funding scraps.

To use one example, in a case study of Egypt's women's movement, it was revealed that "competition and rivalry—often revolving around the wish to guarantee funding and resources ... frequently blocks collective action."[183] The direction of donor resources has also redirected projects—sometimes away from community needs and toward donor priorities. The result is that projects are crippled, no longer meaningful or sustainable, and real needs on the ground remain unmet.

Divisions between women's groups are also fostered by governments. In Tunisia, for instance, the state placed heavy restrictions on the Association of Democratic Women while offering large sums of funding to government-sponsored women's groups.[184] In doing so, they reinforce the groups whose messages align with government priorities, and, by extension, stifle those who oppose. This is not unique to Tunisia. In such settings, the role—and survival—of women's groups is even more critical. Solidarity and collaboration is therefore essential to their survival.

What Happens to Women in Power?

As we have said before, women in power are too few—and often when in positions of power, they tend to sideline feminist causes for party politics. Women in political power are less likely to use their platform for feminism, but rather to serve other interests. The result is further fractures in feminist movements, including a class division, where state *co-opted* feminists disregard the majority—in particular women of minority or vulnerable groups. Indeed, this discrimination transcends politics. For instance, the efforts of early Arab feminists to address women's employment, education, divorce, and inheritance laws, were perceived as lacking voices from rural or underprivileged women.[185]

Further, when feminist movements center women's political participation, this inherently prioritizes women who have the capacity and ability to pursue civic engagement. As one activist from Sudan puts it:

> The concept of a women's movement is sometimes limited to political participation, leading to targeting women from the urban areas and neglecting the rural areas. This means lack of communication between educated and uneducated women.[186]

More than lack of communication, we argue. This actually sets the feminist movement back by rendering it elitist, and therefore irrelevant to local realities.

Governments are also a major dividing force within Arab feminisms. State *co-opted* feminists, or women in power who choose to promote party politics over feminism, are ideal candidates for governments looking to bolster their images by displaying women as prominent figures while ensuring that women's status will not actually change. The UN Arab Human Development report reminds us that "attempts to bring forward women loyal to the ruling party" are not only common, but a key feature "in all the Arab countries, a political peculiarity that springs from the nature of the official ruling regimes."[187] State *co-opted* feminists are not in fact feminists. And therein lies the problem.

What About the Diaspora?

It is estimated that there are up to 20 million Arabs living outside of the region, whether by force or by choice. The diaspora undoubtedly plays a role in impacting the region from abroad. The economic impact of financial remittances to support development "back home" have been well documented.[188] At the same time, political remittances—the transfer of political ideas, norms, and practices—are an increasing phenomenon.[189] Mobilization of the diaspora has an impact on Arab politics and plays a role in accepting or rejecting new ideas. Additionally, those in the diaspora who return to the region bring with them "new" or "foreign" ideas that have an impact on those who remained.

The diaspora are a force that can be mobilized for political purposes. The advocacy work they undertake in their new countries could serve to (re)shape public opinion and foreign policy, including directing the course of development funding. For instance in the U.S., advocacy groups such as the American-Arab Anti-Discrimination Committee and the Arab American Institute, think tanks such as the Middle East Institute, and cultural groups such as Arab America are increasing in popularity, and are helping to bridge the gap between the diaspora and the region.[190] Ultimately, the diaspora may have a strong(er) role to play in supporting Arab feminisms—both "here" and "there."

Are We Intergenerational?

Both the literature and our understanding of feminist movements led us to believe that engaging youth in the region would be a critical aspect of our findings. In fact, this book is built from this very premise.

The Arab region has a very young population—young people (15–29 years) account for 30 percent, or 110 million, of the region's population.[191] This younger generation has proven to be more willing—and more courageous—in their fight for social justice and equality. Their causes and tactics differ, and as such this also results in a growing generational divide. As documented in a case study of Egypt's women's movement:

> Generational differences may be discerned concerning a woman's specific attitudes towards secularism and religion, where younger women tend to be much more open to the idea of reinterpretation of religion in order to counter conservative male interpretations.[192]

Despite the region's overwhelmingly young population, research and evidence shows that youth are still struggling to become "a key driving force for social and economic development of their countries."[193] As Honey Al Sayed, Syrian media consultant and activist says, "local and international political powers and policymakers tend to ignore the power of women and youth in the MENA region, a bountiful power that has not yet been leveraged."[194] Young women in particular are pushing socio-cultural boundaries and struggle to create space and opportunities to influence change and reform policy.[195]

So What? Now What?!

> *A well-developed feminist movement can breach the wall surrounding what is acceptable to society, and liberate both men and women from these shackles. A feminist thought that seeks to destroy the patriarchal systems in conjunction with the political, religious, economic and sectarian structures could provide the opportunity to address all these sexual, bodily, economic and identity issues (that many call human rights)....*
> —Dr. Zeina Zaatari[196]

This chapter lays the foundation for the conversation that is to come.

As we have said, it is true that no country in the world has achieved gender equality. And specifically in the Arab region, women do not enjoy equal rights or equal opportunities as men. In fact, women in the region must fight the same battles time and again.

At the same time, feminism has a rich tradition in the Arab region. Feminist movements in the region have always been present. Feminism did not need to be delivered to the Arab region. It always existed here. It is not singular or homogenous. It is home-grown and indigenous, born from local contexts and driven by denial of rights—and by desperate need. We would argue that feminisms are fueled by anger.

In the Arab region, that anger is righteous—and long overdue.

Even if feminisms are not documented, they exist in the everyday, in the informal, in the spaces we do not always see or hear. Resistance in the seemingly small gestures and acts that, over time, make a big impact. Even when met with major backlash and crackdown, suffocation of space, or stifled activity, the movements exist. Their persistence is also the resistance.

Action in the small spaces is just as valuable, and oftentimes the most powerful resistance is not always a big public display but rather a tiny push for change—micro-movements and micro-rebellions that result in big changes over time. That is not to suggest that progress should move at a snail's pace, nor are we advocating patience while minuscule progress is made. Rather, we acknowledge resistance in all its forms—visible and invisible—and the power it holds.

At the same time, we seek to avoid generalizations. As we stated earlier, there is no one unique Arab region, or Arab perspective, or Arab feminism. There are differences and diversities within countries and communities and families. There are differences in rural and urban areas. There are differences in local and national processes. There are differences in private and public feminisms. There are differences in policy and in practice. There are differences at home and on the streets. All of these are frontlines. All of these have fissures. And all of these are feminisms. And perhaps our difference is our strength.

Each new generation of women has, we hope, been granted greater freedoms and opportunities than their predecessors. They have fought for these gains, standing on the shoulders of our feminist foremothers, including those whose names we may never know. These are women whose work has paved the way and created ripple effects for generations. This story seeks to recognize and acknowledge some of these feminist pioneers and trailblazers, to shine a light on their contributions. In doing so, we can begin to understand our history with its gains and fissures, and our future, with its entry points to equality. We now step back and take a long view, examining the non-linear progressions of feminist phases over the last fifty years.

Across the world, women are charged with the burden of fighting for their own freedoms. For generations, women in the Arab region have been standing up for their rights. And with each generation, new energy and new strategies are gained. And so the fight continues. As Moroccan activist Fatima Ezzahraa El Fattah put it, "The past is a building block that we need to stand on to move to our next future and to adapt to global changes including ... the universalization of human rights."[197]

Is feminism a luxury or a necessity, one writer asks?[198] We argue for the latter. Feminism, ultimately, is a means to an end. It is a catalyst for change. What sort of change, we ask? There need not be any consensus in movement, discourse, or manifestations. There need be consensus in our goal of liberation from the patriarchy and pursuit of full freedom.

The bulk of this book is dedicated to the feminist voices in the region, particularly young people, as they are the strongest force for that freedom. For feminist freedom. We allow the words of young people to determine the direction of our story. It is through their voices and actions that the Arab region will be reimagined.

With all that being said, our story begins fifty years ago, even as we recognize that the foundations of feminism in the region existed before this. A brief background is necessary to explore the origins of feminisms in the Arab region—and the shape it has taken over the last decades. We need to know where we've come from to know where we're going—or to go anywhere at all.

2

Feminist Phases

The Arab woman who is equal to the man in duties and obligations will not accept, in the twentieth century, the distinctions between the sexes that the advanced countries have done away with. The Arab woman will not agree to be chained in slavery and to pay for the consequences of men's mistakes with respect to her country's rights and the future of her children.
—Dr. Huda Shaarawi[1]

The following chapter breaks down the different phases of feminism in the Arab region over the last 50 years.[2] It is not a simple undertaking, to outline common themes and trends in a range of countries with such great diversities. The countries themselves, their occupants, and their journeys toward (or away from) equality are all very distinct stories. Moreover, contrary to popular understanding, women in the Arab region are not an all-encompassing, homogenous category. Their movements are a reflection of their great diversity within the region.

Nonetheless, there are overarching phases that can be gleaned from this diverse history and from conversations with activists and experts. Ultimately, this (re)organization of Arab feminist history orients us and paves the way for discussions that bring in the voices of feminists and activists from the Arab region. They serve as guides to determine what has happened in the region—and what needs to happen—to maintain and fuel a feminist movement.

Overall, our feminist history encompasses some broad trends. Conflict, in all its forms, has undoubtedly played a leading role. Religion, too, has produced disconnects among activists and the pursuit of secular or religious frameworks and agendas. The predominance of state feminism in early state-building, manifesting as state *co-opted* feminism, has also obfuscated a genuine feminist agenda. Additionally, external narratives, often incorrectly viewing women in the region as oppressed, have made an impact. These trends have ebbed and flowed throughout history, creating both challenges and opportunities for national and regional movement-building and solidarity.

Iterations of feminisms in the region have evolved from these patterns, enabling us to delineate feminist phases. So, while we recognize the complexities (and hazards) in making broad generalizations, we can nonetheless flesh out different phases of women's activisms and feminisms in the Arab region. For ease of reference, and for a better understanding of the feminist trajectory in the region, we have chosen to delineate the following phases:

1. Reawakening (1970–1980)
2. Galvanizing (1981–1999)

3. Agitating (2000–2011)
4. Regressing (2012 2022)
5. Collaborating (2023-onwards)

We have dubbed the years 1970 to 1980 as *Reawakening* due to the renewed activity and attention given to women's rights and feminist movements throughout the region during this period. While feminist movements existed prior to this, this period saw increased documentation and action. This section highlights the rise of women's political rights internationally and their impact in the Arab region. The events that took place during this period—and the role women played in mobilizing for these events—redefined Islamic feminism as both liberation and repression.

The period we have called *Galvanizing* covers the early 1980s and extends until the end of the 1990s. Feminist movements and women's activism in the region increased during this period. The reform of personal status laws was a key issue for women's organizations in the region. They had been campaigning for reform before this period, but gained momentum during this time. Women's rights became an important agenda for Arab states, represented by the image of a secular woman, especially on the international stage. Countries made commitments to international entities to address women's rights and human rights in order to present themselves as "modern." As a result, many ratified the Convention on the Elimination of All Forms of Discrimination against Women (CEDAW) in the wake of the Fourth World Conference on Women in Beijing in 1995. At the same time, several states challenged the spirit of the Convention by entering multiple reservations. Reservations are made when states do not wish to comply with certain provisions in the treaty but do not go against the main purpose of the treaty. For example, many states have made reservations to articles in CEDAW that are, in their view, in conflict with national laws, tradition, culture, or religion—in particular *Shari'a* law.[3]

In the 2000s we entered the *Agitating* phase. This decade begins with a long frustration in the region stemming from a desire for better governance and an end to corruption. It ends with region-wide mass mobilization in protest of authoritarian regimes. Fires were ignited across the region. Arab governments attempted to respond to these calls for human rights by creating their own commissions to "put a positive spin on the government's record while trying to divert attention from [ongoing] violations."[4] Collectively, these factors contributed to the eruption of the so-called Arab Spring pro-democracy uprisings of 2011. Women played a leading role in activism and protest, redefining the perception of women's role in the public sphere in a highly visible representation of women exerting their freedom.

The years after the 2011 pro-democracy uprisings led to severe crackdowns—a period we named *Regressing*—characterized by backsliding in many ways, particularly for women's rights. This post–Arab Spring phase, contrary to hopes and expectations, resulted in shrinking civil society space, repression of freedoms, and brutal retaliation to largely unsuccessful democratic transitions. The COVID-19 global health pandemic also played a significant role in reversing gains with regard to violence against women, women's economic empowerment, and the care economy.

This phase leads us to the present day, where the region faces myriad national crises and socio-economic challenges which thwart efforts to move forward. This is further evidenced by the fact that the region as a whole continues to rank among the lowest in terms of all social indicators—particularly gender equality. Protracted crises, deteriorating economic conditions, and fundamentalist movements often go hand in hand. We assert that feminist movements and women's leadership are critical to counter these backsliding trends.

As such, we call this phase *Collaborating* in hopes that feminisms in the Arab region will foster greater collaboration across national, religious, and ideological divides. And there are positive signs of collaboration at the national level that can be scaled. For example, the repeal of the so-called "marry your rapist" law in Lebanon, Tunisia, and Jordan within three weeks of each other after collective civil society efforts. These followed similar moves by Egypt who repealed the "marry your rapist" law in 1999 and Morocco who repealed it in 2014, demonstrating that civil society collaboration and coalition-building are effective.[5] In spite of—or perhaps because of—the numerous feminisms that exist across the region, there is hope for solidarity and collaboration. Arguably, what happens within countries does not stay confined within national borders. Movements are inspired and ignited by one another. If collaboration can be achieved at the national level, then surely it can be replicated and scaled at the regional level. There are already instances of this happening, with organizations like *Musawah* (Equality)—a global movement for equality and justice in the Muslim family—as a prime example of successful collaborative and transnational organizing.

What follows is an overview of each phase along with an explanation of its impact at the regional and national levels, and its resonance with the international arena. More importantly, as we have gleaned from the literature, we address what each phase means for women and for feminist movements in the region overall. These summaries are not meant to be exhaustive historic accounts, but rather an overview of the changes in the region in order to provide the signposts for each phase.

In the chapters that follow, these summaries will be brought to life through the voices and experiences of feminist activists—particularly youth—in the region. It is through their voices that we can best understand feminist activism across the Arab region—by looking back and looking forward.

Phase 1: *Reawakening*

Why Reawakening?

We begin in the 1970s, not because there were no feminisms prior to this period, but because this period presents a reawakening of sorts at both the regional and global levels, and a recognition that more work was necessary to secure the rights that women had historically been denied. From the 1930s to the 1970s, as states in the region gained independence and sought to develop their identities, independent women's activism took the form of non-state organizations—charity groups, women's unions, and religious women's groups.[6]

In the 1970s, women's activism became tightly aligned with state development goals, especially in the aftermath of successful nationalist struggles against colonial powers. Dr. Mervat Hatem's analysis identifies the ways that these nascent postcolonial states were focused on improving women's "developmental citizenship," which included increasing women's access to education, employment, and healthcare.[7] State feminism tended to support women's formal and public citizenship rights but did little to challenge the root causes of inequality. Starting in the 1970s, global conferences inspired the formation of regional alliances and networks with a desire to redress inequalities.[8]

Our story begins here….

While the Arab region sought to engage at the international level during this time, it was also grappling with internal challenges. The moderate openness during this period allowed for some growth in diverse women's movements, especially focused on legal reform—particularly personal status laws. This period also saw the growth of activism and adoption of discourse related to defending women's rights through a religious framework. While there are many religious frameworks interplaying with feminisms, here we refer specifically to what is known as "Islamic feminism." Debates arose as to how Islamic feminism could counter Orientalist and colonial discourses and also whether religion and feminism might coexist. With this growth of feminisms in the region, networks and connections were formed nationally, regionally, and internationally. However, a series of regional setbacks, including serious economic downturns that were not adequately addressed by states, fomented anger and increasing distrust in the government as a safety net. As such, the Arab region saw a rise in conservatism connected to religion in the 1980s and 1990s, often labeled as "political Islam" or "state Islamization." While the religion was a facet of this regional conservatism, for the most part it coalesced with rising conservatism globally.

Women were not immune to this problematic transition and ensuing reforms. As a result, middle class women in the region began to (re)organize because gains made over previous decades were the first targets of reform.[9] Conservatism brought forth new debates on women's presence in the public sphere, as well as the status of legal frameworks governing the so-called private sphere, including discriminatory personal status laws. During this time, women's movements and organizing in the region sought to challenge artificial Western dichotomies between tradition and modernity and between religion and secularism, often labeled as the so-called "woman question."[10]

Thus, this timeframe led to the rise of feminist writers who combined activism with academia; independent women's movements that engaged in the local and the global; nationalist movements with a feminist angle; and Islamic feminists who were well-equipped to critique patriarchal practice in Islamic law. It also prepared the groundwork for women-initiated or women-led human rights and gender equality efforts for the decades to come. A *reawakening*.

Regional and National Landscapes

The 1970s are considered "the most dramatic and important years in recent Middle Eastern history."[11] There were major changes within the region during this decade attributed to political and civil unrest including the impact of oil and related economic development, international involvement, and migration flows.

Proliferation of oil production in several countries had multiple effects and can be cited as an example of "The Dutch Disease," where, despite the influx of wealth, the overall economy and social conditions did not perform as well.[12] Growth of the economy due to oil production and integration into the global economy was volatile and subjected to recession and high inflation—all of which negatively affected gender equality.[13] Moreover, the growing oil economies and their power created "superficially modern-looking societies without solving the dilemmas that rapid Western modernization [had] brought" and meant that "groups with conservative, traditional, and fundamentalist orientations" were encouraged in oil rich countries.[14]

According to Dr. Ghassan Salamé, politologist interviewed for the documentary *Feminism Inshallah: A History or Arab Feminism*, the oil crisis of the 1970s was a turning point for women's rights. "Oil was one of women's worst enemies," he articulates.[15] Oil wealth led to an ultra-monetary and ultra-modern society, but, he elaborates, "at the same time, a lot more conservative with regards to women. Their status regressed while the rest of the society's economy was modernized."[16]

Conflict also defined this period. The 1970s began in the aftermath of the Six-Day War (1967) and the War of Attrition (1967–1970), with tensions running high in the region. The decade started with attempts to quell the Arab-Israeli conflict at the Geneva Conference (1973) in the wake of the October War. Throughout the decade, slow progress was made towards a resolution with the passing of UN Security Council Resolution (UNSCR) 388, calling for a ceasefire in the on-going war between Israel and the Arab countries.[17] In 1978, Egypt's president, Anwar Sadat, and Israel's prime minister, Menachem Begin, met in the U.S. to broker the historic Camp David Accords and build the foundation for the 1979 Egypt-Israel peace treaty between the two countries—the first official recognition of Israel in the region.

Lastly, the 1979 Iranian Revolution and its impact on the Arab region cannot be understated. Ideological shifts and geopolitical tensions swept through the region as a result, with some noting that it "did more to transform the Middle East than any other event in the second half of the 20th century."[18] A significant regional result included increasing securitization within the Gulf region due to a promotion of revolutionary political culture. Several of the monarchies became wary of popular uprisings that would destabilize their states as well as the region. Sunni and Shi'a tensions were further exacerbated, augmented by Iran's increasing support for resistance movements across the region.[19] The success of the Revolution signified the success of increasing conservatism and political Islam, creating concerns about the future of women's rights and women's movements in the region.

The Gulf Region

The Gulf region—comprising Bahrain, Kuwait, Oman, Qatar, Saudi Arabia, the United Arab Emirates (UAE), and Yemen—has been characterized in recent history for its tribalism, religious conservatism, absolute monarchies, and vast oil wealth—with the exception of Yemen. Many Gulf states are relatively young, having gained independence during the 1960s and 1970s. As a result, women's liberation was often viewed as a vehicle for nation-building, rather than as legitimate assertions of women's human rights. For the most part, women's activism was relatively nascent or co-opted by the state. Aside from charitable endeavors, women's rights during this time were broadly attached to the "movements" affiliated with wealthy women or female relatives of the monarchy.

Prior to Bahrain's independence from the United Kingdom in 1971, formal women's groups, like charity and education organizations, were led by elite British and Bahraini women. The decade that followed, however, brought a host of changes that ushered women from all backgrounds into the public sphere and into the movement. More women participated in politics, entered the job market, and engaged in civil society.[20] Efforts to realize an independent Bahrain resulted in feminist activism through women's political engagement, journalism, and advocacy for legal reform, inspired by other efforts in the region.[21] In 1975, Bahrain's attempt to form a parliament was thwarted by ethnic and traditional forces, making it exclusionary and short-lived—with women notably absent. Political participation was suppressed after the 1975 unrest. While the 1970s-1980s were a "liberalizing experience," the movement was unable to enshrine women's rights or alter traditional family laws. The movements failed to be inclusive of rural and lower-class women—arguably the majority of women.[22]

Also established in 1971, the UAE did not see a strong engagement of women in activism in its early years, most likely because as an oil-rich state, many women were not expected to work or engage in the public sphere. However, the promotion of women's education in the 1970s as a state project eventually led them into the workforce. The General Women's Union was established in 1975 and served as an umbrella organization for various women's organizations, ensuring the entrenchment of state feminism.[23]

Kuwait gained independence from the UK in 1961. The women's rights movement began in 1963 with the establishment of the Arab Women Development Society (AWDS) and the Women's Cultural and Social Society (WCSS).[24] Noureya Al-Saddani, in her capacity as head of AWDS, began a national campaign for women's suffrage in 1971.[25] Their proposals were rejected by the National Assembly but social consciousness in favor of women's rights was beginning to shift. The WCSS and AWDS then merged in 1974 and were renamed the Kuwaiti Women's Union in light of their common interests and activities.[26] By 1978, significant gains were made by the Islamist movement, and as a result, the Government of Kuwait announced an official policy of "Islamization." With the increased conservatism, women's rights activists were faced with accusations of being anti-traditional, anti–Islamic, and anti–Kuwaiti.[27]

Modern Oman's identity has been tightly linked to the former Sultan Qaboos, who assumed power in 1970. As such, any and all reforms have been state-led, including efforts to improve the economic, political, educational, and social conditions of women. In 1971, with the permission of Sultan Qaboos, the Omani Women's Society was established.[28] The same year, women were granted the legal right to choose their spouse. Given the top-down and bureaucratic nature of Omani politics, feminist engagement in subsequent reforms has not been well-documented.

Ruled as a hereditary monarchy since 1878, Qatar gained formal independence in 1971.[29] The first higher education institute in Qatar opened in 1973 and enrolled 150 students, both male and female.[30] Similar to other states in the region, the focus was on state-driven women's education as a means of empowerment—but the impact was limited in that it did not necessarily translate into greater socio-economic freedoms.

The Kingdom of Saudi Arabia has formally existed since 1932. Given its commitment to ensure that the state remains socially and religiously conservative and adheres to *Wahhabism*, there is limited documentation of feminist or women's movements in the time under review.[31] However, Saudi Arabian women gained access to formal education in the 1960s, and during this decade, the Saudi Arab Women's Union was formed, headed by the prominent author Samira Khashoggi.[32] Khashoggi also established the Saudi al-Nahda Women's Association with members of the royal family, as well as the al-Jazeera Cultural Girls' Club and Library.[33] Other associations were established, including the Committee of al Sweilem's Saudi Girls School for Literature and Writing in Riyadh. By the 1970s, the University Studies Centre for Girls at King Saud University was founded, creating further opportunities for women's education and academics.[34]

Yemen has had a turbulent modern history. Unified since 1990, the country was originally divided between South Yemen (People's Democratic Republic of Yemen) and North Yemen (also known as the Yemen Arab Republic) after the end of the British occupation in the late 1960s.[35] During this time, South Yemen had a progressive outlook toward women's rights, family law, and the prohibition of polygamy. The General Union of Yemeni Women was established in 1967 in South Yemen. Under the Socialist government, gender equality was codified in the constitution, women had the right to vote, a secular family law was drafted in 1974, and women stood for election in 1977.[36] The General Union's activism was eventually curbed in some governorates due to conservatism.[37] Although the North was less progressive than the South, there was evidence of women thriving in education and employment, and the Yemeni Women's Association took on many of the same activities as the General Union had undertaken in the South.[38]

The Levant Region

The Levant region comprises Iraq, Jordan, Lebanon, Palestine, and Syria, all of which have a shared colonial history. Several of the states within this region also have conflict and/or occupation as defining features of their history and evolution, influencing feminist activism and women's rights movements in very specific ways.

Women in Iraq in the 1960s and 1970s contended with *Ba'athist* state feminism.[39] The General Federation of Iraqi Women served as the main implementer of state policy, running more than 250 rural and urban community centers.[40] In 1970, the Iraqi Provisional Constitution was drafted, outlining equality among all citizens. Some positive changes included making education compulsory, resulting in an increase in women's literacy. In 1978, Iraq amended the personal status law to allow divorced women to have custody of their children until they reached the age of ten. Women were also able to seek divorce, polygynous marriages were regulated, and inheritance was made more equitable.[41]

Under the monarchy in Jordan, women secured the right to vote in 1974 after a long struggle by women's movements and activists.[42] Subsequently, 1978 saw three women—Ina'am al-Mufti, Widad Boules, and Nayla Al-Rashdan—appointed to the 60-seat National Consultative Council, a transitional advisory council in lieu of an official constitution.[43] The following year, in 1979, the first female cabinet minister, Ina'am al-Mufti, was appointed the Minister of Social Development.[44]

In Lebanon, the Civil War defined most of this period. During that time, activism focused on ending the conflict, with women leading important anti-war and anti-violence campaigns. Prior to the war, committees for women were established by political parties, an example being the Lebanese Democratic Gathering of Women.[45] Notably, during this time, the Institute for Women's Studies in the Arab World was established in 1973, under what is now the Lebanese American University. The Institute—now known as The Arab Institute for Women—was the first of its kind in the region, and among the first globally. Its signature feminist journal, *Al-Raida* (The Female Pioneer), was established in 1976, another first in the region.[46]

As a result of Israeli occupation since 1967, Palestinian women struggle with several layers of oppression. During the 1970s, women's movements could not be divorced from the national struggle. In 1965, the General Union of Palestinian Women, affiliated with the Palestine Liberation Organization, was formed to create an active role for women in the social, economic, and political spheres.[47] By 1980, the Union of Palestinian Women Committees was formed (evolving from the Women's Work Committee) to not only empower Palestinian women, but also form an "integral part of the Palestinian national movement."[48]

The Al Assad regime came to power in Syria in 1970 and a period of relative stability initially ensued during this decade. The constitution of 1973 identified Islam as the religion of the majority and aligned the Syrian revolution to the larger Arab revolution.[49] It also stated that men and women were equal and could participate in all political, economic, social, and cultural life. Similar to other states, Syria had institutionalized state feminism, with the first elected female entering parliament in 1973.[50]

The North and Sub–Saharan African Region

The North and sub–Saharan African Region constitutes a diverse set of states, including Algeria, Comoros, Djibouti, Egypt, Libya, Mauritania, Morocco, Somalia, Sudan, and Tunisia. Due to the diversity, we see varying degrees of women's rights activism. The growth of feminist engagement in Algeria, Morocco, and Tunisia involved cross-border networking in similar contexts of political liberalization, increasing Islamism, and economic globalization.[51] Egypt has its own history of prominent feminist engagement, whereas Comoros, Djibouti, Libya, Mauritania, Somalia, and Sudan have distinct manifestations.

Egypt's long history of feminist activism was punctuated in the 1970s by the writings of Dr. Nawal El Saadawi, dismissed from the Ministry of Health in 1972 after publishing *Women and Sex*, which decried female genital mutilation and sexual oppression.[52] She also published *The Hidden Face of Eve* in 1980 which was a translation of the 1977 *Al-Wajh al-'Ari lil-Mar'a al-Arabiyya*. This book was important inspiration for the second wave of Arab and Muslim feminisms, and linked the personal to the political.[53] Her activism stood out in the context of Egypt's state feminism, which only promoted the feminization of the workforce and increased access to education. In 1985, Dr. El Saadawi founded the Arab Women's Solidarity Association (AWSA) and the organization became a focal point for Arab feminisms through information production and dissemination.[54] In terms of political representation, the first female ambassador, A'ishah Rateb, was appointed in 1979, serving in both Germany and Denmark.[55]

Sudan was under military rule from 1969 to 1985, resulting in a silencing of civil society. However, some women's organizations did exist independent of the Sudanese Women's Union, founded in 1971.[56] These include *Raidat al-Mara* (Women's Pioneers), which worked on the *mahr* (dowry) and making marriage more affordable, and the Babiker Badri Scientific Association for Women's Studies, which addressed rural women's needs as well as female genital mutilation.[57] Near the end of the decade, Khartoum University offered an elective course on women's issues through the Department of Sociology.[58] Notably, the Permanent Constitution of 1973 outlined women's equality, including the right to equal education, to hold public office, and to unionize.

In Libya, Muammar Qaddafi's agenda included support for equality between men and women resulting in a number of laws passed throughout the 1970s including a minimum age for marriage, a woman's right to divorce, and equal pay for equal work.[59] While considerable gains were made during this period—especially in relation to education and employment—women still faced discrimination and suffered under the autocratic regime. Most notably, guardianship laws and some aspects of the family law that adhere to *Shari'a* principles placed women at a disadvantage.[60]

Tunisia has historically been considered a pioneer in the region with regard to women's rights, although it was initially a result of state feminism.[61] While abortion was legalized on request in 1973, and several of the progressive steps taken in the 1950s and 1960s remained, some scholars had noted a subtle shift towards Islamic rhetoric and fewer overt state actions with regards to women's rights.[62] As such, it was not until the late 1970s that an independent feminist movement was visible. During this time as well, Islamic feminists who did not trust the state's actions on women also emerged, resulting in "further weakened non-governmental feminist groups [that] facilitated their capitulation to the state."[63]

In the decade after independence, women in Algeria dealt with "patriarchal socialism" resulting in high fertility rates.[64] Women were encouraged to be homemakers with limited employment options. This was despite a new constitution in 1976 declaring all citizens free and equal with no discrimination on the basis of sex. By 1979, the Algerian women's movement emerged as a response to the creation of a commission to draft a family code—two-hundred university women met to influence the process.[65]

Morocco experienced a period of intense state violence, commonly known as "The Years of Lead," under King Hassan II from the 1960s to the 1980s, which resulted in the uprisings of student groups and leftist organizations, denouncing repression in all of its forms through public movements, including feminist ones.[66] The only women's organizations that were not affiliated with or controlled by the state during this time were women's subcommittees within political parties, which were often marginalized. As such, women's rights activists began their own organizations. A notable organization created in 1979 by leftist feminists was the Moroccan Organisation for Human Rights, with the scholar and feminist pioneer Dr. Fatima Mernissi as one of the founders.[67]

Mauritania gained independence from France in 1960. Throughout the 1970s, a system of racial hereditary slavery existed throughout the country, and women's lives differed starkly based on their social class. Freeborn elite *Bidhan* women moved freely throughout society. They were allowed to speak publicly, initiate divorce, act as head of household, and abstain from physical labor.[68] Enslaved women were expected to "produce new slaves" and therefore were less likely to be given or sold their freedom. They were also subjected to sexual violence and other forms of violence.[69] Women's representation in public life was low throughout this period. In 1975, Mauritania appointed its first female cabinet minister with Aïssata Touré Kane as Minister for Protection of Family and Social Affairs.[70]

The 1960s in Somalia were a relatively progressive period, with the beginnings of a Somali feminist movement.[71] A bloodless military coup in 1969 installed the Barre Government and during this period women benefited from free compulsory education, university scholarships, and mobility within the military. The regime created the Somali Women's Democratic Organization (SWDO) to "mobilize women to support and legitimate state policies" and "to make it appear as if women were political actors in the government when in fact they were not."[72] A family law was introduced by presidential decree in 1975, advancing equality in divorce, inheritance, and dowry, contrary to customary and Islamic law.[73] In 1978 women mobilized, by radio, to defend the governmental regime against a failed coup d'état.[74] In just a year's time, by the end of the regime's

1977 war with Ethiopia, women's stance had shifted to resistance toward the regime. A new Constitution in 1979 established equal rights for men and women.[75]

International Synergies and Disconnects

Several international conferences took place in the 1970s that increased international attention on women's rights, highlighting the widening gulf between the West and the Arab region. While many networks transcended national boundaries and expanded international presence, this was largely confined to Western entities. In other words, Western women's international organizations dominated the women's rights discourse and power imbalances persisted between Western and non–Western organizations.[76] Some governments in the Arab region paid attention to this rising international call for human rights—and women's rights—and formed national commissions to address these issues. However, these commissions existed primarily for virtue signaling and even to obscure ongoing rights violations.[77]

Coinciding with International Women's Year in 1975, the first United Nations Conference on Women took place in Mexico City.[78] Overall, the conference helped launch a new era focused on the fight for women's rights and gender equality. In terms of Arab regional representation, all countries were invited to the conference and many Arab states attended except for Bahrain, Comoros, and Djibouti.[79] Notably, the Saudi Arabian delegate viewed the Conference as "potentially disruptive of 'many time-honored institutions.'"[80] Representatives from Egypt and Lebanon stressed the need to focus on assisting women in "majority world" countries, specifically women living in rural and low-income urban areas that needed assistance with education, housing, training, and employment. Countries such as Syria and Egypt emphasized that the problems women faced were also representative of overarching problems in society as a whole. One resolution called upon the international community to express solidarity with women in the Arab region and provide both moral and material assistance.[81] This resolution also expressed concern over the plight of Palestinian women and their inalienable rights.

The conference drew attention to discrimination enshrined in certain laws and aimed to make future-oriented goals that allowed women to continue advancing in society. These efforts laid the foundation for the development of CEDAW, which was subsequently adopted by the UN General Assembly in 1979. As a convention, CEDAW requires nations to take action against the discrimination of girls and women, and crucially, is legally binding for those that accede.[82] The Convention calls upon states to take measures to promote gender equality within their respective societies and to report regularly on such measures to the CEDAW Committee. CEDAW has played a key role in dictating the work of national women's machineries and international organizations in their quest for gender equality, used by many as a benchmark for progress. CEDAW is not a panacea for advancing women's rights and has some major flaws, but it sets international standards and paves the way for greater protections for women.

Many governments at this point implemented policies in line with state feminism, largely through economic inclusion-focused policies such as education and workforce training. International pressure pushed governments to attend to "women's issues," often resulting in policies that did little to ensure women's mobility, safety, and power.

The Islamic Revival

The 1970s saw an emergence of an Islamic "awakening," explained in part as a reaction to Western cultural imperialism.[83] As a result, conservative groups gained popularity as oppositional forces.[84] Aiding their ascent was also the fact that many of these groups also filled a crucial socio-economic gap amidst deteriorating welfare conditions.

The entanglement of women's rights with the perception that feminism is a Western ideology, while not new, became more pervasive during this time. As a result, women had to fight multiple battles—patriarchal structures, societal assumptions, religious interpretations, and Western stereotypes. Moreover, reconciling feminism within Islam became another area for contention. Islam could be seen as a space for liberation or a space for repression—depending on interpretation and external international misconceptions.

Some academics explain that religion is a powerful factor in determining gender in the region because Islam is not simply a code of beliefs, but "a system of identity."[85] At the same time, women from the Arab region were constructing a new identity to fight against the "cultural articulation of patriarchy" through social mores, laws, structures, and political power, which was being exerted by Islam.[86] Women were creating new ways to respond to being silenced in their communities. Women also promoted messaging that Islam is not necessarily more traditional than other religions, and that being a feminist does not mean that they are Western. Rather, it is possible to be both a feminist and a Muslim.

In the words of Dr. Fatima Mernissi, one of the founders of Islamic feminism, "if women's rights are a problem for some modern Muslim men, it is neither because of the Quran nor the Prophet, nor the Islamic tradition, but simply because those rights conflict with the interests of a male elite."[87] Many Muslim feminists have long sought to align women's rights within an Islamic framework, like Dr. Huda Shaarawi, as discussed in Chapter 1. Dr. Nawal El Saadawi argued against Islam being used oppressively, but simultaneously saw Islamic frameworks as a counter to Western misconceptions of Islam.

This phase also brought renewed debates on dress and covering, namely what is—and is not—Islamic, and therefore "appropriate." At the same time, the *hijab* was voluntarily adopted by many Muslim women in countries such as Syria, Egypt, Lebanon, and others, because of its perceived links to cultural identity and the new sense of Arab pride through pan-Arabism that had taken hold in the region.[88]

The debate between secularization and Islamization became central to feminist movements in the region. Questions regarding gender, societal roles, and freedoms were raised during this time. Still today, "there is no agreement across, or even within, different Arab countries, or between different women groups, on how much, or how little, of a role religion should play in gender dynamics in these evolving societies."[89]

What Does This Mean for Women and for Feminist Movements?

Women, and by extension, feminist movements, were impacted by a range of interconnected factors during this time. Overall, there were many "firsts" for women—the first girls' school in Oman, the first Algerian women's magazine, the first Tunisian female ambassador, the first Egyptian female ambassador, and so on. However, recognizing wide regional discrepancies, women remained relatively absent in political representation, decision-making, and economic participation.

Anti-colonial and nationalist movements in several countries fed into the emergence of feminist movements during this time. The struggle for liberation from foreign powers shaped nationalist and reformist agendas, particularly along the lines of culture and religion. And as with all interpretations, the interpretation of liberation took many forms. These debates manifested through the "woman question" where nationalist interests invariably took precedence over women's interests, as expressed by Khamis and Mili:

> Paradoxically and ironically, at the same time as these traditionalists and conservatives were restricting women's freedoms, they were also claiming, with some success and resonance among relatively wide segments of the public, that their efforts were intended to protect and honor women, by honoring and preserving their roles as to vote on mothers and faithful spouses.[90]

The different political systems and models that were adopted also had an influence. Countries like Morocco and Jordan adopted monarchies; Algeria, Egypt, Libya, and Yemen implemented socialist models; and Lebanon and Tunisia adopted Western style democracies.[91] It followed that monarchies were heavily influenced by religious ruling, democracies were more secular, and socialist states were straddling both worlds. Various ideologies—modernist, conservative, secular, Islamist—emerged, impacting the status of women and the feminisms that developed as a result, due to the fact that women were largely absent from the narrative.

The events during this time period highlight the limits with nationalism, state feminism, and neo-liberalization, and bring to the fore the need for more authentic and independent feminist movements, both secular and religious, inspired by regional and international networking and engagement.

Phase 2: Galvanizing

Why Galvanizing?

The following two decades (1981–1999) birthed many organizations and activists focused on women's rights as human rights. This period—*Galvanizing*—is characterized by the creation of formal structures to serve women's needs and interests. The proliferation of such groups was not limited to the region. Arabs in the diaspora, motivated by the ongoing changes in the Arab region, were also galvanizing in favor of change in their home countries.

The 1980s and 1990s would see significant political transformation and international engagement in the Arab region, whether through military invasion and/or occupation, prolonged civil war, or economic downturns and transitions. This was also evidenced through global conferences and participation in United Nations frameworks, including commitment and accession to CEDAW and related events promoting women's rights.

During this time, women's movements became more active and visible, inspired firstly by the need to redress inequalities at the national and regional levels, and also by international women's movements that became a hallmark of the 1990s.[92] As was true globally, this period saw a proliferation of independent women's movements and engagement with transnational feminism spurred by international conferences such as the World Conference on Human Rights in Vienna (1993), the International Conference on Population and Development in Cairo (1994), and the Fourth World Conference on Women in Beijing (1995), with significant presence of women's organizations and activists from the Arab region.[93]

With the increasing influence of activists, women's rights organizations, and other NGOS, many governments began to feel pressured to introduce reforms. These changes, however, would become little more than performative, as state *co-opted* feminism. As such, international engagement became even more pronounced and necessary, with women's rights activists and organizations engaging in transnational feminist networks to reach a broader audience and hold their governments to account.

Regional and National Landscapes

Multiple conflicts throughout this period—namely, the Iran-Iraq war (1980–88) and the Gulf War (1990–91)—had wide ranging implications regionally, affecting national and foreign policy and shaping geopolitical divisions.[94] This legacy of conflict continues to be felt today, impacting peace and stability across the region, to the detriment of women's rights.

Oil wealth in the Gulf region resulted in increases in women's health and education, though not always translating into increased employment or public and political engagement. One academic cited the oil-based growth as a reason for reinforcing a "patriarchal gender contract" where men are the breadwinners and women are wives and mothers.[95]

The 1980s and 1990s did, however, see a more concrete manifestation of women's activism in the region, whether en masse or through individual forms of resistance and reaction. In this section, we highlight instances of such "galvanizing," and in Chapter 3 we go into greater detail on women who pushed boundaries and fought on the feminist frontlines.

The Gulf Region

Advances in women's rights were scant in Saudi Arabia during this time. As one example, in 1980 as oil wealth increased, women's banks opened, allowing women to manage their money without having any contact with men. Frustrations were growing, however, and in 1990, 47 Saudi women drove in Riyadh to protest the driving ban for women. As a result, they were arrested, had their passports confiscated, and were suspended from their jobs.

Omani women faced a series of setbacks in the 1980s as the government retracted certain liberties, while the Omani Women's Association was also stripped of much of its autonomy. A birth spacing program was introduced in 1994 with the aim of improving the wellbeing of women and children, and contraception was also provided as part of the initiative.[96] A written constitution was adopted in 1996 that prohibited gender discrimination but, in reality, many laws continued to restrict and discriminate against women. In 1999, the Al Zahra College for Women was established by royal decree signaling moves towards empowerment, albeit limited.[97]

In 1984, the Kuwait Personal Status Act was established, subjecting women to a harsh guardianship system, among other repressive measures. In 1990, Iraq invaded Kuwait. Women played a significant role in the resistance and, to some extent, changed public perspectives on women's rights in doing so.[98] Overall, however, women's empowerment was not significantly aided by these events.[99] There was an attempt to institute women's suffrage in 1999 by Emir Al-Sabah during a temporary parliamentary dissolution, but this was overturned by the new National Assembly later that same year.

Yemen ratified CEDAW in 1984 but subsequent events were less optimistic. For example, the Nationality Law of 1990 forbade women from passing citizenship on to their children. Additionally, the Personal Status Law came into effect in 1992, which mandated a woman's obedience to her husband and effectively permitted marital rape.[100] Rising food prices led to widespread riots in the early 1990s and the outbreak of civil war in 1994 amplified deteriorating social conditions for women. The same year, 1994, also saw the introduction of Yemen's Penal Code. One article in the Penal Code Law stipulated that compensation for "blood money" (*diya*) for a woman was half that of a man. Another article reduced sentences for those convicted of "honor killings."[101] Amendments to the Personal Status Law in 1998 mandated that women obtain their husband's permission to work outside the home. In 1999, the minimum age of marriage was abolished.[102]

There were several advancements to women's rights in the UAE during this period, driven largely by state policies. The UAE Federal Labour Law (8) of 1980 outlawed discrimination between men and women in terms of equal pay for equal work.[103] In 1992, the first cohort of women graduated from the women's military college, Khawla bint Al Azwar Training College.[104] Throughout the 1990s, women's literacy rates increased and, by 1997, women comprised 72 percent of university students.[105] In 1999, the Federal National Council gave women three months maternity leave with full pay, and another six months at half pay.

In Bahrain, a series of anti-government protests occurred from 1994 to 1999—central to these protests were the political rights and participation of women. For example, in 1995, women started a petition listing their reform concerns, including women's participation in political processes.[106] In 1999, Sheikha Haya Al Khalifa was appointed ambassador to France.[107]

The Qatari government established the Women's Affairs Department in 1996 and then, in 1998, the Supreme Council for Family Affairs created the Women Affairs Committee.[108] The purpose of the Committee was to promote women's rights and encourage women's participation in public life. A women's athletic event was also held in Qatar that year for the first time, highlighting concrete steps to increasing women's public participation. Qatar enfranchised its entire population in 1998, and women voted for the first time in the 1999 municipal elections.[109] Six women contested these elections although none were successful.

The Levant Region

Political divergences around this time in Palestine led to the creation of new "Popular Committees" to oversee civic affairs. Many young women joined the national struggle by entering the political sphere, but not all participation was limited to formal channels.[110] In 1987, the year of the first *Intifada* (uprising), women appeared alongside men and played a key role in resistance. The widespread network of formal and informal organizations—including women's organizations—allowed the resistance to be sustained.[111] In the following year, 1988, the Committees were banned by Israel resulting in, amongst other things, the marginalization of women's groups.[112] The subsequent exclusion of grassroots organizations and the decline of political participation was compounded by two factors: the new political landscape within the Palestinian Liberation Organization (PLO) leadership and the increased international NGO presence throughout the 1990s. Women faced a conservative backlash at this time and experienced discrimination, which the PLO and national women's groups did not challenge.[113]

Women directly participated in the political and parliamentary sphere in Jordan in the 1989 elections but did not manage to gain any seats in the House of Representatives.[114] Jordan ratified CEDAW in 1992, which led to a public debate on policy, signaling a positive step for women's rights.[115] Queen Noor Al-Hussein was an advocate for such advancements and announced the adoption of certain legal reforms to give women equal rights in line with the constitution. Changes came gradually and, in 1993, Tujan Faisal became the first female elected to the Jordanian parliament.[116]

A number of positive milestones mark this period for Iraqi women. For example, women obtained the right to vote in 1980, Iraq became one of the first countries to ratify CEDAW in 1986 and, by 1987, approximately 75 percent of Iraqi women were literate.[117] However, the Gulf War broke out in 1990 sparked by Iraq's invasion of Kuwait and, as a knock-on effect, greater limits were placed on women. As such, women suffered restrictions on their movements and their legal status. For example, an amendment to the law in 1990 allowed so-called "honor killings" without punishment in certain circumstances such as arguing with husbands, committing adultery, or being the victim of rape.[118]

Certain advancements were made in Lebanon for women's organizations during this time, laying the groundwork for future action. In 1990, prominent Lebanese feminist Laure Moghaizel proposed a new constitutional clause to emphasize Lebanon's commitment to human rights.[119] In 1998, the National Commission for Lebanese Women (NCLW) was founded to promote women's rights and enhance gender mainstreaming.[120] Other organizations were also formed around this time, and many organized under the umbrella entity, the Lebanese Council of Women.

The North and Sub–Saharan African Region

Algeria witnessed many instances of women organizing and galvanizing for greater equality during this period. In 1981, women took to the streets in protest of proposed reforms to the Family Code and to demand consultation in any processes regarding new legislation concerning women.[121] These instances of women's resistance were significant, but ultimately the Family Code was adopted in June 1984, informed by a conservative and patriarchal interpretation of Islam. In response, throughout 1988, many took to the streets demanding equality and an end to corruption. In the early 1990s, starting what became known as "The Black Decade," fundamentalists began enforcing stricter interpretations of *Shari'a* law. Mobilization continued, however, with women demonstrating against discriminatory laws and promoting secularism.[122] The *Collectif Maghreb-Égalité 95* was formed in 1992—with women's organizations from around the Maghreb region—and mobilized to promote women's rights.[123] Femmes Algériennes Unies pour L'égalité des Droits was established in 1995 and CEDAW was ratified in 1997, albeit with reservations.[124]

In 1985, Tunisia ratified CEDAW with reservations.[125] Many women's organizations gained official recognition in 1989 such as l'Association Tunisienne des Femmes Démocrates (ATFD) and l'Association des Femmes Tunisiennes pour la Recherche sur le Développement. This paved the way for activism around issues such as violence against women, which ultimately led to the formation of a commission in 1991.[126] Organization and mobilization by women's groups had some positive effects. As a result, the state introduced some amendments to the Code of Personal Status, including women's right to participate in family affairs, and ensuring mothers provide consent for the marriage of their minor child.

In Libya, the status of women regressed somewhat during this period. A number of family laws were passed aimed at improving women's rights in the early 1980s which led to the ratification of CEDAW in 1989.[127] Reservations to the Convention were recorded, however, and most Libyan laws did not comply with its provisions.[128]

The government of Sudan established the Women of Sudan Union in 1991. The General Directorate for Women and Family Affairs was established in 1993, serving as the main state body concerned with women's issues.[129] By 1997, Ahfad University for Women had introduced a master's program on gender and development.[130]

In Djibouti, women were granted the right to stand for election in 1986.[131] In 1995, a Penal Code was passed outlawing violence against women, yet FGM, domestic violence, and marital rape remained unpunished.[132] CEDAW was ratified in 1998 without reservations. In 1999, the Ministry for the Promotion of Women, Family Well-Being, and Social Affairs was established.[133]

The outbreak of civil war in Somalia in 1991 significantly disrupted Somali lives and resulted in mass displacement and migration, increased tribalization, and overall greater danger for women and girls. Female-headed households increased during this period, as did sexual violence and FGM.[134]

Comoros adopted a new constitution in 1992, which enshrined gender equality. In 1994, Comoros acceded to CEDAW.[135] Matriarchal traditions also afforded women some rights, however, gender equality remained out of reach.[136]

The year 1992 was significant in Morocco as many women's organizations banded together to oppose the *Moudawana,* or family code. The group l'Union de l'Action Féminine joined forces with other allies to launch the One Million Signatures campaign, a petition aimed to reform the family code. The campaign was very successful, collecting over one million signatures, inspiring King Hassan II to order the drafting of a new code.[137] CEDAW was ratified in 1993, although with reservations.[138]

In Mauritania, it was not until the late 1980s that women started to enter formal political roles. In 1986, Khadijetou Mint Ahmed was appointed Minister of Mines and Industry. Between 1986 and 1995, only three women represented all Mauritanian women in government.[139] The Association of Women Heads of Households was founded by left-wing activists in 1999 with Aminetou Mint El-Moctar as President. It grew to over 10,000 members and provided training, support services, and assistance to abuse survivors.[140]

International Synergies and Disconnects

Often critiques of Arab States are focused on religion, culture, and autocratic regimes, but international (read: Western) involvement also played a role. Whether through military invasion, imposition of reforms, government interference, or aid intervention, the influence of international Western forces is undeniable.

Internationally, this period saw the fall of the Soviet Union, drastically altering relations and power balances globally. Even though not overly involved, the Arab region "emerged as a critical arena of global superpower confrontation" and, arguably, intervention.[141] An economic crisis impacted the world in the early 1980s. Neoliberal economic reforms were subsequently imposed on many parts of the Arab region by the World Bank and the International Monetary Fund (IMF).

The vast differences across the region in terms of development resulted in varying impacts of neoliberal restructuring policies. The Arab region contains some of the wealthiest and the poorest countries in the world, with countries like the UAE, Kuwait, and Qatar at the top of the spectrum and Mauritania, Sudan, Somalia, and Yemen at the bottom. Overall economic conditions in the region at this time meant increasing poverty, weakening social safety nets, and rising unemployment. In countries like Lebanon and Palestine, these conditions were felt even more acutely due to conflict and occupation.

Enforced economic restructuring had a significant impact on the social landscape and cannot be divorced from feminist activism. As expected, women were severely affected by the reforms and their attendant outcomes. Austerity measures, privatization, and cuts to public services such as education, welfare and health only served to heighten inequalities and exacerbate the "feminization of poverty."[142] Due to increased transport costs, lack of childcare provisions, and absence of decent minimum wage, options for women were limited, if not totally absent. The formation of neoliberal states pushed women away from meaningful economic employment and toward domestic informal occupations. In other words, the types of jobs deemed acceptable for women were based on commonly perceived "feminine traits" in line with the family and what was "appropriate" for women.

The 1980s and 1990s produced a different phase of feminism in response to restrictions on rights and freedoms bolstered by international events. A wave of transnational feminism emerged in the 1990s, alongside international conferences—the World Conference on Human Rights in Vienna (1993) and the Fourth World Conference on Women in Beijing (1995), amongst others—in a bid to unify women's movements and discourses. CEDAW was not universally adopted when it was first introduced in 1979, and by 1980 only three Arab countries had signed on to the Convention—Egypt, Jordan, and Tunisia. Nonetheless, these conferences were critical for state accession to CEDAW, and many countries have since strengthened regulations aimed at ending gender inequality and discrimination on the basis of sex. The road to adoption and implementation in the Arab region, however, has been far from straightforward.

Today, all Arab states—with the exception of Somalia—have acceded to CEDAW. However, many have not fully ratified the Convention due to strict reservations, either related to supposed contradictions with religious law or national law. These numerous reservations not only justify discrimination under religious codes, they also limit the extent of implementation and undermine the purpose of the Convention.

Thus far, Palestine and Djibouti have acceded with no reservations to CEDAW, while Tunisia and Morocco lifted theirs in 2014 and 2018 respectively.[143] On the other hand, Algeria, Bahrain, Egypt, Iraq, Jordan, Kuwait, Lebanon, Libya, Mauritania, Oman, Saudi Arabia, Syria, Tunisia, UAE, and Yemen have all recorded reservations.[144]

What Does This Mean for Women and for Feminist Movements?

The late 1980s and 1990s saw a revival of women's rights consciousness and a proliferation of groups and movements throughout the region. In fact, between 1980 and 2015, the number of women's rights groups in the region nearly tripled.[145] Many emerged due to the political landscape of the time, international events, and state-endorsed activities. Some groups filled a gap by states who did not provide adequate social services. NGOs in countries like Egypt, Palestine, and Lebanon, played a crucial role in this regard and worked alongside national women's groups to provide education, health, and social services.[146] Religious groups providing these services in place of the state led to a new set of challenges for women's rights.

In response to international universalizing discourses on feminism and women's rights, Arab feminist movements sought non–Western frameworks that, instead, built on indigenous and context-specific foundations. As one researcher has noted, for many women in the Arab region, "feminism [is] synonymous with America and fast food."[147] So while social activism for the enhancement of women's rights was growing globally, and international trends had some influence on the Arab region, Arab feminisms sought to be distinct from Western liberal feminism.

However, feminisms in the Arab region were inevitably influenced by these international trends. At the same time, the extent to which they were received was based on socio-political fluctuations in the region and the conflicting values characterizing this period. Just like in any movement, progress is met with regress, and several things exist at the same time that exert influence on one another. For instance, increasing international presence and policy of the period informed a greater awareness of social conditions, which led to the proliferation of international NGOs focused on women. Simultaneously, grassroots groups were battling against this international influence and elite state *co-opted* feminists.

Near the end of the 1990s, the increasing presence of international entities and the proliferation of NGOs, both national and international, resulted in what is known as "NGO-ization."[148] The phenomenon of "NGO-ization" had many effects on feminisms in the region. Feminist organizations and activism became increasingly "NGO-ized" as, in the words of political feminist analyst Farah Daibes, "feminism was hijacked by capitalism and then even more so by neoliberalism."[149] Essentially what this meant was that feminist activism became professionalized and institutionalized, adhering to external standards in order to operate:

> Increased professionalization, larger operational capacity, greater specialization, and international recognition, NGOs quickly became the new *enfants prodige* of the international development system, with more and more support and funds being channeled through them by bilateral and multilateral agencies especially evident when it comes to women's activism.[150]

Organizations became overly reliant on funding from international organizations that was often conditioned, meaning they had to conform to the donor's agenda. What resulted was a noticeable shift where activist efforts became project or issue-based and did not challenge underlying structures like the patriarchal status quo. A dependency cycle then ensued, and feminist organizations molded to fit the new landscape which "…began threatening the integrity and agency of the Arab feminist movement, minimizing mobilization potential and alienating young women from the cause."[151] Implementing programs focused on women's rights was a relatively cheap and easy way to promote democracy and marginally improve standards of living—or at least attempt to—without threatening overall power structures. In other words, women's rights would not pose the same problems to an autocratic regime in the same way democratic elections or freedom of press would.

The introduction of neoliberal policies such as privatization and deregulation during this time did not liberate women or address structural problems. Rather, women become further entrenched in systems of oppression, exploitation, and violence. For example, economic initiatives negated community level dynamics and, as men were assumed to be the breadwinners in patriarchal societies, programs did not consider how women would be treated when they started to engage in economic activities within their communities. Moreover, a lack of economic opportunity is wrongly attributed as the main reason for gender inequality. The reality is far more complex.

Ultimately, not only does this mean it was more difficult for women to advance, it also undermined activism that seeks to break women free from such conditions:

> The dominant neoliberal economic model actively drives values that disempower women, especially those living in poverty and those from certain ethnic and religious groups. In a world where mainstream economic institutions have fixated on growth, feminist economist and women's rights movements have made the case that, while gender equality under certain conditions can support economic growth, economic growth does not necessarily go alongside gender equality.[152]

Another result of the economic conditions was widening class disparities, subsequently reflected in feminist movements. Access to education and resources meant many feminist groups during this period were comprised of well-educated, urban, middle-class, elite women. In many instances, however, this privilege meant that they did not challenge underlying discriminatory structures, choosing instead to focus on issue-based challenges in an *ad hoc* manner. As such, without an intersectional lens, they failed to see the full scope of challenges facing women within their contexts.

One outcome of this was state feminism, usually in the form of national machinery bodies. State feminism refers to the act of governments enforcing policies and legislation that aim to support and promote gender in society. However, more often than not, they focused on women's civil and political rights rather than their social, cultural, and economic rights. And addressing rights in the public sphere typically took precedence over rights in the private sphere. Meaning, women's lives remained fundamentally unchanged.

State feminism or national machineries could be seen as puppets or mouthpieces of the state amounting to mere window-dressing, resulting in little to no actual change and even hindering feminist grassroots movements. These institutions also lacked adequate human and financial resources, and political will from the state. Effectively, state feminism diminished feminist movements by giving them the semblance of progression but hindering them in every capacity:

So-called "state feminism," where women's liberation was taken over by patriarchal, often totalitarian, regimes, limiting the potential for fundamental feminist reforms within countries in the region. Over the years, this tamed feminist discourses, demands and activism, resulting in the de-politicization of the Arab feminist movement.[153]

Similar to NGO-ization, state feminism was flawed in its operation. It did not challenge underlying structures harmful to women. Changes were largely cosmetic if at all, and empowerment was reduced to a buzzword. State feminism focused on issue-based activity, often starting with suffrage. Attention then turned to political participation as it was seen to validate women's public role by giving them a presence, although little power. Changing oppressive structures requires not only sufficient numbers but also political will to implement feminist policy, regardless of who is in power.

Many governments pledged to incorporate women's rights or make changes—albeit small. At the same time, they implemented stricter controls and obstacles for the operation of NGOs as a way to reject what they perceived to be a "Western agenda." As such, NGOs had to advocate strongly and sustain pressure on governments to take action on even the smallest of commitments, in extremely limited circumstances. Superficial changes did not bring women any closer to realizing their rights. Unsurprising, given the fact that "the movement has to call for the protection of human rights by the same authorities which violate those rights in the first place."[154] Ultimately, angling for change within these systems of oppression will always be limited because underlying patriarchal and power structures have not been challenged.

While feminist activism of the 1990s draws much criticism, it nonetheless had an impact. As one example, topics once considered taboo—such as violence against women—were brought into mainstream discussion and consciousness. This in turn led to increased awareness and demands for reform. The activism during this period also provided a framework for feminist organizing and mobilizing, and evidence that changes are possible when women rise up.

At the same time, grassroots movements were still not sufficiently engaged as action during this time was more often top-down and tokenistic. The phenomenon of "first lady syndrome" in the Arab region speaks to this point.[155] First ladies, spouses of men in power, are often figureheads, playing a symbolic role in the state. While at times being a first lady has created new opportunities for women, these women are not known for advancing the causes of women or gender equality.

While the state has a role to play in ensuring equality, they are often also complicit in compromising and violating women's rights. Women's rights are frequently used as bargaining chips, particularly in pursuit of political support from more conservative demographics. Furthermore, state-introduced gender policies have limits in that they do not pose a threat to the patriarchal status quo.

Despite challenges, movements made gains within limited space, and grassroots action paved the way for greater grassroots mobilization to come.

Phase 3: Agitating

Why Agitating?

The next period (2000–2011)—*Agitating*—was characterized by multiple crises in the region, often where the national struggle superseded the feminist struggle. While there are earlier examples of this phenomena in Algeria, Palestine, Lebanon and Iraq, this period saw widespread instances of national agitation, most intensely during the 2011 pro-democracy uprisings. Women were involved in the many pro-democracy protests that occurred during this period, igniting the spark for impassioned advocacy that would be seen in myriad manifestations—for instance the right to drive in Saudi Arabia and pressure in Tunisia leading to the country's first sexual harassment legislation. Women's activism led to significant gains during this time. Some countries attempted gender-based legal reform. In Morocco, Tunisia, and Egypt, for instance, women's rights activists secured legal reform through the amendment of constitutions, penal codes, and personal status laws, as well as the drafting of specialized laws. In Libya, civil society provided gender-sensitive legal expertise to the National Transitional Council and launched the Charter of Libyan Women's Constitutional Rights, which addressed women's rights within an Islamic and human rights framework.[156]

Regional and National Landscapes

Regionally, this period saw greater grassroots action and demand for change, sparked by deteriorating social, economic, and political conditions. Pro-democracy uprisings, commonly referred to as the Arab Spring, swept across the region throughout 2011. Decades of organizing—and dissatisfaction—came to a head in mass mobilization for greater rights and freedoms. And women were at the forefront.

These regional uprisings were inspired by events in Tunisia. Calling for greater social justice and an end to the police state, demonstrations first began in December 2010 after the self-immolation of street vendor Mohamed Bouazizi.[157] Protests ignited across the country in what was dubbed the *Jasmine Revolution*, and after 28 days, 24 years of dictatorial rule came to an end.[158] The ousting of President Zine El Abidine Ben Ali and the subsequent regime overthrow inspired activists across the region to demand change from their own governments.

The uprisings were built from frustration and necessity—an existential demand for a new order; a struggle for survival. Ranging from small demonstrations to mass protests, people in all their diversity rose up against their corrupt governments as they demanded justice, economic improvement, political representation, and—ultimately—regime change.

The region was ignited.

Some actions resulted in the toppling of despots, while others remained contained and were extinguished quickly through concessions from rulers. Countries ruled by monarchies survived due in large part to the wealth of resources and external support. For example, the UAE and Qatar experienced the least civil unrest and challenges to their monarchies.[159] Bahrain experienced more protest and unrest, driven by inequality and spurred by the brutality of the government's response, however this did not result in progressive change.[160] In Tunisia and Egypt, uprisings driven by poverty and unemployment successfully overthrew the ruling governments. In Syria, Yemen, Libya and Iraq, they had a more severe effect, leading to conflict, and even civil war.

The Gulf Region

Protests in Kuwait became more widespread throughout this decade, and women played a significant role. From 2004–2005, women held some of their largest demonstrations in Kuwaiti history and had a significant influence on the National Assembly granting women full political rights.[161] In 2005, women were given the right to vote and run for parliament. That year, Massouma al-Mubarak became the first female government minister.[162] This paved the way for Kuwait's first female parliamentarians—four were elected to parliament in 2009.[163] The same year, women were given the right to obtain passports without a guardian's consent.

In 2000, the Qatar Women's Sport Committee was founded with the aim to achieve gender equality in sport, accredited by the Qatar Olympic Committee in 2001. However, they failed to send a female competitor to the Olympic Games until 2012.[164] A Civil Service Act in 2001 created legal protections for women in the workforce, and the following year women were granted retirement benefits. Women made advancements in the public sphere with the appointment of Sheikha Ahmed al-Mahmoud as Minister of Education in 2003.[165] In the same year, Qatar University appointed its first female president, Sheikha Abdulla Al-Misnad.[166]

Saudi Arabia provided government-issued IDs to women for the first time in 2001, touted as a major step forward.[167] In 2009, the first co-educational university was opened. The first female cabinet minister was appointed—Norah Al Faiz as Vice-Minister of Education.[168] At the same time, the women's movement was not unified, and certain advancements for women were resisted by other women. Rowdha Yousef and other Saudi women launched a petition called "My guardian knows what's best for me," supporting the guardianship system and calling for the punishment of anyone who sought gender equality. The petition received over 5000 signatures in its first two months and signaled a worrying trend for women's rights movements.[169] Authorities preemptively banned public protest amidst the 2011 pro-democracy protests that swept the region. Still, Saudi Arabia did experience unrest, albeit on a much smaller scale.

The first women were appointed to Bahrain's Shura Council in 2000 and the Supreme Council for Women was established in 2001, serving as a central association for all women's organizations.[170, 171] In 2002, the country acceded to CEDAW, and then amended the constitution to grant women the right to vote and stand in national elections.[172] Women played a key role in dialogues leading up to these amendments.[173] Dr. Nada Haffadh became Minister of Health in 2004, making her the first female to head a government ministry.[174] In 2005, women's rights organizations and Al Wefaq, the leading opposition party, called for the introduction of a unified personal status law. There were notable gains for women over the next few years. In 2005, Alees Samaan chaired the Shura Council, becoming the first woman in the Arab region to chair a parliamentary session. In 2006, Haya bint Rashid Al Khalifa was elected President of the UN General Assembly, making her the third woman—and the first Arab woman—to hold the position.[175] Bahrain's first International Women's Day was launched in 2008 by HRH Princess Sabeeka, and continues to be celebrated annually.[176] In 2009, Bahrain codified the Sunni Personal Status Law.[177] The 2011 peaceful pro-democracy uprisings in Bahrain saw massive participation calling for political freedom, equality, and an end to the ruling monarchy. Women were instrumental in the protests.

Oman granted universal suffrage in 2003 to all adult men and women. In 2004, the first female minister, Dr. Rawya Saud Al Busaidi, was appointed to the Ministry of Higher Education.[178] A royal decree in 2008 gave women the right to own land and, later in 2010, the Decent Work Country Program was implemented in collaboration with the International Labour Organisation to increase work opportunities for both women and men.[179] In 2011, inspired by the Arab Spring, an "Omani Spring" spread across the country. An election was held that year amid government promises for reform, but only four women were elected, signaling limited progress for women in the post–Arab Spring landscape.[180]

In 2005, the UAE introduced the Civil Service Law, which provided greater provisions for women regarding maternity leave and gender-based discrimination.[181] Women's economic participation increased and, in 2006, the UAE had the largest number of businesswomen in the region.[182] Conditions for women were improving in certain areas, reinforced by the 2007 UNDP status report stating that the UAE showed positive signs for women's empowerment.[183] Additionally, state legislation did not discriminate against gender with respect to education, services, or employment.

In Yemen in 2008, a symposium titled "Yemeni Woman a Partner in Making Future" [sic] called for the President to introduce a 15 percent quota for women in parliament.[184] The 2011 pro-democracy uprisings—and the aftermath—were significant, particularly regarding the role of women in society. Women were at the heart of these protests, with women's rights activist and journalist Tawakkol Karman awarded the 2011 Nobel Peace Prize in recognition of her nonviolent struggle—the first Yemeni and the first Arab woman to win the award.[185] However, failure to deal with the social conditions that led to the protests eventually gave way to a bloody civil war.

The Levant Region

Iraq enacted a law in 2000 restricting women's freedoms regarding work, travel, and education, reflecting a reversion to conservative norms.[186] Conditions for women were not improving. A report on violence against women released in 2002 stated that since 1991, approximately 4000 women and girls had been the victims of so-called "honor killings."[187] People took action and, in 2003, the Organization of Women's Freedom in Iraq was founded to defend women's rights.[188] Then, during the 2010 national elections, a group of 12 women started their own party centered on women's issues.[189] The Arab Spring began in Iraq in February 2011, including a "Day of Rage" where thousands protested corruption and lack of basic living standards and at least 10 were killed.[190]

Jordan hosted the Arab Women's Summit in 2002, which resulted in improvements to the legislation impacting women's rights in nationality, retirement, and passport allowances.[191] Further changes saw the electoral law amended in 2003 to introduce a women's quota, which in turn boosted women's political participation.[192] In 2008 the Law Regarding Protection from Domestic Violence was adopted to regulate the handling of domestic violence cases.[193]

The early 2000s saw more social upheaval and protest in Palestine. The Second *Intifada* began in 2000 and the women's movement was once again forced to link their agenda to the national struggle.[194] While women's involvement decreased due to mobility restrictions and military presence, they persisted. In fact, as many as 1000 women were arrested during the Second *Intifada,* with some remaining incarcerated for the better part of the decade.[195] In 2000, a new Palestinian Labor Law advanced the rights of women but did not give women equal rights in the workplace or address female-dominated labor sectors. During the period of 1998 until 2009, Palestine had one of the lowest female labor participation rates in the Arab region, below 17 percent.[196] The Ministry of Women's Affairs was created in 2003 to serve as the main governmental agency to protect women's rights, with gender units established throughout all other ministries.[197] In 2006, women's organizations lobbied for a gender quota of 20 percent, and remains successfully upheld.[198]

In Lebanon in 2005, the assassination of Prime Minister Rafik Hariri sparked protests calling for the end of the Syrian occupation of Lebanon in what became known as the Cedar Revolution.[199] The protests and civil resistance efforts were nonviolent, and women played a key role.[200] In 2005, *Kafa* (Enough), a feminist, secular NGO, was established with the aim of eliminating discriminatory structures and practices such as gender-based violence.[201] A women's shelter, *Beit el-Hanane* (Home of Tenderness), was established in 2008 to help survivors of gender-based violence and abuse.[202] In 2011, ABAAD–Resource Centre for Gender Equality, was formed with the aim of advocating for the development and implementation of gender equal policies and laws.[203]

In Syria, civil society faced difficulties during this period as authorities cracked down on organizations that disagreed with government policies. As a result, in 2005 it was reported that members of the Syrian Women's League experienced arrests and detentions.[204] The Arab Spring uprisings took hold in Syria from March to July 2011 when peaceful protesters filled the street demanding a change from the authoritarian regime led by President Bashar Al-Assad. Authorities responded with censorship, and soon after, violence, through the deployment of military forces in an attempt to prevent the protests.[205] Eventually this led to the eruption of the Syrian Civil War which continues to have dire consequences, especially for women and girls. Rebel groups and extremists, such as the Islamic State (IS but also known as ISIS and ISIL), quickly asserted their presence and enforced harsh policies that restricted the freedoms and rights of women in territories under their control.

The North and Sub–Saharan Africa Region

In Tunisia, in 2003, a shelter for women seeking help for domestic violence was established by L'Union Nationale des Femmes Tunisiennes.[206] Then in 2004, with pressure from l'Association Tunisienne des Femmes Démocrates, Tunisia's first legislation combating sexual harassment was passed with an amendment to Article 226 of the penal code.[207] In 2006, many feminist organizations celebrated the 50th anniversary of the Code of Personal Status, although cognizant of the fact that discrimination persisted.[208] The country ratified the Optional Protocol to CEDAW in 2008—one of only two countries in the region to do so—but women's groups continued pressure for full equality.[209] The self-immolation of Mohamed Bouazizi in December 2010 and subsequent "Jasmine Revolution" was credited as being the catalyst and inspiration for what became known as the Arab Spring, pro-democracy uprisings that spread across the Arab region. The transitional government in the aftermath included some women and declared gender parity in elections, promising to lift the remaining reservations to CEDAW.

Moroccan activists, with their rich tradition of organizing, were well-placed to take action throughout this decade. In March 2000, thousands of women gathered for a march promoting women's rights organized by various women's and political groups to coincide with International Women's Day.[210] The women's movement was not unified, however, and an opposition march was organized in response, mainly by Islamist groups.[211] Undeterred, women's organizations rallied and formed an alliance called "The Spring of Equality" in 2004 to agitate for a new family code.[212] They achieved partial success when the law was amended and replaced, but it still fell short in terms of equality. In late 2010, following the events in Tunisia that catalyzed the Arab Spring, Moroccan mother Fadoua Laroui set herself on fire to protest the rejection of her public housing application.[213] Morocco's Arab Spring, also known as the "February 20 Movement," was initiated by youth groups as they protested across numerous cities in 2011. The movement called for constitutional reforms rather than outright regime change, and women were not as present as in other uprisings.

In Somalia, the "Sixth Clan," a women's organization for peace, was founded in 2000 by Asha Hagi Elmi, subverting the typical male clan system where representatives from various clans select members of parliament.[214] The group gained currency, and Elmi led a delegation of women at the 2002 Somali Reconciliation Conference in Kenya. One achievement of the Sixth Clan was securing a 12 percent quota for women in the Transitional Federal Parliament. Elmi also signed a peace agreement in 2004 in Kenya, the first Somali woman to do so.[215] Despite these gains, the situation for women deteriorated throughout the decade. Violence against women became more widespread as gang-related clan attacks increased.

Algeria made several attempts at advancement in the early 2000s, in compliance with CEDAW recommendations. For example, a law reform process was initiated by the government in 2003 to improve gender equality and propose amendments to the Family Code.[216] Conditions for women did not improve, however, as by 2005 there had been insufficient government reforms and continued restrictions on women's legal rights.

Djibouti enacted a 10 percent women's quota in elected offices and administrative positions in 2002.[217] The same year, a Family Code Law was passed guaranteeing certain legal rights to women and girls, such as a minimum age of 18 for marriage.[218] However, many discriminatory practices remained including polygamy, unequal inheritance laws, and marriage of minors with guardian approval. In some positive progress, the quota law helped seven women get elected to Djibouti's Parliament for the first time in 2003.[219]

Conditions for women in Sudan remained precarious during this period. Women continued to be marginalized politically, economically, and socially, with little access to health and education services. A "Women's Strategy" was adopted for the period 2003–2007 with the aim of promoting equality, eliminating disparities, and empowering women.[220] In 2005, a National Action Plan was implemented to combat violence against women and children, but little headway was made. Political representation, on the other hand, experienced some gains as the percentage of women in the Legislative Council increased from 10 percent in 2004 to 25 percent in 2008.[221]

Libya passed the Labor Relations Law in 2010, which reinforced occupational segregation. It also stated that women could not be employed in certain fields, which typically relegated women to lower paid roles.[222] Protests broke out in 2011 inspired by the Arab Spring. This turned into a civil war, with leader Qaddafi killed later that year. Women played a significant role in the revolution by protesting, aiding troops, and forming support groups to advance the revolution.[223]

Mauritania adopted a Family Code in 2001, which provided certain protections but was still discriminatory towards women and girls.[224] For example, even though a minimum age for marriage was set, guardians could still consent to underage marriages. The human rights organization Pour une Mauritanie Verte et Démocratique (For a Green and Democratic Mauritania) was founded in 2009 with Mekfoula Mint

Brahim serving as President.[225] As with other countries in the region, protests erupted in 2011. Dubbed the "February 25 Movement," demonstrators demanded equality and reforms to the political situation. The government responded with some concessions, but also with force.[226]

In Egypt, women's organizations proliferated during this period and more women were publicly involved in challenging oppressive structures. The National Council for Women was created in 2000, a positive advancement but also another example of state feminism, criticized by many for not being representative of all women. The emergence of the *Kefaya* (Enough) movement for workers' rights gained traction from 2004 onwards.[227] Women were at the forefront, which also helped pave the way for women's involvement in the 2011 pro-democracy uprisings.[228] Also in 2011, renowned women's rights activist Dr. Hoda Badran founded the Egyptian Feminist Union, an alliance of women's organizations. This Union was a revival of the organization founded in 1923 by Dr. Huda Shaarawi, banned under President Nasser.[229]

International Synergies and Disconnects

International events in the first decade of the 21st century had significant repercussions in shaping women's rights in the Arab region and internationally. The September 11 attacks in 2001 in the U.S. sparked the so-called "war on terror," which then led to the U.S. invasion of Afghanistan. In 2003, the U.S. then invaded Iraq as part of the war on terror with the aim of toppling Saddam Hussein. This series of events had wide ranging implications on terrorism, extremism, and religion—in particular Islam.[230] Moreover, as a result of the war on terror, countries in the region were plagued by conflict, displacement, and further human rights abuses.

The financial crisis of 2007–2009, originating in the U.S., had global implications resulting in a major economic recession. The Arab region, while strained, was not as badly hit as other parts of the world due in part to their low integration into the global market.[231] Unsurprisingly, oil-producing countries like the GCC states fared better than less resource-rich countries in the region like Egypt, Yemen, and Morocco.[232] Although the region performed comparatively better than others, it remained prone to instability leading to protracted crises, compounding already precarious conditions. Eventually, delayed effects of the crisis manifested in the region, leading to lower remittances, higher inflation, and higher unemployment. In short, existing problems intensified.

International response to the Arab Spring was initially promising—paying lip service but not providing concrete support. The West was reluctant to "interfere" in what was seen as a "home-grown" matter, resulting in perceptions of the West changing within the region.[233] The aftermath signaled shifts both in the Arab region's position on the global stage and in terms of foreign policy between the region and the West.

At the same time, Dr. Nicola Pratt exposes the tendency on the part of the West to view women's protest during the Arab Spring as new and extraordinary, ignoring a long history of women's activism in the region.[234] Yes, the women's engagement in the Arab Spring was an awakening, but it was not the first one. Women in the region have exercised agency and acted in their own interest countless times throughout history, in what Dr. Margot Badran calls "long chains of revolutionary activity."[235] Dr. Mounira Charrad articulates that this was "an explosion of agency on a broad scale and cutting across social classes."[236] And even though democratization did not succeed as was hoped, women's voices were not silenced.

What Does This Mean for Women and for Feminist Movements?

This time period crystallized multiple forms of struggle for women in the Arab region. In what Dr. Deniz Kandiyoti termed the "double jeopardy," women in the Arab region faced political and civic restrictions, as well as social struggle in the form of discriminatory personal status laws.[237] As Dr. Sahar Khamis succinctly put it, "If you are an Arab woman, you are not just struggling for freedom and democracy, rather, you are also struggling to get recognized and to achieve gender equity and equal pay."[238] Even further, women from the region continue to face struggles on several levels: "The political struggle against autocracy and dictatorship, the social struggle against patriarchy and stagnant social traditions, and the legal struggle against discriminatory laws."[239]

As a result of these layered systems of oppression, women were central to the pro-democracy uprisings of 2011. Additionally, they assumed leadership roles and were at the forefront of activity, representing a change in feminist movements towards greater grassroots action. The combination of women's voices, authentic women's leadership, and new grassroots women-led groups together mark a shift in gender politics from a top-down to a bottom-up approach.[240] Dr. Charrad distinguishes between women's rights and women's voices saying, "one does not necessarily lead to the other. Women can voice their concerns and there can be very little change in policy ... voicing your concerns isn't enough for change ... the world doesn't work like that."[241] Rather, state intervention and action by those in power is needed for policy change. But, she contends, this needs to be guided by women's voices.

Additionally, the use of online platforms and social media for spreading awareness, organizing, and agitating led to new forms of cyberactivism for women, enabling them to widen networks quickly, easily, cheaply—and effectively. More on this in Chapter 3.

This period is significant in that it demonstrated not just appetite but *action* for change. Driven largely by necessity, and in spite of risks and dangers, civil society mobilization highlighted the power of collective action and showed women at the forefront of that action. Unfortunately, the momentum of this period was not sustained. Post-revolution disillusionment set in, with women sidelined in transitional processes—despite their prominent role during the uprisings. Many gains were met with strong backlashes and a re-entrenchment of patriarchal prerogatives. The next phase explores this regress.

Phase 4: Regressing

Why Regressing?

The aftermath of the 2011 pro-democracy uprisings led to severe crackdowns, resulting in shrinking of civil society space, repression of freedoms, and the reality of largely unsuccessful democratic transitions. The COVID-19 global health pandemic was also to blame for deteriorating conditions—mostly in terms of increasing violence against women and decreasing women's economic empowerment. Women's rights lost ground during this period, ushering in a phase of *Regressing*.

Regional and National Landscapes

Ignited by the Arab Spring, and in response to brutal regime crackdowns, protests and uprisings continued within the region in this decade. In several states, such as Syria and Yemen, conflict and civil war broke out leading to deaths, injuries, massive displacement, and deepening humanitarian crises. In Palestine, the continued "normalization" of Israel's occupation, bolstered by international deals, saw increased aggression in Gaza by Israeli forces.[242] And in Iraq, the Islamic State experienced a revival during this period and announced an expansion operation that resulted in many deaths and millions displaced. While women's rights in the region regressed, there were some advancements in Gulf countries—although limited and largely cosmetic.

The Gulf Region

Kuwait's first female prosecutors—22 women—were appointed in 2014.[243] Women's status gained prominence again when, in 2019, three women were appointed to cabinet positions, including Mariam Al Aqeel, the first female Minister of Finance in the Gulf region. In 2020, eight female judges were sworn in—the first in the country's history.[244] That same year, a law was passed criminalizing domestic violence, however, it was critiqued for not providing adequate protection.[245]

The UAE received recommendations from the CEDAW Committee in 2015 to further advance women's equality, including repealing discriminatory provisions in the Penal Code and the Personal Status Law.[246] The Labor Law continued to discriminate against domestic workers, the majority of whom are women. Even the 2017 Domestic Worker Law falls short of international standards. In 2019, a new domestic violence law came into effect that enabled women to obtain restraining orders. However, the law was regarded as inadequate in its definition of domestic violence as it reinforces a male guardian's ability to discipline those under his guardianship.[247]

Saudi Arabia introduced more restrictions on women's movements in 2011 with a new program that sent the male guardian a text message whenever the woman under his guardianship leaves the country.[248] At the same time, the next few years saw broadening of women's rights, in an effort to gain international recognition. In 2013, 30 women were appointed to the Shura Council, and legislation required women to hold at least 20 percent of the seats.[249] In 2015, women stood for elections for the first time. In 2017, King Salman allowed women access to government services without the permission of a male guardian, but the guardianship system continued to be the source of aggravation and it remained "largely intact."[250] The Kingdom granted women the right to enter sports events, to drive, and to hold non-combat military positions in 2018. The next few years also saw greater civil rights being granted to women and, in 2019, women were allowed to obtain passports, travel abroad, and register their children's births without the permission of a male guardian.[251] There was also a ban on marriages under 18, and women were no longer required to wear *abayas*, the covering mandated by custom and religion. In 2020, Saudi women used pseudonyms on Twitter to launch Arabic language hashtags "Why I didn't report it" and "Down with remnants of the guardianship system" to report sexual abuse and other oppressions.[252]

In Qatar, there were several progressive milestones for women in public roles. Alya bint Ahmed Al Thani was appointed Permanent Representative of Qatar to the UN in 2013, becoming Qatar's first female ambassador.[253] In 2017, four women were appointed to the Consultative Assembly for the first time.[254] Despite advancements in public life, Qatari women still did not have the same rights as Qatari men, and the guardianship system persisted.[255]

Marginal political gains in Yemen during this period were overshadowed by regressive policies and a deepening humanitarian situation. Yemen's 2014 National Dialogue Conference, which aimed to tackle the ongoing crisis, had 30 percent women's representation.[256] Fears of a crackdown on women's activism spread after female literacy campaigner, Amat al-Aleem al-Asbahi, was killed in a drive-by shooting in 2017.[257] In 2021, the Houthi Ministry of Public Health and Population introduced stricter family planning measures, which included prohibiting a woman from buying contraception without her husband being present.[258] Other crackdowns on women's freedoms appeared as actress and model Intisar al-Hammadi, along with three other women, were sentenced to prison for "indecency." Al-Hammadi's modeling photos were treated as an "act of indecency" and she was labeled a "prostitute."[259] The incident was indicative of escalating crackdowns on women's liberties. As of 2022, Yemen is one of the largest humanitarian crises in the world, with women and children being the most vulnerable.[260]

In 2015, Bahrain introduced some protections from domestic violence for women. In 2017, Family Law no. 19 was passed prohibiting gender discrimination in inheritance.[261] Overall, not enough has been done and conditions have deteriorated, particularly for women. Civil society space continued to shrink and, in 2019, Bahraini women's rights groups protested the detention of women's rights activists.[262] A 2021 report found that activists were denied access to healthcare and fair trials while in custody, and coerced into confessions with threats of rape and death.[263]

In 2015, Oman elected a new Consultative Council, but only one woman gained a seat.[264] In 2016, the country's second municipal elections were held, but again women did not fare well, claiming only seven of a possible 202 available seats.[265] As of 2022, political parties were not allowed in Oman.[266] Unemployment persists, as does the discriminatory *kafala* (sponsorship) system meaning migrant workers, particularly female domestic workers, are exposed to abuse and exploitation.

The Levant Region

In Syria, the Autonomous Administration of North and East Syria in the Kurdish-majority area was created in 2013. There, women enjoy broader political participation. For example, women occupy at least 50 percent of all official and community roles.[267] The Women Now center was opened in 2014 and, in 2015, the feminist organization, A Glimpse of Hope, was founded.[268] In 2016, Hadiya Khalaf Abbas became the first female Speaker of the People's Council of Syria.[269] The Syrian Women's Advisory Board was founded the same year and included an advisory board for gender affairs in political negotiations.[270] Despite these movements, a study conducted in 2017 found 81 percent of Syrian women who were interviewed believed social norms impede women's advancement.[271]

In Iraq, the Islamic State group, renamed as ISIS in 2013, staged an offensive in 2014 in Mosul and Tikrit. The group announced plans to form a caliphate across Syria and Iraq and experienced elements of a revival due to utilization of the internet and its networks of affiliates.[272] Over 2014 and 2015, there were many U.S.-led airstrikes and, by 2017, ISIS had lost 95 percent of its territory.[273] A 2014 law passed in Iraq prohibited women leaving the house without a male relative or spouse's permission, severely curtailing women's free movement.[274] Conditions only worsened for women due to increasing conflict. In 2019, women took part in demonstrations calling for gender equality as well as protesting the broader social, political, and economic situation.[275] Also in 2019, the last ISIS holdout fell, resulting in the mass surrender of ISIS fighters.

In Palestine, this period saw an increase in aggression by Israeli forces, particularly in Gaza. Women continue to be particularly susceptible to poverty and suffering due to the escalations in violence.[276] Egypt closed the tunnel economy in 2013, which had been serving as an economy and trade route to help Gaza cope with the imposed blockade.[277] Israel launched a 50-day military offensive against the Gaza Strip in 2014, which also exacerbated women's vulnerability.[278] In a positive move, Palestine acceded to CEDAW in 2014 without any reservations.[279] In 2018, Palestine repealed the "marry your rapist" law, but this did not apply to Hamas-run Gaza, who enforce a different criminal code.[280] Conditions for women did not improve, however, and the activist group Tal'at called for action in response to increased cases of gender-based violence and so-called "honor killings."[281] In 2018, Palestinians started weekly protests to demand the right to return to their ancestors' homes and an end to the Israeli blockade, known as the "Great March of Return."[282] In 2021, the Israeli government designated six Palestinian civil society groups, including the Union of Palestinian Women's Committees, as "terrorist" organizations.[283] Also in 2021, Israel began forced evictions in the Sheikh Jarrah neighborhood of East Jerusalem which then escalated into brutal crackdowns, culminating in an 11-day military offensive on Gaza.[284]

Jordan repealed their "marry your rapist" law in 2017 after a long campaign by activists.[285] In general, however, women's rights receded during this time. Women continued to be marginalized from the workplace despite high levels of education. Unequal laws persisted in discriminating against women, and political representation remained low. In fact, it was not until 2022 that Jordanian women achieved "linguistic equality" in the constitution, sparking a brawl amongst male parliamentarians over the matter.[286] Real changes to women's status remain elusive.

During this period, Lebanon achieved several key milestones for the advancement of women's rights, but overall the situation was not promising. After great pressure from women's organizations, the "marry your rapist" law was repealed in 2017. In 2020, sexual harassment was criminalized.[287] Women also played a key role in the October 17 Revolution of 2019. Protests erupted amidst deteriorating socio-economic conditions and demonstrators called for an end to rampant political corruption. In the aftermath, however, conditions did not change much and multiple crises compounded matters further. The crippling financial crisis that emerged in 2019 sent unemployment rates soaring, Gross Domestic Product dropped significantly, and the value of the currency plummeted. Furthermore, an explosion at the Port of Beirut in 2020 exposed structural vulnerabilities and social conditions deteriorated even further—all against the backdrop of the COVID-19 pandemic.

The North and Sub–Saharan Africa Region

In 2012, Tunisian women, maintaining the momentum of the Arab Spring, defeated attempts to replace the word "equality" between men and women with "complementarity" in the constitution.[288] In 2014, the new constitution codified gender parity and banned violence against women. That same year, in parliamentary elections, women won 31 percent of the seats, the highest female representation in the region that year.[289] Other milestones of note include passing the strongest law yet on violence against women in 2017, abolishing the "marry your rapist" law, and removing the law prohibiting Tunisian women from marrying non–Muslim men.[290] Despite apparent gains, a 2016 study found that women's rights were still lacking, especially for women in poor and marginalized areas.[291] Moreover, poverty, marginalization, and lack of access to education were cited as the main obstacles to women's political participation. In 2019, there was a major backsliding of progress when only 22 percent of women won seats in the legislative elections—10 percent fewer than in 2014.

The post–Arab Spring landscape did not translate into greater rights for women in Egypt. Women protested the absence of a parliamentary quota for women and demanded greater rights in front of the 2013 Shura Council.[292] Violence against women remained a constant problem and, despite backlash, an online female-led social media campaign was launched in 2014 called "Assault Police" after a group of men gang raped a woman.[293] The campaign sought to highlight the crime and recount other cases of abuse, harassment, and violence Egyptian women suffered without support due to cultural and traditional norms. The campaign also called for judicial reforms so women could more easily seek redress without blame.

In Libya in 2012, a 10 percent quota for women in the new National Assembly was dropped.[294] In 2014, protests erupted when the General National Congress refused to disband after its mandate expired. Later in the year, when a new parliament was formed, clashes broke out.[295] In 2016, the Women's Support and Empowerment Unit was established and was welcomed as a positive development but, in reality, it lacked power to effect meaningful change in gender-related policies.[296] Negative views of women in the public sphere persisted and, in 2019, female parliamentarian Dr. Siham Sergiwa was kidnapped from her home for giving a public TV interview about the ongoing violence in the country.[297] Women faced additional forms of conflict-related violence—particularly sexual violence—after conflict resumed in Tripoli in 2019.[298] The conflict, political division, and lack of police authority meant that, according to a UN Women report, women in the study were four times more likely than men to have never left their homes alone.[299] In 2021, five women were named to the new unity government, including the nation's first female foreign minister, Najla el-Mangoush.[300]

In Mauritania, Aminetou Mint El Moctar, politician and activist, became the first Mauritanian woman to be considered for a Nobel Peace Prize in 2015.[301] In 2016, peaceful protests were held to mark the anniversary of the imprisonment of anti-slavery activists. Police responded with tear gas and arrests while the government denies the existence of slavery in Mauritania.[302] Feminists and activists continued to face obstacles as a 2019 proposal for harsher rape sentences was rejected for contradicting *Shari'a* law.[303] As of 2022, human rights conditions remain a serious issue—freedom of speech and assembly are curtailed and slavery persists, with an estimated 90,000 people enslaved in Mauritania.[304]

A series of events in Djibouti throughout 2013 indicated women's rights were not a high priority. Women staged protests demanding the government fulfill its commitments. In a separate event, 35 women were arrested for protesting supposed fraudulent elections.[305] In 2016, ten Djiboutian women went on hunger strike in Paris to protest the widescale rape inflicted by Djiboutian soldiers and the lack of prosecution.[306] In 2019, as part of the global "16 Days of Activism" campaign, the government and international partners worked to raise awareness on gender-based violence—particularly female genital mutilation.[307] Also in 2019, Moumina Houssein Darar, an anti-terrorism police investigator from Djibouti, was recognized as a Woman of Courage by the U.S. Secretary of State.[308]

The Sudanese revolution began in December 2018 and women played a major role.[309] President Omar al Bashir was eventually toppled in 2019 after a military coup and a new government was then formed. The first female foreign minister, Asma Mohamed Abdalla, was appointed to a cabinet position, along with three other women.[310] The transitional period, however, was not straightforward and a new wave of protests began. By 2022, over 1,000 people had been detained—including 144 women—for opposing a military coup.[311] There were reports of rape during these arrests, 85 people were killed, and many were injured.[312] In 2019, 19-year-old Noura Hussein was sentenced to death by hanging for stabbing her husband to death after he attempted to rape her. A social media campaign—#JusticeForNoura—went viral online and her sentence was overturned following international pressure.[313] In 2020, there were small gains: stricter punishments for FGM were introduced, and the rule requiring permission for a woman to travel was abolished.[314] Now, Sudan is still facing human rights violations, patchy implementation of legislation, and an economic crisis.

Morocco experienced several wins. They repealed their "marry your rapist" law in 2014 after sustained pressure by civil society organizations.[315] In terms of political representation, women won a record 81 seats during the 2016 elections, helped partly by a gender quota, although representation overall was still low.[316] In 2018, a law to combat violence against women came into effect, and in 2020 the Marrakesh Declaration to Eliminate Violence Against Women and Girls was signed, which established standards and protocols to support victims.[317]

A series of strikes, riots, demonstrations, and marches took place in Comoros in 2018 to oppose President Azali Assoumani. Comorians boycotted a referendum on extending the president's term limits and police forces responded with violence, with protests continuing for months.[318] In 2019, the presidential elections were held and protests resulted in at least four people killed. Women were involved in these protests and a march of approximately 100 women was held, resulting in the arrest of 12 female activists.[319]

In Algeria, despite attempts to progress women's status, women experienced marginalization and discrimination. In 2015, an amendment to the penal code criminalized some forms of domestic violence but was inadequate, while child custody and divorce still presented significant problems.[320] Protests in 2019, in which women played a prominent role, signified the dissatisfaction with political, economic, and social conditions.[321] The struggle for better conditions is ongoing, and on International Women's Day in 2021, Algerian women participated in anti-regime protests chanting "We came out for change, not to party."[322]

International Synergies and Disconnects

The rise of right-wing populist political rhetoric across the West marked a worrying trend, most notably among the so-called "superpowers," which saw the instatement of President Donald Trump in the U.S. and Prime Minister Boris Johnson in the UK. Promoting an ideology that perceives "the other" as threatening, discriminatory national policies spilled over into foreign policy, resulting in a rise in Islamophobia, anti-refugee stances, and backsliding of women's rights globally.[323]

The international community also fostered diplomatic ties with the Arab region during this period. These ties, in the interest of trade and profit, reinforced regimes who egregiously and consistently violated human rights. Oil and arms deals with Gulf countries and the continued support of Israel are two clear examples.

This period is also characterized by global climate agreements, such as the 2015 Paris Agreement which came into effect November 2016.[324] The Agreement represents a move away from oil. However, some Arab economies—namely the Gulf—remain heavily oil-dependent. Globally, there has been minimal progress in mitigating climate change. The Arab region is significantly affected, with rising temperatures, water scarcity, food insecurity, displacement, and conflict posing real threats to an already fragile region.

The Russia-Ukraine war has also had a major impact on the Arab region. The region has felt the effects of the war especially in relation to food security and energy prices. Several countries in the region, particularly Egypt, Tunisia, and Libya, rely on wheat imports from Ukraine and Russia.[325] Supplies have now been disrupted and prices have increased, leaving these countries in precarious positions. Energy prices have soared, causing many countries to borrow heavily or descend further into budget deficits. Western double standards have also been exposed, with the international community deciding where to intervene, which issues take precedence, and which populations are deserving of support. Palestine is a case in point.[326] While on one hand international entities mobilized swiftly to aid Ukraine, with Ukrainian resistance touted as heroic, Palestinians continue to experience decades of strife with limited international assistance, and their resistance is often not seen as legitimate.[327] With the Russia-Ukraine war still ongoing at the time of writing, the full outcome for the region—and the world—remains to be seen.

The biggest global shock during this period was the COVID-19 pandemic, which began in December 2019. By March 2020, countries started enforcing strict lockdown measures over the coming months in a bid to curb the spread of infections. Ultimately the virus caused millions of deaths worldwide. The crisis amplified vulnerabilities within societies and between regions. Full effects remain to be seen, but it is clear that vulnerable communities, including women, will continue to face severe challenges in the long term as a result of the pandemic.

What Does This Mean for Women and for Feminist Movements?

This period is characterized by patchy progress and major regress. Overall, certain economies in the region grew, yet disparities between urban, rural, and poorer communities have widened. The least developed countries and conflict-affected countries in particular face increased poverty, especially countries such as Iraq, Yemen, Libya, Palestine, Sudan, and Syria. The 2022 Global Peace Index ranks the region as the least peaceful in the world for the seventh consecutive year.[328] Sudan experienced the largest deterioration in the region, while Yemen is the second least peaceful globally.

And, again, women are disproportionately affected by conflict and crisis.

Women, Peace and Security (WPS) is both a principle and a policy, launched in 2000 with United Nations Security Council Resolution 1325 to promote the inclusion of women in all aspects of peace and security.[329] The WPS Agenda encompasses eight resolutions and includes the need for states to have National Action Plans (NAP) to implement the Agenda. Iraq adopted a WPS National Action Plan in 2014, making it the first country in the region to do so.[330] Djibouti and Palestine followed in 2017 (and Palestine renewed again in 2020); Jordan and Tunisia in 2018; Lebanon in 2019; Yemen and Sudan in 2020; and UAE in 2022.[331] Fifteen years after the WPS Resolution, in 2015, the League of Arab States adopted a Regional Action Plan.[332] This was an important step given the severity of conflict in the region. The issue, however, is that these NAPs are state driven, poorly implemented, under-resourced, and tend to treat women as victims—not empowered and active participants of peace processes.

This phase saw a shift in feminist movements throughout the region. The new phase of feminisms in the region was undoubtedly influenced by the events of the 2011 pro-democracy uprisings. Fissures in feminist movements grew deeper in these years with backsliding of rights, crackdowns by authorities, and the persistence of state feminism. Strong critiques of previous generations of feminisms emerged alongside enhanced polarization between Islamic and secular feminists. New public space carved out by women during the protests and revolutions brought about new waves of feminisms including patterns of micro-rebellions, as Chapter 3 and 4 will highlight.

This new wave engages a wide demographic—religious, secular, youth, grassroots, rural. These groups go "beyond the singular normative liberal feminist view that restricts women's empowerment to their representation in formal politics in accordance with universal international laws and through gender quotas."[333] Instead they seek ways to be community-based and indigenous. At the same time, many criticize their predecessors for sidelining women in rural and poorer communities, as we will see in Chapter 5. Arguably, this wave is more sustainable and inclusive—rooted in community and collective action.

Nevertheless, political engagement remains necessary for capacity building and resource mobilization, and this period also saw the introduction of quotas for women in politics. Indeed, more women in politics is more likely to create legislative change, especially as protection from domestic violence and sexual harassment are priorities for several countries, most notably Jordan, Lebanon, Tunisia, Palestine, and Morocco. However, voters do not have confidence in female politicians, and representation remains low.[334]

This period saw successful civil society campaigns, including repeal of the "marry your rapist" law, laws against domestic violence, expansion of citizenship rights, and less restrictive guardianship laws.[335] It would be easy to assume that these are contagious across the region, with one country creating a ripple effect for others to follow. This is not always clear-cut. What is clear, however, is that more work needs to be done to reform discriminatory legislation, particularly as personal status codes continue to restrict women's bodies and lives in many countries throughout the region.

As this phase, *Regressing*, suggests, the region is still lagging. *Why?*

The aftermath of the 2011 uprisings and the consequent backsliding of women's rights is perhaps unsurprising but remains disappointing. For instance, even new constitutions in places like Egypt and Tunisia that promised equality are not sufficient to protect women's rights.[336] Many reforms were cosmetic, with no real change for women on the ground. Often, as will be explored in subsequent chapters, governments introduce reform or amendments to gain a favorable image on the international stage, without resources, implementation, or monitoring.

Rights and reform on paper will remain hollow as long as education and awareness remain absent. A new phase of collaborating might help build the necessary support to instigate the cultural shifts that could make change meaningful.

Phase 5: Collaborating

Why Collaborating?

And now we speculate. By the time this book is in your hands, there will be no telling what the region—or the world—will look like. We can only imagine based on what we have seen, and what we hope for.

Throughout this chapter, women in the region have actively countered authoritarian regimes, demanded equal rights, and shifted power structures. Through marches, protests, demonstrations, strikes, boycotts, and more, women have been tackling oppression and redefining social norms for generations. This final phase—2023 onwards—could be one of *Collaborating,* suggesting where feminism in the region might now be headed. Challenges across the region are both diverse and pervasive, but in some respects they are similar, ushering in a phase of collaboration.

This does not suggest that there is one unique movement or Pan-Arab Feminism. Collaborating entails solidarity and support in recognition of similarities, without having to agree on all aspects of the movements. The region is home to multiple discourses and multiple feminisms. At the same time, we can exercise difference in implementation and unity in our broader goal—equality.

Moments of success across the region are similar—gains in education and literacy levels, increased political representation, abolition of various discriminatory laws, and increased awareness of subjects previously thought to be taboo. And yet, throughout the region, gains in some of these areas do not necessarily translate into gains in other areas. For example, greater access to education does not necessarily translate into labor force participation.

Challenges, too, are similar—continued violence against women, restricted movements, barriers to participation in public life, and so on. Feminist movements throughout the region are also susceptible to geopolitical developments, the politicization of Islam, restrictions on political activism, and the will of people in the region to fight for greater freedoms.[337]

Based on history, it would be reasonable to assume that the region will continue to face protracted conflicts, economic crises, political instability, and pushback on women's rights.

Will the international community prioritize national interests at the expense of human rights? And similarly, will Arab nations introduce cosmetic measures to comply with international standards to gain leverage? Will international political pressure result in real reform for women in Arab countries?

Evidence suggests that reforms are often window dressing and purplewashing, a term referring to public alignment with women's rights that fails to manifest in reality.[338] Changes are introduced—on paper—in order to climb the rankings of international indices without substantial change.

"Where do we need to go?" asks Dr. Mehrinaz El Awady, Director of the Gender Justice, Population and Inclusive Development cluster at UN ESCWA. "We need to keep pushing the envelope." She continues:

> We need to go for the low hanging fruits because these will help us achieve the hard ones. We need to protect the gains that we had achieved. We need to agree among ourselves on priorities and act as one. We need to address women's rights as societal rights that lead to economic prosperity for all our countries.

Looking ahead for feminist movements in the region, the cycle of marginal gains followed by grave backsliding risks undoing already-precarious rights. There will continue to be a tension between securing rights and freedoms in the long-term, while ensuring that immediate and short-term needs are being met. Ghida Anani, founder and director of ABAAD–Resource Centre for Gender Equality, reminds us that:

> Steps need to be very well studied with different building blocks. Bridging the activism with academia, theories, evidence, data, and research should be the basis of any movement.[339]

In short, activism needs organization. Collectively, the region might benefit from exchanging learnings from within that could advance this organization, sharing strategies and tactics among feminist movements to maximize gains. Feminist movements in the region need to also build strategies to battle on several fronts—neoliberalism, occupation, conflict, displacement—viewed from a gendered lens. In this perhaps-utopian next phase, feminist agendas must prioritize inclusion, appealing to all groups who face vulnerabilities and struggle for fundamental freedoms. All of this could be more easily enabled by cyberfeminism, fueled by a younger, more technology-savvy generation. Central to this is the reminder that, across the region, the obstacle is the same—patriarchy. And the goal is the same—equality.

Women's rights in the Arab region hang in the balance, with an urgent need for "wholesale changes of public perceptions of women" for rights to be won.[340] The following chapters will provide insights as to whether this "wholesale change" is likely and what it might take.

3

Feminisms on the Frontlines of Crisis

Women and feminists in the revolution are calling for a system overhaul, for a shift in power, and for bringing down the patriarchal and religious system with all its social institutions.

—Dr. Lina Abou-Habib[1]

The Arab region is no stranger to upheaval. Conflict and crisis have long characterized the history of this region. In fact, the region's protracted crises—Palestine, Iraq, Syria, Yemen—continue, seemingly for generations, making the story of the region one of inherent conflict.

We believe that conflict cannot be divorced from the story of women's rights. We argue that simply being a woman is enough of a conflict. In Chapter 1, we explained that women continue to be marginalized in Arab societies, whether in conflict or not. They face the greatest barriers to equality and have some of the world's widest gender gaps. Women from the Arab region must fight multiple concurrent battles—from traditional social norms, to discriminatory laws, to sustained violence in all its forms.

Conflict and crisis has a detrimental impact on women and girls—and all marginalized groups. We discussed in Chapter 1 how crises magnify pre-existing vulnerabilities, leaving women worse off than they were before. But we also discussed how women are not just victims of these crises. Crisis presents an opportunity to renegotiate oppressive gender roles, to claim new space, and to push forward boldly for freedom.

This freedom is all the more urgent because women in the region continue to be the greatest victims of various oppressive forces, both from within and beyond national borders. Dictated by heteronormative masculinity, which often manifests as toxic, these regimes have one thing in common: violating human dignity and rights—and women's rights most of all. Women struggle against both patriarchy and colonization, where the former is often trumped by the latter. Meaning, conflicts and occupations in the Arab region are inherently patriarchal—whether they stem from internal problems or external powers. So, women's frontlines are many: they fight autocratic regimes within their countries, occupying forces outside their countries, and their own socio-cultural structures—a triple patriarchal threat.

Women continue to resist this triple threat, actively asserting themselves in public space to reshape in the landscape. In Chapter 2, we discussed women as organizers and agitators—through political parties and grassroots groups, formal and informal channels. Women often assume leadership roles and take on unprecedented levels of engagement and responsibility, particularly in national struggles.

There is ample evidence throughout the region's history to show the critical roles women play in the struggle for freedom. Although they encounter resistance, their efforts have not gone in vain. Research finds this true of every Arab country, even including more conservative states like Yemen, Libya, Bahrain, and Syria.[2] Contexts may differ, but this similarity remains: women in the Arab region courageously push the "boundaries of what is socially acceptable."[3]

National struggles are often not feminist, and adding women does not make them so. But feminist demands are emerging, born from desperate need for reforms, rule of law, democratization, political transparency, and—urgently—human rights.[4] Violations of these often lead to gender-specific demands, because of the gender-specific impacts these challenges expose. Often, once these gendered impacts are revealed, patriarchy becomes an additional frontline.

At the same time, women's *participation* in these struggles often fails to translate into women's *power*. Participation for the duration of the struggle is short-lived, and women are quickly marginalized once the struggle has been deemed "successful." All too often, liberation movements in the region fail to achieve actual liberation, and the national struggle continues for generations.

Ultimately, the national struggle has always superseded the feminist struggle in the region—Palestine, for instance. As a result, women's liberation is suspended—indefinitely—while the national quest continues. In short, we are told that it is "never the right time" for women's rights in the region.

We refute this, along with women's rights activists and many others who are on the frontlines of social change. Now is precisely the time to push more strongly for rights in the region. We need to be at the table—not on the menu.

Global research demonstrates that conflict and crisis can create enabling environments for women's rights to develop. Some scholars assert that conflict can help upend existing gender hierarchies and disrupt their social institutions.[5] Crisis and conflict can often become a vehicle for women's empowerment precisely because instability exposes more women to the public sphere, offering them opportunities to transform their normal social roles in this new space.[6] Protests, uprisings, and revolutions are no different in that they present opportunities to push for progress. Research on Arab women in revolutions tells us that "times of great flux are opportunities for bold decisions."[7] Political events can be those moments, charged with great potential for change. And women can both fight for their own freedom and lead in the fight for national freedom.

There exists a great deal of research on conflicts around the world, and documentation and literature on women's activism and gendered resistance in the Arab region is emerging. The voices of women on the frontlines add to this conversation, reminding us that moments—the "opportunities for bold decisions"—are taking place even as we write, providing an opportunity to advance the battle against patriarchy in favor of equality.

These moments present themselves as opportunities but often fall short in making a sustainable impact. We distinguish here between *moments* of rebellion—an act of resistance—and *movements* of revolution—the battle for a new social order. Although they had revolutionary intent, many rebellious moments did not translate into revolutionary movements. We ask *why?*

Women on the frontlines spoke of "golden moment(s) of unity,"[8] micro-rebellions that aim to challenge the status quo and ignite women. However, these golden moments were too short-lived, too disorganized, and too few. Very often, they remain isolated and viewed as individual incidents that cannot collectively form a movement. They can be seen as scattered, and lacking a long-term strategy or common goal. In some ways, these moments can be considered missed opportunities, failing to scale in ways that could be meaningful and sustainable for women and girls—and for societies overall.

Additionally, spatial politics obstruct gains for women because each rebellion is highly contextualized—situated in a specific place and time, tied to those social conditions. Through upheaval, space becomes redefined and social norms are temporarily disrupted. Looking at what happens in the transitional space in the aftermath of conflict, we believe that everything has changed—but nothing has changed.

In many instances, gains are ephemeral, progress is thwarted, and women are set back—again. Worse, women and girls experience new risks because of new (or renewed) vulnerabilities and new (or increased) forms of violence. Countless examples throughout the Arab region—Egypt, Tunisia, Bahrain, Jordan—show us how these movements never fully materialize and frequently lead to major regression. Women push, society pushes back, and women are left worse off than when they started.

Despite the dangers associated with conflict and resistance, and the disproportionate risk women and girls face, feminists in the region remain active on the frontlines. *But where are those frontlines for women?*

We have learned that these frontlines are public and political, private and creative, existing on all fronts in different forms. There is a burgeoning non-traditional activism emerging, one where the street is not always the frontline. In this chapter and the next, we will examine both—the formal and informal frontlines—to see where change is made and where gains are sustained.

We will not address all conflicts in the region, many other books do this better.[9] Instead, we will highlight key conflicts and crises where women are brought to the fore—whether out of desire or necessity. It is also beyond the scope of this work to assess these varying forms of activism, as time will tell whether these are short-lived rebellious moments or revolutionary feminist movements. We hope for the latter.

Our So-Called Arab Spring

> *Through engaging in these multiple forms of struggle, Arab women were, in fact, contesting and redefining new gendered spaces, politically, legally, and socially, which involved risk-taking and the exercise of agency, despite all forms of intimidation and in the face of many constraints.*
> —Dr. Sahar Khamis and Dr. Amel Mili[10]

Chapter 2 explored the pro-democracy uprisings the region experienced in 2011. Here, we discuss the role of women in the so-called Arab Spring—their actions and consequences before, during, and after.

The unprecedented and highly visible role women played in these uprisings is noteworthy. Women in the region have long been involved in protests, and their activism is not confined to this period, but the Arab Spring marked a noticeable shift in women's movements—for better and for worse. Women gained new leadership roles and recognition, making resistance politics of the region more inclusive. At the same time, they were met with greater resistance and pushback—and new risks.

The uprisings were not necessarily driven by gender equality and the revolutionaries were not necessarily feminists. And yet, these emerged. Gendered demands were present on the agenda from early stages due in large part to the prolific involvement of women.[11] Indeed, women and young people were instrumental in instigating and sustaining the Arab Spring uprisings. As Dr. Margot Badran remarks:

> During the most vibrant period of the uprisings, I observed what I call embedded feminism in the context of all the activities, demonstrations, marches, demands … women were aware of themselves as women … of their rights, of wanting to improve their conditions … this included women of various classes etc. also a feminism across gender divides, united in their demands, empowered, belonging…. I saw feminist aspirations, but not articulated as such.[12]

Women in all their diversity were involved, ushering in a new phase of feminist activism built on desires for national—and regional—solidarity. This women-led action "signifie[d] a new moment of unity, solidarity, and cohesion, mirroring the egalitarian, grassroots movement that they have come out to support."[13] Young women in particular were a driving force both leading to the Arab Spring events and *leading* Arab Spring events.[14] Most were operating individually and not part of formal women's organizations, using social media to gain traction and to galvanize nationally and regionally. These informal-organizers crossed pre-existing divides and engaged with people across social strata to envision a new order.

Women pushed boundaries, joined protests, and redefined what was socially acceptable. They were not only present in demonstrations on the street, they were also key players off the streets, galvanizing action through blogs and social media, arranging food deliveries, and providing medical assistance. Women also contributed to maintaining peaceful protests—as much as was possible. Amidst the chaos, they prevented street fights and worked to unite protesters under shared goals.

The wide participation of women in non-traditional roles was crucial because it contributed both to a renegotiation of public space and to the position of women in public space. Their very public involvement challenged traditional, patriarchal, and conservative norms present in Arab societies. Even more so, exercising agency, albeit with great risk, allowed women to politically and socially redefine these spaces. Women started making gender-specific demands alongside the calls for democracy, legislative reform, political accountability, and an end to corruption.

Ultimately, this came at great cost both during and after the demonstrations. Backlash against women took the form of verbal, physical, and sexual attacks perpetrated by security forces and others. Many were injured or imprisoned—and some lost their lives.[15] Protesters were resolute though, and the systematic targeting of women prompted more women and other social justice activists to coordinate action and make stronger demands for rights and justice.

This does not mean, however, that it was successful.

Country "Springs"

> *The idea of women rising is the idea that women continue to rise. They were rising in the past, they continue to rise today—we see women leading the protests in Lebanon,… in Sudan, in Iraq, in Algeria; and whether in protests or participating in conventional politics, women have shown to the world that they are finally claiming the space that they have always had— now, they have an opening.*
>
>   —Dr. Rita Stephan[16]

Women from all backgrounds participated in the protests demanding rights and justice, even as these demands were different for each context. Local context played a significant role in determining how the uprisings played out, how women participated in them, and how they fared afterwards. Here are a few examples of many throughout the region.

Tunisia

In Tunisia for instance, women were present and visible from the onset, and women's rights were an integral part of protest demands and subsequent transitional efforts. Feminist demands fit into the broader national campaign, calling for a democratic and secular society. Tunisia is often cited as a "success story" of the Arab Spring, given the implementation of free and fair elections, the successful transition of power, and the introduction of a quota for women. However, in 2011, only 49 women were elected to a 217-member group set up to draft a new constitution, and today, women remain significantly underrepresented. Economic deterioration, exacerbated by the COVID-19 pandemic, has created dire conditions for post-revolution Tunisians—particularly young women. In 2021, the female unemployment rate was reported at 24 percent, compared to 14 percent for men.[17] Young women in the country lack viable employment opportunities, resulting in deteriorating socio-economic conditions and increased migration.[18] Tunisia is a prime example, poised for reform but lacking substantial changes.

Egypt

In Egypt, protests were sparked by poverty, corruption, repression, and state violence. Women and young people were on the frontlines, calling for an end to brutalities and for greater opportunities, "just wanting to taste freedom for the first time in their lives."[19] The movement in Egypt cut across social divides because of its roots in labor and grassroots movements, where women played a large part. The *Kefaya* (Enough) Movement was founded in 2004 to call for political reforms and in 2008, working-class women on the margins of Cairo joined factory workers in calling for greater rights. These movements paved the way for the 2011 uprising. Egyptian women brought feminist demands into the revolution, advocating for access to basic services such as education and health, increased opportunities, and political representation.[20] Women demanded an end to violence at the hands of the military and "morality police" who frequently subjected women to detainment, beatings, and rape.[21]

Women bloggers and journalists also played a key role, documenting government brutality and creating spontaneous platforms for activism and solidarity.[22] Egyptian activist Asmaa Mahfouz, whose viral videos called on fellow citizens to join protests in Tahrir Square, is often credited with sparking the mass January protests that initiated the uprising.[23] On Twitter, activists such as Gigi Ibrahim and Nora Shalaby played a great role in crafting the revolution's narrative and influencing public opinion.[24] This provided online agitation beyond the purview of the authorities—at significant risk to their personal safety. The leadership of women in challenging the regime enabled resistance and fueled frequent reporting about the conditions within Egypt and to the world. Despite their efforts, women were "essentially cut out of the political process after playing such a vital role.”[25] Moreover, even though President Hosni Mubarak was deposed, the new regime under Mohamed Morsi undid many reforms of the previous decades.[26]

Yemen

In Yemen, women took to the streets, together with Yemeni men, to overthrow the autocratic regime. Over time, however, divisions appeared along regional, tribal, and sectarian lines.[27] Human rights activist and journalist Tawakkol Karman became a prominent figure throughout the revolution, even winning a Nobel Peace Prize for her involvement. Following the news that Mubarak had been deposed in Egypt, a crowd gathered at Sana’a University with the hope the same could be done to their President Saleh. Known as “the mother of the revolution,” and “the lady of the Arab Spring,” Karman had this to say to a group of women there:

> Now is the time for women to stand up and become active without asking for permission. Women are no longer victims—they have become leaders…. We want to retrieve our nation, we want to become citizens in a new world.[28]

Women’s prolific involvement in Yemen’s uprisings was a reaction to the resurgence of conservatism in society. President Saleh denounced women’s role in protesting his regime, stating that such activity—particularly the mixing of men and women in public—was un–Islamic. Saleh’s comment invoking religious values served to stoke tensions and further fuel anger and dissatisfaction with the government.[29] In response, over 100,000 people, including large numbers of women, demonstrated across Yemen to demand his resignation.[30] Saleh’s comments only emboldened female protesters. Some faced resistance from their families and communities, but many still marched on the frontlines—leading public rallies, sleeping in protest camps, and covering the demonstrations as bloggers and journalists—even as the government continued to restrict them.[31] Undoubtedly, female demonstrators played a key role in forcing Saleh to step down, which he did a year later.

Bahrain

In Bahrain, the pro-democracy uprisings were instigated in response to the Sunni-led Al Khalifa regime’s continued exclusion and discrimination of the Shi’a majority. On 14 February 2011, protesters gathered in the capital, setting up camp and peacefully calling for democratic reform and human rights. Inspired by the revolutions in the region, the main goal of the Bahraini revolution was constitutional reform. However, female activists leveraged the movement to draw attention to issues impacting women, most notably, legal discriminations. While the Sunni Muslim population rely on codified laws for divorce, child custody, and inheritance issues, the Shi’a majority used religious courts headed by clergymen who apply their own interpretations of *Shari’a* law, often to the detriment of women.[32] Women were instrumental in organizing campaigns, documenting human rights abuses, and exerting pressure on the government and international community to address violations. Additionally, women played a critical role in navigating sectarian divides and ideological conflicts, as well as creating an inclusive movement for change.[33] At the same time, Bahraini women experienced harsh backlash for their involvement in the uprisings including arbitrary detention, imprisonment, and torture—some were even killed.[34] Hundreds of young women were dismissed from universities, and many were threatened with rape or were sexually assaulted.[35] The years following have seen revolutionary hopes crushed and a deteriorating human rights situation.[36] The struggle for democracy remains.

In the Aftermath

> *Out of the 2011 revolution did come an explosion of different aspects of feminist awareness and activity—but not in a highly collective sense.*
> —Dr. Margot Badran[37]

In the aftermath, citizens across the region experienced brutal crackdowns, extensive backlash, and repressive countermeasures. Socio-economic conditions worsened, insecurity and state repression increased. The systematic targeting of women did not stop once the protests were over, and women found themselves victims of brutal backlash. Any signs of optimism during the uprisings were swiftly replaced with concern for the future of women's rights.

Women had expected that their participation would lead to inclusion in post-uprising transitions. Having fought side by side with men, many activists—particularly in Tunisia, Egypt, and Libya—imagined as much. This was not the case, however. Women who were at the helm during the uprisings were systematically excluded from decision-making and sidelined from political processes. Women felt the double standard set by men who were "keen to have them on the streets crying freedom [but] may not be so happy to have them in parliament, government, and business boardrooms."[38] Aftermath-exclusion of women is not new to the region and actually has a long, historical pattern.[39] When women have participated in resistance movements, "their gains, in terms of both space and independence, fade quickly."[40] Peace and progress are not possible without the full engagement of women. Globally, women's participation in transition and peace processes ensures that they are meaningful and durable.[41]

Women in the region were not only barred from participating, worse, they were expected to revert to traditional gender roles, despite increasing attacks on their rights. Multiple factors are to blame for this, including political elites excluding women and Islamist movements implementing their view of women's place in society. This has been well documented, with links made between the uprisings and subsequent setbacks of women's rights.

There were, however, differences across the region in the aftermath. Despite its semblance of unity, this women's wave that swept the region resulted in different feminist agendas, products of different contexts and reactions in each country. For countries like Syria, Yemen, and Libya, women's reality was that of failed states in prolonged conflict. For countries like Jordan, Lebanon, Egypt, Tunisia, and Morocco, women's hopes for reforms were thwarted, and discriminations prevailed. For Saudi Arabia, they continued to cloak their "oppressive patriarchal authority with a veneer of modernity."[42] Ultimately, it is safe to assume that women did not fare "better" anywhere after the revolutions.

And yet, there are some sources of optimism to take from the Arab Spring, specifically the emergence of a new wave of feminist activism. It is no small feat to see women participating in protests en masse across the region, visibly and actively redefining their role in society, and asserting their agency and independence. Transitional phases create space for women, and women of all backgrounds in the region claimed that space, providing new—and long overdue—voices and viewpoints to the common struggle for equality and rights.

This so-called "new wave" of feminisms emerging post-revolution marked a shift away from top-down, elite feminism to more grassroots, youth-led, action-oriented feminism. A feature of this wave was the inclusion of women's rights as part of a broader human rights conversation. The older generation of women's organizations were more single-issue focused, emphasizing political representation and economic empowerment while newer movements sought a broad range of human rights activism beyond singular issues.[43]

Additionally, the use of social media and alternative forms of activism during the pro-democracy uprisings informed future movements. Organizing was facilitated through access to information by wider networks, fueling the spread of ideas. While a critical protest tool, social media was also used by governments to track and silence dissenters, presenting new risks to activists.

Despite women's activism across the region, conditions for women remained unchanged at best or deteriorated at worst.[44] The uprisings ultimately failed to result in concrete change, and gender equality fell off the agenda. Expectations were thwarted and inequalities persisted in almost every aspect of life. Myriam Sfeir, Director of The Arab Institute for Women, explains that in times of conflict, women's rights are the first to fall. "It's not as if they ever took center stage," she says, "but they take a blow and they are put on the side."[45] In the years following the 2011 uprisings, protests continued as a result of deteriorating social, economic, and political conditions. And even in the face of resistance, women themselves continue to resist.

Sfeir summarizes the experience of the so-called "false spring" this way:

> Some of the feminist movement has been very active in terms of not accepting the status quo and fighting and being there and being present. For instance, at the time of the Arab uprisings and revolutions all over the Arab world, women were a force to be reckoned with. But at the same time, just like the Palestinian *Intifada*, and all the other movements when women participate in national struggle, so many times when the struggle takes a hit, or when something happens, like the COVID-19 pandemic or the Beirut blast, the movement takes a hit. Movements are crushed, people are crushed, when they worry about other things—look at Roe v. Wade [in the U.S.], look at Afghanistan, look at Iran. It is all related to a push back and a backlash against gender rights. And I don't think the region has enough commitment to change or ameliorate the situation of women simply because they're busy with other things. And never ever are women's rights a priority.

The Revolution Is Female and Resistance Is Everywhere

> *Look at what the feminist groups are doing on the ground. Look how agentic they are, how innovative they are, look at the many examples of amazing work, initiatives, resistance, and revolution. Too many to list.*
> —Dr. Charlotte Karam[46]

The Revolution Is Female—Al-Thawra untha. The motto of many movements in the region. Interestingly, the Arabic word for revolution (*thawra*) is female, as is the word for freedom (*'huriya*) and uprising (*intifada*).[47] We repeat: there is no revolution, no freedom, no peace without women. In the absence of these: uprising.

This long-overdue female revolution marked the moment that women collectively said "Enough!" Women claimed their space at the forefront of activism and protest. They fought, organized, advocated, agitated. In short, they revolted. While these demonstrations of women's activism—and anger—were remarkable, we also recognize the micro-movements, the "little transgressions," in the words of feminist activist Souad Mahmoud, the small everyday spaces in which women challenge oppressive structures. Mahmoud elaborates:

> We reinterpret traditions to create new margins and spaces of freedom, influence, and power, assuring every day our place in public spaces, where we have always been, despite restrictions. This place is built through "little transgressions" that allow us to take spaces of freedom. We move through the city, we produce, we negotiate, we resist, we empower ourselves, and we frustrate relations of domination.[48]

The focus on women in public protests should not undermine the impact of their "little transgressions," often invisible but no less powerful. As gender specialist Anthony Keedi articulates, "it's the simple actions that are taken every day, the ripples that make the waves that make the changes."[49]

Dr. Gabriella Nassif echoes this, adding:

> One of the critical entry points right now which is sad but also exciting is the fact that there's so much crisis and chaos in the region, and crisis always means that there's a potential to challenge the ruling powers, and there's potential to drive a stake at the heart of what is keeping the hegemony in place. So it's been really interesting watching what feminist groups are doing."[50]

The following section details the range of resistance. Protest takes on varied forms, and *all* manner of resistance is important, as long as the target is clear: the patriarchy. Resistance is central to daily life—for women, and in particular for women from the Arab region. Indeed, "nonviolent struggle comes from the life,"[51] when life is built from inequality. As one activist put it:

> You have to be willing to sacrifice for freedom, and above all else, believe in your cause and what you're struggling for. If you believe, you will continue, if you continue, you will succeed."[52]

It would be impossible to list all countries, all women, all resistance. For our purposes, we selected a snapshot each from the Levant, North and sub–Saharan Africa, and the Gulf. And we lament that we could not be exhaustive because there are many cases, and countries, and women who lead causes worth recognizing. This is the subject of a much longer study—we hope someone reading our words will take it on!

At the same time, we cannot speak of women on the frontlines without making special mention of Palestine, the region's longest running and most tragic conflict—for human rights and for women's rights. In the words of Palestinian feminist Muna Nassar:

> There's no resisting from the "frontlines" because the frontlines are different depending on where you are—but also because they are everywhere. All Palestinians are resisting because it is a constant, everyday thing. You are resisting even just by existing.[53]

Activist and academic Dr. Nadera Shalhoub-Kevorkian writes of the cultivating of "resistance-based knowledge" for women in Palestine, "taking into account what it means to be 'born under a system of state terrorism.'"[54] She "calls on feminists to support the non-negotiable right of Palestinian feminists to resist the occupation by indigenizing feminist knowledge, and by working towards 'building a feminist strategy for resistance.'"[55]

Arguably, Palestinian feminists are already doing this. Women have always played an integral role in Palestinian resistance, despite violent backlash and attacks. Struggle and resistance is a legacy, passed from generation to generation, because existence itself is the struggle. Muna El Kurd, an activist from Sheikh Jarrah—an area constantly subjected to Israeli attacks and forced evictions—says, "every Palestinian woman is a kind of teacher of resistance and struggle. Every Palestinian woman is a symbol."[56]

The following country stories are women's stories, built around the story of a singular woman and her fight for freedom. These women are extraordinary, but they are not unique. They likely serve as an amalgam for all women, women whose existence symbolizes resistance.

We argue that, whether in conflict or not, there remains a conflict for women. We do not define war in the traditional sense. Rather, we look at the war that we face in every space and time—the war against women. For women, the frontlines are at home, on the streets, and in personal spaces just as much as in communities and countries. Even if peace for a nation exists, peace for women is illusive.

Here we focus on the story of one woman to illustrate the journey of the individual in this collective struggle. "Wars" can be fought behind the wheel and in basements just as much as on the streets. We present a snapshot of this wide range. These stories reveal the importance of individual actions and micro-moments, and also remind us of the perpetual need to turn these moments of rebellion into movements of revolution—no matter what form they take.

Most importantly, we invite you to imagine the many, many women who exist beyond these pages.

Building a Women's Political Movement in Syria

Mariam Jalabi starts her story this way:

> The Syrian women's political movement was formed because myself and few other women realized, after working with the Syrian opposition for almost seven years, that there was no way for us to become part of the official opposition or be in the official corridors of negotiations, or be in high-level meetings, if we were part of a body that is already led by men. There was a meeting for the opposition in Riyadh and it did not include any women. Seventy men. So at the time, we created a statement by Syrian women that was signed by over 500 people and said that over 75 civil society organizations and others felt that this was unacceptable. As a catalyst to that statement, a few of us women came together. We were seven....[57]

Jalabi is, amongst many other things, the Co-Founder of the Syrian Women's Political Movement.[58] Jalabi is fueled by the injustice and inequality she sees around her, in every country and every context. "The world is built for men—young, abled, men. No one thinks of anything else that does not fit into that stereotypical man's world," she asserts. "Men don't think to include us. They assume because they have access, that is enough. They do not realize that not everyone has this access!"

The 2011 uprising in Syria against President Assad's regime escalated into a full-blown war—a war now in its eleventh year. Peace negotiations have proven unsuccessful, and women were sidelined in the process. In fact, UN peace talks did not even include women until 2016—and still women have not been adequately represented.[59]

Jalabi continues:

> The seven became twenty-eight. Twenty-eight co-founders. In consultation with many, many other women. We decided that we needed to establish something for us, a bloc for us, a body for us, the Syrian women, and the feminists, the ones who wanted to change how policy was being made for Syria. And we realized also that policy being made for Syria was not just specific to Syria. We are part of a global structure, a global economy, global politics, that is rooted and led by very patriarchal systems and very patriarchal priorities. And we wanted to create something that steps outside of all of those systems and all those ways of working.

Syrian women have long experienced marginalization and must shoulder incredible burdens as a result of the conflict. High numbers of male casualties have resulted in more women heads of households, struggling to provide for their families.

Jalabi continues, animated:

> We wanted to start our own bloc, our own work, our own movement. At the beginning, it wasn't going to be a movement, actually. We were thinking like a bloc, a party, but then we realized, being in the diaspora and spread all over the world, it will be better to be more in the structure of a movement. And so we became a movement.

The Syrian Women's Political Movement describes itself as composed of "political women and men who have struggled against the tyrannical regime." Collectively, they demand freedom, justice, dignity for all Syrians—particularly for women, whose rights and freedoms have been dramatically impacted. The movement is inclusive, and represents all Syrians who "believe in the same principles including women's rights, gender equality and the importance of women empowerment and active participation in all aspects of life and decision-making circles for the future of Syria."[60]

Jalabi explains how the movement grew and gathered support:

> We focused on the work that we needed to do, because we needed all of the possible support for all of the women who believed in this, in the principles of feminist policy. So the motto for it when we started at the beginning was very basic. Each one of us, on our own, trying so hard, making very little progress. We believed that the whole of us—together—will be so much stronger and so much better than the sum of our parts.

Coming together gave the movement the strength it needed, a multiplication of power, Jalabi calls it. Coming together under one banner, one umbrella, enabled the moment to become a movement—and to become powerful.

> And that's how the Syrian women's political movement was established in October 2017. So now we're five years old! And now we are recognized and known in the political scene. We go to meetings at the highest levels with the international community. We have pushed and raised women's participation in the political process. We doubled the participation. It was about seven percent. And now it's 15 percent.

Jalabi explains that not all members of the movement come from the same places, or subscribe to the same processes. Their strength is in their diversity.

> Many of the members of the Syrian women's political movement are included in the different bodies that work at the UN in the political process, or in all of the different political bodies that are working with Syria. So we have members in this political opposition, and

that political opposition. Among us are also many women who are leading in civil society work and who work on the ground. All of us. And together, it is fruitful. We give each other support.

It is through this support that the movement remains solid, even in the face of challenges. Jalabi talks about her personal experience engaging with the UN:

Every panel I go to, every political meeting, it's all men! And then what do they say when they see one Syrian woman?! "Oh we are so happy to see a woman here, to see women's representation!" while they are an entire room of men!

These imbalances galvanize her into action. She continues to tell the story of the movement:

We help each other, train each other. For women who want training on media, training on writing. We have our website, we have so many different elements that keep women engaged at different levels. We get funding from Canada, from France, from the UK…

Syrian women's movements have a rich history—and Jalabi finds energy in this movement. "I personally find that being part of such a movement is what keeps me going," she says. "It is very difficult to keep doing the kind of work we're doing, as women." The movement gives her strength. She explains that they needed a structure that brought them together. Their events and annual meetings keep the movement connected and energized. "I find that keeps me going," Jalabi explains, "because I keep seeing these women and there's always something to do with them." They work collectively, she says, adding that "there's a lot of openness in how to bring forward opportunities and projects that we work on."

Every year they formulate a plan, request funding, take action. "This takes a lot of work and a lot of time to get anything done," Jalabi says, but the effort is worth it. "This is a collaborative effort between all of the different women, which creates this very crazy, very nice atmosphere. We fight a lot!"

Indeed, the Syrian crisis needs a collaborative effort. The devastating humanitarian impact of the war cannot be understated. It is estimated that 6.9 million Syrians are internally displaced, while 5.6 million are refugees, and figures from 2022 indicate that 14.6 million Syrians require assistance.[61] The country faces increasing poverty, food insecurity, economic deterioration, political instability, and constant violence.

Jalabi explains that, despite the differences, they learn how to solve them collectively. "We learn how to talk to each other, we learn how to be together." Jalabi continues:

It's been inspiring for me, and for many other women. We address the issues, the problems, that we as women have, to be part of policymaking globally, policymaking for Syria. Because, policymaking for Syria is directly connected to policymaking globally. We see how the global political structure is formed, how things are getting done, for every country, every corner in the world.

And that is how they engage, by ensuring that women have a role in Syrian—and global—policymaking. "We think of these things, like more projects, more resources, more access for women," Jalabi says, "to get them to decision-making places." She adds:

After we started the political body, we realized that a lot of women can't be part of politics, can't be part of all these different places and spaces because they don't have access to resources, they don't have access to connections, to people, to power structures. Not like men do. Men already have wealth, have the time, have the connections, to powerful people.

How can we create something like that? How can women be more involved in think tanks and writing and in having access to different policymakers, access to governments, access to funding, access to all kinds of resources?

Jalabi explains that this is one thing, among many, that has come out of their work with the Syrian Women's Political Movement, the realization that, for a movement to take hold, "we need to think a little more deeply and put a little more effort if we want to have women in policy-making and decision-making places."

Jalabi adds that men assume women need to be taught and educated, as if "we are witnesses—not the ones who create knowledge, make knowledge, produce knowledge." Her feminism starts here, with the belief that women have the knowledge they need, but need the resources and support to gain access.

In her work, she builds the movement by asking: "What are the things that we need to provide women with? And we provide those things."

Saudi Arabia, a Driving Force

A notable example of moment-to-movement is the agitation and activism employed to lift the driving ban on Saudi Arabian women. Saudi Arabia is well known for constraining women by extreme interpretations of religious texts that deny their freedom of mobility and bodily autonomy. And the driving ban served as a symbol of the country's repressive attitude towards women and their denial of women's rights and fundamental freedoms. Yet Saudi Arabian women have long resisted their government's edicts— on and off the roads.

The initial protests of the driving ban date back to 1990 when 47 women drove in Riyadh, Saudi Arabia, in a coordinated attack against the patriarchy. The women were all subsequently arrested and had their passports confiscated. In response to the demonstration, authorities passed an official decree outlawing driving for women where previously it had been a customary ban.[62] Undeterred, momentum grew with a petition in 2007 and later the "Women2Drive" campaign in 2011 led by Manal al-Sharif, inspired by the Arab Spring protests. Many women activists took to the road but were detained, arrested, and sentenced. Despite violent backlash and crackdowns, the movement remained active over the next few years, with women taking videos of themselves driving and uploading them to social media.

We spoke to a Saudi Arabian women's rights activist who was arrested, imprisoned, and tortured by authorities for her participation in the driving protests. She said the driving campaign divided people, with one group believing in the rights but not the methods. They saw it as a very confrontational strategy and said other channels should have been used. There was another group against the driving campaign, harder to convince of the goal because they believed that the women were going against Islam. The violent response and the arrest of activists brought about a shift. Many could now see the unfairness and the brutality which slowly made them question their situation. They could see that the women did nothing wrong, but were still punished.

What they did not know, she explained, was that the activists had exhausted every available avenue up to that point with parallel aspects of the campaign. Since the 1990s, they had been communicating with the King and had been speaking to the government as they were legally entitled, but it had to be done in secret. A lot of the work was done behind closed doors, and most people were unaware. They eventually reached a point where there was no other option, as efforts did not yield results, and activists had nothing left to lose. Public pressure was the last resort, and it worked. But the consequences were brutal. The lifting of the ban was introduced in 2017 but was not official until 2018. This marked a turning point with activists getting arrested. Our contact disclosed: "The day they announced women could legally drive, I was in a secret prison getting tortured."[63] She was subjected to torture, sexual harassment, solitary confinement, and more.

In August 2022, a few days before we spoke, a video surfaced of authorities storming an orphanage, beating and chasing girls down.[64] The girls had been protesting conditions and demanding rights. The footage has served a separate purpose insofar as people who did not initially believe the activist now started to believe her brutal experience of imprisonment, seeing the abuse and hypocrisy with their own eyes. Greater documented evidence will paint a clearer picture, and she believes that exposing more violations will be better for the wider cause.

The lifting of the driving ban did not mean freedom was granted. In fact, many women found themselves trapped more than they had been when the ban was in place. Previously, women could go anywhere with a driver. After the new law, men resisted and women were imprisoned in their own homes, not able to leave. Legalizing driving did not change some parts of society, and inverted it in some cases. They blamed the activists, and this hurt the movement. She felt it to be a betrayal by women who were blaming the wrong people, failing to see the efforts for the collective good.

Meanwhile, Crown Prince Mohammed bin Salman is rapidly introducing changes, although people are unaware—or unprepared. Saudi Arabia's so-called transformation strategy could be viewed as a calculated political exercise to repair a fractured reputation and score public relations points with the international community.[65] For women, these transformations remain as tokenistic and cosmetic, rather than actual changes in the name of fundamental human rights.

The activist explained how there are two very different realities in the country existing in parallel. While the shiny artificial international image is being projected, there is a climate of fear and silence due to brutal crackdowns. "Darkness is spreading," she said. There are less people involved, less documentation, and any organizing in civil society has effectively been thwarted.

Feminists and activists are, however, tying to utilize this to their advantage. She hopes that exposing the government's violations will continue, and that the authorities will be forced to allow civil society to organize as a result. If even on a small scale initially, this will be a start, she says. "It's about existence," she says, "to prove it's always been there. It's not novel, it's not Western, it's not foreign—and this is an opportunity to build a cumulative experience so we are not repeating the same mistakes."

It is this loss of cumulative experience that she laments. Knowledge, she articulates, must be upheld by civil society space and the ability to document work in solidarity and safety. In the absence of this, mistakes are repeated, and the movement is set back.

This plays out clearly online, in the new phase of cyberfeminism in Saudi Arabia:

> They are repeating the same conversations—and mistakes—of the past which means there is no growth or progress in the community. There is no management, no organization, no discourse, no sharing, no continuity. It's superficial.

There has also been a return to anonymity due to the danger of using their names in public:

> We have gone back to before when the same thing happened with the driving campaign and authorities could say those with no names are not Saudi, and it worked and killed the movement.

While this is built from fear and lack of civil society space, it is also because "we also don't know who is who, there's always new faces." Many of the women who were imprisoned felt abandoned and turned their backs on the movement. But our contact explained it was difficult for activists to help because they did not know who was imprisoned.

The activist hopes that civil society space can once again be built to share knowledge, learnings, and stories. And she says women are not giving up.

A Sudanese Dream

Sudan is a consistently fragile state. Protracted conflict has brought economic instability, increasing humanitarian needs, and volatile peace deals, all of which compound to make women and marginalized groups even more vulnerable. Forms of gender-based violence such as girl-child marriage, female genital mutilation, and others continue unabated. Malnutrition and school drop-out disproportionately affect women and girls.[66] Women are the first and last victims. Yet they continue to resist.

We spoke to Yosra Akasha, a Sudanese journalist and feminist, galvanized into activism in university. The political climate at the time was opening as a result of a comprehensive peace agreement, but there was still little space for women. As a result, Akasha launched her blog *Sudanese Dream* to highlight this absence and address the myriad struggles faced by women in Sudan.[67]

Akasha faced enormous backlash for her commentary. Here she speaks of the threats she received:

> I got the first big attack when I wrote an article about my life without hijab, in 2014. People on Twitter started a hashtag to call for my rape in public. Last year too, I had a couple of incidents. One time I went on national TV with a short skirt and afterwards, people all over social media were saying those are the fruits of having a civilian-led government, we don't want those images to be in our houses, and so on. And that was the light in comparison to other instances. Another time I received death threats from someone affiliated with ISIS after participating in a couple of campaigns. I filed a police report and informed the Prime Minister's office at that time, but no one did anything.[68]

Towards the end of 2017, Akasha was forced to leave the country for security reasons. "It affected my mental health," she said. "It affected my safety. If something happened, I had to be really careful and think about where I went and at what time." But she returned after the revolution. "Now I feel more resilient," she continued, "it's not affecting me as it was before."

The 2018 revolution that successfully overthrew Omar al-Bashir would not have been possible without women. The generation that took to the streets was born and raised under al-Bashir's 30-year oppressive reign, which was particularly harsh to women. Examples of discrimination include dress and behavior codes targeting women, gender segregation, and determining appropriate jobs for women. Al-Bashir's regime came to an end thanks in large part to the "Women's Revolution"—women were 70 percent of protesters.[69]

Akasha says she was impressed by feminist activists—young feminists in particular. Even women who did not directly participate joined the cause by organizing networks, encouraging other women to join as well as cooking and donating food. At the same time, women experienced great risk in the form of arrests, rape, torture, and even death.[70] There were harsh crackdowns as government forces responded to protests with violence against the women activists in a bid to silence them. One official even said, "Break the girls, because if you break the girls, you break the men."[71]

In the end, women did not benefit from significant gains post-revolution. Transitional processes lacked women, with women given only two of the 11 seats on the Sovereign Council, an entity designed to lead Sudan through a three-year political transition.[72] There was still work to be done. Akasha once again became actively involved and helped organize a march in 2021. Women were agitating for change. Akasha continues:

> There is no protection whatsoever for women at any level and there is a high level of impunity. Women are facing gender-based violence within the family, on the streets, in the workplace, even in the protest areas. Everywhere. Even in conflict they face it from not only the enemy but also from people within their communities and from the humanitarian workers. The lack of protection and gender-based violence is endemic in Sudan.

A number of entities drafted what was called the Feminist Manifesto, presented to the Minister of Justice in April 2021.[73] It included numerous demands such as equality in inheritance, that children born out of wedlock to be registered under the name of their mothers if they wish, the right to adoption, and many others. The Feminist Manifesto was the result of two years' work and consultations by various civil society and grassroots groups who hoped it would serve as an intersectional feminist agenda for all Sudanese women. It opened up space for much needed dialogue and highlighted the desire for common ground among women's groups.

However, women's rights as articulated in the Manifesto succumbed to what is commonly referred to as the "tyranny of the urgent," meaning that women's rights were sidelined due to supposedly more pressing concerns.

When asked about the interplay between women's rights and humanitarian needs, Akasha shares one example:

> During one particular inter-communal conflict, there was a campaign started to collect donations to buy sanitary pads for refugee and internally displaced women. Then, on social media, there was a backlash with people saying things like "why don't you provide them with food or shelter?" Of course, that's beyond our capacity, and there are so many other organizations providing things like food and shelter and other important stuff. But the issue of sanitary pads is also important. And every time I get taken aback by the audacity of politicians and activists, who would say, "this is not important." But you do not have a woman's body to judge what is important and what is not.

International organizations also fell short for women in failing to prioritize the agendas articulated by feminist movements. Akasha explains that they are "trying to impose certain agendas" on the movement, which "does not work." She explained that they exert pressure and dictate the agenda "because they are donors they are coming with money, they have the money."

What is your "Sudanese Dream" now, we ask her?

Akasha wants radical change—total reform of laws, policies, and structures. Her biggest dream is this:

> I want the care work women provide for their families to have an economic value, because
> if that happens, then they will be economically independent, they would have the ability to
> walk away from abusive relationships, they would be able to participate politically.

And they would be powerful. Although she does not believe it will happen in her life-time, Akasha says, "I would be optimistic, but I don't think I'll witness this. It might not happen before I die."

And she adds: "But from now until that day, I will do everything possible for this to happen."

Fighting for Women in Jordan

Jordanian culture—like other Arab states—is patriarchal, restricting women to traditional gender roles, with women in the domestic sphere and men as the providers and protectors. Jordan is also largely tribal, contributing to traditional attitudes and also placing women at risk of violence—particularly domestic and sexual violence. Little exists in the way of protection or support services, and perpetrators are rarely punished.

Sometimes, the frontlines are personal.

Lina Khalifeh was galvanized into action in university. A friend of hers showed up with bruises as a result of violence meted by her father and brother, violence she was forced to endure daily. Seeing the impact of this, Khalifeh was angry.

At the same time, she recognized that the trappings of patriarchy prevented many women from acknowledging and acting upon this abuse. She explains:

> It is not only about the existence of domestic violence, or harassment in Jordan. It's that
> women do not know they are oppressed. They think they are free, but they are oppressed in
> all ways. They have been controlled by one man their whole lives, and they think that is the
> norm.

In a bid to help women protect themselves, and in the absence of social safety nets, Khalifeh founded SheFighter in 2012—the first self-defense studio for women in Jordan. Growing up, Khalifeh witnessed war, poverty, and injustice. And for women—rampant inequalities and violence. At that time, she did not understand why, but she understood that she must defend herself. "You either learn to fight because you are about to live a life of challenges, or you quit and follow their system."[74]

Competitive and physically active from a young age, Khalifeh found her passion in Taekwondo. She actively resists socio-cultural stereotypes, saying, "I have never believed that women were weak. In fact, I have always believed that women are so strong that they can change the world, they just don't know it yet."[75] And so SheFighter began, with Khalifeh teaching Taekwondo to women in the basement of her parents' home.

SheFighter embodies the message of women's strength and teaches women to fight on two fronts: physical defense and the fight against social oppression. Khalifeh believes approaches to violence against women are reactionary instead of precautionary. As a feminist and activist, she sees self-defense as a way to combat this. SheFighter has since grown to partner with many networks for the empowerment of women and youth, becoming a successful enterprise recognized nationally, regionally, and internationally.

But it has not always been easy.

Khalifeh speaks about her struggle and the backlash she experienced. She explains that toxic masculinity fuels the patriarchal attitudes that force men to suppress their emotions and abuse their power, allowing violence against women to happen.

> Men are not allowed to express their emotions and then they explode totally. When they explode they commit crimes. Men believe the statement "We are men" is the explanation of the way they lead their lives. And in a way it is, but it is moreover the root of the crimes.[76]

In response, Khalifeh advocates for working side by side with men, and has created men's workshops for this purpose. At the same time, she argues that women need to support each other more strongly, to prepare to act without their inherited and indoctrinated fear. Khalifeh works for women to be strong, proactive, and unafraid to use their voice to become influencers, change-makers, and leaders.

Rana Husseini, author of *Years of Struggle: The Women's Movement in Jordan*, reminds us that:

> History has shown us that any breakthrough in the women's rights space was the result of long and sustained collective effort and advocacy over many years and by multiple organizations, individuals or groups.[77]

Husseini confirms that "the women's movement must find a way to 'repoliticize its agenda' to achieve strategic rights for women." And sometimes this starts in a basement.

Khalifeh fights on, asserting that every woman has the right to "stand up, defend herself, and live."

Lebanon's Revolution Is Women's Revolution

Feminist activist Hayat Mirshad starts this way:

> For the first time in the history of Lebanon, there's a movement, a revolution, from the people. Unplanned. Organic. Women on the ground, women leading. This movement was grassroots and popular, not organized by any political side or religion, as we are used to in Lebanon, that's why there was space for women to be present, to lead.[78]

The October 2019 revolution in Lebanon was an inevitable force, built from many transgressions. The last straw came after the government proposed a tax for use of WhatsApp.[79] Protests began as a demand to put an end to corruption. Slogans such as *Kellon Yaani Kellon* (all of them means all of them) blamed all of those in power and demanded radical change.

"October 17 was our day, our moment," one young activist said. "Our glory. People got tattoos of this date. It changed us forever. Because it gave us hope."

Mirshad tells the story:

> In this revolution, women were present everywhere. Against the usual image that says women are not in conflict. We were there! Road blockages, facing the police and army, demonstrations and chants. Women were everywhere. The Revolution is Female. That was the name of our movement, to mainstream feminist causes. People on the ground joined us. We told them "Women's demands are part of this revolution." There's no revolution without women, and no reform without women.

Feminist activist and academic Dr. Carmen Geha writes that Lebanese women had been "living under apartheid" and at last, this was their revolution. "We had to be at the heart of it," she writes, because "more than anyone else, we women know what it means to be discriminated against, beaten, thrown in jail, refused custody, raped, paid less, and treated differently...."[80]

Indeed, Lebanon was on the brink of revolution before this, and women were on the frontlines before this. "Women have always been leading," Mirshad says. "Women were involved in all political stages during the Civil War and involved in trying to make peace between the factions.[81] And in the *You Stink* movement, and in every other movement since."[82]

Mirshad explains that the deteriorating economic situation was a driver, but the revolution was built from the "social struggles of all the people, all the struggles they've been living with."

"We as a people," she continues, "we've been working on building this movement." Feminists have long been fighting the government, Mirshad says, because it is "corrupt and patriarchal and practices violence and repression against women and minority groups."

On October 17, women finally claimed their rightful place on the frontlines. Geha writes of those early days with optimism:

It has now been over 100 days, and women have transformed political life as we know it. We did not wait for any donor, NGO, or government to come and empower us. We waited for each other and looked out for each other. We knew intuitively that the only way to organize was a feminist one, through inclusive, horizontal, and decentralized forms of leadership. We did not let the men monopolize the scene and tell us what to do. Actually, that part was easy—because we were the majority and they could not monopolize the spaces, and because frankly they did not know what to do and so could not mansplain the revolution to us.[83]

Mirshad continues:

As women, we're concerned with social, political, and economic causes. Our causes are political causes. Women organized movements all around the country, especially young women, in all of Lebanon, even in areas where it was thought that it would not happen. And in all of Lebanon, women were demanding rights to identity, to political roles, to peace talks, for LGBT, for migrant workers, for refugees.

During the revolution, women infiltrated male-dominated spaces. This was, Mirshad explains, "an opportunity for us to stress that our causes are a vital part of the demands of the people."

Women remained steadfast in the face of violent backlash, "literally placing their bodies between other protesters and state forces."[84] Female protesters were subjected to sexual harassment and all forms of misogyny. Geha articulates that "...women have experienced this revolution very differently than men, because our struggles with the system are so existential. It is about our livelihoods, bodies, and voices."[85]

"But sadly, history does not give us justice." Mirshad explains that women were not mentioned in the media, unless it was to objectify them. One newspaper article even ran with the title: "Lebanese babes: all beautiful women are revolting."[86]

Worse, Mirshad says, "women did not get rights in the revolution. We were excluded from making decisions." And today, the struggle continues, Mirshad explains. The continued economic crisis, COVID-19, and the Beirut blast put their revolutionary plans on hold.[87] "It was a big hit and took us backwards years, especially as the women's rights movement, especially because before that, we were on the frontlines." Women were lobbying, advocating, struggling to change laws, change mentalities, change old traditions, Mirshad says.

"We had a big influence," she explains, "and we were able to get lots of laws changed—domestic abuse, Article 522, and pass a law to protect from sexual harassment."[88]

Unfortunately, there was not enough change afterwards, despite their prominent role. And women in Lebanon must continue to fight for basic rights. For instance, Lebanese women still cannot pass their citizenship onto their spouses or children, depriving their families of critical citizenship rights.[89] Civil marriage, or a marriage recorded and recognized by a government official instead of a religious cleric, is still not recognized within the country.[90] Lebanese women remain subjected to unfair rulings in child custody cases, which are determined exclusively in religious courts with little to no government oversight.[91]

The revolution continues. Today, Lebanon faces unprecedented levels of poverty. This once-middle income country now has 78 percent of its population below the poverty line.[92]

"Sadly, now we are back to service delivery, which in my opinion is very dangerous," Mirshad continues. It is a great setback for the women's movement, especially after having been on the frontlines. The new reality for women and girls in Lebanon is one of poverty, and as a result, basic needs trump strategic change. Rather than focusing on long-term goals, women's groups are filling a gap in the absence of a viable government—providing humanitarian support for women and girls.

Mirshad explains that "even when there is peace and stability, women's issues are not a priority. So now when the situation is more challenging and we're in crisis, women's issues are even more deprioritized."

Even though the revolution was not what women had hoped, there were promising outcomes. Women realized their power to make change, and their power on Lebanon's frontlines. That revolution was female. And, arguably, the next one will be also. Geha summarizes it this way:

> Surely the personal is political, and in our case, as Lebanese women, the political is revolutionary. For it is only through revolutionary, radical change that we will have the chance to be properly heard and meaningfully represented.[93]

Mirshad concludes:

> For me, the revolution did not end when it was stopped. For me, the seeds are there in one way or another, no matter how long. I have big hope that we will rise again and women will be part of it. And as women's organizations, we did not stop organizing, meeting, discussing, moving. In spite of it all.

Women as Symbols and Icons

> *I am a woman, and that is my weapon.*
> —Malak Alaywe-Herz[94]

From many revolutions, singular images of individuals were embraced as icons of the moment. Images have the power to capture the energy of a revolution, a historic snapshot of a moment, preserved. They are powerful in their organic state. Often these moments were made immortal by chance. No one posed for these pictures. They happened, and they were captured at the right time, in all their raw power.

The women in these images became icons because they strike a chord close to the heart, because these women are at once exceptional and ordinary. They are familiar, yet they wear openly the passion, courage, and hope that so many feel and wish to embody. They unite and inspire. They capture our imagination. And so they become symbols of the movement. To be sure, there are so many people on the frontlines in those moments showing the same passion and courage. Their photos may have been taken—or not. Even if their revolutionary acts go unnoticed by the mainstream media, they are no less revolutionary.[95] And their moment is no less powerful. Here are only a few examples.

Algeria

In 2019, just prior to International Women's Day, protests erupted on the streets of Algeria against President Bouteflika. The demonstrations involved women and youth and included large nationwide strikes affecting transportation and schooling.[96] The country was at a standstill. In Algiers, women were largely visible in the movement, issuing a manifesto against the restrictive family code, fighting for equal rights, and even establishing a "feminist square" in the University of Algiers.[97] Women in the feminist square were threatened, but not deterred.

During the protests, Rania G, a photographer from Algeria, captured Melissa Ziad dancing in the street. Ziad was dubbed the "Ballerina of Hope" and the photo became a symbol of the revolution. On Instagram, Ziad shared the photo with the caption: "An alternative to the dominant system can be expressed through artistic creativity, thus initiating a revolution in ways of thinking."[98] The photographer shared that "art can be a source of political change." She went on to say that the "more Algerian women see women participating in this movement, the more it will encourage them to participate."[99] This illustrates the ways in which women and youth are conceptualizing protest in new ways through art and hope, resonating with the population at large.

Sudan

In 2019, Sudanese photographer Lana Haroun captured a photo of then 22-year-old student Alaa Salah in a white thobe standing atop a car with a finger in the air addressing a crowd of women. The image of Salah inspired many women and spurred on revolutionary efforts during nationwide uprisings against leader Omar al-Bashir. These protests, like many across the region, featured women at the forefront. In fact, 70 percent of the protesters on the streets during those months of revolution were female.[100] Women's protest in Sudan has a long history, with women leading the October Revolution in 1964 and the 1985 revolt against the Nimeiri regime, two peaceful revolutions in the country.[101]

Salah took part in the protests because she dreamed of a better Sudan. For her, the popularity of the image was useful in that it spread awareness of the revolution not just in Sudan, but internationally.[102] And internationally, it served as a reminder that women throughout the region are leading the charge for change. Salah does not, however, call herself an icon of the revolution. "All Sudanese people are the icons of the revolution," she says.[103]

Lebanon

Malak Alaywe-Herz was filmed kicking an armed bodyguard during the protests in Lebanon. That moment was captured, and she became the iconic "Kick Queen," a symbol for the revolution. The video of her went viral and was reproduced in images, memes, and even as merchandise. One art historian remarked that Alaywe-Herz's kick became so iconic because the image is not only aesthetically impressive, it also fits the mold of "women fighting against oppression," popular in photography and paintings.[104] Alaywe-Herz's video and image rallied people to action.

Alaywe-Herz said that Lebanon is a "non-functioning country." She went on to say that "it might have been better had he killed me. It would have been really symbolic. This is the only way for things to change."[105] The image summed up the struggles protesters fought against, symbolizing both hope and futility for their cause. Months later, Alaywe-Herz was summoned to military court to stand trial.

Her message to all Lebanese women was to never underestimate their power, to be strong, and to bring down the system. "In this part of the world," Alaywe-Herz said "women's rights are not given, they are taken."[106]

Iraq

Anti-government protests erupted in October 2019 in Iraq due to rising unemployment levels, deteriorating living conditions, and political corruption. Prime Minister Adil Abdul-Mahdi resigned as a result of public pressure, but conditions have not improved and unrest continues. Here too, women are at the forefront, risking their lives.

Saba al Mahdawi, volunteer medic and women's human rights defender, was abducted by an unidentified militant group on her way home from a demonstration in Baghdad's Tahrir Square. She had been volunteering at the anti-corruption demonstrations, providing medical attention to protesters.[107]

Global advocacy groups mobilized, calling for her release. The photo used to campaign for her release shows al Mahdawi standing in front of a row of protesters on a Baghdad street, making the peace sign with each hand.[108] Al Mahdawi was released after eleven days.

In an article aptly titled "Civil disobedience, not terrorism, is the biggest threat to Iraq's elites," Tallha Abdulrazaq writes:

> The beauty of the current protests is that the people of Iraq are themselves leading the charge for deep-rooted reform in their country…. People like Saba have legitimacy. Because they are peaceful, known to their community, and are willing to stand bravely in the face of fire to call for the collective rights of all Iraqis….[109]

Al Mahdawi became a national symbol for her bravery, and spurred women around the country into action.[110] Today, women and youth continue to be a driving force of the demonstrations, "for the collective rights of all."

Singular Heroines

While we celebrate these images—and imagine the many others we did *not* see—there are criticisms of these "singular heroines." Academic Dr. Ibtesam Al Atiyat writes that the feminist agenda has "adopted an extreme form of individual salvation: New forms of feminist activism embody neoliberal ideals as shown in individual struggles and singular heroines."[111]

We recognize that "individual struggles" and "singular heroines" are a *moment*— not a *movement*. At the same time, we recognize that their image has value, and their presence has power. In the end, history will judge....

These images serve a purpose: they are visual, translatable, relatable—nationally and internationally. Not only do these images galvanize and mobilize other women in revolution, but they deconstruct pervasive international stereotypes of the oppressed Arab woman in need of saving. Instead, they highlight women in the Arab region actively resisting, saving themselves—and their countries.

The same argument can be made for Iran, a country which, at the time of writing, is experiencing a revolution led by young women who, after decades of oppression, will seemingly stop at nothing until they achieve reforms. In other words, women of the region are not now—nor have ever been—as helpless as the world thinks. And, here too, like its Arab neighbors, people have begun to accept women as the face of revolutions. At the same time, activism is still individual, the so-called singular heroine. Once again, we ask: *Is this a moment—or a movement?*

Across the region, feminists are taking up space in new ways and demanding visibility. Even if the long-term goals remain out of reach, we hang onto these women-as-symbols because their anger, courage, and hope is contagious. And there is hope that even more women will stand up and speak out in the face of patriarchy.

Cyberfeminism

> *Through social media shedding light on these issues [of inequality in the law], this reached the targeted authorities and they are looking into changing the laws around that.*
>
> —Young Bahraini activist

The rapid spread of technological advances, coupled with the younger generations of feminists, has helped propel feminism in the region into the online sphere. The utilization of online platforms, and social media in particular, brings people together to spread a message, gain visibility, and garner support and solidarity. As such, cyberfeminism is becoming "an increasingly effective tool to denounce misogyny and social injustices against women."[112]

Online activism can be a powerful tool in spreading awareness with ease and speed across borders—geographic, ideological, or otherwise. Cyberfeminism specifically has been cited as an equalizer in this regard, contributing to generating transnational solidarities amongst women's movements in the region.[113] Cyberfeminism also creates space for those in less open societies to express themselves with anonymity— to a certain extent. This opens avenues for new dialogue, community-building, sharing, and learning.

Even though there are many positives, online activism is not without drawbacks or dangers. These exist, magnifying vulnerabilities. Participation for many women is dangerous and brings new risks: death threats, harassment, cyberstalking, bullying, and more. In a bid to shrink online activism and silence dissent, authorities have introduced or expanded cybercrime laws, targeting activists.

Cyberactivism is not a panacea. It can be fickle and disorganized. Our attention is short-lived; there is always another incident, another video, and another hashtag to distract us. And migrating from words on a screen to actions on the street is not necessarily linear. Cyberfeminism is, however, worth examining in the region, especially as it has been touted by many as the "fourth-wave of feminism."[114] While not always the case, many global feminist campaigns have succeeded in raising awareness and making positive change. As these campaigns gain traction, they also exert influence on the region, spreading in their original—or regionally-adapted—form.

The #MeToo movement is often used as the most obvious example. Founded by Tarana Burke in 2006, this movement creates space for survivor voices in the fight against sexual violence. While the #MeToo campaign became a global phenomenon, its impact was quieter in the Arab world. As one activist in the region describes, "we've been whispering 'me too!' to each other for generations, but don't dare post it because the risks far outweigh the benefits…."

In the Arab region, similar to other parts of the world, the movement could not take hold with the same fervor due to safety concerns, lack of legal recourse, cultural taboos and shame, or technological barriers.

At the same time, many Arab versions of this movement were born as a result.[115] For instance, #AnaKamen (Me Too) helped women in the region reclaim and contextualize this space, using their own language and experiences. #Ismaani (Hear Me) also emerged as a complement to #MeToo to further engage Arabic-speaking women in this global conversation.[116] In Tunisia #EnaZeda (Me Too) emerged as a localized version of the broader movement to encourage survivors to post their stories of sexual assault. Within two months, there were over 500 personal stories.[117]

There are many examples of regional and national cyberfeminist campaigns, critically bringing women in the Arab region into conversation and opening space to address otherwise-taboo issues.

Digital technology was particularly advantageous for feminist organization during the Arab Spring in 2011 because it allowed for anonymity, privacy, and increased accessibility for women of all social classes. Egyptian female bloggers like Asmaa Mahfouz mobilized online and called for women to participate, while Tunisian Lina Ben Mhenni started a blog called *A Tunisian Girl* which also played a role in the start of protests and spreading of information of violations.[118]

In October 2011, a movement called "The Uprising of Women in the Arab World" was launched virtually by Yalda Younes, Diala Haidar, Farah Barqawi and Sally Zohney via a Facebook page.[119] Inspired by the Arab Spring, the group wanted to use the power of social media to support women's struggle for equal rights, to spread awareness, and to create a community of solidarity. The premise was to post a picture of yourself holding a sign that read "I am with the uprising of women in the Arab world because…" and fill in the rest. The campaign was a success as thousands upon thousands of photos—from women *and* men—poured in, with the page receiving over 40,000 likes in less than three weeks. Lines were powerful and impactful. For instance, a Syrian girl wrote: "My body is mine. It doesn't belong to the liberals whose only aim is to undress it, nor to the radicals whose only aim is to cover it." These lines were not without controversy, however. Some Facebook users reacted aggressively: "If she was my sister I'd fire a dozen rifle cartridges at her," one man from Yemen commented.[120]

The campaign persevered. "More than just a web page: it has become an *intifada* in its own right."[121] Young feminists from across the region succeeded in collaborating beyond their countries. Younes, interviewed for *Feminism Inshallah: A History of Arab Feminism* documentary said, "This feminine solidarity is essential for changes to come about in the Arab world."[122] She cited the importance of working together to share learning, in the spirit of the slogan on the *Uprising* page: "Together for fearless, free, independent women in the Arab world."[123]

In 2012, while in high school, Xena Amro started a Facebook page called *True Lebanese Feminist* to "raise awareness about women's issues not just in Lebanon, but also globally."[124] The page garnered over 11,000 followers and covers topics such as domestic violence, sexuality, religion, and more. It has served to help women and encourages more people to join the feminist cause.

The #NotYourAshta campaign began in Lebanon in 2016.[125] Launched by the Knowledge is Power project at the American University of Beirut, the campaign sought to shed light on the issue of street and sexual harassment. The next year, they launched #Mesh_Basita (Not Okay) with the Women's Affairs Ministry, a six-week national campaign raising awareness about sexual assault and confronting how pervasive it is within society.[126] By encouraging women to share their stories, they highlighted the need for legislation to combat sexual harassment in Lebanon.[127]

Palestinian-Jordanian Laila Hzaineh started using social media to raise awareness on women's continued struggle for rights and freedoms. Through a series of Facebook and YouTube videos, Hzaineh called out sexism, discrimination, and harassment both in Jordan and the wider Arab region. One video responded to a Jordanian man who said women's choice of clothing resulted in sexual harassment. Another video from 2016 addressed a Moroccan woman who posted a make-up tutorial on how to cover up bruises received from intimate partner violence.[128] Hzaineh's video touched the core of gender inequalities in the region. "We don't solve problems, but cover them up," she said. "What we need is advice for the entire community on how to protect women that get beaten by their husbands."[129]

Hzaineh chooses videos and social media as the most direct and honest way to communicate her message, and to reach a wide audience. Her face and her name are visible, which she says gave her greater traction, but also greater messages of criticism, threats, and hate. She has since stopped subtitling her videos in English so her message does not become misconstrued. "Culture works as an authority," Hzaineh says, and social norms exert a huge amount of pressure.[130] While she encourages women to report incidents, she understands if they choose not to, because of the risks they face in doing so. In the future, Hzaineh would like to see more women reporting and publicly sharing their stories, further exposing—and ultimately ending—the problem.

In 2018, Yasmeen Mjalli, a Palestinian designer, founded #NotYourHabibti (Not Your Darling) to confront sexual violence in Palestine. Also in 2018, feminist journalist Mona Eltahawy launched the hashtag #MosqueMeToo to organize the discussion on sexual assault and harassment during the Islamic pilgrimage to Mecca. Eltahawy recounted her own assault while at *hajj* as a young girl, and her viral post sparked hundreds of stories exposing the extent of sexual violence at holy sites.[131] Reflecting on it years later, she describes the shame and silencing of these experiences, coming from men at *hajj* and from Saudi authorities:

I buried my sexual assault. I had no words for it. No one I knew had ever shared a similar horror. Who would believe that something so awful had happened to me at such a sacred place? It was better to stay silent. I was 15, and all I knew was that I wanted to hide my body from men.[132]

One Sudanese feminist explains how the rise of social media and online activism, while helpful especially in her work, is not without its dangers. She elaborates:

Back then, there was no social media. So the effects were less or the threats were less. You would know that some group would target you, they will follow you and so on. But the work didn't get threats as much as it does now.

Arguably, the work has always been dangerous, but online threats and dangers are pervasive and omnipresent. They are also global, and can mobilize the masses, gaining force as they go "viral." It is harder to remain anonymous, and remain safe, in this new medium. Online activism presents grave security risks—sometimes manifesting offline.

In 2018, women of Morocco created their own version of the #MeToo movement in the form of the #Masaktach (I will not be silenced) movement.[133] The highly publicized rape and torture of a seventeen-year-old identified only as Khadija catalyzed the movement. Khadija was mistreated by the Moroccan media, who aired quotes from the perpetrators' families slandering her reputation and accusing her of lying.[134] Her story sparked a public outcry, bringing together the collective behind the #Masaktach movement, mobilizing to counter this narrative in the media.[135] They published anonymous stories from victims in solidarity, with women using the #Masaktach hashtag to condemn violence and impunity.[136]

Podcasts have also created opportunities for women to document their experiences, share stories, and spread awareness in ways that are accessible to a wide range of women. Debuting in 2019, the podcast *Khilqit Binit* (A Girl is Born) spotlighted inspiring women and their stories, tackling taboo topics and challenging stereotypes.[137] These podcasts have become critical for unpacking identity and speaking about the hidden injustices that impact women.[138]

In 2019, Lebanese-American actor Rana Alamuddin founded *Bayne W Baynek* (Between Me and You), a podcast and online platform for Arab women to share personal stories about sensitive topics and experiences without judgment.[139] "It started as a conversation series and then it turned into an online platform, growing organically, and now looks towards the future on how we can find our own place and redefine life as Arab women on our own terms," Alamuddin says.[140]

Alamuddin then created the movement #IForgiveMyself, focused on empowering women to break free of the guilt and societal expectations that hold them back. Alamuddin says she "bring(s) women together in a safe space of sisterhood away from societal shaming and judgment." Her campaign invited women to write what they wanted to forgive themselves for on their bodies. And a movement was created, going viral on International Women's Day.

Alamuddin explains:

It's like an intimate act of inking yourself, committing to yourself, making a pledge to yourself. Through this campaign, young women have been forgiving themselves daily for not believing in their own worth, to hating their bodies, rejecting societal rules, having depression and anxiety, wanting to make themselves a priority, having premarital sex, not getting married or having children or getting married too young.[141]

During the COVID-19 lockdowns throughout 2020 and onward, social media became increasingly popular with activists. This was further amplified by deteriorating social conditions and dire need, for instance, to address increased intimate partner violence as a result of COVID-19. Online platforms were useful in providing information, as well as access to services and support during the pandemic. Organizations in the region from Iraq, Jordan, Libya, and Lebanon, ran online counseling sessions and shared crucial information such as hotline numbers and other lifesaving services.[142]

In 2021, Kuwait launched its online campaign against sexual harassment with #LanAsket (I will not be silent), with women sharing accounts of sexual harassment and assault. One of the most prominent came from influential Kuwaiti-American fashion blogger Ascia Al Faraj, whose video calling out the damaging impact of sexual harassment sparked a nationwide conversation. A social media page launched by Dr. Shayma Shamo began anonymously posting stories of sexual harassment across Kuwait.[143] While women shared their stories of harassment and abuse online, activists rallied offline to call for reforms to the legal and judiciary systems that had failed to protect women.[144]

In July of 2022, several incidents of femicide caused feminist groups across the region to use social media in calling for a transnational strike, encouraging women to stay home from work.[145] Organizers held protests in Beirut, Tunis, and Amman to show solidarity and condemn violence against women. Through social media campaigns, protesters demanded accountability for perpetrators and called for reform.

While these virtual movements are critical for instigating conversations and pushing boundaries, they remain hindered by obstacles that limit their effectiveness. Women face targeted backlash, and governments restrict online civil space. Boundaries between the virtual and the physical are increasingly blurred. These accounts, and the women behind them, are subject to censorship, bans, and threats of violence and death—some of which materialize.

For instance in Egypt, authorities arrested groups of women—famous on social media, mainly TikTok—for so-called "immoral behavior." Gulf states like the UAE, Saudi Arabia, and Bahrain have particularly harsh punishments for voicing or supporting dissent online, with jail time of up to 15 years. In Bahrain, simply "following" a dissident on social media will result in imprisonment. And Saudi Arabia deploys "troll armies" to silence dissidents and activists.[146]

Ultimately, there are benefits and drawbacks to cyberfeminism. Its uses will continue to be limited as long as, for some women, the risks outweigh the benefits. Moreover, the digital divide and digital illiteracy will continue to be impediments in the region.

On the positive side, more women in the region are taking ownership of this medium and using it to tell their own stories. They are:

> …breaking new ground and taking their gender activism to the next level, by influencing the agenda of mainstream media and shaping their content, through a spillover from the realm of citizen journalism, which placed gender-related issues and concerns at the center stage of media coverage.[147]

Online activism may more often be a moment than a movement. While these start conversations, they are not the end of the fight. Activists lament that more work is not done to translate these online moments into sustained movements—with tangible "offline" results.

So What? Now What?!

We know now that some powerful groups will do whatever they can to maintain the unacceptable status quo and enforce their agenda of eliminating women from the political, economic and social scene. These groups are waiting for the chance to put women in their place, which is no place.
—Hibaaq Osman[148]

Despite the pushback, academic Dr. Aitemad Muhanna-Matar points out that:

The fact that women in some of the most conservative Arab societies have rallied in large numbers for many months under threatening and dangerous conditions signals a new era in the history of feminism in this region.[149]

In all its forms, revolution and resistance creates social and political space, a historical moment with hope for this "new era." However, history reveals that, for women's movements, such new eras are hard won, often resulting in setbacks and backlash. Feminist scholars have long documented the "limited possibilities of major social transformations" arising from revolution.[150]

Transitional processes are moments of opportunity, an open door. However, the door swiftly closes on women, often with significant setbacks. Research and "cross-cultural and historical evidence suggests that unless women explicitly insist on their gender-specific needs, rights and problems, these will be sidelined, ignored and swept under the carpet."[151] We argue that even when women *explicitly* insist on their gender-specific needs, they are *still* swept under the carpet. While countries look ahead, they leave women behind.

Feminist activist scholar Dr. Charlotte Karam theorizes on what is holding women and women's movements back:

The history of bloodshed in various parts of the region creates a distrust that's tied to community. And I think that seeps into the feminist agenda, so the political and socio-economic factors, and in particular the history of feudalism, and the history of religious trends create a distrust and create a division that's tied to identity, that's stronger than gender identity, stronger than being an Arab woman. That creates a lot of misconceptions, too. It's tied to biases, it's tied to prejudice against different religious sects. And ultimately, it leads to stopping us.

Women's rights are actively violated before, during, and after revolutions. It has been said time and again that "women are one of the greatest casualties of crises," and women's bodies are the battlegrounds.[152] The battle for women is never over. And the battle for women is fought everywhere.

This is not just about the so-called Arab Spring. Yes, the Arab Spring was a turning point for the region—and for women's rights and roles in the region. Public and private, masculine and feminine spaces were blurred. And women fought battles on many fronts, against many oppressions—that "threatened their livelihood as citizens on the one hand, and as gendered and racialized citizens on the other."[153]

Women on the frontlines of activism and resistance defied norms and rewrote history, which has translated into increased agency and power, still visible over a decade later.[154] Dr. Lina Abou-Habib, Director of the Asfari Institute for Civil Society and Citizenship at the American University of Beirut, puts it this way:

Feminists re-created participatory spaces for discussions, learning, exchanges, as well as planning for ways to disrupt the patriarchy which manifests itself in all forms of social institutions.... Strategies that feminists had used over decades were now transported as tools of the revolution.[155]

Although she is referring to Lebanon in particular, this re-creation applies across the region. And in times of so-called peace just as much as in times of crisis. As we have said—we see frontlines at home and in war as different manifestations of the same battle against patriarchy.

This chapter sought to demonstrate the range of activist expression against that patriarchy. Our fight against patriarchy must be as diverse as we are—all forms, all fronts, all the time. This remains true in the home just as much as on the streets. The frontlines are everywhere. In the words of one young activist: "I fight on the streets against the patriarchy, and then I fight at home against my fathers and brothers—the micro-patriarchy."

Understandably, much of this fight is born from anger. Anger fuels activist energy. Rage gives us courage. As Soraya Chemaly, feminist and author of *Rage Becomes Her: The Power of Women's Anger* asserts: "A society that does not respect women's anger is one that does not respect women—not as human beings, thinkers, knowers, active participants, or citizens."[156]

At the same time, some of those profiled in this chapter, and the ones that follow, would argue that anger is not effective or sustainable. We do not necessarily equate anger with violence. Kuwaiti women's rights activist Dr. Alanoud Alsharekh adds: "I strongly believe that people need to get angry for change to happen.... As long as that anger doesn't become a destructive force."[157]

Ultimately, whatever path is chosen, the end goal must be clear. Feminist journalist Mona Eltahawy reminds us that "patriarchy knows that when we nurture anger in girls, they will hold patriarchy accountable, and that those girls will grow up to be women who demand a reckoning."

This chapter has shown the many forms of resistance and revolution in the region. A reckoning—one of many. Micro-rebellions and everyday resistance can sometimes lay the foundation for a movement. But this is not enough. To effectively dismantle patriarchal structures—the real battle—what can be done to sustain that movement?

Around the world, nonviolent resistance has been used to topple autocratic regimes, end colonial rule, resist foreign powers, and secure human rights. Nonviolent resistance necessitates two characteristics: it must be collective action and it must avoid violence.[158] It can be an effective method for populations to overcome repression and achieve liberation when we lack access to formal political channels or where regimes are oppressive. One major advantage of nonviolent resistance is the low barriers to participation, which lead to higher levels of mobilization.[159] In other words, it is far easier for people to join a collective demonstration than reach positions of political power, for example.

The choice of method very much impacts outcomes.[160] Combining protest with noncooperation and strategic intervention are a tested recipe for success.[161] And it must be grassroots, as Rasha Younes, LGBTQ+ rights researcher, puts it:

> Approaching it from a critical lens theoretically is very important, but also how to accomplish [resistance] on the ground has to be very much grassroots, and has to be very much within these neighborhoods, and within these families [...] you can't detach that from the reality.[162]

While this resistance is organic and grassroots, it also must be organized and strategic. At the same time, even failed attempts lay the groundwork for further reform and inspire future actions.

What now? How might we capitalize on collective action fueled by anger and sustain it? Patriarchy must not only be challenged—it must be dismantled. Activists face the enduring problem of all revolutionary politics: how to "transform the egalitarian spirit of a brief uprising into a long-lasting revolution, in this case, for women's equality."[163]

The next chapter presents one avenue of transformation: creatively transforming mindsets.

4

Feminisms on the Frontlines
of Creativity

The resistance is one mind at a time.
—Dr. Bahia Shehab[1]

What is *activism*? And what does *revolution* look like?

In conversations with many activists, we learned that activism evolves, taking on whatever shape best fits the space and time. Activism morphs to suit the moment—and the movement. Activism does not need the label—it often exists in subtle and non-confrontational ways. But we can name it, even if we do not see it.

Activism in the Arab region has never been limited to street demonstrations or mass protest. In fact, these are the exceptions, not the norm. Protest and revolution exist in the small spaces, and subversive activism is often the strongest tool women have to express their discontent and advocate for change. While some activists took to the streets to march, others used the streets in different ways. We assert that both are essential, and that there is room for both.

One of the biggest challenges to sustaining change in the region is "the culture and the mindset of people," according to a young Bahraini activist. How, then, to change mindsets? How to capture people's imaginations and remind them that yes, a better world is possible? Art—in all its forms—does precisely this. It works at the "profound levels of culture," because, as feminist activist Kavita Ramdas tells us, art touches "our heart, not just our brain."[2]

Alternative forms of activism have long been present in the region. Much has been written about the role of arts and literature in defining struggle and resistance throughout the Arab world. Palestinian resistance poets, such as Mahmoud Darwish, Samih al-Qasim, and Fadwa Tuqan, have actively participated in Palestinian liberation efforts while also writing extensively about dispossession from their homeland and Palestinian oppression under occupation.[3] In many cases, older poetry is adapted and recontextualized for modern resistance. For example, verses from the early-twentieth-century Tunisian poet Abdul Qasim al Shabi became unofficial rallying cries in Egypt and Tunisia.[4] Poetry and prose have also given women the opportunity to express social commentary and reimagine the worlds they live in—creating a collective narrative for those who experience oppression.[5]

Art-activism has also been a significant feature of revolutions and resistance in the region, creatively conveying political messages through music, literature, theater, street art, and more. There are countless examples of artist-activists throughout the Arab region, politicizing their art and capturing our imaginations.

One of the most obvious examples is street art, often very bold visuals, quickly absorbed and easily relatable. Their intent is to be widely understood and accepted, and to make an immediate impact. Artist-activists engage with the urban environment by placing deliberate rebellion in the everyday. They take the pulse of the people, capturing a historic snapshot of the social climate. This art is usually temporary, but no less disruptive. In fact, it has an enduring impact as a physical manifestation of the collective, oppressed consciousness. In this way, it is effective in building community, showing support or remembrance, challenging social beliefs, spreading political messages, and changing mindsets:

> Protest graffiti is a critical intervention in urban space, especially as municipalities and police attempt to shut down the streets. Even after protests have dispersed, graffiti stands as a testament to the protestors' collective voice.[6]

Art can claim physical space as well as the space of people's imaginations. As one musician articulated to us, "broken societies create artists."[7] Revolutions are both destruction and creation, with the latter inspiring creativity and possibility. Art-activism is important as an alternative avenue of expression, particularly in instances of disorder or dissent:

> Political graffiti always signals the potential for social change. The graffiti may soon be washed away, but not before it is documented, becoming part of history. Graffiti in times of crisis can also offer hope, echoing on walls across the city and country: "Another World Is Possible."[8]

While the above refers to graffiti in particular, we believe that this applies to the full range of art forms. In all its forms, art-activism drives conversations in areas often off-limits or taboo, bringing forward emotions in both audience and artist. Through their chosen medium, artist-activists claim space and express thoughts that are often dangerous, particularly in contexts when dialogue is thwarted.[9] Art-activism is particularly effective when civil society space is restricted and fundamental freedoms—especially speech and expression—are monitored or controlled by authorities. While not unique to the Arab region, a prominent feature of Arab revolutions and resistances is the proliferation of art conveying struggles against oppressive power structures. Artist-activists often only realize the power in their art when governments start to cover it up—or crack down on the artists themselves. Subversive activism thrives in these restrictive environments.

What follows is a sample of artists-activists from the region and their use of different media to advocate for change. Their work navigates resistance and creates conversations on feminist politics. Feminist-artist-activists.

The Birth of the Artist-Activist

Assil Diab, or *Sudalove*, was the first street artist in Sudan—male or female—meaning Diab fought, and persevered, on two fronts. Not only was she breaking ground in a male-dominated space, she was also breaking out of stereotypical roles ascribed to women in Sudan. She recounted an exchange with a close family member who said:

> The reason why you're not married is because you reach a certain age and you're roaming the streets, and any man who sees that is not going to respect you, because a respectable profession is one that's behind four walls, not in the street.[10]

As we have said, too many women in the Arab region remain bound by traditional gender roles fueled by patriarchy. The farther they stray from these roles, the greater challenges—and risks—they face. Diab says "that's the Sudan they don't want. That's too advanced. That's too … too much freedom."

Diab and others have explained that these restrictions—reinforcements of the patriarchal social order—come from women as well. We explore this challenge further in Chapter 5. In Diab's words:

> I have females who come up to me and ask me how I convinced my husband or my brother or my father to do this as a profession. How did you do it? And the question itself was, how do I tell them that I didn't really have to convince anyone? But I can't say that, it's too harsh to their situation, so I kind of sometimes made up a story just so I can relate it to them.

Diab recognizes that pushing these patriarchal boundaries and defying social mores is challenging, but it must be done.

Similar to Diab, Haifa Subay was the first female artist to use street graffiti to convey her message on the streets of Yemen. Subay paints murals to raise awareness for women and children, and more specifically, what it means to be a woman and a mother during war. The murals she creates symbolize female power and women's ability to create peace in the most violent situations:

> Through my art I am trying to transmit a positive message to other women to wage the war with non-violent alternatives. Hopefully street art can contribute to see the world in a different way to end this pointless war. We should not surrender.[11]

She started creating this type of art on the walls of Sana'a, Yemen's capital, with her brother, Murad Subay, a well-known street artist, soon after the Arab Spring erupted. When she first became involved, there was a great deal of stigma attached to women painting in the street. Years later, in 2017, when she launched her own campaign, this was less shocking because people had grown accustomed to it.

Her campaign included a series of murals depicting the horrors of the war and the suffering of civilians. She bravely depicted the worst outcomes of the war—disease, violence, famine, poverty, and more. One mural titled *Women Make Peace* gained particular attention. It was split in half with one half showing a woman with arm raised, bent at the elbow, and a closed fist: a sign of power. The other half was the peace symbol merged with the symbol for women. Women, peace, power—all in one. This is the piece that graces the cover of this book. Subay was happy to lend her work to this book because she says, "As a woman who believes in the great power of women to make change and bring peace wherever they are, I consider women to be the force of peace in this world."[12]

Dr. Bahia Shehab is an artist, activist, and educator from Egypt. She credits her interdisciplinary background for giving her a unique perspective on problem-solving. Art helps her to see structural problems and to translate them into activism. To that end, she has launched numerous resistance campaigns throughout her career to ignite social change and educate the next generation of creators.

Like Subay, the 2011 Revolution had a massive impact on Shehab's work. As part of an exhibition commemorating 100 years of Islamic art in Europe, Shehab was tasked with using the Arabic script for her work. She was inspired by one word: No. As an artist, a woman, an Arab, she wanted to claim and use this word more strongly. An Arabic expression for no is: *No, and a thousand times no,* so Shehab created work to reflect the need to say no.[13]

The project then became a campaign in reaction to the brutal retaliation of the authorities after the Revolution. Witnessing the crackdown on liberties and the various atrocities meted out, Shehab started adding a message to every "No" she spray painted in the streets to convey the sense that people had enough of injustice, discrimination, and violence. It became a series: No to military rule, No to a new *Pharaoh* (leader), No to violence, No to killing, No to burning books, No to barrier walls, No to stripping people. This last one included a spray-painted blue bra in reference to the woman publicly stripped and beaten by members of the military in Tahrir Square during the 2011 uprising. The image of "the girl in the blue bra" became symbolic of the state-sanctioned violence and served as a rallying cry, inciting women around the country to protest.

Shehab's piece *Mokhak Awra* was also in response to sexual harassment of women protesters in Tahrir Square. It featured a brain made up of women's body parts with the Arabic message that translates to "your brain is shameful and it should be covered."[14] It was directed at men who claim women's faces, hair, and bodies are sources of temptation and therefore of shame, to be covered in order to safeguard women's honor.

These themes around women's bodies, honor, and sexuality are also common to the work of author Alya Mooro. Born in Egypt and raised in London, Mooro breaks many cultural and societal taboos in her book *The Greater Freedom: Life as A Middle Eastern Woman Outside the Stereotype*. Starting out as a journalist, Mooro found writing the natural medium for her to challenge patriarchal structures, resist stereotypical concepts, and crucially, represent women from the Arab region. Her work primarily centers around sexual repression—both her own and that of all women.

> There's an endless list of things that happen off the back of shame and lack of conversation that we have around these things. And that's what bothers me, and that's what made me want to talk about it. Even me, who grew up in London and has been having sex, I was having panic attacks like, why was I having panic attacks? Why did I say to a guy "Do you think less of me?" It was almost by osmosis that I had adopted this mentality, so imagine the women who literally have no clue.[15]

She started questioning all the messages throughout her life:

> I started to really realize there is a disconnect between what I personally believe and the messages that I've received since I was a baby. I don't think sex is wrong or a sin but I felt so much shame for believing that. It made me begin to question the vast inequality across the board, because why do I feel like this and men in my life do not?

Mooro was supported fully by her, "extremely, extremely liberal" family, enabling her to approach her work with the honesty she felt was needed. In fact, it was her father who told her to "either do it and be honest, or don't bother." This liberated Mooro, because much attention in Arab societies is given to what other people think, especially when it comes to notions of shame and honor. But it did not matter to her father—or to her.

> His main thing is, "I don't care what other people think," which I think a big problem in the region is everyone cares about what their neighbor is gonna say and what people are gonna think. But my dad doesn't care about that. So that really enabled me to be honest in the ways that I needed to.

Soultana, the first female rapper not only in Morocco but in the Arab region, became involved in hip hop from the age of 13.[16] She said it was unusual for people to see "a small, tiny girl with curly hair" in a scene that was predominantly male, and also quite a bit older.[17] She was dismissed and accused of being western and not Arab, not in line with tradition. Like Mooro, her family was supportive. As a result she carved out a career in music inscribed with social messages.

Yazz Ahmed is a British-Bahraini jazz musician, using her mixed heritage as a source of inspiration to create her own fusion of Arabic music and jazz. Reflecting on her career to date, Ahmed explained she found it difficult as a woman in the music scene and put it down to, among other reasons, representation. As with Soultana, the music industry was heavily dominated by men, with very few female role models. Ahmed puts it this way:

> Growing up, I wasn't aware of any female jazz musicians, I didn't see any women on the scene. I wasn't taught that people like me could become professional jazz musicians or composers. I later realised that this was mainly down to visibility. When we don't see people like ourselves, one automatically thinks "Oh, I can't be that," which is what I grew up thinking.[18]

Mooro also believes in the significance of representation for women in the Arab region. "It's easier to be yourself if you can see yourself," she says. Mooro has built her life around this principle and feels passionate about presenting alternative ways of living for women. A huge part of the process is unlearning the messages society teaches, and broadening ideas that restrict us to narrow gender roles:

> I feel like we really need representation across mediums and trying to provide alternative ways of living, because I think that traditionally women, but especially Arab women, have been given a very narrow idea of what life can even look like, which is usually only marriage and kids.

With a wide view of what life can look like, sisters Michelle and Noel Keserwany from Lebanon are known for their satirical takes on socio-political issues through music. The sisters capitalize on music's ability to inform, rouse, and unite people. In 2010 Michelle Keserwany released *Jagal el Usek*, a satirical song critiquing Lebanese dating and male-female relations in the Arab region, exposing the double standard and hypocrisy. Since then both sisters have released other songs denouncing the ills of the country. Both Michelle and Noel studied advertising in university, and therefore understood the potential of their music to spread awareness on social issues that would captivate wider audiences. "With the release of this first song, we found our medium. We just needed to find what stirred us, and proceed to share it," they said.[19] They are moved by social issues like corruption, oppression, and deteriorating living conditions—all increasingly relevant in Lebanon.

The Artist as a Political Actor

In Morocco, Soultana's song *Sawt Nsaa* (Woman's Voice) was inspired by the story of an old classmate who was exploited by her partner.[20] He would force her into prostitution to pay off his gambling debts. He left her after she became pregnant, and social shame forced her into prostitution. Her lyrics tell the story:

> She gave him everything—money, love and life.
> He gave her lies and violence and made her turn tricks for quick cash.

Even though this story inspired the song, the meaning runs much deeper, as it is also a commentary on wider social issues. The song embodies the fact that women are not treated equally, are silenced, and are held to hypocritical standards, as seen in the chorus:

> Woman's voice that I'm calling
> Girl's voice that is lost in my country
> The voice of those who wanna talk who wanna say
> A voice for all the women who want a sign.

Using music to amplify their voice was equally important to the Keserwany sisters in Lebanon. They became politicized by the desire to wake people up—to advocate against passivity. For them, silence was not an option:

> We feel that if we say what we want to say, we will feel better, by connecting with people who feel the same way. It is in this emotional connection that we garner the force to sustain a movement towards being more satisfied with our environments.

They feel Lebanon has a multitude of problems—for everyone. Their songs courageously tackle difficult issues such as class, wealth gaps, power, injustice, violence, corruption, and so on. They explain it this way:

> We can't see problems independently. It's a circle of problems in a complex system. In other words, we don't choose topics based on how urgent they may or may not be. What we will speak about depends on what we are living. Life is a big range of issues.

Their song *3al Jamal Bi Wasat Beirut* (A Camel in Downtown Beirut) satirically describes riding a camel through the downtown, typically an area of gratuitous displays of wealth. The song is a commentary on major class distinctions, wealth disparities, and how power relations are played out, as told by the following lyrics:

> I want to go cruising on a camel in downtown Beirut
> Let those who don't have the amount for gas have hope.[21]

Tackling topics that are taboo informs much of the work of the artist-activists. One such example is the film *Open Wound*, produced by Elie Youssef and directed by Georgi Lazar. The film is about the systematic use of rape as a weapon of war and the permanent destruction of women, the family, and society. They acknowledge their positionality as two men directing and producing a film about women, a common question they receive, but Youssef maintains:

> We don't matter, what matters is the film and the topic. The real driving force which made this film possible is the women who told us their stories and the leading woman (Hiam Abbass) whose view and emotional and artistic input made the film what it is.[22] Plus, everybody should be talking about this subject matter. Especially men.[23]

While they did not label the film as feminist or activist, it is both of these things. For Youssef and Lazar, it is firstly about women survivors, about humanity, and about a specific humanitarian cause. It is, however, a political act and "activist by default," Youssef says. "Of course it's political," he explains, "but our tool is artistic." They choose to fictionalize the film to protect survivors, building on real incidents with a view to impacting a wider audience.

In Sudan, while Diab's work started out as art, it quickly became political, and she was lured into activism:

> It really starts off with the artwork, and then we were forced into these dialogues and conversations about what's happening in Sudan, whether it's the economy, or politics, or women.

> It was so funny to me because it wasn't about the subject of the artwork anymore. It became about people's ingrown opinions and backgrounds, on religion, on politics, and their cultural differences and personal differences.

She describes how people's reactions were revealing of their political persuasion. While some people offered suggestions for her next work, others erased the pieces and failed to see the significance. To them "it's just a portrait and it's just art" she says, but that negates the power of street art. In response, Diab leaned into activism and the political nature of her work more strongly, saying:

> I made it a mission to always touch on these subjects and make it a point to become a subject myself as a female. It slowly became not about the artwork anymore. And now with the internet shutdowns, especially with the protests, I make it a point to keep posting and keep sharing and stuff like that.

Lebanon has also seen similar forms of politicized art. Many have taken to the streets to express themselves on so-called "revolution walls" through art.[24] Urban spaces throughout Lebanon are dotted with murals and graffiti, capturing and narrating the social climate. One such artist is Roula Abdo, who believes this form of art has been instrumental in revolutions:

> We live in a "visual era," and when people see a "visual," it affects them faster and they can relate to it easily; not everyone focuses on speeches, but they focus on visuals more easily and quickly.[25]

The impact of visual pieces are often more memorable than speeches. On one hand these pieces exist in everyday space, part of the landscape. On the other hand, they can be disruptive and deliver a quick shock factor. Either way, they exist to portray the current situation. Abdo's most famous piece, *Revolution Is Female,* showcases the power of revolutionary art. She created it during the *Nour el-thawra* (Light of the Revolution) march led by women. She says:

> The idea of producing activism art during the feminist march began with an association called Arts of Change, which had been promoting art on streets and walls for a long time, even before the revolution.[26]

Similar to Diab and Abdo, Shehab explains her work in Egypt this way:

> The work was a reaction to what was going on on the streets. Everything I sprayed was a reaction to what was going on. Every "No" was a reaction to an injustice that I was witnessing.[27]

In every "No," Shehab's art became an important way to document and record events. This, coupled with the use of social media during the revolution, led to the uploading and wide sharing of art-activism online. The result, Shehab says, was an "online/offline dialogue" whereby artwork would be uploaded, people would rush to the location of the art to retaliate, new photos would be circulated, and so the cycle would continue. These exchanges allowed an urban, visual conversation between artists unknown to each other. There is meaning in this event—a liberating and liberal sharing of art, and art seen as a public conversation, particularly given the constraining political climate.

Shehab explains it this way:

> I don't think I will ever live anything that intense or beautiful again in my life because I felt like I was part of a collective. Every time an event would happen, we'd all rush down to the streets to have the same reaction in 100 different voices—but visually, without a curator,

without a gallery, without funding, without all these mechanisms. This raw, visceral reaction to an artwork is what was really beautiful about the revolution. For me that is an experience that can never be recreated.

The organic nature of this exchange and the freedom from formal channels allowed for creation—and recreation. The art lived beyond the artist. Such is the impact revolution can have.

Art can create space—moments—but revolutions without strategy do not create change. Shehab acknowledges that "revolutions are wonderful spaces of discoloration and expression, but," she continued "they do not create social change." She explains that social change necessitates "working tirelessly, having an agenda, organizing, meeting, talking, disseminating."

"And it's not the work of one group of people," she concludes, "but of everybody."

Art can be a powerful instigator, but without "everybody" and without structure and strategy, it cannot be sustained.

The Artist as Feminist

Deena Mohamed is a female Muslim Egyptian artist, and her character Qahera is "a female visibly Muslim superhero who combats misogyny and Islamophobia amongst other things."[28] The name "Qahera" is the female Arabic word for "Vanquisher" or "Conqueror" or "Triumphant" and it also holds a double meaning because when you add "al" to make it "al Qahera," the meaning changes to Cairo, Egypt's capital. On why Mohamed started this project, she says:

> I've always kind of wanted to do a webcomic starring a badass Muslim superhero who defends women against the kind of stupid idiocy we have to put up with every day whilst shutting up all the white feminists who try to co-opt the struggle … [plus] the potential behind a *hijabi/niqabi* superhero like her outfit comes with a ready-made abaya-cape and a mask.[29]

Saudi Arabian musician Tamtam explained how feminism has inspired her work.[30] She strongly believes in equality, and growing up in Saudi Arabia, she felt there were certain rigid roles society placed on women—and men. Tamtam described her parents as being open minded and supportive of her music. Others were slightly more hesitant when it came to online exposure, saying that she can only post videos that do not show her face or share her name. And so she adopted the stage name Tamtam. Undeterred, Tamtam released her song on YouTube. Those words stuck with her, and she concluded that their concern was informed by societal expectations since, at the time, no one was openly singing in Saudi Arabia—at least not in English, nor as a woman.

Her song *Gender Game* was inspired by the incident and is reflected in the lyrics:

> I won't share my face
> I won't share my name
> In this gender game
> If I say my name or I show my face
> I should be ashamed
>
> What hurts the most is if she were
> A boy it would be fine
> But doing it when you're a girl
> You really cross the line.

Following the release of the song, Tamtam asked herself: "Why did I feel the need to ask permission?" She continued:

> I feel if I was a Saudi guy, I wouldn't ask permission. I wouldn't ask my dad. I wouldn't ask anyone. I would just do it with little consequence. That was the biggest thing. I was like, Why did I have to ask?[31]

Tamtam explains that she struggled to reconcile social and familial obligations. She recognized that no law says that she cannot do it, but cultural and societal pressure force conformity, leading women to believe they are doing something wrong. In recognizing this, she concluded: "And then in the end of the video of *Gender Game*, I reveal my face. And this time I didn't ask, I just did it."

That moment was also an awakening:

> I was like, this is all in my head, I'm not doing anything wrong. Every time I talk about my country, I'm proud and I want to help the Saudi people have these opportunities too. I want to pave the way and I'm so happy that now things are shifting and people can do this now. And it's okay, you know?

British-Bahraini Ahmed is hoping to be a force for change for women everywhere, so representation is a significant element of her work. "I hope that this might change people's perceptions, seeing a woman on stage performing complex music that is inspired by other women," she says.

Being a female artist in a male-dominated field is a reflection of women's position in society. To navigate this, Ahmed feels the need to be subtle and non-confrontational because that is also an expectation that society places on women, "otherwise, you're branded as being an angry person." She describes how she sometimes tries to find subtle ways, "a gentle nudge in helping people open their minds" through her music.

In Egypt, one of Shehab's artworks represents what she calls "the voice of the feminine rising." In 2014, Shehab reimagined the *Adhan* (Muslim call to prayer) with a female voice by having a mezzo soprano from Cairo Opera House raise the call. To find the right sound, they enlisted the help of the singer's mother—also a singer. Her advice to them was:

> "Don't imitate the voice notes of men. We are women. Our voices are different. The way we go about life is different. Don't imitate, we have our voices. We use our voice."

This sentiment inspired Shehab's work. She continues:

> To me, this artwork is very subtle, but really, conceptually speaking, it speaks to everything I want to say. It's women's voice. It's daily. It's consistent. It's ancient. But it's the future.

To her, the artwork also functions as an apt metaphor for women in society and serves as a constant reminder of her calling to do this work, compelled by the need to challenge oppressive patriarchal structures:

> We want justice, and women deserve better. For centuries, we have been enslaved by the patriarchy, and the few of us who have resisted were burned and written out of history books. We are excluded. We are excluded if we don't marry, if we don't have children, if we don't comply, if we don't serve, if we don't accommodate, if we don't fit the role.

Not everyone is willing to resist. Shehab argues that while this is a barrier to advancing women's rights in Egypt—and arguably in the entire region—she recognizes the difficulties and risks. She continues:

With systematic oppression, it's normalized. You accept your life because you just want to live, you don't want to challenge, you just want to fit in. You don't want to stand out because it's already hard. You are barely making ends meet, your kids need to eat and you have more basic priorities. So I really understand. I really understand why people don't want to challenge.

All the artist-activists we spoke with used their art to fight back, united in their commitment to social justice and to women's rights—even when not overtly "feminist." For instance, Diab does not call herself a feminist, but acknowledges that her presence and her work is in line with feminist goals as she defies stereotypes of what a Sudanese woman can or cannot do.

In Lebanon, the Keserwany sisters resist the label "feminist" and prefer the term humanitarian. One explains:

Feminism is misleading. I don't like this word which is excluding other human rights. For me, it's normal to interact with your environment, not to stay passive, and I don't need to put a definition on this. Humanitarian is a better word because it is including all human rights.

And she continues:

I don't even consider myself to be an outright activist. Our aim is to not just stand passively in our environment. As a human being, you automatically react to what is happening around you. We are only expressing ourselves about what we think is bad in our country.

In other words, the Keserwany sisters are similar to many activists in that they eschew labels and generalizations, opting instead to address social issues that concern them in a way that is organic. They prefer to tackle a range of issues as they emerge, rather than focus exclusively on one sector, or sit squarely under one label.

Songs by the Keserwany sisters are not feminist per se, at least not on the surface. But the issues they raise affect women profoundly. For instance, the song *Beghalat* (Cinderella) is a reimagining of the fairytale and a call for women to not be passive. It speaks strongly to gender equality:

We wanted to express that we are annoyed by the fact that fairytales encourage girls to wait passively for someone to come and save their lives instead of taking charge, following their goals, and even saving the world.

The sisters acknowledge that rejecting the feminist label has much to do with their personal circumstances, but they recognize the deep gendered discrimination that remains pervasive in Lebanese society.

We feel that nothing ever prevented us to do what we want when it comes to being a girl or being a woman. So, basically, we don't see the obstacle in our personal life. But if you look at the law, there is big discrimination. This discrimination is absurd.

With that absurd discrimination in mind, they agreed to collaborate with The Arab Institute for Women (AiW) to create a song about gender equality. The animated song, *Bi'Ideh* (In My Hand) is a duet between two young people—male and female—debating the existence of discrimination against women. The chorus says:

By my own hand I write, and I demand on my own
By my own hand I ask, and I'll vote on my own
With my own vote, I will change things, tables I will turn
And unjust rules I'll overrule, to hell with no return

As the song continues, the young man is convinced that women are discriminated against. It continues:

> Someone whispered in front of me, he said:
> "When it forgot its other half, society has bled"
> When insults are our facts to face
> And inhuman deeds burdens to brace

The song concludes with this call to action:

> If you've seen injustice and you did not move
> Then through the years, what will improve?

The Keserwany sisters add:

> We were very happy to work with AiW and talk about those law discriminations through the voices of one boy and one girl. Because we think that's how change comes. We need to be all of us together talking about this.

> AiW Director Myriam Sfeir explains it this way:

> This is a great example of something positive we did for Arab youth. The song doesn't lament the situation of women or paint her as fragile or vulnerable. Instead it says, "in my hand, I can change things, and if I use my voice, change will happen." The point is to remind youth that they have a voice and they can use it for change.

The sisters actively refuse to relegate themselves to *just* women's issues. One of them explains further:

> My problems are not solely if at all related to the fact that I am a woman. We have many needs as people living in this region. We must understand all points of view.

By engaging with intersecting human rights issues in Lebanon, they avoid the divisions that cripple the country. They spoke of the need to defy all forms of sectarianism—religious, economic, racial—in order to reach a wider audience and to have meaning. And, ultimately, to instigate change.

Art Breaking Conversation Barriers

Many artist-activists see their work as a conversation—on the present, and for the future—a way to create dialogue and pave the way for otherwise taboo topics and critical conversations at the crux of social evolution. Sometimes these conversations are uncomfortable, but they open spaces for dialogue that did not previously exist. And in doing so, they create opportunities for growth. Keeping conversations alive and allowing women to express themselves in that space is one step towards creating change.

In Saudi Arabia, Tamtam says that even when she receives negative comments, she feels that she is succeeding in changing that person's subconscious a little bit—planting the seed at the very least. She continues by saying it is important to have respect and to appreciate that people are going to have different opinions, but being open to that conversation will foster gradual change:

> I really believe that in order to change something, it shouldn't be in an aggressive way. I really think it's about a conversation and that's what I feel like I'm doing … having a conversation. And there's nothing wrong with that.

However, she recognizes that not everyone can express themselves freely, especially on topics that are still considered taboo. "It's not perfect yet," she says. "There's a long way to go."

For Diab, the revolution and the art it birthed has opened up a space for much needed dialogue in Sudan. She speaks of her art as a tool to create this critical conversational space:

> These conversations I have with people are our way of really talking about or forcing that dialogue, talking about everything. And it's knowledge that is shared between us, as Sudanese people.

She continues by emphasizing the impact these conversations can have:

> These conversations became the whole point of why I love doing this. It really isn't about the artwork anymore. I feel like there's change happening every time we have a conversation with somebody. And if I can convince one person of one thing or they can do the same for me, that's more powerful than protesting, that's more powerful than hate. That's powerful because it's talking to strangers. Nobody owes anyone anything but the truth.

In Egypt, Shehab perseveres through art, conversations, mentoring, and dialogues—building a community that will not, and should not, accept injustice. In order to engage communities, artists would arrange for nannies so mothers could safely leave their children and come to paint. They would provide soup kitchens as well. Eventually, communities responded to these initiatives, joining with the artists at the wall to have conversations and ask questions. In this way, the art took on a life of its own beyond the words on the wall. Together, artists and communities not only discussed and debated issues, but they were able to document atrocities. Eventually, this also helped them to heal:

> The way of bringing the community together with this healing, this talking. The conversation to me is more important than the artwork. It's really not the wall, it's not the design. Yeah, the designs and the words are nice. But it's really the people who come and talk together on the wall. That is really the point, the artwork is about that dialogue. This is for conversation, the spaces for healing, the spaces for processing.

The film *Open Wound* speaks to emotions, exposing the real damage of sexual violence—for the survivor and for communities. Youssef and Lazar made the creative choice not to include the violent act of rape in the film. The topic itself is violent—and the film is not easy to watch. And the difficulty in watching is precisely the point. The film was informed by interviews with survivors, but there is no specific language and no specific location—another deliberate choice. "Because it is all women," Youssef explains. "We have one main character in the film that embodies all of the women that we interviewed, all the women that refused to talk to us, and all the women that we don't know about."

The film was funded by various non-profit and for-profit entities, but it was not always easy to secure funding, even from organizations specifically dealing with the topic. Youssef remarks that one organization in particular said it was too difficult to watch and they would not use the film because "they did not want people to be shocked." Rape as a weapon of war *must* be shocking. This finding was shocking to Youssef and Lazar, exposing the hypocrisy of those who allegedly claim to help rape survivors.

"As people who do not suffer this kind of abuse, men and women alike, we will never fully understand the experience of survivors," Youssef says, "nor will a lot of these NGOs or people interacting and working with women survivors." Still, he hopes that the film will help portray the gravity of the violence and the irreversible damage it causes. They still believe in the power of fiction built on truth to expose this crime.

Mooro also speaks of the freedom of fiction, saying, "there's a power in fiction where maybe you have a bit more freedom to say whatever you want." The topics of bodily autonomy and sexual liberation are of great significance to Mooro and central to her work. "If you're not able to own your own body, how are you going to really be an empowered human in the world?" she laments. "It starts with you and the vessel that you're in."

With these conversations, artists recognize that social change will happen slowly, but also that they cannot afford to be passive. "We should be aggressive about protecting the rights we already have," Shehab explains, "but we also need to fight for more rights." We need to create laws but, she warned, even if laws are created, they are useless without enforcement. The challenge is in ensuring law enforcement within Arab communities, creating awareness within the community and the government about the need for these laws, and investing in restructuring systems to protect those laws.

Mooro thinks there is a certain shift, particularly around the topic of sex and women's bodily autonomy, attributed mostly to social media. In the process of writing her book, Mooro interacted with many women on social media, helping to advance her research as well as her own learning and empowerment. She describes how feeling part of a community gave her courage, support, and validation. It also opened up space for conversations and sharing, which ultimately helped women feel less alone. "There is power in numbers, and there is power in realizing it's not just me. That's very much what I'm trying to harness."

Shehab is committed to disrupting and documenting oppression while at the same time remembering and celebrating women. Remembering is a form of resistance, telling the untold stories of women who came before lets people know "that we have a tree, we have roots, it's not a desert." In other words, resistance runs deep and has always been there—whether or not we see it. Being a woman, Shehab has learned, means that nothing is guaranteed and nothing can be taken for granted. Rights and freedoms can be stripped away from one moment to the next. "It's a lot of work. We still have a lot of work," Shehab says. "It's a lifelong process."

And she adds: "The resistance is one mind at the time."

The same sentiment was put forth by Youssef when he said:

> You hope for a change. You know, you hope for a strong impact that will mobilize people and turn them into advocates and maybe initiate action. Even if I change one person's mind, if I only turn one person into an advocate, I'm happy I have gained one advocate. You just need the opportunity for people to listen and change could happen.

The Artist at Risk

Building resistance one mind at a time is a slow but necessary process. And it does not come without great risks. Every artist-activist with whom we spoke also mentioned the risks they take in their art—fear, threats, intimidation, and worse. They were aware of these risks, and still they persisted.

Navigating a limited space with grave consequences is the reality for so many artist-activists. As a result, the social changes activists seek are not only extremely difficult, but come at great personal risk. Even more challenging, any rights granted are hardly guaranteed and can be withdrawn at any stage. Nothing is certain. The result is a survival mindset that penetrates both the artist and their work, making their efforts more precarious—and more urgent.

Diab speaks about the backlash, harassment, and violence she experiences in Sudan as a result of her art-activism. She was extremely active during the 2019 revolution creating murals to honor martyrs of the revolution. But this brought a whole new level of danger:

> The rapid security forces were everywhere, literally every corner. And for them, it's as easy as shooting you. Like they're not gonna lock you up for vandalism. They're gonna kill you. I mean, best case scenario is that they kill you. That's the best case scenario. There's other stuff that happens. But I've been locked up. I've been harassed. I've been threatened. You know, there are so many stories there.

She also expresses concern for the safety of the communities who helped her and were supportive of her work. People made human barricades and created distractions so Diab could finish the portraits. But, "I put a lot of families in danger because of the artwork," Diab laments. The authorities "raided the houses, threatened the families, threw tear gas and beat them up, broken fingers and stuff like that, like real threats." They demanded Diab be turned in, but these communities continued to protect her. "It's not just me fighting or defending myself, but society. It's now actual danger."

Diab believes that the authorities would not have been threatened if her work was not having an impact. And she believes that the protection she received from communities was also a sign that her work had worth.

In Morocco, Soultana's song was well-received by other women who were grateful that their problems were being talked about openly. However, Soultana received criticism and faced severe backlash. The line in the song "tell me how many mosques were built on ruins" came under scrutiny for the religious reference even though the intent was to express the history and beauty found in us all, despite the past. She recounts:

> They were like "Why did you talk about the mosque in your music?" Already they have this idea that music is *haram*, especially for women.[32] But I really didn't care because I had this rage inside me and I wanted to talk not just about women, but about our generation, about all the problems that we have. We have a lot of problems.

The government made life difficult for Soultana and her family. She was warned not to speak poorly of the country and was banned from performing. Soultana maintains that she was not criticizing but rather pointing out that the government was failing to fulfill its commitments to citizens. The punishment was harsh:

> It happened to me because of my message. I was locked down for five years. I couldn't do music, I couldn't do anything, I didn't go out. I was really frightened. I was scared. Sometimes people would come up to me telling me they are the government, and they threatened to hurt me or my family if I didn't stop.

Soultana's forced hiatus made her feel disconnected from the music scene in Morocco, and now she feels somewhat forgotten, archived. She points out the lack of solidarity among artists and blames the competition on a scarcity mindset. There is no collaboration, she says, and others feel that they "can't get in touch with other female rappers because they need to be the queen. But," she continues, "the problem is that they don't know that each one of us is a queen of her own."

At the same time, Soultana's experience and her message sets her apart from other artists. By marrying the worlds of activism, academia, and art, Soultana's work has a depth and a maturity that she feels is currently lacking from the music scene. The younger generation of rappers and hip hop musicians are not facing the same backlash, nor have they struggled in the same way. She explains it like this:

> The younger artists don't care about the problems or the social issues. All they care about is making money. And this suits the government because they know that those new generations are not going to talk about problems. So, for the government, it's good to ban all the rappers that are talking about social issues, and just keep artists that say nothing.

In Egypt following the revolution, the authorities systematically and aggressively attempted to shut down civil society. Shehab spoke of the dangers she faced as an activist, an artist, and a woman:

> When I was spraying on the street, I would use stencils because they're faster, they're safer, and I could run. I was really jealous of male artists, my counterparts, because they could stay on the street months painting huge murals. And I couldn't do that. I wouldn't feel safe. And that idea of me not having to run when I do art, did not sink in. I was still scared. Every time I sprayed, I was looking at who's going to come get me.

Despite the backlash, Shehab was not afraid to break taboos or push boundaries. Her 2014 reimaging of the *Adhan* was perhaps the most controversial because, for the past 1400 years, only men have raised the call to prayer.[33]

The time since the revolution has seen drastic changes for artist-activists in terms of shrinking civil society space. At present, Shehab's work in Egypt cannot be political—she must self-censor, otherwise the consequences are severe:

> I don't do art in Cairo. I do art for the world out of Cairo. I can't speak to the local audience—unless it's not political, but unfortunately most of my work is political. It's very subtle and non-confrontational because I want to stay here in Egypt.

In Yemen, Subay also experienced backlash and crackdowns. Since 2019, she has not been able to paint—there is no space for any activism:

> There's no rights here, you cannot say anything, you can't raise your voice. They will arrest you, really. They threatened me many times and they also threatened my family. So no, I cannot do anything. This is sad—really.[34]

This also meant the healing aspect of her art—for both herself and for Yemeni communities—is now missing. She put it this way:

> For me, as a woman I've started facing many troubles, especially in the war. The art was healing for me when I was facing hard times. I was going to this space to put the colors on the canvas or on the walls. I was healing myself and it was a good treatment for me, my soul. But unfortunately, I cannot do this anymore. I cannot put the happiness that is in my heart and to introduce it to the people on the walls because of some armed people that at any time, at any minute, they will arrest me.

Walking around Sana'a now, she describes how she cannot find her murals anymore. They have scratched the walls or repainted over them with their own logos and words. They may have erased her art, but not her determination to return to it someday.

When Soultana was restricted from using her voice and her art, she became despondent. As a result, she began to hate music and was sure she would never create again. Slowly though, she found her voice and inspiration through listening to different artists across different genres:

> It obviously woke up something inside me because my life before was a lot of black but then I started to see colors. I started to enjoy the moments and not worry about the future like I used to. I was able to leave the house again, exercise, go out into the world. I went out from the darkness that I was living in. I feel like I gave myself confidence again. I feel young.

She still faces multiple challenges in returning to music and rebuilding her career. Patriarchal powers persevere within society—and within the music industry. Although she has found her sound again, she does not necessarily have the freedom to use her voice—at least not yet. As a result, she must self-censor. She remains determined to infuse her music with social and political messages.

Social media is another obstacle. "I hate social media" Soultana says, "I hate social networks. You can do nothing without it." She acknowledges the power of it though, and how crucial it is to utilize social media to get across her message, saying:

> I need this base of a lot of people following me so I can have the power to talk about whatever I need, whatever I want to say. If you don't have this base of followers and people that know you, you can do nothing. You can't even change one percent.

Changing one percent is made all the more challenging in countries that restrict freedom of expression. Reaction to Mooro's book has been largely positive, although she was anticipating greater backlash. She explains that this is likely because she wrote in English, and outside of Egypt. Even from the outside, however, safety remains a concern. But her style avoids antagonism, preferring instead to pose questions and open space for dialogue and critical thinking saying, "I try to approach things by being honest and sharing my own experiences, and doing it in a way I hope doesn't feel aggressive or confrontational. It's more like, 'Can we think about this?'"

British-Bahraini Ahmed admits that it would be much harder to write protest music or be critical of certain organizations if she was living in Bahrain or anywhere in the Arab region:

> If I were living in these regions, sadly, I wouldn't have been able to have written this music. And when I do perform there, I'm always sort of worried that maybe I might cause some problems. It's been taken well, but I've tried to be careful in some ways as well.

Nonetheless, Ahmed believes it is important for her music to have a deeper message, especially considering the history of jazz music itself. "It's expressive music, protest music," she says, "and I think it's really important to carry on that tradition."

Art and the Aftermath

The impact of art and art-activism in all its forms cannot be understated. Art continues to exist and exert influence, even when revolution does not. It lives, reincarnates, and takes on new meaning. It offers space for change, reflection, conversation, and healing. The spirit of revolution and resistance endures in the minds of many artist-activists. However, Shehab explains that the aftermath of the revolution in Egypt led to serious depression and disenchantment, including greater social problems and a rise in youth suicide. She reflects on this time with frankness:

> It was too much to handle the loss, the elation that we were feeling, the dream of a better future and then having all that dropped again. It was extremely naive of us to think that we were possibly creating social change and that we were not being manipulated. That we were being used as tools of pressure within power dynamics. That we were not aware of all that in the back.

Despite the sense of loss and disenchantment, *can art still heal*, we wanted to know?

"I'm not sure," Youssef says. He continues:

> I mean I hope it can help in the healing process, but from what I've seen, and what the product is trying to say, this damage of rape is irreversible. Unfortunately, it is irreversible. That is why it's so important to talk about it. That is why it's so important to do films about it.

In Yemen, Subay spoke about how painting the murals put "hope and happiness" in her heart. This is particularly powerful given that there were great hopes for a new Yemen during the revolution—a Yemen that has unfortunately failed to materialize. Instead, the situation deteriorated dramatically. Yemen has been at war since 2015 and is one of the world's worst, and least funded, humanitarian crises.[35] As of 2022, nearly three quarters of the population—over 23 million people—are in need of humanitarian assistance.[36] A reality that international actors tend to neglect, but Yemenis cannot escape from. "If you go to the streets and be with the people, you'll see the real life," Subay says.

Subay speaks of her motivation and the dire situation:

> I did it because I am a woman, and like every woman in Yemen, the world that we are facing with war issues is terrible. The people are starving, the Houthi militias are controlling the north, the women are facing domestic violence, there's no electricity, children can't finish their education and many, many other issues here.

These "many other issues" show no sign of abating. For women and children, the situation only appears to worsen. In fact, during our conversation, a starving child knocked on the door begging for food and support. The people of Yemen are *still* waiting for the war to end. While there was a brief lull in the shelling, unfortunately it was short lived. During our conversation in August 2022, Subay heard the news that violence had resumed. She laments:

> My hope—I think it is broken. Something broke. They broke every happiness, every hope in our hearts. Nothing is getting better at all.

Whatever dreams people had are now thwarted. For those of us who seek to record voices, document experiences, amplify causes, this makes our work more urgent. Activists are propelled by hope—hope that something will change, hope that things can improve. *But what do you do when there is no hope?* Everyone we spoke with walked the tightrope between hope and hopelessness.

Youssef also speaks of this, especially given the current climate in Lebanon:

> In regards to this place, I have no hope at the moment. But if you ask me, do you think it's totally hopeless, it can never change? I'll say no. It is possible. It's not hopeless, but right now, I have no hope.

He continues:

> Change is possible, you just need the opportunity for people to listen and the masses need to unlearn what they have learned by challenging belief systems. And I've seen it. So it's

possible. But at the same time, I'm telling you, I have no hope. I don't have much hope right now in this moment.

Activist-Art to Imagine What Is Possible

As Youssef and others articulate, having no hope now does not mean that it is entirely hopeless. Art-activism can also be symbolic of rebirth, regeneration, rebuilding. Art births dialogues, reactions, conversations—this plays a part and fills a gap.

Diab spoke about how her art became a rebuilding process in Sudan because the state and international organizations were not providing adequate services. "It wasn't just about the streets," she said. "Now we're rebuilding. The whole process of protesting and rebuilding, but building a new Sudan."

This "new Sudan," according to Diab, is one that separates religion from politics and governance. Just as her art is subject to various interpretations, so too is religion, and certain interpretations should not determine people's lives, livelihoods, or futures. She hopes in the future Sudan can:

> Remove religion from the state and from governing the country. I don't think they work together. It's a very personal thing. So I hope that we get to do that and Sudan can reach our democracy and our civilian rule. And let people be.

In Yemen, work from artists like Subay are increasingly important as they serve as motivation and reminder that women have the power to instigate change and ignite hope:

> Street art touches directly people on the streets, it is democratic because it is available for everyone without any kind of censure. It is not TV, you can touch the experience. People can also react with you right away and speak out about their feelings. People like to join me while I am drawing. They feel powerful to be part of the experience.[37]

Without space to advocate for women's rights in Yemen, Subay must now focus on her safety and that of her family. With a grant from the Artist Protection Fund in support of artists from conflict-affected areas, Subay, her husband, and their baby will travel abroad to safety—and to opportunity.[38] Subay hopes to further her education in art, as thus far she has been self-taught. She will also continue to focus her work on Yemen without fear:

> I will do some projects that will be the same as I do here. It will be about the situation in Yemen because I was in it and I will still be in it even if I am abroad because my family, and the people I love, will still be in it. I must talk about it and I must draw it because the people need it. And me and the other artists do not speak about it here because we are afraid of the situation. So who will be talking about this? The politicians? No, actually no one is talking about it.

Such an opportunity comes at a cost, however, and Subay admits it is bittersweet:

> It's very sad for me to leave my country, to leave my family here. I don't know if I will be back or see my family again. And my father, he loves my daughter so much, but he said to me: "Please do not come back. For your daughter. Do not come back here again." This broke my heart that I don't know if I can see him again.

Soultana in Morocco says the Arab Spring "revolution" was no revolution but rather oppression in another form: "We were the puppets and the master was playing with us," she says. Conditions in Morocco have not improved and Soultana says she has seen no meaningful change beyond the superficial:

> In this society, I lost hope. This is for sure. There's a lot of hypocrisy, there's a lot of contradictions and it's so hard to change those things. You can't change those things, they need something big.

And yet, despite it all, Soultana cannot remain passive and is determined to continue in her mission. "I'm going to fight," she says. "I'm still gonna keep fighting—because I have to."

On the future in Sudan, Diab was more optimistic. In her activism, she witnessed the emergence of many artists, musicians, and photographers—especially women. And while it has always been there, albeit privately or secretly, she believes there has been an outburst of creativity after the revolution:

> I get this feeling that people are not afraid anymore. They're just being themselves, inexcusably. So it's really beautiful to see what should have always been okay. We're not asking for a bunch you know, just personal freedom. But seeing the amount of women do various things and really just coming together supporting each other versus in the beginning … they really couldn't do it at the time. So it's frustration, I would say. So for females to come on and for them to support each other now, it's a beautiful thing to witness.

Overall, Tamtam is hopeful for the future and believes times are changing, especially among Saudi Arabian youth, "I just feel like it's different, definitely. And Saudi Arabia is a young country so things are changing." She celebrates the burgeoning creative scene and new opportunities now present in Saudi Arabia. "Saudi has its own scene, it has its own flavor, and I love that people are starting to do their own thing. To me that's the true culture in the country." Tamtam is happy with the direction of change: "My hope is that it keeps moving this direction. And in a steady way."

So What? Now What?!

> *Feminism, it seems to me, should be guiding and illuminating the women's movements by providing wide arguments for radically broad change, expressed in the new and powerful language.*
> —Jean Said Makdisi[39]

It can be argued that art is one of those new and powerful languages.

Earlier in this chapter, Egyptian artist Dr. Bahia Shehab spoke of revolutions as "wonderful spaces of discoloration and expression," but she questions whether these spaces create social change. She explains that social change comes from waking up every day and doing the work you know needs doing. But without platforms for this kind of organizing, she asks rhetorically, "how do you do it?"

This chapter presents an alternative to traditional activism—through art. It asks us to question what "revolution" looks like, and what forms it takes? *Can it look different? And—will that work?!*

In the words of artist-activists—yes. Art is often political, and feminism certainly is political. The evolution from artist to activist is an act of reconnecting feminism to its political roots.

Artist-activists create conversations, break barriers, and take great risks in doing so. They imagine what is possible, and depict it for us in ways that are easy to understand and absorb.

Artist-activists continue to find alternative avenues of expression—to document, record, protest, object—in subtle and not-so-subtle ways. These ways are a reflection of a moment, a snapshot of a social statement.

Artist-activists are, by virtue of their medium, communal and inclusive. These are building blocks of a movement. In using art for political comment, they remind us that changing minds is just as important as changing laws. More than change, art provides space for healing. All of this is revolutionary.

In research featured in *New Trends of Women's Activism after the Arab Spring*, Dr. Aitemad Muhanna-Matar reveals that:

> Arab women's forms of activism and resistance oscillate between binary opposites, such as tradition vs modern, the online vs the offline, the religious vs the secular, the top-down vs the bottom-up, the official vs the popular, the formal vs the informal, the private vs the public, and the local vs the global.[40]

Art is one of these seeming-opposites, bringing a new angle to the resistance. All forms—from songs to street art—are welcome, and necessary. This, along with the more traditional forms of protest—marches, protests, boycotts—creates a rich body of work upon which we can build a feminist movement. There is room for us all on the frontlines—crisis activist and creative activist.

5

Fragmented Feminisms

When we talk about the feminist movement, its reach, its fractures, its entry points, its challenges, I don't think the whole world is doing well these days, especially the region. It is not doing well at all.

—Myriam Sfeir[1]

To start, there is no one unique feminism that exists. It is possible to argue that, since the inception of this term, there have been varying definitions of what it is, who represents it, and how to express it. As such, every feminism can be fragmented, in a way. For our purposes, it is worth recalling that we are using feminism to denote the understanding that women are unequal in every space and place, that this inequality stems from patriarchy, and that concrete action is required to combat patriarchy and remedy this inequality.

What this concrete action is, and what result is expected, are the subject of much debate. Being feminist and *doing* feminism are fundamentally different things. Ideally they coexist, but in many cases they might not. The latter—*doing* feminism—is usually met with tangible action that is inherently political. Anything less is performative.

But, *what is Arab feminism—if such a term exists? And how might it be different?* We've been exploring this question throughout this book. Dr. Rita Stephan, Visiting Researcher at North Carolina State University, says that "Arab feminism is a series of disconnected experiences in silos and closed spaces," as the voices in these pages will illustrate. "It feels as if the movement is not mature," feminist activist and academic Dr. Carmen Geha adds. Meaning, there are isolated incidents one might describe as "feminist"—but these are often overpowered by the rifts and disconnects. Palestinian scholar Jean Said Makdisi expresses it this way:

> Because of the absence of masses of women committed to feminist principles, the feminist movement in the Arab world, and consequently the women's movement as well, have remained marginal to the major political currents of society, easily ignored by the powers that be in organizing the world in which we live.[2]

In order to understand the disconnects, or what we call the fissures in feminisms in the Arab region, one must first assume that there are, in fact, feminisms. We would argue that, even when the label is shunned, the actions are present. As such, one can *do* feminism without *being* feminist—at least in the Arab region. This chapter will highlight the challenges. While it might be argued that these are well documented, there is a difference between documenting and understanding, understanding and applying. That is a finding in and of itself. In other words, we assume to know what is wrong—*but do we? And even in knowing, do we act on it? How are we fixing it? Are we moving*

134

forward—and in which direction? After all, *what is a movement, unless we are willing to move—and move in the same direction?*

We reached over 200 people in our interviews, correspondence, surveys, and informal conversations to understand where we're moving. These conversations exposed fissures specific to the Arab region. Here we try to distill these in order to build stronger feminisms for the future of the region. This list is not meant to be exhaustive, but rather what emerged from our findings. They present a good starting point for conversation, consideration, and ultimately—change.

Further, we present this not in order of priority but as a list of aspects to consider—and eventual challenges to address—as we march forward. We have chosen to leave as much as possible in the authentic voice and words of those who expressed it in order to retain the integrity of the sentiment.

Surveying Young Feminists from the Arab Region

I believe in feminism because I believe in gender equality. Everyone should be empowered no matter what their gender might be, especially for people who identify as women in societies that marginalize them.
—Young feminist

This chapter begins with data from our survey of 113 people from 18 countries in the region as a starting point. For the survey, we deliberately sought the perspectives of young people of all genders from the region and the diaspora because, as we explained in Chapter 1, the Arab region has an overwhelmingly young population. And, young people have been on the frontlines of social movements in recent years. They are on the streets calling for change, not just in terms of women's rights and equality, but for all issues affecting their lives.

For instance, in Libya, where youth make up 60 percent of the country's population, young people have been at the forefront of conflict prevention, peacebuilding dialogues, and civic engagement initiatives since the end of the Libyan revolution in 2011.[3] The protests in Lebanon against government corruption were ignited by young people in light of frustration with longstanding social and economic inequalities. Students and youth took to the streets and refused to return to the classroom until demands for election reforms and an overhaul of the country's ruling elite were met.[4] Similarly, in Iraq, young Iraqis are mobilizing to make their voices heard by joining in mass protest and organizing civic engagement. Young people arguably hold the most political will in the country and have played an increasingly crucial role in attempting to change Iraq's political systems.[5] And, as described in Chapter 3, Tunisian youth ignited the "Jasmine Revolution" through protests and calls for political reform, ushering in a period of democratic transition set in motion by young people's vision for a more just state.[6] Following the revolution, youth mobilized spaces for civic engagement and debate, hosted skills-building workshops for their peers, and launched websites to monitor elected officials and hold them to account.

Further evidence abounds, but the point is that young people hold a unique and necessary perspective. Their opinions are a foundation for understanding feminisms in the region—both present and future. There is no agreed upon definition or age group for youth. For our purposes, however, we define "young people" as those who are 30 years and under.

For this book, we actively sought young people's voices for the survey, with both qualitative and quantitative questions. Their voices inform all of the responses below, but are most prominent in the following chapter when we talk about our Feminist Future. They are, after all, our Feminist Future.

It is worth noting that women, men, and gender non-conforming people completed the survey. We sought all perspectives in an effort to be as inclusive as possible. While the responses do not reflect the actual demographics of the region, they provide a useful snapshot and entry point into understandings of, and engagement with, the term feminist—and its underlying actions.

The survey began with the deliberately provocative question: *Do you consider yourself a feminist?* Eighty-nine percent of study participants answered yes, they did. That, already, is a positive sign. It might be interesting to conduct a survey with those who are over 30, asking them the same question. But that is the subject of different research. Of the 12 young men who completed the survey, nine said that yes, they are feminists. One young man from Egypt says he believes "women are equal to men in importance to society." Another says that yes, he believes in feminism "in its original purpose."

A young man from Lebanon writes that "feminism is one of the most pressing causes that support the inclusion of half of our community," while another from Egypt explains that, for him, feminism is about "equality between all genders," but is mostly about "elevating the rights that women currently have." A young Lebanese man explains that he had grown up with female role models, and a working mother. And, he adds, "being gay also helped." A young man from Bahrain writes that he believes in "equal political, social, and economic rights between men and women."

Of the three men who said no, they are not feminists, one says that while he supported feminism, he does not actively demonstrate it. Another prefers to be neutral and "not advocate more towards one gender." Ultimately, the views of this Lebanese man probably sums up the thoughts of many: "I don't really know enough about what a feminist is to claim I am one." A Lebanese woman who says she is not a feminist echoed the same sentiment. "This word is used so broadly," she writes, "I don't understand it completely, and feel it's used left and right." This was repeated by a few women who felt that they were not well informed about the movement, and did not particularly act in a way that supported the movement. For instance, a young woman from Libya explains that she is not a feminist because she does not engage in activities "that would advocate women's rights and gender justice."

One young woman from Jordan explains it this way:

> Feminist activism is a big word built on many attempts and challenges, especially in the Arab world. Although I consider myself a feminist, I do not participate in many activities that help and aim to improve the situation in the region.

And another young woman from Jordan feels that the term is a "Western ideology" built on the belief that "men are equal to women and are the same even though there are physiological and psychological differences." Her belief is built on specific roles for each gender, "not to say one gender is better," but rather "to assure us that one gender completes the other in order to establish a well sustained society based on well sustained families." Her traditional viewpoint is perhaps fueled by her perception that feminism is Western ideology or against family structure. An ideology that, she says, is "trying to liberalize women even though in reality, it's doing exactly the opposite."

Some women who argued against being feminists still believe that women's rights is an important issue for consideration. For instance, one woman from the UAE who says "I'm not into this stuff," still feels that women's rights and equality was a key issue in her country. And she selected "ending violence against women" as one way to achieve that equality.

Some make the distinction between being feminists and being advocates for women's rights or women's empowerment. For instance, one young woman from Saudi Arabia explains that the term has been politicized, and as a result she would not adopt the label and would instead "always participate in women empowerment." A young Moroccan woman reinforces this view, stating that she advocates for women's rights but is "not a fan of labels nor of modern and white feminism." She went on to explain that while labels create complications, she cares "very deeply about equality between women and men."

Of the 90 young women and one non-binary person who says they identified as feminists, their answers were similar, and equally passionate. Words and phrases like "human rights" and "equal rights" and "opportunities" and "dignity" and "respect" were all used frequently. Words like "equality" and "equity" and "inclusion" were also used often.

A feminist is one who believes in gender equality, many argue. Women "should be treated equally to men—which includes having the same economic and social opportunities and rights," one states. This sentiment was shared by many. In addition to believing in equality, one woman from Egypt explains that her feminism was born from the realization that "we suffer as women from discrimination and cultural and systematic violence because of the patriarchal society." And another from Lebanon defines her feminism as striving "for a world based on social, ecological and gender justice," because, she continues, all of these things are "lack[ing] in our societies today."

Some women argue on the basis of "common sense," and that feminism is a "natural response to the patriarchy," or a "natural thing to be, simple as that." How could I *not* be a feminist, many express. "Because I believe women deserve rights," one woman from Kuwait says, "I can't imagine people not being feminists."

Many explain their feminism as built from the reality of inequality and discrimination, having been denied opportunities or experiences. They blame "this patriarchal system" and refer to the misogyny they have experienced firsthand. And many state that equality must be on all fronts—social, economic, political. One young Jordanian-Palestinian woman explains that she is "passionate about fighting for our social and political rights that the patriarchy has deprived us from."

Others see a responsibility in teaching their children "how to support and encourage feminism" and "instilling feminist values" in their daughters. Many others were teachers in their own ways, supporting feminist activities and educating others about feminism. For instance, one young Syrian woman explains that she works "with human rights organizations that publish articles and texts on women's rights and gender equality" and another young woman from Lebanon actively engages in projects and campaigns advocating for women's rights, using her platform "to voice issues of women." And in the words of another Lebanese woman, "I have been advocating for justice and against gender imbalance for as long as I can remember."

One young Arab woman living in the United States sums it up simply: "Feminism is about equality and liberation. I'm all for that." One young feminist from Lebanon explains her views this way:

First, I do believe that women are discriminated against based on their sex and second, I firmly believe in the necessity of challenging gender roles, and dismantling the patriarchy for a more prosperous future.

This was echoed by another young woman from Lebanon who adds that "we live in a world where men have been making decisions for us," and, she continues, "in order to see change, we (women) must fight for our rights."

A Tunisian feminist echoes this sentiment. "Why are you a feminist?" we ask. Here are her words:

I'm a feminist because I believe in equality and equity and I think that women are a subject of a multitude of domination systems. I'm a feminist because I believe that the fight is necessary to protect, empower, and push all the women and the queers from the margin to the center. I want to identify myself as a feminist because the word is stigmatized and I want to be one of the women who dare take this label and deconstruct all the misconceptions about it.

A young Yemeni activist explains that her feminism is built on support for "women's independent thinking, life, and voice as a living and global voice that matters." Because men have created chaos, she explains, women's contributions are essential. "Women are a power that can't be denied," she says, "and it is time for women's policies to be applied."

She goes on to say that she works with women because, given the same resources and opportunities as men, women can "save the planet" and build a future that generations will celebrate and say "they made it and we wouldn't be able to live this life without their persistence to take the risk to fight for their rights and the rights of others."

She concludes with this: "I am a feminist … and have worked so hard to get where I am today…. I am a woman and believe we can do it once we realize how valuable we are." A young Lebanese feminist builds on this view, adding that "by being empowered, women can achieve so much." She advocates for the abolition of sexism "so that men and women can live without a divide in the society that considers one gender as superior to the other." And another young Lebanese-American adds that "true equality will only be achieved when such terms only exist in history books and there is no need to justify them—similar to racism."

One feminist from Libya explains her belief this way:

I believe in feminism because I believe in gender equality. Everyone should be empowered no matter what their gender might be, especially for people who identify as women in societies that marginalize them. They and we can do so much more if we can only unite and shatter the glass ceiling. I believe that the moment I became a feminist was the day I was born in a society that does not grant me my full rights just because of my assigned sex. I knew early on that if I didn't fight for myself and my rights no one will take this fight for me. This conviction was reinforced during the civil wars that unfolded in my country, where females were the primary victims of gender-based violence and secondary war effects, I knew that feminist thought and being a feminist scholar will provide me with the right tools and theories to tackle what had happened to those females and hopefully prevent it from happening again.

A young woman in Tunisia calls herself a "decolonial feminist." She explains it this way:

Beyond my theoretical and practical understanding of feminist scholarship… "I live my politics." I obsessively and vocally interrogate how the most mundane or political aspects of women's existence are constrained by patriarchy. I am particularly interested in the ways in which class, race, and sexism interplay. I am helplessly outspoken and passionate about fostering subversive feminist solidarity.

This echoes the sentiments of the authors and reflects the foundations on which this book is built. To conclude, in the powerful words of one Lebanese feminist:

> No one is born believing that women deserve less rights than others—the patriarchy teaches us that. Everyone is born a feminist and you either remain a feminist or you become a misogynist.

The survey responses brought many topics to light. The sense of hope, positivity, and ability to effect change was encouraging. But, realistically, there are still many factors inhibiting progress such as patriarchal structures, discriminatory laws, and prohibitive social norms—all of which we have documented. Another reason is lack of cohesion within feminist movements themselves. As we will see below, disagreements around the compatibility of feminism and religion, the definition of feminism itself, and the methods to achieve feminist goals are all barriers to the change that many wish to see.

The categories below emerged directly from interviews and survey questions, helping us to better understand where the fissures are in feminisms in the Arab region.

What Is Feminism?

> *There are hundreds of reasons that make me mad every day. As women and girls, we have hundreds of reasons to be feminists.*
>
> —Hayat Mirshad[7]

We start with the critical question *What is feminism?* because the term itself is so contentious in the region, and so poorly understood. For those who embrace the term, it is meant to signify equality and a counter to patriarchy. For others, they prefer to use a different term rather than identifying with feminism and with the movement. Often, the actions are the same, but the words used vary. We highlighted this as a potential disconnect in Chapter 1, and now we return to it here through the voices of feminists themselves.

Saudi Arabian musician Tamtam expresses it simply: "Feminism is equality between men and women ... definitely I'm a feminist because I do believe in equality."[8]

Takatoat, a non-governmental, independent feminist collective based in Jordan puts it this way:

> We are feminists because the personal is political. We all suffer from this system, from patriarchy, from these norms, traditions, and it's always oppressing us and limiting us from expressing ourselves completely.[9]

Bochra Bel Haj Hmida, Tunisian lawyer and politician, explains that, to her, "feminism is a societal choice which implies the equality of all people." She argues against discrimination and elaborates to say that "the discriminations that are most shared across the world are those founded on sex, given that even in the most developed countries the patriarchy is still strongly implanted." She continues to say that the changes that we can see today are significant, "but no society can claim to have put an end to patriarchy."[10]

Dr. Hosn Abboud, Lebanese academic and author, builds on this to add that her feminism includes the understanding of "the oppression inflicted on girls and women because of a long history of authoritative patriarchy and misogyny" and includes "the effort made to change this injustice by women and men."[11]

Dr. Mehrinaz El Awady, Director, Gender Justice, Population and Inclusive Development cluster at UN ESCWA, explains feminism this way:

> Feminism is about the movement to achieve equal socio-political rights for all types of women. It is not only about the results but also about the process of how we achieve those rights. It's also not just about working with women to achieve the rights but rather a whole of society approach.

Feminism, many have said, is about solidarity in the fight to achieve equal rights. Ghida Anani, Founder and Director of ABAAD–Resource Centre for Gender Equality, explains it as "solidarity with women working on access to resources" and a duty to live our values, working on the rights agenda, working to counter patriarchy, working to ensure safety and dignity and protection. "It's really living something you believe in and really practice in every single word and detail of your daily lives."[12]

Many noted that there are multiple ways to "do feminism"—many of which have yet to be fully explored. And yet there is an assumption that there is only one unique demonstration of feminism. This belief needs to be challenged. Nada Darwazeh, who works with the UN and other partners on gender equality in the MENA region, explains it this way:

> I don't think it's only a misunderstood concept. The whole concept of feminism is a concept that could be interpreted in many ways. It's not a binary where you're either a feminist, or not feminist. There's a wide spectrum of commitment towards women's rights that are located on this spectrum. I don't think there is one place where you could say, this is my only definition of feminism. It doesn't work like that. It's basically how far people are committed, what sorts of actions they're taking.[13]

Banan Abu Zain Eddin, Jordanian co-founder of Takatoat, identifies as a feminist—in both name and practice. She looks not only at the word but also at her own feminist activism and how she demonstrates her commitment to the movement. It is how she chooses to live her life, she explains. "It's not a label. It's how you practice this value and the solidarity and support each other. And the meaning of the words."

Diana Moukalled, Lebanese journalist and co-founder of Daraj Media, calls the feminist movement "the new manifestation of women's rights." While it might not be new globally, she explains, it is new terminology for the region, and it is "shaking lots of what some considered a solid brand."[14]

Even if the terminology is novel, the action is not. Dr. Hatoon Al Fassi, Saudi Arabian historian and activist contends that feminism—as a concept that believes there are discriminatory rules, notions, and practices against women—has always existed in Saudi Arabia, even if not overtly referred to as feminism. Arguably, this holds true across the region. She acknowledges that while the movements themselves were not comprehensive, women have always taken stands against patriarchal discriminatory structures to varying degrees.

Sossi Boladian, member of the National Commission of Lebanese Women (NCLW),[15] explains it this way, "I like women to have their rights equal to men, to respect laws. And I believe in the rights of everybody."[16] Her feminism is about the freedom every individual has to express their thoughts and live their lives.

Rym Badran, Lebanese student and Girl Up Middle East and North Africa Regional Leader, was galvanized into action in a classroom where a boy said, "I can't imagine a country being led by a woman."[17] She explains this moment as the first time she became personally aware of inequalities. As a result, she joined her school's feminist club and learned about the movement. Shortly thereafter, she became president of the feminist club and ignited the founding of many other feminist clubs.

To conclude this section, Chérine Kurdi, artist and women's leadership expert, says

Feminism is the stance of siding with humanity all over the world. It's an integral part of being humane, to make sure women and girls have access to basic human rights, freedom of choice, education and opportunities. To me it's a way for us to all care for each other because there are socio-economic injustices in the world. Some of them are very outraging in the 21st century. Just having that care of wanting to do something in whatever way we can is incredibly powerful and impactful.

What Is Gender and Gender Equality?

Feminism not only liberates women but also liberates men from social pressures.

—Young Lebanese woman

Some of those we spoke to made the distinction between feminism and gender equality. In order to better understand these perspectives, we explored the question *What is gender?* and, by extension, *What is gender equality?* Many felt that the goal should not be to alienate men, but rather to recognize the inequalities faced by men—and women—and to build better societies for all of us.

Dr. Noura Al Obeidli, Research Fellow at New York University Abu Dhabi, explains that "the term gender is quite alien to Emirati societies" as it was "pushed into our mindset and our culture through the state's recent initiative to achieve Gender Balance."[18] She compares this to the traditional top-down development approaches used by many governments, lacking broad buy-in and application. The UAE, she explains, has "certain schemes and agendas that we want to target, especially with the United Nations." In other words, the state has certain politicized development goals—like reducing its gender gap—that it wants to achieve. She continues:

They use gender to look into these numbers and then use it as a propaganda for the state initiatives concerning women's representation in vital sectors such as politics, in which they are visibly represented as ministers and Members of the Parliament.

Dr. Azza Charara Baydoun, Lebanese professor and feminist activist, shares how her feminism evolved over the years in a way that is "strikingly similar" to many other women across a range of affiliations and cultures. She explains this as an evolution from the "anger that fueled our '60s and '70s feminist discourse" into something that better reflected the concerns and wellbeing "of all women and men of all ages, races, creeds, sexual orientations" and other marginalized identities. She continues:

It seemed to me that these women strove for equality in order to participate more efficiently in the development of their societies and create more space and better opportunities for them to be tougher around world peace. Demands for gender equality by way of asserting themselves seemed to me much less of a preoccupation.[19]

Feminist activist Hayat Mirshad speaks to the micro-transgressions, even at an early age, that inspired her feminism:

> I grew up in a conservative society, a village in Lebanon, where girls were bound by patri-archal norms and traditions and culture. From a young age, I felt discrimination between me as a girl and any boy in society, including my own brothers. Small restrictions as a small girl. For example, you cannot play in the village playground because you are a girl, and that playground and all public spaces were dominated by boys and men. It was in these very small details, I felt this was wrong, while society told us this was normal. This answer "you are a girl and he is a boy" was not convincing at all. And that's why I started asking questions.

Sossi Boladian echoes this and builds her feminism on advocating for equality for both women and men, which she believes, starts at home. "For example, with my children, if my son needs a cup of water, why should my daughter bring it? This is how it starts," she says "from minute, simple things."

Yara Ghanem, Girl Up Syria founder, explains that her interest is in social justice and gender equality, "more than saying I'm a feminist."[20] Her activism is built on equal-ity and includes support for men, "because as a feminist I believe in the equality between all genders." For her, it is about freedom, and the right to live free from violations—and violence—regardless of who experiences it.

Moroccan rapper Soultana builds on this, saying that in her music she "wasn't just talking about feminism, or the problems of women."[21] Rather, she continues, "the prob-lem is bigger. And this is not good. And I'm sure that it's not just in our world, but it's worldwide."

A young Lebanese feminist from our survey sums it up perfectly:

> We live in an unequal world and that needs to change. Feminism is the theory of the political, economic, and social equality of the sexes. Feminism not only liberates women but also liber-ates men from social pressures. And it has tangible economic and social benefits for the world as a whole.

In a conversation with Fatima Al Mokaddem, a young student from Lebanon, she starts this way:

> I believe that everyone would begin by saying "I'm a feminist because I am an advocate of gender equality." But it is far more than this. The reality is that we still live in a world that is replete with discrimination, injustice, suffering, and inequality because of the unequal distri-bution of power, and because of the dissolving sense of humanity.[22]

Al Mokaddem explains that her feminism is not simply about women's rights and free-doms, it is built on the belief that everyone "deserves to live a life of dignity, free of discrimination and injustice regardless of their social identity." Her feminism is built on inclusion. "I cannot be a feminist," she says, "if I advocate for equal opportunities for women, while completely disregarding other individuals that fall outside the gen-der binary." She continues to say that, to her, being a feminist entails "constant exam-ination" of her biases and assumptions, and how they impact her view of the world and its individual occupants. She builds this on a foundation of respect, tolerance, and compassion.

Al Mokaddem explains herself as "someone who wishes to make life better and more equitable for people who are suffering from multiple oppressions." She concludes powerfully:

I firmly believe that everyone inhabiting this planet deserves to have equal opportunities to choose the life that they want; a life that is free from oppression and suffering. For these reasons, I consider myself to be a feminist.

Ultimately, it is clear that there are strong pushes for supporting equality—for everyone. Feminists and activists above are arguing for a holistic approach to equality. Research reinforces this push as well, with reports advocating for better engagement with families and communities, rather than viewing individuals in isolation, as if they exist separate from their social structures. Women's organizations, as one report advises, should view women's rights as interconnected with the "rights of men, children and the elderly within households, local communities or at the national level."[23]

Misconceptions of Feminism

The F-word. Is it a bad word? Too many people think so. Good thing I'm not those people.
—Young feminist activist

There is a common misconception throughout the Arab region of the word "feminist" and the negative connotations that travel with it. The age-old trope of the raging, man-hating feminist leaves many deterred from the label and the movement. When feminism is misunderstood, feminist movements suffer as a result.

Haneen Hadi, Iraqi activist and co-founder of domestic violence awareness campaign Speak Up, did not consider herself a feminist until a couple of years ago. She says it was "because of the wrong concept of feminism in Iraq and the whole region." She explains that people "think feminists are women who want to be liberated in a very sexual way," which detracts what feminism is truly about, namely, "equality and justice" she says.[24]

"I see how men roll their eyes when I say I am a feminist," one activist says. "And I see how some women refuse to say they are feminists because they don't want to be branded that way."

"Even if they *are* feminists!" she exclaims. "How are we ever going to create a movement if we can't even say the word?!"

Author Alya Mooro builds on this, adding that "for a long time I shied away from it because we don't want to be seen as scary, or angry, or against men because we care about the male gaze so much."[25]

Hadi continues:

I always argue with a lot of my friends who say they are not feminists, including men who say they are not feminists because they are not women, but I ask them if they believe in equality and they say "of course, I do" and then I call them a feminist and they push back. Other people seem to think that it questions the roles of men and women so they won't support it.

Assil Diab, Sudanese street artist and activist, explains the dynamic this way:

People confuse feminists with people who not just fight for women's empowerment but hate men and are loud and obnoxious and we mix everything together with religion and politics and certain lines and certain laws and certain verses, and tackle it in the name of feminism. And they just have a bad rep.[26]

Dr. Noura Al Obeidli from the UAE adds that language of gender and feminism is misinterpreted in the Gulf, explaining that "the first thing the conservatives accuse us with is that we are men haters. They don't really get what the concept of feminism is," she adds. They just assume that "we are fighting against men and the religious traditions."

Yara Ghanem of Syria used to introduce herself as a feminist even though she recognizes that it is likely to be misunderstood. Now, she says, she thinks about who she might be talking to, recognizing that when she uses the label, "not everyone realizes what a feminist is." Changing or diluting feminist language is not uncommon. And yet, *will this bring about greater understanding of the term itself? Or should we continue to dilute the term for the sake of the movement?* The verdict is unclear.

"For example," she continues, "they think that feminist means hatred of men and being superior and having the superpower and ruling the whole thing." This is built on the deep-seated belief that men run communities—and countries—because they are superior to women. Therefore, she explains, if feminists seek this equality, "then we are seeking for this priority and to be better or to be stronger."

The misconceptions and stereotypes that follow the term "feminist" are clear barriers to what feminist movements are trying to achieve, and are performed by both men and women. This, coupled with the assumption that feminists are sexualized, angry, loud, man-hating, and so on, prevents many women from identifying as feminists.

What About Everyone Else?!

> *Because of the divide between different human rights and feminist organizations, we need to be educated more on those concepts ... so we come to a common understanding of the functions.*
>
> —Ghida Anani

There is a tension, many argue, between the feminist agenda and a broader human rights agenda. Feminism does not sufficiently advocate for the full range of human rights, they feel. Feminism as it is understood is only about women, many say. And they prefer to address human rights in their totality, particularly considering the grave human rights needs in the Arab region.

"Yes, I consider myself a feminist," Abir Chebaro, Lebanese gender consultant and activist, explains.[27] "I'm a human rights defender." Feminism is not only about women, she continues. It is about "equal access to opportunities, to the right to expression, to bodily autonomy for everyone—not only for feminists." For feminists, she continues, they might focus more closely on women's rights, "but this at the end will benefit everyone around you. Not only women."

Dr. Charlotte Karam, feminist activist scholar puts it this way:

A lot of efforts fail to recognize other women who come from historically marginalized communities, or migrant women, or refugee women, and they tend to not make the link, often on purpose and consciously, in order not to politicize the conversation in a direction that would undermine their primary aim, which is to push for a demographic that looks more like them, ignoring all other demographic categories. Sometimes it's conscious and it's political, other times, it's racist. It's important in terms of the boundaries of who's included and who's excluded in some Arab feminisms.

When we speak of those who are historically excluded, many feminists found a red line when it concerns LGBTQ+ rights—where there is resistance to addressing (or even acknowledging) the full range of sexual orientations, gender identities, and expressions. For instance, Randa Siniora, Director of the Women's Centre for Legal Aid and Counseling in Palestine, explains the resistance feminists face in "trying to allow for LGBTQ+ rights."[28] She continues to say that "while all rights are universal and indivisible, social and cultural constraints are often a major obstacle in addressing LGBTQ+ rights within Palestinian society." Many feminists are also advocates of LGBTQ+ rights, which are resisted by conservative elements who accuse them of "bringing in Western ideas to our society." The rejection of LGBTQ+ rights then results in rejection of the feminist movement as a whole. Even attempts to address other forms of inequality such as gender-based violence are then also resisted, according to Siniora.

Globally, there are divergences in the discourse emerging around gender norms. The Arab region still has not fully accepted this critical dialogue. Dr. Kristin Diwan, Senior Resident Scholar at The Arab Gulf States Institute in Washington, puts it like this:

> There is a lot of attention being paid to the political debate within the United States on gender. This is generating a lot of fear about gender normativity and transgender rights, and this is entering the political discourse in the Gulf region as well. This kind of moral panic is generating a backlash that is sure to hurt feminist movements as well and to hinder their acceptance and advancement.[29]

Dr. Tarek Zeidan, Executive Director of Helem, an NGO focused on LGBTQ+ justice and equality, has this to say:

> The past three years have been extremely difficult for LGBTQ movements and organizations in the MENA region. The COVID-19 pandemic, as well as shifting geopolitics, have led to a large number of organizations closing down or contracting to offering basic services, if any. The mainstreaming of LGBTQ issues in MENA, whether through deliberate advocacy or through insidious manipulation by states and the religious establishment, have led to devastating backlash against queer individuals in the Middle East without the necessary infrastructure of protection and support in order to withstand the onslaught. The current mode is survival in most of the region, with a few pockets fighting to keep what difficult gains they have made.[30]

Fatima Al Mokaddem, a young woman from Lebanon, put it this way when speaking of challenges to equality in the Arab region:

> I haven't touched on the subject of the LGBT community because the presence of these individuals is seen as a threat to the heteronormative mentality and many are dehumanized for their divergent lifestyle and sexual orientation.[31]

The call for a feminist future requires an intersectional movement. One that recognizes the unique strengths and needs of its members and the power of solidarity. But this is not without its challenges. Diwan continues to say:

> The current polarization within the United States itself makes it difficult to advance unifying strategies. In fact, it seems more likely that there will be transnational coalitions against these openings. This will make things a lot tougher.

This is playing out in real time, as Yosra Akasha from Sudan explains. She recounts an instance where various groups were participating in a symposium. "Women's rights activists from Sudan were not happy … because they were sitting in the room with sex workers and the LGBTQ+ community. Many of them withdrew. Only a few of us remained," she says.[32]

Anthony Keedi of ABAAD explains that they tried to employ an "intersectional feminist approach" in Lebanon, "because there are so many different subcultures."[33] Indeed, it is not only impossible but also irrelevant to ignore intersecting needs and realities. Our feminist agenda needs to look beyond these boundaries and binaries.

Intersectionality is critical, and needs to form part of our understanding of vulnerabilities in the region. Dr. Gabriella Nassif, feminist researcher, explains the challenges this way:

> Legally, around the region, women are second class citizens. Period. And then you double down on that marginalization as you go down. The hierarchical ladder of how people of varying genders and sexualities are valued. So, women are second class citizens then LGBTQ+ folks are third class citizens, trans folks are fourth class citizens. And if you add any type of intersectional identity like say you're trans and a black woman living in Egypt, it's nearly impossible to navigate those intersectional identities in places where parts of your identity are practically made illegal. And you're rendered invisible by the state.[34]

Ultimately, Myriam Sfeir, Director of The Arab Institute for Women, summarizes it this way: "There are many fractures related to the fact that there is no buy-in on the level of intersectionality, and gender rights or women's rights are viewed as split."

Young activist Rym Badran says that while she is still at the beginning of her activist journey, she is "learning every single day." "But yes," she continues, "I would consider myself a feminist, and especially an intersectional feminist." The young feminists who shared their views in the survey felt strongly about the need for intersectional approaches that are inclusive of all human rights. One young woman explains that her feminism includes a need for "intersectional knowledge production that highlights underrepresented voices and marginalized communities." Another young woman adds that many groups "women, transgender and non-binary people, people of color, etc." encounter multiple discriminations and oppressions, "...which is why I constantly advocate for feminism and equality." One young "ecofeminist" explains that patriarchy exploits "both women and nature." And that we must address these issues as intersecting.

Finally, another young feminist from Lebanon explains it this way:

> Speaking up for equality in all its forms is not just a responsibility but a fundamental part of my core values. Feminism encompasses many intersectional issues that I believe need to be highlighted and changed in my community and society.

Is Sisterhood Global?

> *Sisterhood is not global. It might not even be local. Women do not necessarily act in solidarity with each other, just because they are women.*
> —Dr. Nadje Al-Ali[35]

As much as we would like to believe that sisterhood is global, this is naive. As academic and activist Dr. Nadje Al-Ali rightly stated, sisterhood might not even be local. In other words, unfortunately we do not support each other just because we are women. In fact, we can be each other's harshest critics and biggest obstacles.

One woman from the UAE shares her professional experience about the "condescending attitude" she experiences from women. "It breaks my heart," she says. "Women will always compliment the way I look—my hair, my makeup, my shoes—but not what I do."

Her experience with men in her profession is not the same, she explains, because "it has been established over the past 15 years that I'm not to be messed with." But she laments the treatment she receives from other women, "especially European and American." She adds: "I find them very condescending towards me that I come from the GCC."[36]

She actively defies gender norms. "I represent everything that's *haram*," she says. "I don't cover my head, which for them is *haram*. It has nothing to do with what I say," she adds, "And it's not about what I bring to the table. It's how I *look* when I'm bringing it to the table."[37]

Dr. Noura Al Obeidli from the UAE explains it well: "Women actually are fighting each other like we're our worst enemies and because of that, we don't have a collective mindset of feminism." She is not the only one who shares this sentiment. Abir Chebaro adds that it is "not only men who are attacking women's issues," and ultimately Chebaro explains, "we need women to stop being misogynistic."

Yosra Akasha from Sudan has also been under personal attack. She explains that she chooses not to be a part of any group that does not respect her personal freedoms. She puts it this way:

> If they are slut shaming, this is not an entity I'd like to be a part of. And I received this slut shaming myself for dressing inappropriately, specifically from women who are women's rights activists, but also affiliated with some political groups. They would shame how you appear, how you behave in the public eye, sometimes even in the private sphere.

Clearly, women acting in support of other women cannot be assumed, and, in fact, is at risk. There are more statements of opposition than solidarity, meaning that our commonly assumed "global sisterhood" is perhaps not so common after all.

Are We Victims of the Patriarchy?

Women are part of the problem and part of the solution.

—Soultana

It is naive—and in fact, dangerous—to put the onus on women for perpetuating a system of male domination. And yet, our conversations revealed that there women who choose to not disrupt the status quo, to—in the words of feminist academic Dr. Deniz Kandiyoti—"bargain with patriarchy." Meaning, there are women who resist radical change because they receive benefits by subscribing to the status quo.[38] Patriarchy will protect them—or so they are led to believe. Such women are, in feminist journalist Mona Eltahawy's words, "foot soldiers of the patriarchy."[39] Eltahawy goes on to say, "if you are not actively dismantling the patriarchy, you are factually benefiting from it."[40]

While these women benefit from the existing system—patriarchy—they might also be victims of that system, whether or not they choose to recognize it. Women we spoke with explained that other women not only reinforce their patriarchal bargains, but also try to force others to conform. Too often, while these women assume they benefit, they do not recognize the oppression they suffer—and the oppression they perpetrate as a result.

It is partly in their upbringing and socialization, Abir Chebaro explains, and built from the lack of knowledge about their rights. As mentioned in Chapter 3, Lina Khalifeh from Jordan echoes this view and explains that not only do all forms of violence against women exist, women "do not know they are oppressed." Rather, they maintain the illusion that they are free. Being under patriarchal control their whole lives, Khalifeh explains, "they think that is the norm."[41]

Takatoat, the feminist collective from Jordan, added that they receive "messages and comments from women and girls attacking us." They explain that these women are "victims of the patriarchal system because they are not aware of these things as problems."

Some spoke of the need to tap into the power of the matriarchy and address the messages and behaviors women themselves are perpetuating, especially in raising children according to prevailing norms and traditions. In the domestic sphere, women tend to have greater agency and can therefore use their maternal role to influence their children by reinforcing patriarchal messages—or challenging them.

Surely, a woman's ability to rewrite social norms is linked with the extent to which she has agency in home and community. Soultana of Morocco explains it this way: "Women are part of the problem and part of the solution" and she uses child rearing as an example to illustrate the point. It is a socio-cultural given that the woman is the primary caretaker and therefore she bears a responsibility in forming a child's ideas. Traditional ideals that reinforce male entitlement and women's "place" begin at home, resulting in upbringings that perpetuate the patriarchy.[42]

Or, these ideals can be rewritten at home.

"We are building them. We are creating them. We make that difference between the boy and the girl," Soultana continues:

> When I was a kid, my mom never bought me dolls, and I was always with my dad, or in soccer fields, or running on the street with the guys. She never told me that my place is in the kitchen instead. She always said you need to be responsible and you need to be independent, so that's what made me like this. But I know a lot of girls now whose dream is to get married, have children, do the laundry, and raise the babies. How is it still like this?

It might "still be like this" for some girls because they cannot imagine having more, or actively fear demanding more. Further, in contexts of conflict or insecurity, survival instincts prevail, and demanding more does not feature because people are less inclined to break the status quo in favor of the safety that established (albeit oppressive) patterns provide.

For instance, Alya Mooro of Egypt and the UK explains the "scarcity mindset" as an element of "ingrained misogyny." She explains it as fear—in particular the fear of chaos and disorder that could result by defying "the ways that things are." She elaborates:

> If too many people step outside of this system that we've known, that's been hundreds of years and passed down mother to daughter, what the hell is going to happen? It's going to be anarchy.

The fear of defying the established social order helps keep women in line. Even Mooro's own mother would argue in favor of marriage, although she is divorced. Mooro explains that her mother, like many others, think that following this prescribed path guarantees a better life, "which is ultimately what people want for their kids." Conversely, "there's a fear that if you don't follow this path, you're going to live a really difficult life and you're not going to have anyone who's going to have your back." She continues, "traditionally women in the Arab region—and across the world—have not been able to work and have therefore not known how to fend for themselves or exist in the world." As a result, they depend on men for survival. "If it's not your father, it has to be your husband," she says. So ultimately, you must ensure that you have a husband. To do so, Mooro continues, "you need to be nice, you need to not speak too loudly, and you need to not be a sexual person."

Additionally, she explains that there is an element of jealousy when daughters are defying rules that mothers had no choice but to follow. Initially, she explains, her mother envied her daughter's freedom, and tried to restrict her further. "Now," she says, "[my mother] is like, you go girl, but I think a big piece of it used to be jealousy."

"Was that heartbreaking to hear?" we ask her.

"It was also like 'Thank you.' Because it means that I'm doing things differently."

Another trap of the patriarchal system expressed by many was the pressure to conform to Arab gender norms, and the fallout experienced when failing to fit the stereotypical woman mold. Moreover, some described needing to emulate traditionally "male" qualities to get ahead. One study found this practice to be especially present in workplace environments where "masculine defaults" are the norm.[43]

One woman we spoke to feels that she had to adopt a certain persona in order to succeed in her chosen (male-dominated) field:

> I had to work more than anybody. I stayed at the office longer than everybody. I had to be so loud. I had to be so rude. I had to take insensitive jokes. I had to listen to curse words, to derogatory terms, and pretend they didn't hurt me. I had to just move on against my good judgment.

It was necessary, she explains, in order to establish a path for other women:

> I am ambitious. I knew that, in order for me to be a voice for women, to hire more women, to establish committees concerning women and children—I had to reach. I had to reach. And in order for me to reach, I swallowed a lot of pride and also I sometimes deviated from my value system. I'm against derogatory terms. I'm against sexist jokes, but I had to take it.

She continues:

> I'm not proud of it, but I'm also not ashamed of it. Where I am right now, I have an equal say on a table with people three times higher rank than me. If I did not go through that journey, I wouldn't be able to influence the decision-making for women right now. I had to do it for them to come in.

It has served its purpose but the stakes are high, as she is well aware. Higher for her than any other man:

> If I don't succeed in my position, there will not be another female after me. I know that I'm not proud of it. I'm being very frank and honest with you. I'm not proud of it. But I have zero regrets. I have zero shame. Because fuck them. Yeah, fuck them. Really. It's a boys-club.

Another activist explains that, with Arabs, it is "different." "With our culture women are looked upon as more nurturing, and professionally we have to pay the price." She elaborates, "I am often given files on women and children because I am a female."

Women continue to be victims of gendered stereotypes and their perceived maternal nature.

Ultimately, it can be argued that if women are indeed perpetuating patriarchy, it is because they are victims of the patriarchal system. They use their maternal roles as social influencers, to reinforce patriarchal messages that they themselves were forced to subscribe to. On one level there is a reproduction of stereotypes and behaviors—due in part to being victims—and on the other there remains a (potentially-untapped) power in exercising a matriarchal role for relearning and defiance.

There is truth in the old adage: "It starts at home." Many of those we spoke to were able to defy social norms because they had families who did not subscribe to strict societal expectations. In short, there is room to challenge the traditional order, starting at home, with the space we occupy. There is untapped power in everyday resistance.

While this holds true at the household level, the Jordanian feminist collective Takatoat advocates for a system-wide rethink. "The whole system needs to reflect and to think about it again and how to proceed."

We are all programmed by patriarchy, they explain, and as a result it is hard to defy what is so deeply ingrained. "To liberate ourselves from these beliefs and from these thoughts was really hard. And this is what we expect from others. But we know that it's really hard and it takes a lot of time."

Feminist activist and academic Dr. Carmen Geha adds a layer of nuance to the conversation at the macro level:

> No, I wouldn't say that we are guilty of perpetuating the patriarchy. The patriarchy is so enshrined through insidious ways like sectarianism, corruption, militarization. There is a cooptation by the state that is bigger than us right now. I wouldn't be so binary, or so quick to judge us. I think we're working within the structures as best we can. But I don't think we're guilty. I think we're oppressed. And within those structures of oppression, we're trying. We're trying through civil society, academia, journalism, art, culture, we're trying. But it's very difficult to break those shackles.

Let's Not Rock the Boat

> *Although we have the Women's Council, they are not adopting a progressive approach anymore. With all due respect to their history, with all due respect to whatever they do, but they are not taking a progressive approach as they did historically.*
>
> —Abir Chebaro

Many of those we spoke to explained that entities that appear to be "feminist"—or even claim to be feminist—are in fact not progressive, not pushing boundaries, not pressing for political space. Instead, they are toeing the line, avoiding so-called sensitive issues, and watering down the agenda. By eschewing political battles, they are in fact undermining the entire raison d'être of feminism. It is, after all, a political battle.

"There are things that our women would advocate for," Myriam Sfeir explains, "but they're hush-hush, no-no. The subjects that they wouldn't talk about."

Yosra Akasha from Sudan speaks to what she calls the "gap in the country" in terms of willingness to push boundaries and to embrace a feminist agenda. She explains that issues like the right to work and to have an education are discussed, while the barriers keeping women and girls from these are ignored. For instance, discussions around unpaid labor that have been "nonexistent until the past few years after the revolution and the involvement of a new generation of feminists."

"There's been a long long history in the region of elite co-optation of the women's rights discourse," Dr. Gabriella Nassif argues. "These people aren't even feminist. They don't even claim to be feminists."

She continues:

A lot of these agencies that are allowed to exist in the government, that's part of the so-called patriarchal bargain, to reference Deniz Kandiyoti. These elite women's groups, educated women, their bargain in order to reach the state and to be in the state was to compromise on the more political issues of feminism. So like issues of racial equality. Issues of labor equality. They weren't interested in that because those patriarchal and male-dominated spaces would have just tossed them out if they brought that stuff up.

Akasha recounts an incident that uncovered the hypocrisy of these entities for her. After a state-led massacre which resulted in deaths and injuries, a women's organization that records such information questioned the legitimacy of women's stories of sexual violence. Akasha describes it like this:

When it's sexual violence there is a huge stigma. Those two ladies were literally in operation having surgery [as a result of their injuries] and you want to go to them to ask if that happened to you or not? So for me that was a huge disappointment from public figures within the women's rights movement.

There is a sense that entities and activists such as these, avoid—or lack the courage to address—critical issues. As another example, she explains that these women's rights activists focus on political participation while "not addressing the root causes why women are participating in politics"—or not. These movements ask for a quota, "but then refrain from discussing the barriers or discussing their policies and regulations that affect women's access to resources and also the power balance within the family institution." Challenging the unequal power structures and pushing boundaries is a non-negotiable imperative. Without this, there is no feminism.

Dr. Carmen Geha explains that the obstacle is political:

It's the state structure and the form of feminism or women's rights that is tolerated by the regimes in the region. And it is regime-serving, elitist, sectarian that is the mainstream type of feminism that the state accepts, and anything outside of it meaning feminism to include gender equality, pertaining to our bodies, to include members of LGBTQ community, to include migrant domestic workers, anything outside, anything that is seen by the state as "deviant," is not considered part of state feminism or women's inclusion agendas by the Arab governments.

Diana Moukalled from Lebanon sums it up perfectly:

If you want to present yourself as a feminist with the feminist agenda, you are challenging religion, politics. You're challenging class, you're challenging many of the pillars that society is built on. So that's why its access and ability to work is not easy and not easily granted. You need fighters for that.

The Cult of the Elite Feminist

State feminism ... cannot change the rules of the game.
—Dr. Carmen Geha[44]

Many women we spoke with did not feel adequately represented by the state *co-opt*ed-feminists, political-feminists, or celebrity-feminists who appeared to speak for the movement. These women were often family members of political men, or in politics themselves, but who did not necessarily bring a feminist agenda to their role.

"There is a decline in the feminist approach," Dr. Mehrinaz El Awady explains. "The feminist movement had been politicized and there is a shift towards state-led feminism. Such an approach has its pros and cons."

One feminist explains the situation in Lebanon this way:

> At the time of the 2019 revolution, activists felt that the NCLW did not represent them, because they were not representative of their people.[45] Especially as they were appointed because they were in good relation with the President of the Commission—who is the daughter of the President of the Republic.

Feminist activist and academic Dr. Carmen Geha puts it strongly, reminding us that:

> State feminism in Lebanon, like elsewhere, cannot change the rules of the game. Real change cannot seek approval from men, and cannot be gender-mainstreamed according to some international legal standard.[46]

Dr. Hatoon Al Fassi describes how the government in Saudi Arabia selectively supported women on the condition that they fit the state's image. Meaning, conforming to the status quo and not supporting real change for women—the real, radical change that is very much needed. She explains:

> The state has done a lot and there have been good changes. But all in all, women have been used. The national state had always held that the country's image was her women's image. Today as the state is renovating and reinventing its image, it is using women in a different way, by applying state feminism to its choice of representative women—state women who meet its criteria of loyalty and obedience. However, some of them are more aware of their status and keep a low profile on their role trying to accomplish it slowly. But I believe that, little by little, hopefully, things will be better for the next generation.[47]

Diana Moukalled builds on this and explains that yes, there is a problem with the movement being hijacked by elite women. "I cannot be part of the same political elite who robbed us. We need more women from the spectrum," she says. At the same time, she recognizes the phenomenon of those in power adding women simply because they are women. She will not support such elite tokenism. For instance, she explains, in the context of the investigations of the Beirut explosion of August 2020, "I cannot go to streets to protest those who stopped Beirut port investigations and clap for them because they brought women. I would be failing myself, frankly I cannot."

Nada Darwazeh also speaks to the politicization of the agenda, and the challenge when women in political positions toe the party line, at the expense of a feminist agenda. "The women's movement is not a very coherent movement," she says, "because they have their variances and differences based on where they stand and what political party they support." She goes on to explain that, on many occasions, women members of political parties are political, above all else. Even at the expense of feminism.

In her experience working across the region, she found divisions within the movement to be debilitating. She explains that women of rival political parties would still not be able to reach agreement on the women's rights agenda. "They need to keep in mind what's common between them," she says. And she continues:

In terms of supporting women, you have women who are being represented in peace talks or negotiations on the women's quota, but they are also part of the Islamic party, or part of other ideologies. Then when the discussion is related to women's rights, instead of working together to advise or to make a breakthrough, they would stay divided to talk about the political faction that they belong to. Eventually, what is really lost is women's chance to gain more rights.

Darwazeh goes on to explain that when she talks about the women's movement, "I would not include national women machinery."[48] These structures are mandated by their governments, meaning their loyalty is in line with the political agenda rather than women's rights. National women's machineries, ironically established to support "women's interests," still relegate women's rights to the backseat.

There is also a phenomenon common across the region of the cult of the celebrity-feminist. This person becomes the (often) self-appointed spokesperson and media darling for "all things women." The result is that we come to see her agenda as synonymous with the feminist agenda.

We latch onto that idea that it is her model of feminism or nothing—she becomes the inadvertent face of feminism. Ultimately, if we like her, we accept feminism. If not, the movement suffers.

Haneen Hadi of Iraq explains that "famous feminists" have done a disservice to the movement, and Iraqis have distanced from feminism as a result. "I've noticed that the shock approach for Iraqis does not work," she adds. And now the population is less inclined to "accept that feminism is actually about equality."

Hadi points out that the elite feminists in Iraq "are not even looking for solutions because [that] would remove them from the spotlight." She continues. "Some say that the pioneers of this movement are tackling this the wrong way, trying to look like the center of attention and the heroes." Such methods only serve to delay progress. "They fight with each other instead of cooperating. It is a competitive approach and they shouldn't treat it like a race as people are dying out there," she concludes. In other words, while these women are competing, other women are quite literally dying. As such, cooperation is a matter of urgency.

Ultimately, women's organizations in the Arab region are too few and too far between. And cooperation is the exception, unfortunately too often *not* part of the region's psyche. Whether political-feminist or celebrity-feminist, these elite women do not represent the masses. When feminist causes are restricted to higher levels, with women's rights only addressed by political parties and political-feminists, cooperation and solidarity become even more essential. There is also an emerging generational element here—the older generation engaging in "women's work" as a charitable endeavor while the activists on the street see the struggle as non-negotiable and existential.

Female Presence Is Not Feminist Power

> *It's not about quantity only. We want more women, good women, or a good feminist agenda on the table. It's not about having any woman at the table.*
> —Diana Moukalled

Being a woman does not mean being a feminist. More specifically, being a woman in government certainly does not mean being a feminist. While there are feminists in government, these are few, and the majority of women in power do not espouse feminist values or support a feminist agenda.

Journalist Diana Moukalled spoke about the debates being raised in feminist circles after eight female parliamentarians were elected to the Lebanese Parliament in 2022. Moukalled says:

> I don't believe I should support a woman just because she's a woman. I will support her because she has a feminist agenda. I find it degrading to discuss numbers and how many women we have when they don't have feminist agenda. I don't want feminist issues to be transformed into something superficial and naive. So to me, you need to be clear what type of messaging you have and what political agenda you have.

A feminist from the UAE similarly believes that feminism is "being empowered because you are capable, not because your gender is female." She goes on to describe how the UAE mandated a 50 percent female quota in parliament, which she does not necessarily agree with because:

> Initially, that will only generate female representatives but not capable female representatives. Just because they are female ministers does not mean I see them as feminists. I admire that they are in these positions but they follow mandates and are not breaking ground. I understand it's a journey and after the first five to 10 years we will see more capable people, but I wish I could see them more expressive of themselves and that the initiatives they present when it comes to empowering women is something more than paid maternity leave.

Dr. Noura Al Obeidli, also of the UAE, echoes the fact that the government is pushing for women's emancipation in politics and economics, but it remains an artificial imposition, top-down and tokenistic due to the pressures imposed by the patriarchal society:

> When feminism is examined and discussed, the patriarchs at home and at the workplace would often be resistant of the state-led progressive initiatives, pointing out that "we have female ministers in the country," or that we've been granted with emancipation, and equal salaries, neglecting core societal problems by simply commenting "what else do women need?" But we [women] are not happy. Women battle privately with mental health issues, struggle with arranged marriages, health risks with consanguineous marriages, high divorce rates, and issues concerning citizenship. Let alone the domestic workload that adds to the challenge of balancing personal and professional life. So in the workplace, yes, we have equal salaries but we are misrepresented, institutionally clustered, and lack access to career opportunities.

She concludes by saying:

> There are changes happening and a push towards women's emancipation, but we still have the patriarchy.

This sentiment was built upon by Nada Darwazeh, who, through her work in the region, sees countries improving their rankings on international gender indices. But, she warns, these numbers don't measure real change on the ground. "So you would see a country high up in the ranks," she explains, "but that does not reflect on the reality of women's situation." This is further impeded by lack of data to verify and measure the impact, but "it's still early," she says. And since some countries have recently amended their laws, Darwazeh explains that we need to see what they are going to do and how the daily lives of women might actually change.

Chasing international rankings often means cosmetic changes that do not result in changes in women's lives. Artificially inserting women into positions of power without addressing the root causes of gender inequality is performative—and dangerous. The result is that countries smugly climb the ladder of various global indices reflecting "equality," while the reality remains vastly unequal.

Similarly, the mere existence of women's organizations does not mean that the work being done is beneficial to women. It may in fact marginalize other women further. One study finds that certain organizations can be considered elitist, utilizing their networks to get close to donors or policymakers. What often happens, however, is just a reinforcement of status quo, and the study concludes that "women may have *presence*, but not a *role*."[49]

Dr. Gabriella Nassif sums up the challenge this way, explaining that cosmetic changes are woefully inadequate, or at best a starting point to what should be a far more meaningful fight for real rights:

> A lot of people who claim to be feminists are not feminist. They are just advocates for cisgendered women, they are only advocates for women's rights and in that sense, only legal rights. And once the law is passed, they think they finished their work. No, that's not done at all. You need to make sure it's implemented. You need to make sure people have equal access to the law. And so on.

The Nation Is Divided

> *Class and location make a huge difference and they advocate for the problems they see around them so there is not a lot of crossover.*
> —Haneen Hadi

It goes without saying that not all feminists—or feminist organizations—agree on the same agenda or approaches. There are vast diversities within movements. Some of those diversities included rural/urban divides and class differences. At the sub-national level, what happens in the capital is often far removed from the rural areas—arguably where the more conservative elements of society reside.

In addition, the challenge becomes even greater when there is conflict within the country. We summarize: In conflict and instability, challenges are magnified. Firstly, the feminist struggle is often sidelined for the national struggle. Feminist interests are shelved, often never to be addressed, even after supposed-peace has been achieved. And women are left out of peace processes. Additionally, when only part of a nation is in conflict, there is a disconnect between the conflict-affected areas and the rest of the country.

Sudan presents a good example, as Yosra Akasha explains in an effort to build consensus and "one movement":

> Last year, before the military coup, we had been having discussions with both women's rights activists and feminists in war-affected areas in order to say, ok we are one movement. But the needs of people in Khartoum are very different from the people in North Darfur. So we need to have this connected agenda.

She goes on to say that organizations should not necessarily unify as "there is power in diversity of views, agendas, and identities." Organizations should, however, support each other's agendas and she explains that the movement has to consider the issues specific to conflict-affected areas. At the moment, she sees "poor networking, dialogue, and communication" between women in conflict areas and those in Khartoum but would like to see the movement get to a place where they can "respect the uniqueness of each group and advocate collectively," she elaborates.

Yara Ghanem, a young feminist from Syria, explains how cultural differences present across the governorates in Syria:

> Our community is hungry for [feminist] workshops and education, we need this. But the thing is that we have limits that prevent us from going further. They all believe in the importance of empowering girls and they all believe in the importance of trying to end what we are suffering from. But the thing is, when it comes to what we are doing, there are kind of differences in cultures. This is something important in our community that we have diversity and we have people from different backgrounds.

She continues to share how this affects her work, and the ways she adapts:

> Sometimes you have to just edit, or delete information, or explain less. It depends on the people that you are dealing with and what cultural background they have. I try as much as possible to be flexible with other people and just deal with them, or talk to them the way they want because this can create less conflict. Especially in a country that is suffering from war for 11 years now, it adds another layer of complexity. So, I learned this and I try to implement this in my work.

Akasha also explains that class differences present challenges to unifying the feminist movement. Her example is from Sudan, but it likely applies across the Arab region. "Within Khartoum itself, and other urban centers," she says, you can see the divisions, "the class division between the women who are upper middle class and the working class women."

To further illustrate the point on class divisions in the region, Nada Majdalani from Palestine says, "I see our region like the *Titanic*." She continues, "There are people sitting in first class with the champagne and the ballrooms, and people who are at the bottom of the ship. But once the iceberg hits: everybody sinks."[50] Dr. Fatima Sadiqi of Morocco echoes this sentiment, adding that she is deliberate in her efforts to support both marginalized and rural women in order to build a concerted feminist agenda that honors diversity:

> Being both an academic and an activist, I believe in promoting marginalized (rural) women by underlining their historical and current agency in the construction of their communities and societies. This goal is part and parcel of the overarching aim of feminism in the region, which seeks to promote women in their heterogeneity.[51]

Feminist movements cannot afford to be elitist, or alienate their rural base. As Dr. Kaltham al-Ghanim puts it, "…for the dream to become a reality, ordinary women must be brought into the feminist project."[52]

One young Lebanese activist builds on this and hopes feminism will be:

> …less exclusive to a group of niche, highly educated Westernized feminists, and become more inclusive of religious women, less educated, from rural areas, refugees and other marginalized women.

Haneen Hadi explains the situation in Iraq:

> There are a lot of differences and a lot of different classes. Women from the upper class want to discuss issues that they consider more important like the way they dress, or if they can smoke Shisha in public.[53] In rural areas, a lot of women are being killed or people are wanting greater education and health rights, or fighting to stop women from being married to their

cousins. So class and location make a huge difference and they advocate for the problems they see around them so there is not a lot of crossover. Some [organizations] go more on a broader scope and try to tackle all of these issues together, but it can be confusing.

Hadi describes how "people in the city are more open to change," but their aims drastically differ from people in rural areas. In one example, Hadi says there was a movement around women riding bicycles but she says, "that is easy because it's not something that questions traditions like girls marrying cousins or allowing women to go to universities. They're the biggest issues, and they do not get success."

This observation is important in highlighting different needs for different groups and different areas. At the same time, it exposes a reality: patriarchal structures will only allow certain space for change. The so-called low-hanging fruit. The easy, non-threatening, cosmetic changes. Often at the expense of the strategic, real changes. Take Saudi Arabia for example. Allowing women to drive does little to indicate a sea-change for women's rights, rather it serves as an isolated "gift" from a benevolent patriarchy—not a fundamental right that grants women freedom over their lives and choices.

A young Bahraini activist echoed this sentiment and says:

Bahrain has been progressive when it came to women's rights in comparison to its neighboring countries—growing up there I never felt restricted, we had freedom as long as it was "within reason." It is a patriarchal religious country and I'd say the cultural restrictions are what's not working the most.

The notion that freedoms are granted "within reason" is common across the region. But this is not reasonable to women.

Myriam Sfeir of The Arab Institute for Women puts this in context:

When states want to appease women's movements, they do this by changing laws at a superficial level that don't have major political consequences. Particularly if the law is in line with international conventions that countries have signed, so there's international pressure to comply. Countries removed the "marry your rapist" law because of pressure of the feminist campaigns. However, it was easy to remove—or easier to remove—because it is not as complicated as laws that are related to religion or nationality, because those have wider political implications. Low-hanging fruit legal reform.

When it comes to feminist gains, we noted divisions on several front. Firstly, needs and demands of rural and urban areas differ—and often do not speak to one another. The same argument goes for class divisions. These exist as separate spheres with their own interpretations of "feminisms." Indeed, research and experience remind us that movements need to be "responsive to local women's needs and dynamics of action in their daily lives" with a view to "reconfiguring gender relations in traditional local communities that are barely reached by elitist feminist organisations."[54] At the same time, the nation grants feminist "concessions" in cosmetic areas of women's lives, in an effort to detract from the lack of strategic and meaningful gains. Meaning, the government is divided from the very people it has a duty to protect.

Feminism as a "Western Agenda"

Feminism should be about women to do what they want to do. It's not the Western idea of feminism.

—Salma Khalaf[55]

Feminism in the Arab region has been resisted for many reasons, not the least of which is the accusation that it is "Western." In fact, one method to shut feminism down is to attach the label Western to it. There is nothing inherently Western about feminism. It exists everywhere and is indigenous. It exists as long as patriarchy exists. Nonetheless, the perception that feminism is an evil arm of a "Western agenda" continues to permeate.

On the other hand, there is a Western perception that women from the Arab region are miserable and downtrodden and in need of saving. This also fuels resistance. Neither of these are true: feminism is not Western, and women from the Arab region do not need to be saved. In the words of human rights campaigner Tala Harb, work is needed to "bridge the misconception generated by the West and the voices of the region."[56]

Nada Darwazeh explains that "the concept of feminism is not a concept that is very much accepted and agreed upon." Part of the resistance comes because "people just take the concept of feminism as a Western concept."

Dr. Hatoon Al Fassi of Saudi Arabia, says the term "gender," and by extension, feminism, has negative connotations in Saudi Arabia. She explains there is even an association of the terms with a "plot by the United Nations and its organizations to Westernize Saudi Arab Muslim society to break down its solidarity."[57] She continues:

> The plot and conspiracy theory used to be by the religious, traditional, and soft official state stand but recently the state has made her stand firmer in backing up the UN conventions, especially on the term of "feminism."

There are many attempts to tarnish and discredit the feminist movement in Saudi Arabia, explains another Saudi Arabian activist. Women are intimidated by these smear campaigns, and fear being associated with something perceived to be "shameful" as a result. The image is destroyed, and consequently people are reluctant to call themselves feminists, refusing to understand the true meaning of the term. "They become illiterate in feminism and unity is destroyed," she says.

Alya Mooro brings in another perspective on how harmful this can be, explaining that she initially "shied away" from the term and its "negative connotations." She articulates that she finds it difficult to have these conversations because of the impression from the West that "our women are so oppressed, and we [the West] have to save them." This "othering" builds resistance, and makes it difficult to speak about issues that affect us, without proving these stereotypes right.

She puts it this way:

> These are our problems as a world. And I find it really important to always stress that actually. We live in a patriarchal world, obviously, and these are issues that we can very often feel and see everywhere. It just sometimes might be heightened or played out in different ways in our region.

At Takatoat, Al-Taher says "we have a problem with this word." She adds, "at the end of the day, you look at the action that you can do." Indeed, feminism is—and must be— about action. But the word comes across as Western, she explains, while Takatoat works to counter that. She continues:

> We work in Arabic to produce knowledge in Arabic and produce feminist knowledge
> from Arabic activists. So we have our stories and we rephrase the concepts and causes and

contextualize them based on our region or on our identities. This is what we do to avoid this fear people have of identifying themselves as feminists.

She tells the story of Takatoat this way:

> We co-founded Takatoat because we wanted something inclusive and comprehensive and something for all women. It's hard to be identified as a feminist organization. I believe that we are the first [in Jordan] who identified themselves as a feminist organization.

Another activist explains that organizations—especially grassroots, women-led groups—are often forced to direct their agendas based on donor dictates. She explains that some organizations working on women and girls do not publicly identify as feminist as this might deter donors. Most of these organizations depend on external funding to sustain their work, and as a result, they are compelled to deviate from their mandate in order to receive donor-dictated funding. The activist says that very few organizations have turned down essential funding in order to stay true to their feminist goals. Those who have not only risk operational uncertainty, they risk the future of the organization itself. This is a stance that most grassroots groups cannot afford to take.

Haneen Hadi of Iraq describes the detrimental effect of dismissing feminist issues as Western. Speaking specifically about domestic violence, she says:

> Legislators do not pay attention to this. Domestic violence law has been on the table since 2015 but they didn't vote because they said it was a Westernized law. A lot of the religious parties in the parliament said that the law would make families struggle more and it doesn't work with the culture, habits, and traditions of Iraqis, which is why they refused the law.

Not only has Western labeling prevented potential life-saving legislation, it also entrenches the notion that domestic violence is shameful and *haram* meaning "no one wants to talk about this. People do not consider honor crimes or rape as being connected to domestic violence." As a result, Hadi says, "there are also no official records because most of the cases are changed and not listed as a result of domestic violence." Diverting attention toward Westernization and away from the real issue—violence—hinders feminist advancement in the region. And so the real problems remain unaddressed.

Salma Khalaf, a young Palestinian-Lebanese woman, says that social media has helped expose people to ideas of feminism, and as a result they try to "take this and translate it into their own communities."

"Sometimes I would say I'm feminist," she says, "but I'm very conscious of what the term could hold or mean or how people could interpret that." Khalaf argues that there is a predominant image of "Western feminism" that could be constraining for women in the region. "It depends on what a woman needs and depends on the culture and the social context."

She continues to explain that "there's feminism, but there's also other terms that you could identify as that hold the same concept as feminism, but they may be more inclusive or diverse."

Ultimately, she argues that the perception of feminism as Western detracts from the core message of feminism. A neoliberal emphasis on women as workers, business leaders, and politicians can miss the mark. She explains it like this:

> It's not the Western idea of feminism of "we should be workers." Feminism should be about women to do what they want to do. So just being aware of what women need, what every

individual woman needs, and then helping by providing this woman with the resources, knowledge, whatever tools that she needs to reach these places.

Religion as Vehicle and Obstacle

The biggest issue is the patriarchal system that uses religion as a way to control women.

—Young Bahraini activist

While religion did not emerge as an overwhelmingly prevalent category of concern for those we spoke with, we elected to leave space for it here, given the significant role it plays in the Arab region. We admit to having been surprised by these findings. At the same time, a study conducted by UN Women and Search for Common Ground identified the ideological divide between secular and non-secular organizations as one of the most prominent divides across countries.[58]

Religious elements are often used to undermine or deny the women's rights agenda. In the Arab region, it is firstly worth noting that there are different religions—contrary to popular assumptions. And, at their core, these religions are theoretically equal in their treatment of women. Although many feminists will argue that certain religious interpretations, and their manifestations, in fact perpetuate misogyny.

Additionally, there are those—both women and men—who prefer to understand and examine their lives within their religious frameworks. Their religions outline the gendered rights, roles, responsibilities to which they must adhere, most notably through personal status laws. As explained in Chapter 1, personal status laws are the discriminatory structures that determine many aspects of women's lives.

Randa Siniora of Palestine, explains that there is a strong force in favor of having "family issues" addressed "only within the context of *Shari'a*." Some view this as problematic as it does not allow for women's full rights given the conservative confines of religious interpretations.

Siniora continues to explain that there are multiple discourses that animate the feminist movement in Palestine and in the rest of the Arab region. "There's the secular movement," she begins, "which strongly believes that we have to separate religion from the state, and we have to develop modern secular laws based on human rights standards and conventions." She elaborates that "people generally have the right to their religious beliefs and its manifestations as a basic human right but in the adoption of laws, human rights principles should be our reference point." There are strong passions and politics on both sides of this debate, she explains. "Others are saying there's no place for secular laws, and they always dismiss our calls for these things, saying that we are bringing in Western ideas alien to our society and culture."

Indeed, the accusation that secular means Western is an effective way to undermine any attempt for change. Religion and culture are extremely intertwined, and caught in the crossfire are women's rights—sacrificed as a result.

On the other end of the spectrum, one young woman—also from Palestine—explains that she prefers to see her rights within her religious framework:

I am a Palestinian Christian and Jesus made it clear when the woman was caught in adultery that the first Pharisee who hasn't sinned should throw the first stone at her. Of course none of them did. My faith is important to me and it is abundantly clear that God created the different genders to have equal rights. Even from a non-religious perspective, people from all genders face death. We were not created unequally, thus we should not treat individuals differently based on their gender.

Religion is always a highly polarized topic—particularly in the Arab region. Religious differences, as well as political beliefs, often interfere with the agendas of women's groups. *Are there still ways to bridge these gaps and work together across religious and political lines?* Sometimes. The answer is unclear. Or, rather, it depends.

Research on obstacles to women's rights in the region revealed that there was a consensus within women's civil society that "the ideological divide prevents organizations and individuals from getting to know each other, respect each other, and, most importantly, work together."[59] While the strong difference in opinion on the compatibility of religion and feminism make it immensely difficult to foster collaboration and consensus, outright rejection of Islam or religious frameworks risks alienating many in the region.

To prevent some of these losses, organizations like *Musawah* (Equality) is a global movement for equality and justice in the Muslim family. The organization is doing important work to combat discrimination in laws by working alongside Islamic activists, scholars, NGOs, and policymakers. The organization's knowledge-building work touches on women's rights and equality in Muslim families, offering resources that reframe conversations on equality in the context of Muslim values, legal traditions, and international standards.[60]

Dr. Gabriella Nassif advocates for utilizing more of these organizations in the interest of collaboration:

> We need to start looking transnationally. And there are great examples. Think of *Musawah*, that transnational Islamic feminism group, as an amazing model for thinking about how a transnational feminist movement might work in the region.

While female religious figures are scarce, faith leaders are an important part of communities and wield significant power. Often, many people turn to faith leaders before authorities in times of trouble. This means engaging faith leaders could actually be an untapped area that creates new space for learning and collaboration. In 2013, ABAAD–Resource Centre for Gender Equality, based in Lebanon, engaged religious leaders of all faiths—Christian, Druze, Muslim—across Egypt, Iraq, Jordan, Syria, and Lebanon to find common ground in addressing violence against women. The result was a critical conversation and an innovative campaign—unique in the region—that brought religious leaders together for women's rights.

There is potential through religion to advance feminist goals, it seems. Salma Khalaf, Palestinian-Lebanese youth activist, agrees. She believes that since many women subscribe to an Islamic feminism, this could be a good entry point into more critical conversations. She explains it like this:

> Because now you're bringing to the people something that's rooted in their belief system and something they are used to—it can't be passed off as "Western feminism." We're just taking what we have in Islam and using it in the right way to support the idea that women deserve rights.

She sums up succinctly by saying:

> It's really important when we're talking about gender equality to listen to everyone. We have to be open to hearing these [religious] voices. Because these voices exist. We cannot just eliminate them or just disregard them because we wouldn't be solving this problem.

Khalaf, however, acknowledges some obstacles, mainly regarding LGBTQ+ rights. "There is a huge gap because I feel like secular feminism pushes more for the rights of the LGBTQ+ community, but Islamic feminism not as much," she says.

The bottom line is this: the Arab region places an enormous emphasis on religion, and this permeates politics, which in turn creates inevitable fractures across feminist movements. While we have seen that these fractures are not irreparable, it will take a great deal of dialogue to determine the extent to which feminisms and religions can coexist. This will be a perpetual struggle in the region, we were told, and a perpetual impediment to the feminist movement.

We Can't Fight if We Can't Eat

How can you even move towards putting together a cohesive mobilization
on behalf of feminist demands if you have people that aren't even eating?
—Dr. Gabriella Nassif

In early chapters, we explained that the region faces multiple protracted crises and increased insecurities. Socio-economic conditions cannot be divorced from feminist movements. Similar to national struggles, it is conveniently easy, and seemingly "justifiable," to park feminist interests in the face of a national struggle. If nation trumps feminism, people argue, then so too does poverty.

What is stopping us from advancing? We asked those we spoke to. Here is Dr. Gabriella Nassif's answer:

Based on my vantage point from Lebanon—poverty. People can't afford bread, because it's just too expensive. People aren't going out. We're not interacting, everybody is stuck in their homes, no electricity. How can you even move towards putting together a cohesive mobilization on behalf of feminist demands if you have people that aren't even eating?

Youth activist Yara Ghanem describes how, in Syria, there are "some obstacles that may not exist in other countries." She goes on to explain how her city is one of the safest in the country, and how they were "lucky to only have one explosion in the 11 years of war." Such circumstances are not even a consideration for so many others.

Humanitarian needs in the region are extreme, and getting worse. Protracted crises continue, economies spiral, and the COVID-19 pandemic amplifies gaps that will take generations to close. In such contexts, women's rights deteriorate. They are the first to be stripped and the last to be revived. In the words of Somali global political strategist Hibaaq Osman: "Women's rights are a test for universal rights, yet women's rights are usually the first ones to be challenged and negotiated out. Loss of women's rights would be loss of everyone's rights."[61]

We know from research and experience that women, already vulnerable prior to crisis, experience magnified vulnerabilities and new insecurities. These do not end when the emergency ends. In fact, for women, the crisis continues. So women not only are expected to suspend their feminist demands, but they also experience new risks and abuses as part of the crisis. Women's human rights defenders are at even greater risk. If they speak out, they are further criticized for highlighting women's concerns when "everyone is suffering."

Diana Moukalled describes it like this:

When you raise up the feminist agenda many will claim you are privileged, it's not the time. But it's all a priority. I want electricity and I want my rights all at the same time because they're basic rights—as a woman and as a citizen.

It also becomes increasingly difficult to mobilize for these rights. Feminist activist and academic Dr. Carmen Geha elaborates:

There's a lot of rifts that don't find a way to work themselves out because we're fighting multiple crises, multiple disasters, so it's very hard to mobilize. When you start mobilizing around something like COVID, then there's a financial crisis, and then there's an explosion, and then there's emigration, and then there's a refugee disaster, and then there are people dying at sea. It's this constant rushing that is not allowing a transnational movement to take place.[62]

Arguably, even without a crisis, there is a wide divide across the region between those who have access and opportunity and those who have next to nothing. Additionally, in the Arab region, the middle class is negligible, meaning that the disparity between those who have and those who do not is even wider. How might feminism cross socio-economic divides, as they continue to widen?

Dr. Nassif also argues that "we need to be taking care of those issues as part of a holistic approach to feminism and women's rights." She explains that, undeniably, socio-economic class plays a role. Those in poverty are hardly able to meet basic needs—much less strategic interests. "Take a survivor of violence, for instance," Dr. Nassif explains. She continues:

If she's going to take her case to court, that's really expensive. For starters, she needs to have the legal wherewithal to know that she can prosecute her case. And then she must be able to afford the lawyer, the legal fees. And then there is probably no justice at the end. How many women can navigate that?

Ultimately, it is about having basic needs met. Activism can appear to be a luxury when there is no food. Can we focus on both simultaneously—addressing the pressing problems of poverty while also not losing sight of our feminist demands, "so that we can start having these bigger conversations," Dr. Nassif concludes, "like, how do we overthrow all of this stuff that's in power?"

Where Is the Collaboration?!

Any change in women's status is, however, subject to three conditions: having a clear objective, the desire and the ability to achieve it.
—Dr. Suad Zayed Al-Oraimi[63]

An academic noted that "Arab feminists would do better if they sought the support of, and solidarity with, other women."[64] Many said the same. "We need more collaboration from everyone," Abir Chebaro of Lebanon unequivocally states. *Why are feminists not collaborating*, we ask? "Because they're not supported. They're independent. They are working in small groups." Diana Moukalled explains.

"I'm not suggesting that the movement on women's rights should basically lose their identity for the collective good," Nada Darwazeh adds. She elaborates:

I'm just saying that different movements with the aim of advancing women's rights need to find common grounds because otherwise they are perceived by the community and decision-makers as a group of different voices with no common agenda and agreed upon vision. And I think a collective voice could be a much more heard voice.

She continues to say that if each group has different definitions of gender equality, how will they convince those who do not even see the importance of gender equality? "And I'm not saying that one of us should compromise our views," she explains, "but I think at least we need to agree on some key messages, relating to where we should be heading and how to move forward and avoid competition."

In Sudan, Akasha says it is "issue-based, ad-hoc collaboration." But, she continues, "if it happens more frequently it will be very beneficial." She uses an example of regional collaboration to illustrate the point:

> There was the African Feminist Forum, in which feminists on the African continent gather in one place every three years discuss their issues, come up with strategies and action plans and take it back home, to follow up with other feminist movements across the region.

While such instances of unification are encouraging, they do not represent the reality. Being a feminist is challenging enough—and an Arab feminist perhaps harder still. We are already too few, but coordination would make us far stronger.

Still, the disconnects are many: *Is organizing intentional or organic? Are there structured campaigns or spontaneous actions? Is work at the level of grassroots or government? Should they be confrontational or subtle? Conventional or alternative?* And on it goes.

Darwazeh also laments the "competition" inside the women's movement. "Even with all these fissures, we still "waste so much time in not working together," one activist states. "It's our fault, but it's donors' fault too." Here she refers to donor-driven competition for resources, adding that "the pots of money are so small, and we're all scrambling to get the money to do the projects because, how else will our organization stay alive?"

Moreover, donor-driven agendas fail to represent or respond to local needs. Somali-American activist Degan Ali reminds us that local women must always determine the direction of aid, and that "we should never have an outsider, whether a donor or international humanitarian actor, drive the design of aid programmes."[65] Feminist groups must have agency in determining their own agendas.

Another rift exists between feminists who are organized versus those who are organic. There is a nascent informal network that remains largely invisible because it is not organized—or documented—in conventional ways. The real work is happening—even if we are unable to see it or define it.

Anthony Keedi of ABAAD in Lebanon puts it this way:

> I think feminists have been building more formal and informal networks and basing movements and narrative for movement-building in those spaces. It's the invisible work by the feminist movement that doesn't get acknowledged.

Feminist activist and academic Dr. Carmen Geha offers this:

> I also think that we as a movement are not organized, and we are not doing justice by each other. We are allowing a lot of these political rifts—left or right, pro- or anti-government, and so on—come between us. And it has become impossible to get organized around gender issues.

She continues to say, "It feels as if the movement is not mature. And it's not mature because of structural issues, because of the state."

Collaboration is critical for movement-building. Feminist voices repeat it, and studies reinforce it. One study on Arab states found that collaboration can be useful in strengthening efforts and momentum, avoiding duplication of campaigns, offering key learnings, enabling activists to advance their agendas, and enhancing impact.[66] The study—aptly named "Across Divides to Advance Women's Rights Through Dialogue"—reminds us that feminist collaboration is critical, and challenging:

> It involves the risk of failure from the start. It is threatened when contentious topics are addressed, strong positions are taken on the basis of principles, and accusations are levelled on either side. While it may take some time to mature and become effective on the ground, its importance is recognized as crucial in reducing misunderstandings, stereotypes, and stigmatization of opposite sides.[67]

The study states that lack of coordination results in missed opportunities in working and building relations with others in order to foster "a better and more localised meaning of feminist leadership and empowerment."[68] What is needed, therefore, is for movements to reach across ideological differences and party lines, across other political and activist groups. There is an undeniable need "to exhibit more evidence of coordination, unity, organization, and solidarity within, and across, gender equity movements" if we hope for meaningful and sustainable results.[69]

Research and experience on women's movements in the Arab region reveal that "we have not yet figured out how to coordinate efforts between women, countries, scholars, and disciplines, nor have we carefully thought out the process toward or the broader implications and requirements of social transformation."[70]

We Need Our Own Arab Feminism

> *I wish we had a defined Arab Feminism because I feel like our struggles as Arab women are erased and never defended by other feminists.*
> —Young Feminist from Morocco

With all its diversities, it might appear to be impossible to have one understanding of feminism in the Arab region, or even within individual countries in the region. At the same time, it might be possible to have some aspects of a shared agenda. Our fight is the same, for instance. We all (hopefully) agree that women deserve equality. We all (hopefully) agree that women have been denied equality. We all (hopefully) agree that patriarchy is the greatest impediment to our equality. We might not all agree on how to address it, however.

Bochra Bel Haj Hmida from Tunisia explains that "feminist movements in the Arab world generally share the same visions and objectives. What differs sometimes are the strategies put in place, which of course take into consideration the local specificities and the environment."[71]

Dr. Noura Al Obeidli from the UAE puts it as follows:

> I call it woman bargaining—we're bargaining with the state, we're bargaining with the patriarchy, with ourselves, as well as women. We [Arab women] have to push for that collective mindset of feminism because we have a lot of issues to discuss and try to solve. But then again, we have a lot of psychological embedding of perspectives about traditions, religion, the varying ideologies, and with the way we were raised—it's really complicated.

Despite our differences, there might be greater opportunities for regional collaboration, exchange, and understanding. Arguably, we are not capitalizing on these as much as we should be.

Rym Badran from Lebanon tells the story of her engagement with Girl Up, a global movement focusing on girls' leadership. She was selected as one of a small group of "teen advisors" who guide the strategy of the organization. Badran was "one of the first advisors from the region and living in the region."

She continues:

> I was hearing a lot that "oh the Middle East is a very difficult region. We don't know how to approach it." I was just 17 and I felt like I had the responsibility of bringing the movement to the region. I started with founding Girl Up Lebanon in 2019. And then girls from other Arab countries were reaching out. And they were asking about the process. How can we start a club and how can we do advocacy? So from that kind of spirit, we decided to found the Arab region coalition. And now we have about nine countries represented.

Yosra Akasha of Sudan explains that when there is collaboration across the region, it brings a sense of solidarity, a connection to feminist movements in other Arab countries, and a sense that yes, maybe a regional movement is possible:

> I feel there is some source of support that comes through regional groups. For instance, I really appreciate the Revolutionary Socialists in Egypt. They reached out last year, and they connected us with the Moroccan movement. We exchanged views and contexts, and we even did a symposium together on Facebook. There are some elements of coordination. And for us, we learned so much from the experiences of the women's movement across the region.

Randa Siniora from Palestine explains that "we don't have a unified discourse in the Arab region." From her perspective, the differences are vast. Her call for "secularism and democracy and separation of powers" is not heeded by all. She continues:

> I don't think that without an environment of democracy and pluralism you can really speak about the possibility of achieving much in feminism or in women's rights. But at the same time, I think that we are not agreeing on one discourse, and I don't think there should be one discourse.

Siniora recognizes that "there are different opinions about how we should address it." And she adds, "We never have agreed, actually, and I don't think we will ever agree. There will be differences. I should accept and live with these differences in our region."

Ultimately, Nada Darwazeh puts it this way: "I don't think there is a unified movement throughout the region or in countries. I think there are multi-layered challenges that hinders the adoption of a unified agenda that is agreed upon by all actors to advance women's rights."

We do not need to advocate for one sole discourse, but at the same time, diversity should not obstruct equality. Surely we can find common ground on that front. And perhaps we will find strength on that front, assuming there is a foundation of understanding on which to build solidarity.

Some young feminists felt that issues in the Arab region were unique enough in their challenges that they needed this greater solidarity.

In the words of one woman from Lebanon:

> I am a feminist because women don't have rights anywhere in the world, but especially in the Arab world. Women's life standards are terrible, expectations of us are terrible, laws don't protect us, men don't respect us, we are murdered and raped and held in hostage marriages and relationships and it is all normalized. Our worth is tied to our body and our reproductive abilities.

Another reinforces this, adding that women in the region are victims of violence and inequality, and her role as a feminist is "trying to bring them, and all oppressed groups, on equal grounds with all other individuals."

Another young Palestinian feminist echoes this, adding that we need to strengthen feminism in the region because women "are treated less than men and are not able to decide their own destiny."

And finally, in the words of one Syrian living in Kuwait, she argues that feminism is a requirement rather than an option in the region. In fact, she says, "you have to when living in the Middle East, to survive."

Divided by the Diaspora

Even if you are born or raised in a certain Arab country and moved abroad, especially to the West, the wealthy West, the wealthy, white West—recognize that your voice is no longer as powerful or accurate as those on the inside.

—Tala Harb[72]

Living in the diaspora presents its own set of unique challenges. On the one hand, distance is created to gain perspective. "I grew up in Canada," one young activist explains, "and I love being Canadian because here, I am more free. When I go to Lebanon, I wonder how women do it? Their freedoms? It's like going back in time."

Another explains the tensions this way:

Every summer we go "back home," and it's like I go through cultural rewiring. For ten months of the year, I am allowed one set of freedoms, but then for two months I have to be Arab again.

A young Arab woman living outside the region had this to add:

I will always have a love-hate relationship with the Arab region. As a woman, I am free here, where I am. I'll never go back. But I feel guilty. Should I do more? What am I supposed to do? Sometimes I just wish that all the women—especially the young women—would leave the region, start their lives elsewhere, and find freedom.

While that particular woman sees leaving the region as an opportunity for greater freedom, for most this is not an option. Moreover, leaving is no guarantee of freedom.

The complex feelings associated with leaving and returning to the Arab region from abroad represent the challenges of existing in two spaces. The contradictory notion of not being enough or being too much for either place is a constant struggle. Being both too Western in the Arab region and not Arab enough—and vice versa—means occupying the liminal space of insider-outside. Juggling these hybrid identities and straddling two worlds is a struggle that resonated with many—whether in the diaspora or of mixed heritage.

A young Kuwaiti woman feels the double bind deeply and says even though she studies abroad, her family still thinks she should abide by norms of women in Kuwait. "I live two separate lives," she says, "and I don't know how to reconcile them."

Many women from the Arab region pursue education or career opportunities abroad, but, when they return home are met with criticism. Dr. Noura Al Obeidli from the UAE experienced other women accusing her of coming back "Westernized." Al Obeidli, however, says she came back with "a growth mindset" and is determined to utilize that. She goes on to say:

I lived in a broken home, I understand what domestic violence means, I understand what manipulation and abuse means. I've seen friends who have gone through sexual abuse. I've known lots of women going through a lot of abuse, and they're silent about it. And we need to do something about that. It's not about fighting men, I'm not fighting my religion as Muslim.

Doing something about it, however, can prove difficult. A young Iraqi feminist in exile put it like this:

I look on wondering what I'm supposed to do. I hardly ever lived there. I could do more, I should do more. But I don't know how to be useful.

The feeling of powerlessness came up in conversation with some Arab-American women when we asked if the diaspora is doing enough to help advance women's rights in the Arab region. One woman says, "It's tough. We're sort of paralyzed but also obligated." She continued, "But we sort of paralyze ourselves too—if we don't see it then we don't have to deal with it."

Another added, "emotionally we don't even feel connected, but we feel bad. We need to switch our thinking but not a lot of people care to do that."

This sentiment was built upon by one woman who says, "We sit and watch shit happen. So, how do we feel? A bit schizophrenic, surely."

It certainly is a complicated landscape to navigate. The diaspora is challenged by being both disconnected and obligated. The challenge now is how to translate this into concrete action.

A Generational Disconnect

We're really grateful that you're doing something, but you don't have our experience.

—Rym Badran

As we touched upon earlier, youth in the Arab region are increasingly taking action on issues they care about, often on the frontlines of movements, revolutions, and subsequent reconstructions. This passion, however, is sometimes disconnected from older generations, causing ideological rifts between generations. Overall, youth are driven by anger, while the older generation often fight patriarchy politely.

Yosra Akasha of Sudan explains that she is saddened to see "the old generation not willing to support the younger generation that much. And sometimes criticize them," she adds. She says there is a "shaming of personal behavior and appearance" coupled with a denial of feminism, "as if feminist is a bad word," she says. "It's something that still continues unfortunately, sometimes within the women's rights movement itself."

Akasha tells the story of the need for intergenerational feminist activism:

For some time towards the end of 2017 I had to leave the country for security reasons. I didn't come back until the revolution happened. And I lost connection with the movement. But when I returned, I was so impressed that there are so many women's activists who identify as feminists, and most of them are their early 20s. But I felt ashamed because I see that they are struggling with the older generation. Because I'm not part of any organization and I had been away for a while, and I was not able to provide them with any kind of support, the support that I wish I could have had back in the day.

Are we doing enough to cross generational divides? No.

Rym Badran, a young Lebanese feminist, recounts her experience participating in a region-wide dialogue:

> I really found it hard to communicate with them. They're all older and are the ones who founded their very own feminist movement in the region. So we're talking about feminists age 70. And then, for example, when I would be talking with them, they weren't even making eye contact. And they won't give recognition because you're super young and their idea is like, okay, we're really grateful that you're doing something, but you don't have our experience.

There is an acknowledgment that yes, the previous generations of feminists were bound by the socio-cultural mores of their time. Despite these restrictions, they managed to make gains for the movement, particularly given the limited space they had. At the same time, they were not without shortcomings.

Diana Moukalled describes past feminist movements in Lebanon:

> It was very classical. There were always women's movements which were progressive at that time, so I cannot deny what they have accomplished. But they were not feminists and you will find contradictions. For example, women activists looking to stop violence against women and to improve laws, but they were still under the umbrella of religion, norms, and traditions. Again, I don't want to criticize because within the context that they were working on 30–50 years ago, at that time, they were progressive.

Haneen Hadi had something similar to say in Iraq:

> How can I say this without insulting a whole generation? They are still taking an old approach and not taking direct action against the authorities. It hasn't been working and that is my problem with this old approach. To even say that they are feminists, they don't advocate for the cause of feminism but more advocate for women's rights in an old fashioned way which I think prevented real cooperation.

We should do better to have cross-generational discussions; mentoring and support; learning that goes both ways; and better engagement with young activists, especially those who are not organized in the so-called old-fashioned ways. A Saudi Arabian activist says there is a generational disconnect whereby "the youth are growing up with certain freedoms their parents did not have, and the progressiveness is a shock to their value systems," she says.

If the new generation of feminism is not being supported by their predecessors, they could end up reproducing this exclusivity, alienating the next generation. The point here is that the younger generation is more progressive—a good thing—but this liberal stance also becomes exclusive, narrowing the parameters of who is—or is *not*—a feminist. In a region that is overwhelmingly Muslim, and in a socio-political context where veiling and Western values are highly charged, alienating a large segment of the population would be a loss for feminism.

Even though youth are a major presence and a major power, one academic notes:

> It remains to be seen whether the new generation of youth and women activists will manage to continue their organising and mobilising efforts and build a genuine, organic women's movement which better responds to women's lived realities and their socio-economic problems and needs.[73]

In conversations with many feminists and activists, we learned that they felt older feminists were not engaged with their younger counterparts. There was no mentoring, no intergenerational collaboration, no proverbial "passing of the torch." In fact, many young feminists saw the opposite—an older generation that clung to their power and refused to share. Additionally, these older feminists were viewed as elitist, often the wives of politicians or men in power for whom "doing feminism" was a charitable endeavor to be discussed at a ladies' luncheon.

Director of The Arab Institute for Women, Myriam Sfeir, laments that "young people feel cornered. They're hopeless and they're leaving the Arab region and emigrating, or they're staying and accepting the status quo."

In the words of one young Syrian activist: "The older generation of feminists, they were top-down. This younger generation of feminists—my generation—we are inclusive. We are about every woman."

So What? Now What?!

> Crisis opens opportunities and we have seen women's rights organizations and girl-centered groups rise to the occasion: meeting child protection challenges that increased child marriage risks, as well as nutrition declines, impeded access to education, health and sanitation. Local organizing found solutions—despite consistent under-resourcing including in Lebanon, Sudan, Syria and Yemen. Women's organizations create opportunities and possibilities and they should be fully engaged.
>
> —Maha Muna[74]

This chapter is fueled by the voices of feminists and activists. It begins with findings from our survey of young people in the region, and continues with their voices and views in order to better understand where our disconnects are.

In Chapter 1, we provided context on the region and on the status of women's rights. There, we imagined what the disconnects might be—and explained our rationale for thinking so. Here, we see where the disconnects actually are.

Surely, the fissures in feminisms are plenty. *Are we inclusive? Are we a "sisterhood"? Are we elite? Are we present—or powerful? Are we divided? Are we "Western"? Are we addressing poverty? Are we engaging the diaspora? Are we working across generations? Are we collaborating?*

The one question we return to time and again is this: *Are we feminists!?* The largest fissure we noted is the question we have asked throughout: *What is feminism? What is a feminist?* And, following from these: *How does one actually* do *feminism?* These questions came up often enough in conversation that they required further reflection.

To better grasp the various levels of understanding of and engagement with feminism, we created several broad categories. We recognize that, in situating this as a "feminist" book, we might be inadvertently excluding those who do not identify as feminist.

We dislike labels and in no way wish to restrict, brand, or confine activity. Rather we present these as a starting point for analysis, to help us better understand how feminisms manifest in the region (and perhaps globally) and how, in pushing toward equality, we might advance to more robust understandings of the word. And ultimately, how we might *do feminism* better.

We should all be feminists, after all.[75]

As we hear the voices and understand the experiences of those on the feminist frontlines, we begin to see some broad categories emerge. On one end of the spectrum is what we will call the Activist-Feminist—the individual who not only *gets it*, but also *does it*. This is the young woman on the streets, the iconic image of 22-year-old Alaa Salah of Sudan, as she stands on top of a car, rising above the crowd. She defiantly holds her arm in the air, finger pointing to the sky.

The Acceptance-Feminist understands the principles, espouses the values, but does not take to the streets—whether literal or figurative. This role is a reminder that we do not need to be formal activists to be active in our daily lives. Change is made and progress is won in the small spaces, as we have said.

In the words Haneen Hadi of Iraq:

> I did not consider myself a feminist because I thought you had to be more active with calling it out.… I was a feminist in the short quarters of my life—arguing with my family and male friends about women's rights. Now I consider myself an activist. But that is also a misconception, because you don't need to be an activist to be a feminist.

Moving further along the spectrum are the Elitist-Feminists. We dedicated a section to this caricature, the political or celebrity feminist who perhaps panders to the patriarchy, or conforms to the "women's activism" trend, at risk of being "easily coopted and instrumentalised by the larger political actors and state elites."[76]

The Untapped-Feminists are those who might accept the principles, but who have yet to understand or embrace the label. We presume this category to be significant—with vast, untapped potential.

Again, Haneen Hadi explains it best:

> Whenever I say I am a feminist I get laughs and then weird looks but I think a lot of the time, these people around me are feminists in their actions. They are living the life of an actual feminist but they don't acknowledge that because they don't understand what the term feminism is actually about. It's sad because if we get those people to support the idea of feminism, we would have a lot of good people supporting us.

Finally, on the opposite end of the spectrum are the Anti-Feminists, the staunch opposition, those for whom feminism will always be a battle, and a resistance.

Ultimately, we close this section with the words of Dr. Rita Stephan, Visiting Researcher at North Carolina State University, who offers her view of the fragments and fissures, and a call to action for what must lie ahead:

> Arab feminism is a series of disconnected experiences that run parallel to each other. We are both similar and diverse and these two features must be captured in our narrative. We are similar in the fight against patriarchal structures, laws, and decision-makers. We are similar in being systematically excluded and constantly being put on the defensive front to pass the test of authenticity and popularity. We are diverse because of our ethnic, religious, ideological, geographic, class, and transnational experiences. Feminist conversations are happening in silos and closed places. My experience with Arab feminists is that they are committed to the perfect, and ideals that make the perfect the enemy of the good. They view their inability to build and sustain coalitions within and across ideological lines as prohibiting them from forming a successful movement. However, the movement is happening despite their reservation. Finally, cross-generational dialogue is very much needed. Today, in the age of technology, globalization, and broken boundaries, Arab feminists face the challenge of

embracing diversity within their ranks. The young must embrace the pioneers as their heritage, and the reform feminists must embrace the young revolutionaries as the future of Arab feminism.[77]

In looking at what divides us, this chapter actually seeks to bring us closer to what unites us. Ultimately, highlighting these fissures in feminisms help us better prepare for a feminist future.

6

Feminist Futures

Yes there are changes, but yes, we want more.
—Yara Ghanem

This story has spanned fifty years, looking back to understand what the foundations of Arab feminisms might have been, covering five phases of our feminist trajectory, understanding feminisms on the frontlines of war and insecurity, and highlighting the fissures in our feminist movements. Here we begin to explore what the future holds. Here we center youth in galvanizing Arab feminisms going forward. Here we bring their voices and hopes—and their challenges and concerns.

While Chapter 5 was a deep dive into the challenges from the perspectives of those on its frontlines, Chapter 6 zooms out, looking to the horizon to explore what our future might look like, and if it might be feminist. *What are the most important issues? How are we to address them? How might we achieve equality? And, is it even possible? Ultimately, what do we hope for the future? Do we dare hope for a feminist future?*

We asked young people to tell us what needed to change, and whether or not things were actually changing. Ultimately, we seek to expedite that change.

In the words of Yara Ghanem, one young Syrian woman, "Yes, there are changes, but yes, we want more." The changes happening are not strong, solid, or sustainable enough. And it is ok to demand more. In fact, it is necessary to do so!

"There are a lot of people who don't even believe that we need something," Ghanem explains. "What's going on with you?" people ask her. "What's the problem with your life? You have everything you want. You're not having any problems."

She explains that people do not realize the extent of the challenges. And the need to ensure that any gains made are sustained. "They think that these mere and basic human rights are something huge for us and we should be thankful for letting us have it," Ghanem continues. In other words, why arc wc not satisfied yet? She explains that she is not fighting for herself as an individual, but rather for *all* women and girls and the rights they should have:

> The thing is that it's not about what I'm suffering from just because I am lucky not to suffer from this and this and this. I realized the importance of it and I realize how important it is that all girls in our community don't suffer from the same thing.

It is bold and powerful to recognize that we deserve more, to ask for more, and to demand more. Undoubtedly, there is a great deal of work to do, and incredible challenges to surmount. At the same time, there are elements of cautious optimism. In Chapter 1, we talked about the region's social indicators and the forces fighting against feminism. Despite these hurdles, there is good news, there are gains, and there are signs of hope. Myriam Sfeir of The Arab Institute for Women elaborates:

> It is true that we are lagging behind but this is widespread across the globe and not restricted to any region. I have to admit that the feminist movement has achieved a lot. Understanding of intersectionality, adoption of the quota, amendment of nationality law—even work within the religious system, that is something! And to amend laws is something positive but amendments require applicability and so the importance of putting pressure on countries to implement what is there on paper—removal of clauses that are very discriminatory, like the marry your rapist law, and issues related to marital rape are now being discussed.[1] Improvements have been made, especially considering that the women's movement had to negotiate these with ruling elites or government. Extracting these gains is something!

More than this, there is strength and conviction and commitment to not stop fighting. Young people are clearer in their rights and more determined to achieve them. In short, they know what they deserve and will stop at nothing to get it. Feminist movements in the region are the "good news" stories that need to be told, as we have seen through these pages and many others. Women in the region continue to create and lead these movements. They have agency, and they fight tirelessly and relentlessly for their rights. Civil society organizations and women's movements have been a leading force in shaping advancements in women's rights—and human rights—across Arab states.

Stories from the region show that there have been changes, and that change is possible. We have covered changes in legislation, reform of discriminatory laws, and the creation of new laws in favor of women's rights and equality. We have also seen changes in culture, recognizing that laws and culture do not evolve at the same pace and often do not even speak to each other.

Changes in culture start with us, and with our families, in the small spaces we occupy. Overwhelmingly, the younger generation views the fight as one against oppression, and one in which men are involved—on the same side. Working alongside men reminds us that this is not a war of the sexes but rather a war against patriarchy and oppression. Bringing in the men and working within the family is a critical prerequisite for a contagious movement, making transformation more likely and more sustainable.[2]

We have addressed the interconnections between social justice issues—because they cannot be addressed in silos. Advances for feminism are advances for all human rights. Young people are embracing the full range of social justice causes in their work. For example, one report tells us how Arab feminists are smashing the patriarchy:

> Their discourses are maturing into an anti-racist, anti-authoritarian, anti-homophobic, anti-transphobic, anti-colonial, and anti-neoliberal force that links feminism with all other social justice movements. The intersectional Arab feminism that is currently evolving goes beyond understanding how systems of oppression interact to shape the realities of women of different backgrounds. It recognizes how all systems of oppression are sustaining the patriarchy, and therefore, how all systems of oppression need to be eliminated to achieve true justice.[3]

In order to achieve true justice, there is work to be done in communities as well. And here too, sustained advocacy can lead to positive change. While there are conservative and fundamentalist forces holding us back, we must work with the understanding that anti-fundamentalism is not anti-religion.[4] Islamophobia, particularly in the West, creates an image of women in the region as passive victims, as we have documented in Chapter 5. Women—and men—who fight against patriarchy and for feminism are refuting these images, highlighting their power and agency, rather than feeding into cliches and stereotypes.[5]

Expressions of Arab feminisms are omnipresent, even if they are not always obviously so. Feminists in the region must creatively and sometimes covertly operate. So, it is there even if we do not see it, as we have demonstrated in previous chapters.

Arab feminisms also offer ample evidence of strong collective action and advocacy strategies, as highlighted throughout the book. But most importantly, *young* women are leading movements around the region, pushing for change in new, non-traditional ways. They are committed to freedom and justice, and through them we can imagine a regional feminist movement on the rise, leading to a revolutionary new chapter that fearlessly demands an equitable and dignified future for all.[6]

The younger generation are not simply leaders of tomorrow. They are leaders today, in their own right. And when women—especially young women—have real opportunity, it makes a real difference. Liberation brings out the best in everyone.[7]

The inspiration for this chapter lies in their stories.

The Future Is…. Listening to Young People

> *This is what they tell us: "Where have you been in 1987 when I was doing this and that?" Well I wasn't here … but now I'm here and I have something to say.*
>
> —Engy Ghozlan[8]

New generations of young activists are taking a less compromising stance and challenging the status quo by pushing for equal rights in non-formal ways. They are adamant that state gender frameworks be adapted to respond to their needs—a real reflection of the voices on the ground. They view these frameworks as the lowest common denominator, a starting point upon which real change must be built. It is clear that young feminists are at the center of transformational change. But, we need to support them with the knowledge, skills, and resources to make that change. We also, crucially, need to listen to them.

In the words of Dr. Gabriella Nassif:

> Where to now? Listen to younger folks. They're out all the time, even when we can't see them. They're on the streets. They don't buy into this bullshit rhetoric that the generation before us in this region thought about women in the house and men in the public sphere, there's none of that now.

There is a need for more research on youth activism in the region. To be sure, it is growing, especially after the Arab Spring, given the huge role of youth and marginalized communities on the frontlines. A number of organizations have conducted studies to understand the state of youth organizing in the Arab region and around the world. These studies show that Arab youth are creating innovative solutions, despite being dramatically under-resourced.[9] At the same time, the climate is not always open to their demands for change. Young activists face stigma, discriminations, and often serious threats to their safety—impediments to successful movements.

We need to better understand their obstacles in order to help overcome these impediments—using their own solutions to do so. This starts with including youth in organizing and decision-making from the onset. We must remove structural barriers to access, and foster enabling environments for their activism. This also necessitates educating youth about human rights from the earliest possible opportunity.[10]

We have argued here for the need to more strongly champion these activists, amplify their causes, and help support their future successes. Listening to them is a good start.

Here, we aim to spotlight their voices.

When we set out to listen to their voices, we did so in multiple ways—surveys, focus group discussions, informal exchanges, interviews—so we could reach them where they are, and reach them through multiple channels. In Chapter 5, we highlighted our region-wide survey of young people, with 113 responses from across the region. We used the findings of the survey as a starting point to outline the issues that are presented here in Chapter 6.

To start, the survey found that 85 percent of study participants did *not* believe there was gender equality in their country, meaning there is an extraordinary amount of work to do at the level of communities, countries, and the region. This finding is unsurprising.

Young people who responded were then asked to list the most important social issues in their country. The options were: "Climate Change"; "Education"; "Healthcare"; "Good Governance"; "LGBTQ+ Rights"; "Peace and Security"; "Poverty Reduction and Economic Opportunity"; and "Women's Rights and Gender Equality." We recognize that all of these issues are interlinked, and that progress—or regress—in one area impacts all others. The most important social issue at the country level, according to 71 percent of study participants, was "Poverty Reduction and Economic Opportunity" with "Women's Rights and Gender Equality" ranking second. "Good Governance" and "Peace and Security" were tied in third place.

This finding is consistent with other studies showing that economic issues are of high priority for youth in the Arab region. One study found that "developing the economy and reducing unemployment" was the second highest priority for Arab youth after "guaranteeing civil and political rights."[11] Focusing on reform and economic opportunity speaks well to the impetus behind Arab feminist organizing and the Arab Spring protests. The so-called Arab Spring saw millions protest against economic inequalities—with protesters sharing slogans such as "economic justice is a feminist issue."[12] A focus on economic reform and poverty reduction speaks to what movements require to be sustainable. Activism is built from instability, but also benefits from a stable foundation—because people cannot march on empty stomachs.

Economic reform rises to the top to reflect people's most pressing insecurities, while gender justice, as we have seen many times before, is relegated to the back seat. This instinct is at once deeply human and deeply troubling. Individual and immediate needs often cloud our vision of root causes of injustice and obstruct our focus from the more existential issues.

We then zoomed out to ask about the region. *What is the most important social issue at the regional level*, we wanted to know. The options were the same as for the country level, mentioned above. As we might expect, however, regional answers differ from the country level as individuals are more likely to respond in line with their daily needs. Here, 74 percent of study participants selected "Women's Rights and Gender Equality" as the most important issue. "Peace and Security" and "Poverty Reduction and Economic Opportunity" followed second and third respectively. "Good Governance" was fourth, followed by "Healthcare," "Climate Change," and "LGBTQ+ Rights."

Focus then turned to solutions. We asked what the best way might be to achieve gender equality at the country level, and 69 percent of study participants marked "Change Social/Cultural/Religious Traditions that Discriminate Against Women" as their top choice. The other options—"Provide Greater Economic Opportunities for Women"; "End Discrimination in the Law"; "End Violence Against Women"; "Increase Women's Political Participation"; and "Ensure Full Sexual and Reproductive Health and Rights"—were all close behind.

We then asked again what the best way was to achieve gender equality in the region. Here too, the answer was the same as the country level responses for 70 percent of young people: "Change Social/Cultural/Religious Traditions that Discriminate Against Women." Clearly there are common barriers to overcome at the country and regional levels—we need to change the social, cultural, religious traditions that discriminate against women.

In short, all of these solutions are interconnected. Prioritizing one over the other is not an easy choice, given that improvements in all of these areas are desperately needed, and have spillover effects into other aspects of our lives. Feminist inquiry is built on listening and acting on those responses. We heard time and again that the agenda should be set by those most impacted—young people—and not by those with influence, power, or resources.

Are we listening, we asked?

A young Lebanese woman, Rym Badran, answers. "It's getting way better. A lot of international organizations give opportunities to youth … and do work on including young people." She continues: "There's this movement to include more girl-led initiatives. This is at first being forced on regional organizations, like if they want to get funding." At first there is some resistance, or maybe a lack of interest, but young people are persevering in these settings. Badran continues to explain that "once they get to know you, then they will listen to you, but at first it will be hard." It is possible to access opportunities through these organizations, but, Badran repeats, "at first I would say it's really difficult."

Yara Ghanem of Syria echoes this sentiment:

> We are trying so hard to be heard. And if you compare the efforts that we are doing, with how much attention we are getting, it's not that fair. But if we continue to create this effort and to make this effort, I think this attention will increase day by day, and I think it's worth it so I don't mind working so hard to be heard. And then even if one, then two, then two becomes four, and four becomes eight. Count on it to make a change, even if it's small.

Is there collaboration? Are the older generation opening the door to these dynamic young voices? "I really hope for more collaboration," Badran explains. The older generation of feminists are "closed to new perspectives," although, she says:

> The situation in Lebanon is better than the one in other Arab countries, where young feminists are able to contribute to some extent and established organizations will be open to the idea of collaborating with the new generation once they identify young people they can rely on.

Still, she continues, "I really hope for more collaboration and also getting more recognition, especially as youth activists. In our region we often go unnoticed." In some countries in the region, young people are very engaged, Badran explains, "because we know that our present and our future is at stake. To some extent we don't really have the choice or privilege to stay on the sidelines and not get involved."

Another activist put it this way:

> As the ancestors did, the new generation is also trying to defend a feminism that stems from their personal ideological and intellectual background. The new generation has its ways and methods to participate in political life which can mainly be described as non-traditional.

In a podcast conversation about youth activism in Libya, peace activist Hajer Sharief explains that "we all need to do our bit."[13] She adds that young women from the region need the "opportunity to write our own narrative, speak openly and freely, not censored, and not having someone else telling our story on our behalf."

Badran concludes with this:

> I really hope women have more collaboration and use the "competition" that might exist between the different organizations not to eliminate each other, but rather to complete each other, learn from each other, and advance the movement as a whole.

Yes, every country has its struggles, but the Arab region has greater challenges, she explains, and therefore greater need to work together, especially across generations. She remains "open to all the new things happening" and motivated to prove wrong the belief that "the region is very resistant to change."

In the documentary *Feminism Inshallah: A History of Arab Feminism*, a young activist on the street in Tunisia says this: "And I say to the previous generation of feminists, don't close the door. Leave dialogue open between the generations. We mustn't get weaker and become divided!"[14]

The Future Is…. Reigniting Feminism

> *What are your hopes for the future of Arab feminism?*
> *I hope we are still not fighting the same battles in fifty years.*
> —Young feminist activist

Many of those we surveyed and spoke with addressed the need to better understand the definition of feminism, not as a Western import and imposition, but rather as an indigenous, grassroots movement born from the inequalities that exist in every country, in every context. Yes, the form can be adapted for context, but the need for feminism in the Arab region was undeniable.

Many people in this book—women and men—were hesitant to identify as feminists, preferring terms such as activist, gender equalist, or even humanist. We highlighted these disconnects in Chapter 5.

Author Alya Mooro puts it simply, hoping that eventually we may all exist as ourselves and "…not feel beholden to stereotypes of what they should do and how they should be, and what a life should look like." Her call is compelling in its simplicity:

> Basically, I feel like what we really need is to broaden so that everyone can live freely and safely and happily as themselves. We really need to broaden all of our ideas of what it means to be a human in the world and not feel that we need to ascribe to what are very often outdated ideas.

Many recognize that there was also a battle to be won with women themselves. *Do they understand the definition of feminism?* There was still resistance to the term across the region, even if the concepts were supported. Some activists did not see this nuance, arguing that women are either active as feminists or they are in the opposition, as we elaborated in Chapter 5. The latter, they argued, were likely not aware of what the concept meant and how it might apply to their lives.

In an effort to demystify—and reclaim—the word feminist, The Arab Institute for Women (AiW) at the Lebanese American University forged a collaboration with House of Paisley, a small fashion label owned by two women, Noha Dimitri and Rima Mardini. Together they created a t-shirt with the word "feminist"—the English word written in Arabic script. The intent was to create conversation around this contentious word. Both the t-shirt and the campaign were touted as a success and were worn by women throughout the region and in the diaspora.

At the same time, pushback remains a concern. Many feminists and activists had hope for their movements in the future, but also expressed concern about a strong opposition. A young Syrian woman says she wishes that Arab feminism would achieve "a high level of awareness" and that women in the region would become feminists and would claim their rights. "But," she fears, "political and religious systems push feminist development backwards and spread the culture of misogyny." One young Libyan feminist says she hopes "that Arab feminism will succeed in playing its role, as it has a great responsibility, but there is no promising sign in the near future."

Activists asked how we might better understand, apply, and expand feminism, while also fighting off resistance. *How could they counter the opposition?*

In a conversation with young Arab activists, they explain that they are well aware of the opposition's arguments against a feminist agenda. Any calls for equality would be rebutted by centering culture, religion, society, values, tradition, and more. "What can we say?" they ask, "We want a 'cheat sheet' to be able to respond to the arguments we know we'll hear. The arguments we already hear, all the time."

"We know we are right," they explain, "but we want to shut down the opposition with facts. We want to be firm, clear, and context-relevant. We want an argument that will penetrate patriarchal ears."

Clearly there are strong counter-forces in the region that risk derailing any progress made. Another young Syrian woman adds that communities should not misunderstand feminism, and should stop seeing it as a threat. "The feminist movement is getting stronger," she concludes, "and the coming generations will carry on with it."

Another woman from the UAE adds that, in the future, she expects that feminism "stands tall, thrives, and dominates." Many said they hope for equality and for freedom—and for feminism to cease to be necessary. Meaning, equality would be a given. Women's rights are not just a "trending term," one young woman from the Kurdistan region of Iraq argues, "but an actual value held by community members." One young Lebanese woman says that feminism should be "a matter of *fact*, and not a matter of *fight*."

An activist from Bahrain says:

I'm hopeful but it is still only a minority who are willing to speak about these issues. For most, they are still taboo (except in narrow issues like employment and equal pay) so engaging more with the public is vital for the future of Arab feminism.

I hope that feminism is "recognized as a good thing instead of rebellious crazy act," one Moroccan activist exclaims.

Below are the powerful words of one Libyan activist who summarizes it best:

We shift away from the discourse of West versus Arab feminists, ensuring that we have a unified ground to stand on to tackle problems that similarly unfold everywhere in the world. Ending the stigma of feminism both in our home countries and in the eyes of the West should pave the way for a future with inclusive dialogue where everyone has an equal opportunity and seat at the table. It is time to end the attached negativities surrounding the word "feminism" within our Arabian societies, we must educate our youth and especially our girls that it's not a bad word, or a crazy "woman" rather it is a reputable field of study and activism that ensures proper treatment of all genders on all levels.

The feminist fire is being reignited. And we need to stoke it.

The Future Is…. Exercising Our Power

We need to advocate for independence when it comes to choices in our lives.
—Kuwaiti activist

Building on the need to unlearn and reframe, feminists explained that they must boldly (re)claim their power, exercise their voice, and live to their full potential. Feminism, they argue, would bring agency and greater decision-making for women. Activists talked about elevating women to their rightful place in society, and the need to ensure that women are viewed as full, equal, autonomous, empowered individuals.

Women should be looked up to, valued, and respected, one young activist explains. This sentiment was echoed by many who believe that women have no option but to unite in their quest for equality and to counter patriarchy. Women from all parts of the world have the right to protest for their rights, one explains. Women in the Arab region should do the same.

Dr. Gabriella Nassif believes those that have power to express themselves need to continue to do so, especially on behalf of those who cannot:

For me, I'm a bit more radical. For me, where to now is the streets. We need to be on the streets. We need to be yelling and screaming all the time, all the time, all the time, all the time. Those of us who have privilege need to be screaming even louder on the behalf of those who can't, on the behalf of those who can't get to the streets for any number of reasons.

At the same time, one young Lebanese feminist explains, we need "to continue working on multiple aspects of inequality at the same time." We need to view our challenges as multidimensional and intersectional, and fight on all fronts. "All rights are intertwined," she continues, "and there is no hierarchy in terms of which fight we need to win first." The feminist quest must be viewed alongside all other efforts to achieve social justice. But there is no justice without gender justice. She continues: "We need to keep reminding ourselves that change (social, cultural, political, and legal) needs time, effort, and lots of sacrifices."

A Kuwaiti woman adds that she hopes the future entails "giving women a voice and creating safe spaces for agency." She continues:

Women need to unite against patriarchy and not fall victim to it. We need to stop believing our worth is reliant on men. We need to advocate for independence when it comes to choices in our lives.

Indeed, many activists we spoke with seek equal opportunities and access in terms of basic needs like health and education, and many others also demand their rights to economic and political opportunity—and power. Women should have "a stronger voice within the socio-cultural political power," one Jordanian-Palestinian activist states. In order to achieve this, all communities in the region need to be committed to "equality, humanity, and education on how women contribute to life (health, emotional, political, financial)." Too many women felt held back by their societies—they demanded reform.

One Lebanese feminist says, "my hope is that, through education and cultural evolution, more people realize the opportunities and benefits of having a more diverse society." And another adds that Arab women should have "freedom to dictate their own lives, and impact the society they live in."

Many speak of the frustration they feel for not being able to live full, free, rich lives and exercise their potential. One Lebanese activist hopes that women in the Arab region would one day "be able to just be themselves and … express themselves freely and contribute like any other person to their communities where they feel safe and accepted."

Another, an Egyptian male, adds:

I hope that women are no longer judged before showing what they have to provide. Everyone should be able to at least show what they are capable of without the fear of the premeditated thoughts of others.

For women to claim their rightful place and power, one Saudi Arabian feminist hopes that women would be able to heal "from what they've learned in the past," with a future that offers "a limitless brain and foresight."

Many see the challenges in the quest for equality, hoping that women are able to "stay strong and fight for their rights," because the road will not be an easy one. Some view education and economic access as the best path to equality, like one Lebanese activist who explains that in order to effect real change in the Arab world, women need full suffrage, greater access to education, equitable pay, and a "better chance for leading roles." In addition, others argue that the quest should be "truly intersectional" if it is to achieve meaningful policy and social change.

In terms of economic empowerment, some wish for "transparency and economic opportunities," while others see the future as more political, with "equal representation in public spaces" and "more leadership and legal representatives." Women need more expanded—and more effective—political participation, one explains. And advocacy should be stronger, and more practical, in order for it to make an impact.

One Lebanese activist summarizes it this way:

I can see a lot of progress made throughout the years, but it's slow and it's not enough. I would like to believe that we will achieve equality in my lifetime, however social, cultural, and legislative change needs to be faster and more efficient.

One woman wishes "to have the chance to go back and have women make a change," meaning to go back in time and give power to women, with the belief that the present would be better if the past had been equal. It was interesting to note that although this question asked about the future, her answer was to go back and change the system— going back to move forward. This raised the question: *Is it actually possible to change the systems we have now? Or are they so fundamentally flawed that they must first be destroyed to be rebuilt?*

Another feminist speaks to this, explaining that we need to build the movement starting with girls and young women, giving them space to speak and reminding them that they have power—and they need to claim it. She wants "girls to know that the only person who's telling them no, you cannot do that, is themselves. Just as simple as this."

With regards to young women specifically, she says she "always tell[s] them that there is nothing in the books that forbids you from speaking up, you are doing it for yourself."

Jordanian feminist collective Takatoat share this view:

> Women and girls expressing themselves completely without fear, without violence without threats, and to be safe—safe from inside first. To not think twice what to wear in the morning, or to take what street to avoid harassment.

Are you optimistic that this might happen, we ask?

> At times no, big no. It depends. Sometimes when we see the girls and the participants and all the sharing, yeah. And the next day there is a femicide so, yeah, it depends. I can't say that I will see major change anytime soon. But yeah, we do our best to pave the way.

Ultimately, *how might women—especially young women—exercise their power?* A young Qatari woman puts it powerfully:

> As an Arab woman, I can only hope that one day I shouldn't have to hide how I think, or how I really feel about certain topics, just because I am a woman. I am so tired of staying quiet. I feel like I am suffocating.

The Future Is…. Learning About Feminism

> *I had started to pay more attention and, in doing so, I saw inequality everywhere.*
>
> —Ayla Mooro

How do young people learn about feminism? Is it taught at schools? At home? Not likely. Anything related to feminism or gender equality is seldom taught in education systems, in the Arab region and globally. "We don't have that basic education in schools," says Dr. Noura Al Obeidli from the UAE. Often, feminism in the region is born from practical experience rather than technical knowledge. Feminism is built on justice and equality, and often born of both tragedy and necessity.

How might we bring young feminists into the movement without tragedy as initiation? How, then, are feminist teachings and understandings conveyed, and what forms do they take? How might we look to a future where we institutionalize these teachings, embedding understandings of feminist and human rights approaches in lessons about patriarchy, oppression, discrimination?

Young people who spoke to us share that they absorbed feminist messages through informal channels. At the same time, they lament that those who lack awareness, or those who oppose, might have misconceptions about feminism and what it seeks to achieve. So, *what is feminist education? And how do young activists obtain it?*

It was agreed that a lack of formal understandings was an obstacle—not only in advancing feminist movements but also in the perpetuation of beliefs and behaviors that actively work against female emancipation. Feminist education is about knowledge-sharing and movement-building, breaking patriarchal shackles in doing so.

Many activists speak of needing to go through processes of unlearning in order to make room for feminist learning. Alya Mooro, in her book *The Greater Freedom*, puts it like this:

> I had started to pay more attention and, in doing so, I saw inequality everywhere. I began to understand that we are all products of societies that teach us that men are more important than women.[15]

This patriarchal perspective is not unusual. It is transmitted through all our institutions and permeates our belief systems. Academic institutions are no exception, in fact they can be viewed as microcosms of societies. They are often highly patriarchal, and can perpetuate or reproduce discriminatory beliefs, often meaning unequal structures are unchallenged and gender norms remain entrenched. More needs to be done to hire women in academic posts, to raise awareness about inequality in these spaces, to open up curricula to gender programs, and to embed feminist principles across all disciplines.

At the same time, studies or research on gender and women's rights is still in its infancy in the region.[16] The result is that a critical feminist lens on issues is scant—or wholly absent. Feminism therefore continues to be seen as a somewhat controversial or threatening topic. Failure to provide formal education opportunities prevents the creation of indigenous knowledge on feminism.

Feminist academic Dr. Hoda Elsadda believes that gender studies are critical, as "an intellectual cultural project that involves a set of resistance strategies, including defining the biases and contradictions within the prevailing discourse, and learning from worldwide experiences in resisting these biases and producing feminist knowledge in Arabic."[17]

One key counter to address the gap in feminist knowledge production and sharing is The Arab Institute for Women. Established in 1973 in what is now the Lebanese American University, the Institute is the first of its kind in the Arab region and one of the first globally. The Institute advances women's rights and gender equality in the region, operating at the intersection of academia and activism. It is a pioneer and serves as both a producer and disseminator of feminist knowledge, such as through its bi-annual feminist journal *Al-Raida* (The Female Pioneer), established in 1976. AiW serves as a regional leader, having ignited the creation of similar institutes in the Arab world.[18]

There are many examples to celebrate, and this list is by no means exhaustive. For instance, Bahithat, the Lebanese Association of Women Researchers, established in 1992; CAWTAR, established in 1993, in Tunisia; and the Institute of Women's Studies at Birzeit University, Palestine, established in 1994. The American University in Cairo also has its Cynthia Nelson Institute for Gender and Women's Studies. The Center for Women's Studies at The University of Jordan was founded in 2006. Women's studies programs also operate at the American University of Sharjah, UAE, and the American University of Beirut, Lebanon. As one example outside of the region, the Association for Middle East Women's Studies (AMEWS) is comprised of scholars and individuals with an interest in women and gender studies in the Arab region. It was founded in 1985 by the well-known scholar Dr. Suad Joseph.

Institutions such as these, however, are in the minority meaning, yet again, feminist education remain inaccessible for too many women in the region. Moreover, these institutes must constantly struggle to defend their space and their programming.

Yara Ghanem, a youth activist from Syria, tries to fill that gap and creates a community for learning and sharing on feminism and activism:

> The most important thing here is to share what I learn with my community. For example, I attended GBV sessions through Girl Up and I just shared what I learned. I shared it with my peers, the club members, everyone.

The most important thing for her in her activism is learning. As founder of Girl Up Syria, Ghanem hosts events with a dual purpose for members: to raise awareness of social issues and as a free way to practice speaking English. She explains that, despite the need to learn English, a lot of girls cannot afford private classes and so this became a way to speak, listen, and learn in English. A *feminist* English.

Abir Chebaro, Lebanese gender consultant and activist, speaks of needing to teach herself:

> I have practically learned. I did not learn in the books, or in schools, or universities about it. I learned practically by experimenting, learning on the ground with women, and, of course, I started reading and educating myself, attending workshops, and getting involved in projects.

Saudi Arabian novelist Badriah al-Beshr also speaks to this saying, "From a young age, I felt that I would like to live in a better environment for women, so I started reading and writing, and expressing my ideas as a first step in that journey of change."[19]

Chebaro mentions the importance of generational knowledge transfer, saying she learned from the women around her. "It was like passing from one generation to another," she explains. "They used to surround me and to love me and communicate lots of their experiences with me. So I have learned from their experiences."

Dr. Bahia Shehab, Egyptian artist and educator, speaks about passing on knowledge and ideas to the next generation.

> In my case, I'm trying to organize at the very micro level. Even if it's educating the one percent, at least I feel like I'm giving back and I know that it's going to be a very long time before anything happens. Creating the next generation of designers for me is very rewarding. I feel like my teaching and activism overlap in a way because I'm giving to the next generations the ideas that my generation gave to me in very small doses, but also that I collected from my perception of what's going on around me.

Feminist activist Hayat Mirshad reveals how she discovered feminism, and the importance of passing on this knowledge:

> The turning point for me was the first time I read *Women and Sex* by Nawal El Saadawi.[20] It was an eye-opener for me. Reading El Saadawi was the turning point that launched my revolution. That awareness directed my activism. That's why now my activism is built on spreading awareness among women and girls.[21]

Many feminists tend to learn informally by creating a circle of influence in order to perpetuate these learnings. Jordanian feminist organization Takatoat also learned from other feminists in the region, now many of those women are on their board of trustees. Takatoat sees the importance of producing and passing on feminist knowledge through cultivating spaces to talk, share, learn:

What we do is disseminate knowledge because we believe that gaining knowledge and having knowledge is the tool to reclaim and to have these discussions with decision-makers, or your family, or whatever.

They operate with this in mind and have built feminist knowledge into their programs, filling a critical gap not being met by formal education channels:

We design programs for members to have basic knowledge. This is the first step in being a feminist collective. We explore what feminism is, the diversity, the different schools of thought, discriminatory laws in Jordan, the price feminists pay, and more.

In late 2022, Helem, the region's "first LGBTQIA+ rights organization," launched its Gender and Sexuality Library with hundreds of resources focused on queer, feminist, and intersectional issues.[22] Sources were crowdsourced, offering a space for knowledge that, in Executive Director Dr. Tarek Zeidan's words, would "bring in knowledge that is purposefully left out of our curricula, our media, and our school libraries." This massive contribution to our knowledge is for "anyone who wants to learn more about themselves and others" and for those who want to "make up their own minds."[23]

In addition to learning about ourselves and others, feminist learning brings awareness of rights, laws, and support services. Often this information is lifesaving. Iraqi domestic violence activist Haneen Hadi speaks of constantly having conversations with friends, dispelling certain deeply ingrained beliefs:

And I said [domestic violence] is not your fault. I had these discussions with my friends who were all trying to make her think it was her fault and I realized that women and girls in this society need to understand that it is not their fault.

Combating ingrained ideas and behaviors is crucial, and feminist education is the answer. But this is not just for feminists to take on. Education systems and governments need to inform citizens about human rights from the youngest age, empowering them "to be active participants in their own lives and in public affairs."[24]

The Future Is…. Education and Economic Empowerment

A feminist education starts with a basic education.
—Young Lebanese activist

The right to education is a critical entry point to being active participants in our own lives. This begins with basic education, Moroccan rapper Soultana explains:

The revolution is not going to be demonstrations because you can't fight war with war. The revolution is going to be with education, the people need to be educated so then they can talk about their rights peacefully, and know how to do it.

Laila Hzaineh, Jordanian-Palestinian activist, is a firm believer in educating women on their rights, and undoing patriarchal ideals. Education, she says, is key in creating a supportive network of women who understand their own rights, and work together in the movement towards greater female freedom.[25]

Kuwaiti women's rights activist Dr. Alanoud Alsharekh reminds us that "the progression of feminism in the Arab world … is intertwined with two things: post-independence struggles, and education for women."[26]

Soultana argues that lack of education is the biggest obstacle. "The people," she says, "they know nothing about it because they're not educated. There's no education. They don't even know their rights." Soultana explains that feminist knowledge must be built on a very basic foundation, starting with rudimentary understandings of our bodies and their natural processes. She uses an example from her country to illustrate the point, explaining that in Morocco, even the simple act of buying menstrual products is met with discomfort and shame, "as if you are selling drugs," she says. "It's crazy." She adds: "So how can you talk about feminism and about social issues in this situation?"

Many young people explain that they lack awareness of their own bodies and what can be considered "normal." There is no sex education curriculum taught in schools around the region, and most young people are not taught these things at home either. Upon further questioning, some young people—young men, specifically—say they learned about sex and human bodies through pornography—not the best teacher, surely. There must be a base of education in general—for both women and men—and knowledge of our sexual and reproductive lives in particular. This knowledge must be built through a rights-based approach that prioritizes consent and addresses women's rights to sexual pleasure. This did not emerge from the findings, but should be a topic for another book!

Arguably, we need to start with basic education. A young Bahraini activist believes education for all is the best tool for the future of feminism:

> I would say that our best approach is through educating people and raising awareness. I believe that our generation and the next have the education, understanding and tools to move this movement forward.

At the same time, as we saw Chapter 1, more girls than boys are denied an education. "I am surprised," says one young mother, "that so many women raise their girls thinking that marriage is more important than education." She continues to say this:

> I am shocked at how society views the difference in girls and boys. A boy gets a degree, and there is a big celebration. A girl gets an engagement, and there is a big celebration. We are guilty of reinforcing messages that marriage is the goal for women, not education.

"I hear this all the time," another activist adds, "young girls saying they want to grow up to be wives and mothers. There's nothing wrong with that," she says, "but we never ever say to those little girls that yes, that is an option, but it's not the *only* option...."

Education is a critical entry point to better our lives. We know this to be true. What is more, countless studies show that educated people are more likely to hold "emancipated social values which can influence and slowly change social norms."[27] This brings increased autonomy and enables the "young generation to feel more liberated and more hopeful about the future than their parents."[28]

Education is also a tool of liberation. Here again, countless studies have shown that women's education is directly linked to economic empowerment, and economically empowered women are more free to make their own choices. Educated women entering the workforce are not simply workers—they are agents of reform. These women will be more likely to encourage women's greater participation in the labor market, "especially in leading positions," as one Lebanese activist states. At the same time, she explains, in the current climate, the working world itself needs to take on those reforms and create an enabling environment for women before these patriarchal boundaries are crossed.

Educated and financially secure women are not only more free—they are more safe.

Some women mentioned that economic empowerment brings both financial and personal security in that they would be better able to avoid "bad situations"—or to swiftly leave and still land on their feet.

Some linked education and empowerment to intimate partner violence, and the belief that education brings money, brings control, brings safety. Here too, ample evidence shows that women in violent situations are less likely to leave if they are financially dependent on their partner. With their own income—or the *ability* to earn an income, an important distinction—leaving becomes an option. This option could be lifesaving.

One father of a young daughter explains it this way:

> I tell my daughter that education is important, not only for the sake of it, but because it is a tool for her. In the end, she may choose not to work, but she will always have the power to do so if she needs to. Education is a weapon that no one can take from her. And if one day she finds herself in a situation that is dangerous or unwelcome, this weapon can save her life. With education, she will always be able to stand on her feet.

The Future Is.... Abolishing Discrimination and Solidifying Our Rights

> *Women in the Arab world one day will be able to control their own lives without any intervention.*
>
> —Palestinian activist

Activists recognize that it might be futile to demand participation in systems that are fundamentally flawed. Institutions such as the economy, politics, religion were already built on patriarchal grounds and therefore "adding women" will *not* solve the problem. Many demand that these outdated institutions be reformed in order to build more equitable structures. This includes reform of socio-cultural norms as well as political, religious, and economic frameworks.

Women should "raise our voices regarding the discrimination" and challenge the institutions that hold them back. "The social, cultural, and religious traditions need to change," one Lebanese woman states. "Cultural boundaries [should not] interfere with women's rights," an Egyptian woman adds. Discrimination is layered, complex, and too often invisible. It is hard to fight what we cannot see.

Many activists lament the extent of discriminations, with some feeling overwhelmed about where to start. Others feel that the setting of home and family was a good entry point. They argue that social expectations and patriarchal boundaries are designated at home, and that we should start there. "I hope for social pressures on women to be completely abolished," one Lebanese woman states. And that "women will be free from the burden of family expectations," a man adds.

Those who saw the pathway for change in economic or political reform argued that women's lives have been restricted by these systems. One Palestinian activist says that she hopes "women in the Arab world one day will be able to control their own lives without any intervention."

Many saw the road to equality lay in legal reform, with one Palestinian activist stating that she hopes "the law in our countries will change in favor of women and people will stop thinking less of them." And legal reform is not possible without coordination and the active involvement of all feminist groups. Ghida Anani of ABAAD advocates for "an umbrella entity" under which all organizations can sit "at equal distance from each other" in order to regulate work being done. The lack of coordination is an impediment to any feminist advocacy in favor of reform. Anani goes on to explain that this entity could take on the heavy load of building coherent messages on legal and civil rights so that organizations—and the communities they serve—might "speak the same language" when it comes to demanding rights. This is particularly relevant when advocating to abolish discrimination in the law. If we are not clear on our demands, and using language that makes sense at that level, we will get nowhere, Anani explains.

Those who advocate for legislative reform also talk about "radicalism in terms of access to equality in inheritance," which should be applied both in law and practice. It was recognized that what exists on paper does not often apply in practice. Further, one Tunisian activist states that pervasive inequalities in inheritance specifically were, as she puts it, "a root-cause/driver of inequality." In the future, one respondent states that he hopes laws would have changed to allow for greater equality "in social life compared to men."

Dr. Bahia Shehab argues the point strongly:

> What I hope for is more rights for women. We should not take our rights for granted, like the right to vote. Anything could be taken any minute away from us and we should be aggressive about protecting the rights we already have. But also fighting for more rights. So for that to happen we really need to rally, network, and speak out more with each other and create the laws. How do you create law enforcement within Arab communities and how do you create awareness within the government for the needs of law? Enforcement and protection of women against violence? How do you make police systems safer spaces for women?

Dr. Hatoon Al Fassi, Saudi Arabian historian and women's rights activist, argues that yes, there is progress, but our work is not done. She uses the example of Saudi Arabia and its recent reforms to illustrate her point:

> I find that most of what women have asked for is coming to light. One after the other. The last thing was family personal law. Definitely, that was one of the main demands that we were after. Still missing is women passing their nationality to their children. However, so many rules have been permitted. And I can't tell you how much we are making very good use of that today. We are breaking the ceiling and beyond as much as possible, so we don't leave it only to what they provide us or what they permit us. Now we also respond in a very strong, positive way.

An anonymous activist says that there are also risks, and that activists must be careful. There is a history of restricting human rights defenders, particularly those focused on women's rights. She explains that "anybody who tries to critique or criticize anything, they will be behind bars immediately. Critique is intolerable." She elaborates that yes, laws did change from the top down, but "first they were our demands. That's how they are received, even if they come from top to down. They didn't come from the void." Ultimately, she says, "I'm happy with the changes, but should always stand on my toes."

Another Saudi Arabian activist agrees that the changes are good, and in line with activist demands. However, the issue she explains "is that it is not organic and there is no public involvement." If the public is not involved, they are unlikely to understand or support the process. Without their support, changes will be hollow. And swiftly undone. She continues:

> Previous activism brought discourse, conversation, and even argument but it was all building the movement, bringing people together. Now, it is by force. It was always top-down but this only becomes a problem when it is top-down without the bottom pushing. Before, the top-down changes came because grassroots pushed from the bottom-up.

When reforms are imposed, they lack community buy-in. Without this critical prerequisite, changes are cosmetic and likely to be resisted. Worse, this resistance could lead to a stronger patriarchal backlash. The fear of going back—and brutally so—is very real. "I fear as a woman, a liberal, and a public figure. These are changes we have asked for, but not in this way," she concludes.

Building on this, one woman from the UAE laments that young women in her country are "not aware of their rights." She goes on to say this:

> I don't understand why women don't act upon it. We need to act upon the rights, our rights. We don't need to be given rights, we have rights. Why do we always operate as if we need to be given rights to operate? This always frustrates me personally. And that's my hope, my hope that more awareness happens, and education in universities and in schools, and that this is not taboo. It needs to happen. And for [women] to understand that.

One Lebanese activist sums it up perfectly:

> I hope that we as women can be united together against the religious and political institutions governed by men that oppress us, rather than defending them and using them as tools to oppress other women. I hope women have the autonomy over their life financially and legally, and that we can make decisions that affect us, not sit helplessly while those decisions are made for us. I hope we can be united against the oppressive religious and non-religious men that utilize every tool they have (religion, tradition, the law, the media) to oppress us.

Ultimately, the sentiment was that radical reform is needed across all aspects of women's lives in the region. Without such drastic change, equality will always be imaginary.

The Future Is…. Intersectional and Interconnected

> *The intersectional Arab feminism that is currently evolving goes beyond understanding how systems of oppression interact to shape the realities of women of different backgrounds. It recognizes how all systems of oppression are sustaining the patriarchy, and therefore, how all systems of oppression need to be eliminated to achieve true justice.*
>
> —Farah Daibes[29]

While this theme appropriately cuts across all our findings, we felt the need to highlight here again that feminism must be intersectional, that our movements are interconnected, and that we should all be feminists—as we so often say! This means widening the support base, building bridges between networks, and creating conversations across identity lines, generational divides, socio-economic differences.

The Arab region is home to a diverse population. Conversations about diversity, and acceptance of it, are increasingly becoming mainstream. While certain things remain contentious, we argue that these diversities present opportunities for coalition-building founded on inclusion. In the words of one young Tunisian activist, we need to "be united and to have an intersectional approach."

Being "intersectional" is a phrase that has become part of our contemporary discourse. To us it means not only that we are inclusive, but that each of our freedoms is bound to one another's. Coalition-building that is intersectional, inclusive, and interconnected will build better, stronger movements. And better, stronger movements will increase the likelihood that we succeed in abolishing patriarchy.

Dr. Tarek Zeidan, Executive Director of Helem, an NGO focused on LGBTQ+ justice and equality, explains it best:

> Intersectionality isn't just a buzzword, it is a massive responsibility and extremely difficult to achieve. When two marginalized groups come together to ensure protection and survival, there is not only a confluence of interests but also that of suspicion, stigma, and deep-held trauma. It is to be expected that oppressed communities would attempt to reject and nullify one another due to these dynamics, and do enormous amounts of harm in the process. The chronic lack of spaces and resources makes it excruciatingly difficult and painful to do this work because violence is so easily transmittable—but we have no other choice but to face one another with courage and compassion. Feminist movements that do not factor in race and class, that have a heteronormative and binary view of sexuality and gender, risk replicating the same prejudice and inequity that sparked their impulse to organize and resist oppression in the first place. Queer liberation movements that do not purposefully inculcate their ranks, values, and action with feminist principles are destined to do the same. Bastions of oppression will never fall if those besieging them are constantly bickering at the gates.

Being "intersectional" also requires that we decolonize our movements. We cannot build on structures designed to destroy us. Decolonizing systems of oppression requires actions of unlearning and learning, challenging the status quo, and centering indigenous feminist objectives. In the words of one young Tunisian feminist, "I hope that we could connect with each others and create our own narrative and decolonize our fight."

Dr. Gabriella Nassif recommends the movement also looks to "so-called non-traditional influence and actors." She explains it like this:

> Historically, women's rights organizations and women's rights leaders did not really look to non-citizen and informal workers, gender and sexual minorities, and so on. But the way they're doing work in such a hostile environment, we need to model our own work after that. And we need to work with them. And we need to see them. And we need to give proper respect to their strategies. It has to be bottom-up. It certainly can't be top-down. A more holistic approach to what feminism means.

A more holistic, inclusive feminism is a more sustainable feminism. After all, our feminist fight is one for human rights and equality for all.

Across the region, rights-based organizations are building coalitions. For instance the Arab Foundation for Freedoms and Equality and MantiQitna, are regional networks coordinating multi-country campaigns. *My.Kali* is an online pan-Arab LGBTQ+ magazine established in Jordan. And Ahwaa, the regional online platform, is an LGBTQ+ support community for the Middle East. AiW also has an online platform focused LGBTQ+ youth featuring information, animations, Q&A, and a glossary, amongst other things.

In Tunisia, the Collective for Individual Freedoms is a coalition of 37 organizations, including feminist groups, have come together in support of equality for women and LGBTQ+ people.[30] An activist working with Chouf, a feminist organization in

Tunisia that works with women of all sexualities, says: "The feminist movement in Tunisia was not previously gay-friendly, but it's changed. They were afraid to get involved before. The change came from within associations. Young lesbian and bi women joined [feminist associations], and changed things from within."[31]

There are many organizations at the country level—alQaws and Aswat in Palestine, Haven and Marsa in Lebanon, Mawjoudin in Tunisia, Bedayaa and Mesahat in Egypt, TransHomosDZ in Algeria—working to empower sexual and gender minorities and provide representation and visibility. IraQueer advocates for LGBTQ+ rights in Iraq from outside the country. The existence of these groups is promising—and an act of resistance in and of itself—and yet challenges remain. There are, of course, different levels of risk across the region, but overall LGBTQ+ rights remain a concern for the future. Some of those who speak out are in the diaspora or must use pseudonyms. It is still not fully safe within the region itself.

According to the Equaldex LGBT Equality Index, no Arab state is even in the top 100 countries for being friendly to LGBTQ+ people in terms of legal rights and public attitudes.[32] Yemen and Saudi Arabia rank last and second last respectively, while Somalia, Mauritania, and Libya are also in the bottom ten countries on the index.

The lack of more comprehensive data, coupled with the lack of civil society space for LGBTQ+ activism, is a finding in itself. The silence and restriction around the topic means more needs to be done. To be sure, there are organizations working to fill this gap but real progress remains distant.

The Future Is.... Engaging Men and Redefining Masculinities

> *Patriarchy is not about men ... feminism is not about "hating men." Patriarchy is about power, and feminism is about destroying patriarchy.*
> —Mona Eltahawy[33]

We argue that, when talking about feminisms, we must include masculinities in our conversation. To that end, Chapter 1 highlighted efforts to engage men and explore healthy masculinities. While the majority of men in the region likely support traditional masculinities and hold inequitable views, there are entry points to working with men, and to supporting those men who seek alternative masculinities. This is a growing field, with significant studies presenting evidence that engaging men and boys in gender equity movements contributes to deconstructing patriarchal hierarchies and gendered power asymmetries.[34] To achieve real feminist goals, men must be included.

Anthony Keedi is a gender specialist and masculinities technical advisor at ABAAD–Resource Centre for Gender Equality. It is one of the first masculinities programs of its kind in the region, built to support men while also responding to the needs of women. He acknowledges that often there is a counter argument when including masculinities, and a concern that women's voices will be sidelined as a result.

Keedi explains it like this:

> This becomes a difficult conversation because it requires more resources, and does engaging men come at the expense of providing services to engage women? It shouldn't, but somehow that becomes the narrative because there's not enough money to go around after paying for missiles and bullets and guns.

Many young activists feel that engaging men and reforming masculinities are critical to ending patriarchy. Dr. Noura Al Obeidli of the UAE points out that when it comes to gender, it is not just about women alone. "It's also about educating men," she says.

Elie Youssef, actor and producer of the film *Open Wound*, thinks that the worst thing feminism can do is exclude men. "The feminist movement needs allies," he says. But crucially, he explains, "the movement needs allies from the other camp to change mindsets. I think men are essential as allies to change the narrative, to change the way of thinking of men."

Salma Khalaf, Palestinian youth activist, has a similar outlook saying "whether we like it or not, men do affect each other." To her, men's movements for positive masculinities could be contagious across the region.

Our survey respondents also recognize the need for engaging men. One Tunisian activist wants "greater focus on changing male attitudes and behavioral norms" while a Lebanese activist wants "men to recognize and take accountability for ignoring us" in order for "our voices to be heard," she says.

Another young feminist from Egypt wants "women to be able to express their rightful need for equal rights without backlash, and for women to be treated with the same respect that men are treated with."

In the words of one young Egyptian feminist, she seeks "a future where the male is not the default." In order for that to happen, there needs to be "full support from both men and women to secure opportunities and freedoms for all genders" according to a Saudi-Emirati feminist. A Palestinian feminist says she "hopes that Arab men fight for Arab women." Saudi Arabian musician Tamtam echoes this and says she hopes "that more men will stand up for women."

Promisingly, our interviewees and our survey respondents indicate that this is increasingly taking place with the next generation. Khalaf is encouraged by what she sees among her peers:

> People my age, it's crazy how much I see them talk about women's rights. Even young boys or men my age. I see them speaking about these things, arguing about these things. And that's really important. I've never heard older men speak about women's rights, but seeing these younger men talking about women's rights, that shows me there's some sort of change.

One woman from the UAE also speaks of her sons and the difference she sees with the younger generation and how they treat girls and women. "I'm very proud of my boys and their friends," she says. "It's a different generation. I see respect. It's a different ballgame, believe me. It's not the way it was with me in school."

But, as with everything, more needs to be done. Narrow definitions of what it means to "be a man" need to be destroyed. Alya Mooro, Egyptian author based in the UK, had this to say:

> A lot of the time, especially in the Arab region, there's very toxic ways in which men are told they need to be men. So feminism is good for men too, because men are also beholden to very stringent ideas of what it means to be a man which is a huge burden and also where a lot of the control comes in. At the end of the day, we all want to be ourselves, unrestricted, without having to ascribe to specific gender roles.

Keedi agrees that rigid, traditional gender norms are destructive:

> From a masculinity perspective, I would almost argue that the number one identity that we still promote for men is being a provider and protector. What kind of hopes do we have for

male youth in the future? There's a lot of hope in female youth but maybe not as much in the men, and that's why we need to engage them more.

When we asked about youth, Keedi makes a valid point in asking: "When we say youth, who are we talking about?"

He goes on to explain it like this:

I think you can look at it as a double-edged sword. And this is maybe where I look at it from a masculinities perspective. So when we think about youth and we think about young women, yes, absolutely. I think that's the place where we can exclusively put our hopes with these topics. But what about young men? Are they learning anything different or are young men also becoming stronger in their devotion to the patriarchy?

Keedi explains that their devotion is due to a lack of alternatives, and a lack of understanding of the implication of hypermasculinity, militarism, confessionalism, and other oppressive-isms.

Keedi shares his impressions of, as he puts it, being "astounded by the power of women" while also "always looking for male role models and never really ... finding an adequate one," except for his father, he explains. Keedi remarks that while he was "always searching" for the right male role model, he nonetheless found "so many women with open arms accept me" within the movement. From them, he explains, he learned a great deal. Women's strength has "always been powerful," he says, "but it's in the dark space that you see how powerful they are."

While Keedi's experience has been positive, it has not yet caught on. There is room for more here. And men can more visibly serve as allies to women, and as mentors to other men. One Syrian activist sums it up this way:

We talk so much about "engaging men" but doesn't that also put the responsibility on women again, as if it is women's "job" to reach out to men, to open the door, to include them, to bring them to the work and say "look, this will be good for you, too!" I say that men also need to step up and show that they are ready and willing and want to change, to be allies and to be in support of rights and equality. Without this, we are doing all the work. Again. And more unpaid work and emotional labor is not what we need right now.

The Future Is.... Protecting Our Bodies[35]

> *We have bigger issues like the normality of underage girls getting married, and a culture of victim shaming when it comes to sexual assault or harassment and general prejudice around women and their bodies. There is a saying in our culture that a man can't be shamed or faulted for anything, this implies that women are the ones who carry the guilt and shame, so if anything happens to them it's their fault and their own doing.*
> —Young Bahraini activist

In Chapter 1 and throughout this book, we spoke of women's safety—in the form of bodily integrity and autonomy—as a critical prerequisite to progress. If we are not safe from violence or do not have autonomy over our own bodies, then we do not have freedom. Without women's safety in public and private space, all other rights are rendered meaningless and will not be attainable. Protecting our bodies is the cornerstone of the feminist movement, we argue, but it is also the most contested and hardest to win.

Sophie Bessis, Tunisian-French historian and feminist, articulates it this way:

The feminists of the Arab world fight about rights, jurisdiction, socio-economic issues, but speaking about the body is very difficult. There are taboo subjects like the body and sex. And ... if we don't talk about the body and sex, we'll never talk about the heart of the question of women.[36]

As documented in previous chapters, women in the Arab region face severe limitations that restrict their freedoms—to move freely, to speak freely, to make their own choices, to learn, to be healthy, to marry or not—the list goes on. Bodily autonomy is threatened in every sphere—by social norms that view women as property, by restrictive laws and discriminatory courts built from those social norms, and through high levels of gender-based violence to enforce those social norms.

Many of those we spoke with and surveyed cite violence against women as a major inhibitor to their freedom. "End GBV," they say. This came up time and again, in all its forms. As long as violence exists, freedom will be impossible.

Yara Ghanem, youth activist from Syria, says "we have such difficulties with people's mindset with violence and harassment," which makes her all the more determined to help end violence against women and girls:

I want to work with international organizations to help Syrian girls. I would like to represent Syrian youth—and young women in general—in international organizations so that girls in my country stop suffering from what they are suffering from, which is early marriage and gender-based violence. They're really suffering from a lot of obstacles and problems that we can't even think about.

Many felt that legal provisions are one way to end gender-based violence. Bodily autonomy and integrity cannot be divorced from the full range of sexual rights, some explain. And "women's sexual and reproductive rights must be ensured and guaranteed by the law," one young Lebanese feminist says. A young Jordanian-Palestinian feminist echoes this sentiment, adding that the law needs to provide protection from "dangers that any woman may face, such as honor killings," while a Yemeni activist advocates for raising awareness among policy makers to ensure the protection of women.

Another young woman from Jordan would rather society reach a place "to not need intervention for women's rights and GBV." Building on this, a young Egyptian feminist hopes that "ensuring full sexual and reproductive health and right is no longer debatable and that violence against women is not tolerated." She continues to acknowledge that socio-cultural and religious traditions need to change for that to happen, which she says, "will take a long time."

"We have such difficulties with people's mindsets with violence and harassment," Ghanem explains. "You can feel there is friction in our community." And yes, this will take a long time. Accessing the full range of sexual and reproductive health and rights continues to be a challenge in the region.

Violence against women is pervasive, and no space is safe for women—public or private. At the same time, we can claim whatever space we have that might bring us closer to bodily autonomy and integrity. We cannot be *safe* in our bodies if we are not *free* in our bodies. Activist Rana Alamuddin reminds us that, in the Arab region, guilt, honor, and shame hold women back from owning their bodies:

You're guilty for being comfortable in your body, you're guilty for enjoying your sexuality, feeling powerful. You're just guilty for ruffling feathers around you as women and we're born into that. That's a way of controlling women because if you remove the pressure of honor from women's shoulders, women are free.[37]

Helping women find that freedom starts with eliminating all forms of violence against women. Women's right to be safe and to have full bodily autonomy is the foundation upon which all other freedoms must be built. Access to education and healthcare, politics and the economy, and every other right will be hollow as long as violence against women persists.

The Future Is…. Healing from Collective Trauma

> *It's hard to fight and grieve at the same time.*
> —Dr. Tarek Zeidan[38]

While feminisms are often born from crisis, it is hard to build sustainable movements on shaky ground. The region's protracted crises at the macro level fuel traumas at the micro level that endure long after the crisis has subsided. We touched upon notions of healing briefly in Chapter 4, and it emerged again in conversations with activists as a prerequisite for a feminist future.

Yemeni street artist Haifa Subay speaks frankly on the subject of healing and hope, colored by the ever-present war in her country. While her hopes center on education, she explains that mental health is just as critical "because our mental health problems go on." Activists spoke of the difficulties in struggling to deal with their own trauma while also trying to support others. This creates an environment of insecurity upon which it is difficult to build a movement.

Subay continues:

> Actually, I don't have hope. I don't have hope for this war to end. And actually, I don't know what the future will bring for us. We live day by day. We don't know what tomorrow is hiding for us.

The use of the word "hiding" is particularly powerful. In Subay's context, and for so many others, threats come from all angles—fostering greater fear for the future. Healing is, quite literally, day by day, leaving little room to advance the feminist agenda.

Individual and collective trauma is pervasive in the Arab region. There are insufficient understandings of the nature of ongoing trauma that characterizes the Arab region. Post-traumatic stress disorder (PTSD), for example, is a diagnosis grounded in the aftermath or "post" traumatic stage. *What does this have to offer people living a region of perpetual upheaval and trauma? A region where there is no "post" trauma?*

It is well documented that mental health services in the region are underdeveloped and underfunded.[39] And there is a greater risk of mental health issues developing into chronic conditions. Trauma manifests in many ways, but lack of awareness and research means that figures likely underrepresent reality. Furthermore, diagnoses are based on international standards, and there is a growing movement around decolonizing mental health structures to apply to local contexts.[40] Diagnostics should be grounded in socio-cultural realities and treatments should reflect communities' needs. As such, one approach recommended is a joint effort between Arab states to develop guidelines for diagnosis, treatment, or management.[41]

Healing should be prioritized, with special considerations for those on the front-lines who struggle with having to heal themselves while also supporting others. Activists felt that even putting voice to these issues raises more challenges than solutions. Dr. Tarek Zeidan, in a documentary about LGBTQ+ activism in the region, explains it perfectly by saying, "it's hard to fight and grieve at the same time."

One activist puts it this way: "We live in a train wreck on repeat. Every day I wake up and I don't know what I will find. I cannot look, but I cannot look away, either." She continues to explain that she cannot work under these conditions, but she has no choice. "I pick up my broken self and I try to help other people. And for a moment, I forget that I am broken. But not for very long."

She says that it comes back to her in the quiet, private moments. "I cannot stop grieving," she says, "for all of us." The cumulative effect of violence and insecurity that she experiences have worn her down. "Every time I hear of someone's story, it is like it is happening to me all over again. And it never seems to stop."

She concludes with this:

> There is personal trauma that we each have as individuals. Yes, every single one of us. And then there is the collective trauma. The collective trauma is not just the sum of our personal traumas, no. There are other traumas we have as a community, these remain unaddressed. How can we heal as individuals when our community is broken? How can a community heal when its individuals are broken? How can we think of the future when we cannot even survive the present. I cannot find my balance.

In the words of Rana Alamuddin, "true healing is a collective journey. We heal together, and that's what makes it so much stronger."[42]

The Future Is…. Mobilizing Online

> *The virtual openness that we are living in is something unbelievable.*
> —Dr. Hatoon Al Fassi

Social media is a huge asset in feminist organizing. This is generational—older activists did not have the ability to galvanize the masses at a moment's notice or spread advocacy messages with the same speed. Experience shows that the internet has offered unlimited potential for cross-border solidarity and movement-building, unprecedented just two decades ago. Feminists and other human rights activists create and share knowledge and spread their messages more readily, and to a more receptive audience. This also helps bridge a gap between feminist theory and feminist action, bringing our understandings of *being* feminist together with actually *doing* feminism. Fueled by social media, "young Arab feminists are taking the reins of developing radical feminist discourses and have scaled up their ability to organize and mobilize."[43]

This new way of organizing also offers young feminists a way of organizing outside of traditional avenues—avenues in which young feminists have little faith. Yalda Younes, part of the group who launched the *Uprising of Women in the Arab World* on social media, puts it this way:

> What I'm interested in is the networking with people, and what these new social media technologies offer us. I don't really have a lot of faith unfortunately in NGOs, nor in political organizations.[44]

Feminist researcher Dr. Gabriella Nassif notes this dynamic:

> One of the interesting things that's emerging around the region is the local feminist work either through using social media platforms or just really working along community lines, more or less under the notion that the state is very oppressive and instigates feminist backlash. So it's this move where women's rights groups and feminists kind of move away from their dependence on the state and to function in their own communities.

There are many positive elements to this. Social media is a huge tool, especially among youth groups. It affords anonymity and is a supposedly "safe space" in climates where there are civil society restrictions. There are risks, certainly, and new forms of violence that have emerged as a result of this new medium. Many activists experience online harassment and bullying, threats to their safety, restriction of speech, and invasion of privacy.

Dr. Hatoon Al Fassi of Saudi Arabia has been severely restricted by authorities in both her academic work and in her freedom of expression. Even though her platform and contribution have been curtailed, she still finds hope and inspiration in the digital sphere.

Online "presence" carries significant weight in the Arab region because it is inherently connected to whatever presence is deemed acceptable in society. This speaks to women's identity and existence overall. In societies where women carry the burden of familial reputation—and therefore honor and shame—revealing oneself online through image or name becomes even more symbolic. This is particularly relevant in questions of covering and veiling, and the question of whether "presence" needs to be visual.

Al Fassi explains:

> With social media, the online connection, and COVID-19 restrictions, women have become more adept at voicing their opinions as well as their images, much more than they used to. Little by little you see that more women are breaking this taboo. It has enabled us, those trapped by our inaccessibility to work, become exposed to the world with just the click of a keyboard's button. It's a great advantage and a great opportunity as well for a new reality. One has new creative ways of communication, production, connecting to the world, and continuing researching and working. I can't describe this moment and how precious I find it. I can't really can't find the right words. The virtual openness that we are living in is something unbelievable.

Social media is not without its flaws, however. She continues:

> On the other hand, the problem of freedom of expression is the one that is holding us back from ameliorating the current status or from correcting the flaws. There are many things that need to be done.

A young Bahraini activist echoes this sentiment and says that digital activism does not necessarily reach audiences outside of the echo chamber. She explains:

> With digital activism, yes you do reach a wider target, but it's people that are genuinely interested in it so it's really hard to be that organic. It's usually people who know about the topic and are interested in the topic already.

Overall though, young activists argue that the net result is positive. There is space for a multiplicity of narratives and voices. When used effectively, social media has provided a space to address taboo topics and build an accessible platform for activism. Online campaigns have taken hold, and are likely to increase.

Salma Khalaf, an activist in the Palestinian diaspora, advocates for tagging and pushing out stories, spreading them so as to "force the country indirectly to take steps." She explains that through the internet people are "getting exposed to how the ideas of feminism are in the Western world. And they tried to take this and translate it into their own communities."

While Kahlaf agrees that connectivity can be a problem, she also feels that it is not an impediment. And we are more connected than we think. She continues:

> Whether we like to admit it or not, despite the electricity, the internet or whatever, everyone has access to social media in one way or another. Almost everyone. Even people who are in a bad economic situation. They would own phones, even if just the cheapest phone and some form of data to access the internet.

Khalaf elaborates on the potential this holds:

> When someone sees multiple posts, or multiple people talking about, say, a certain case of domestic violence, and then seeing people arguing why this is wrong. Because people need to get exposed to this because sometimes a lot of people who live in a certain community will think, Oh, it's fine. If I hit my wife, it's fine … then when they get exposed to these ideas, they might be like, Oh, maybe I shouldn't do that … what I'm doing is wrong.

She concludes by saying that "it is really important to have this content out there. And it's going to reach people, trust me, whether someone wants to see it or not."

In a conversation about the need to use kindness in the face of great harm, Dr. Bahia Shehab asks, "can we find more intelligent tools, kind tools, that can cripple systems?" She sees the internet, and social media specifically, as this tool. "The medium is the message," she says, "and it is called *social* media." Shehab continues:

> It's about bringing people together. So it has delivered that. The problem with social media is that it is being manipulated and it is also ephemeral, it has very short-term memory. People forget. But we've created space. I think what we've established now is the collective memory and reaction and pressure, people can come together. They can plan big things together. Social media has provided a tool. But now, how do you make it effective? How do you make that tool drive real social change?

The internet is both an organizing and a learning tool. Many we spoke to, particularly young activists, said they use the internet to learn about feminism because this learning is otherwise not available. Further, feminists learn from each other online, and find inspiration in each other's movements.

Shehab speaks to this point as well, saying that social media allows for "learning from each other's experiences." She explains that "the revolution in Sudan learned a lot from what happened in Egypt, there was a lot of experiential exchange between activists in Egypt and Sudan, thanks to social media." This cross-pollination and cross-border collaboration is promising, and may be a good sign of things to come in the region.

Ghanem explains the particular situation in Syria, where online "gatherings" are subjected to government scrutiny and skepticism. "This might be very simple in different countries," she says "but [in Syria] I have to justify everything and try to do everything legally." Ghanem is part of the Girl Up campaign, affiliated with the UN Foundation, meaning there is suspicion that this is an NGO and therefore needs a government license. She explains that "it is just as simple as a club of some members who belong to a global campaign and working towards achieving certain goals."

Despite this, "it is complicated here," she laments. "We're trying to do a lot of things online."

To make matters more complicated, connectivity is a challenge. "In Syria, it's not very helpful with this internet situation," she says. "It is very important for people who have access." But having access is one thing, and having a stable internet connection is another. And having electricity is harder still. For activists, Ghanem says, "we have a bigger problem, which is electricity. If you don't have electricity to charge your phone, your laptop, and light to see and so that people see you, it's a problem."

Ghanem is finding ways to overcome these obstacles while also learning, teaching, and spreading a message. She concludes with this:

> I see this opportunity as no boundaries, no limits. I just feel like we all belong to the same coalition. And most people are very young. It means I can work with girls from different countries. And then I got to know girls from our countries who are living abroad and Syrian girls who are moving or who are living abroad. And I learn with online activism because most of the people who I deal with online are from other countries.

Ultimately, human rights campaigner Tala Harb explains that even those who are not activists or not in the region have a role to play. She advises that we all keep our "social media platforms populated with Arab voices, experts, academics, representatives, activists, journalists, especially women, girls, and non-cis men."

Digital mobilization is, in the words of one young activist, "rising among Gen Z."[45] Here, there is massive potential for building communities and fostering feminisms across issues, backgrounds, and borders.

The Future Is.... Collaborating Across the Region

I hope for strong feminist grassroots movements across the region.
—Young activist

There is no unique discourse or movement for the entire Arab region. Socio-cultural, historical, and political diversities divide us, and therefore strategies will take on different forms in different spaces. However, there is room for greater collaboration, and ultimately for solidarity. *What, then, does collaboration across the region look like?*

Rym Badran, a young Lebanese activist, speaks of a "very beautiful idea of other countries coming together," happening more and more, she says.

She admits that collaboration may be "easier between North Africa and the Levant than with the Gulf" because she personally has found this difficult through her activism work. "I think it has to do with the history of the movement and the regions," she explains, "but I would say definitely, it's getting easier. And it's not just the feminist movement," she adds. "Climate activism is also benefiting from regional collaboration."

Badran also explains that socio-economic similarities make cross-border collaboration easier. "It's something we've seen," she explains, referring to her experience with Girl Up. "I think it's easier to talk with someone when you both have maybe the same economic and social status, although we're not from the same country."

Responses from our survey and conversations with young activists indicate similar desires for collaboration. One young Lebanese activist expressed her hope for feminism "to grow around the region." Another particularly wanted to see "strong feminist grassroots movements across the region."

In Chapter 3, we covered the story of a Saudi Arabian activist who shared her thoughts on regional collaboration. She explained that common issues, such as violence against women, would surely benefit from a unified or pan-Arab feminism. However, she cautioned that geopolitics can impede regional collaborations. She asked a rhetorical question about whether national or regional movements should be pursued first. "We have hardly built ourselves [nationally]," she said, making regional collaboration an even greater challenge. She concluded by advocating for regional solidarity—when causes gain regional momentum, they are more likely to receive national attention.

An activist from Bahrain explains it this way:

> I think about how people in the Middle East are not so connected to other causes or issues. Maybe coming from the Gulf it's an even smaller bubble, and the restrictions on protests or any form of activism doesn't allow us to do much.

She uses action for Palestine to illustrate the point and to explain that organizing for any social cause is near impossible with such government restrictions:

> I remember when everyone was protesting around the world for Palestine. I think that's the first time in Bahrain they were trying to organize a protest, and the government just shut it down. Any form [of protest] that goes out on social media—like meeting points or whatever—police were there and nobody was allowed to gather.

At the same time, she laments that people are "just not that interested," regardless of the issue, saying it is "more of an out of sight, out of mind thing." Those who take action are the minority, and likely do so because they are "exposed to alternative media." But for the majority, she explains, "everyone else was just discarding it, saying no we don't have this problem or we don't care about this problem or it's not as important [as other issues]."

One example of a movement that can gain regional traction is the repeal of the so-called "marry your rapist" law, the provision in country penal codes that allows rapists to escape punishment by marrying their victims. In a matter of weeks in 2017, Tunisia, Jordan, and Lebanon all did away with this discriminatory law. Palestine followed suit in 2018, although the ruling cannot be applied to Gaza as it is controlled by Hamas. This presents evidence that, to a certain extent, progress can cross national borders and also could propel other reforms in the region. Other countries with this law in place —Algeria, Bahrain, Iraq, Kuwait, Libya, and Syria—will ideally follow suit, no longer allowing rapists to escape punishment. [46]

There have been many attempts to foster regional collaboration. There are too many to list here, but one good example is the "Inclusive Dialogue Within Women Rights Movements in MENA" founded by Search for Common Ground."[47] This program aims to facilitate dialogue between various female civil society organizations from different backgrounds. Despite divisions, the initiative has been able to produce recommendations for the advancement of women's rights in the region aimed at policy makers, women's organizations, and donors. Women's organizations in Morocco, Lebanon, and Tunisia adopted collaborative agency campaigns after involvement in the dialogue process.[48]

The first ever Arab Girls' Summit was held in Amman, Jordan in 2022 to promote regional cooperation in tackling gender inequality and to provide support tailored to girls.[49] Several organizations cooperated to host the event in order to collectively highlight the unique challenges facing girls in the region, help drive targeted investment, and provide space for learning and sharing.

Findings from these events and others suggested that issue-based dialogue was effective in bridging divisions and establishing common courses of action. In order to create an environment for regional collaboration to thrive, activists can start by recognizing the socio-cultural and political differences that animate the diverse countries in the region. A charter of values could be established for this purpose. It is not impossible to find common entry points for work.

The 2016 conference "Towards prioritizing women, peace and security on the Arab agenda" can be used as case in point. It brought together experts, academics, practitioners, civil society representatives, government officials and United Nations representatives from the region, culminating in the Beirut Call for Action.[50] The Arab Institute for Women has been instrumental in creating space for conversations on women, peace, and security across the region. AiW Director Myriam Sfeir elaborates:

> The Institute provides space for gathering, for debate, for understanding what is happening in theory and practice, for critique. The Institute builds a regional dialogue for this, for how to use this agenda in ways that are truly feminist and truly regional.

Bringing regional activists together means fostering communication built in a safe space, and establishing what might be the entry-level or lowest common denominator issues to launch discussions. Creating issues-based coordination mechanisms is one useful strategy to ensure that conversations continue beyond the duration of the conference or event, retaining that collaborative spirit after activists have returned to their home countries. Joint campaigns and social media messaging could be another regional action, at a minimum.

Young people are perhaps more willing to collaborate across national divides. Myriam Sfeir explains how the Institute succeeded in reaching youth through creativity and competition:

> When it comes to young people in the region, we reach them with creative things like our annual art-for-activism competition, our animated song, our panels and lectures, our film festivals to name a few. The competition gets more and more submissions every year from throughout the region, and the song is the first of its kind in the region, it is a positive call to young people. They have a voice, they need to use their voice. Regional messages for young people are the ones that spread.

Regional learnings, synergies, and collaborations allow for a stronger voice from the region in global fora. And they can impact countries and communities in new ways. Ultimately these regional collaborations could serve to strengthen existing movements and establish new ones at the country level, enabling activists to work as part of a regional collective, but focusing within their own countries and communities where critical change begins.[51]

The Future Is.... Galvanizing the Diaspora

We exist in the diaspora more than in our country ... we are strong wherever we go.... Our women are incredible and successful and strong. This at least should change the way the world thinks of Arab women. We represent the region and it is how people come to understand what Arab is—and what an Arab woman is. The diaspora are the ambassadors.
—Young Lebanese man

In Chapter 5, study participants raised the diaspora as a challenge—"those who left don't get it," those who remained explained. And those who left felt like the perpetual insider-outsiders, forever balancing the tensions of being part of two worlds. In our conversations, the diaspora was raised as an opportunity, an entry point, a galvanizer for action. Those within felt as if there was an important role the diaspora could play in supporting those on the inside—channeling attention and resources and generating greater action for social change.

Alya Mooro, Egyptian author raised in the UK, discusses navigating an identity straddling two worlds that comes with being a member of the diaspora and the impact that has on her activism. While existing in a space of "both and neither" can raise its own challenges, it also offers an opportunity and a freedom to have these conversations.

Living in the diaspora provides space to voice criticism or agitate for change when such space is restricted within the region. For example, in instances of stifled civil society activity, crackdowns, or internet censorship, people living outside the region can use their voice to push boundaries and social norms by being the insider-outsider.

A Syrian feminist explains how she "participate[s] in all the Arab events and speak[s] out at every opportunity." She went on to say that she lives in an area where there is a large and diverse Arab community. "We keep talking about it and sending money and connecting with each other," she says, explaining that she was "raised in an Arab bubble." While this has created some tensions for her, her commitment to the region—inherited, imposed, or deliberate—is unwavering. "When I am able," she says, "I will spend some time there and work. I don't know when but I will do it."

A Palestinian woman echoes this sentiment, using her activism for Arab-American causes and participating in various advocacy and awareness groups. "I'm a member of Arab America and the Arab-American Anti-Discrimination Committee and all that stuff," she says.[52] "Every single group there is. I'm there. They have events all the time." And when asked about how these organizations support women in the region, or Arab women in the diaspora, she explains: "They talk about and celebrate Arab women's achievements, like extraordinary Arab-American women and stuff. It's important to celebrate those things."

A Palestinian activist explains that she uses the cause of Palestine as her entry point into all social justice issues. She says:

I was raised on the narrative of Palestine, so my activism starts there, but equality is part of this story and so I do what I can for equal rights for Palestinians and for everyone. Women's rights too. The power of Palestinian women—I believe in us! I march and donate and keep focus on this. Everyone knows this is my strongest belief and whatever I do will mention Palestine—this is my North Star.

A young Lebanese man celebrates the successes of the diaspora. In the case of Lebanon in particular, the diaspora is global, and has often been well integrated into society. He explains it this way:

> We exist in the diaspora more than in our country—look at Brazil, there are more Lebanese there than in Lebanon! My point is that we are strong wherever we go, and we defy stereotypes that we're backwards or conservative. Our women are incredible and successful and strong. This at least should change the way the world thinks of Arab women. We represent the region and it is how people come to understand what Arab is—and what an Arab woman is. The diaspora are the ambassadors.

In conversations with Arab-Americans, we asked what they thought the role of the diaspora might be in helping to advance women's rights in the region. One speaks of the tedium in having to explain to American activists why this matters, and why it isn't "as backwards as they think." "Grassroots education and conversation is needed," one says. "Or maybe sending money somewhere," another adds. "But where?!" a few responded. Often the causes are overwhelming, and as a result the diaspora send money to personal contacts—family first—rather than to causes.

The exception is a major catastrophe, some say. "The Beirut blast was my catalyst," one says. "I just couldn't send enough money, sending money everywhere, giving to any fund I saw, to anyone who asked." But, fortunately, these dramatic crises are few. And while feminism (or lack thereof) is a crisis, it does not hold the same power over our purse strings.

How, then, to galvanize the "outsiders" to amplify and fund feminist causes? Human rights campaigner Tala Harb has many excellent and actionable recommendations. Stay in contact, she says, especially with the activists on the frontlines. Check in on them, ask what they need, and—to the best of your ability—deliver it. Ensure that they are the spokespeople on the issues.

Echoing this sentiment, Dr. Rita Stephan, Visiting Researcher at North Carolina State University, explains that Arab feminisms are "still not represented in global discussion." "And when it happens," she continues, it is driven by "diaspora scholars and activists who carry the voices of Arab feminists from their home countries." Ultimately, the voices from the frontlines need to be at the forefront.

Harb continues. Concretely, "mobilize yourself and others digitally and offline for protests, for signing petitions," she suggests. "Work with the diaspora and galvanize shipments of items people need, and ensure that there's continuity of goods coming in." Harb also urges the diaspora to provide education support through scholarships, starting with the most marginalized communities. "Too many people are really, really oppressed," she says. "Under layers and layers of patriarchy. So education is the way to really empower them."

Harb also advocates for helping local businesses scale up, or at least withstand crises. She explains that economic opportunities are critical for the region's survival. The diaspora can use its business knowledge to provide guidance, or at least to support local businesses from abroad. "Share your skills," she says. "Don't educate people on the inside but rather share what you learned and follow their lead on what works or doesn't on the inside, work together to tailor the approach."

For the women's movement specifically, "become an organizer and a campaigner to support their causes," and provide technical knowledge and financial contributions,

Harb recommends. When it comes to women's rights in the region, we can do a lot to "fight stereotypes and discrimination abroad through discussion, and invite a speaker who is on the inside," she insists. We must think, work, and act together in solidarity to support the needs of women in the region. She continues, "Remember, their voices matter more. You are led and guided by the inside voices. Respect their process."

Harb reminds us to "recognize your relative privilege," and the resentment that this may bring. At the same time, "do not feel guilty, that doesn't do anyone any favors." Harb concludes with this powerful call to action:

> Act. Take action. And when in doubt, turn to those powerful voices on the inside. You're working together. You're thinking together. Ask those on the inside what they want. Ask them what they need. And remember that you are working in collaboration, you are not educating, you are not helping them, you are not saving them, you are working together. Both parties have a lot to learn from each other.

And a young Lebanese woman explains it this way:

> I talk about it a lot. I find that I am put in a position to defend the region sometimes, here in the States when people assume that we are backwards and oppressive. Sure, amongst ourselves I don't disagree with that, but if anyone from the outside tries to insult us, I put them in their place. Anyway, look at what is happening to women in the US. I don't see equality here either.

Despite the absence of equality everywhere, Dr. Stephan shares this powerful call to galvanize the diaspora:

> Arab women in the diaspora can do several things to advance women's rights in the region. First and foremost, they can celebrate the diversity of their ethno-sectarian and regional identities as a symbol of power. Instead, today they are divided across religious affiliations and ethnic identities. Next, diaspora feminists work in silos, across sectors and national boundaries. Canadian feminists rarely collaborate with Americans, and feminist scholars are not connected with practitioners. Thus, they can push beyond their comfort levels, national boundaries, and professional circles to achieve global credibility, which they can later leverage to elevate and amplify the voices of Arab women from the region.

The Future Is…. Preparing for the Long Fight

It is true that the road is still too long.
—Young activist

Diana Moukalled reminds us that "there's a long road to go and it's a serious challenge." But she sees space for hope. She continues:

> We need to build and invest in the political movements and the rights movements that are here already in the region. I believe in the voice of this civil society. And we're here to stay, we're not leaving.

No, we are not leaving. *But are we moving fast enough?* A common refrain throughout this book has been that we need time. Changes we seek will not come quickly, and if they do, they have failed to penetrate the surface. Those we spoke to shared caution when it came to optimism. Their hopes were for the future, for the next generation, perhaps not in our lifetime.

Randa Siniora of Palestine shares her hopes for "a more just society with equality, with respect to our rights, our dignity." She went on to say that "it might not be happening in my age," but adds this: "I really think that perhaps our daughters and our sons would have a better future."

Alexander Nehme of Arab.org,[53] a platform for social good, shares his view:

I look after platforms that are at the heart of MENA civil society and also identify new channels of empowering giving by people and organizations to do good. Our region is synonymous for its legendary hospitality and its giving charitable mentality. But—as hospitable and giving as the people of this region are, the region remains somewhat fearful of change and therefore resist any deviation of ancient teachings, learnings and norms. Such timeless values may need to be revisited and I think it's all waiting for the right circumstances and alignment to give birth to a real renaissance of sorts. For women's rights causes in particular, clearly something is missing or we wouldn't be having this conversation. I think as long as there is a problem such as unfairness and injustice, then there will always be hills to overcome. But the key question is: on what timeline? For one thing, women's rights go hand-in-hand with human rights so, depending from where and how you're looking at it, it may take years or generations but the momentum is surely there, embedded and engraved in people's minds just waiting to manifest itself. But, what's holding us back? Customs and traditions perhaps? Or maybe superstitions and fear of modern clandestine ideas? What's for sure is the lack of understanding of the modern role of men and women and their part in the households and societies of today with their respective challenges in ever changing dynamics. Without a doubt, we need better education that includes in its curriculum: rights—human rights specifically—as well as humanity's constant thirst for freedom and knowledge. And to put it simply, at the end of the day, anyone is free to make or not to make sandwiches.

What is the future of Arab feminisms, we asked. *What hopes do you have? Where do we go from here? What is holding us back?* Myriam Sfeir reminds us that "we need to be more united in terms of our asks, and we need to be more intersectional in terms of our demands." Fatima Al Mokaddem, a young Lebanese woman, expresses the frustrations of many:

I am going to be quite frank about this one. Though this might sound cynical, I do not hold much hope for feminism in the Arab world for many reasons. First of all, the culture in the Arab world is not a culture that advocates for gender equality. I cannot generalize (Tunisia, for example, has made huge progress with regards to women's rights and female representation in political positions) but Arab societies are still characterized by a heteronormative way of thinking. Second, women are still seen as inferior to men because "they are born this way." Gender is viewed as something that is inherited rather than performed. Another major reason is that any form of change that is directed towards women's rights is seen as deviating from Eastern traditions and Islamic laws (despite the presence of Christians in many Arab countries, the dominant religion is Islam). Third, women are extremely sexualized and shamed. Fourth, many laws that violate international agreements (CEDAW for example) still exist such as the presence of laws that criminalize abortion. Not to mention that women's involvement in the labor market is generally low and there exists a large gender pay gap (many women who are employed work in jobs that are considered to be "feminine"). However, I cannot project a universalizing view because the women of the Arab world have diverse social identities. In short, the culture, the politics, and religion present large obstacles towards achieving gender equality in the Arab world.

Surely there's reason to be cynical. But the majority of those we spoke to—particularly young activists—felt that yes, there *is* change. But, they add, "we won't see it in our lifetime."

How to bring changes to fruition in our lifetimes? Young activists, and in fact *all* activists, say that they remain committed to doing whatever is within their power to bring about the changes they demand—whether for this generation or the next.

Tamtam of Saudi Arabia explains that she is "happy with the changes that are happening." She tells the story of how she responded to someone who accused her of being overly positive. "Nothing's ever going to change, she told me. Nothing's gonna change."

Tamtam shares her response:

> I think positive people like me are going to change it. And I think it is going to change. And I believe in it. Maybe it's gonna take 10 years, I don't know how long it's gonna take, but it's gonna change sooner than you think.

Changes are already underway in Saudi Arabia, she explains. "Honestly, everyone is shocked by what's happening and what's been happening. It's amazing." Tamtam goes on to say this:

> My hope is to keep these changes, these shifts, happening slowly. I think slow is okay, we don't have to rush. I mean, it's already rushed, things were changed really fast. And that's great. Now for people to adapt. It's okay that it's slow. I'd rather be slow and steady and in the right direction, than things going too quickly.

She adds that she hopes "people just have an open mind." This applies at home as well as in social institutions that mold beliefs and behaviors:

> I hope that schools encourage curiosity. I hope that they teach them about other religions and other people. I think that's going to change a lot of things. And even if schools don't do that, it's okay. I hope that the youth are going to do that. I know they're already doing that. They're already talking and they're already having those conversations. That's my hope.

Mediation Advisor Karma Ekmekji put it this way:

> You're writing a book looking at 50 years of Arab feminism. That's what we should do— take the long view. 50 years. Where were we back then? Was it better? Of course not. It was crappy. And now? Is it better? Marginally. It is still crappy—but maybe less crappy? You ask if I have hope. Yes. I have no choice but to have hope. I always lean positive. What choice do we have? Hope is a choice. I will continue to fight for hope, because without it we have nothing. If I didn't have hope, I couldn't do this work. I myself search for inspiration every day to be able to continue in this field of conflict resolution. At times I am drained. How can I give the younger generation hope? Who's giving me hope? We move so slow. My students ask me if I have hope. Well I tell them it depends on what our timeframe for hope is. Is it selfish of us to expect immediate change, instant gratification, satisfaction in our lifetime? I struggle with this a lot. I look at the next generation. I look at my children. I'm doing it for them, not for me. Social change takes time. We live in an age of speed. We hit the refresh button over and over, expecting something new, change. But change takes time, especially social change. As a first step, we must accept and acknowledge that the impact we are trying to make, the change we are working so hard to achieve, we may not witness in our lifetime. But we should also firmly believe that the change that will come will not be possible without the work, the advocacy, the mobilization we are doing today. Think of it 50 years from now. What will we say about today, about our rights, about our fight? You want to be a feminist? An activist? An advocate for equality?

Well, this is long term. Be patient, it's going to take a while. Feminist aims take generations to achieve. But what effort is more deserving of the fight? None but this.[54]

So What? Now What?!

The Arab world demands a reassessment of what feminist revolutions can do.
—Xena Amro

Every single person we consulted for this book was asked the same question: *What is your hope for the future?* Their voices are the ones that bring us hope. Hope is fundamental—the belief in a better future propels us to continuously and tirelessly fight for greater rights and freedoms. Despite great challenges and impossible conditions, people managed to believe in a better future.

But what happens when hope cannot be sustained? How, then, do you reclaim hope? And more importantly, *how do you build a movement from that hope when it wanes with every setback?*

Elie Youssef explains that what he really hopes for "is that we stop talking about feminism, stop talking about gender-based violence, stop talking about racism because as long as we're talking about it, it means it's still there."

He hopes for a future where we don't need to have conversations about feminism, because it is "just life … equality, no one is marginalized, no second class citizens." A young Palestinian-Kuwaiti echoes this, hoping that one day it might be "alien to imagine a world with such drastic inequality."

Are you hopeful? we ask.

Yes and no, many answer. Change is happening, many say. More change is possible, many agree. But too often that change is hard to see.

Anthony Keedi ends on a more hopeful note. The women's movement is so brave, he celebrates, "and I think these days are showing the strength of the women's movement and its sustainability." He continues to explain that "it's not that I believe that *The Future is Female* is just a slogan. It's not just about putting women in [leadership] positions that will solve the problem. It is *feminist* leadership that will solve the problem."

When asked about the future of Arab feminisms, Dr. Rita Stephan summarizes it this way:

> The future of Arab feminisms is its plurality. Embracing gender equity, sexual rights, and intersectionality are three critical points that we must embrace and advance widely. Arab feminists must focus on working within systems, increasing their visibility in public spaces, and support the next generation as they make their own claims using their own voices. Finally, the future of Arab feminisms must be crafted within a global context reaching out East and West, North and South, regardless of colonial heritage and current politics.

Ultimately, feminist movements *are* our hope. Even if they look different, this plurality is ok—as long as we remain connected in our shared goal for equality, and freedom.

Dr. Gabriella Nassif explains that "there does not need to be a consensus to build a movement." She reminds us that movements are built on plurality, on setting goals, on "clearly identifying where we want to go broadly in the future, but also leaving room and space for different opinions and different attitudes."

"By definition a movement cannot stand still," Somali feminist activist and political strategist Hibaaq Osman articulates, "it has to be renewed ... durable ... inclusive ... truly representative."[55] And sometimes, it is moving in the small spaces. Feminist movements cannot only be measured through public proclamations and leadership but also through "the actual experiences and dynamics of activism undertaken by women to gain social and political recognition, both in formal and informal politics"[56] In other words, activism at every level.

In Chapter 5 we said that sisterhood might not be global, but that does not mean we should not at least try—we are stronger together and should aim to build systems of solidarity. Women need to coordinate and collaborate. Without this, our movement will not move. Ultimately, we need more women supporting women, especially the younger generations. As Egyptian artist Dr. Bahia Shehab says:

> Women for women, there's no other way. We have to be there for each other. We have to be the backbone that we never had. So if you never were supported, find a younger woman, support her. Be for others what you did not have. It's a lot of work. We still have a lot of work. It's a lifelong process.

One young Palestinian woman speaks powerfully and eloquently about her hopes for the region:

> My hope is that Arab women will continue to fight for their rights, all their rights, in a way that does not bring them personal harm. I understand that is a difficult task. My hope is to see more Arab women in office, as real change will never happen without policy change. My hope is to see Arab women with the same job, educational, and other opportunities that men are offered. My hope is to see Arab women have a voice that is not silenced by the patriarchy that surrounds them at every turn. My hope is that Arab women living in diaspora, like me, will fight for the rights of women living back home, because their rights matter just as much as ours. I hope that Arab men who have outdated ideas about a woman's place in this world will open their eyes and see that women are their equals and should be treated as such. I hope that Arab men fight for Arab women to hold office, and for discriminatory laws against women to change. I have many hopes for the future of Arab feminism.

Indeed, building feminist futures is an exercise of effort and imagination—sweat and hope—in equal measure. The precarious balance of hope and fear, joy and frustration is a tension felt by so many in the region.

But how to expedite hope? Feminist Mona Eltahawy says that every day she wakes up and thinks "today's the day I will destroy the patriarchy." She explains that her feminism is "not a T-shirt, it's not a 9 to 5 job. Feminism for me is every day. It's my existence."[57] She holds onto the belief that she will dismantle the patriarchy, but also that it probably will not happen in her lifetime.

"That's what we need going forward," Dr. Nassif concludes. "Oh, yeah, and also, we need to burn it all down."

True Lebanese Feminist, Xena Amro, gives us these closing words:

> The Arab world demands a reassessment of what feminist revolutions can do. Emphasizing the overwhelming number of problems can be disorienting, and it continues to discourage us from the fight that we do not know how to begin, find its middle, or anticipate its end. Rather than observing all issues at once, let us focus our energies on one problem at a time, starting with the painful truth that domestic violence persists without consequences. We must unite and shelter women regardless of their feminist lineages. There can be no revolution if we do

not guarantee the safety of every woman who will join us on the streets. We need to prioritize our battles. We can no longer listen to the repetitive narrative that excuses men for the violence they enact on women. We have had enough time to discuss; we must now act. It starts in a neighborhood and stretches to other neighborhoods. It starts with one woman's cruel fate for other women to realize their moral obligation to fight, fight, fight. The Arab world has been waiting impatiently, eager for destruction. Let us destroy.[58]

Conclusion

So What? Now What?!

I support the uprising of women in the Arab world because the liberation of women will liberate society.
—Feminist activist[1]

This undertaking began with an inquiry: *What are Arab feminisms?* We returned to this question again and again.

And building from that: *What has been its role?*

Qatari academic Dr. Kaltham al-Ghanim suggests that we "…ask ourselves about the role of Arab feminism in offering Arab women an alternative to their present reality. Has it contributed to raising Arab women's awareness of their rights and importance?"[2] We believe that it has—in all of its manifestations. And we believe that feminism belongs to the region as much as it belongs to any other. Feminism belongs to everyone. Dr. Alanoud Alsharekh reminds us that "because feminism is a global movement, wherever you live in the world, you can be influenced by what's happening."[3]

At the same time, there might well be a new—or renewed—Pan-Arab Feminism taking hold in the region. In the Preface, we began with Maria Najjar's call to revive Pan-Arabism in feminist activism, defining Pan-Arab Feminism as a movement "characterized by difference whilst united in a goal of dismantling patriarchal structures of oppression and exploitation."[4] This notion is built on collaboration and common goal-setting for solidarity and accountability. This framework anchors social justice and intersectionality, and is not about denying our differences and diversities, but rather working with them as a source of strength. Collaboration, we have articulated, is our best way forward for a feminist future.

Concretely, what do we need to succeed?

Emirati academic Dr. Suad Zayed al-Oraimi lists several ingredients: a strong base of support; a political and economic revival that puts an end to dependency and subordination; an intellectual widening; an ability to meet basic needs in order to be able to focus on strategic goals; a recognition that there is no single Arab nation and no single Arab feminism; and stronger agreement among women. In short: a feminist consciousness.[5]

And: feminist action.

Dr. al-Oraimi asserts that "Arab feminism today needs a popular *intifada* (uprising); no feminist thought can develop and prosper if it does not have a strong base of support."[6]

And a strong base of support is built from having a clear opponent: patriarchy.

Scholar Dr. Suad Joseph explains that "the continuities of patriarchal structures, modes of operation, and idioms of discourse in different social spheres are expressions of the power of patriarchy in Arab states."[7]

Clearly, patriarchy continues to thrive—everywhere.

To counter this formidable opponent, we hope, along with Palestinian scholar Jean Said Makdisi, for "a wise, brave, clear-sighted, imaginative kind of feminism that can overcome the problems and proclaim itself fearlessly."[8]

Our **Feminist Foundations** showed us that social indicators are not on our side, and our journey for equality—at least on paper—will be a long one. We explored progress and regress both within the region and on the international stage across thematic areas—health, education, economics, politics, legislation, and violence. We posited explanations as to why the region still lags behind, and posed key questions that were explored throughout the book. The questions emerged from research, experience, and our curiosities—and the answers emerged from the voices in this book.

Is there a genuine Arab feminist movement? the book *Arab Feminisms: Gender and Equality in the Middle East* asks. *Is it genuine?* Yes—without a doubt. *Is it singular?* No. The region and the movement are not monoliths. The book elaborates:

> There are different kinds and degrees of Arab feminisms, each with its own set of issues and questions.... The concerns and problems of Arab women in their various regions, the various political systems under which they live and work, and their various cultural histories, are translated into theoretical questions, as they have been far more obviously and publicly translated into an active women's movement.[9]

Feminist activist scholar Dr. Charlotte Karam puts it perfectly:

> So is there such a thing as an Arab feminism? I think as in any place, any time, there are multiple feminisms. I don't think that there's one type of feminism in the Arab world that can carry the banner of Arab feminism on its own. It's too complex and there's too many important voices. And the dissonance or the tensions between those voices and what emerges in terms of irreconcilable differences or hot points are in and of themselves feminists messages, it's just too complex. And so I would say, there are many, many, many Arab feminisms, and not just one.

Ultimately, "there is no single, all-encompassing form of Arab feminism—just as there is no such single form anywhere else in the world."[10] We endeavored to recognize this difference with all its challenges—and strengths. Contexts vary, but patriarchy underpins all. Academic and activist Maria Najjar summarizes it clearly: "We can acknowledge our diversity while also maintaining our 'common ideological opponent'—patriarchy."[11] This sentiment drove our efforts.

The **Feminist Phases** oriented us and offered a historical foundation on which we might build our future feminisms. We cannot know where we are going, after all, if we do not know where we have been. This chapter served, in many respects, as a review of literature, events, and research from the last 50 years. It was not meant to be exhaustive, rather it provides a snapshot and context upon which we might build.

Khamis and Mili, in *Arab Women's Activism and Socio-Political Transformation: Unfinished Gendered Revolutions,* see three stages of Arab feminism(s): post–World War II feminism, top-down state feminism, and Arab Spring feminism.[12] We saw more, and named them *Reawakening, Galvanizing, Agitating, Regressing, Collaborating.*

Our investigation prompted us to ask: *What phase will come next?* Collaborating is our hope. And yet it is too early to tell.

Our vision of collaboration is in line with Palestinian scholar Jean Said Makdisi:

> I in no way mean to imply by what I have said that there are no courageous Arab feminists or bold Arab feminist writings. There are many. But we need more, and we need them to coordinate—not necessarily to agree with each other's definitions, visions, aims and strategies, but at least not to work against each other, or to sabotage each other's efforts, but to coordinate so as to form what we can call a feminist movement—and we need to disseminate this bold feminism through the women's movement that is so active on the ground in order to reach the women who are most in need of support.[13]

Director of the Asfari Institute for Civil Society and Citizenship at the American University of Beirut Dr. Lina Abou-Habib adds to this, speaking of "a feminist co-creation process that is distinct from business as usual. Within such a project, individuals and structures in power would no longer be able to co-opt spaces, voices, and resources, or ensure that the status quo remains unscathed."[14] This collaboration and co-creation is more challenging—and more urgent—in the context of conflict, crises, and insecurities.

We then explored **Feminisms on the Frontlines of Crisis**—because our feminist history is both intertwined with conflict and is a history of conflict. And, in studying conflict, we also learn about resistance. Resistance not only in public movements, but also in private spaces. Resistance in the face of significant restriction—and backlash.

While there have been other waves, we use our so-called Arab Spring as evidence in our recent history. This experience was also pivotal for women in the region, igniting the next phase of their activism.[15] In understanding the impact of the Arab Spring on feminist movements, Dr. Sahar Khamis refers to two camps—optimists and those who are less optimistic. The optimists believe that Arab women's resilience and determination will ward off any potential backlash against women's rights.[16] The optimists comprise the younger generation, who see women's rights as only one component of broader human rights. The other camp—the less optimistic—see women's rights as distinct from other issues. This camp—the older generation—believe that women's rights should be highlighted and fought for. This book shows evidence of both.

At the same time, conflict brings opportunity. Feminist activist and journalist Nay El Rahi tells us that the dire situation "proves the validity of some of the drastic changes that feminists have long asked for." And while the road is long and the goals appear distant, she feels that "this is the change in discourse that is happening, albeit painfully slowly."[17] The change is happening, feminist activist and academic Dr. Carmen Geha asserts:

> This time, our private political actions are revolutionary. The mere fact of marching down the streets with banners making feminist demands makes our personal choice to engage with politics revolutionary. The idea that the new political system must espouse gender equality is born out of our conviction that we have a personal duty to shape the trajectory of the revolution. Our visualization of the current system as a gender apartheid means that this revolution can only succeed to the extent that it is revolutionary enough to enable women to sit at the table and decide about the future. The revolution falters if we go back to a version of NGOization and state feminism that blames women for the system's long-standing discrimination.[18]

Dr. Geha refers to Lebanon, but she could be talking about any place, any Arab country—in fact, any country at all.

Looking at the Arab region from the outside, the world only now sees women in the region as having greater agency and exercising their right to resist. Meanwhile, it had been there all along. They did not need to be "taught" this. They did not need to be "saved." They rose up, and resisted. As they have done before. And, as they continue to do—in many forms.

From the frontlines of crisis, we journeyed to **Feminisms on the Frontlines of Creativity**, meeting a range of artists engaged in civil resistance. Through art, literature, film, music, street art, and more, artist-activists constantly push boundaries, spread messages, and ignite movements. Activism is not limited to demonstrations or street protests. Resistance is powerful—and durable—when it "get[s] to the heart, not just the head."[19]

Historian Dr. Margot Badran explains that expression exists more than ever in the arts, and "in seeing this we understand what they are living and aspiring for."[20] Indeed, art is resistance, and also hope. It shows us what is not working—and invites us to imagine how it might work instead.

"We don't think of ourselves as activists or as feminists when we wake up in the morning," the Keserwany sisters explain. "We don't start our day thinking we want to change the world. But we have things to say, and we want our voices to be heard."[21]

The following chapter brought us the voices and experiences of over 200 people who guided us in identifying the fissures and challenges within women's movements and locally, nationally, and regionally. Learning about our **Fragmented Feminisms** helps us understand where the disconnects are—and where the (re)connects must be built.

In the words of gender historian Dr. Joan W. Scott, good things can come from difference and disconnect:

> The reassuring thing in this moment of high tension is that, historically, feminists have been extremely adept at addressing the problem of difference; not by solving it, but by working with it, by making it a critical tool of the theory we practice.[22]

Dr. Karam explores what is stopping us from having a unified movement:

> Our embodied experience of the world and the differences between us, between different communities, our starting points and embodied experiences and the ways in which we understand the world and the ways in which we study the world and the ways in which we live in the world, require political avenues that are different for change. Yes, there's a basic message and a basic agenda and a basic Northern Star for feminism. But I think the complexity of the lived experience in Baghdad versus Kurdistan, or in Beirut versus Akkar, or in Haifa versus Jerusalem, is too complex and too tied within the system. That's really what's stopping us from having a homogenous movement.

Harnessing difference could be key to enhancing collaboration, despite the challenges. At the same time, the environment continues to thwart feminist movements. Movements are stifled when civil society is restricted—and constantly under threat. Movements are stifled when gains are precarious—and frequently undone. We risk reversals at every turn, as we have seen all over the world. Women's rights are not on solid ground—and feminist movements risk being undone.

The story of the region seems to be one of "yes, but…."

Yes there's feminism, but….

Yes there's progress, but….

Yes there's hope, but….

In short, there is always a caveat. So, *where do we go from here?*

Finally, we focus on our **Feminist Futures**. Here too, we allow the voices and experiences of activists and feminists—particularly young feminists—to guide us. Their voices are the greatest authority. Research tells us that "little is known about how ordinary Arab women have experienced the changes...."[23] We set out to do precisely this.

Diana Moukalled, Lebanese journalist and co-founder of Daraj Media, reminds us that "the feminist movement is more loud and more confident. More assured. And it's there to stay. Again the road is not easy, but we see good movement happening."[24] This echoes the sentiment of the young Lebanese activist who wants feminism to be "a matter of *fact*, and not a matter of *fight*."

Yes, we say, feminism *should* be matter of fact—but we also need to prepare ourselves for the fight.

We believe, in line with Somali activist Hibaaq Osman, that "the biggest resources women have is themselves."[25] And we hope, in line with a young Bahraini activist, that women in the region will have "the freedom of choice ... knowing they'd be safe to make those choices."

What might we now say that has not already been better said by the voices who animate this book? It is in these voices that the future of feminism in the Arab region is (re) imagined.

Feminist futures are both grassroots and government, online and offline, before/during/after our so-called Spring. It must be possible to go wide *and* to aim high, to build a support base with every-woman and to ensure political will with policymakers.

Ultimately, feminist movements are built on—and from—the lives of real women, real people, who advocate for rights, equality, justice, and dignity. And they are the ones who can bring about change in their own lives. Part of this starts from within.

Founder of women's platform *Bayneh W Baynek* Rana Alamuddin shares this personal piece about her own feminism from within:

My perspective on Arab feminism is intuitive. I find myself not needing to use the word because I feel it's something that I just embody. By embodying who we are as women and being the type of women we want to be—that is the greatest display of Arab feminism. I think what's missing is embodied women. Are women really owning their choices? Doing their inner work really boldly? Listening to their inner voice really boldly? Making decisions based on that intuition and on that bold vision of who they want to be, and leading by example? Yes we're all angry, each one in her own way, for the injustices and the oppression, the ancestral generational historic abuse that we've been through as women collectively and individually. But to me, every day is an opportunity for us to reinvent ourselves in our feminine identity. It's the journey of introspection that is more exciting than the journey of anger. What hasn't worked is the type of feminism that says that we are strong all the time. I think that that's almost as bad as the historic notion that we're weak as women. We've been taught, we've been conditioned, to see ourselves as women as either weak, or the opposite spectrum to say, we're so strong, we're not weak. We're strong. And I think that we've been denied the initiation to our true nature as women, our natural design, which has to be multifaceted. We get to truly co-create our femininity, which is such a privilege. We embody a spectrum of femininity from self-confidence to self-doubt, from courage to anxiety, from glories to defeats, from breakthroughs to breakdowns—we get to wear each one of them as a badge of honor. And that is the hardest thing about being a woman—really being able to accept the spectrum.

And that every nuance in the spectrum is just as powerful. Feminism that is also embodied will help the other facets of feminism—the intellectual, the research, the structured. We need women who are embodied, who are happy, who are comfortable in their skin, who are living their lives, who are not trying to explain too much or justify too much. There's infinite ways of being a woman, and there's also infinite ways of being feminist. And I think that once that is done, women are unstoppable. Because you can't box anybody, you can't label anybody. It becomes way too much power to control. But I think that no matter how strong of a feminist you are, and how accomplished and well read and outspoken and well-spoken, I think that all of us, as long as we have deep guilt and shame, we will always be held back as women in our power and our beauty, in living our full potential. I feel that self-forgiveness is a huge one because sometimes our anger as feminists is more directed at ourselves than at others or the system. I'll speak for myself—that was my own experience. Oftentimes I found myself having this unbearable anger towards people, mostly men in the system. And I realized that my anger was actually more directed towards myself—for betraying myself. I was angry and resentful and deeply ashamed of myself, either for things that I thought I had done, that I was shamed for in society or just anger because I hadn't stood up for myself or showed up for myself or defended myself or protected myself. So I think that once we forgive ourselves, it's a game-changer. I really see this as a shifting or a reframing of our mindset, every woman taking charge of her own life and not waiting for anyone. She's not waiting to forgive anyone on the outside or waiting for anyone to forgive her. Not a mother or a father, not an ex, not a man, not a woman, not an institution, not a system, not a society. She's taking charge of her own liberation. And what's beautiful is it's completely self-generated and self-controlled, which is an immense act of power.

Now What … Rebecca

Throughout the process of researching and writing this book, and from my experiences in the region, certain themes kept appearing again and again such as rebirth, regrowth, resilience—and they gave me pause.

Admittedly, I have a love-hate attitude towards these words.

While supposed to evoke a sense of strength in overcoming great obstacles, they implicitly infer that something was taken away or lost, that something has to be gained back. Nobody should *have* to be resilient. Nobody should *have* to recover and rebuild—whether that is from rights being stripped away, unimaginable atrocities, or grave injustices; occurrences all too common in this region.

And yet, this book has shown time and again people doing just that. Feminism fueled, in part, by necessity. I started this book hoping to be a vessel for these stories, to open space for necessary conversations, to amplify and applaud, to stand in solidarity and support.

Now I end this book resolute because I also kept coming across resistance, rebellion, and revolution. The region is ignited and is overflowing with passion, determination, creativity, curiosity, and *hope*. Old processes and systems are being challenged and torn down. In balancing anger with kindness, righteous rage is being channeled nonviolently to seek the change needed.

So yes the region is rebuilding—but reimagined.

And reimagined through an intersectional *feminist* lens. As we have repeated throughout, peace and feminism are synonymous so yes, the future absolutely must be feminist.

And that future is in good hands with the next generation.

Give it to them.

Now What ... Lina

This book began with a question: *What is going on here?*

Here's what I was seeing: young people, new ways of acting and organizing and being—new angers and new energies. I saw activism that looked less formal, more fluid, less rigid, more horizontal, less organized, more responsive, less issues-based, more inclusive.

Is this a movement? And how does it move?!

Instead of asking *myself* these questions, we asked young people these questions—and this book is their answers.

This book has started (and stopped) a million times, because I could not let it go—I wanted to know! And just like the young feminist movements themselves, the process has been extremely fluid. It is as chaotic as young people on the street, out there demanding change!

I love their anger, because I feel it too. The world seems like it's spinning in the wrong direction. Patriarchy is as strong as ever. Conflicts continue. Conservative movements gain strength. Development is not really ... developing. And feminism was starting to feel feeble. Depoliticized. I think this young anger and energy is just what the movement has been waiting for.

And in the Arab region, peace is elusive—at least for women. Meanwhile, women's rights are sidelined and sideswiped, relegated to a mythical land called "Later." While we linger in Later, we are slapped with a backlash against our own rights and freedoms. Not just the Arab region—EVERYWHERE.

At the same time, here are the boundary-pushers, the disruptive-mobilizers. They are building a new activist infrastructure. They are ... resisting.

So where does the region go from here? Will these moments become movements, as we've asked? Will these movements connect with each other? Will they connect with the world?!

To me, feminist activism needs three things: fuel, fire, focus. We—the collective—are the fuel. We are the tribe. Feminists who believe in equality. Who fight the patriarchy. Who are simply sick of all this crap!

The fire is the feminist foundation on which we stand, the beliefs we all hold, the foremothers who paved the way for us. It is our struggle against systems—not people. Against injustice—not individuals. It is our righteous rage, the rage that gives us courage, the courage that is contagious. And because, for so many of us, this fight is personal—that's what makes the fire spread!

And then our focus—our shared direction. It's in the pressure points, where we invest our energy, how we disrupt, what strategies we use, how we go bigger—even as spaces grow smaller.

We need to start where we stand, to pull together our fire, fuel, focus—and fight. And I want us to win this thing.

YALLA.

Now What?!

Khamis and Mili write of "unfinished revolutions."[26] This book hopes to add one piece to the story of our unfinished revolution. *What are Arab feminisms if not an evolving story?* A story of history and political and social contexts. A story that is by no means complete. This story continues to unfold and will take whatever shape Arab feminists determine. It was not born with the so-called Arab Spring—and it certainly did not die when the Spring died.

Arab feminisms create room for all of us—from the 22 Arab states and the diaspora, from religious or secular backgrounds, from activists to artists to academics. Their identities are different. Their realities are different. Their issues and concerns are often different. The forms they take can be different. The tools of their resistance are different. But they share one thing: they resist.

They resist because this revolution is unfinished.

The question is: *What will they do now?*

Rather: *What will we do now?* After all, this resistance is collective.

This is our conclusion—the final *so what?* And yet, it leaves the *now what?!* open. Now… *what?* There are so many directions this book can continue to take. It is one part of a very long story—one that, in our opinion, has many chapters yet to be written. Women are writing their own chapter, dictating the direction of feminisms in the region.

We look forward to what the next book will hold…

Afterword

BY AYA CHEBBI

At nine years old I was cornered in a cemetery and abused, put through *"Tasfih,"* a ritual that claims to protect my virginity.[1]

I went on to university, I was touched in public transport, harassed online and bullied.

I went on to protest in uprisings, I was beaten, humiliated and arrested by hostile police brutality for speaking up and knowing my rights. In fact, the darkest truth about being female is that it is always the people who are supposed to protect you who end up abusing you.

My story is like many in this book, it's about *fighting*! So I turned into a rebel in my family and my village. I found power in my voice and stood up to *fight* patriarchy.

I have become angry and fearless.

Lucky for me, I had a feminist father who was there to take the punch for me and had my back.

Why am I who I am? Why do we risk our lives?

Why do we wake up every day to continue the struggle?

It is about female liberation, and it's worth it.

We're not asking for favors—it's our right, it's my generation's mission.

We have been protesting this past decade starting from my country Tunisia back in 2011 with a simple slogan "Jobs, Freedom, Dignity." We protested because the future our leaders are talking about is related to monetary value but the future we need has to be about freedom.

The freedom as a girl to be safe, to make choices, to have access to reproductive and sexual health, to have education, to unlock financial freedom, to just be, to become and to belong as an equal human being. That is my feminism.

Liberation is personal and collective, and in Kimberlé's words—*intersectional*.[2]

We are a new wave of feminists in the region, some call us "Fourth-wave feminism." We are intersectional because *my liberation is your liberation*. I cannot fight for equality without jobs with dignity, or fight the pandemic without social justice.

Revolutions happen when we have no choice but to *fight*! What would be the alternative? It is the *state of waithood*, waiting for representation, for leadership, for rights, for change. I was not one to wait. My generation deserved better than endless waiting. We were going to make the change happen ourselves. We cannot continue to rely on the neo-liberal, neo-colonial patriarchal systems. When systems don't work anymore, we must change them.

And yes, let's recognize that women of all generations, especially young women like me have been at the frontline of these movements, unafraid to die for freedom. I am the daughter of women warriors, thinkers, scientists, queens, and governors outlined in this book over the span of five decades. In Dr. Nawal El Saadawi's words, "you cannot have a revolution without women."

Our revolution lit the flame—and the region was alive. The most empowering landscape the revolution provided is that *your voice matters*; that every voice in the movement is a political voice, that being a feminist is being an everyday activist.

Your voice matters especially that we turned social media into a tool for social change and we drastically shaped the face of journalism and youth activism.

I was not just blogging or protesting, but participating. Not just participating, but organizing. Not just organizing, but leading. We must stop blaming systems of oppression and actually take responsibility for our future.

In fact, we are the youngest generation in human history, which means we have some superpowers: the demographic power, the voting power, the mobilization power, and the innovation power. We take to the streets when no one listens because our struggle is a struggle for voice. My generation is simply calling for intergenerational co-leadership. We don't want a torch passed to us, we want to co-lead now.

It is exhausting to fight! It's suffocating to be silenced! It's disheartening to be excluded from leadership seats we deserve.

But against all odds, we rise, we occupy.

People might not be ready to accept young women leaders. But I believe in myself and the young women leaders of Nala Feminist Collective (Nalafem) who are shaking things up in the corridors of power.[3]

Female solidarity is both possible and powerful. In fact, radical.

We may have our differences but we need our solidarity in the feminist movement across ages. We can stop arguing about the obvious and start making an endless impact.

This revolution demands all of us. This fourth-wave feminism must be intersectional and multigenerational. We must all find our calling. That's when we find who we are, and what we are capable of. We find our power.

I have said before and I will say again, again, again: Your power is your radical self.

Fight! But don't fight back or fight against. Fight *for*.

Fight for liberation.

Aya Chebbi is an award-winning pan–African feminist. She gained popularity as a prominent political blogger during the 2010/11 Tunisian Revolution. Chebbi served as the first ever African Union Special Envoy on Youth and is a founder of the Nala Feminist Collective. She was named in Forbes' *Africa's 50 Most Powerful Women as well as in the* New African Magazine *List of 100 Most Influential Africans.*

Glossary

Adhan—Muslim call to prayer

Al Raida—Academic journal meaning "The Female Pioneer" produced by the Arab Institute for Women

Al-Thawra untha—The Revolution is Female

Ayb—Shame

Ba'athist—An Arab nationalist ideology that resists colonialism and promotes pan-Arab socialism

Diya—Blood money

Fatwa—A ruling handed down by authorities based on religious interpretations

Hajj—Islamic pilgrimage to the holy city of Mecca that Muslims must make at least once

Haram—Any action or practice that is forbidden by Islamic law

Hijab—A veil that covers the head and hair

Intifada—Uprising

Kafala—A system that allows individuals or companies to sponsor visas for migrant workers

Kefaya—Egyptian movement for workers' rights, literally means "Enough"

Mahr—Dowry

Mahram—Male guardian

Mosque—Muslim house of prayer

Moudawana—Morocco's family code

Musawah—Equality

Niqab—A veil that covers the face

Sharia—Islamic legal system based on the Qur'an

Shia—A major branch of Islam

Shisha—A water pipe used for smoking tobacco

Sunni—A branch of Islam comprising the majority of Muslims

Tasfih—A practice in Tunisia, Algeria, and Morocco performed on young girls with the intention of discouraging pre-marital sex and maintaining "purity"

Wahhabism—A Sunni fundamentalist movement, the foundational doctrine of Saudi Arabia

Wali—Male guardian

Chapter Notes

Acknowledgments

1. Hatem, Mervat. "What Do Women Want? A Critical Mapping of Future Directions for Arab Feminisms." *Contemporary Arab Affairs* 6, no. 1 (2013): 91–101, 11. https://www.jstor.org/stable/48600672.

Preface

1. Mona Eltahawy, *Headscarves and Hymens* (New York: Farrar, Straus and Giroux, 2015).

2. Nawaal El Saadawi and Sherif Hetata (Translator), *Woman at Point Zero (Imra'ah 'Inda Nuqtat Al-Sifr)* (1979; repr., London: Zed Books, 2015).

3. Samira Rafidi Meghdessian, *The Status of the Arab Woman* (Greenwood, 1980).

4. Hanan Al-Shaykh, *One Thousand and One Nights* (London: Bloomsbury, 2011), Pg. 190.

5. Khamis, Sahar. "The Arab 'Feminist' Spring?" *Feminist Studies* 37, no. 3 (2011), P. 694. http://www.jstor.org/stable/23069929.

6. Fatima Mernissi, *Scheherazade Goes West: Different Cultures, Different Harems* (New York: Washington Square Press, 2001).

7. SWANA Alliance, "What Is SWANA?," SWANA Alliance, n.d., https://swanaalliance.com/about.

8. Yassine Temlali, "The 'Arab Spring' Rebirth or Final Throes of Pan-Arabism?," *Perspectives, Political Analysis and Commentary from the Middle East*, 2011, 46–49.

9. Maria Najjar, "Reviving Pan-Arabism in Feminist Activism in the Middle East," *Kohl: A Journal for Body and Gender Research* 6, no. 1 (2020): 119–32, https://kohljournal.press/reviving-pan-arabism-feminist.

10. Zeina Zaatari, "From Women's Rights to Feminism: The Urgent Need for an Arab Feminist Renaissance—Zeina Zaatari," in *Arab Feminisms: Gender and Equality in the Middle East*, ed. Jean Said Makdisi, Noha Bayoumi, and Rafif Rida Sidawi (London & New York: I.B. Tauris, 2014), P. 58

11. Salmah Eva-Lina Lawrence, "The Majority World—What's in a Phrase?," Philanthropy Australia, November 4, 2022, https://www.philanthropy.org.au/blog/view/The-Majority-World-whats-in-a-phrase.

12. Dorothy E. McBride and Amy G. Mazur, "Women's Policy Agencies and State Feminism," in *The Oxford Handbook of Gender and Politics*, ed. Georgina Waylen et al. (Oxford University Press, 2013), 654–78, https://doi.org/10.1093/oxfordhb/9780199751457.001.0001.

13. Birte Siim, "Helga Maria Hernes: Welfare State and Woman Power. Essays in State Feminism, Norwegian University Press, Oslo 1987, 176 Pp.," *Scandinavian Political Studies*, no. 3 (January 1, 1988), https://tidsskrift.dk/scandinavian_political_studies/article/view/32609/30667.

14. For more information please see: Sawer, Marian. 1990. *Sisters in suits, women and public policy in Australia.* Sydney: Allen & Unwin.; Eisenstein, Hester. 1996. *Inside agitators: Australian femocrats and the state.* Philadelphia: Temple University Press.; Pringle, Rosemary, and S. Watson. 1992. "Women's interests and the post structuralist state." In M. Barrett and A. Phillips, eds., *Destabilizing theory: Contemporary feminist debates.* Cambridge, UK: Polity Press, 53–73.; Franzway, S., D. Court, and R. W. Connell. 1989. *Staking a claim: Feminism, bureaucracy and the state.* Sydney: Allen & Unwin.

15. Amy G. Mazur and Dorothy E. McBride, "State Feminism," in *Politics, Gender, and Concepts*, ed. Gary Goertz and Amy G. Mazur (Cambridge: Cambridge University Press, 2008), 244–69, https://doi.org/10.1017/cbo9780511755910.011.

16. Dorothy E. McBride and Amy G. Mazur, "Women's Policy Agencies and State Feminism," in *The Oxford Handbook of Gender and Politics*, ed. Georgina Waylen et al. (Oxford University Press, 2013), 654–78, https://doi.org/10.1093/oxfordhb/9780199751457.001.0001.

17. Johanna Kantola and Judith Squires, "From State Feminism to Market Feminism?," *International Political Science Review* 33, no. 4 (April 13, 2012): 382–400, https://doi.org/10.1177/0192512111432513.

18. Renata Pepicelli, "Rethinking Gender in Arab Nationalism: Women and the Politics of Modernity in the Making of Nation-States. Cases from Egypt, Tunisia and Algeria," *Oriente Moderno* 97, no. 1 (2017): 201–19, https://doi.org/10.11 63/221 38617-12 340145.

19. Alanoud Alsharekh quoted in Nada Ghosn,

"Kuwait's Alanoud Alsharekh, Feminist Groundbreaker," The Markaz Review, December 6, 2020, https://themarkaz.org/kukuwaits-alanoud-al-sharekh-feminist-groundbreaker/.

Chapter 1

1. Hatoon Al Fassi, in discussion with the author, online, September 2022.

2. Nawal El Saadawi quoted in Joseph Mayton, "Nawal El Saadawi Interview," Progressive.org, December 12, 2011, https://progressive.org/magazine/nawal-el-saadawi-interview/.

3. Parts of this section were previously published in this article by the author available here: Lina AbiRafeh, "Want to Help the Arab Region? Put It in the Hands of Women.," AP NEWS, January 30, 2021, https://apnews.com/press-release/kisspr/war-and-unrest-sustainable-development-rebellions-and-uprisings-coronavirus-pandemic-environment-97f8a816f0a6ca2c9de6afd1ca698953.

4. Hoda Badran quoted in Claudia Mende, "Egyptian Women's Rights Activist Hoda Badran: Women as Losers of the Revolution?," Qantara.de—Dialogue with the Islamic World, 2012, https://en.qantara.de/content/egyptian-womens-rights-activist-hoda-badran-women-as-losers-of-the-revolution.

5. SIDA, "Multidimensional Poverty Analysis for the Middle East and North Africa" (Swedish International Development Cooperation Agency, 2019), https://cdn.sida.se/app/uploads/2021/08/24151349/MDPA-For-MENA-2019.pdf.

6. Adel Abdellatif and Ellen Hsu, "A Crisis on Top of a Crisis; the Fragility of Arab States," *UNDP* (blog), April 9, 2020, https://www.undp.org/blog/crisis-top-crisis-fragility-arab-states.

7. Yezid Sayigh, "The Crisis of the Arab Nation-State," Carnegie Middle East Center, November 19, 2015, https://carnegie-mec.org/2015/11/19/crisis-of-arab-nation-state-pub-62002.

8. Rosemary Sayigh, "Current Challenges Facing the Arab Women's Movements," *Al-Raida Journal* 20, no. 100 (2003): 49–92, https://doi.org/10.32380/alrj.v0i0.444.

9. Sahar Khamis and Amel Mili, eds., *Arab Women's Activism and Socio-Political Transformation : Unfinished Gendered Revolutions* (USA: Palgrave Macmillan, 2018), Pg. 263.

10. Mahnaz Afkhami, and Lina Abou-Habib, et al. "Equality: It's All in the Family" (*Video*, English). Women's Learning Partnership. https://learningpartnership.org/resource/equality-its-all-family-video-english.

11. UNICEF, "Situational Analysis of Women and Girls in the MENA and Arab Region: A Decade Review 2010–2020" (New York: UNICEF, November 2021)

12. WEF, "Global Gender Gap Report 2022" (Geneva: World Economic Forum, 2022), https://

www.weforum.org/reports/global-gender-gap-report-2022/.

13. 2022 Global Gender Gap Rankings for the MENA region (out of 146 countries): UAE 68, Lebanon 119, Tunisia 120, Jordan 122, Saudi Arabia 127, Egypt 129, Kuwait 130, Bahrain 131, Comoros 134, Morocco 136, Qatar 137, Oman 139, Algeria 140

14. UNDP, "Latest Human Development Composite Indices Tables," hdr.undp.org (UNDP, 2022), https://hdr.undp.org/data-center/documentation-and-downloads.

15. GDI and GII 2021/2022 ranking of Arab states: UAE 26, Bahrain 35, Qatar 42, Kuwait 50, Oman 54, Algeria 91, Egypt 97, Tunisia 97, Jordan 102, Libya 104, Palestine 106, Lebanon 112, Iraq 121, Morocco 123, Saudi Arabia 150, Syria 150, Comoros 156, Mauritania 158, Djibouti 171, Sudan 172,Yemen 183.

16. GIWPS and PRIO, "Women, Peace, and Security Index 2021/22" (Washington D.C.: GIWPS, 2021).

17. Maria Fernanda Espinosa, "Peace Is Synonymous with Women's Rights," UN Chronicle (United Nations, September 21, 2020), https://www.un.org/en/un-chronicle/peace-synonymous-women%E2%80%99s-rights.

18. WPS 2021/22 Arab region rankings: UAE 24, Bahrain 97, Qatar 97, Saudi Arabia 102, Oman 110, Tunisia 117, Kuwait 123, Jordan 127, Lebanon 132, Comoros 135, Egypt 136, Morocco 138, Algeria 141, Libya 150, Djibouti 151, Mauritania 157, Somalia 159, Palestine 160, Sudan 162, Iraq 166, Yemen 168, Syria 169.

19. Fragile States Index, "Global Data | Fragile States Index," fragilestatesindex.org, 2022, https://fragilestatesindex.org/global-data/.

20. Fragile States Index, "Fragile States Index | the Fund for Peace," Fragilestatesindex.org (The Fund for Peace, 2022), https://fragilestatesindex.org/.

21. UNHCR, "Regional Summaries: The Middle East and North Africa" (UNHCR, 2020).

22. Maha Yahya and Marwan Muasher, "Refugee Crises in the Arab World," Carnegie Endowment for International Peace, 2018, https://carnegieendowment.org/2018/10/18/refugee-crises-in-arab-world-pub-77522.; Amnesty International, "The World's Refugees in Numbers," Amnesty.org, 2019, https://www.amnesty.org/en/what-we-do/refugees-asylum-seekers-and-migrants/global-refugee-crisis-statistics-and-facts/.

23. Lina AbiRafeh, "What's Holding Arab Women Back from Achieving Equality?," The Conversation, March 8, 2017, https://theconversation.com/whats-holding-arab-women-back-from-achieving-equality-74221.

24. UNICEF, "Situational Analysis of Women and Girls in the MENA and Arab States Region" (UNICEF Middle East and North Africa, October 2022).

25. UNICEF, "Situational Analysis of Women

and Girls in the MENA and Arab States Region: Pillar 1 Health and Wellbeing" (UNICEF Middle East and North Africa, October 2022).

26. Lina Abou-Habib and Zeina Abdel Khalik, "Sexual and Reproductive Health and Rights in the Arab Region" (Arab States Civil Society Organizations and Feminists Network and UN Women, 2021), https://arabstates.unwomen.org/sites/default/files/Field%20Office%20Arab%20States/Attachments/2021/07/SRHR-Policy%20Paper-EN.pdf.

27. UNICEF, "Situational Analysis of Women and Girls in the MENA and Arab States Region: Pillar 1 Health and Wellbeing" (UNICEF Middle East and North Africa, October 2022).

28. Irene Maffi and Liv Tønnessen, "Editorial the Limits of the Law: Abortion in the Middle East and North Africa," Health and Human Rights Journal, December 9, 2019, https://www.hhrjournal.org/2019/12/editorial-the-limits-of-the-law-abortion-in-the-middle-east-and-north-africa/#_ednref4.

29. UNICEF, "Situational Analysis of Women and Girls in the MENA and Arab States Region: Pillar 1 Health and Wellbeing" (UNICEF Middle East and North Africa, October 2022).

30. UNFPA, "Navigating Comprehensive Sexuality Education in the Arab Region," 2020, https://arabstates.unfpa.org/sites/default/files/pub-pdf/situational_analysis_final_for_web.pdf.

31. Jamila Abuidhail, Sanaa Abujilban, and Lina Mrayan, "Arab Women's Health Care: Issues and Preventive Care," Handbook of Healthcare in the Arab World, 2021, 41–54, https://doi.org/10.1007/978-3-030-36811-1_3.

32. Hala Aldosari, "The Effect of Gender Norms on Women's Health in Saudi Arabia" (Washington, D.C.: The Arab Gulf States Institute in Washington, 2017), https://agsiw.org/wp-content/uploads/2017/05/Aldosari_Womens-Health_Online-1.pdf.

33. United Nations, "Policy Brief: The Impact of COVID-19 on the Arab Region an Opportunity to Build Back Better" (New York: United Nations, July 2020), https://unsdg.un.org/resources/policy-brief-impact-covid-19-arab-region-opportunity-build-back-better.

34. UN Women, "The Impact of COVID-19 on Gender Equality in the Arab Region" (UN Women Arab States, April 2020), https://arabstates.unwomen.org/sites/default/files/Field%20Office%20Arab%20States/Attachments/Publications/2020/04/Impact%20of%20COVID%20on%20gender%20equality%20-%20Policy%20Brief.pdf.

35. FAO, "Near East and North Africa—Regional Overview of Food Security and Nutrition 2021" (Cairo: FAO, 2021), https://doi.org/10.4060/cb7495en.

36. FAO, "Near East and North Africa—Regional Overview of Food Security and Nutrition 2021" (Cairo: FAO, 2021), https://doi.org/10.4060/cb7495en.

37. UNICEF, "Situational Analysis of Women and Girls in the MENA and Arab States Region: Pillar 1 Health and Wellbeing" (UNICEF Middle East and North Africa, October 2022).

38. UNICEF, "Situational Analysis of Women and Girls in the MENA and Arab States Region: Pillar 1 Health and Wellbeing" (UNICEF Middle East and North Africa, October 2022), https://www.unicef.org/mena/media/14321/file/Pillar-1_V2.pdf.pdf

39. EMR Mental Health Collaborators, "The Burden of Mental Disorders in the Eastern Mediterranean Region, 1990–2015: Findings from the Global Burden of Disease 2015 Study," International Journal of Public Health 63, no. S1 (August 3, 2017): 25–37, https://doi.org/10.1007/s00038-017-1006-1.

40. Caroline Freund, "The Surprising Rates of Depression among MENA's Women," World Bank Blogs, March 17, 2013, https://blogs.worldbank.org/arabvoices/surprising-rates-depression-among-mena%E2%80%-99s-women#:~:text=On%20average%2C%20globally%2C%20depression%20ranks.

41. GAGE, "Countries," GAGE, n.d., https://www.gage.odi.org/research/countries/.

42. World Bank, "Literacy Rate, Adult Total (% of People Ages 15 and Above)—Arab World | Data," data.worldbank.org, 2022, https://data.worldbank.org/indicator/SE.ADT.LITR.ZS?locations=1A.

43. Maysa Jalbout, "Unlocking the Potential of Educated Arab Women," Brookings, March 12, 2015, https://www.brookings.edu/blog/education-plus-development/2015/03/12/unlocking-the-potential-of-educated-arab-women/#:~:text=Echoing%20the%20trend%20observed%20globally.

44. Bessma Momani, "Equality and the Economy: Why the Arab World Should Employ More Women" (Washington D.C.: Brookings Doha Center, December 2016).

45. Yara M Asi, "The (Slowly) Changing Gender Dynamics in Arab Countries," Arab Center Washington DC, May 11, 2021, https://arabcenterdc.org/resource/the-slowly-changing-gender-dynamics-in-arab-countries/.

46. UNICEF, "Situational Analysis of Women and Girls in the MENA and Arab Region: A Decade Review 2010–2020" (New York: UNICEF, November 2021), https://www.unicef.org/mena/reports/situational-analysis-women-and-girls-middle-east-and-north-africa.

47. UN Women, "The Impact of COVID-19 on Gender Equality in the Arab Region" (UN Women Arab States, April 2020), https://arabstates.unwomen.org/sites/default/files/Field%20Office%20Arab%20States/Attachments/Publications/2020/04/Impact%20of%20COVID%20on%20gender%20equality%20-%20Policy%20Brief.pdf.

48. UNESCWA and ILO, "Towards a Productive and Inclusive Path: Job Creation in the Arab Region" (UNESCWA and ILO, August 2021).

49. ILO, "Recovery in Youth Employment Is Still Lagging, Says ILO," www.ilo.org, August 11, 2022, https://www.ilo.org/global/about-the-ilo/newsroom/news/WCMS_853078/lang—en/index.htm.

50. Artur Bala and Héla Ben Fayala, "Across Divides to Advance Women's Rights through Dialogue: Experiences from the Ground" (Search for Common Ground and UN Women, 2017).

51. World Bank, "Labor Force Participation Rate, Female (% of Female Population Ages 15+) (Modeled ILO Estimate)—Middle East & North Africa | Data," Worldbank.org, 2019, https://data.worldbank.org/indicator/SL.TLF.CACT.FE.ZS?locations=ZQ.; World Bank, "Labor Force Participation Rate, Female (% of Female Population Ages 15+) (Modeled ILO Estimate) | Data," data.worldbank.org, 2022, https://data.worldbank.org/indicator/SL.TLF.CACT.FE.ZS?name_desc=false.

52. Yara M Asi, "The (Slowly) Changing Gender Dynamics in Arab Countries," Arab Center Washington DC, May 11, 2021, https://arabcenterdc.org/resource/the-slowly-changing-gender-dynamics-in-arab-countries/.

53. Naderah Chamlou, "Women's Rights in the Middle East and North Africa | Global Policy Journal," Globalpolicyjournal.com, 2000, https://www.globalpolicyjournal.com/blog/03/10/2017/women%e2%80%99s-rights-middle-east-and-north-africa.

54. Yara M Asi, "The (Slowly) Changing Gender Dynamics in Arab Countries," Arab Center Washington DC, May 11, 2021, https://arabcenterdc.org/resource/the-slowly-changing-gender-dynamics-in-arab-countries/.

55. United Nations, "Policy Brief: The Impact of COVID-19 on the Arab Region an Opportunity to Build Back Better" (New York: United Nations, July 2020), https://unsdg.un.org/resources/policy-brief-impact-covid-19-arab-region-opportunity-build-back-better.

56. Meera Senthilingam, "Sexual Harassment: How It Stands around the Globe," CNN, 2017, https://www.cnn.com/2017/11/25/health/sexual-harassment-violence-abuse-global-levels/index.html.

57. UNESCWA, "The Impact of COVID-19 on Gender Equality in the Arab Region" (ESCWA and UN Women, 2020).

58. Ibtesam Al-Atiyat, "The Current Faces of Arab Feminism," *Friedrich Ebert Stiftung*, 2020, https://mena.fes.de/publications/e/the-current-faces-of-arab-feminism; PWC, "MENA Women in Work Survey 2022: Young Women, Powerful Ambitions" (PWC, 2022.), https://www.pwc.com/m1/en/publications/images-new/woman-in-work/-mena-women-in-work-survey-2022.pdf.

59. IPU. "Women's Suffrage: A World Chronology of the Recognition of Women's Right to Vote and to Stand for Election," Inter-Parliamentary Union, http://archive.ipu.org/wmn-e/suffrage.htm

60. IPU, "IPU Comparative Data on Women's Right to Vote," Parline: the IPU's Open Data Platform, accessed October 22, 2022, https://data.ipu.org/compare?field=country%3Afield_suffrage%3Afield_right_to_vote*ion=middle_east_and_north_africa#map.

61. IPU. "Comparative Data on Women's Right to Vote"

62. Fatima Tawfik, "Rising in the Rankings, Arab Women Dream of Gender Equality" msmagazine.com, February 18, 2022, https://msmagazine.com/2022/02/18/arab-women-politics-gender-equality/.

63. Arab Barometer, "Opinion on Arab Women and Political Power," Arab Barometer, 2020, https://www.arabbarometer.org/2020/02/opinion-on-arab-women-and-political-power/.

64. WEF, "Global Gender Gap Report 2022" (Geneva: World Economic Forum, 2022), https://www.weforum.org/reports/global-gender-gap-report-2022/.

65. Represent Women, "Country Brief: Arab States Brief," representwomen.app.box.com, 2021, https://representwomen.app.box.com/s/2rt8ot8qo32nbv3k7bbembqwus1u5kr9.

66. IPU, "Women in Parliament in 2021" (Geneva: Inter-Parliamentary Union, 2022).

67. IPU, "Women in Parliament in 2021" (Geneva: Inter-Parliamentary Union, 2022).

68. Ahmed Marwane, "Women and Politics in Algeria: One Step Forward, Two Steps Back," The Washington Institute (Fikra Forum, September 15, 2021), https://www.washingtoninstitute.org/-policy-analysis/women-and-politics-algeria-one-step-forward-two-steps-back.

69. IPU, "Women in Parliament in 2021" (Geneva: Inter-Parliamentary Union, 2022).

70. Andrea Lopez-Tomas, "Lebanon Elects Record Number of Women to Parliament—Al-Monitor: Independent, Trusted Coverage of the Middle East," www.al-monitor.com, June 19, 2022, https://www.al-monitor.com/originals/2022/06/lebanon-elects-record-number-women-parliament.

71. IDEA, "Gender Quotas Database: Iraq," International IDEA, 2022, https://www.idea.int/data-tools/data/gender-quotas/country-view/148/35.

72. Huda Al-Tamimi, "Effects of Iraq's Parliamentary Gender Quota on Women's Political Mobilization and Legitimacy Post-2003," *Contemporary Arab Affairs* 11, no. 4 (December 2018): 41–62, https://doi.org/10.1525/caa.2018.114003.

73. IPU, "Women in Parliament in 2021" (Geneva: Inter-Parliamentary Union, 2022).

74. Scott Neuman, "Tunisia's New Prime Minister Is the 1st Woman to Lead a Government in the Arab World," *NPR*, September 29, 2021, sec. Middle East, https://www.npr.org/2021/09/29/1041431089/-tunisias-new-prime-minister-is-the-first-woman-to-lead-an-arab-world-government.

75. Hanen Jebli, "Tunisians Outraged after Female Parliamentarian Slapped by Islamist Colleague—Al-Monitor: Independent, Trusted

Coverage of the Middle East," www.al-monitor. com, July 8, 2021, https://www al-monitor.com/originals/2021/07/tunisians-outraged-after-female-parliamentarian-slapped-islamist-colleague.

76. World Bank, "Nearly 2.4 Billion Women Globally Don't Have Same Economic Rights as Men," *Press Release*. World Bank, March 1, 2022, https://www.worldbank.org/en/news/press-release/2022/03/01/nearly-2-4-billion-women-globally-don-t-have-a-same-economic-rights-as-men.

77. According to Amina Said, "Huda Shaarawi is without any contention the leader of the Woman's Rights Movement in all Islamic countries." A quoted in: Rula Quawas, "'A Sea Captain in Her Own Right': Navigating the Feminist Thought of Huda Shaarawi," *Journal of International Women's Studies* 8, no. 1 (January 11, 2013): 219–35, https://vc.bridgew.edu/jiws/vol8/iss1/17.; Huda Sha'arawi, "Huda Sha'arawi, Speech at the Arab Feminist Conference, 1944," Speech, *TBR Reading* (Arab Feminist Conference, March 20, 2019), https://www.tbr.fun/huda-shaarawi-speech-at-the-arab-feminist-conference-1944/.

78. Mohammad Amin Al-Midani, "The League of Arab States and the Arab Charter on Human Rights," ACIHL, n.d., https://acihl.org/articles.htm?%20article_id=6.

79. OHCHR, "Arab Charter on Human Rights (Unofficial Translation)," *Https://Www.ohchr.org/Sites/Default/Files/Documents/Issues/IJudiciary/-Arab-Charter-On-Human-Rights-2005.Pdf* (OHCHR, 2005).

80. Johnny Wood, "104 Countries Have Laws That Prevent Women from Working in Some Jobs," World Economic Forum, August 13, 2018, https://www.weforum.org/agenda/2018/08/104-countries-have-laws-that-prevent-women-from-working-in-some-jobs/.

81. Personal status laws and personal status codes are occasionally used interchangeably throughout the text, acknowledging that they have different terminology across the region but refer to the same general structure.

82. Souad Mahmoud, "The Challenges of Grassroots Feminism in Arab Countries," Capire, March 25, 2021, https://capiremov.org/en/analysis/the-challenges-of-grassroots-feminism-in-arab-countries/.

83. Antonio-Martín Porras-Gómez, "Constitutional Transformation and Gender Equality: The Case of the Post-Arab Uprisings North African Constitutions," *Oxford Journal of Legal Studies* 42, no. 1 (September 29, 2021), https://doi.org/10.1093/ojls/gqab028.

84. UNESCWA et al., "Gender Justice & Equality before the Law," 2019, https://www.undp.org/arab-states/publications/gender-justice-equality-law.

85. Hussein Yassine·Explained·January 5 and 2021, "What Is Civil Marriage and Does It Work in Lebanon?," The961, January 4, 2021, https://www.the961.com/civil-marriage-in-lebanon-explained/.

86. Mahnaz Afkhami, and Lina Abou-Habib, et al. "Equality: It's All in the Family" (*Video*, English). Women's Learning Partnership. https://learningpartnership.org/resource/equality-its-all-family-video-english.

87. Gulf News, "Lebanese Women Wage Painful Custody Battles," gulfnews.com, March 26, 2017, https://gulfnews.com/world/mena/lebanese-women-wage-painful-custody-battles-1.2000613.; Human Rights Watch, "Lebanon: Laws Discriminate against Women," HRW, January 2, 2019, https://www.hrw.org/news/2015/01/19/lebanon-laws-discriminate-against-women.

88. Nadia Ait-Zai, "Reforms in Family Law in the Maghreb," IEMed, 2005, https://www.iemed.org/publication/reforms-in-family-law-in-the-maghreb/.

89. SIGI, "Social Institutions and Gender Index," Genderindex.org, 2019, https://www.genderindex.org/.

90. We note the difference in terms referring to guardians due to varying dialects in the region; Human Rights Watch, "'Everything I Have to Do Is Tied to a Man' Women and Qatar's Male Guardianship Rules" (HRW, March 2021).

91. Afkhami, Mahnaz, "Equality: It's All in the Family."

92. César Chelala, "Domestic Violence in the Middle East," The Globalist, September 16, 2019, https://www.theglobalist.com/middle-east-domestic-violence-gender-equality/#:~:text=Of%20the%2022%20United%20Nations.

93. Human Rights Watch, "Lebanon: Domestic Violence Law Good, but Incomplete," Human Rights Watch, April 3, 2014, https://www.hrw.org/news/2014/04/03/lebanon-domestic-violence-law-good-incomplete.

94. UNFPA, "State of the World Population 2021" (UNFPA, 2021), https://www.unfpa.org/sowp-2021.

95. UNESCWA et al., "Gender Justice & Equality before the Law," 2019, https://www.undp.org/arab-states/publications/gender-justice-equality-law.

96. UNESCWA et al., "Gender Justice & Equality before the Law," 2019, https://www.undp.org/arab-states/publications/gender-justice-equality-law.

97. BBC, "Tunisian Women Free to Marry Non-Muslims," *BBC News*, September 15, 2017, sec. Africa, https://www.bbc.com/news/world-africa-41278610.

98. Zeina Zaatari, "From Women's Rights to Feminism: The Urgent Need for an Arab Feminist Renaissance—Zeina Zaatari," in *Arab Feminisms: Gender and Equality in the Middle East*, ed. Jean Said Makdisi, Noha Bayoumi, and Rafif Rida Sidawi (London & New York: I.B. Tauris, 2014), 62.

99. World Health Organization, "Devastatingly Pervasive: 1 in 3 Women Globally Experience

Violence," www.who.int (World Health Organization, March 9, 2021), https://www.who.int/news/item/09-03-2021-devastatingly-pervasive-1-in-3-women-globally-experience-violence.

100. UN Women Arab States, "Facts and Figures: Ending Violence against Women and Girls," UN Women—Arab States, accessed October 29, 2022, https://arabstates.unwomen.org/en/what-we-do/ending-violence-against-women/facts-and-figures-0#:~:text=37%25%20of%20Arab%20women%20have.

101. Equality Now, "Family Laws in MENA Fail to Protect Women and Girls," *Equality Now*, May 12, 2022, https://www.equalitynow.org/news_and_insights/family-laws-in-mena-fail-to-protect-women-and-girls/?utm_source=Equality%2BNow&utm_campaign=f221eecf6d-EMAIL_CAMPAIGN_2022_04_27_05_09_COPY_01&utm_medium=email&utm_term=0_1a58d68771-f221eecf6d-238337152.

102. Equality Now, "Family Laws."

103. Equality Now, "Family Laws."

104. *Feminism Inshallah: A History of Arab Feminism*, Film (Women Make Movies, 2014).

105. Nada Ghosn, "Kuwait's Alanoud Alsharekh, Feminist Groundbreaker," The Markaz Review, December 6, 2020, https://themarkaz.org/kukuwaits-alanoud-al-sharekh-feminist-groundbreaker/.

106. The Economist, "Arab Governments Are Doing Too Little to End Honour Killings," *The Economist*, 2021, https://www.economist.com/middle-east-and-africa/2021/02/06/arab-governments-are-doing-too-little-to-end-honour-killings.

107. Adam Coogle, "Recorded 'Honor' Killings on the Rise in Jordan," Human Rights Watch, October 27, 2016, https://www.hrw.org/news/2016/10/27/recorded-honor-killings-rise-jordan.

108. Dadouch, Sarah. "Killings of Women at Mideast Universities Provoke Outrage and Worry." The Washington Post. WP Company, July 10, 2022. https://www.washingtonpost.com/world/2022/07/08/killings-university-women-egypt-jordan/.

109. Egypt Independent, "Court to Consider Annulling Death Sentence against Naira Ashraf's Murderer in January," Egypt Independent, September 12, 2022, https://egyptindependent.com/court-to-consider-annulling-death-sentence-against-naira-ashrafs-murderer-in-january/.

110. Cathrin Schaer, "Murdered because of Snapchat? Social Media Uptick in Honor Crime," *DW.com*, January 29, 2021.

111. Arab Barometer, "The Arab World in Seven Charts: Are Arabs Turning Their Backs on Religion?—Arab Barometer," BBC News, June 24, 2019, https://www.arabbarometer.org/2019/06/the-arab-world-in-seven-charts-are-arabs-turning-their-backs-on-religion/.

112. "Facts and figures: Female genital mutilation in the Middle East and North Africa." 2020. UNICEF. https://www.unicef.org/mena/reports/facts-and-figures-female-genital-mutilation-middle-east-and-north-africa.

113. UNICEF MENA, "Facts and Figures: Female Genital Mutilation in the Middle East and North Africa," www.unicef.org, February 2020, https://www.unicef.org/mena/reports/facts-and-figures-female-genital-mutilation-middle-east-and-north-africa.

114. UNFPA, "Female Genital Mutilation," UNFPA Egypt, April 11, 2016, https://egypt.unfpa.org/en/node/22544#:~:text=However%2C%20the%20recent%20history%20of.

115. Ganiyu O. Shakirat et al., "An Overview of Female Genital Mutilation in Africa: Are the Women Beneficiaries or Victims?," *Cureus* 12, no. 9 (September 4, 2020), https://doi.org/10.7759/cureus.10250.

116. UNFPA and UNICEF, "Child Marriage in the Context of COVID-19: MENA Regional Analysis" (UNFPA, June 2021).

117. UNFPA and UNICEF, "Child Marriage in the Context of COVID-19: MENA Regional Analysis" (UNFPA, June 2021).

118. UNESCWA, "The Arab Gender Gap Report 2020" (UNESCWA, 2020), https://publications.unescwa.org/projects/aggr/index.html#%5C31.

119. UNICEF MENA, "UNICEF Middle East and North Africa," Unicef.org, accessed October 20, 2022, https://www.unicef.org/mena/.

120. UNESCWA et al., "Gender Justice & Equality before the Law," 2019, https://www.undp.org/arab-states/publications/gender-justice-equality-law.

121. Salvador Santino Jr. Fulo Regilme and Elisabetta Spoldi, "Children in Armed Conflict: A Human Rights Crisis in Somalia," *Global Jurist* 0, no. 0 (March 16, 2021), https://doi.org/10.1515/gj-2020-0083.

122. Etenesh Abera and Zecharias Zelalem, "'Two Thirds' of Female Migrant Workers in Lebanon Survivors of Sexual Harassment," Middle East Eye, October 17, 2022, https://www.middleeasteye.net/news/lebanon-two-thirds-migrant-worker-women-survivors-sexual-harassment.

123. A system that allows individuals or companies to sponsor visas for migrant workers.; Kali Robinson, "What Is the Kafala System?," Council on Foreign Relations, March 23, 2021, https://www.cfr.org/backgrounder/what-kafala-system.

124. Zeina Zaatari, "From Women's Rights to Feminism: The Urgent Need for an Arab Feminist Renaissance," in *Arab Feminisms: Gender and Equality in the Middle East*, ed. Jean Said Makdisi, Noha Bayoumi, and Rafif Rida (I.B. Tauris, 2014), 104.

125. Wassyla Tamzali quoted in: *Feminism Inshallah: A History of Arab Feminism*, Film (Women Make Movies, 2014).

126. UNESCWA, "ESCWA Marks International Women's Day with Call to Action: The Time Is Now," ESCWA, March 5, 2019, https://www.

unescwa.org/news/escwa-marks-international-women%E2%80%99s-day-call-action-time-now.

127. Suad Zayed alOraimi, "Arab Feminism—Obstacles and Possibilities: An Analytical Study of the Women's Movement in the Arab World," in *Arab Feminisms Gender and Equality in the Middle East*, ed. Jean Said Makdisi, Noha Bayoumi, and Rafif Rida Sidawi (London & New York: I.B. Tauris, 2014), P. 132.

128. CCCB, "Mona Eltahawy: 'Patriarchy Is the Form of Oppression with Which the Entire World Struggles,'" *Video*. www.youtube.com, 2019, https://www.youtube.com/watch?v=08DW7edwWyY.

129. UNICEF, "Situational Analysis"

130. Lina AbiRafeh and Rachel Dore-Weeks, "Opinion: A Month after the Blast, Let's Rebuild Beirut as the Arab Region's First Feminist City," *The Independent*, September 4, 2020, https://www.independent.co.uk/voices/beirut-explosion-lebanon-blast-news-women-feminism-a9703546.html.

131. Gabriella Nassif, in conversation with the author, online, October 2022.

132. Najla Hamadeh, "Recognition of Difference: Towards a More Effective Feminism," in *Arab Feminisms Gender and Equality in the Middle East*, ed. Jean Said Makdisi, Noha Bayoumi, and Rafif Rida Sidawi (London: I.B. Tauris, 2014), 21.

133. Lila Abu-Lughod, "Do Muslim Women Really Need Saving? Anthropological Reflections on Cultural Relativism and Its Others," American Anthropologist 104, no. 3 (2002): 783–90, http://www.jstor.org/stable/3567256.

134. Wendy S. Hesford, "Do Muslim Women Need Saving? By Lila Abu-Lughod. Cambridge, MA: Harvard University Press, 2013.," *Signs: Journal of Women in Culture and Society* 40, no. 4 (June 2015): 985–87, https://doi.org/10.1086/680405.

135. Aida Edemariam, "Joumana Haddad: 'I Live in a Country That Hates Me,'" The Guardian, August 21, 2010, https://www.theguardian.com/theguardian/2010/aug/21/joumana-haddad-interview.

136. Mervat Hatem, "What Do Women Want? A Critical Mapping of Future Directions for Arab Feminisms," *Contemporary Arab Affairs* 6, no. 1 (2013): 91–101, https://www.jstor.org/stable/48600672.

137. Zeina Zaatari, "From Women's Rights to Feminism: The Urgent Need for an Arab Feminist Renaissance," in *Arab Feminisms: Gender and Equality in the Middle East*, ed. Jean Said Makdisi, Noha Bayoumi, and Rafif Rida (London: I.B. Tauris, 2014), p.99

138. Yvonne Singh, "What Does It Take to Be an Arab Feminist in 2019?," Middle East Eye, July 5, 2019, https://www.middleeasteye.net/discover/what-does-it-take-be-arab-feminist-2019.

139. Sarah El-Shaarawi, "Women's Activisms and the Future of Feminist Movements in the Arab Region," Arab Media & Society, March 3, 2022, https://www.arabmediasociety.

com/womens-activisms-and-the-future-of-feminist-movements-in-the-arab-region/.

140. Maya Mikdashi, "How to Study Gender in the Middle East," CCAS, June 3, 2020, https://ccas.georgetown.edu/2020/06/03/how-to-study-gender-in-the-middle-east/.

141. Charlotte Karam, in conversation with the author, online November 202.

142. Zarqa Parvez, "Is 'Feminism' Really Helping Women's Rights in the Middle East?," *Middle East Monitor*, January 31, 2019, https://www.middleeastmonitor.com/20190131-is-feminism-really-helping-womens-rights-in-the-middle-east/.

143. Rosemary Sayigh, "Current Challenges Facing the Arab Women's Movements," *Al-Raida Journal* 20, no. 100 (2003): 49–92, https://doi.org/10.32380/alrj.v0i0.444.

144. "Translating Gender." Samia Mehrez. *Journal of Middle East Women's Studies*, Vol. 3, No. 1, Special Issue: *Transnational Theory, National Politics, and Gender in the Contemporary Middle East / North Africa*. (2007), pp. 106–127. Published by Duke University Press

145. Gabriel Semerene, "The Words to Say It," *Language* (Mashallah News, 2016), https://www.mashallahnews.com/language/words-to-say.html.

146. Jean Said Makdisi, Noha Bayoumi, and Rafif Rida Sidawi, eds., *Arab Feminisms : Gender and Equality in the Middle East* (London ; New York: I.B. Tauris, 2014), P.95–6

147. Jean Said Makdisi, "Huqouq Almar'a: Feminist Thought and the Language of the Arab Women's Movement," in *Arab Feminisms Gender and Equality in the Middle East*, ed. Jean Said Makdisi, Noha Bayoumi, and Rafif Rida Sidawi (London; New York: I.B Tauris, 2014), p.123

148. Jean Said Makdisi, "Huqouq Almar'a: Feminist Thought and the Language of the Arab Women's Movement," in *Arab Feminisms Gender and Equality in the Middle East*, ed. Jean Said Makdisi, Noha Bayoumi, and Rafif Rida Sidawi (London; New York: I.B Tauris, 2014), p.123

149. Maria Najjar, "Reviving Pan-Arabism in Feminist Activism in the Middle East," *Kohl: A Journal for Body and Gender Research* 6, no. 1 (2020): 119–32, https://kohljournal.press/reviving-pan-arabism-feminist.

150. Raneem Al-Afifi, "Feminism in Egypt: A Brief Overview," MedFemiNiswiya, April 8, 2021, https://medfeminiswiya.net/2021/04/08/contexte-egypte/?lang=en.

151. Elsadda is also co-founder of the Women and Memory Forum, a group of women scholars, researchers, and activists who produce and share knowledge on Arab women.; Hoda Elsadda, "Gender Studies in the Arab World: Reflections and Questions on the Challenges of Discourses, Locations and History," in *Arab Feminisms Gender and Equality in the Middle East*, ed. Jean Said Makdisi, Noha Bayoumi, and Rafif Rida Didawi (London: I.B. Tauris, 2014), p.68

152. Myriam Sfeir, email message to author, October 2022.

153. Najjar, "Reviving Pan-Arabism."

154. Nawar Al-Hassan Golley, "Is Feminism Relevant to Arab Women?," *Third World Quarterly* 25, no. 3 (March 2004): 521–36, https://doi.org/10.1080/0143659042000191410.

155. Hasan Ismaik, "Arab Feminism: A Luxury or a Necessity?," *Egypt Independent*, April 1, 2021, https://egyptindependent.com/arab-feminism-a-luxury-or-a-necessity/.

156. Saskia Glas and Amy Alexander, "Explaining Support for Muslim Feminism in the Arab Middle East and North Africa," *Gender & Society* 34, no. 3 (May 19, 2020): 437–66, https://doi.org/10.1177/0891243220915494.

157. UC Press, "Author Spotlight: Nicola Pratt on Women's Activism in the Middle East," UC Press Blog, October 13, 2020, https://www.ucpress.edu/blog/52517/author-spotlight-nicola-pratt-on-womens-activism-in-the-middle-east/.

158. Nada Ghosn, "Kuwait's Alanoud Alsharekh, Feminist Groundbreaker," *The Markaz Review*, December 6, 2020, https://themarkaz.org/kukuwaits-alanoud-al-sharekh-feminist-groundbreaker/.

159. Ghassan Salame, *The Foundations of the Arab State* (Routledge, 2013).

160. Said, Edward. *Orientalism* (New York: Pantheon Books, 1978).

161. Therese Saliba, "Arab Feminism at the Millennium," *Signs* 25, no. 4 (2000): 1087–92, https://www.jstor.org/stable/3175492.

162. Nicola Pratt quoted in: UC Press, "Author Spotlight: Nicola Pratt on Women's Activism in the Middle East," UC Press Blog, October 13, 2020, https://www.ucpress.edu/blog/52517/author-spotlight-nicola-pratt-on-womens-activism-in-the-middle-east/.

163. Larbi Touaf. Review of "Touaf on Charrad, 'States and Women's Rights: The Making of Postcolonial Tunisia, Algeria, and Morocco,'" *H-Gender-MidEast* (H-net Reviews, 2003), https://networks.h-net.org/node/6386/reviews/6614/-touaf-charrad-states-and-womens-rights-making-postcolonial-tunisia.

164. Al-Hassan Golley, "Is Feminism Relevant to Arab Women?"

165. Nicola Pratt quoted in: UC Press, "Author Spotlight: Nicola Pratt on Women's Activism in the Middle East," UC Press Blog, October 13, 2020, https://www.ucpress.edu/blog/52517/author-spotlight-nicola-pratt-on-womens-activism-in-the-middle-east/.

166. Jean Said Makdisi, Noha Bayoumi, and Rafif Rida Sidawi, eds., *Arab Feminisms : Gender and Equality in the Middle East* (London ; New York: I.B. Tauris, 2014), 16–17.

167. Al-Hassan Golley, "Is Feminism Relevant to Arab Women?"

168. Saliba, "Arab Feminism."

169. Al-Hassan Golley, "Is Feminism Relevant to Arab Women?"

170. Lina AbiRafeh, "Going Backward Is Not an Option: The Challenge of Equality for Arab Women," Arab Center Washington DC, April 22, 2022, https://arabcenterdc.org/resource/going-backward-is-not-an-option-the-challenge-of-equality-for-arab-women/.

171. Al-Hassan Golley, "Is Feminism Relevant to Arab Women?"

172. Soukaina Rachidi, "Huda Sharawi: A Remarkable Egyptian Feminist Pioneer," *Inside Arabia*, July 6, 2019, https://insidearabia.com/-huda-sharawi-a-remarkable-egyptian-feminist-pioneer/.; Jennifer Jaffer, "Huda Sharawi | Egyptian Feminist and Nationalist," in *Encyclopædia Britannica*, 2019, https://www.britannica.com/biography/Huda-Sharawi.

173. Al-Hassan Golley, "Is Feminism Relevant to Arab Women?"

174. Al-Hassan Golley, "Is Feminism Relevant to Arab Women?"

175. Margot Badran, "Nawal El-Saadawi: A Fearless Feminist without Borders" *Blog Post,* Wilson Center, March 8, 2022, https://www.wilsoncenter.org/blog-post/nawal-el-saadawi-fearless-feminist-without-borders.

176. Amal Amireh, "Framing Nawal El Saadawi: Arab Feminism in a Transnational World," *Signs: Journal of Women in Culture and Society* 26, no. 1 (October 2000): 215–49, https://doi.org/10.1086/495572.

177. Nawal El Saadawi, *The Hidden Face of Eve: Women in the Arab World*, trans. Sherif Hetata (London: Zed, 1980).

178. One example of this study carried out in Egypt: Tarek Masoud, Amaney Jamal, and Elizabeth Nugent, "Using the Qur'ān to Empower Arab Women? Theory and Experimental Evidence from Egypt," *Comparative Political Studies* 49, no. 12 (July 9, 2016): 1555–98, https://doi.org/10.1177/0010414015626452.

179. UN Women, "Working with Men and Boys for Gender Equality: State of Play and Future Directions" (New York: UN Women, 2021).

180. Shereen El Feki, Gary Barker, and Brian Heilman, eds., "Understanding Masculinities: Results from the International Men and Gender Equality Survey (IMAGES)—Middle East and North Africa" (UN Women and Promundo, 2017).

181. Human Rights Watch, "Audacity in Adversity | LGBT Activism in the Middle East and North Africa," Human Rights Watch, April 16, 2018, https://www.hrw.org/report/2018/04/16/audacity-adversity/lgbt-activism-middle-east-and-north-africa.

182. Human Rights Watch, "Audacity in Adversity | LGBT Activism in the Middle East and North Africa," Human Rights Watch, April 16, 2018, https://www.hrw.org/report/2018/04/16/audacity-adversity/lgbt-activism-middle-east-and-north-africa.

183. Al-Ali, "Women's Movement in the Middle East."

184. "The Arab Women's Movement: Struggles and Experiences" (ADHR, 2005).

185. UNESCWA, "Operationalizing

Intersectionality in the Arab Region: Challenges and Ways Forward" (Beirut: UNESCWA, 2019).

186. Rosemary Sayigh, "Current Challenges Facing the Arab Women's Movements," *Al-Raida Journal* 20, no. 100 (2003): 49–92, https://doi.org/10.32380/alrj.v0i0.444.

187. "The Arab Women's Movement: Struggles and Experiences" (ADHR, 2005). https://arab-hdr.org/wp-content/uploads/2007/11/-ahdr-report_2005-en-chapter_5.pdf

188. Sarah Anne Rennick, "Introduction: What Is New about Post-2011 MENA Diasporas?," *Arab Reform Initiative*, July 26, 2021, https://www.arab-reform.net/publication/introduction-what-is-new-about-post-2011-mena-diasporas/.

189. Sarah Anne Rennick, "Introduction: What Is New about Post-2011 MENA Diasporas?," *Arab Reform Initiative*, July 26, 2021, https://www.arab-reform.net/publication/introduction-what-is-new-about-post-2011-mena-diasporas/.

190. ADC, "American Arab Anti Discrimination Committee," Adc.org, 2022, https://www.adc.org.; Arab American Institute, "Arab American Institute Foundation," Arab American Institute Foundation, n.d., https://www.aaiusa.org/.; MEI, "Middle East Institute," Middle East Institute, n.d., https://www.mei.edu.; Arab America, "Arab American Community Resources | Arab World News & Events," *Arab America*, accessed October 29, 2022, https://www.arabamerica.com.

191. UNFPA, "Youth Participation & Leadership," UNFPA Arabstates, 2022, https://arabstates.unfpa.org/en/topics/youth-participation-leadership.

192. Nadje Al-Ali, "Gender and Civil Society in the Middle East," *International Feminist Journal of Politics* 5, no. 2 (January 2003): 216–32, https://doi.org/10.1080/1461674032000080576.

193. Artur Bala and Héla Ben Fayala, "Across Divides to Advance Women's Rights through Dialogue: Experiences from the Ground" (Search for Common Ground and UN Women, 2017).

194. AbiRafeh, "Going Backward Is Not an Option."

195. Artur Bala and Héla Ben Fayala, "Across Divides to Advance Women's Rights through Dialogue: Experiences from the Ground" (Search for Common Ground and UN Women, 2017).

196. Zeina Zaatari, "Women's Rights to Feminism: The Urgent Need for an Arab Feminist Renaissance," in *Arab Feminisms: Gender and Equality in the Middle East*, ed. Jean Said Makdisi, Noha Bayoumi, and Rafif Rida Sidawi (London & New York: I.B Tauris, 2014), 54–65.

197. This quote was taken, with permission, from an essay submitted to AiW.

198. Ismaik, "Arab Feminism: A Luxury or a Necessity?"

Chapter 2

1. Huda Sha'arawi, "Huda Sha'arawi, Speech at the Arab Feminist Conference, 1944," *Speech* (Arab Feminist Conference, March 20, 2019), https://www.tbr.fun/huda-shaarawi-speech-at-the-arab-feminist-conference-1944/.

2. The authors would like to express their thanks to everyone who advised and helped bring this chapter to life, particularly Dr. Stephanie Chaban, whose knowledge of Arab feminist history is exemplary.

3. United Nations, "United Nations Treaty Collection," treaties.un.org, accessed October 29, 2022, https://treaties.un.org/pages/ViewDetails.aspx?src=IND&mtdsg_no=IV-8&chapter=4&clang=_en#EndDec.

4. Eric Goldstein, "Before the Arab Spring, the Unseen Thaw," *Human Rights Watch*, 2012, https://www.hrw.org/node/259729.

5. Equality Now, "Not Backing down against 'Marry-Your-Rapist' Laws," *Equality Now*, August 21, 2017, https://www.equalitynow.org/news_and_insights/not_backing_down_against_marry_your_rapist_laws/.; IPS World Desk, "Lebanon Joins Jordan and Tunisia in Fight against Rapists Impunity," *Inter Press Service*, August 23, 2017, http://www.ipsnews.net/2017/08/lebanon-joins-jordan-and-tunisia-in-fight-against-rapists-impunity/.

6. For further information see: Mervat F. Hatem, "In the Shadow of the State: Changing Definitions of Arab Women's 'Developmental' Citizenship Rights," *Journal of Middle East Women's Studies* 1, no. 3 (2005): 20–45, https://www.jstor.org/stable/40326870.; Valentine M Moghadam, "Gender Regimes in the Middle East and North Africa: The Power of Feminist Movements," *Social Politics: International Studies in Gender, State & Society* 27, no. 3 (2020): 467–85, https://doi.org/10.1093/sp/jxaa019.; Pernille Arenfeldt and Nawar Al-Hassan Golley, eds., *Mapping Arab Women's Movements: A Century of Transformations from Within* (Cairo: American University in Cairo Press, 2012).;

7. Mervat F. Hatem, "In the Shadow of the State: Changing Definitions of Arab Women's 'Developmental' Citizenship Rights," *Journal of Middle East Women's Studies* 1, no. 3 (2005): 20–45, https://www.jstor.org/stable/40326870.

8. Specifically, the First World Conference on Women in Mexico City (1975), which resulted in the designation of International Women's Year and then the UN Decade for Women (1975–1985). Notably, the decade also saw the International Tribunal on Crimes against Women (1976) in Brussels.

9. For a more detailed description of the factors influencing women's organizing during this time, see: Mervat Hatem, "Toward the Development of Post-Islamist and Post-Nationalist Feminist Discourse in the Middle East," in *Arab Women: Old Boundaries, New Frontiers*, ed. Judith E. Tucker (Bloomington: Indiana University Press, 1993), 29–48.

10. Lila Abu-Lughod, *Remaking Women: Feminism and Modernity in the Middle East* (Princeton: Princeton University Press, 1998).

11. Roger Owen, "The Arab Economies in the 1970s," *MERIP Reports* XI, no. 8–9 (1981), https://merip.org/1981/11/the-arab-economies-in-the-1970s/.

12. The Dutch Disease, named after the impact of Netherlands' gas discovery, is an economic term describing the negative effect natural resource discovery has on the economy.

13. Michael Ross, *The Oil Curse: How Petroleum Wealth Shapes the Development of Nations* (Princeton, NJ: Princeton University Press, 2013).

14. May Seikaly, "Women and Social Change in Bahrain," *International Journal of Middle East Studies* 26, no. 3 (1994): 416, http://www.jstor.org/stable/163696.

15. *Feminism Inshallah: A History of Arab Feminism*, Film (Women Make Movies, 2014).

16. *Feminism Inshallah: A History of Arab Feminism*, Film (Women Make Movies, 2014).

17. Al Jazeera, "Timeline: The Middle East Conflict," *Al Jazeera*, January 21, 2008, https://www.aljazeera.com/news/2008/1/21/timeline-the-middle-east-conflict.

18. Giorgio Cafiero, "Iran and the Gulf States 40 Years after the 1979 Revolution," Middle East Institute, February 8, 2019, https://www.mei.edu/publications/iran-and-gulf-states-40-years-after-1979-revolution.

19. Seyed Hossein Mousavian, "A Revolution and a War: How Iran Transformed Today's Middle East," *The Cairo Review of Global Affairs* 45 (June 7, 2022), https://www.thecairoreview.com/essays/-a-revolution-and-a-war-how-iran-transformed-todays-middle-east/.

20. May Seikaly, "Women and Social Change in Bahrain," *International Journal of Middle East Studies* 26, no. 3 (1994): 415–26, http://www.jstor.org/stable/163696.

21. Sabika Muhammad Al-Najjar, "The Feminist Movement in the Gulf," *Al-Raida* 20, no. 100 (2003): 29–37, https://doi.org/10.32380/alrj.v0i0.441.

22. May Seikaly, "Women and Social Change in Bahrain," *International Journal of Middle East Studies* 26, no. 3 (1994): 415–26, http://www.jstor.org/stable/163696.

23. Laila Prager, "Emirati Women Leaders in the Cultural Sector from 'State Feminism' to Empowerment?," *Hawwa* 18, no. 1 (2020): 51–74, https://doi.org/10.1163/15692086-12341370.

24. Haya Al-Mughni, "Women's Organizations in Kuwait," *Middle East Report*, no. 198 (1996), https://merip.org/1996/03/womens-organizations-in-kuwait/.

25. An-Chi Hoh Dianu, "Contemporary Short Stories by Kuwaiti Women: A Study of Their Social Context and Characteristics," *MELA Notes*, no. 75/76 (2002): 69–84, https://www.jstor.org/stable/29785770.

26. An-Chi Hoh Dianu, "Contemporary Short Stories by Kuwaiti Women: A Study of Their Social Context and Characteristics," *MELA Notes*, no. 75/76 (2002): 69–84, https://www.jstor.org/stable/29785770.

27. Mary Ann Tétreault, Helen Rizzo, and Doron Shultziner, "Fashioning the Future: The Women's Movement in Kuwait," in *Mapping Arab Women's Movements: A Century of Transformations from Within*, ed. Pernille Arenfeldt and Nawar Al-Hassan Golley (Cairo: American University in Cairo Press, 2012), 253–80.

28. Arab.org, "Omani Women Association at Muscat | Arab.org," Directory, January 19, 2017, https://arab.org/directory/omani-women-association-at-muscat/.

29. Qatar National Day Committee, "History of Qatar," SNDCOC—The State National Day Celebration Organizing Committee, accessed October 20, 2022, https://www.qatar.qa/en/qatar/history-of-qatar-qatar-national-day-committee/.

30. Gulf Times, "Celebrating Qatar's Rich History of Education," *Gulf-Times*, December 18, 2012, https://www.gulf-times.com/story/335895/-Celebrating-Qatar-s-rich-history-of-education.

31. Wahhabism is a Sunni fundamentalist movement associated with the 18th-century scholar Muhammad ibn Abd al-Wahhab. It has served as the foundational doctrine of Saudi Arabia.

32. Hatoon Al Fassi, "Does Saudi Feminism Exist?," in *Arab Feminisms: Gender and Equality in the Middle East.*, ed. Jean Said Makdisi, Noha Bayoumi, and Rafif Rida Sidawi (London: I.B. Tauris, 2014), 121–31.

33. Al Nahda, "Al Nahda—النهضة," www.alnahda.org, accessed October 28, 2022, https://www.alnahda.org/about/?lang=en.

34. Hatoon Al Fassi, "Does Saudi Feminism Exist?," in *Arab Feminisms: Gender and Equality in the Middle East.*, ed. Jean Said Makdisi, Noha Bayoumi, and Rafif Rida Sidawi (London: I.B Tauris, 2014), 121–31.

35. Robert Burrowes and Manfred W Wenner, "Yemen | People, History, & Facts," in *Encyclopædia Britannica*, February 6, 2019, https://www.britannica.com/place/Yemen.

36. Pernille Arenfeldt and Nawar Al-Hassan Golley, eds., *Mapping Arab Women's Movements* (American University in Cairo Press, 2012), https://doi.org/10.5743/cairo/9789774164989.001.0001.

37. Amel Nejib Al-Ashtal, "A Long, Quiet and Steady Struggle: The Women's Movement in Yemen," in *Mapping Arab Women's Movements: A Century of Transformations from Within*, ed. Pernille Arenfeldt and Nawar Al-Hassan Golley (Cairo: American University in Cairo Press, 2012), 197–252.

38. Margot Badran, "Unifying Women: Feminist Pasts and Presents in Yemen," *Gender & History* 10, no. 3 (1998): 498–518, https://doi.org/10.1111/1468-0424.00115.

39. Ba'athism is an Arab nationalist ideology that resists colonialism and promotes pan-Arab socialism.

40. Human Rights Watch, "Background on Women's Status in Iraq prior to the Fall of the Saddam Hussein Government" (Human Rights

Watch, 2003), https://www.hrw.org/legacy/backgrounder/wrd/iraq-women.pdf.

41. Human Rights Watch, "Background on Women's Status in Iraq prior to the Fall of the Saddam Hussein Government" (Human Rights Watch, 2003), https://www.hrw.org/legacy/backgrounder/wrd/iraq-women.pdf.

42. Maisoon Al-Amarneh, "Jordanian Feminist Movement and the Struggle for Social and Political Change: Achievements and Challenges," *Sayaran—WE4L Knowledge and Learning Platform*, no. 1 (2018), https://www.sayaran.org/jordanian-feminist-movement-and-the-struggle-for-social-and-political-change/.

43. The Hashemite Kingdom of Jordan Parliament, "Freezing Parliamentary Life and Forming National Consultative Councils (1974–1984)," Parliament.jo, accessed October 27, 2022, http://parliament.jo/en/node/148.

44. Jamal Al Shalabi and Tareq Al-Assad, "Political Participation of Jordanian Women," *Égypte/Monde Arabe*, no. 9 (January 1, 2012): 211–30, https://doi.org/10.4000/ema.3033.

45. Rita Stephan, "Four Waves of Lebanese Feminism," E-International Relations, 2014, https://www.e-ir.info/2014/11/07/four-waves-of-lebanese-feminism/; Bernadette Daou, "Feminisms in Lebanon: After Proving Loyalty to the 'Nation,' Will the 'Body' Rise within the 'Arab Spring'?," *Civil Society Review*, no. 1 (2015): 55–66.

46. Arab Institute for Women, "About | the Arab Institute for Women | LAU," The Arab Institute for Women, accessed November 2, 2022, https://aiw.lau.edu.lb/about/.

47. Arab.org, "General Union of Palestinian Women | Arab.org," Directory, June 1, 2016, https://arab.org/directory/general-union-of-palestinian-women/.

48. UPWC, "UPWC about Us," accessed October 14, 2022, http://upwc.org.ps/.

49. IDEA, "Constitutional History of Syria," ConstitutionNet, 2021, https://constitutionnet.org/country/syria.

50. Arab Women Organization, "Milestones in the History of Arab Women" (Cairo: Arab Women Organization, n.d.), http://elibrary.arabwomenorg.org/Content/2840_milestones%20in%20the%20history%20of%20arab%20women.pdf.

51. Islamism refers to the ideology and belief system whereas Islamization is a societal shift towards Islam.

52. Heba Saleh, "Nawal El Saadawi, Feminist Author and Political Activist, 1931–2021," *Financial Times*, March 26, 2021, https://www.ft.com/content/44db1483-4a0f-4e0e-a611-aad6a132adfb.

53. Margot Badran, "Nawal El-Saadawi: A Fearless Feminist without Borders" *Blog Post,* Wilson Center, March 8, 2022, https://www.wilsoncenter.org/blog-post/nawal-el-saadawi-fearless-feminist-without-borders.

54. Margot Badran, "Nawal El-Saadawi: A Fearless Feminist without Borders" *Blog Post,* Wilson Center, March 8, 2022, https://www.wilsoncenter.org/blog-post/nawal-el-saadawi-fearless-feminist-without-borders.

55. Arab Women Organization, "Milestones in the History of Arab Women" (Cairo: Arab Women Organization, n.d.), http://elibrary.arabwomenorg.org/Content/2840_milestones%20in%20the%20history%20of%20arab%20women.pdf.

56. UNHCR, "Refworld | Sudan: The Sudanese Women's Union (SWU) Including Activities, Roles, Organization and Problems Faced in Sudan," Refworld, 2002, https://www.refworld.org/docid/3df4bea84.html.

57. Bashir A Abdelqayoum Ali, "Non-Governmental Organizations and Development in the Sudan: Relations with the State and Institutional Strengthening" (Doctoral Thesis, 2010), https://core.ac.uk/download/pdf/161880511.pdf.

58. Balghis Badri, "Feminist Perspectives in the Sudan: An Analytical Overview." A paper presented on the workshop *"Feminist Perspectives,"* Free University Berlin, 26th-27th May 2005, https://www.fu-berlin.de/sites/gpo/tagungen/tagungfeministperspectives/balghis_badri.pdf.

59. Judith Miller, "Libya's Women: Era of Change (Published 1986)," *The New York Times*, 2022, https://www.nytimes.com/1986/02/03/style/libya-s-women-era-of-change.html.

60. Freedom House, "Women's Rights in the Middle East and North Africa 2010—Libya," *Refworld*, 2010, https://www.refworld.org/docid/4b99012091.html.

61. Kira Jinkinson, "State Feminism and the Islamist-Secularist Binary: Women's Rights in Tunisia," E-International Relations, 2020, https://www.e-ir.info/2020/07/27/state-feminism-and-the-islamist-secularist-binary-womens-rights-in-tunisia/.

62. International Campaign for Women's Safe Right to Abortion, "ALGERIA—Abortion Has Not Been Legalised in Algeria," International Campaign for Women's Right to Safe Abortion (SAWR), August 21, 2018, https://www.safeabortionwomensright.org/news/algeria-abortion-has-not-been-legalised-in-algeria/.; Mounira Charrad, "Policy Shifts: State, Islam, and Gender in Tunisia, 1930s-1990s," *Social Policy* 4, no. 2 (1997): 284–319.

63. Imen Yacoubi, "Sovereignty from Below: State Feminism and Politics of Women against Women in Tunisia," *The Arab Studies Journal* 24, no. 1 (2016): 254–74.

64. Valentine M. Moghadam, "Algerian Women in Movement," in *Confronting Global Gender Justice: Women's Lives, Human Rights*, ed. Deborah Bergoffen et al. (London & New York: Routledge, 2011), 180–99.

65. Valentine M. Moghadam, "Organizing Women: The New Women's Movement in Algeria," *Cultural Dynamics*, no. 13 (2001): 131–54.

66. Abdelaziz Radi, "Protest Movements and Social Media: Morocco's February 20 Movement," *Africa Development / Afrique et Développement*

42, no. 2 (2017): 31–55, https://www.jstor.org/stable/90018190.

67. Fatema Mernissi, "About Fatema," Fatema Mernissi, n.d., https://fatemamernissi.com/about-us.

68. Katherine Ann Wiley, "Women in Mauritania," *Oxford Research Encyclopedia of African History*, July 30, 2020, https://doi.org/10.1093/acrefore/9780190277734.013.529.

69. Stephen J. King, "Ending Hereditary Slavery in Mauritania: Bidan (whites) and Black "slaves" in 2021," *Arab Reform Initiative,* August 26, 2021, https://www.arab-reform.net/publication/ending-hereditary-slavery-in-mauritania-bidan-whites-and-black-slaves-in-2021/

70. Oumar Kane, "Première Femme Ministre En Mauritanie," ACTUME, February 5, 2013, https://actume.org/en/blog/aissata-kane-premiere-femme-ministre-en-mauritanie/.

71. Mohamed Haji Ingiriis, "Sisters; was this what we struggled for?': The Gendered Rivalry in Power and Politics," *Journal of International Women's Studies,* Vol. 16, No. 2 January 2015. https://vc.bridgew.edu/cgi/viewcontent.cgi?article=1803&context=jiws

72. Iman Abdulkadir Mohamed, "Somali Women and the Socialist State," *Journal of Georgetown University-Qatar Middle Eastern Studies Student Association*, no. 1 (2015), 4 https://doi.org/https://doi.org/10.5339/messa.2015.4.

73. Mohamed Haji Ingiriis, "Sisters; was this what we struggled for?': The Gendered Rivalry in Power and Politics," *Journal of International Women's Studies,* Vol. 16, No. 2 January 2015, 383 https://vc.bridgew.edu/cgi/viewcontent.cgi?article=1803&context=jiws

74. Mohamed Haji Ingiriis, "Sisters; was this what we struggled for?': The Gendered Rivalry in Power and Politics," *Journal of International Women's Studies,* Vol. 16, No. 2 January 2015, 383 https://vc.bridgew.edu/cgi/viewcontent.cgi?article=1803&context=jiws

75. Judith Gardner and Judy El Bushra, eds., *Somalia the Untold Story: The War through the Eyes of Somali Women* (London: Pluto Press, 2004).

76. Melanie M. Hughes et al., "Does the Global North Still Dominate Women's International Organizing? A Network Analysis from 1978 to 2008," *Mobilization: An International Quarterly* 23, no. 1 (March 1, 2018): 1–21, https://doi.org/10.17813/1086-671x-23-1-1.

77. Eric Goldstein, "Before the Arab Spring, the Unseen Thaw," *Human Rights Watch,* https://www.hrw.org/node/259729

78. Women's World Conference, *1975 World Conference on Women,* Mexico City, 19th June—2nd July 1975. http://www.5wwc.org/conference_background/1975_WCW.html

79. The Arab countries that chose to attend include: Algeria, Egypt, Iraq, Jordan, Kuwait, Lebanon, Libya, Morocco, Mauritania, Oman, Qatar, Saudi Arabia, Somalia, Sudan, Syria, Tunisia, UAE. *Representatives from the Palestine Liberation Organization were present as observers during the conference

80. Judith P. Zinsser, "From Mexico to Copenhagen to Nairobi: The United Nations Decade for Women, 1975–1985," *Journal of World History* 13, no. 1 (2002): 139–68, https://www.jstor.org/stable/20078945.

81. United Nations, "Report of the World Conference of the International Women's Year," in *The World Conference of the International Women's Year* (New York: United Nations, 1976), 1–199.

82. Pooja Khanna and Zachary Kimmel, "Convention on the Elimination of All Forms of Discrimination against Women (CEDAW) for Youth" (New York: UN Women, 2016).

83. Therese, Saliba. "Arab Feminism at the Millennium." *Signs* 25, no. 4 (2000): 1087–92. http://www.jstor.org/stable/3175492.

84. Nawla Darwiche, "Women in Arab NGOs: A Publication of the Arab Network for Non-Governmental Organizations, December 1999," *Feminist Review* 69, no. 1 (2001): 15–20, https://doi.org/https://doi.org/10.1080/014177800110070094.

85. Stephanie Maravankin, "Arab Feminism in the Arab Spring: Discourses on Solidarity, the Socio-Cultural Revolution, and the Political Revolution in Egypt, Tunisia, and Yemen.," *Clocks and Clouds* 7, no. 2 (2017), http://www.inquiriesjournal.com/a?id=1632.

86. Miriam, Cooke. "Women, Religion, and the Postcolonial Arab World." *Cultural Critique*, no. 45 (2000): 150–84. https://doi.org/10.2307/1354370.

87. Fatima Mernissi, *The Veil and the Male Elite : A Feminist Interpretation of Women's Rights in Islam* (1987; repr., New York: Basic Books, 1991).

88. Sherifa Zuhur, "Women and Empowerment in the Arab World," *Arab Studies Quarterly* 25, no. 4 (2003): 17–38.

89. Sahar Khamis and Amel Mili, eds., *Arab Women's Activism and Socio-Political Transformation : Unfinished Gendered Revolutions* (New York: Palgrave Macmillan, 2018).

90. Sahar Khamis and Amel Mili, eds., *Arab Women's Activism and Socio-Political Transformation : Unfinished Gendered Revolutions* (New York: Palgrave Macmillan, 2018), 10.

91. Sahar Khamis and Amel Mili, eds., *Arab Women's Activism and Socio-Political Transformation : Unfinished Gendered Revolutions* (New York: Palgrave Macmillan, 2018), 10.

92. Pernille Arenfeldt and Nawar Al-Hassan Golley, eds., *Mapping Arab Women's Movements: A Century of Transformations from Within* (Cairo: American University in Cairo Press, 2012).

93. Stephanie Chaban, "Women's Organizations, International Norms and the Emergence of Domestic Violence Legislation in the Middle East and North Africa: An Examination of Activism in Egypt and Lebanon" (PhD Thesis, 2016).

94. Ranj Alaaldin, "How the Iran-Iraq War Will Shape the Region for Decades to Come," *Brookings*, October 9, 2020, https://www.brookings.edu/

blog/order-from-chaos/2020/10/09/how-the-iran-iraq-war-will-shape-the-region-for-decades-to-come/.

95. Valentine M. Moghadam, "Women's Economic Participation in the Middle East: What Difference Has the Neoliberal Policy Turn Made?," *Journal of Middle East Women's Studies* 1, no. 1 (2005): 110–46, https://www.jstor.org/stable/40326851.

96. WHO, "Review of the Birth Spacing Programme," World Health Organization—Regional Office for the Eastern Mediterranean, accessed October 28, 2022, https://www.emro.who.int/omn/oman-news/review-of-the-birthspacing-programme.html.

97. Al Zahra, "Al-Zahra College for Women—about Us," Zcw.edu.om, 2022, http://www.zcw.edu.om/About-ZCW/About-Us.aspx.

98. Kim Murphy, "Kuwait Women Resist Iraq, Seek Recognition of Role : Gulf Crisis: Chants, Posters and Peaceful Marches Are Their Arms against Invaders. Three Have Died so Far.," *Los Angeles Times*, October 16, 1990, https://www.latimes.com/archives/la-xpm-1990-10-16-mn-2519-story.html.

99. Maria Juliá and Hadi Ridha, "Women and War: The Role Kuwaiti Women Played during the Iraqi Occupation," *Journal of International Development* 13, no. 5 (July 2001): 583–98, https://doi.org/10.1002/jid.782.

100. Equality Now, "Yemen—the Personal Status Act No. 20 of 1992," Yemen—The Personal Status Act No. 20 Of 1992, 2021, https://www.equalitynow.org/discriminatory_law/yemen_the_personal_status_act_no_20_of_1992/.

101. National legislative Bodies/National Authorities, "Yemen: Republican Decree, by Law No. 12 for 1994, Concerning Crimes and Penalties," Refworld, 1994, https://www.refworld.org/docid/3fec62f17.html.

102. World Bank, "Republic of Yemen the Status of Yemeni Women: From Aspiration to Opportunity Poverty Reduction and Economic Management Department Middle East and North Africa Region" (World Bank, 2014), http://documents1.worldbank.org/curated/en/640151468334820965/pdf/878200REVISED00Box0385200B00PUBLIC0.pdf.

103. Baker McKenzie, "Middle East: Baker McKenzie MENA Employment Newsletter—Labour Law Updates in the GCC Promoting Gender Equality—Ensure Your Current Salary Practices Are Compliant," Insight Plus, October 19, 2020, https://insightplus.bakermckenzie.com/bm/employment-compensation/middle-east-labour-law-updates-in-the-gcc-promoting-gender-equality-ensure-your-current-salary-practices-are-compliant#:~:text=8%20of%201980%20(the%20%22UAE.

104. UAE MFNCA, "Women in the United Arab Emirates: A Portrait of Progress" (OHCHR, 2008), https://www.google.com/url?q=https://www.ohchr.org/sites/default/files/lib-docs/HRBodies/UPR/Documents/Session3/AE/UPR_UAE_ANNEX3_E.pdf&sa=D&source=docs&ust=1668532711517486&usg=AOvVaw09U6f0nWy0-XMYfaczkG5f.

105. Rachid Zeffane and Linzi Kemp, "Emiratization: Benefits and Challenges of Strategic and Radical Change in the United Arab Emirates," in *Case Studies in Work, Employment and Human Resource Management*, ed. Tony Dundon and Adrian Wilkinson (Prahan, Vic., Australia: Tilde University Press, 2019), 245–53, https://doi.org/10.4337/9781788975599.00049.

106. Marwa Shalaby and Ariana Marnicio, "Women's Political Participation in Bahrain," in *Women Rising: In an beyond the Arab Spring*, ed. Rita Stephan and Mounira M. Charrad (New York: New York University Press, 2020), 321–29, https://doi.org/10.18574/nyu/9781479846641.003.0036.

107. Fakir Al Gharaibeh, "Women's Empowerment in Bahrain," *Journal of International Women's Studies* 12, no. 3 (2011): 96–113, https://vc.bridgew.edu/jiws/vol12/iss3/7.

108. Helen Ziegler & Associates, "The Role of Women in Qatar," Hziegler.com, 2019, https://www.hziegler.com/articles/role-of-women-in-qatar.html.

109. Ebtisam Al Kitbi, "Women's Political Status in the GCC States," Carnegie Endowment for International Peace, August 20, 2008, https://carnegieendowment.org/sada/21229.

110. Élisabeth Marteu, "Féminismes Israéliens et Palestiniens : Questions Postcoloniales," *Revue Tiers Monde* 209, no. 1 (2012): 71, https://doi.org/10.3917/rtm.209.0071.

111. Maura K. James, "Women and the Intifadas: The Evolution of Palestinian Women's Organizations," *Strife Journal*, no. 1 (2013): 18–22.

112. CEIRPP, "Report of the Committee on the Exercise of the Inalienable Rights of the Palestinian People" (United Nations, October 27, 1988), https://www.un.org/unispal/document/auto-insert-179999/.

113. Maria Holt, "Palestinian Women, Violence, and the Peace Process," *Development in Practice* 13, no. 2/3 (2003): 223–38, https://www.jstor.org/stable/4029594.

114. Maisoon Al-Amarneh, "Jordanian Feminist Movement and the Struggle for Social and Political Change: Achievements and Challenges," *Sayaran—WE4L Knowledge and Learning Platform*, no. 1 (2018), https://www.sayaran.org/jordanian-feminist-movement-and-the-struggle-for-social-and-political-change/.

115. OHCHR, "UN Treaty Body Database," Ohchr.org, accessed October 1, 2022, https://tbinternet.ohchr.org/_layouts/15/TreatyBodyExternal/Treaty.aspx?CountryID=88&Lang=EN.

116. Fasia Faqir, "Engendering Democracy and Islam in the Arab World," *Third World Quarterly* 18, no. 1 (1997): 165–74.

117. IPU, "Women's Suffrage," Ipu.org, 2019, http://archive.ipu.org/wmn-e/suffrage.htm;

Human Rights Watch, "Background on Women's Status in Iraq prior to the Fall of the Saddam Hussein Government" (Human Rights Watch, 2003), https://www.hrw.org/legacy/backgrounder/wrd/-iraq-women.pdf.

118. Open Societies Foundations, "Casualties of War: Iraqi Women's Rights and Reality Then and Now," Opensocietyfoundations.org, 2003, https://www.opensocietyfoundations.org/events/-casualties-w=ar-iraqi-womens-rights-and-reality-then-and-now.

119. Civil Society Knowledge Centre, "Giving Precedence to International Treaties," The Centre for Social Sciences Research and Action, May 23, 2019, https://civilsociety-centre.org/content/giving-precedence-international-treaties.

120. NCLW, "Mission and Vision," NCLW, accessed October 4, 2022, https://nclw.gov.lb/en/mission-and-vision-2/.

121. Zahia Smail Salhi, "Algerian Women, Citizenship, and the 'Family Code,'" *Gender and Development* 11, no. 3 (2003): 27–35, http://www.jstor.org/stable/4030558.

122. Aili Mari Tripp, "Women Are Deeply Involved in the Algerian Protests—on International Women's Day, and All the Time," The Washington Post, March 8, 2019, https://www.washingtonpost.com/politics/2019/03/08/-women-are-deeply-involved-algerian-protests-international-womens-day-all-time/.

123. UIA, "Collectif 95 Maghreb Égalité | UIA Yearbook Profile | Union of International Associations," uia.org, 2004, https://uia.org/s/or/en/1100003794.

124. Malika Remaoun, "Les Associations Féminines Pour Les Droits Des Femmes," *Insaniyat / إنسانيات*, no. 8 (August 31, 1999): 129–43, https://doi.org/10.4000/insaniyat.8331.

125. Association tunisienne des femmes démocrates, "Women's Rights in Tunisia Declaration" (ATFD, 2010), https://tbinternet.ohchr.org/Treaties/CEDAW/Shared%20Documents/TUN/INT_CEDAW_NGO_TUN_47_10160_E.pdf.

126. Valentine M. Moghadam, "The State and the Women's Movement in Tunisia: Mobilization, Institutionalization, and Inclusion" (New York: James A. Baker III Institute for Public Policy of Rice University, 2018).

127. Jazaya Gebril, "Women's Rights in Libya: Preserving Past Gains, Fearing for the Future—Legal Agenda," *Legal Agenda*, December 18, 2015, https://english.legal-agenda.com/womens-rights-in-libya-preserving-past-gains-fearing-for-the-future/.

128. Mohamed Karbal, "Human Rights in Libya: During and after Gaddafi," Mondaq, October 12, 2020, https://www.mondaq.com/-human-rights/993460/human-rights-in-libya-during-and-after-gaddafi-#:~:text=Human%20Rights%20in%20Practice%20under%20Gaddafi&text=Gaddafi.

129. JICA, "The Republic of Sudan: Country Gender Profile" (JICA, 2012), https://www.jica.go.jp/english/our_work/thematic_issues/gender/background/c8h0vm0000anjqj6-att/sudan_2012.pdf.

130. Balghis Badri, "Feminist Perspectives in the Sudan: An Analytical Overview," in *"Feminist Perspectives"* (Free University Berlin, 2005), https://www.fu-berlin.de/sites/gpo/tagungen/tagungfeministperspectives/balghis_badri.pdf.

131. IPU, "Women's Suffrage," Ipu.org, 2019, http://archive.ipu.org/wmn-e/suffrage.htm.

132. UNDP, "Gender Justice and the Law: Djibouti," *UNDP.org* (UNDP, 2019), https://www.undp.org/sites/g/files/zskgke326/files/migration/arabstates/Djibouti.Summary.19.Eng.pdf.

133. United Nations, "Ministry for the Promotion of Women, Family Well-Being, and Social Affairs National Ten-Year Evaluation Report on Implementation of the Beijing Platform for Action," *Republic of Djibouti Office of the Prime Minister* (UN, 2004), https://www.un.org/womenwatch/daw/Review/responses/DJIBOUTI-English.pdf.

134. Debra M. Timmons, "The Sixth Clan -Women Organize for Peace in Somalia: A Review of Published Literature," ed. Mary E. King (Geneva: University for Peace, 2004), http://maryking.info/wp-content/TheSixthClanWomenOrganizeforPeaceinSomalia.pdf.

135. UCA, "Comoros (1975-Present)," uca.edu, accessed November 4, 2022, https://uca.edu/politicalscience/dadm-project/sub-Saharan-africa-region/comoros-1975-present/.

136. United States Department of State, "U.S. Department of State Country Report on Human Rights Practices 2004—Comoros," Refworld, 2005, https://www.refworld.org/docid/4226d9698.html.

137. Centre for Public Impact, "Reforming Moroccan Family Law: The Moudawana," Centre For Public Impact (CPI), 2016, https://www.centreforpublicimpact.org/case-study/moroccan-moudawana-reform.

138. Human Rights Watch, "Letter to the King of Morocco on His Commitment to Withdraw Reservations to CEDAW," Human Rights Watch, April 14, 2010, https://www.hrw.org/news/2010/04/14/-letter-king-morocco-his-commitment-withdraw-reservations-cedaw.

139. Céline Lesourd, "The Lipstick on the Edge of the Well: Mauritanian Women and Political Power (1960–2014)," in F. Sadiqi, *Women's Rights in the Aftermath of the Arab Spring* (London: Palgrave Macmillan, 2016), 77–93.

140. Courants de Femmes, "AFCF—Association Des Femmes Chefs de Famille," courantsdefemmes.free.fr, accessed November 6, 2022, http://courantsdefemmes.free.fr/Assoces/Mauritanie/AFCF/AFCF.html.

141. Anna Borshchevskaya, "How the Death of the Soviet Union Transformed the Middle East," *Policy Analysis* The Washington Institute, December 21, 2021, https://www.washingtoninstitute.org/policy-analysis/how-death-soviet-union-transformed-middle-east.

142. Ibtesam Al Atiyat, "Current Faces of Arab Feminisms: Micro-Rebels, Art Activists and Virtual Heroines," *Friedrich Ebert Stiftung*, 2020, https://mena.fes.de/publications/e/the-current-faces-of-arab-feminism.

143. OHCHR, "Experts of the Committee on the Elimination of Discrimination against Women Praise Morocco for Legislation Prohibiting Discrimination, Ask about High Maternal Mortality and Female Illiteracy Rates in Rural Areas," *Press Release*. OHCHR, 2022, https://www.ohchr.org/en/press-releases/2022/06/experts-committee-elimination-discrimination-against-women-praise-morocco.; WUNRN, "Tunisia—Lifting of CEDAW Reservations Is Landmark Step for Gender Equality," Wunrn.com, 2014, https://wunrn.com/2014/05/tunisia-lifting-of-cedaw-reservations-is-landmark-step-for-gender-equality/.

144. United Nations, "United Nations Treaty Collection," treaties.un.org, accessed October 29, 2022, https://treaties.un.org/pages/ViewDetails.aspx?src=IND&mtdsg_no=IV-8&chapter=4&clang=_en#EndDec.

145. Union of International Associations, "The Yearbook of International Organizations | Union of International Associations," uia.org (Brill, 2021), https://uia.org/yearbook?qt-yb_intl_orgs=3.

146. Lina Abou-Habib, "The 'Right to Have Rights': Active Citizenship and Gendered Social Entitlements in Egypt, Lebanon and Palestine," *Gender & Development* 19, no. 3 (November 2011): 441–54, https://doi.org/10.1080/13510347.2011.625633.

147. Elizabeth Fernea, 1998 quoted in Saliba, Therese. "Arab Feminism at the Millennium." *Signs* 25, no. 4 (2000): 1087–92. http://www.jstor.org/stable/3175492.

148. Term used to describe the institutionalization and professionalization of organizations or movements.

149. Farah Daibes, "Smashing the Patriarchy & Co: How Arab Feminists Are Re-Politicizing Their Movement," (blog), July 5, 2021, https://mena.fes.de/press/e/smashing-the-patriarchy-co-how-arab-feminists-are-re-politicizing-their-movement.

150. Nicolas Gianni, Francesco Michele, and Chiara Lozza, "From 'Liberal' to 'Liberating' Empowerment: The Community Protection Approach as Best Practice to Address NGO-Ization," *Civil Society Review*, November 2021, https://doi.org/10.28943/csr.005.003.

151. Daibes, "Smashing."

152. COAR, "The Business of Empowering Women: Insights for Development Programming in Syria," COAR, May 15, 2020, https://coar-global.org/2020/05/15/the-business-of-empowering-women/.

153. Daibes, "Smashing."

154. Abdullahi Ahmed An-Na'im, "Human Rights in the Arab World: A Regional Perspective," *Human Rights Quarterly* 23, no. 3 (2001): 701–32, https://doi.org/10.1353/hrq.2001.0026.

155. Khamis and Mili, "Arab Women's Activism.," 13.

156. Stephanie Chaban, "Addressing Violence against Women through Legislative Reform in States Transitioning from the Arab Spring," in *Gender, Human Rights and the Limits of Legal Frameworks: Challenging the Place of Women's Rights in Post-Transition Countries*, ed. John Lahai and Khanyisela Moyo (London: Palgrave, 2018), 113–41.

157. Joseph Hincks, "Heirs of the Arab Spring," *Time*, January 2021, https://time.com/5927349/heirs-of-the-arab-spring/.

158. Hincks, "Heirs of the Arab Spring."

159. Yasmina Abouzzohour, "Heavy Lies the Crown: The Survival of Arab Monarchies, 10 Years after the Arab Spring," Brookings, March 8, 2021, https://www.brookings.edu/blog/order-from-chaos/2021/03/08/heavy-lies-the-crown-the-survival-of-arab-monarchies-10-years-after-the-arab-spring/.; Kelly McEvers, "Bahrain: The Revolution That Wasn't," *NPR*, January 5, 2012, https://www.npr.org/2012/01/05/144637499/-bahrain-the-revolution-that-wasnt.

160. Abouzzohour, "Heavy Lies the Crown."

161. Steve Coll, "In the Gulf, Dissidence Goes Digital," *The Washington Post*, March 29, 2005, https://www.washingtonpost.com/archive/politics/2005/03/29/in-the-gulf-dissidence-goes-digital/ad4fb146-f495-4399-ab91-c5d6df77779a/.

162. Associated Press in Kuwait City, "Kuwait Gets First Female Minister," *The Guardian*, June 13, 2005, https://www.theguardian.com/world/2005/jun/13/1.

163. Mark Tran, "First Women Elected to Kuwait Parliament," *The Guardian*, May 17, 2009, https://www.theguardian.com/world/2009/may/17/kuwait-women-elected-parliament.

164. Team Qatar, "Programmes and Initiatives | Team Qatar," www.olympic.qa, accessed August 28, 2022, https://www.olympic.qa/programmes-and-initiatives#:~:text=The%20Qatar%20Women.

165. Feminist Majority Foundation, "First Woman Minister Appointed in Qatar," Feminist Majority Foundation, May 15, 2003, https://feminist.org/news/first-woman-minister-appointed-in-qatar/.

166. MEI, "Sheikha Abdulla Al-Misnad," Middle East Institute, accessed November 6, 2022, https://www.mei.edu/profile/sheikha-abdulla-al-misnad.

167. BBC News Middle East, "Saudi Women Get Identity Cards," news.bbc.co.uk, December 10, 2001, http://news.bbc.co.uk/2/hi/middle_east/1702342.stm.

168. Norah Al-Faiz, "Norah Al-Faiz Faces, Vice-Minister at the Ministry of Education," *Faces of Saudi* (Arab News, April 19, 2020), https://facesofsaudi.com/19/04/2020/norah-al-faiz-ministry-of-education-faces-of-saudi-by-arab-news/.

169. Katherine Zoepf, "Talk of Women's Rights Divides Saudi Arabia (Published 2010)," *The New York Times*, May 31, 2010, sec. World, https://www.

nytimes.com/2010/06/01/world/middleeast/01iht-saudi.html.

170. Ebtisam Al Kitbi, "Women's Political Status in the GCC States," Carnegie Endowment for International Peace, August 20, 2008, https://carnegieendowment.org/sada/21229.

171. The National Portal of the Kingdom of Bahrain, "Women in Bahrain," Bahrain.bh, 2011, https://www.bahrain.bh/new/en/equality-women_en.html.

172. Ministry of Foreign Affairs, "The Kingdom of Bahrain Has Acceded and Ratified to Core Human Rights Instruments," www.mofa.gov.bh, accessed November 1, 2022, https://www.mofa.gov.bh/Default.aspx?tabid=9725&language=en-U.S..

173. Bahrain News Agency, "Bahrain News Agency," www.bna.bh, February 13, 2022, https://www.bna.bh/en/NationalActionCharter2002ConstitutionconfirmlegitimacyofBahrainiwomensrights.aspx?cms=q8FmFJgiscL2fwIzON1%2BDmNtPWA4PtwLWj6RV9fMoNw%3D.

174. Houda Nonoo, "Bahrain's Women Pioneers: Dr. Nada Haffadh," Ambassador Houda Nonoo, March 11, 2012, https://houdanonoo.wordpress.com/2012/03/11/bahrains-women-pioneers-dr-nada-haffadh/.

175. Woman This Month, "Sisters Doing It for Themselves," womanthismonth.com, May 1, 2018, https://www.google.com/url?sa=t&rct=j&q=&esrc=s&source=web&cd=&cad=rja&uact=8&ved=2ahUKEwiepsns7Iv7AhXwEEQIHZyiAgEQFnoECAoQAQ&url=https%3A%2F%2Fwomanthismonth.com%2Fsisters-doing-it-for-themselves%2F&usg=AOvVaw1C8RcxKpAnuRAGy30EA2XY.; WUNRN, "First Arab Woman President of UN General Assembly—Shaikha Haya of Bahrain," WUNRN, September 12, 2006, https://wunrn.com/2006/09/first-arab-woman-president-of-un-general-assembly-shaikha-haya-of-bahrain/.

176. The National Portal of the Kingdom of Bahrain, "Women in Bahrain," Bahrain.bh, 2011, https://www.bahrain.bh/new/en/equality-women_en.html.

177. Bureau of Democracy, Human Rights, and Labor, "Bahrain," U.S. Department of State, November 17, 2010, https://2009-2017.state.gov/j/drl/rls/irf/2010/148815.htm.

178. Ahlam Khalfan Al Subhi and Amy Erica Smith, "Electing Women to New Arab Assemblies: The Roles of Gender Ideology, Islam, and Tribalism in Oman," *International Political Science Review* 40, no. 1 (2019): 90–107, https://doi.org/10.2139/ssrn.2827795.; TAS News Service, "After Nearly 17 Years, Oman's First Woman Minister Dr Rawya al Busaidi Steps Down," *The Arabian Stories News,* August 25, 2020, https://www.thearabianstories.com/2020/08/25/after-nearly-17-years-omans-first-woman-minister-dr-rawya-al-busaidi-steps-down/.

179. UNICEF, "Universal Periodic Review—Human Rights Council Oman" (OHCHR), accessed September 21, 2022, https://www.ohchr.org/sites/default/files/lib-docs/HRBodies/UPR/Documents/Session10/OM/UNICEF_

UnitedNationsChildren%27sFund_eng.pdf.; International Labour Organisation, "Sultanate of Oman Signs Decent Work Country Programme, the Second Gulf Country after the Kingdom of Bahrain," www.ilo.org, June 15, 2010, https://www.ilo.org/global/about-the-ilo/newsroom/news/WCMS_141756/lang—en/index.htm.

180. Quentin Müller and Sebastian Castelier, "Omani Elections: Women Making Small Leaps in Politics," *Middle East Eye*, 2016, https://www.middleeasteye.net/features/omani-elections-women-making-small-leaps-politics.

181. OHCHR, "Women in the United Arab Emirates: A Portrait of Progress" (OHCHR, 2008), https://www.ohchr.org/sites/default/files/lib-docs/HRBodies/UPR/Documents/Session3/AE/UPR_UAE_ANNEX3_E.pdf.

182. OHCHR, "Women in the United Arab Emirates: A Portrait of Progress" (OHCHR, 2008), https://www.ohchr.org/sites/default/files/lib-docs/HRBodies/UPR/Documents/Session3/AE/UPR_UAE_ANNEX3_E.pdf.

183. UNDP, "Making Globalization Work for All" (UNDP, 2007), https://www.undp.org/publications/undp-annual-report-2007.

184. Yemen News Agency (Saba), "Yemeni Women Call for Their 15 Percent Quota," www.saba.ye, August 21, 2008, https://www.saba.ye/en/news162183.htm.

185. Tawakkol Karman, "About," tawakkolkarman.net, n.d., https://www.tawakkolkarman.net/enabout.

186. Human Rights Watch, "Background on Women's Status in Iraq prior to the Fall of the Saddam Hussein Government" (Human Rights Watch, 2003), https://www.hrw.org/legacy/backgrounder/wrd/iraq-women.pdf.

187. Radhika Coomaraswamy, "Report of the Special Rapporteur on Violence against Women, Its Causes and Consequences," (ECOSOC, 2002), https://digitallibrary.un.org/record/459009?ln=en.

188. MADRE, "Organization of Women's Freedom in Iraq," MADRE, accessed November 1, 2022, https://www.madre.org/partners/organization-womens-freedom-iraq#:~:text=The%20Organization%20of%20Women.

189. John Leland and Riyadh Mohammed, "Iraqi Women Are Seeking Greater Political Influence," *The New York Times,* February 17, 2010, sec. World, https://www.nytimes.com/2010/02/17/world/middleeast/17iraqwomen.html.

190. Khalid al-Ansary, "Thousands Rally in Iraq's 'Day of Rage' Protests," *Reuters,* February 25, 2011, sec. World News, https://www.reuters.com/article/us-iraq-protests-idUSTRE71O1RN20110225.

191. Ibtesam Al-Atiyat, *The Women's Movement in Jordan: Activism, Discourses, and Strategies* (Amman: Friedrich Ebert Stiftung, 2003).

192. OECD, "Women's Political Participation in Jordan" (MENA OECD, 2018), https://www.oecd.org/mena/governance/womens-political-participation-in-jordan.pdf.

193. Laith K. Nasrawin, "Protection against Domestic Violence in Jordanian Law and International Conventions," *Arab Law Quarterly* 31, no. 4 (2017): 363–87, https://www.jstor.org/stable/26567164.

194. Maura K. James, "Women and the Intifadas: The Evolution of Palestinian Women's Organizations," *Strife*, no. 1 (2013): 18–22, https://www.strifejournal.org/wp-content/uploads/2020/05/STRIFE_1_3_JAMES_M_18_22.pdf.

195. Najla M. Shahwan, "The Ongoing Struggle of Palestinian Women | Opinion," *Daily Sabah*, March 20, 2020, https://www.dailysabah.com/opinion/op-ed/the-ongoing-struggle-of-palestinian-women.

196. Sophie Richter-Devroe, "Gender Equality and Women's Rights in Palestinian Territories" (Policy Department Citizens' Rights and Constitutional Affairs, 2011), https://www.europarl.europa.eu/document/activities/cont/201110/20111027ATT30536/20111027ATT30536EN.pdf.

197. Euro-Mediterranean Women's Foundation, "Palestine—Ministry of Women's Affairs," Euromedwomen.foundation, May 17, 2015, https://www.euromedwomen.foundation/pg/en/resources/view/4364/palestine-ministry-of-womens-affairs.

198. Najla M. Shahwan, "The Ongoing Struggle of Palestinian Women | Opinion," *Daily Sabah*, March 20, 2020, https://www.dailysabah.com/opinion/op-ed/the-ongoing-struggle-of-palestinian-women.

199. Ersun N. Kurtulus, "'The Cedar Revolution': Lebanese Independence and the Question of Collective Self-Determination," *British Journal of Middle Eastern Studies* 36, no. 2 (2009): 195–214, https://www.jstor.org/stable/40593253.

200. Rita Stephan, "Lebanese Women's Rights beyond the Cedar Revolution," in *Arab Women's Activism and Socio-Political Transformation: Unfinished Gendered Revolutions*, ed. Sahar Khamis and Amel Mili (London: Palgrave Macmillan, 2018), 73–88, https://doi.org/10.1007/978-3-319-60735-1_4.

201. Kafa, "About KAFA," كفى, n.d., https://kafa.org.lb/en/about.

202. Beit el-Hanane, "Beit El Hanane," Beit el Hanane, accessed October 28, 2022, https://beitelhanane.wordpress.com/.

203. ABAAD, "About | ABAAD," www.abaadmena.org, n.d., https://www.abaadmena.org/about.

204. Catherine Bellafronto, "Refworld | Women's Rights in the Middle East and North Africa—Syria," Refworld (Freedom House, 2005), https://www.refworld.org/docid/47387b70c.html [accessed 15 August 2022].

205. OHCHR, "Human Rights Council Debates Situation of Human Rights in Syrian Arab Republic in Special Session," OHCHR, August 22, 2011, https://www.ohchr.org/en/press-releases/2011/08/-human-rights-council-debates-situation-human-rights-syrian-arab-republic.

206. Canada: Immigration and Refugee Board of Canada, "Tunisia: Protection and Resources Available to Women Fleeing Family Abuse; Whether a Single Woman Could Find Safety in Any Part of the Country (2000-July 2004)," Refworld, 2004, https://www.refworld.org/docid/41501c6423.html.

207. The Advocates for Human Rights and MRA Mobilising for Rights Associates, "Tunisia: Submission to the Committee on Economic, Social and Cultural Rights," Ohchr.org, 2016, https://tbinternet.ohchr.org/Treaties/CESCR/Shared%20Documents/TUN/INT_CESCR_CSS_TUN_24991_E.docx.

208. Iman Zayat, "Tunisia Marks Long Struggle for Women's Rights | Iman Zayat," *The Arab Weekly*, August 15, 2020, https://thearabweekly.com/tunisia-marks-long-struggle-womens-rights.

209. HRW, "Tunisia: Government Lifts Restrictions on Women's Rights Treaty," Human Rights Watch, September 6, 2011, https://www.hrw.org/news/2011/09/06/tunisia-government-lifts-restrictions-womens-rights-treaty.

210. Bruce Maddy-Weitzman, "Women, Islam, and the Moroccan State: The Struggle over the Personal Status Law," *Middle East Journal* 59, no. 3 (2005): 393–410, https://www.jstor.org/stable/4330155.

211. Bruce Maddy-Weitzman, "Women, Islam, and the Moroccan State: The Struggle over the Personal Status Law," *Middle East Journal* 59, no. 3 (2005): 393–410, https://www.jstor.org/stable/4330155.

212. Katja Žvan Elliott, "Morocco and Its Women's Rights Struggle," *Journal of Middle East Women's Studies* 10, no. 2 (2014): 1–30, https://doi.org/10.2979/jmiddeastwomstud.10.2.1.

213. Reuters, "Moroccan Single Mother Burns Herself in Protest," *Reuters*, February 23, 2011, sec. Top News, https://www.reuters.com/article/cnews-us-morocco-protest-idCATRE71M4ZF20110223.

214. "Asha Hagi Elmi—Right Livelihood," Right Livelihood, August 10, 2021, https://rightlivelihood.org/the-change-makers/find-a-laureate/asha-hagi-elmi/.

215. Debra M. Timmons, "The Sixth Clan—Women Organize for Peace in Somalia: A Review of Published Literature," 2004, http://maryking.info/wp-content/TheSixthClanWomenOrganizeforPeaceinSomalia.pdf.

216. UNHCR, "Preventing and Reducing Statelessness: Good Practices in Promoting and Adopting Gender Equality in Nationality Laws" (UNHCR, 2014), http://www.unhcr.org/531a001c9.pdf.

217. United Nations, "Ministry for the Promotion of Women, Family Well-Being, and Social Affairs National Ten-Year Evaluation Report on Implementation of the Beijing Platform for Action," Republic of Djibouti Office of the Prime Minister (UN, 2004), https://www.un.org/womenwatch/daw/Review/responses/DJIBOUTI-English.pdf.

218. United Nations, "Ministry for the Promotion of Women, Family Well-Being, and Social Affairs National Ten-Year Evaluation Report on Implementation of the Beijing Platform for Action," Republic of Djibouti Office of the Prime Minister (UN, 2004), https://www.un.org/womenwatch/daw/Review/responses/DJIBOUTI-English.pdf.

219. IDEA, "Gender Quotas Database: Djibouti," International Institute for Democracy and Electoral Assistance, accessed November 7, 2022, https://www.idea.int/data-tools/data/gender-quotas/country-view/93/35.

220. Japan International Cooperation Agency, "The Republic of Sudan: Country Gender Profile" (JICA, 2012), https://www.jica.go.jp/english/our_work/thematic_issues/gender/background/-c8h0vm0000anjqj6-att/sudan_2012.pdf.

221. Japan International Cooperation Agency, "The Republic of Sudan: Country Gender Profile" (JICA, 2012), https://www.jica.go.jp/english/our_work/thematic_issues/gender/background/-c8h0vm0000anjqj6-att/sudan_2012.pdf.

222. International Labour Organisation, "Law No. 12 of 1378 [2010] on Labour Relations." (ILO, 2010), https://www.ilo.org/dyn/natlex/natlex4.detail?p_isn=86041&p_lang=.

223. Chris Stephen, Irina Kalashnikova, and David Smith, "Libyan Women: It's Our Revolution Too," *The Guardian*, September 16, 2011, https://www.theguardian.com/world/2011/sep/16/libyan-women-our-revolution-too.

224. Musawah, "Mauritania: Overview of Family Laws and Practices" (Musawah, 2017), https://www.musawah.org/wp-content/uploads/2019/03/-Mauritania-Overview-Table.pdf.

225. Front Line Defenders, "Mekfoula Mint Brahim," *Front Line Defenders*, February 21, 2020, https://www.frontlinedefenders.org/en/profile/mekfoula-mint-brahim.

226. Hassan Ould Moctar, "Social Movements and Unrest in Mauritania since the Arab Uprisings," openDemocracy, June 2013, https://www.opendemocracy.net/en/social-movements-and-unrest-in-mauritania-since-arab-uprisings/.

227. Nadia Oweidat et al., "The Kefaya Movement: A Case Study of a Grassroots Reform Initiative," *Rand*, October 26, 2008, https://www.rand.org/pubs/monographs/MG778.html.

228. Rana Magdy, "Egyptian Feminist Movement: A Brief History," *openDemocracy*, March 8, 2017, https://www.opendemocracy.net/en/north-africa-west-asia/egyptian-feminist-movement-brief-history/.

229. Claudia Mende, "Egyptian Women's Rights Activist Hoda Badran: Women as Losers of the Revolution?—Qantara.de," translated by Nina Coon, *Qantara—Dialogue with the Islamic World*, 2012, https://en.qantara.de/content/egyptian-womens-rights-activist-hoda-badran-women-as-losers-of-the-revolution.

230. Wilson Center, "The Global Impact of 9/11: Twenty Years on | Wilson Center,"

Video, *Wilson Center*, September 9, 2021, https://www.wilsoncenter.org/event/global-impact-911-twenty-years.

231. Intissar Fakir, "Snapshot of the Economic Crisis in the Arab World," Carnegie Endowment for International Peace, July 7, 2009, https://carnegieendowment.org/sada/23357.

232. Shalendra D. Sharma, "The Arab World amidst the Global Financial Crisis of 2008–2009," *Contemporary Arab Affairs* 3, no. 1 (2010): 38–52, https://www.jstor.org/stable/48599700.

233. Helle Malmvig and Christina Markus Lassen, "The Arab Uprisings: Regional Implications and International Responses," *IEMed Mediterranean Yearbook* (IEMed, 2013), https://www.iemed.org/publication/the-arab-uprisings-regional-implications-and-international-responses/.

234. Nicola Pratt quoted in: UC Press Blog, "Author Spotlight: Nicola Pratt on Women's Activism in the Middle East," UC Press Blog, 2020, https://www.ucpress.edu/blog/52517/author-spotlight-nicola-pratt-on-womens-activism-in-the-middle-east/.

235. Margot Badran quoted in: Wilson Center, "Book Talk: 'Women Rising: In and beyond the Arab Spring,'" Wilson Center, 2020, https://www.wilsoncenter.org/event/book-talk-women-rising-and-beyond-arab-spring.

236. Mounira Charrad quoted in: Wilson Center, "Book Talk: 'Women Rising: In and beyond the Arab Spring,'" Wilson Center, 2020, https://www.wilsoncenter.org/event/book-talk-women-rising-and-beyond-arab-spring.

237. Deniz Kandiyoti as quoted in Naomi Sakr, "Seen and Starting to Be Heard: Women and the Arab Media in a Decade of Change," *Social Research: An International Quarterly* 69, no. 3 (September 2002): 821–50, https://doi.org/10.1353/sor.2002.0033.

238. Sahar Khamis quoted in Sarah El-Shaarawi, "Women's Activisms and the Future of Feminist Movements in the Arab Region," Arab Media & Society, March 3, 2022, https://www.arabmediasociety.com/womens-activisms-and-the-future-of-feminist-movements-in-the-arab-region/.

239. Khamis in "Women's Activisms."

240. Khamis and Mili, *Arab Women's Activism*," 17.

241. Mounira Charrad quoted in: Wilson Center, "Book Talk: 'Women Rising: In and beyond the Arab Spring,'" Wilson Center, 2020, https://www.wilsoncenter.org/event/book-talk-women-rising-and-beyond-arab-spring.

242. Narjas Zatat, "10 Events That Drastically Changed the Middle East," *Https://English.alaraby.co.uk/*, December 23, 2019, https://english.alaraby.co.uk/news/10-events-drastically-changed-middle-east.

243. Kuwait News Agency (KUNA), "22 Female Prosecutors Take Oath," www.kuna.net.kw, November 6, 2014, https://www.kuna.net.kw/ArticleDetails.aspx?id=2406968&language=en.

244. Gulf Business, "New Kuwait Cabinet Has GCC's First Female Finance Minister," Bloomberg, December 17, 2019, https://gulfbusiness.com/-new-kuwait-cabinet-gccs-first-female-finance-minister/.

245. Rothna Begum, "Domestic Violence Law Signals Hope for Kuwait's Women," Human Rights Watch, September 29, 2020, https://www.hrw.org/news/2020/09/29/domestic-violence-law-signals-hope-kuwaits-women.

246. Committee on the Elimination of Discrimination against Women, "CEDAW/C/ARE/CO/2–3: Concluding Observations on the Combined Second and Third Periodic Reports of the United Arab Emirates" (United Nations, 2015), https://www.ohchr.org/en/documents/concluding-observations/cedawcareco2-3-concluding-observations-combined-second-and-third.

247. Official Portal of the UAE Government, "Family Protection Policy," u.ae, n.d., https://u.ae/en/about-the-uae/strategies-initiatives-and-awards/federal-governments-strategies-and-plans/family-protection-policy.

248. Human Rights Watch, "Boxed in | Women and Saudi Arabia's Male Guardianship System," Human Rights Watch, June 6, 2017, https://www.hrw.org/report/2016/07/16/boxed/women-and-saudi-arabias-male-guardianship-system.

249. BBC, "Saudi Arabia's King Appoints Women to Shura Council," *BBC News*, January 11, 2013, https://www.bbc.com/news/world-middle-east-20986428.

250. Human Rights Watch, "Saudi Arabia: 'Unofficial' Guardianship Rules Banned," HRW, May 9, 2017, https://www.hrw.org/news/2017/05/09/saudi-arabia-unofficial-guardianship-rules-banned#:~:text=(Beirut)%20%E2%80%93%20Saudi%20Arabia.

251. Human Rights Watch, "Saudi Arabia: Important Advances for Saudi Women," HRW, August 2, 2019, https://www.hrw.org/news/2019/08/02/saudi-arabia-important-advances-saudi-women.

252. Human Rights Watch, "Saudi Women Are Speaking up Online," Human Rights Watch, April 14, 2020, https://www.hrw.org/news/2020/04/14/-saudi-women-are-speaking-online.

253. Permanent Mission of the State of Qatar to the United Nations, "Word from the Permanent Representative," Mission.qa, accessed November 8, 2022, https://ny.mission.qa/en/the-embassy/the-permanent-representative.

254. Al Jazeera, "Qatar Appoints Four Women to Shura Council," www.aljazeera.com, November 9, 2017, https://www.aljazeera.com/news/2017/11/9/qatar-appoints-four-women-to-shura-council.

255. Human Rights Watch, "Everything I Have to Do Is Tied to a Man," Human Rights Watch (HRW, March 29, 2021), https://www.hrw.org/report/2021/03/29/everything-i-have-do-tied-man/women-and-qatars-male-guardianship-rules

256. Charles Schmitz, "Yemen's National Dialogue," Middle East Institute, March 10, 2014, https://www.mei.edu/publications/yemens-national-dialogue.

257. Sofia Petkar, "Woman Who Campaigned for Female Literacy Shot Dead in Broad Daylight," *Metro*, January 7, 2017, https://metro.co.uk/2017/01/07/woman-who-campaigned-for-female-literacy-shot-dead-in-broad-daylight-6366535/#:~:text=A%20female%20charity%20worker%20who.

258. Safia Mahdi, "Yemen: Women in Houthi Area No Longer in Control of Their Own Body | Daraj," daraj.com, February 3, 2021, https://daraj.com/en/66573/.

259. Ahmed Al-Haj and Samy Magdy, "Yemeni Rebels Sentence Actor, Her 3 Companions to Prison," *AP NEWS*, November 8, 2021, https://apnews.com/article/middle-east-iran-yemen-sanaa-human-rights-watch-0a7683396afff468322faed3b49d629d.

260. UNICEF, "Yemen Crisis," Unicef.org (UNICEF, 2022), https://www.unicef.org/emergencies/yemen-crisis.

261. Supreme Council for Women, "National Strategy to Protect Women from Domestic Violence," www.scw.bh, 2015, https://www.scw.bh/en/InformationCenter/Pages/nsdv.aspx.; Kingdom of Bahrain, "Law No. (19) of 2017," *Bahrain.bh* (The National Portal of the Kingdom of Bahrain, 2019), https://www.google.com/url?q=https://bahrain.bh/wps/wcm/connect/1edd4432-107d-4cfa-8e2c-6aabeec852fa/LAW%2BNO.%2B%252819%2529%2BOF%2B2017.pdf?MOD%3DAJPERES&sa=D&source=docs&ust=1667902536471322&usg=AOvVaw0xuJLnUqFpUp8Rc8eCa2n8.

262. Jihan Abdalla, "Rights Groups Slam Bahrain over Detention of Female Activists," www.aljazeera.com, October 29, 2019, https://www.aljazeera.com/news/2019/10/29/rights-groups-slam-bahrain-over-detention-of-female-activists.

263. ADHRB and BIRD, "Breaking the Silence: Bahraini Women Political Prisoners Expose Systemic Abuses" (Washington DC: ADHRB, 2019), https://www.adhrb.org/wp-content/uploads/2019/09/ADHRB_BreakingTheSilence_Web.pdf.

264. The Arab Weekly, "One Woman to Represent All Women in Oman Shura Council," *AW*, October 23, 2015, https://thearabweekly.com/-one-woman-represent-all-women-oman-shura-council.

265. Quentin Müller and Sebastian Castelier, "Omani Elections: Women Making Small Leaps in Politics," *Middle East Eye*, 2016, https://www.middleeasteye.net/features/omani-elections-women-making-small-leaps-politics.

266. Freedom House, "Oman: Freedom in the World 2020 Country Report," Freedom House, 2020, https://freedomhouse.org/country/oman/freedom-world/2020.

267. Alaa Nassar, "Keeping Hope, but Still Waiting: Syrian Feminism and a Decade of Revolution," *Syria Direct*, March 4, 2021, https://

syriadirect.org/in-a-decade-of-hopes-and-hopes-dashed-the-syrian-feminist-movement-mirrors-the-trajectory-of-the-revolution/.

268. Alaa Nassar, "Keeping Hope, but Still Waiting: Syrian Feminism and a Decade of Revolution," *Syria Direct*, March 4, 2021, https://syriadirect.org/in-a-decade-of-hopes-and-hopes-dashed-the-syrian-feminist-movement-mirrors-the-trajectory-of-the-revolution/.

269. Taarek Refaat, "Syria's 1st Parliament Speaker 'Hadiya Abbas' Dies of Heart Attack" see. news, November 14, 2021, https://see.news/syrias-1st-parliament-speaker-hadiya-abbas-dies-of-heart-attack.

270. UN Women, "A Group of Women Has Bridged Differences towards Peace in Syria," UN Women—Arab States, November 1, 2022, https://arabstates.unwomen.org/en/stories/feature-story/2022/11/a-group-of-women-has-bridged-differences-towards-peace-in-syria.

271. Daniel Hilton, "The Shifting Role of Women in Syria's Economy" (The Tahrir Institute for Middle East Policy, 2017), https://timep.org/syrias-women/economy/the-shifting-role-of-women-in-syrias-economy/.

272. Wilson Center, "Timeline: The Rise, Spread and Fall of the Islamic State," Wilson Center, October 28, 2019, https://www.wilsoncenter.org/article/timeline-the-rise-spread-and-fall-the-islamic-state.

273. Wilson Center, "Timeline: The Rise, Spread and Fall of the Islamic State," Wilson Center, October 28, 2019, https://www.wilsoncenter.org/article/timeline-the-rise-spread-and-fall-the-islamic-state.

274. Borgen Magazine, "Remaining Barriers to Women's Rights in Iraq," Borgen, November 25, 2020, https://www.borgenmagazine.com/remaining-barriers-to-womens-rights-in-iraq/.

275. Taif Alkhudary, "Iraqi Women Are Engaged in a Struggle for Their Rights," LSE Middle East Centre, June 15, 2020, https://blogs.lse.ac.uk/mec/2020/06/15/iraqi-women-are-engaged-in-a-struggle-for-their-rights/.

276. UNESCWA, "Social and Economic Situation of Palestinian Women and Girls: July 2012—June 2014" (New York: United Nations, 2015).

277. United Nations, "Special Focus: Gaza Strip—Is the Closure of the Tunnels from Egypt Further Suffocating the Gaza Economy?—WFP Food Security Analysis," *Question of Palestine*, February 2014, https://www.un.org/unispal/document/auto-insert-196041/.

278. UNESCWA, "Social and Economic Situation of Palestinian Women and Girls: July 2012—June 2014" (New York: United Nations, 2015).

279. Human Rights Watch, "Human Rights Watch, Women's Centre for Legal Aid and Counselling, and Equality Now, Joint Submission to the CEDAW Committee on the State of Palestine, 70th Session," Human Rights Watch, June 11, 2018, https://www.hrw.org/news/2018/06/11/human-rights-watch-womens-centre-legal-aid-and-counselling-and-equality-now-joint#:~:text=Palestine%20acceded%20to%20the%20UN.

280. Human Rights Watch, "Palestine: 'Marry-Your-Rapist' Law Repealed," Human Rights Watch, May 10, 2018, https://www.hrw.org/news/2018/05/10/palestine-marry-your-rapist-law-repealed.

281. Fidaa Al Zaanin, "Feminist Protests in Palestine—Rosa-Luxemburg-Stiftung," www.rosalux.de, March 8, 2021, https://www.rosalux.de/en/news/id/44203.

282. Huthifa Fayyad, "Gaza's Great March of Return Protests Explained," *Al Jazeera*, March 30, 2019, https://www.aljazeera.com/news/2019/3/30/gazas-great-march-of-return-protests-explained.

283. OHCHR, "Israel/Palestine: UN Experts Call on Governments to Resume Funding for Six Palestinian CSOs Designated by Israel as 'Terrorist Organisations,'" Press Release OHCHR, April 25, 2022, https://www.ohchr.org/en/press-releases/2022/04/israelpalestine-un-experts-call-governments-resume-funding-six-palestinian.

284. Nasim Ahmed, "Remembering Israel's 2021 Onslaught on Gaza," *Middle East Monitor*, May 6, 2022, https://www.middleeastmonitor.com/20220506-remembering-israels-2021-onslaught-on-gaza/.

285. DW, "Jordan Repeals 'Marry the Rapist' Law—DW—08/01/2017," dw.com, January 8, 2017, https://www.dw.com/en/jordan-repeals-marry-the-rapist-law/a-39924374.

286. Hanna Davis, "'Elephant in the Room': Jordanian Women and Equal Rights," www.aljazeera.com, February 18, 2022, https://www.aljazeera.com/news/2022/2/18/elephant-in-the-room-jordanian-womens-struggle-for-rights.

287. UN Women, "Historic Day for Women in Lebanon as Parliament Repeals Rape Law," UN Women, August 18, 2017, https://www.unwomen.org/en/news/stories/2017/8/news-lebanon-parliament-repeals-rape-law; Human Rights Watch, "Lebanon: Sexual Harassment Law Missing Key Protections," HRW, March 5, 2021, https://www.hrw.org/news/2021/03/05/lebanon-sexual-harassment-law-missing-key-protections.

288. Najet Tnani, "Tunisian Women at the Crossroad: Between a Feminist Spring and an Islamist Winter," *Al-Raida Journal*, no. 151 (July 17, 2020): 35–44, https://doi.org/10.32380/alrj.vi.1768.

289. Salsabil Chellali, "Tunisia Tramples Gender Parity ahead of Parliamentary Elections," Human Rights Watch, November 2, 2022, https://www.hrw.org/news/2022/11/02/tunisia-tramples-gender-parity-ahead-parliamentary-elections.

290. Maaike Voorhoeve, "The Tunisian Law on Violence against Women," *Cahiers D'Études Africaines*, no. 242 (2021): 377–94, https://doi.org/https://doi.org/10.4000/etudesafricaines.34304.; Elspeth Dehnert, "As Lebanon, Jordan, Tunisia End 'Marry-Your-Rapist' Laws, Where Next?," *The New Humanitarian*, August 22, 2017, https://

deeply.thenewhumanitarian.org/womenandgirls/articles/2017/08/22/as-lebanon-jordan-tunisia-end-marry-your-rapist-laws-where-next.; BBC, "Tunisian Women Free to Marry Non-Muslims," *BBC News*, September 15, 2017, sec. Africa, https://www.bbc.com/news/world-africa-41278610.

291. Michael Drinkwater, Hanan Kwinana, and Awny Amer, "Final Evaluation of the AMAL Programme: 'Supporting Women's Transformative Leadership at Changing Times in the MENA Region'" (Oxfam, 2016), https://oxfamintermon.s3.amazonaws.com/sites/default/files/documentos/files/EF-%20Marruecos%20abr16.pdf.

292. Aaron T. Rose, "Protesters Demand Women's Rights in the Constitution," dailynewsegypt.com, November 13, 2013, https://dailynewsegypt.com/2013/11/13/protesters-demand-womens-rights-in-the-constitution/.

293. Nadda Osman, "Egypt Orders Arrest of Hotel Rape Suspects Following Investigation," *Middle East Eye*, August 25, 2020, https://www.middleeasteye.net/news/egypt-metoo-cairo-hotel-rape-arrest-suspects.

294. Oliver Holmes, "Libya Drops Election Quota for Women," *Reuters*, January 20, 2012, sec. Commodities News, https://www.reuters.com/article/libya-women-idAFL6E8CK1SF20120120.

295. BBC News, "Libya Profile—Timeline," *BBC News*, September 3, 2018, https://www.bbc.com/news/world-africa-13755445.

296. UNSMIL, "Martin Kobler: Establishment of Women's Empowerment Unit a Key Step to Include Women in Politics," UNSMIL, September 9, 2016, https://unsmil.unmissions.org/martin-kobler-establishment-women%E2%80%99s-empowerment-unit-key-step-include-women-politics.

297. Amnesty International, "Libya: Abducted Politician's Fate Remains Unknown a Year On, amid Ongoing Disappearances," www.amnesty.org, July 17, 2020, https://www.amnesty.org/en/latest/news/2020/07/libya-abducted-politicians-fate-remains-unknown-a-year-on-amid-ongoing-disappearances/.

298. UNSC, "United Nations Support Mission in Libya: Report of the Secretary General" (UNSC, January 7, 2019).

299. https://arabstates.unwomen.org/en/digital-library/publications/2020/04/the-economic-and-social-impact-of-conflict-on-libyan-women

300. The Arab Weekly, "Libya's New Cabinet Includes Five Women, Still below Pledge," *AW*, March 12, 2021, https://thearabweekly.com/libyas-new-cabinet-includes-five-women-still-below-pledge.

301. Women's Learning Partnership, "Aminetou Ely (Mint El-Moctar) Oral History Audio Files | Women's Learning Partnership," learningpartnership.org, 2015, https://learningpartnership.org/resource/aminetou-ely-mint-el-moctar-oral-history-audio-files.

302. Annie Kelly, "Anti-Slavery Activists in Mauritania Face Violent Clampdown, Rights Groups Warn," *The Guardian*, January 20, 2016, https://www.theguardian.com/global-development/2016/jan/20/anti-slavery-activists-in-mauritania-face-violent-clampdown-rights-groups-warn.

303. Kuwait Times, "Confronting Sexual Violence in a Conservative Mauritania," *Kuwait Times*, March 7, 2019, https://www.kuwaittimes.com/confronting-sexual-violence-in-a-conservative-mauritania/.

304. Global Slavery Index, "Global Slavery Index" (Walk Free Foundation, 2018), https://www.globalslaveryindex.org/resources/downloads/#gsi-2018.

305. International Federation for Human Rights, "Djibouti: Political Opponents Shot Dead by Security Forces during Demonstration," Press Release. International Federation for Human Rights, February 28, 2103, https://www.fidh.org/en/region/Africa/djibouti/Djibouti-Political-opponents-shot-13063.

306. AfricaNews, "France: Djiboutian Activists Continue Hunger Strike against Rape by Soldiers," *Africanews*, 2016, https://www.africanews.com/2016/04/05/france-djiboutian-activists-continue-hunger-strike-against-rape-by-soldiers/.

307. '16 Days of Activism' is an international campaign to raise awareness and take action to combat gender-based violence.; UNFPA, "Closing of the 16 Days of Activism against Gender-Based Violence Including FGM," UNFPA Djibouti, September 4, 2020, https://djibouti.unfpa.org/en/news/closing-16-days-activism-against-gender-based-violence-including-fgm.

308. Ismail Akwei, "U.S. Honours Three African Women from Djibouti, Egypt and Tanzania for Courage," *Face2Face Africa*, March 13, 2019, https://face2faceafrica.com/article/u-s-honours-three-african-women-from-djibouti-egypt-and-tanzania-for-courage.

309. Liv Tønnessen, "Sudanese Women's Revolution for Freedom, Dignity and Justice Continues," *Chr. Michelsen Institute* (blog), 2020, https://www.cmi.no/publications/7355-sudanese-womens-revolution-for-freedom-dignity-and-justice-continues.

310. France 24, "Sudan PM Hamdok Unveils First Cabinet since Fall of Bashir," *France 24*, September 5, 2019, https://www.france24.com/en/20190905-sudan-pm-hamdok-first-cabinet-bashir.

311. Michelle Bachelet, "Oral Update on the Situation of Human Rights in the Sudan," https://www.ohchr.org/en/statements/2022/03/-oral-update-situation-human-rights-sudan#:~:text=They%20are%20reported%20to%20be,144%20women%2C%20and%20148%20children..

312. Michelle Bachelet, "Oral Update on the Situation of Human Rights in the Sudan," https://www.ohchr.org/en/statements/2022/03/-oral-update-situation-human-rights-sudan#:~:

text=They%20are%20reported%20to%20be,144
%20women%2C%20and%20148%20children..

313. Justice For Noura, "About," *Justice For Noura*, 2018, https://www.justicefornoura.com/about.

314. UNICEF, "Sudan Enters New Era for Girl Rights with Criminalization of FGM," www.unicef.org, 2020, https://www.unicef.org/mena/press-releases/sudan-enters-new-era-girl-rights-criminalization-fgm.; Naba Mohiedeen, "Sudanese Women Welcome Freedom to Travel Abroad with Children," VOA, July 14, 2020, https://www.voaafrica.com/a/africa_sudanese-women-welcome-freedom-travel-abroad-children/6192759.html.

315. Al Jazeera, "Morocco Repeals 'Rape Marriage Law,'" *Al Jazeera*, 2014, https://www.aljazeera.com/news/2014/1/23/morocco-repeals-rape-marriage-law#:~:text=Controversial%20article%20previously%20allowed%20rapists.

316. Abderrafie Zaanoun, "The Impact of the Quota System on Women Parliamentary Representation in Morocco: A Series of Reforms or a Regressive Path?," *Arab Reform Initiative*, April 14, 2022, https://www.arab-reform.net/publication/the-impact-of-the-quota-system-on-women-parliamentary-representation-in-morocco-a-series-of-reforms-or-a-regressive-path/.

317. OHCHR, "Experts of the Committee on the Elimination of Discrimination against Women Praise Morocco for Legislation Prohibiting Discrimination, Ask about High Maternal Mortality and Female Illiteracy Rates in Rural Areas," Press Release, OHCHR, June 22, 2022, https://www.ohchr.org/en/press-releases/2022/06/experts-committee-elimination-discrimination-against-women-praise-morocco.

318. Al Jazeera, "Comoros: Civilians Flee Strife-Torn City on Anjouan Island," *Al Jazeera*, 2018, https://www.aljazeera.com/news/2018/10/18/-comoros-civilians-flee-strife-torn-city-on-anjouan-island.

319. Press TV, "Police Arrest 12 Female Protesters in Comoros," *PressTV*, March 28, 2019, https://www.presstv.ir/Detail/2019/03/28/592068/-Comoros-Police-Protestors.

320. The Borgen Project, "5 Things to Know about Women's Rights in Algeria," *The Borgen Project*, December 8, 2020, https://borgenproject.org/womens-rights-in-algeria/.

321. Aili Mari Tripp, "The Fight for Democracy & Women's Rights in Algeria: A Long Legacy of Struggle," *Transatlantic Policy Quarterly* (TPQ), June 26, 2019, http://turkishpolicy.com/article/957/the-fight-for-democracy-womens-rights-in-algeria-a-long-legacy-of-struggle.

322. Lydia Haddag, "Hirak and Feminism: An Equation with Two Unknowns," *Arab Reform Initiative*, June 22, 2021, https://www.arab-reform.net/publication/hirak-and-feminism-an-equation-with-two-unknowns/.

323. Corina Lacatus and Gustav Meibauer, "'Saying It like It Is': Right-Wing Populism,

International Politics, and the Performance of Authenticity," *The British Journal of Politics and International Relations* 24, no. 3 (May 27, 2022): 437–57, https://doi.org/10.1177/13691481221089137.

324. United Nations, "The Paris Agreement," United Nations, n.d., https://www.un.org/en/climatechange/paris-agreement#:~:text=The%20Agreement%20is%20a%20legally.

325. Amr Hamzawy et al., "What the Russian War in Ukraine Means for the Middle East," *Carnegie Endowment for International Peace*, March 24, 2022, https://carnegieendowment.org/2022/03/24/-what-russian-war-in-ukraine-means-for-middle-east-pub-86711.

326. Amr Hamzawy et al., "What the Russian War in Ukraine Means for the Middle East," Carnegie Endowment for International Peace, March 24, 2022, https://carnegieendowment.org/2022/03/24/what-russian-war-in-ukraine-means-for-middle-east-pub-86711.

327. Amr Hamzawy et al., "What the Russian War in Ukraine Means for the Middle East," Carnegie Endowment for International Peace, March 24, 2022, https://carnegieendowment.org/2022/03/24/what-russian-war-in-ukraine-means-for-middle-east-pub-86711.

328. Institute for Economics and Peace, "Global Peace Index 2022" (Sydney: IEP, 2022), https://www.visionofhumanity.org/resources/global-peace-index-2022/.; This ranking is for the Middle East and North Africa which includes Israel and Iran. It classifies Mauritania, Djibouti, and Comoros in the Sub–Saharan category, while Comoros is excluded from the index.

329. UNSC, "Resolution 1325" (New York: UNSC, 2000), http://unscr.com/en/resolutions/doc/1325.

330. WILPF, "Iraq—1325 National Action Plans," 1325 NAPS, n.d., http://1325naps.peacewomen.org/index.php/iraq/.

331. WILPF, "1325 National Action Plans—an Initiative of the Women's International League for Peace and Freedom," 1325 NAPS, n.d., https://1325naps.peacewomen.org/.

332. UN Women, "Arab League Presents Regional Action Plan for Women, Peace and Security," UN Women—Arab States, October 13, 2015, https://www.google.com/url?q=https://arabstates.unwomen.org/en/news/stories/2015/10/-arab-league-presents-regional-action-plan&sa=D&source=docs&ust=1667930886822053&usg=AOvVaw3j74I-t_iGKPFlfvjjQ2Ik.

333. Aitemad Muhanna-Matar, "New Trends of Women's Activism after the Arab Uprisings: Redefining Women's Leadership," *LSE Middle East Centre Paper Series* 5 (2014), http://www.lse.ac.uk/middleEastCentre/home.aspx.

334. Sherifa Zuhur, "Women and Empowerment in the Arab World," *Arab Studies Quarterly* 25, no. 4 (2003): 17–38, https://doi.org/https://www.jstor.org/stable/41858460.; Rebecca O'Keeffe and Karma Ekmekji, "Women at the Table:

Insights from Lebanese Women in Politics" (Beirut: UN Women and ESCWA, December 2022).

335. Benjamin G. Bishin and Feryal M. Cherif, "The Big Gains for Women's Rights in the Middle East, Explained," *Washington Post*, July 23, 2018, https://www.washingtonpost.com/news/monkey-cage/wp/2018/07/23/womens-rights-are-advancing-in-the-middle-east-this-explains-why/.

336. Muhanna-Matar, "New Trends."

337. Amel Mili (2005) cited in Sahar Khamis and Amel Mili, eds., *Arab Women's Activism and Socio-Political Transformation: Unfinished Gendered Revolutions* (New York: Palgrave Macmillan, 2018).

338. Purplewashing refers to publicly aligning with gender equality but in reality practices are not supportive of gender equality, feminism, or women's rights.

339. Ghida Anani, in discussion with the author, Beirut, June 2022.

340. Zuhur, "Women and Empowerment."

Chapter 3

1. Lina Abou-Habib, "Co-Optation versus Co-Creation: Reflections on Building a Feminist Agenda," *Feminist Revolutions* 5, no. 3 (2019).

2. Nadje Al-Ali, "Gendering the Arab Spring," *Middle East Journal of Culture and Communication* 5, no. 1 (2012): 26–31, https://doi.org/10.1163/187398612x624346.

3. Al-Ali, "Gendering the Arab Spring."

4. Al-Ali, "Gendering the Arab Spring."

5. Kaitlyn Webster, Chong Chen, and Kyle Beardsley, "Conflict, Peace, and the Evolution of Women's Empowerment," *International Organization* 73, no. 02 (2019): 255–89, https://doi.org/10.1017/s0020818319000055.

6. Punam Yadav, "Can Women Benefit from War? Women's Agency in Conflict and Post-Conflict Societies," *Journal of Peace Research* 58, no. 3 (June 19, 2020): 449–61, https://doi.org/10.1177/0022343320905619.

7. Elise Salem, "Shaking Things up in Lebanon: Women, Revolution, and the University," *Al Raida* 44, no. 1 (2020): 93–98, https://doi.org/10.32380/alrj.v44i1.1826.

8. Sahar Khamis, "The Arab 'Feminist' Spring?," *Feminist Studies* 37, no. 3 (2011): 692–95, https://www.jstor.org/stable/23069929. P. 692.

9. There are too many examples to list but a good place to start is: Mark L Haas, *The Arab Spring : The Hope and Reality of the Uprisings* (London: Routledge, 2018); Robert Fisk et al., *Arab Spring Then and Now* (Mango Media Inc., 2017).

10. Sahar Khamis and Amel Mili, eds., *Arab Women's Activism and Socio-Political Transformation : Unfinished Gendered Revolutions* (New York: Palgrave Macmillan, 2018), P. 2.

11. Sahar Khamis and Amel Mili, eds., *Arab Women's Activism and Socio-Political Transformation : Unfinished Gendered Revolutions* (New York: Palgrave Macmillan, 2018).

12. Margot Badran quoted in: Wilson Center, "Book Talk: 'Women Rising: In and beyond the Arab Spring,'" Wilson Center, 2020, https://www.wilsoncenter.org/event/book-talk-women-rising-and-beyond-arab-spring.

13. Sahar Khamis, "The Arab 'Feminist' Spring?," *Feminist Studies* 37, no. 3 (2011): 692–95, https://www.jstor.org/stable/23069929. P. 692.

14. United Nations, "Women and the Arab Spring," *UN Chronicle* 53, no. 4 (December 2016), https://www.un.org/en/chronicle/article/women-and-arab-spring.

15. Elham Manea, "The Arab Popular Uprisings from a Gender Perspective," *Zeitschrift Für Politik* 61, no. 1 (2014): 81–100, https://www.jstor.org/stable/24229172.; Nadje Al-Ali, "Gendering the Arab Spring," *Middle East Journal of Culture and Communication* 5, no. 1 (2012): 26–31, https://doi.org/10.1163/187398612x624346.

16. Wilson Center, "Book Talk: 'Women Rising: In and beyond the Arab Spring,'" Podcast, Wilson Center, June 30, 2020, https://www.wilsoncenter.org/event/book-talk-women-rising-and-beyond-arab-spring.

17. World Bank, "Unemployment, Total (% of Total Labor Force) (Modeled ILO Estimate)—Tunisia | Data," data.worldbank.org, accessed June 9, 2022, https://data.worldbank.org/indicator/SL.UEM.TOTL.ZS?locations=TN&fbclid=-IwAR1V4GLsL2T0Y7ivmUckfMZAJZ9OU7-WFrtaVo83G2drlu6-f-js5S1PdzY.

18. World Bank, "Tunisia: Breaking the Barriers to Youth Inclusion" (Washington DC: World Bank, 2014), https://www.worldbank.org/content/dam/Worldbank/document/MNA/tunisia/breaking_the_barriers_to_youth_inclusion_eng.pdf.

19. Democracy Now!, "Uprising in Egypt: A Two-Hour Special on the Revolt against the U.S.-Backed Mubarak Regime," Video, *Democracy Now!*, February 5, 2011, http://www.democracynow.org/2011/2/5/uprising_in_egypt_a_two_hour.

20. Nadine Naber, "Women and the Arab Spring: Human Rights from the Ground Up," *International Institute Journal at University of Michigan* 1, no. 1 (2011): 11–13, https://www.peacewomen.org/assets/file/women_in_the_arab_spring-human_rights_from_the_ground_up.pdf.

21. Morality police refers to authorities who ensure (religious) values and codes of conduct are being adhered to including dress code, for example.

22. Frontline, "Revolution in Cairo Day-To-Day Jan. 25," *PBS Frontline*, February 22, 2011, http://www.pbs.org/wgbh/pages/frontline/revolution-in-cairo/day-to-day/.; Nadia Idle and Alex Nunns, eds. *Tweets from Tahrir: Egypt's Revolution as It Unfolded, in the Words of the People Who Made It* (New York: OR Books, 2011).

23. Democracy Now!, "Asmaa Mahfouz & the

YouTube Video That Helped Spark the Egyptian Uprising," Video, *Democracy Now!*, February 8, 2011, https://www.democracynow.org/2011/2/8/asmaa_mahfouz_the_youtube_video_that.

24. Manal al-Natour, "The Role of Women in the Egyptian 25th January Revolution," *Journal of International Women's Studies* 13, no. 5 (2012), https://vc.bridgew.edu/jiws/vol13/iss5/7.

25. James Podgers, "Arab Spring Brings No Thaw for Women's Rights," *ABA Journal*, April 1, 2013, https://www.abajournal.com/magazine/article/arab_spring_brings_no_thaw_for_womens_rights.

26. Following the uprising and ousting of Hosni Mubarak, Mohamed Morsi of the Muslim Brotherhood organization served as President of Egypt from 2012–2013. The new constitution he pushed through took a conservative stance on gender and did not protect women, especially in areas such as child marriage and FGM.

27. Elham Manea, "The Arab Popular Uprisings from a Gender Perspective," *Zeitschrift Für Politik* 61, no. 1 (2014): 81–100, https://www.jstor.org/stable/24229172.

28. Tom Finn, "Yemen's Women Revolutionaries," *Dissent Magazine*, January 2015, https://www.dissentmagazine.org/article/yemen-women-revolutionaries-arab-spring-2011-tawakkol-karman.

29. Tom Finn, "Yemen's Women Revolutionaries."

30. Associated Press Sana'a, "Yemeni Women Join Street Protests against President Saleh," *The Guardian*, April 17, 2011, https://www.theguardian.com/world/2011/apr/17/yemeni-women-protest-against-president-saleh.; Mohammed Jamjoom and Hakim Almasmari, "Yemeni Women Protest against Saleh's Remarks for Second Day," *CNN*, April 19, 2011, http://edition.cnn.com/2011/WORLD/meast/04/17/yemen.women.protest/index.html.

31. Tom Finn, "Saleh Is Gone, but Yemen Women's Struggle Goes On," *Reuters*, April 11, 2012, https://www.reuters.com/article/us-yemen-politics-women-idUSBRE83A0SX20120411.

32. Samyah Alfoory, "The 2011 Bahraini Uprising: Women's Agency, Dissent and Violence" (Washington DC: Georgetown Institute for Women, Peace and Security, 2014), https://giwps.georgetown.edu/resource/the-2011-bahraini-uprising-womens-agency-dissent-and-violence/.

33. Magdalena Karolak, "Bahraini Women in the 21st Century: Disputed Legacy of the Unfinished Revolution," *Journal of International Women's Studies* 13, no. 5 (2012), https://vc.bridgew.edu/jiws/vol13/iss5/3.

34. Farah Kader, "The Role of Women in the 2011 Bahraini Uprising," *Blog* Americans for Democracy & Human Rights in Bahrain, July 2, 2016, https://www.adhrb.org/2016/07/role-women-2011-bahraini-uprising/.

35. Alfoory, "The 2011 Bahraini Uprising."

36. BIRD, "Bahrain Human Rights Report: Events of 2020" (London: The Bahrain Institute for Rights and Democracy, 2021), https://birdbh.org/-wp-content/uploads/2021/02/BIRD-Annual-HR-Report-2021-FINAL.pdf.

37. Margot Badran quoted in: Wilson Center, "Book Talk: 'Women Rising: In and beyond the Arab Spring,'" Podcast, Wilson Center, 2020, https://www.wilsoncenter.org/event/book-talk-women-rising-and-beyond-arab-spring.

38. Xan Rice et al., "Women Have Emerged as Key Players in the Arab Spring," *The Guardian*, April 22, 2011, https://www.theguardian.com/world/2011/apr/22/women-arab-spring.

39. Manea, "The Arab Popular Uprisings."

40. Manea, "The Arab Popular Uprisings." P. 90.

41. Desirée Nilsson, "Anchoring the Peace: Civil Society Actors in Peace Accords and Durable Peace," *International Interactions* 38, no. 2 (April 2012): 243–66, https://doi.org/10.1080/03050629.2012.659139.

42. Ibtesam Al Atiyat, "The Current Faces of Arab Feminism," *Publication* Friedrich Ebert Stiftung, January 27, 2021, https://mena.fes.de/publications/e/the-current-faces-of-arab-feminism.

43. Aitemad Muhanna-Matar, "New Trends of Women's Activism after the Arab Uprisings: Redefining Women's Leadership," *LSE Middle East Centre Paper Series* 5 (2014), http://www.lse.ac.uk/middleEastCentre/home.aspx.

44. Michael Safi, "Life Has Got Worse since Arab Spring, Say People across Middle East," *The Guardian*, December 17, 2020, https://www.theguardian.com/global-development/2020/dec/17/arab-spring-people-middle-east-poll.

45. Myriam Sfeir, in discussion with the author, online, October 2022.

46. Charlotte Karam, in conversation with the author, online, October 2022.

47. Sara Abbas, "Revolution Is Female: The Uprising of Women in the Arab World," *OpenDemocracy*, 2012, https://www.opendemocracy.net/en/5050/revolution-is-female-uprising-of-women-in-arab-world/.

48. Souad Mahmoud, "The Challenges of Grassroots Feminism in Arab Countries," Capire, March 25, 2021, https://capiremov.org/en/analysis/the-challenges-of-grassroots-feminism-in-arab-countries/.

49. Anthony Keedi, in discussion with the author, online, May 2022.

50. Gabriella Nassif, in discussion with the author, online, October 2022.

51. Katherine Hughes-Fraitekh, "Nonviolent Resistance in Palestine: Steadfastness, Creativity and Hope," *Blog* openDemocracy, July 14, 2015, https://www.opendemocracy.net/en/civilresistance/nonviolent-resistance-in-palestine-steadfastness-creativity-and-hope/.

52. Quoted in: Hughes-Fraitekh, "Nonviolent Resistance in Palestine."

53. Muna Nassar, in discussion with the author, October 2022.

54. Nadera Shalhoub-Kevorkian, "Indigenizing

Feminist Knowledge: Palestinian Feminist Thought between the Physics of International Power and the Theology of Racist 'Security,'" in *Arab Feminisms: Gender and Equality in the Middle East*, ed. Jean Said Makdisi, Noha Bayoumi, and Rafif Rida Sidawi (London & New York: I.B. Tauris, 2014) P. 208.

55. Shalhoub-Kevorkian, "Indigenizing Feminist Knowledge." P. 215

56. Muna El Kurd quoted in: Esat Firat, "Palestinian Women Lead Resistance against Israeli Occupation," Anadolu Agency, May 16, 2021, https://www.aa.com.tr/en/middle-east/-palestinian-women-lead-resistance-against-israeli-occupation/2243469.

57. Mariam Jalabi, in conversation with the author, October 2022.

58. The Syrian Women's Political Movement, "SWPM: Mariam Jalabi," SWPM, 2020, https://syrianwomenpm.org/members/mariam-jalabi/.

59. Abby O'Keefe, "A Patriarchal Peace in Syria," Carnegie Endowment for International Peace, November 6, 2020, https://carnegieendowment.org/sada/83158.

60. SWPM, "About Us," The Syrian Women's Political Movement, accessed November 9, 2022, https://syrianwomenpm.org/abous-us/.

61. European Civil Protection and Humanitarian Aid Operations, "Syria Factsheet," ECHO, accessed November 9, 2022, https://civil-protection-humanitarian-aid.ec.europa.eu/where/middle-east/syria_en#facts--figures.

62. Rothna Begum, "The Brave Female Activists Who Fought to Lift Saudi Arabia's Driving Ban," Human Rights Watch, October 11, 2017, https://www.hrw.org/news/2017/09/29/brave-female-activists-who-fought-lift-saudi-arabias-driving-ban.

63. Anonymous, in discussion with the author, September 2022.

64. ALQST for Human Rights @ALQST_En, "ALQST Tweet: Footage from Khamis Mushait Orphanage," *Twitter*, August 31, 2022, https://twitter.com/ALQST_En/status/1564935743117660160.

65. Saudi Vision 2030, "رؤية المملكة العربية 2030 السعودية," Vision 2030, 2022, https://www.vision2030.gov.sa/.

66. UNICEF Sudan, "Sudan Gender Report" (Khartoum: UNICEF Sudan, 2021), https://www.unicef.org/sudan/media/8516/file/UNICEF%20Sudan-%20Gender-%20Report%20(2021).pdf.

67. Yosra Akasha, "Sudanese Dream," *Blog* kandakegranddaughter.blogspot.com, accessed July 9, 2022, http://kandakegranddaughter.blogspot.com/.

68. Yosra Akasha, in discussion with the author, online, July 2022.

69. Sydney Young, "The Women's Revolution: Female Activism in Sudan," *Harvard International Review*, May 25, 2020, https://hir.harvard.edu/the-womens-revolution-female-activism-in-sudan/.

70. Nagwan Soliman, "Sudan Spring: Lessons from Sudanese Women Revolutionaries," *Blog*

GIWPS, April 11, 2020, https://giwps.georgetown.edu/sudan-spring-lessons-from-sudanese-women-revolutionaries/.

71. Young, "The Women's Revolution."

72. Soliman, "Sudan Spring."

73. SIHA, "توضيح ☪," *Facebook*, April 10, 2021, https://www.facebook.com/SIHAInArabic/posts/260396912449060.

74. *Because I'm a Fighter! | Lina Khalifeh | TEDxPragueWomen*, YouTube, TEDxPragueWomen (TEDx Talks, 2017), https://www.youtube.com/watch?v=tIDwTmYR1Cs.

75. TEDx Talks, "Because I'm a Fighter! | Lina Khalifeh | TEDxPragueWomen," *Video* www.youtube.com, January 18, 2017, https://www.youtube.com/watch?v=tIDwTmYR1Cs.

76. Quote from an interview with Lina Khalifeh conducted by AiW in 2018 and used with their permission.

77. 'Rana Husseini, *Years of Struggle: The Women's Movement in Jordan* (Amman: Friedrich-Ebert-Stiftung, 2021).

78. Hayat Mirshad, in discussion with the author, online, October 2022.

79. Mara Mordecai, "Protests in Lebanon Highlight Ubiquity of WhatsApp, Dissatisfaction with Government," Pew Research Center, November 19, 2019, https://www.pewresearch.org/fact-tank/2019/11/19/protests-in-lebanon-highlight-ubiquity-of-whatsapp-dissatisfaction-with-government/.

80. Carmen Geha, "Our Personal Is Political and Revolutionary," *Al Raida* 44, no. 1 (2020): 23–28, https://doi.org/10.32380/alrj.v44i1.1818.

81. The Lebanese Civil War lasted from 1975 until 1990 arising from sectarian tensions, socioeconomic disparity, and political disagreement.

82. "You Stink" referred to both the waste management crisis that saw streets teeming with rubbish, and also the corruption of the ruling powers.

83. Carmen Geha, "Our Personal Is Political and Revolutionary," *Al Raida* 44, no. 1 (2020): 23–28, https://doi.org/10.32380/alrj.v44i1.1818.

84. Alya Abdulhakim Humran, "Revolution Is Female," *Al Raida* 44, no. 1 (2020): 29–36, https://doi.org/10.32380/alrj.v44i1.1819.

85. Carmen Geha, "Our Personal Is Political and Revolutionary," *Al Raida* 44, no. 1 (2020): 23–28, https://doi.org/10.32380/alrj.v44i1.1818.

86. WILPF, "In Lebanon, the Revolution Is a Woman," *WILPF*, December 11, 2019, https://www.wilpf.org/in-lebanon-the-revolution-is-a-woman/.

87. The 2019 economic crisis has been touted as one of the most severe financial crises globally and on August 4, 2020, a massive explosion at the Port of Beirut killed 218 people, injured 7,000, and displaced 300,000.

88. An anti-domestic violence law was passed in 2014, Article 522 or the "marry your rapist law" was repealed in 2017, and sexual harassment became a crime in 2020.

89. Mahnaz Afkhami et al., "Equality: It's All in the Family," *Video* Women's Learning

Partnership, 2017, https://learningpartnership.org/resource/equality-its-all-family-video-english.

90. Hussein Yassine, "What Is Civil Marriage and Does It Work in Lebanon?," *The 961*, January 5, 2021, https://www.the961.com/civil-marriage-in-lebanon-explained/.

91. Gulf News, "Lebanese Women Wage Painful Custody Battles," *Gulf News*, March 26, 2017, https://gulfnews.com/world/mena/-lebanese-women-wage-painful-custody-battles-1.2000613.3; Human Rights Watch, "Lebanon: Laws Discriminate against Women," *HRW*, January 19, 2015, https://www.hrw.org/news/2015/01/19/lebanon-laws-discriminate-against-women.

92. Kareem Chehayeb, "'Living Nightmare': UN Says Lebanon Faces Growing Starvation," *Al Jazeera*, October 1, 2021, https://www.aljazeera.com/news/2021/10/1/un-lebanon-reforms-extreme-poverty-economic-crisis.

93. Carmen Geha, "Our Personal Is Political and Revolutionary," *Al Raida* 44, no. 1 (2020): 23–28, https://doi.org/10.32380/alrj.v44i1.1818.

94. Malek Alaywe-Herz quoted in: Mira Matar, "NAYA| Woman of the Month: Malak Alaywe Herz, Lebanon's Uprising Icon," *An-Nahar*, November 9, 2019, https://www.annahar.com/english/article/-1065303-naya-woman-of-the-month-malak-alaywe-herz-lebanons-uprising-icon.

95. Maria Najjar, "Reviving Pan-Arabism in Feminist Activism in the Middle East," *Kohl: A Journal for Body and Gender Research* 6, no. 1 (2020): 119–32, https://kohljournal.press/reviving-pan-arabism-feminist.

96. Chamseddine Bouzghaia, "'Poetic Protest': How the Photo of a Ballet Dancer Became a Symbol of Algeria's Protests," *France 24*, March 10, 2019, https://www.france24.com/en/20190310-algeria-poetic-protest-photo-dancer-ballet-ballerina-teenager-bouteflika.

97. Terry Moon, "Woman as Reason: Algerian Women at the Forefront," *News & Letters*, April 23, 2019, https://newsandletters.org/woman-reason-algerian-women-forefront/.

98. Melissa Ziad, "@Melziad Instagram Post," Instagram, March 4, 2019, https://www.instagram.com/p/BulgCDUnn97/.

99. Bouzghaia, "Poetic Protest"

100. BBC, "Letter from Africa: 'We're Not Cleaners'—Sexism amid Sudan Protests," *BBC News*, April 1, 2019, https://www.bbc.com/news/world-africa-47738155.

101. Hakim Bishara, "The Viral Photograph That Has Come to Symbolize Sudan's Uprising," *Hyperallergic*, April 12, 2019, https://hyperallergic.com/494770/the-viral-photograph-that-has-come-to-symbolize-sudans-uprising/.

102. Zeinab Mohammed Salih, "'I Was Raised to Love Our Home': Sudan's Singing Protester Speaks Out," *The Guardian*, April 10, 2019, https://www.theguardian.com/global-development/2019/apr/10/alaa-salah-sudanese-woman-talks-about-protest-photo-that-went-viral.

103. BBC, "Sudan Protests: The Women Driving Change in Sudan," *BBC News*, April 24, 2019, https://www.bbc.com/news/av/world-africa-48027451.

104. Marwan Chahine, "The Icon of the Lebanese Revolution," *L'Orient Today*, October 26, 2019, https://today.lorientlejour.com/article/1192726/-the-icon-of-the-lebanese-revolution.html.

105. Marwan Chahine, "The Icon of the Lebanese Revolution," *L'Orient Today*, October 26, 2019, https://today.lorientlejour.com/article/1192726/-the-icon-of-the-lebanese-revolution.html.

106. Malak Alaywe-Herz quoted in: Mira Matar, "NAYA| Woman of the Month: Malak Alaywe Herz, Lebanon's Uprising Icon," *An-Nahar*, November 9, 2019, https://www.annahar.com/english/article/1065303-naya-woman-of-the-month-malak-alaywe-herz-lebanons-uprising-icon.

107. MENA Rights Group, "Female Human Rights Defender Saba al Mahdawi Subjected to Reprisals after Providing Medical Assistance to Anti-Government Protestors," *MENA Rights Group*, November 14, 2019, https://www.menarights.org/en/caseprofile/female-human-rights-defender-saba-al-mahdawi-subjected-reprisals-after-providing.

108. Frontline Defenders, "Saba al Mahdawi," Front Line Defenders, November 6, 2019, https://www.frontlinedefenders.org/en/profile/saba-al-mahdawi.

109. Tallha Abdulrazaq, "Civil Disobedience, Not Terrorism, Is the Biggest Threat to Iraq's Elites," *TRT World*, November 13, 2019, https://www.trtworld.com/opinion/civil-disobedience-not-terrorism-is-the-biggest-threat-to-iraq-s-elites-31344.

110. Aaya Al-Shamahi, "Iraqi Women Are Leading Protests in Iraq despite the Dangers," Video, *Middle East Eye*, December 13, 2019, https://www.middleeasteye.net/video/iraqi-women-are-leading-protests-iraq-despite-dangers.

111. Ibtesam Al Atiyat, "The Current Faces of Arab Feminism," Friedrich Ebert Stiftung, January 27, 2021, https://mena.fes.de/publications/e/the-current-faces-of-arab-feminism.

112. Maha Tazi and Kenza Oumlil, "The Rise of Fourth-Wave Feminism in the Arab Region? Cyberfeminism and Women's Activism at the Crossroads of the Arab Spring," *CyberOrient* 14, no. 1 (January 2020): 44–71, https://doi.org/10.1002/j.cyo2.20201401.0002.

113. Sahar Khamis and Amel Mili, eds., *Arab Women's Activism and Socio-Political Transformation: Unfinished Gendered Revolutions* (USA: Palgrave Macmillan, 2018).

114. Maha Tazi and Kenza Oumlil, "The Rise of Fourth-Wave Feminism in the Arab Region? Cyberfeminism and Women's Activism at the Crossroads of the Arab Spring," *CyberOrient* 14, no. 1 (January 2020): 44–71, https://doi.org/10.1002/j.cyo2.20201401.0002.

115. Heidi Basch-Harod, "#MeToo and the

History of 'Hashtag Feminism' in the MENA Region" (IEMed Mediterranean, 2019), https://www.iemed.org/publication/metoo-and-the-history-of-hashtag-feminism-in-the-mena-region/.

116. UN Women, "#Ismaani—a Hashtag for Women from the Arab States," UN Women Arab States, February 13, 2019, https://arabstates.unwomen.org/en/news/stories/2019/2/a-hashtag-for-women-from-the-arab-states.

117. Tunisia Office Center for Middle Eastern Studies Harvard University, "#EnaZeda, the Birth of a Movement against Sexual Harassment in Tunisia," cmestunisia.fas.harvard.edu, January 8, 2020, https://cmestunisia.fas.harvard.edu/event/-enazedathe-birth-movement-against-sexual-harassment-tunisia.

118. Maha Tazi, "The Arab Spring and Women's (Cyber)Activism: 'Fourth Wave Democracy in the Making?' Case Study of Egypt, Tunisia, and Morocco," *Journal of International Women's Studies* 22, no. 9 (September 17, 2021): 298–315, https://vc.bridgew.edu/jiws/vol22/iss9/20.

119. "The Uprising of Women in the Arab World انتفاضة المرأة في العالم العربي," Facebook, 2011, https://www.facebook.com/intifadat.almar2a.

120. Lara Overmeyer, "The Uprising of Women in the Arab World: Fighting Patriarchal Tyranny," Qantara.de—Dialogue with the Islamic World, 2013, https://en.qantara.de/content/the-uprising-of-women-in-the-arab-world-fighting-patriarchal-tyranny.

121. Noreen Sadik, "The Uprising of Women in the Arab World," *New Internationalist*, March 8, 2013, https://newint.org/blog/2013/03/08/womens-rights-campaign-arab-world.

122. *Feminism Inshallah: A History of Arab Feminism*, Film (Women Make Movies, 2014).

123. Noreen Sadik, "The Uprising of Women in the Arab World," *New Internationalist*, March 8, 2013, https://newint.org/blog/2013/03/08/-womens-rights-campaign-arab-world.

124. Xena Amro, "True Lebanese Feminist," Facebook, accessed November 9, 2022, https://www.facebook.com/TrueLebaneseFeminist.; JC, "Xena the True Lebanese Feminist," *Blog* Sweden and the Middle East Views, April 25, 2013, https://swedenmiddleeastviews.com/2013/04/25/xena-the-true-lebanese-feminist/.

125. "Ashta," or sugar apple, is known for its sweet taste and is commonly used as part of a street harassment phrase: "shu ya ashta." The campaign aimed to subvert the derogatory phrasing. Read more at: https://thekipproject.info/not-your-ashta/

126. The Kip Project, "#Mesh_Basita "مش_بسيطة" Campaign," KIP, accessed November 9, 2022, https://thekipproject.info/mesh-basita/.

127. The New Arab, "Mesh Basita (It's Not Ok): Lebanese Women Stand up to Sexual Harassment," *The New Arab*, August 3, 2017, https://english.alaraby.co.uk/features/mesh-basita-lebanese-women-stand-sexual-harassment.

128. Laila Hzaineh, "'ستر 'الفضيحة' في الوطن العربي,"

Video Facebook, June 21, 2019, https://www.facebook.com/100006739657111/videos/1873040889597215/.

129. Laila Hzaineh, "'ستر 'الفضيحة' في الوطن العربي'."

130. Quote from an interview conducted by AiW with Laila Hzaineh and used with their permission.

131. Malaka Gharib, "#MosqueMeToo Gives Muslim Women a Voice about Sexual Misconduct at Mecca," *NPR*, February 26, 2018, https://www.npr.org/sections/goatsandsoda/2018/02/26/588855132/--mosquemetoo-gives-muslim-women-a-voice-about-sexual-misconduct-at-mecca.; Laignee Barron, "'A Revolutionary Moment.' Activist Mona Eltahawy Talks Sexual Assault and #MosqueMeToo," *Time*, March 7, 2018, https://time.com/5170236/mona-eltahawy-mosquemetoo/.

132. Mona Eltahawy, "#MosqueMeToo: What Happened When I Was Sexually Assaulted during the Hajj," *The Washington Post*, February 15, 2018, https://www.washingtonpost.com/news/global-opinions/wp/2018/02/15/mosquemetoo-what-happened-when-i-was-sexually-assaulted-during-the-hajj/.

133. Maedeh Sharifi, "#MeToo in MENA: The Women Shake Region out of Its Silence on Sexual Harassment," *The New Arab*, March 9, 2021, https://english.alaraby.co.uk/features/mena-women-shake-region-out-sexual-harassment-silence.

134. Ella Williams, "#Masaktach: Social Media and Sexual Violence against Women in Morocco," *Oxford Middle East Review (OMER)*, July 3, 2020, https://omerjournal.com/2020/07/03/masaktach-social-media-and-sexual-violence-against-women-in-morocco/.

135. Euronews, "#Masaktach, How the Moroccan #MeToo Began," *Euronews*, October 17, 2018, https://www.euronews.com/2018/10/17/-masaktach-how-the-moroccan-metoo-began.

136. Alessandra Bajec, "Moroccan #MeToo Helps Women to Break Their Silence against Sexual Harassment and Rape," The New Arab, March 7, 2020, https://english.alaraby.co.uk/analysis/-moroccan-metoo-helps-women-break-silence.

137. Scene Arabia, "A Girl Is Born: The Podcast Dialing up the Voices of Arab Women," *Scene Arabia*, March 8, 2021, https://scenearabia.com/Life/A-Girl-Is-Born-The-Podcast-Dialling-Up-The-Voices-Of-Arab-Women.

138. Mirna Abdulaal, "8 Arab Women Podcasters You Should Listen To," *Egyptian Streets*, July 31, 2020, https://egyptianstreets.com/2020/07/31/-a-journey-of-self-realization-8-arab-women-podcasters-you-should-listen-to/.

139. Mayada Srouji, "'Bayneh W Baynek': A Place Where Arab Women Can Speak about Their Struggles without Any Judgement!," *MVSLIM*, February 27, 2019, https://mvslim.com/bayneh-w-baynek-a-place-where-arab-women-can-speak-about-their-struggles-without-any-judgement/.

140. Mirna Abdulaal, "8 Arab Women Podcasters You Should Listen To," *Egyptian Streets*, July 31, 2020, https://egyptianstreets.com/2020/

07/31/a-journey-of-self-realization-8-arab-women-podcasters-you-should-listen-to/.

141. Rana Almuddin, "'You're Guilty for Enjoying Your Sexuality.' Actress on Her Campaign for Women to Accept Themselves," Video, *CNN*, 2022, https://edition.cnn.com/videos/world/2022/08/03/-rana-alamuddin-as-equals-lon-orig.cnn.

142. Ben Barkawi and Menna A. Farouk, "Seek Help, Say Middle East Women's Groups as Domestic Violence Surges," *Reuters*, April 7, 2020, sec. Coronavirus, https://www.reuters.com/article/us-health-coronavirus-women-mideast-trfn-idUSKBN21P23M.; Sara K. Andrews et al., "Responding to Rising Intimate Partner Violence amid COVID-19: A Rapid Global Review" (Washington DC: GIWPS, 2021).

143. Nourah Al-Oseimi, "Women in Kuwait Stand against Harassment," *The Times Kuwait*, February 13, 2021, https://timeskuwait.com/news/we-will-not-be-silenced/.

144. The New Arab, "In Conservative Kuwait, Women Launch Their Own #MeToo Movement," *The New Arab*, February 9, 2021, https://english.alaraby.co.uk/news/conservative-kuwait-women-launch-their-own-metoo-movement.; Shaistha Khan, "'I Will Not Be Silenced': Women in Kuwait Fight Back against Violence," *Women's Media Center*, July 14, 2021, https://womensmediacenter.com/news-features/i-will-not-be-silenced-women-in-kuwait-fight-back-against-violence.

145. Lara Bellone d'Altavilla, "Solidarity across Borders: Arab Women Demand Action after Series of Femicides Bleed Society Dry," *The New Arab*, July 8, 2022, https://english.alaraby.co.uk/features/-arab-women-demand-action-after-femicides-bleed-society-dry.

146. Hincks, "Heirs of the Arab Spring."

147. Sahar Khamis and Amel Mili, eds., *Arab Women's Activism and Socio-Political Transformation : Unfinished Gendered Revolutions* (New York: Palgrave Macmillan, 2018), P 244.

148. Hibaaq Osman, "Special Statement from Hibaaq Osman: Democracy IS Women's Rights," Press Release, Karama, March 8, 2011, https://www.elkara.ma/news/content/special-statement-from-hibaaq-osman-democracy-is-womens-rights.

149. Aitemad Muhanna-Matar, "New Trends of Women's Activism after the Arab Uprisings: Redefining Women's Leadership," *LSE Middle East Centre Paper Series* 5 (2014), http://www.lse.ac.uk/middleEastCentre/home.aspx.

150. Therese Saliba, "Arab Feminism at the Millennium," *Signs* 25, no. 4 (2000): 1087–92, https://www.jstor.org/stable/3175492.

151. Nadje Al-Ali, "Gendering the Arab Spring," *Middle East Journal of Culture and Communication* 5, no. 1 (2012): 26–31, https://doi.org/10.1163/187398612x624346.

152. Alanoud Alsharekh and Azadeh Pourzand, Women and power in the Middle East, interview by Gitika Bhardwaj, *Chatham House*, May 21, 2021, https://www.chathamhouse.org/2021/05/women-and-power-in-the-middle-east.

153. Maria Najjar, "Reviving Pan-Arabism in Feminist Activism in the Middle East," *Kohl: A Journal for Body and Gender Research* 6, no. 1 (2020): 119–32, https://kohljournal.press/reviving-pan-arabism-feminist.

154. Maria Najjar, "Reviving Pan-Arabism in Feminist Activism in the Middle East," *Kohl: A Journal for Body and Gender Research* 6, no. 1 (2020): 119–32, https://kohljournal.press/reviving-pan-arabism-feminist.

155. Lina Abou-Habib, "Co-Optation versus Co-Creation: Reflections on Building a Feminist Agenda," *Kohl: A Journal for Body and Gender Research* 5, no. 3 (December 18, 2019): 9–9, https://kohljournal.press/Cooptation-versus-cocreation..

156. Soraya Chemaly, *Rage Becomes Her: The Power of Women's Anger* (New York: Atria Books, 2018)., P xxii.

157. Alanoud Alsharekh quoted in Nada Ghosn, "Kuwait's Alanoud Alsharekh, Feminist Groundbreaker," The Markaz Review, December 6, 2020, https://themarkaz.org/kukuwaits-alanoud-al-sharekh-feminist-groundbreaker/.

158. Michael Randle, *Civil Resistance*, 1st ed. (London: Fontana Press, 1994).

159. Kurt Schock, "The Practice and Study of Civil Resistance," *Journal of Peace Research* 50, no. 3 (May 2013): 277–90, https://doi.org/10.1177/0022343313476530.

160. Erica Chenoweth and Maria J. Stephan, *Why Civil Resistance Works: The Strategic Logic of Nonviolent Conflict* (New York: Columbia University Press, 2011); Maia Carter Hallward and Julie M. Norman, *Understanding Nonviolence* (Cambridge: Polity, 2015).

161. Gene Sharp, *Politics of Nonviolent Action: Power and Struggle (Vol 1)* (Boston: Porter Sargent, 1973).

162. Gabriella Nassif, "Resistance, Gender, and Identity Politics: A Conversation with Rasha Younes," *Civil Society Review*, 2021, https://doi.org/10.28943/csr.005.005.

163. Tom Finn, "Yemen's Women Revolutionaries," *Dissent Magazine*, 2015, https://www.dissentmagazine.org/article/yemen-women-revolutionaries-arab-spring-2011-tawakkol-karman.

Chapter 4

1. Bahia Shehab, in discussion with the author, online, August 2022.

2. Mahnaz Afkhami et al., "Equality: It's All in the Family," Women's Learning Partnership, 2017, https://learningpartnership.org/resource/equality-its-all-family-video-english.

3. Salam Mir, "Palestinian Literature: Occupation and Exile," *Arab Studies Quarterly* 35, no. 2 (2013): 110–29, https://doi.org/10.13169/arabstudquar.35.2.0110.

4. NPR, "Tunisian Poet's Verses Inspire Arab Protesters," NPR, January 30, 2011, https://www.

npr.org/2011/01/30/133354601/Tunisian-Poets-Verses-Inspire-Arab-Protesters.

5. Reham Zughair, "Fiction as a Tool of Resistance against the Reality of Womanhood: Arab Women Writers' Approach to Truth," *Honi Soit*, August 17, 2021, https://honisoit.com/2021/08/fiction-as-a-tool-of-resistance-against-the-reality-of-womanhood-arab-women-writers-approach-to-truth/.

6. Susan A. Phillips, "Op-Ed: 'Say Their Names': How Graffiti Is Cutting to the Heart of the Protests," *Los Angeles Times*, June 14, 2020, https://www.latimes.com/opinion/story/2020-06-14/graffiti-protests-los-angeles.

7. Danny Bou-Maruon, musician and composer with Ostura, in conversation with the author, June 2022.

8. Phillips, "Op-Ed: 'Say Their Names.'"

9. Alya Abdulhakim Humran, "Revolution Is Female," *Al Raida* 44, no. 1 (2020): 29–36, https://doi.org/10.32380/alrj.v44i1.1819.

10. Assil Diab, in discussion with the author, online, August 2022.

11. Susana F. Molina, "Female Street Art Defies War in Yemen. No Peace without Women," *The Urban Activist*, January 12, 2021, https://theurbanactivist.com/idea/female-street-art-defies-war-in-yemen-no-peace-without-women/.

12. Haifa Subay, in conversation with the author, online, November 2022.

13. TED, "Bahia Shehab: A Thousand Times No," Video, *YouTube*, September 28, 2012, https://www.youtube.com/watch?v=R_U9GUlSOC4.

14. Bahia Shehab, "Mokhak Awra," Bahia Shehab, accessed November 10, 2022, https://www.bahiashehab.com/graffiti/mokhak-awra.

15. Alya Mooro, in discussion with the author, online, August 2022.

16. Soultana's real name is Youssra Oukaf.

17. Soultana, in discussion with the author, online, August 2022.

18. Yazz Ahmed, in discussion with the author, online, September 2022.

19. Quotes from an interview conducted by AiW with Michelle and Noel Kersewany and used with permission.

20. In Arabic the song is: صوت النساء

21. مؤلف, "Michelle & Noel Keserwany: 3al Jamal Bi Wasat Beirut (عالجمل بوسط بيروت)," Lebanese Arabic Institute, February 12, 2018, https://www.lebanesearabicinstitute.com/3al-jamal-bi-wasat-beirut/.

22. Hiam Abass is a Palestinian actor playing the lead role in the film.

23. Elie Youssef, in conversation with the author, August 2022.

24. Since the 2019 revolution, walls around the city have become adorned with art and graffiti portraying images of both dissent and hope.

25. Humran, "Revolution Is Female."

26. Humran, "Revolution Is Female."

27. Bahia Shehab, in discussion with the author, online, August 2022.

28. Deena Mohamed, "Qahera—About," Tumblr, 2013, https://qaherathesuperhero.com/about.

29. A niqab is a veil that covers the face, while a hijab is a veil that covers the head and hair.; Deena Mohamed, "Qahera," qaherathesuperhero.com, June 13, 2013, https://qaherathesuperhero.com/post/64031330049.

30. Tamtam is a stage name.

31. Tamtam, in discussion with the author, online, August 2022.

32. *Haram* describes any action or practice that is forbidden by Islamic law. We acknowledge it has come to take on a range of meanings in society and often is employed to put women in their place

33. Bahia Shehab, "Adhan (Call to Prayer)," Fine Acts, 2014, https://fineacts.co/bahia-shehab.

34. Haifa Subay, in discussion with the author, online, August 2022.

35. OCHA, "Yemen | Global Humanitarian Overview," OCHA, 2022, https://gho.unocha.org/yemen.

36. UNFPA, "Yemen: One of the World's Largest Humanitarian Crises," United Nations Population Fund, October 11, 2022, https://www.unfpa.org/yemen#:~:text=largest%20humanitarian%20crises-.

37. Subay quoted in Molina, "Female Street Art Defies War in Yemen."

38. IIE, "Artist Protection Fund," www.iie.org, accessed November 10, 2022, https://www.iie.org/programs/artist-protection-fund.

39. Jean Said Makdisi, "Huqouq Almar'a: Feminist Thought and the Language of the Arab Women's Movement," in *Arab Feminisms Gender and Equality in the Middle East*, ed. Jean Said Makdisi, Noha Bayoumi, and Rafif Rida Sidawi (London; New York: I.B Tauris, 2014), P. 83.

40. Aitemad Muhanna-Matar, "New Trends of Women's Activism after the Arab Uprisings: Redefining Women's Leadership," *LSE Middle East Centre Paper Series* 5 (2014), http://www.lse.ac.uk/middleEastCentre/home.aspx. P. 7.

Chapter 5

1. Myriam Sfeir, in discussion with the author, online, October 2022.

2. Jean Said Makdisi, "Huqouq Almar'a: Feminist Thought and the Language of the Arab Women's Movement," in *Arab Feminisms Gender and Equality in the Middle East*, ed. Jean Said Makdisi, Noha Bayoumi, and Rafif Rida Sidawi (London; New York: I.B. Tauris, 2014), P. 84.

3. UNOY, "Policy Brief: Beyond Dividing Lines in Libya" (UNOY, 2018), https://unoy.org/downloads/policy-brief-beyond-dividing-lines-in-libya/.

4. Suleiman Al-Khalidi and Eric Knecht, "Young, Angry Lebanese Ditch Their Differences to Target 'Unjust' System," *Reuters*, October 23, 2019, sec. Industry, Materials and Utilities, https://www.reuters.com/article/lebanon-protests-youth/

young-angry-lebanese-ditch-their-differences-to-target-unjust-system-idUSL3N2771XN.

5. Hayder Al-Shakeri, "The Aspirations and Disillusionment of Iraq's Youth," Chatham House—International Affairs Think Tank, July 27, 2022, https://www.chathamhouse.org/2022/07/-aspirations-and-disillusionment-iraqs-youth.

6. Shadi Rouhshahbaz, "Youth Agency in Peacebuilding in Post-Jasmine Revolution Tunisia," *Journal of Youth, Peace and Security* 1, no. 1 (2021): 22–26, https://unoy.org/ypsrn/shadirouhshahbaz/.

7. Hayat Mirshad, in conversation with the author, online, October 2022.

8. Tamtam, in discussion with the author, online, August 2022.

9. Takatoat founders Aya Al-Taher and Banan Abu Zain Eddin, in discussion with the author, online, July 2022.

10. Author's translation from French. Original quotation from email correspondence, July 2022: "Le féministe c'est un choix sociétal qui suppose l'égalité de tous et de toutes. Aucune discrimination ne peut être tolérée au nom d'une quelconque différence .C'est vrai que les discriminations les mieux partagées à travers le monde demeurent celles fondées sur le sexe vu que même dans les pays les plus avancés le patriarcat est fortement implanté."

11. Hosn Abboud, email message to author, July 2022.

12. Ghida Anani, in discussion with the author, Beirut, June 2022.

13. Nada Darwazeh, in discussion with the author, online, June 2022.

14. Diana Moukalled, in discussion with the author, Beirut, June 2022.

15. The National Commission for Lebanese Women is a group of 24 rotating women members that convene to cover issues ranging from economics, education, health, and gender equality in Lebanon.

16. Sossi Boladian, in discussion with the author, Beirut, June 2022.

17. Rym Badran, in discussion with the author, online, June 2022.

18. Noura Al Obeidli, in discussion with the author, online, June 2022.

19.Aazza Charara Baydoun عزّه شرارة بيضون, "Azzachararabaydoun," azzachararabaydoun.word press.com, 2019, https://azzachararabaydoun.wordpress.com/.

20. Yara Ghanem, in discussion with the author, online, June 2022.

21. Soultana, in discussion with the author, online, August 2022.

22. Fatima Al Mokaddem, in discussion with the author, Beirut, June 2022.

23. Aitemad Muhanna-Matar, "New Trends of Women's Activism after the Arab Uprisings: Redefining Women's Leadership," *LSE Middle East Centre Paper Series* 5 (2014), http://www.lse.ac.uk/middleEastCentre/home.aspx.

24. Quotes taken with permission from an interview AiW conducted with Haneen Hadi.

25. Alya Mooro, in discussion with the author, online, August 2022.

26. Assil Diab, in discussion with the author, online, August 2022.

27. Abir Chebaro, in discussion with the author, online, June 2022.

28. Randa Siniora, in discussion with the author, online, June 2022.

29. Kristin Diwan, in discussion with the author, online, September 2022.

30. Tarek Zeidan, in conversation with the author, online, October 2022.

31. Fatima Al Mokaddem, in conversation with the author, online, August 2022.

32. Yosra Akasha, in discussion with the author, online, July 2022.

33. Anthony Keedi, in discussion with the author, online, May 2022.

34. Gabriella Nassif, in discussion with the author, online, October 2022.

35. Nadje Al-Ali, "Gendering the Arab Spring," *Middle East Journal of Culture and Communication* 5, no. 1 (2012): 26–31, https://doi.org/10.1163/187398612x624346.

36. The GCC refers to the Gulf Cooperation Council, a regional political, economic, and social organization comprising Bahrain, Kuwait, Oman, Qatar, Saudi Arabia, and the United Arab Emirates.

37. *Haram* describes any action or practice that is forbidden by Islamic law. We acknowledge it has come to take on a range of meanings in society and often is employed to put women in their place.

38. Deniz Kandiyoti, "Bargaining with Patriarchy," *Gender and Society* 2, no. 3 (1988): 274–90, http://www.jstor.org/stable/190357.; We recognize that the circumstances have changed since the original theory but the references remain valid. See: Columbia Global Centers, "Interview with Emeritus Professor Deniz Kandiyoti on Gender and Politics," globalcenters.columbia.edu, January 31, 2022, https://globalcenters.columbia.edu/news/-interview-emeritus-professor-deniz-kandiyoti-gender-and-politics.;

39. Mona Eltahawy, *The Seven Necessary Sins for Women and Girls* (Boston: Beacon Press, 2019).

40. Eltahawy, *The Seven Necessary Sins*.

41. Taken with permission from an interview AiW conducted with Lina Khalifeh in 2018.

42. Alanoud Alsharekh and Azadeh Pourzand, Women and power in the Middle East, interview by Gitika Bhardwaj, *Chatham House*, May 21, 2021, https://www.chathamhouse.org/2021/05/women-and-power-in-the-middle-east.

43. Sapna Cheryan and Hazel Rose Markus, "Masculine Defaults: Identifying and Mitigating Hidden Cultural Biases.," *Psychological Review* 127, no. 6 (November 2020): 1022–52, https://doi.org/10.1037/rev0000209.

44. Carmen Geha, "Our Personal Is Political and Revolutionary," *Al Raida* 44, no. 1 (2020): 23–28, https://doi.org/10.32380/alrj.v44i1.1818.

45. The National Commission for Lebanese

Women is a group of 24 rotating women members that convene to cover issues ranging from economics, education, health, and gender equality in Lebanon.

46. Carmen Geha, "Our Personal Is Political and Revolutionary," *Al Raida* 44, no. 1 (2020): 23–28, https://doi.org/10.32380/alrj.v44i1.1818.

47. Hatoon Al Fassi, in discussion with the author, online, September 2022.

48. National Women Machinery refers to mechanisms set up by the government to promote gender equality.

49. Artur Bala and Héla Ben Fayala, "Across Divides to Advance Women's Rights through Dialogue: Experiences from the Ground" (UN Women Arab States, 2016), https://arabstates.unwomen.org/en/digital-library/publications/2016/all/-across-divisions-to-advance-womens-rights-upd.

50. Joseph Hincks, "Heirs of the Arab Spring," *Time*, January 2021, https://time.com/5927349/heirs-of-the-arab-spring/.

51. Fatima Sadiqi, email message to the author, July 2022.

52. Kaltham Al-Ghanim, "The Intellectual Frameworks and Theoretical Limits of Arab Feminist Thought," in *Arab Feminisms: Gender and Equality in the Middle East*, ed. Jean Said Makdisi, Noha Bayoumi, and Rafif Rida Sidawi (London & New York: I.B. Tauris, 2014), Pg. 152.

53. Shisha, or hookah, is a water pipe used for smoking tobacco that is usually flavored. Shisha is a common form of entertainment in the region.

54. Aitemad Muhanna-Matar, "New Trends of Women's Activism after the Arab Uprisings: Redefining Women's Leadership," *LSE Middle East Centre Paper Series* 5 (2014), http://www.lse.ac.uk/middleEastCentre/home.aspx.

55. Salma Khalef, in discussion with the author, online, July 2022.

56. Tala Harb, in discussion with the author, online, October 2022.

57. Hatoon Al Fassi, "Does Saudi Feminism Exist?," in *Arab Feminisms: A Critical Comparative Study, Gender and Equality in the Middle East*, ed. Jean Said Makdisi, Noha Bayoumi, and Rafif Rida Sidawi (London & New York: I.B. Tauris, 2014), 121–31.

58. Artur Bala and Héla Ben Fayala, "Across Divides to Advance Women's Rights through Dialogue: Experiences from the Ground" (UN Women Arab States, 2016), https://arabstates.unwomen.org/en/digital-library/publications/2016/all/-across-divisions-to-advance-womens-rights-upd.

59. Artur Bala and Héla Ben Fayala, "Across Divides to Advance Women's Rights through Dialogue: Experiences from the Ground" (UN Women Arab States, 2016), https://arabstates.unwomen.org/en/digital-library/publications/2016/all/-across-divisions-to-advance-womens-rights-upd.

60. Musawah, "About," Musawah, accessed November 9, 2022, https://www.musawah.org/about/.

61. Hibaaq Osman quoted in: Karama, "Hibaaq Osman's Remarks to Generation Equality Forum Mexico," Karama, March 31, 2021, https://www.elkara.ma/news/hibaaq-osmans-remarks-to-generation-equality-forum-mexico.

62. Carmen Geha, in conversation with the author, online, October 2022.

63. Suad Zayed Al-Oraimi, "Arab Feminism—Obstacles and Possibilities: An Analytical Study of the Women's Movement in the Arab World," in *Arab Feminisms: Gender and Equality in the Middle East*, ed. Jean Said Makdisi, Noha Bayoumi, and Rafif Rida Sidawi (London & New York: I.B. Tauris, 2014), P. 139.

64. Nawar Al-Hassan Golley, "Is Feminism Relevant to Arab Women?," *Third World Quarterly* 25, no. 3 (2004): 521–36, https://www.jstor.org/stable/3993823.

65. Degan Ali and Deqa Saleh, "Addressing the Systematic Barriers Facing Women and Girls in the Aid System in Somalia," *Humanitarian Practice Network*, no. 75 (May 31, 2019), https://odihpn.org/publication/addressing-systematic-barriers-facing-women-girls-aid-system-somalia/.

66. Artur Bala and Héla Ben Fayala, "Across Divides to Advance Women's Rights through Dialogue: Experiences from the Ground" (UN Women Arab States, 2016), https://arabstates.unwomen.org/en/digital-library/publications/2016/all/-across-divisions-to-advance-womens-rights-upd.

67. Artur Bala and Héla Ben Fayala, "Across Divides to Advance Women's Rights through Dialogue: Experiences from the Ground" (UN Women Arab States, 2016), https://arabstates.unwomen.org/en/digital-library/publications/2016/all/-across-divisions-to-advance-womens-rights-upd.

68. Aitemad Muhanna-Matar, "New Trends of Women's Activism after the Arab Uprisings: Redefining Women's Leadership," *LSE Middle East Centre Paper Series* 5 (2014), http://www.lse.ac.uk/middleEastCentre/home.aspx.

69. Sahar Khamis and Amel Mili, eds., *Arab Women's Activism and Socio-Political Transformation: Unfinished Gendered Revolutions* (New York: Palgrave Macmillan, 2018). P. 247

70. Sherifa Zuhur, "Women and Empowerment in the Arab World," *Arab Studies Quarterly* 25, no. 4 (2003): 17–38, https://www.jstor.org/stable/pdf/41858460.pdf. P. 17.

71. Author's translation from French. Original quote in email message to author: "le mouvement féministe dans le monde arabe notamment en Afrique et au moyen orient partagent généralement les mêmes visions et les mêmes objectifs. Ce qui diffère parfois ce sont les stratégies mises en place qui bien sûr prennent en considération les spécificités locales et l'environnement."

72. Tala Harb, email message to the author, October 2022.

73. Aitemad Muhanna-Matar, "New Trends of Women's Activism after the Arab Uprisings: Redefining Women's Leadership," *LSE Middle East Centre Paper Series* 5 (2014), http://www.lse.ac.uk/middleEastCentre/home.aspx.

74. Maha Muna is a women's and girls' rights advocate with UNICEF. Quote is from conversation with the author, online, November 2022.

75. Chimamanda Ngozi Adichie, *We Should All Be Feminists* (London: Fourth Estate, 2014).

76. Aitemad Muhanna-Matar, "New Trends of Women's Activism after the Arab Uprisings: Redefining Women's Leadership," *LSE Middle East Centre Paper Series* 5 (2014), http://www.lse.ac.uk/middleEastCentre/home.aspx.

77. Rita Stephan, email message to the author, October 2022.

Chapter 6

1. As mentioned in Chapter 1, the "marry your rapist" law allows a rapist to avoid prosecution if they marry their victim.

2. Mahnaz Afkhami et al., "Equality: It's all in the family," Women's Learning Partnership, 2017, video. https://learningpartnership.org/resource/equality-its-all-family-video-english.

3. Farah Daibes, "Smashing the Patriarchy & Co: How Arab Feminists Are Re-Politicizing Their Movement," July 5, 2021, https://mena.fes.de/press/e/smashing-the-patriarchy-co-how-arab-feminists-are-re-politicizing-their-movement.

4. Afkhami, Women's Learning Partnership, Video.

5. Fatima Sadiqi, "New Feminists in Morocco Are Innovating Cultural Change," *The Wilson Center Middle East Women's Initiative* (blog), March 8, 2020, https://www.wilsoncenter.org/blog-post/-new-feminists-morocco-are-innovating-cultural-change.

6. Daibes, "Smashing."

7. Afkhami et al., "Equality" Video.

8. Engy Ghozlan quoted in: Heba El-Sherif, "Young Arab Feminist Network Hopes to Build Dialogue with Older Generations, Non-Feminists," *Daily News Egypt*, May 5, 2010, https://dailynewsegypt.com/2010/05/05/young-arab-feminist-network-hopes-to-build-dialogue-with-older-generations-non-feminists/.

9. Deepa Ranganathan, "'Girls Know What's Best for Them': A Conversation about the Power and Agency of Girl-Led Activism on International Day of the Girl, 2021," FRIDA | Young Feminist Fund, October 11, 2021, https://youngfeministfund.org/girls-know-whats-best-for-them-a-conversation-about-the-power-and-agency-of-girl-led-activism-on-international-day-of-the-girl-2021/;FRIDA and AWID, "The Global State of Young Feminist Organizing" (FRIDA, 2016), https://www.awid.org/sites/default/files/atoms/files/frida-awid_field-report_final_web_issuu.pdf.; Rafiah Al Talei, "The Arab Youth: Aspirations for the New Year," Carnegie Endowment for International Peace, January 11, 2022, https://carnegieendowment.org/sada/86063.; Arab Reform Initiative, "Youth Activism & Livelihoods," Arab Reform Initiative, accessed November 9, 2022, https://www.arab-reform.net/area_of_work/youth-activism-livelihoods/, FRIDA and Mama Cash, "Girls to the Front: A Snapshot of Girl-Led Organising" (FRIDA The Young Feminist Fund, 2018), https://www.mamacash.org/media/publications/girlstothefront_report_web.pdf..

10. OHCHR, "Girls' and Young Women's Activism—Report of the Working Group on Discrimination against Women and Girls" (United Nations, May 9, 2022), https://www.ohchr.org/en/documents/thematic-reports/ahrc5025-girls-and-young-womens-activism-report-working-group.

11. Rafiah Al Talei, "The Arab Youth: Aspirations for the New Year," Carnegie Endowment for International Peace, January 11, 2022, https://carnegieendowment.org/sada/86063.

12. Daibes, "Smashing."

13. Karma Ekmekji, "Thinking out Loud with Hajer Sharief" *Podcast* (Diplowomen, June 2021), https://soundcloud.com/diplowomen/dw5.

14. *Feminism Inshallah: A History of Arab Feminism*, Film (Women Make Movies, 2014).

15. Alya Mooro, *The Greater Freedom: Life as a Middle Eastern Woman Outside the Stereotypes* (New York: Little A, 2019), 172.

16. Huda Alsahi, "The Challenges of Teaching Women's and Gender Studies in the Gulf Region," *Gender (Im)Balance in Gulf Societies*, 2018, 2–4.

17. Hoda Elsadda quoted in: Jean Said Makdisi, Noha Bayoumi, and Rafif Rida Sidawi, eds., *Arab Feminisms: Gender and Equality in the Middle East* (London & New York: I.B. Tauris, 2014) P. 17.

18. At the 1944 Arab Women's Conference in Cairo, Lebanese delegate Zahiyya Dughan called upon Arab universities to formally study women's writing which feminist scholar Margot Badran documents as the earliest instance for such a call. Now, more than seventy years later, it is clear that gender studies in the region has expanded greatly. (See more at: https://al-fanarmedia.org/2020/10/-teaching-gender-womens-studies-in-the-middle-east/).

19. Yvonne Singh, "What Does It Take to Be an Arab Feminist in 2019?," *Middle East Eye*, July 5, 2019, https://www.middleeasteye.net/discover/what-does-it-take-be-arab-feminist-2019.

20. Nawal El Saadawi and نوال السعداوي، المرأة والجنس *(Woman and Sex)* (1972; repr., دار و مطابع المستقبل (بالفجالة و الإسكندرية، 2006).

21. Hayat Mirshad, email message to the author, October 2022.

22. Helem, "LGBTQIA+ Non-Profit Organization | Helem Lebanon | About," www.helem.net, accessed November 9, 2022, https://www.helem.net/about.

23. Tarek Zeidan, "Gender and Sexuality Library," Facebook, October 23, 2022, https://www.facebook.com/Tarek.Zeidan/posts/pfbid02A422nMZz5rjCQLLX6iDqJkA5iytJshgGAZD1b68diPJqYcEvLkBwunGPQRfXU4v4l.

24. OHCHR, "Girls' and Young Women's Activism—Report of the Working Group on Discrimination against Women and Girls" (United

Nations, May 9, 2022), https://www.ohchr.org/en/documents/thematic-reports/ahrc5025-girls-and-young-womens-activism-report-working-group.

25. Taken with permission from an interview AiW conducted with Laila Hzaineh in 2018.

26. Alanoud Alsharekh quoted in Nada Ghosn, "Kuwait's Alanoud Alsharekh, Feminist Groundbreaker," The Markaz Review, December 6, 2020, https://themarkaz.org/kukuwaits-alanoud-al-sharekh-feminist-groundbreaker/.

27. Oussama Safa, "Social Development Report 2—Inequality, Autonomy and Change in the Arab Region" (UNESCWA, 2018), https://archive.unescwa.org/sites/www.unescwa.org/files/publications/files/social-development-report-2-english.pdf. P. 61

28. Oussama Safa, "Social Development Report 2—Inequality, Autonomy and Change in the Arab Region" (UNESCWA, 2018), https://archive.unescwa.org/sites/www.unescwa.org/files/publications/files/social-development-report-2-english.pdf. P. 86.

29. Farah Daibes, "Smashing the Patriarchy & Co: How Arab Feminists Are Re-Politicizing Their Movement," July 5, 2021, https://mena.fes.de/press/e/smashing-the-patriarchy-co-how-arab-feminists-are-re-politicizing-their-movement.

30. Human Rights Watch, "Audacity in Adversity: LGBT Activism in the Middle East and North Africa" (Human Rights Watch, April 2018), https://www.hrw.org/report/2018/04/16/audacity-adversity/lgbt-activism-middle-east-and-north-africa.

31. Human Rights Watch, "Audacity in Adversity: LGBT Activism in the Middle East and North Africa" (Human Rights Watch, April 16, 2018), https://www.hrw.org/report/2018/04/16/audacity-adversity/lgbt-activism-middle-east-and-north-africa.

32. Equaldex, "LGBT Equality Index," Equaldex, 2022, https://www.equaldex.com/equality-index.

33. Mona Eltahawy, *The Seven Necessary Sins for Women and Girls* (Boston: Beacon Press, 2019).

34. Michael Flood and Alan Greig, "Working with Men and Boys for Gender Equality: State of Play and Future Directions," April 2022, https://www.unwomen.org/sites/default/files/2021-11/-Policy-brief-Working-with-men-and-boys-for-gender-equality-en.pdf.

35. Parts of this section are paraphrased from previous publications by the author: Lina AbiRafeh, interview by SheDecides, accessed November 9, 2022, https://www.shedecides.com/champions/lina-abirafeh/.;

Lina AbiRafeh, We Have No Choice but to Win: An Interview with Lina AbiRafeh, interview by Ron Scapp, *Ethnic Studies Review 44 (2)*, July 2021, https://online.ucpress.edu/esr/article/44/2/57/118433/We-Have-No-Choice-but-to-Win An-Interview-with-Lina.

36. *Feminism Inshallah: A History of Arab Feminism*, Film (Women Make Movies, 2014).

37. Rana Alamuddin, "'You're Guilty for Enjoying Your Sexuality.' Actress on Her Campaign for Women to Accept Themselves," Video, *CNN*, 2022, https://edition.cnn.com/videos/world/2022/08/03/rana-alamuddin-as-equals-lon-orig.cnn.

38. Tarek Zeidan quoted in: *Beirut Dreams in Color*, Film (The Guardian Documentaries, 2022).

39. Suad Joseph et al., "Whose Trauma? De-Colonizing Post-Traumatic Stress Disorder and Refugee Mental Health Frameworks," Harvard Medical School Primary Care Review, January 2022, https://info.primarycare.hms.harvard.edu/review/whose-trauma-.

40. Suad Joseph et al., "Whose Trauma? De-Colonizing Post-Traumatic Stress Disorder and Refugee Mental Health Frameworks," Harvard Medical School Primary Care Review, January 2022, https://info.primarycare.hms.harvard.edu/review/whose-trauma-.

41. Joseph El-Khoury, Andres Barkil-Oteo, and Lynn Adam, "Addressing Psychiatric Care in Conflict Zones: Recommendations for the Arab Region," *BJPsych International* 18, no. 1 (August 26, 2020): 2–4, https://doi.org/10.1192/bji.2020.41.

42. Alamuddin, "You're Guilty for Enjoying Your Sexuality."

43. OHCHR, "Girls' and Young Women's Activism—Report of the Working Group on Discrimination against Women and Girls" (United Nations, May 9, 2022), https://www.ohchr.org/en/documents/thematic-reports/ahrc5025-girls-and-young-womens-activism-report-working-group.

44. Yalda Younes quoted in: Sara Abbas, "Revolution Is Female: The Uprising of Women in the Arab World," *OpenDemocracy*, 2012, https://www.opendemocracy.net/en/5050/revolution-is-female-uprising-of-women-in-arab-world/.

45. Gen Z is short for Generation Z and refers to people born in the late 1990s to early 2010s.

46. Arthur Erken, ed., "State of the World Population: My Body Is My Own" (UNFPA, 2021), https://www.unfpa.org/sowp-2021.

47. Search for Common Ground and UN Women, "Across Divides to Advance Women's Rights through Dialogue: Experiences from the Ground" (UN Women, 2017), https://www.sfcg.org/inclusive-dialogue-womens-rights-mena/.

48. Search for Common Ground and UN Women, "Across Divides to Advance Women's Rights through Dialogue: Experiences from the Ground" (UN Women, 2017), https://www.sfcg.org/inclusive-dialogue-womens-rights-mena/.

49. UNICEF, "Arab Girls' Summit: A Space for Girls and Young Women to Make Their Voices Heard," Press Release www.unicef.org, October 11, 2022, https://www.unicef.org/mena/-press-releases/arab-girls-summit-space-girls-and-young-women-make-their-voices-heard.

50. LAU et al., "Beirut Call for Action," 2016, https://aiw.lau.edu.lb/research/books-publications/beirut-call-for-action-prioritiz.php.

51. Equality Now, "Family Laws in MENA Fail to Protect Women and Girls," *Equality Now*,

May 12, 2022, https://www.equalitynow.org/news_and_insights/family-laws-in-mena-fail-to-protect-women-and-girls/?utm_source=Equality+Now&utm_campaign=f221eecf6d-EMAIL_CAMPAIGN_2022_04_27_05_09_COPY_01&utm_medium=email&utm_term=0_1a58d68771-f221eecf6d-238337152.

52. Arab America and the Arab American Anti-Discrimination Committee are organizations that share Arab-related resources, promote Arab heritage, and defend rights of Arab descendants.

53. Arab.org, "About," arab.org, accessed November 9, 2022, https://arab.org/about-u.

54. Karma Ekmekji, in discussion with the author, October 2022.

55. Hibaaq Osman quoted in: Karama, "Hibaaq Osman's Remarks to Generation Equality Forum Mexico," Karama, March 31, 2021, https://www.elkara.ma/news/hibaaq-osmans-remarks-to-generation-equality-forum-mexico.

56. Aitemad Muhanna-Matar, "New Trends of Women's Activism after the Arab Uprisings: Redefining Women's Leadership," *LSE Middle East Centre Paper Series* 5 (2014), http://www.lse.ac.uk/middleEastCentre/home.aspx.

57. Sirin Kale, "Mona Eltahawy: 'Feminism Is Not a T-Shirt or a 9 to 5 Job. It's My Existence,'" The Guardian, April 23, 2021, https://www.theguardian.com/books/2021/apr/23/mona-eltahawy-feminism-is-not-a-t-shirt-the-seven-necessary-sins-for-women-and-girls.

58. Xena Amro, email correspondence to the author, October 2022.

Conclusion

1. *Feminism Inshallah: A History of Arab Feminism*, Film (Women Make Movies, 2014).

2. Kaltham Al-Ghanim, "The Intellectual Frameworks and Theoretical Limits of Arab Feminist Thought," *Contemporary Arab Affairs* 6, no. 1 (2013): 200, https://www.jstor.org/stable/48600671.

3. Alanoud Alsharekh quoted in: Nada Ghosn, "Kuwait's Alanoud Alsharekh, Feminist Groundbreaker," The Markaz Review, December 6, 2020, https://themarkaz.org/kukuwaits-alanoud-al-sharekh-feminist-groundbreaker/.

4. Maria Najjar, "Reviving Pan-Arabism in Feminist Activism in the Middle East," *Kohl: A Journal for Body and Gender Research* 6, no. 1 (2020): 119–32, https://kohljournal.press/reviving-pan-arabism-feminist.

5. Suad Zayed Al-Oraimi, "Arab Feminism—Obstacles and Possibilities: An Analytical Study of the Women's Movement in the Arab World," in *Arab Feminisms: Gender and Equality in the Middle East*, ed. Jean Said Makdisi, Noha Bayoumi, and Rafif Rida Sidawi (London & New York: I.B. Tauris, 2014), 132–44.

6. Suad Zayed alOraimi, "Arab Feminism—Obstacles and Possibilities: An Analytical Study of the Women's Movement in the Arab World," in *Arab Feminisms Gender and Equality in the Middle East*, ed. Jean Said Makdisi, Noha Bayoumi, and Rafif Rida Sidawi (London: I.B. Tauris, 2014), P. 182.

7. Suad Joseph, "Gender and Citizenship in the Arab World," *Al-Raida Journal*, no. 129–130 (January 1, 2010): 8–18, https://doi.org/10.32380/alrj.v0i0.50.

8. Jean Said Makdisi, "Huqouq Almar'a: Feminist Thought and the Language of the Arab Women's Movement," in *Arab Feminisms Gender and Equality in the Middle East*, ed. Jean Said Makdisi, Noha Bayoumi, and Rafif Rida Sidawi (London; New York: I.B Tauris, 2014). P.88

9. Jean Said Makdisi, Noha Bayoumi, and Rafif Rida Sidawi, eds., *Arab Feminisms : Gender and Equality in the Middle East* (London; New York: I.B. Tauris, 2014), P. 15.

10. Jean Said Makdisi, Noha Bayoumi, and Rafif Rida Sidawi, eds., *Arab Feminisms : Gender and Equality in the Middle East* (London; New York: I.B. Tauris, 2014), P. 15.

11. Maria Najjar, "Reviving Pan-Arabism in Feminist Activism in the Middle East," *Kohl: A Journal for Body and Gender Research* 6, no. 1 (2020): 119–32, https://kohljournal.press/reviving-pan-arabism-feminist.

12. Sahar Khamis and Amel Mili, eds., *Arab Women's Activism and Socio-Political Transformation : Unfinished Gendered Revolutions* (New York: Palgrave Macmillan, 2018).

13. Jean Said Makdisi, "Huqouq Almar'a: Feminist Thought and the Language of the Arab Women's Movement," in *Arab Feminisms Gender and Equality in the Middle East*, ed. Jean Said Makdisi, Noha Bayoumi, and Rafif Rida Sidawi (London; New York: I.B. Tauris, 2014), Pg. 89.

14. Lina Abou-Habib, "Co-Optation versus Co-Creation: Reflections on Building a Feminist Agenda," *Feminist Revolutions* 5, no. 3 (2019).

15. Sahar Khamis and Amel Mili, eds., *Arab Women's Activism and Socio-Political Transformation : Unfinished Gendered Revolutions* (New York: Palgrave Macmillan, 2018), Pg. 244–5.

16. Sahar Khamis, "The Arab 'Feminist' Spring?," *Feminist Studies* 37, no. 3 (2011): 692–95, http://www.jstor.org/stable/23069929.

17. Nay El Rah, email message to the author, October 2022.

18. Carmen Geha, "Our Personal Is Political and Revolutionary," *Al Raida* 44, no. 1 (2020): 23–28, https://doi.org/10.32380/alrj.v44i1.1818.

19. Michael Collins, "Beirut Dreams in Colour," Video, *The Guardian*, 2022, https://www.theguardian.com/world/ng-interactive/2022/jun/22/one-good-song-can-do-more-than-5000-protests-the-queer-revolution-in-the-middle-east#:~:text=While%20this%20violent%20repression%20against.

20. Margot Badran quoted in: Wilson Center, "Book Talk: 'Women Rising: In and beyond the Arab Spring,'" Wilson Center, 2020, https://www.wilsoncenter.org/event/book-talk-women-rising-and-beyond-arab-spring.

21. Michelle and Noel Keserwany, in conversation with the author, Beirut, 2016.

22. Joan W. Scott, "Feminism's Difference Problem," in *Arab Feminisms Gender and Equality in the Middle East*, ed. Jean Said Makdisi, Noha Bayoumi, and Rafif Rida Sidawi (London & New York: I.B. Tauris, 2014), Pg. 163.

23. Sahar Khamis and Amel Mili, eds., *Arab Women's Activism and Socio-Political Transformation : Unfinished Gendered Revolutions* (New York: Palgrave Macmillan, 2018), Pg. 247.

24. Diana Moukalled, in conversation with the author, Beirut, June 2022.

25. Hibaaq Osman, "Hibaaq Osman Twitter Profile," Twitter, December 8, 2021, https://twitter.com/hibaaq/status/1468654469554610180.

26. Sahar Khamis and Amel Mili, eds., *Arab Women's Activism and Socio-Political Transformation: Unfinished Gendered Revolutions* (USA: Palgrave Macmillan, 2018).

Afterword

1. Tasfih is a practice in Tunisia, Algeria, and Morocco performed on young girls with the intention of discouraging pre-marital sex and maintaining "purity." Actual rituals vary between countries but usually the girl will repeat seven times: *"wald el nas khet wa ana haït,"* which can be translated as "People's son is a string and I'm a wall." In other words, the girl is said to be tied or closed and can only be undone on her wedding by her husband.

2. Feminist and activist Kimberlé Crenshaw coined the term in 1989 to describe how multiple factors such as race, class, gender, sexuality, disability, etc., intersect to create unique forms of inequality.

3. NalaFem is a pan–African feminist collective that seeks to embolden and mobilize women and girls for transformative feminist change.

Bibliography

ABAAD. "About | ABAAD." www.abaadmena.org, n.d. https://www.abaadmena.org/about.

Abbas, Sara. "Revolution Is Female: The Uprising of Women in the Arab World." *OpenDemocracy,* 2012. https://www.opendemocracy.net/en/5050/-revolution-is-female-uprising-of-women-in-arab-world/.

Abdalla, Jihan. "Rights Groups Slam Bahrain over Detention of Female Activists." www.aljazeera.com, October 29, 2019. https://www.aljazeera.com/news/2019/10/29/rights-groups-slam-bahrain-over-detention-of-female-activists.

Abdellatif, Adel, and Ellen Hsu. "A Crisis on Top of a Crisis; the Fragility of Arab States." *UNDP* (blog), April 9, 2020. https://www.undp.org/blog/crisis-top-crisis-fragility-arab-states.

Abdelqayoum Ali, Bashir A. "Non-Governmental Organizations and Development in the Sudan: Relations with the State and Institutional Strengthening." Doctoral Thesis, 2010. https://core.ac.uk/download/pdf/161880511.pdf.

Abdulaal, Mirna. "8 Arab Women Podcasters You Should Listen To." *Egyptian Streets,* July 31, 2020. https://egyptianstreets.com/2020/07/31/-a-journey-of-self-realization-8-arab-women-podcasters-you-should-listen-to/.

Abdulrazaq, Tallha. "Civil Disobedience, Not Terrorism, Is the Biggest Threat to Iraq's Elites." *TRT World,* November 13, 2019. https://www.trtworld.com/opinion/civil-disobedience-not-terrorism-is-the-biggest-threat-to-iraq-s-elites-31344.

Abera, Etenesh, and Zecharias Zelalem. "'Two Thirds' of Female Migrant Workers in Lebanon Survivors of Sexual Harassment." *Middle East Eye,* October 17, 2022. https://www.middleeasteye.net/news/lebanon-two-thirds-migrant-worker-women-survivors-sexual-harassment.

AbiRafeh, Lina. "Going Backward Is Not an Option: The Challenge of Equality for Arab Women." Arab Center Washington, D.C., April 22, 2022. https://arabcenterdc.org/resource/going-backward-is-not-an-option-the-challenge-of-equality-for-arab-women/.

AbiRafeh, Lina. "Want to Help the Arab Region? Put It in the Hands of Women." AP NEWS, January 30, 2021. https://apnews.com/press-release/kisspr/war-and-unrest-sustainable-development-rebellions-and-uprisings-coronavirus-pandemic-environment-97f8a816f0a6ca2c9de6afd1ca698953.

AbiRafeh, Lina. "What's Holding Arab Women Back from Achieving Equality?" The Conversation, March 8, 2017. https://theconversation.com/whats-holding-arab-women-back-from-achieving-equality-74221.

AbiRafeh, Lina, and Rachel Dore-Weeks. "Opinion: A Month after the Blast, Let's Rebuild Beirut as the Arab Region's First Feminist City." *The Independent,* September 4, 2020. https://www.independent.co.uk/voices/beirut-explosion-lebanon-blast-news-women-feminism-a9703546.html.

AbiRafeh, Lina. Lina AbiRafeh. Interview by SheDecides. Accessed November 9, 2022. https://www.shedecides.com/champions/lina-abirafeh/.

AbiRafeh, Lina. We Have No Choice but to Win: An Interview with Lina AbiRafeh. Interview by Ron Scapp. *Ethnic Studie Review 44 (2),* July 2021. https://online.ucpress.edu/esr/article/44/2/57/118433/We-Have-No-Choice-but-to-WinAn-Interview-with-Lina.

Abou-Habib, Lina. "Co-Optation versus Co-Creation: Reflections on Building a Feminist Agenda." *Kohl: A Journal for Body and Gender Research* 5, no. 3 (December 18, 2019): 9–9. https://kohljournal.press/Cooptation-versus-cocreation.

Abou-Habib, Lina. "The 'Right to Have Rights': Active Citizenship and Gendered Social Entitlements in Egypt, Lebanon and Palestine." *Gender & Development* 19, no. 3 (November 2011): 441–54. https://doi.org/10.1080/13510347.2011.625633.

Abou-Habib, Lina, and Zeina Abdel Khalik. "Sexual and Reproductive Health and Rights in the Arab Region." Arab States Civil Society Organizations and Feminists Network and UN Women, 2021. https://arabstates.unwomen.org/sites/default/files/Field%20Office%20Arab%20States/Attachments/2021/07/SRHR-Policy%-20Paper-EN.pdf.

Abouzzohour, Yasmina. "Heavy Lies the Crown: The Survival of Arab Monarchies, 10 Years after the Arab Spring." Brookings, March 8, 2021. https://www.brookings.edu/blog/order-from-chaos/2021/03/08/heavy-lies-the-crown-the-survival-of-arab-monarchies-10-years-after-the-arab-spring/.

Abu-Lughod, Lila. "Do Muslim Women Really

Need Saving? Anthropological Reflections on Cultural Relativism and Its Others." *American Anthropologist* 104, no. 3 (2002): 783–90. http://www.jstor.org/stable/3567256.

Abu-Lughod, Lila. *Remaking Women: Feminism and Modernity in the Middle East.* Princeton: Princeton University Press, 1998.

Abuidhail, Jamila, Sanaa Abujilban, and Lina Mrayan. "Arab Women's Health Care: Issues and Preventive Care." *Handbook of Healthcare in the Arab World,* 2021, 41–54. https://doi.org/10.1007/978-3-030-36811-1_3.

ADC. "American Arab Anti-Discrimination Committee." Adc.org, 2022. https://www.adc.org.

ADHRB, and BIRD. "Breaking the Silence: Bahraini Women Political Prisoners Expose Systemic Abuses." Washington, D.C.: ADHRB, 2019. https://www.adhrb.org/wp-content/uploads/2019/09/ADHRB_BreakingTheSilence_Web.pdf.

Adichie, Chimamanda Ngozi. *We Should All Be Feminists.* London: Fourth Estate, 2014.

The Advocates for Human Rights, and MRA Mobilising for Rights Associates. "Tunisia: Submission to the Committee on Economic, Social and Cultural Rights." Ohchr.org, 2016. https://tbinternet.ohchr.org/Treaties/CESCR/Shared%20Documents/TUN/INT_CESCR_CSS_TUN_24991_E.docx.

Afkhami, Mahnaz, Lina Abou-Habib, Karima Bennoune, Yakin Ertürk, Anne Gahongayire, Allison Horowski, Soraida Hussein, et al. "Equality: It's All in the Family." Women's Learning Partnership, 2017. https://learningpartnership.org/resource/equality-its-all-family-video-english.

AfricaNews. "France: Djiboutian Activists Continue Hunger Strike against Rape by Soldiers." Africanews, 2016. https://www.africanews.com/2016/04/05/france-djiboutian-activists-continue-hunger-strike-against-rape-by-soldiers/.

Ahmed, Nasim. "Remembering Israel's 2021 Onslaught on Gaza." *Middle East Monitor,* May 6, 2022. https://www.middleeastmonitor.com/-20220506-remembering-israels-2021-onslaught-on-gaza/.

Ait-Zai, Nadia. "Reforms in Family Law in the Maghreb." IEMed, 2005. https://www.iemed.org/publication/reforms-in-family-law-in-the-maghreb/.

Akasha, Yosra. "Sudanese Dream." kandakegranddaughter.blogspot.com. Accessed July 9, 2022. http://kandakegranddaughter.blogspot.com/.

Akwei, Ismail. "U.S. Honours Three African Women from Djibouti, Egypt and Tanzania for Courage." *Face2Face Africa*, March 13, 2019. https://face2faceafrica.com/article/u-s-honours-three-african-women-from-djibouti-egypt-and-tanzania-for-courage.

Al Atiyat, Ibtesam. "Current Faces of Arab Feminisms: Micro-Rebels, Art Activists and Virtual Heroines." *Friedrich Ebert Stiftung,* 2020. https://mena.fes.de/publications/e/the-current-faces-of-arab-feminism.

Al Fassi, Hatoon. "Does Saudi Feminism Exist?" In *Arab Feminisms: A Critical Comparative Study, Gender and Equality in the Middle East,* edited by Jean Said Makdisi, Noha Bayoumi, and Rafif Rida Sidawi, 121–31. London & New York: I.B. Tauris, 2014.

Al Gharaibeh, Fakir. "Women's Empowerment in Bahrain." *Journal of International Women's Studies* 12, no. 3 (2011): 96–113. https://vc.bridgew.edu/jiws/vol12/iss3/7.

Al Jazeera. "Bahrainis Protest Unemployment." www.aljazeera.com, April 1, 2005. https://www.aljazeera.com/news/2005/4/2/bahrainis-protest-unemployment.

Al Jazeera. "Comoros: Civilians Flee Strife-Torn City on Anjouan Island." *Al Jazeera*, 2018. https://www.aljazeera.com/news/2018/10/18/-comoros-civilians-flee-strife-torn-city-on-anjouan-island.

Al Jazeera. "Morocco Repeals 'Rape Marriage Law.'" *Al Jazeera*, 2014. https://www.aljazeera.com/news/2014/1/23/morocco-repeals-rape-marriage-law#:~:text=Controversial%20article%20previously%20allowed%20rapists.

Al Jazeera. "Qatar Appoints Four Women to Shura Council." www.aljazeera.com, November 9, 2017. https://www.aljazeera.com/news/2017/11/9/-qatar-appoints-four-women-to-shura-council.

Al Jazeera. "Timeline: The Middle East Conflict." www.aljazeera.com, January 21, 2008. https://www.aljazeera.com/news/2008/1/21/timeline-the-middle-east-conflict.

Al Kitbi, Ebtisam. "Women's Political Status in the GCC States." Carnegie Endowment for International Peace, August 20, 2008. https://carnegieendowment.org/sada/21229.

Al Nahda. "Al Nahda—النهضة." www.alnahda.org. Accessed October 28, 2022. https://www.alnahda.org/about/?lang=en.

Al Sahi, Huda. "The Challenges of Teaching Women's and Gender Studies in the Gulf Region." *Gender (Im)Balance in Gulf Societies,* 2018, 2–4.

Al Shalabi, Jamal, and Tareq Al-Assad. "Political Participation of Jordanian Women." *Égypte/Monde Arabe,* no. 9 (January 1, 2012): 211–30. https://doi.org/10.4000/ema.3033.

Al Subhi, Ahlam Khalfan, and Amy Erica Smith. "Electing Women to New Arab Assemblies: The Roles of Gender Ideology, Islam, and Tribalism in Oman." *International Political Science Review* 40, no. 1 (2019): 90–107. https://doi.org/10.2139/ssrn.2827795.

Al Talei, Rafiah. "The Arab Youth: Aspirations for the New Year." Carnegie Endowment for International Peace, January 11, 2022. https://carnegieendowment.org/sada/86063.

Al Zaanin, Fidaa. "Feminist Protests in Palestine—Rosa-Luxemburg-Stiftung." www.rosalux.de, March 8, 2021. https://www.rosalux.de/en/news/id/44203.

Al Zahra. "Al-Zahra College for Women—about Us." Zcw.edu.om, 2022. http://www.zcw.edu.om/About-ZCW/About-Us.aspx.

Al-Afifi, Raneem. "Feminism in Egypt: A Brief Overview." MedFemiNiswiya, April 8, 2021. https://medfeminiswiya.net/2021/04/08/contexte-egypte/?lang=en.

Al-Ali, Nadje. "Gender and Civil Society in the Middle East." *International Feminist Journal of Politics* 5, no. 2 (January 2003): 216–32. https://doi.org/10.1080/1461674032000080576.

Al-Ali, Nadje. "Gendering the Arab Spring." *Middle East Journal of Culture and Communication* 5, no. 1 (2012): 26–31. https://doi.org/10.1163/187398612x624346.

Al-Ali, Nadje, and Nicola Pratt, eds. *Women and War in the Middle East: Transnational Perspectives.* London & New York: Zed Books, 2013.

Al-Amarneh, Maisoon. "Jordanian Feminist Movement and the Struggle for Social and Political Change: Achievements and Challenges." *Sayaran—WE4L Knowledge and Learning Platform*, no. 1 (2018). https://www.sayaran.org/jordanian-feminist-movement-and-the-struggle-for-social-and-political-change/.

Al-Ansary, Khalid. "Thousands Rally in Iraq's 'Day of Rage' Protests." *Reuters*, February 25, 2011, sec. World News. https://www.reuters.com/article/us-iraq-protests-idUSTRE71O1RN20110225.

Al-Ashtal, Amel Nejib. "A Long, Quiet and Steady Struggle: The Women's Movement in Yemen." In *Mapping Arab Women's Movements: A Century of Transformations from Within,* edited by Pernille Arenfeldt and Nawar Al-Hassan Golley, 197–252. Cairo: American University in Cairo Press, 2012.

Al-Atiyat, Ibtesam. *The Women's Movement in Jordan: Activism, Discourses, and Strategies.* Amman: Friedrich Ebert Stiftung, 2003.

Al-Faiz, Norah. "Norah Al-Faiz Faces, Vice-Minister at the Ministry of Education." Faces of Saudi. *Arab News*, April 19, 2020. https://facesofsaudi.com/19/04/2020/norah-al-faiz-ministry-of-education-faces-of-saudi-by-arab-news/.

Al-Ghanim, Kaltham. "The Intellectual Frameworks and Theoretical Limits of Arab Feminist Thought." In *Arab Feminisms: Gender and Equality in the Middle East,* edited by Jean Said Makdisi, Noha Bayoumi, and Rafif Rida Sidawi, 145–56. London & New York: I.B. Tauris, 2014.

Al-Haj, Ahmed, and Samy Magdy. "Yemeni Rebels Sentence Actor, Her 3 Companions to Prison." *AP NEWS*, November 8, 2021. https://apnews.com/article/middle-east-iran-yemen-sanaa-human-rights-watch-0a7683396afff468322faed3b49d629d.

Al-Khalidi, Suleiman, and Eric Knecht. "Young, Angry Lebanese Ditch Their Differences to Target 'Unjust' System." *Reuters*, October 23, 2019, sec. Industry, Materials and Utilities. https://www.reuters.com/article/lebanon-protests-youth/young-angry-lebanese-ditch-their-differences-to-target-unjust-system-idUSL3N2771XN.

Al-Midani, Mohammad Amin. "The League of Arab States and the Arab Charter on Human Rights." ACIHL, n.d. https://acihl.org/articles.htm?%20article_id=6.

Al-Mughni, Haya. "Women's Organizations in Kuwait." *Middle East Report,* no. 198 (1996). https://merip.org/1996/03/womens-organizations-in-kuwait/.

Al-Najjar, Sabika Muhammad. "The Feminist Movement in the Gulf." *Al-Raida* 20, no. 100 (January 1, 2003): 29–37. https://doi.org/10.32380/alrj.v0i0.441.

Al-Natour, Manal. "The Role of Women in the Egyptian 25th January Revolution." *Journal of International Women's Studies* 13, no. 5 (2012). https://vc.bridgew.edu/jiws/vol13/iss5/7.

Al-Oraimi, Suad Zayed. "Arab Feminism—Obstacles and Possibilities: An Analytical Study of the Women's Movement in the Arab World." In *Arab Feminisms Gender and Equality in the Middle East,* edited by Jean Said Makdisi, Noha Bayoumi, and Rafif Rida Sidawi, 132–44. London & New York: I.B. Tauris, 2014.

Al-Oseimi, Nourah. "Women in Kuwait Stand against Harassment." *The Times Kuwait,* February 13, 2021. https://timeskuwait.com/news/we-will-not-be-silenced/.

Al-Shakeri, Hayder. "The Aspirations and Disillusionment of Iraq's Youth." Chatham House—International Affairs Think Tank, July 27, 2022. https://www.chathamhouse.org/2022/07/-aspirations-and-disillusionment-iraqs-youth.

Al-Shamahi, Aaya. "Iraqi Women Are Leading Protests in Iraq despite the Dangers." Video. *Middle East Eye,* December 13, 2019. https://www.middleeasteye.net/video/iraqi-women-are-leading-protests-iraq-despite-dangers.

Al-Shaykh, Hanan. *One Thousand and One Nights.* London: Bloomsbury, 2011.

Al-Tamimi, Huda. "Effects of Iraq's Parliamentary Gender Quota on Women's Political Mobilization and Legitimacy Post-2003." *Contemporary Arab Affairs* 11, no. 4 (December 2018): 41–62. https://doi.org/10.1525/caa.2018.114003.

Alaaldin, Ranj. "How the Iran-Iraq War Will Shape the Region for Decades to Come." *Brookings,* October 9, 2020. https://www.brookings.edu/blog/order-from-chaos/2020/10/09/how-the-iran-iraq-war-will-shape-the-region-for-decades-to-come/.

Alamuddin, Rana. "'You're Guilty for Enjoying Your Sexuality.' Actress on Her Campaign for Women to Accept Themselves." Video. *CNN,* 2022. https://edition.cnn.com/videos/world/2022/08/03/rana-alamuddin-as-equals-lon-orig.cnn.

Aldosari, Hala. "The Effect of Gender Norms on Women's Health in Saudi Arabia." Washington, D.C.: The Arab Gulf States Institute in Washington, 2017.

Alfoory, Samyah. "The 2011 Bahraini Uprising: Women's Agency, Dissent and Violence." Washington, D.C.: Georgetown Institute for Women, Peace and Security, 2014. https://giwps.

georgetown.edu/resource/the-2011-bahraini-uprising-womens-agency-dissent-and-violence/.

Ali, Degan, and Deqa Saleh. "Addressing the Systematic Barriers Facing Women and Girls in the Aid System in Somalia." *Humanitarian Practice Network,* no. 75 (May 31, 2019). https://odihpn.org/publication/addressing-systematic-barriers-facing-women-girls-aid-system-somalia/.

Alkhudary, Taif. "Iraqi Women Are Engaged in a Struggle for Their Rights." LSE Middle East Centre, June 15, 2020. https://blogs.lse.ac.uk/mec/2020/06/15/iraqi-women-are-engaged-in-a-struggle-for-their-rights/.

ALQST for Human Rights @ALQST_En. "ALQST Tweet: Footage from Khamis Mushait Orphanage." Twitter, August 31, 2022. https://twitter.com/ALQST_En/status/1564935743117660160.

Alsharekh, Alanoud, and Azadeh Pourzand. Women and power in the Middle East. Interview by Gitika Bhardwaj. Chatham House, May 21, 2021. https://www.chathamhouse.org/2021/05/-women-and-power-in-the-middle-east.

Amireh, Amal. "Framing Nawal El Saadawi: Arab Feminism in a Transnational World." *Signs: Journal of Women in Culture and Society* 26, no. 1 (October 2000): 215–49. https://doi.org/10.1086/495572.

Amnesty International. "Libya: Abducted Politician's Fate Remains Unknown a Year On, amid Ongoing Disappearances." www.amnesty.org, July 17, 2020. https://www.amnesty.org/en/latest/news/2020/07/libya-abducted-politicians-fate-remains-unknown-a-year-on-amid-ongoing-disappearances/.

Amnesty International. "The World's Refugees in Numbers." Amnesty.org, 2019. https://www.amnesty.org/en/what-we-do/refugees-asylum-seekers-and-migrants/global-refugee-crisis-statistics-and-facts/.

Amro, Xena. "True Lebanese Feminist." Facebook. Accessed November 9, 2022. https://www.facebook.com/TrueLebaneseFeminist.

Andrews, Sara K., Jean Gabat, Georgia Jolink, and Jeni Klugman. "Responding to Rising Intimate Partner Violence amid COVID-19: A Rapid Global Review." Washington, D.C.: GIWPS, 2021.

Arab.org. "About." arab.org. Accessed November 9, 2022. https://arab.org/about-u.

Arab.org. "General Union of Palestinian Women | Arab.org." Directory, June 1, 2016. https://arab.org/directory/general-union-of-palestinian-women/.

Arab.org. "Omani Women Association at Muscat | Arab.org." Directory, January 19, 2017. https://arab.org/directory/omani-women-association-at-muscat/.

Arab America. "Arab American Community Resources | Arab World News & Events." Arab America. Accessed October 29, 2022. https://www.arabamerica.com.

Arab American Institute. "Arab American Institute Foundation." Arab American Institute Foundation, n.d. https://www.aaiusa.org/.

Arab Barometer. "The Arab World in Seven Charts: Are Arabs Turning Their Backs on Religion?—Arab Barometer." BBC News, June 24, 2019. https://www.arabbarometer.org/2019/06/the-arab-world-in-seven-charts-are-arabs-turning-their-backs-on-religion/.

Arab Barometer. "Opinion on Arab Women and Political Power." Arab Barometer, 2020. https://www.arabbarometer.org/2020/02/opinion-on-arab-women-and-political-power/.

Arab Institute for Women. "About | the Arab Institute for Women | LAU." The Arab Institute for Women. Accessed November 2, 2022. https://aiw.lau.edu.lb/about/.

Arab Reform Initiative. "Youth Activism & Livelihoods." Arab Reform Initiative. Accessed November 9, 2022. https://www.arab-reform.net/area_of_work/youth-activism-livelihoods/.

The Arab Weekly. "Libya's New Cabinet Includes Five Women, Still below Pledge." *AW,* March 12, 2021. https://thearabweekly.com/libyas-new-cabinet-includes-five-women-still-below-pledge.

The Arab Weekly. "One Woman to Represent All Women in Oman Shura Council." *AW,* October 23, 2015. https://thearabweekly.com/one-woman-represent-all-women-oman-shura-council.

Arab Women Organization. "Milestones in the History of Arab Women." Cairo: Arab Women Organization, n.d. http://elibrary.arabwomenorg.org/Content/2840_milestones%20in%20the%20history%20of%20arab%20women.pdf.

Arenfeldt, Pernille, and Nawar Al-Hassan Golley, eds. *Mapping Arab Women's Movements: A Century of Transformations from Within.* Cairo: American University in Cairo Press, 2012. https://doi.org/10.5743/cairo/9789774164989.001.0001.

Asi, Yara M. "The (Slowly) Changing Gender Dynamics in Arab Countries." Arab Center Washington, D.C., May 11, 2021. https://arabcenterdc.org/resource/the-slowly-changing-gender-dynamics-in-arab-countries/.

The Associated Press. "Sudan Overturns Moral Policing Law and Disbands Al-Bashir's Party." *The New York Times,* November 29, 2019, sec. World. https://www.nytimes.com/2019/11/29/world/africa/sudan-moral-policing-law-al-bashir.html.

Associated Press Kuwait City. "Kuwait Gets First Female Minister." The Guardian, June 13, 2005. https://www.theguardian.com/world/2005/jun/13/1.

Associated Press Sana'a. "Yemeni Women Join Street Protests against President Saleh." *The Guardian,* April 17, 2011. https://www.theguardian.com/world/2011/apr/17/yemeni-women-protest-against-president-saleh.

Association tunisienne des femmes démocrates. "Women's Rights in Tunisia Declaration." ATFD, 2010. https://tbinternet.ohchr.org/

Treaties/CEDAW/Shared%20Documents/TUN/INT_CEDAW_NGO_TUN_47_10160_E.pdf.

ATFD. "Women's Rights in Tunisia: Alternative Report." ATFD, 2010. http://www2.ohchr.org/english/bodies/cedaw/docs/ngos/ATFD_Tunisia_CEDAW47_en.pdf.

Bachelet, Michelle. "Oral Update on the Situation of Human Rights in the Sudan." Presented at the 49th Session of the Human Rights Council, March 7, 2022. https://www.ohchr.org/en/statements/2022/03/oral-update-situation-human-rights-sudan#:~:text=They%20are%20reported%20to%20be,144%20women%2C%20and%20148%20children..

Badran, Margot. "Nawal El-Saadawi: A Fearless Feminist without Borders | Wilson Center." Wilson Center, March 8, 2022. https://www.wilsoncenter.org/blog-post/nawal-el-saadawi-fearless-feminist-without-borders.

Badran, Margot. "Unifying Women: Feminist Pasts and Presents in Yemen." *Gender & History* 10, no. 3 (1998): 498–518. https://doi.org/https://doi.org/10.1111/1468-0424.00115.

Badri, Balghis. "Feminist Perspectives in the Sudan: An Analytical Overview." In *"Feminist Perspectives."* Free University Berlin, 2005. https://www.fu-berlin.de/sites/gpo/tagungen/tagungfeministperspectives/balghis_badri.pdf.

Bahrain News Agency. "Bahrain News Agency." www.bna.bh, February 13, 2022. https://www.bna.bh/en/NationalActionCharter2002ConstitutionconfirmlegitimacyofBahrainiwomensrights.aspx?cms=q8FmFJgiscL2fwIzON1%2BDmNtPWA4PtwLWj6RV9fMoNw%3D.

Bajec, Alessandra. "Moroccan #MeToo Helps Women to Break Their Silence against Sexual Harassment and Rape." *The New Arab*, March 7, 2020. https://english.alaraby.co.uk/analysis/moroccan-metoo-helps-women-break-silence.

Baker McKenzie. "Middle East: Baker McKenzie MENA Employment Newsletter—Labour Law Updates in the GCC Promoting Gender Equality—Ensure Your Current Salary Practices Are Compliant." *Insight Plus*, October 19, 2020. https://insightplus.bakermckenzie.com/bm/employment-compensation/middle-east-labour-law-updates-in-the-gcc-promoting-gender-equality-ensure-your-current-salary-practices-are-compliant#:~:text=8%20of%201980%20(the%20%22UAE.

Bala, Artur, and Héla Ben Fayala. "Across Divides to Advance Women's Rights through Dialogue: Experiences from the Ground." UN Women Arab States, 2016. https://arabstates.unwomen.org/en/digital-library/publications/2016/all/across-divisions-to-advance-womens-rights-upd.

Barbuscia, David, and Hadeel Al Sayegh. "Kuwait's Debt Law Gridlock Poses First Economic Test for New Emir." *Reuters*, September 30, 2020, sec. Middle East & Africa. https://www.reuters.com/article/kuwait-emir-economy-int-idUSKBN26L1XN.

Barkawi, Ben, and Menna A. Farouk. "Seek Help, Say Middle East Women's Groups as Domestic Violence Surges." *Reuters*, April 7, 2020, sec. Coronavirus. https://www.reuters.com/article/us-health-coronavirus-women-mideast-trfn-idUSKBN21P23M.

Barron, Laignee. "'A Revolutionary Moment.' Activist Mona Eltahawy Talks Sexual Assault and #MosqueMeToo." *Time*, March 7, 2018. https://time.com/5170236/mona-eltahawy-mosquemetoo/.

Basch-Harod, Heidi. "#MeToo and the History of 'Hashtag Feminism' in the MENA Region." IEMed Mediterranean, 2019. https://www.iemed.org/publication/metoo-and-the-history-of-hashtag-feminism-in-the-mena-region/.

Baydoun, Azza Charara عزّه شرارة بيضون. "Azzachararabaydoun." azzachararabaydoun.wordpress.com, 2019. https://azzachararabaydoun.wordpress.com/.

BBC. "Letter from Africa: 'We're Not Cleaners'—Sexism amid Sudan Protests." *BBC News*, April 1, 2019. https://www.bbc.com/news/world-africa-47738155.

BBC. "Libya Profile—Timeline." *BBC News*, September 3, 2018. https://www.bbc.com/news/world-africa-13755445.

BBC. "Man Dies after Setting Himself on Fire in Saudi Arabia." *BBC News*, January 23, 2011, sec. Middle East. https://www.bbc.com/news/world-middle-east-12260465.

BBC. "Saudi Arabia's King Appoints Women to Shura Council." *BBC News*, January 11, 2013. https://www.bbc.com/news/world-middle-east-20986428.

BBC. "Sudan Protests: The Women Driving Change in Sudan." *BBC News*, April 24, 2019. https://www.bbc.com/news/av/world-africa-48027451.

BBC. "Tunisian Women Free to Marry Non-Muslims." *BBC News*, September 15, 2017. https://www.bbc.com/news/world-africa-41278610.

BBC. "Yemeni Model Jailed for Indecency by Rebel Authorities." *BBC News*, November 8, 2021, sec. Middle East. https://www.bbc.com/news/world-middle-east-59205765.

BBC News Middle East. "Saudi Women Get Identity Cards." news.bbc.co.uk, December 10, 2001. http://news.bbc.co.uk/2/hi/middle_east/1702342.stm.

Begum, Rothna. "The Brave Female Activists Who Fought to Lift Saudi Arabia's Driving Ban." *Human Rights Watch*, October 11, 2017. https://www.hrw.org/news/2017/09/29/brave-female-activists-who-fought-lift-saudi-arabias-driving-ban.

Begum, Rothna. "Domestic Violence Law Signals Hope for Kuwait's Women." Human Rights Watch, September 29, 2020. https://www.hrw.org/news/2020/09/29/domestic-violence-law-signals-hope-kuwaits-women.

Beirut Dreams in Color. Film. The Guardian Documentaries, 2022.

Beit el-Hanane. "Beit El Hanane." Beit el Hanane.

Accessed October 28, 2022. https://beitelhanane. wordpress.com/.

Bellafronto, Catherine. "Refworld | Women's Rights in the Middle East and North Africa— Syria." *Refworld.* Freedom House, 2005. https:// www.refworld.org/docid/47387b70c.html.

BIRD. "Bahrain Human Rights Report: Events of 2020." London: The Bahrain Institute for Rights and Democracy, 2021.

Bishara, Hakim. "The Viral Photograph That Has Come to Symbolize Sudan's Uprising." *Hyperallergic,* April 12, 2019. https://hyperallergic. com/494770/the-viral-photograph-that-has-come-to-symbolize-sudans-uprising/.

Bishin, Benjamin G., and Feryal M. Cherif. "The Big Gains for Women's Rights in the Middle East, Explained." *Washington Post,* July 23, 2018. https://www.washingtonpost.com/ news/monkey-cage/wp/2018/07/23/womens-rights-are-advancing-in-the-middle-east-this-explains-why/.

Black, Ian. "Emergence of Saudi-Style 'Morality Police' Causes Alarm in Yemen." the Guardian, September 2, 2008. https://www.theguardian. com/world/2008/sep/03/yemen.

Borgen Magazine. "Remaining Barriers to Women's Rights in Iraq." *Borgen,* November 25, 2020. https://www.borgenmagazine.com/remaining-barriers-to-womens-rights-in-iraq/.

The Borgen Project. "5 Things to Know about Women's Rights in Algeria." The Borgen Project, December 8, 2020. https://borgenproject. org/womens-rights-in-algeria/.

Borshchevskaya, Anna. "How the Death of the Soviet Union Transformed the Middle East." *The Washington Institute,* December 21, 2021. https://www.washingtoninstitute.org/policy-analysis/how-death-soviet-union-transformed-middle-east.

Bouzghaia, Chamseddine. "'Poetic Protest': How the Photo of a Ballet Dancer Became a Symbol of Algeria's Protests." *France 24,* March 10, 2019. https://www.france24.com/en/20190310-algeria-poetic-protest-photo-dancer-ballet-ballerina-teenager-bouteflika.

Bureau of Democracy, Human Rights, and Labor. "Bahrain." U.S. Department of State, November 17, 2010. https://2009-2017.state.gov/j/drl/rls/ irf/2010/148815.htm.

Burrowes, Robert, and Manfred W. Wenner. "Yemen | People, History, & Facts." In *Encyclopædia Britannica,* February 6, 2019. https:// www.britannica.com/place/Yemen.

Cafiero, Giorgio. "Iran and the Gulf States 40 Years after the 1979 Revolution." Middle East Institute, February 8, 2019. https://www.mei.edu/ publications/iran-and-gulf-states-40-years-after-1979-revolution.

Canada: Immigration and Refugee Board of Canada. "Tunisia: Protection and Resources Available to Women Fleeing Family Abuse; Whether a Single Woman Could Find Safety in Any Part of the Country (2000-July 2004)." Refworld, 2004.

https://www.refworld.org/docid/41501c6423. html.

Carter Hallward, Maia, and Julie M. Norman. *Understanding Nonviolence.* Cambridge: Polity, 2015.

CCCB. "Mona Eltahawy: 'Patriarchy Is the Form of Oppression with Which the Entire World Struggles.'" www.youtube.com, 2019. https://www. youtube.com/watch?v=08DW7edwWyY.

CEIRPP. "Report of the Committee on the Exercise of the Inalienable Rights of the Palestinian People." United Nations, October 27, 1988. https://www.un.org/unispal/ document/auto-insert-179999/.

Centre for Public Impact. "Reforming Moroccan Family Law: The Moudawana." Centre For Public Impact (CPI), 2016. https://www. centreforpublicimpact.org/case-study/ moroccan-moudawana-reform.

Chaban, Stephanie. "Addressing Violence against Women through Legislative Reform in States Transitioning from the Arab Spring." In *Gender, Human Rights and the Limits of Legal Frameworks: Challenging the Place of Women's Rights in Post-Transition Countries,* edited by John Lahai and Khanyisela Moyo, 113–41. London: Palgrave, 2018.

Chaban, Stephanie. "Women's Organizations, International Norms and the Emergence of Domestic Violence Legislation in the Middle East and North Africa: An Examination of Activism in Egypt and Lebanon." PhD Thesis, 2016.

Chahine, Marwan. "The Icon of the Lebanese Revolution." *L'Orient Today,* October 26, 2019. https://today.lorientlejour.com/article/1192726/-the-icon-of-the-lebanese-revolution.html.

Chamlou, Naderah. "Women's Rights in the Middle East and North Africa | Global Policy Journal." Globalpolicyjournal.com, 2000. https:// www.globalpolicyjournal.com/blog/03/10/2017/ women%e2%80%99s-rights-middle-east-and-north-africa.

Charrad, Mounira. "Policy Shifts: State, Islam, and Gender in Tunisia, 1930s-1990s." *Social Policy* 4, no. 2 (1997): 284–319.

Charrad, Mounira M. *States and Women's Rights: The Making of Postcolonial Tunisia, Algeria, and Morocco.* Berkeley: University of California Press, 2001.

Chebbo, Karima. "Women's Rights and Gender Equality in Lebanon: Denying the Basic Right of Nationality." *Al Rawiya,* January 24, 2022. https://al-rawiya.com/human-rights/womens-rights-and-gender-equality-in-lebanon-denying-the-basic-right-of-nationality/.

Chehayeb, Kareem. "'Living Nightmare': UN Says Lebanon Faces Growing Starvation." *Al Jazeera,* October 1, 2021. https://www.aljazeera.com/ news/2021/10/1/un-lebanon-reforms-extreme-poverty-economic-crisis.

Chelala, César. "Domestic Violence in the Middle East." *The Globalist,* September 16, 2019. https://

www.theglobalist.com/middle-east-domestic-violence-gender-equality/#:~:text=Of%20the%2022%20United%20Nations.

Chellali, Salsabil. "Tunisia Tramples Gender Parity ahead of Parliamentary Elections." Human Rights Watch, November 2, 2022. https://www.hrw.org/news/2022/11/02/tunisia-tramples-gender-parity-ahead-parliamentary-elections.

Chemaly, Soraya. *Rage Becomes Her: The Power of Women's Anger.* New York: Atria Books, 2018.

Chenoweth, Erica, and Maria J Stephan. *Why Civil Resistance Works: The Strategic Logic of Nonviolent Conflict.* New York: Columbia University Press, 2011.

Cheryan, Sapna, and Hazel Rose Markus. "Masculine Defaults: Identifying and Mitigating Hidden Cultural Biases." *Psychological Review* 127, no. 6 (November 2020): 1022–52. https://doi.org/10.1037/rev0000209.

Civil Society Knowledge Centre. "Giving Precedence to International Treaties." The Centre for Social Sciences Research and Action, May 23, 2019. https://civilsociety-centre.org/content/giving-precedence-international-treaties.

COAR. "The Business of Empowering Women: Insights for Development Programming in Syria." COAR, May 15, 2020. https://coar-global.org/2020/05/15/the-business-of-empowering-women/.

Coll, Steve. "In the Gulf, Dissidence Goes Digital." The Washington Post, March 29, 2005. https://www.washingtonpost.com/archive/politics/2005/03/29/in-the-gulf-dissidence-goes-digital/ad4fb146-f495-4399-ab91-c5d6df77779a/.

Columbia Global Centers. "Interview with Emeritus Professor Deniz Kandiyoti on Gender and Politics." globalcenters.columbia.edu, January 31, 2022. https://globalcenters.columbia.edu/news/interview-emeritus-professor-deniz-kandiyoti-gender-and-politics.

Committee on the Elimination of Discrimination against Women. "CEDAW/C/ARE/CO/2–3: Concluding Observations on the Combined Second and Third Periodic Reports of the United Arab Emirates." United Nations, 2015. https://www.ohchr.org/en/documents/concluding-observations/cedawcareco2-3-concluding-observations-combined-second-and-third.

Coogle, Adam. "Recorded 'Honor' Killings on the Rise in Jordan." Human Rights Watch, October 27, 2016. https://www.hrw.org/news/2016/10/27/recorded-honor-killings-rise-jordan.

Cooke, Miriam. "Women, Religion, and the Postcolonial Arab World." *Cultural Critique,* no. 45 (2000): 150–84. https://doi.org/10.2307/1354370.

Coomaraswamy, Radhika. "Report of the Special Rapporteur on Violence against Women, Its Causes and Consequences." ECOSOC, 2002. https://digitallibrary.un.org/record/459009?ln=en.

Courants de Femmes. "AFCF—Association Des Femmes Chefs de Famille." courantsdefemmes.free.fr. Accessed November 6, 2022. http://courantsdefemmes.free.fr/Assoces/Mauritanie/AFCF/AFCF.html.

Dadouch, Sarah. "Killings of Women at Mideast Universities Provoke Outrage and Worry." *The Washington Post,* July 10, 2022. https://www.washingtonpost.com/world/2022/07/08/killings-university-women-egypt-jordan.

Daibes, Farah. "Smashing the Patriarchy & Co: How Arab Feminists Are Re-Politicizing Their Movement," July 5, 2021. https://mena.fes.de/press/e/smashing-the-patriarchy-co-how-arab-feminists-are-re-politicizing-their-movement.

Daily Jubba. "Somalia's Successful Mass Literacy Campaign of 1973–1975." *Daily Jubba,* October 24, 2022. https://www.dailyjubba.com/2022/10/24/somalias-successful-mass-literacy-campaign-of-1973-1975/.

D'Altavilla, Lara Bellone. "Solidarity across Borders: Arab Women Demand Action after Series of Femicides Bleed Society Dry." *The New Arab,* July 8, 2022. https://english.alaraby.co.uk/features/arab-women-demand-action-after-femicides-bleed-society-dry.

Daou, Bernadette. "Feminisms in Lebanon: After Proving Loyalty to the 'Nation,' Will the 'Body' Rise within the 'Arab Spring'?" *Civil Society Review,* no. 1 (2015): 55–66.

Darwiche, Nawla. "Women in Arab NGOs: A Publication of the Arab Network for Non-Governmental Organizations, December 1999." *Feminist Review* 69, no. 1 (2001): 15–20. https://doi.org/https://doi.org/10.1080/014177800110070094.

Darwish, Adeed. "Rebellion in Bahrain." *Middle East Review of International Affairs* 3, no. 1 (1999).

Davis, Hanna. "'Elephant in the Room': Jordanian Women and Equal Rights." www.aljazeera.com, February 18, 2022. https://www.aljazeera.com/news/2022/2/18/elephant-in-the-room-jordanian-womens-struggle-for-rights.

Dehnert, Elspeth. "As Lebanon, Jordan, Tunisia End 'Marry-Your-Rapist' Laws, Where Next?" *The New Humanitarian,* August 22, 2017. https://deeply.thenewhumanitarian.org/womenandgirls/articles/2017/08/22/as-lebanon-jordan-tunisia-end-marry-your-rapist-laws-where-next.

Democracy Now! "Uprising in Egypt: A Two-Hour Special on the Revolt against the U.S.-Backed Mubarak Regime." Video. *Democracy Now!,* February 5, 2011. http://www.democracynow.org/2011/2/5/uprising_in_egypt_a_two_hour.

Democracy Now! "Asmaa Mahfouz & the YouTube Video That Helped Spark the Egyptian Uprising." Video. *Democracy Now!,* February 8, 2011. https://www.democracynow.org/2011/2/8/asmaa_mahfouz_the_youtube_video_that.

Dianu, An-Chi Hoh. "Contemporary Short Stories by Kuwaiti Women: A Study of Their Social Context and Characteristics." *MELA Notes,* no. 75/76 (2002): 69–84. https://www.jstor.org/stable/29785770.

Drinkwater, Michael, Hanan Kwinana, and Awny Amer. "Final Evaluation of the AMAL Programme: 'Supporting Women's Transformative Leadership at Changing Times in the MENA Region.'" Oxfam, 2016. https://oxfamintermon. s3.amazonaws.com/sites/default/files/doc umentos/files/EF-%20Marruecos%20abrl6.pdf.

DW. "Jordan Repeals 'Marry the Rapist' Law—DW—08/01/2017." dw.com, January 8, 2017. https://www.dw.com/en/jordan-repeals-marry-the-rapist-law/a-39924374.

The Economist. "Arab Governments Are Doing Too Little to End Honour Killings." *The Economist,* 2021. https://www.economist. com/middle-east-and-africa/2021/02/06/arab-governments-are-doing-too-little-to-end-honour-killings.

Edemariam, Aida. "Joumana Haddad: 'I Live in a Country That Hates Me.'" *The Guardian,* August 21, 2010. https://www.theguardian. com/theguardian/2010/aug/21/joumana-haddad-interview.

Egypt Independent. "Court to Consider Annulling Death Sentence against Naira Ashraf's Murderer in January." Egypt Independent, September 12, 2022. https://egyptindependent.com/court-to-consider-annulling-death-sentence-against-naira-ashrafs-murderer-in-january/.

Eisenstein, Hester. 1996. *Inside agitators: Australian femocrats and the state.* Philadelphia: Temple University Press.

Ekmekji, Karma. "Thinking out Loud with Hajer Sharief." Diplowomen, June 2021. https:// soundcloud.com/diplowomen/dw5.

El Feki, Shereen, Gary Barker, and Brian Heilman, eds. "Understanding Masculinities: Results from the International Men and Gender Equality Survey (IMAGES)—Middle East and North Africa." UN Women and Promundo, 2017.

El Saadawi, Nawaal, and Sherif Hetata (Translator). *Woman at Point Zero (Imra'ah 'Inda Nuqat Al-Sifr).* 1979. Reprint, London: Zed Books, 2015.

El Saadawi, Nawal. *The Hidden Face of Eve: Women in the Arab World.* Translated by Sherif Hetata. London: Zed, 1980.

El Saadawi, Nawal. *The Nawal El Saadawi Reader.* London: Bloomsbury, 1998.

El-Khoury, Joseph, Andres Barkil-Oteo, and Lynn Adam. "Addressing Psychiatric Care in Conflict Zones: Recommendations for the Arab Region." *BJPsych International* 18, no. 1 (August 26, 2020): 2–4. https://doi.org/10.1192/bji.2020.41.

El-Shaarawi, Sarah. "Women's Activisms and the Future of Feminist Movements in the Arab Region." Arab Media & Society, March 3, 2022. https://www.arabmediasociety.com/-womens-activisms-and-the-future-of-feminist-movements-in-the-arab-region/.

El-Sherif, Heba. "Young Arab Feminist Network Hopes to Build Dialogue with Older Generations, Non-Feminists." *Daily News Egypt,* May 5, 2010. https://dailynewsegypt. com/2010/05/05/young-arab-feminist-network-hopes-to-build-dialogue-with-older-generations-non-feminists/.

Elise, Salem. "Shaking Things Up in Lebanon: Women, Revolution, and the University." *Al-Raida Journal* 44, no. 1 (August 20, 2020): 93–98, https://doi.org/10.32380/alrj.v44i1.1826.

Elliott, Katja Žvan. "Morocco and Its Women's Rights Struggle." *Journal of Middle East Women's Studies* 10, no. 2 (2014): 1–30. https://doi. org/10.2979/jmiddeastwomstud.10.2.1.

Elsadda, Hoda. "Gender Studies in the Arab World: Reflections and Questions on the Challenges of Discourses, Locations and History." In *Arab Feminisms Gender and Equality in the Middle East,* edited by Jean Said Makdisi, Noha Bayoumi, and Rafif Rida Didawi. London: I.B. Tauris, 2014.

Eltahawy, Mona. *Headscarves and Hymens.* New York: Farrar, Straus and Giroux, 2015.

Eltahawy, Mona. "#MosqueMeToo: What Happened When I Was Sexually Assaulted during the Hajj." *The Washington Post,* February 15, 2018. https://www.washingtonpost. com/news/global-opinions/wp/2018/02/15/-mosquemetoo-what-happened-when-i-was-sexually-assaulted-during-the-hajj/.

Eltahawy, Mona. *The Seven Necessary Sins for Women and Girls.* Boston: Beacon Press, 2019.

EMR Mental Health Collaborators. "The Burden of Mental Disorders in the Eastern Mediterranean Region, 1990–2015: Findings from the Global Burden of Disease 2015 Study." *International Journal of Public Health* 63, no. S1 (August 3, 2017): 25–37. https://doi.org/10.1007 /s00038-017-1006-1.

Equaldex. "LGBT Equality Index." Equaldex, 2022. https://www.equaldex.com/equality-index.

Equality Now. "Family Laws in MENA Fail to Protect Women and Girls." *Equality Now,* May 12, 2022. https://www.equalitynow.org/news_ and_insights/family-laws-in-mena-fail-to-protect-women-and-girls/?utm_source= Equality+Now&utm_campaign=f221eecf6d-EMAIL_CAMPAIGN_2022_04_27_05_09_ COPY_01&utm_medium=email&utm_term=- 0_1a58d68771-f221eecf6d-238337152.

Equality Now. "Not Backing down against 'Marry-Your-Rapist' Laws." *Equality Now,* August 21, 2017. https://www.equalitynow. org/news_and_insights/not_backing_down_ against_marry_your_rapist_laws/.

Equality Now. "Yemen—the Personal Status Act No. 20 of 1992." Yemen—The Personal Status Act No. 20 Of 1992, 2021. https://www.equalitynow. org/discriminatory_law/yemen_the_personal_ status_act_no_20_of_1992/.

Erken, Arthur, ed. "State of the World Population: My Body Is My Own." UNFPA, 2021. https:// www.unfpa.org/sowp-2021.

Euro-Med Human Rights Monitor. "One War Older: Israeli Violations against Children and Women during the Military Attack on Gaza (10– 21 May 2021)." Geneva: Euro-Med, July 2021.

Euro-Mediterranean Women's Foundation. "Palestine—Ministry of Women's Affairs." Euromedwomen.foundation, May 17, 2015. https://www.euromedwomen.foundation/pg/en/resources/view/4364/palestine-ministry-of-womens-affairs.

Euronews. "#Masaktach, How the Moroccan #MeToo Began." *Euronews*, October 17, 2018. https://www.euronews.com/2018/10/17/-masaktach-how-the-moroccan-metoo-began.

European Civil Protection and Humanitarian Aid Operations. "Syria Factsheet." ECHO. Accessed November 9, 2022. https://civil-protection-humanitarian-aid.ec.europa.eu/where/middle-east/syria_en#facts—figures.

Facebook. "The Uprising of Women in the Arab World 2011 ",العربي العالم في المرأة انتفاضة. https://www.facebook.com/intifadat.almar2a.

Fakir, Intissar. "Snapshot of the Economic Crisis in the Arab World." Carnegie Endowment for International Peace, July 7, 2009. https://carnegieendowment.org/sada/23357.

FAO. "Near East and North Africa—Regional Overview of Food Security and Nutrition 2021." Cairo: FAO, 2021. https://doi.org/10.4060/cb7495en.

Faqir, Fasia. "Engendering Democracy and Islam in the Arab World." *Third World Quarterly* 18, no. 1 (1997): 165–74.

Fayyad, Huthifa. "Gaza's Great March of Return Protests Explained." *Al Jazeera*, March 30, 2019. https://www.aljazeera.com/news/2019/3/30/-gazas-great-march-of-return-protests-explained.

Feminism Inshallah: A History of Arab Feminism. Film. Women Make Movies, 2014.

Feminist Majority Foundation. "First Woman Minister Appointed in Qatar." Feminist Majority Foundation, May 15, 2003. https://feminist.org/news/first-woman-minister-appointed-in-qatar/.

Fernanda Espinosa, Maria. "Peace Is Synonymous with Women's Rights." UN Chronicle. United Nations, September 21, 2020. https://www.un.org/en/un-chronicle/peace-synonymous-women%E2%80%99s-rights.

Finn, Tom. "Saleh Is Gone, but Yemen Women's Struggle Goes On." *Reuters*, April 11, 2012, sec. Emerging Markets. https://www.reuters.com/article/us-yemen-politics-women-idUSBRE83A0SX20120411.

Firat, Esat. "Palestinian Women Lead Resistance against Israeli Occupation." Anadolu Agency, May 16, 2021. https://www.aa.com.tr/en/middle-east/palestinian-women-lead-resistance-against-israeli-occupation/2243469.

Fisk, Robert, Patrick Cockburn, Kim Sengupta, and *The Independent. Arab Spring Then and Now.* Mango Media Inc., 2017.

Flood, Michael, and Alan Greig. "Working with Men and Boys for Gender Equality: State of Play and Future Directions," April 2022. https://www.unwomen.org/sites/default/files/2021-11/Policy-brief-Working-with-men-and-boys-for-gender-equality-en.pdf.

Fragile States Index. "Fragile States Index | the Fund for Peace." Fragilestatesindex.org. The Fund for Peace, 2022. https://fragilestatesindex.org/.

Fragile States Index. "Global Data | Fragile States Index." fragilestatesindex.org, 2022. https://fragilestatesindex.org/global-data/.

France Inter. "Kamel Daoud Livre Son Analyse Des Manifestations En Algérie et Sur Le Régime Bouteflika." Video. *YouTube*, March 8, 2019. https://www.youtube.com/watch?v=KDBaCmlwxk4.

France 24. "Sudan PM Hamdok Unveils First Cabinet since Fall of Bashir." *France 24*, September 5, 2019. https://www.france24.com/en/20190905-sudan-pm-hamdok-first-cabinet-bashir.

France 24. "Djibouti Police Clash with Anti-Regime Protesters." *France24*, February 19, 2011. https://www.france24.com/en/20110219-police-clash-with-anti-government-protesters-djibouti.

Franzway, S., D. Court, and R.W. Connell. 1989. *Staking a claim: Feminism, bureaucracy and the state.* Sydney: Allen & Unwin.

Freedom House. "Oman: Freedom in the World 2020 Country Report." Freedom House, 2020. https://freedomhouse.org/country/oman/freedom-world/2020.

Freedom House. "Women's Rights in the Middle East and North Africa 2010—Libya." *Refworld*, 2010. https://www.refworld.org/docid/4b99012091.html.

Freedom House. "Women's Rights in the Middle East and North Africa—Libya." *Refworld*, October 14, 2005. https://www.refworld.org/docid/47387b6dc.html.

Freund, Caroline. "The Surprising Rates of Depression among MENA's Women." World Bank Blogs, March 17, 2013. https://blogs.worldbank.org/arabvoices/surprising-rates-depression-among-mena%E2%80%80-99s-women#:~:text=On%20average%2C%20globally%2C%20depression%20ranks.

FRIDA, and AWID. "The Global State of Young Feminist Organizing." FRIDA, 2016. https://www.awid.org/sites/default/files/atoms/files/-frida-awid_field-report_final_web_issuu.pdf.

FRIDA, and Mama Cash. "Girls to the Front: A Snapshot of Girl-Led Organising." FRIDA, The Young Feminist Fund, 2018. https://www.mamacash.org/media/publications/girlstothefront_report_web.pdf.

Front Line Defenders. "Mekfoula Mint Brahim." Front Line Defenders, February 21, 2020. https://www.frontlinedefenders.org/en/profile/mekfoula-mint-brahim.

Frontline. "Revolution in Cairo Day-To-Day Jan. 25." *PBS Frontline*, February 22, 2011. http://www.pbs.org/wgbh/pages/frontline/revolution-in-cairo/day-to-day/.

Frontline Defenders. "Saba al Mahdawi."

Front Line Defenders, November 6, 2019. https://www.frontlinedefenders.org/en/profile/saba-al-mahdawi.

GAGE. "Countries." GAGE, n.d. https://www.gage.odi.org/research/countries/.

Gardner, Judith, and Judy El Bushra, eds. *Somalia the Untold Story: The War through the Eyes of Somali Women.* London: Pluto Press, 2004.

Gebril, Jazaya. "Women's Rights in Libya: Preserving Past Gains, Fearing for the Future—Legal Agenda." *Legal Agenda,* December 18, 2015. https://english.legal-agenda.com/womens-rights-in-libya-preserving-past-gains-fearing-for-the-future/.

Geha, Carmen. "Our Personal Is Political and Revolutionary." *Al Raida* 44, no. 1 (2020): 23–28. https://doi.org/10.32380/alrj.v44i1.1818.

Gharib, Malaka. "#MosqueMeToo Gives Muslim Women a Voice about Sexual Misconduct at Mecca." *NPR,* February 26, 2018. https://www.npr.org/sections/goatsandsoda/2018/02/26/588855132/-mosquemetoo-gives-muslim-women-a-voice-about-sexual-misconduct-at-mecca.

Ghosn, Nada. "Kuwait's Alanoud Alsharekh, Feminist Groundbreaker." *The Markaz Review,* December 6, 2020. https://themarkaz.org/-kukuwaits-alanoud-al-sharekh-feminist-groundbreaker/.

Gianni, Nicolas, Francesco Michele, and Chiara Lozza. "From 'Liberal' to 'Liberating' Empowerment: The Community Protection Approach as Best Practice to Address NGO-Ization." *Civil Society Review,* November 2021. https://doi.org/10.28943/csr.005.003.

GIWPS, and PRIO. "Women, Peace, and Security Index 2021/22." Washington, D.C.: GIWPS, 2021.

Glas, Saskia, and Amy Alexander. "Explaining Support for Muslim Feminism in the Arab Middle East and North Africa." *Gender & Society* 34, no. 3 (May 19, 2020): 437–66. https://doi.org/10.1177/0891243220915494.

Global Slavery Index. "Global Slavery Index." Walk Free Foundation, 2018. https://www.globalslaveryindex.org/resources/downloads/#gsi-2018.

Goldstein, Eric. "Before the Arab Spring, the Unseen Thaw." *Human Rights Watch,* 2012. https://www.hrw.org/node/259729.

Golley, Nawar Al-Hassan. "Is Feminism Relevant to Arab Women?" *Third World Quarterly* 25, no. 3 (2004): 521–36. https://www.jstor.org/stable/3993823.

Gouvy, Constantin. "A Decade after Revolution, Tunisia's Women Face an Uphill Battle." www.aljazeera.com, January 17, 2021. https://www.aljazeera.com/news/2021/1/17/a-decade-after-revolution-tunisias-women-face-an-uphill-battle.

Gulf Business. "New Kuwait Cabinet Has GCC's First Female Finance Minister." Bloomberg, December 17, 2019. https://gulfbusiness.com/new-kuwait-cabinet-gccs-first-female-finance-minister/.

Gulf News. "Lebanese Women Wage Painful Custody Battles." *Gulf News,* March 26, 2017. https://gulfnews.com/world/mena/lebanese-women-wage-painful-custody-battles-1.2000613.

Gulf Times. "Celebrating Qatar's Rich History of Education." *Gulf-Times,* December 18, 2012. https://www.gulf-times.com/story/335895/-Celebrating-Qatar-s-rich-history-of-education.

Haas, Mark L. *The Arab Spring: The Hope and Reality of the Uprisings.* London: Routledge, 2018.

Haddag, Lydia. "Hirak and Feminism: An Equation with Two Unknowns." *Arab Reform Initiative,* June 22, 2021. https://www.arab-reform.net/publication/hirak-and-feminism-an-equation-with-two-unknowns/.

Haji Ingiriis, Mohamed. "'Sisters; Was This What We Struggled For?': The Gendered Rivalry in Power and Politics." *Journal of International Women's Studies* 16, no. 2 (2015). https://vc.bridgew.edu/jiws/vol16/iss2/24.

Hamadeh, Najla. "Recognition of Difference: Towards a More Effective Feminism." In *Arab Feminisms Gender and Equality in the Middle East,* edited by Jean Said Makdisi, Noha Bayoumi, and Rafif Rida Sidawi. London: I.B. Tauris, 2014.

Hamzawy, Amr, Karim Sadjadpour, Aaron David Miller, Frederic Wehrey, Zaha Hassan, Yasmine Farouk, Kheder Khaddour, et al. "What the Russian War in Ukraine Means for the Middle East." *Carnegie Endowment for International Peace,* March 24, 2022. https://carnegieendowment.org/2022/03/24/what-russian-war-in-ukraine-means-for-middle-east-pub-86711.

The Hashemite Kingdom of Jordan Parliament. "Freezing Parliamentary Life and Forming National Consultative Councils (1974–1984)." Parliament.jo. Accessed October 27, 2022. http://parliament.jo/en/node/148.

Hatem, Mervat. "Toward the Development of Post-Islamist and Post-Nationalist Feminist Discourse in the Middle East." In *Arab Women: Old Boundaries, New Frontiers,* edited by Judith E. Tucker, 29–48. Bloomington: Indiana University Press, 1993.

Hatem, Mervat. "What Do Women Want? A Critical Mapping of Future Directions for Arab Feminisms." *Contemporary Arab Affairs* 6, no. 1 (2013): 91–101. https://www.jstor.org/stable/48600672.

Hatem, Mervat F. "In the Shadow of the State: Changing Definitions of Arab Women's 'Developmental' Citizenship Rights." *Journal of Middle East Women's Studies* 1, no. 3 (2005): 20–45. https://www.jstor.org/stable/40326870.

Helem. "LGBTQIA+ Non-Profit Organization | Helem Lebanon | About." www.helem.net. Accessed November 9, 2022. https://www.helem.net/about.

Helen Ziegler & Associates. "The Role of Women in Qatar." Hziegler.com, 2019. https://www.

hziegler.com/articles/role-of-women-in-qatar. html.

Hesford, Wendy S. "Do Muslim Women Need Saving? By Lila Abu-Lughod. Cambridge, MA: Harvard University Press, 2013." *Signs: Journal of Women in Culture and Society* 40, no. 4 (June 2015): 985–87. https://doi.org/10.1086/680405.

Hilton, Daniel. "The Shifting Role of Women in Syria's Economy." The Tahrir Institute for Middle East Policy, 2017. https://timep.org/-syrias-women/economy/the-shifting-role-of-women-in-syrias-economy/.

Hincks, Joseph. "Heirs of the Arab Spring." *Time,* January 2021. https://time.com/5927349/heirs-of-the-arab-spring/.

Holmes, Oliver. "Libya Drops Election Quota for Women." *Reuters,* January 20, 2012, sec. Commodities News. https://www.reuters.com/article/libya-women-idAFL6E8CK1SF20120120.

Holt, Maria. "Palestinian Women, Violence, and the Peace Process." *Development in Practice* 13, no. 2/3 (2003): 223–38. https://www.jstor.org/stable/4029594.

Hughes, Melanie M., Pamela Paxton, Sharon Quinsaat, and Nicholas Reith. "Does the Global North Still Dominate Women's International Organizing? A Network Analysis from 1978 to 2008." *Mobilization: An International Quarterly* 23, no. 1 (March 1, 2018): 1–21. https://doi.org/10.17813/1086-671x-23-1-1.

Hughes-Fraitekh, Katherine. "Nonviolent Resistance in Palestine: Steadfastness, Creativity and Hope." openDemocracy, July 14, 2015. https://www.opendemocracy.net/en/civilresistance/-nonviolent-resistance-in-palestine-steadfastness-creativity-and-hope/.

Human Rights Watch. "Audacity in Adversity | LGBT Activism in the Middle East and North Africa." Human Rights Watch, April 16, 2018. https://www.hrw.org/report/2018/04/16/-audacity-adversity/lgbt-activism-middle-east-and-north-africa.

Human Rights Watch. "Background on Women's Status in Iraq prior to the Fall of the Saddam Hussein Government." Human Rights Watch, 2003. https://www.hrw.org/legacy/backgrounder/wrd/iraq-women.pdf.

Human Rights Watch. "Boxed in | Women and Saudi Arabia's Male Guardianship System." Human Rights Watch, June 6, 2017. https://www.hrw.org/report/2016/07/16/boxed/women-and-saudi-arabias-male-guardianship-system.

Human Rights Watch. "'Everything I Have to Do Is Tied to a Man' Women and Qatar's Male Guardianship Rules." HRW, March 2021.

Human Rights Watch. "Human Rights Watch, Women's Centre for Legal Aid and Counselling, and Equality Now, Joint Submission to the CEDAW Committee on the State of Palestine, 70th Session." Human Rights Watch, June 11, 2018. https://www.hrw.org/news/2018/06/11/human-rights-watch-womens-centre-legal-aid-and-counselling-and-equality-

now-joint#:~:text=Palestine%20acceded%20to%20the%20UN.

Human Rights Watch. "Lebanon: Domestic Violence Law Good, but Incomplete." Human Rights Watch, April 3, 2014. https://www.hrw.org/news/2014/04/03/lebanon-domestic-violence-law-good-incomplete.

Human Rights Watch. "Lebanon: Laws Discriminate against Women." HRW, January 19, 2015. https://www.hrw.org/news/2015/01/19/lebanon-laws-discriminate-against-women.

Human Rights Watch. "Lebanon: Laws Discriminate against Women." HRW, January 2, 2019. https://www.hrw.org/news/2015/01/19/lebanon-laws-discriminate-against-women.

Human Rights Watch. "Lebanon: Sexual Harassment Law Missing Key Protections." HRW, March 5, 2021. https://www.hrw.org/news/2021/03/05/lebanon-sexual-harassment-law-missing-key-protections.

Human Rights Watch. "Letter to the King of Morocco on His Commitment to Withdraw Reservations to CEDAW." Human Rights Watch, April 14, 2010. https://www.hrw.org/news/2010/04/14/letter-king-morocco-his-commitment-withdraw-reservations-cedaw.

Human Rights Watch. "Palestine: 'Marry-Your-Rapist' Law Repealed." Human Rights Watch, May 10, 2018. https://www.hrw.org/news/2018/05/10/palestine-marry-your-rapist-law-repealed.

Human Rights Watch. "Saudi Arabia: 'Unofficial' Guardianship Rules Banned." HRW, May 9, 2017. https://www.hrw.org/news/2017/05/09/saudi-arabia-unofficial-guardianship-rules-banned#:~:text=(Beirut)%20%E2%80%93%20Saudi%20Arabia.

Human Rights Watch. "Saudi Arabia: Important Advances for Saudi Women." HRW, August 2, 2019. https://www.hrw.org/news/2019/08/02/-saudi-arabia-important-advances-saudi-women.

Human Rights Watch. "Saudi Women Are Speaking up Online." Human Rights Watch, April 14, 2020. https://www.hrw.org/news/2020/04/14/-saudi-women-are-speaking-online.

Human Rights Watch. "Tunisia: Government Lifts Restrictions on Women's Rights Treaty." Human Rights Watch, September 6, 2011. https://www.hrw.org/news/2011/09/06/tunisia-government-lifts-restrictions-womens-rights-treaty.

Humran, Alya Abdulhakim. "Revolution Is Female." *Al Raida* 44, no. 1 (2020): 29–36. https://doi.org/10.32380/alrj.v44i1.1819.

Husseini, Rana. *Years of Struggle: The Women's Movement in Jordan.* Amman: Friedrich-Ebert-Stiftung, 2021.

Hzaineh, Laila. "ستر 'الفضيحة' في الوطن العربي." Facebook, June 21, 2019. https://www.facebook.com/100006739657111/videos/1873040889597215/.

IDEA. "Constitutional History of Syria." ConstitutionNet, 2021. https://constitutionnet.org/country/syria.

IDEA. "Gender Quotas Database: Djibouti." International Institute for Democracy and Electoral Assistance. Accessed November 7, 2022. https://www.idea.int/data-tools/data/gender-quotas/country-view/93/35.

IDEA. "Gender Quotas Database: Iraq." International IDEA, 2022. https://www.idea.int/data-tools/data/gender-quotas/country-view/148/35.

Idle, Nadia, and Alex Nunns, eds. *Tweets from Tahrir: Egypt's Revolution as It Unfolded, in the Words of the People Who Made It.* New York: OR Books, 2011.

IIE. "Artist Protection Fund." www.iie.org. Accessed November 10, 2022. https://www.iie.org/programs/artist-protection-fund.

ILO. "Recovery in Youth Employment Is Still Lagging, Says ILO." www.ilo.org, August 11, 2022. https://www.ilo.org/global/about-the-ilo/newsroom/news/WCMS_853078/lang—en/index.htm.

ILO. "Sultanate of Oman Signs Decent Work Country Programme, the Second Gulf Country after the Kingdom of Bahrain." www.ilo.org, June 15, 2010. https://www.ilo.org/global/about-the-ilo/newsroom/news/WCMS_141756/lang—en/index.htm.

Institute for Economics and Peace. "Global Peace Index 2022." Sydney: IEP, 2022.

International Campaign for Women's Safe Right to Abortion. "ALGERIA—Abortion Has Not Been Legalised in Algeria." International Campaign for Women's Right to Safe Abortion (SAWR), August 21, 2018. https://www.safeabortionwomensright.org/news/algeria-abortion-has-not-been-legalised-in-algeria/.

International Federation for Human Rights. "Djibouti: Political Opponents Shot Dead by Security Forces during Demonstration." International Federation for Human Rights, February 28, 2103. https://www.fidh.org/en/region/Africa/djibouti/-Djibouti-Political-opponents-shot-13063.

International Labour Organisation. "Law No. 12 of 1378 [2010] on Labour Relations." ILO, 2010. https://www.ilo.org/dyn/natlex/natlex4.detail?p_isn=86041&p_lang=.

IPS World Desk. "Lebanon Joins Jordan and Tunisia in Fight against Rapists Impunity." *Inter Press Service,* August 23, 2017. http://www.ipsnews.net/2017/08/lebanon-joins-jordan-and-tunisia-in-fight-against-rapists-impunity/.

IPU. "IPU Comparative Data on Women's Right to Vote." Parline: the IPU's Open Data Platform. Accessed October 22, 2022. https://data.ipu.org/compare?field=country%3Afield_suffrage%3Afield_right_to_vote°ion=middle_east_and_north_africa#map.

IPU. "Women in Parliament in 2021." Geneva: Inter-Parliamentary Union, 2022.

IPU. "Women's Suffrage: A World Chronology of the Recognition of Women's Right to Vote and to Stand for Election." Ipu.org, 2019. http://archive.ipu.org/wmn-e/suffrage.htm.

IPU. "Women's Suffrage." Ipu.org, 2019. http://archive.ipu.org/wmn-e/suffrage.htm.

Ismaik, Hasan. "Arab Feminism: A Luxury or a Necessity?" Egypt Independent, April 1, 2021. https://egyptindependent.com/arab-feminism-a-luxury-or-a-necessity/.

Jaafari, Shirin. "Here's the Story behind the Iconic Image of the Sudanese Woman in White." *The World from PRX,* April 10, 2019. https://theworld.org/stories/2019-04-10/heres-story-behind-iconic-image-sudanese-woman-white.

Jaffer, Jennifer. "Huda Sharawi | Egyptian Feminist and Nationalist." In *Encyclopædia Britannica,* 2019. https://www.britannica.com/biography/Huda-Sharawi.

Jalbout, Maysa. "Unlocking the Potential of Educated Arab Women." Brookings, March 12, 2015. https://www.brookings.edu/blog/-education-plus-development/2015/03/12/-unlocking-the-potential-of-educated-arab-women/#:~:text=Echoing%20the%20trend%20observed%20globally.

James, Maura. "Women and the Intifadas: The Evolution of Palestinian Women's Organizations." *Strife,* 2013, 18–22. https://www.strifejournal.org/wp-content/uploads/2020/05/STRIFE_1_3_JAMES_M_18_22.pdf.

James, Maura K. "Women and the Intifadas: The Evolution of Palestinian Women's Organizations." *Strife,* no. 1 (2013): 18–22. https://www.strifejournal.org/wp-content/uploads/2020/05/STRIFE_1_3_JAMES_M_18_22.pdf.

Jamjoom, Mohammed, and Hakim Almasmari. "Yemeni Women Protest against Saleh's Remarks for Second Day." *CNN,* April 19, 2011. http://edition.cnn.com/2011/WORLD/meast/04/17/yemen.women.protest/index.html.

Japan International Cooperation Agency. "The Republic of Sudan: Country Gender Profile." JICA, 2012. https://www.jica.go.jp/english/our_work/thematic_issues/gender/background/-c8h0vm0000anjqj6-att/sudan_2012.pdf.

JC. "Xena the True Lebanese Feminist." Sweden and the Middle East Views, April 25, 2013. https://swedenmiddleeastviews.com/2013/04/25/xena-the-true-lebanese-feminist/.

Jebli, Hanen. "Tunisians Outraged after Female Parliamentarian Slapped by Islamist Colleague—Al-Monitor: Independent, Trusted Coverage of the Middle East." www.al-monitor.com, July 8, 2021. https://www.al-monitor.com/originals/2021/07/tunisians-outraged-after-female-parliamentarian-slapped-islamist-colleague.

Jinkinson, Kira. "State Feminism and the Islamist-Secularist Binary: Women's Rights in Tunisia." *E-International Relations,* 2020. https://www.e-ir.info/2020/07/27/state-feminism-and-the-islamist-secularist-binary-womens-rights-in-tunisia/.

Joseph, Suad. "Gender and Citizenship in the Arab World." *Al-Raida Journal,* no. 129–130 (January 1, 2010): 8–18. https://doi.org/10.32380/alrj.v0i0.50.

Joseph, Suad, Osama Tanous, Nadine Hosny, and Patrick Marius Koga. "Whose Trauma? De-Colonizing Post-Traumatic Stress Disorder and Refugee Mental Health Frameworks." Harvard Medical School Primary Care Review, January 2022. https://info.primarycare.hms.harvard.edu/review/whose-trauma-.

Juliá, Maria, and Hadi Ridha. "Women and War: The Role Kuwaiti Women Played during the Iraqi Occupation." *Journal of International Development* 13, no. 5 (July 2001): 583–98. https://doi.org/10.1002/jid.782.

Juneau, Thomas. "Yemen and the Arab Spring: Elite Struggles, State Collapse and Regional Security." *Orbis* 57, no. 3 (June 2013): 408–23. https://doi.org/10.1016/j.orbis.2013.05.004.

Justice For Noura. "About." Justice For Noura, 2018. https://www.justicefornoura.com/about.

Kader, Farah. "The Role of Women in the 2011 Bahraini Uprising." Americans for Democracy & Human Rights in Bahrain, July 2, 2016. https://www.adhrb.org/2016/07/role-women-2011-bahraini-uprising/.

Kafa. "About KAFA." كفى, n.d. https://kafa.org.lb/en/about.

Kale, Sirin. "Mona Eltahawy: 'Feminism Is Not a T-Shirt or a 9 to 5 Job. It's My Existence.'" *The Guardian*, April 23, 2021. https://www.theguardian.com/books/2021/apr/23/mona-eltahawy-feminism-is-not-a-t-shirt-the-seven-necessary-sins-for-women-and-girls.

Kandiyoti, Deniz. "Bargaining with Patriarchy." *Gender and Society* 2, no. 3 (1988): 274–90. http://www.jstor.org/stable/190357.

Kane, Oumar. "Première Femme Ministre En Mauritanie." ACTUME, February 5, 2013. https://actume.org/en/blog/aissata-kane-premiere-femme-ministre-en-mauritanie/.

Kantola, Johanna, and Judith Squires. "From State Feminism to Market Feminism?" *International Political Science Review* 33, no. 4 (April 13, 2012): 382–400. https://doi.org/10.1177/0192512111432513.

Karama. "Hibaaq Osman's Remarks to Generation Equality Forum Mexico." Karama, March 31, 2021. https://www.elkara.ma/news/hibaaq-osmans-remarks-to-generation-equality-forum-mexico.

Karbal, Mohamed. "Human Rights in Libya: During and after Gaddafi." Mondaq, October 12, 2020. https://www.mondaq.com/human-rights/993460/human-rights-in-libya-during-and-after-gaddafi-#:~:text=Human%20Rights%20in%20Practice%20under%20Gaddafi&text=Gaddafi.

Karman, Tawakkol. "About." tawakkolkarman.net, n.d. https://www.tawakkolkarman.net/enabout.

Karolak, Magdalena. "Bahraini Women in the 21st Century: Disputed Legacy of the Unfinished Revolution." *Journal of International Women's Studies* 13, no. 5 (2012). https://vc.bridgew.edu/jiws/vol13/iss5/3.

Kaufman, Rachel. "Women and Social Media: Key Drivers of Protest in Iraq." Wilson Center, December 22, 2021. https://www.wilsoncenter.org/article/women-and-social-media-key-drivers-protest-iraq.

Kelly, Annie. "Anti-Slavery Activists in Mauritania Face Violent Clampdown, Rights Groups Warn." The Guardian, January 20, 2016. https://www.theguardian.com/global-development/2016/jan/20/anti-slavery-activists-in-mauritania-face-violent-clampdown-rights-groups-warn.

Khamis, Sahar. "The Arab 'Feminist' Spring?" *Feminist Studies* 37, no. 3 (2011): 692–95. http://www.jstor.org/stable/23069929.

Khamis, Sahar, and Amel Mili, eds. *Arab Women's Activism and Socio-Political Transformation : Unfinished Gendered Revolutions*. New York: Palgrave Macmillan, 2018.

Khan, Shaistha. "'I Will Not Be Silenced': Women in Kuwait Fight Back against Violence." *Women's Media Center,* July 14, 2021. https://womensmediacenter.com/news-features/i-will-not-be-silenced-women-in-kuwait-fight-back-against-violence.

Khanna, Pooja, and Zachary Kimmel. "Convention on the Elimination of All Forms of Discrimination against Women (CEDAW) for Youth." New York: UN Women, 2016.

Kingdom of Bahrain. "Law No. (19) of 2017." *Bahrain.bh*. The National Portal of the Kingdom of Bahrain, 2019. https://www.google.com/url?q=https://bahrain.bh/wps/wcm/connect/1edd4432-107d-4cfa-8e2c-6aabeec852fa/LAW%2BNO.%2B%252819%2529%2BOF%2B2017.pdf?MOD%3DAJPERES&sa=D&source=docs&ust=1667902536471322&usg=AOvVaw0xuJLnUqFpUp8Rc8eCa2n8.

The Kip Project. "#Mesh_Basita" "#مش_بسيطة Campaign." KIP. Accessed November 9, 2022. https://thekipproject.info/mesh-basita/.

Kurtulus, Ersun N. "'The Cedar Revolution': Lebanese Independence and the Question of Collective Self-Determination." *British Journal of Middle Eastern Studies* 36, no. 2 (2009): 195–214. https://www.jstor.org/stable/40593253.

Kuwait News Agency (KUNA). "22 Female Prosecutors Take Oath." www.kuna.net.kw, November 6, 2014. https://www.kuna.net.kw/ArticleDetails.aspx?id=2406968&language=en.

Kuwait Times. "Confronting Sexual Violence in a Conservative Mauritania." Kuwait Times, March 7, 2019. https://www.kuwaittimes.com/-confronting-sexual-violence-in-a-conservative-mauritania/.

Lacatus, Corina, and Gustav Meibauer. "'Saying It like It Is': Right-Wing Populism, International Politics, and the Performance of Authenticity." *The British Journal of Politics and International Relations* 24, no. 3 (May 27, 2022): 437–57. https://doi.org/10.1177/13691481221089137.

Lawrence, Salmah Eva-Lina. "The Majority World—What's in a Phrase?" Philanthropy Australia, November 4, 2022. https://

www.philanthropy.org.au/blog/view/The-Majority-World whats-in-a-phrase

Lebanese American University, UNESCWA, Institute for Women's Studies in the Arab World, and KVINFO. "Beirut Call for Action," 2016. https://aiw.lau.edu.lb/research/books-publications/-beirut-call-for-action-prioritiz.php.

Leland, John, and Riyadh Mohammed. "Iraqi Women Are Seeking Greater Political Influence." *The New York Times*, February 17, 2010, sec. World. https://www.nytimes.com/2010/02/17/world/middleeast/17iraqwomen.html.

Lesourd, Céline. "The Lipstick on the Edge of the Well: Mauritanian Women and Political Power (1960–2014)." In *Women's Rights in the Aftermath of the Arab Spring*, 77–93. Palgrave Macmillan, 2016.

Lopez-Tomas, Andrea. "Lebanon Elects Record Number of Women to Parliament—Al-Monitor: Independent, Trusted Coverage of the Middle East." www.al-monitor.com, June 19, 2022. https://www.al-monitor.com/originals/2022/06/lebanon-elects-record-number-women-parliament.

Maddy-Weitzman, Bruce. "Women, Islam, and the Moroccan State: The Struggle over the Personal Status Law." *Middle East Journal* 59, no. 3 (2005): 393–410. https://www.jstor.org/stable/4330155.

MADRE. "Organization of Women's Freedom in Iraq." MADRE. Accessed November 1, 2022. https://www.madre.org/partners/organization-womens-freedom-iraq#:~:text=The%20Organization%20of%20Women.

Maffi, Irene, and Liv Tønnessen. "EDITORIAL the Limits of the Law: Abortion in the Middle East and North Africa." *Health and Human Rights Journal*, December 9, 2019. https://www.hhrjournal.org/2019/12/editorial-the-limits-of-the-law-abortion-in-the-middle-east-and-north-africa/#_ednref4.

Magdy, Rana. "Egyptian Feminist Movement: A Brief History." openDemocracy, March 8, 2017. https://www.opendemocracy.net/en/north-africa-west-asia/egyptian-feminist-movement-brief-history/.

Mahdi, Safia. "Yemen: Women in Houthi Area No Longer in Control of Their Own Body | Daraj." daraj.com, February 3, 2021. https://daraj.com/en/66573/.

Mahmoud, Souad. "The Challenges of Grassroots Feminism in Arab Countries." *Capire*, March 25, 2021. https://capiremov.org/en/analysis/the-challenges-of-grassroots-feminism-in-arab-countries/.

Makdisi, Jean Said. "Huqouq Almar'a: Feminist Thought and the Language of the Arab Women's Movement." In *Arab Feminisms Gender and Equality in the Middle East*, edited by Jean Said Makdisi, Noha Bayoumi, and Rafif Rida Sidawi, 78–89. London; New York: I.B. Tauris, 2014.

Makdisi, Jean Said, Noha Bayoumi, and Rafif Rida Sidawi, eds. *Arab Feminisms: Gender and Equality in the Middle East*. London; New York: I.B.Tauris, 2014.

Malmvig, Helle, and Christina Markus Lassen. "The Arab Uprisings: Regional Implications and International Responses." *IEMed Mediterranean Yearbook*. IEMed, 2013. https://www.iemed.org/publication/the-arab-uprisings-regional-implications-and-international-responses/.

Manea, Elham. "The Arab Popular Uprisings from a Gender Perspective." *Zeitschrift Für Politik* 61, no. 1 (2014): 81–100. https://www.jstor.org/stable/24229172.

Maravankin, Stephanie. "Arab Feminism in the Arab Spring: Discourses on Solidarity, the Socio-Cultural Revolution, and the Political Revolution in Egypt, Tunisia, and Yemen." *Clocks and Clouds* 7, no. 2 (2017). http://www.inquiriesjournal.com/a?id=1632.

Marteu, Élisabeth. "Féminismes Israéliens et Palestiniens: Questions Postcoloniales." *Revue Tiers Monde* 209, no. 1 (2012): 71. https://doi.org/10.3917/rtm.209.0071.

Marwane, Ahmed. "Women and Politics in Algeria: One Step Forward, Two Steps Back." The Washington Institute. Fikra Forum, September 15, 2021. https://www.washingtoninstitute.org/-policy-analysis/women-and-politics-algeria-one-step-forward-two-steps-back.

Masoud, Tarek, Amaney Jamal, and Elizabeth Nugent. "Using the Qurān to Empower Arab Women? Theory and Experimental Evidence from Egypt." *Comparative Political Studies* 49, no. 12 (July 9, 2016): 1555–98. https://doi.org/10.1177/0010414015626452.

Matar, Mira. "NAYA | Woman of the Month: Malak Alaywe Herz, Lebanon's Uprising Icon." *An-Nahar*, November 9, 2019. https://www.annahar.com/english/article/1065303-naya-woman-of-the-month-malak-alaywe-herz-lebanons-uprising-icon.

Mayton, Joseph. "Nawal El Saadawi Interview." Progressive.org, December 12, 2011. https://progressive.org/magazine/nawal-el-saadawi-interview/.

Mazur, Amy G., and Dorothy E. McBride. *State Feminism*. Edited by Gary Goertz and Amy G. Mazur. *Politics, Gender, and Concepts*. Cambridge: Cambridge University Press, 2008. https://doi.org/10.1017/cbo9780511755910.011.

McBride, Dorothy E., and Amy G. Mazur. "Women's Policy Agencies and State Feminism." In *The Oxford Handbook of Gender and Politics*, edited by Georgina Waylen, Karen Celis, Johanna Kantola, and S. Laurel Weldon, 654–78. London: Oxford University Press, 2013. https://doi.org/10.1093/oxfordhb/9780199751457.001.0001.

McEvers, Kelly. "Bahrain: The Revolution That Wasn't." NPR, January 5, 2012. https://www.npr.org/2012/01/05/144637499/bahrain-the-revolution-that-wasnt.

Meghdessian, Samira Rafidi. *The Status of the Arab Woman*. Westport, CT: Greenwood, 1980.

MEI. "Middle East Institute." Middle East Institute, n.d. https://www.mei.edu.

MEI. "Sheikha Abdulla Al-Misnad." Middle

East Institute. Accessed November 6, 2022. https://www.mei.edu/profile/sheikha-abdulla-al-misnad.

MENA Rights Group. "Female Human Rights Defender Saba al Mahdawi Subjected to Reprisals after Providing Medical Assistance to Anti-Government Protestors." *MENA Rights Group,* November 14, 2019. https://www.menarights.org/en/caseprofile/female-human-rights-defender-saba-al-mahdawi-subjected-reprisals-after-providing.

Mende, Claudia. "Egyptian Women's Rights Activist Hoda Badran: Women as Losers of the Revolution?" Qantara.de—Dialogue with the Islamic World, 2012. https://en.qantara.de/content/-egyptian-womens-rights-activist-hoda-badran-women-as-losers-of-the-revolution.

Mernissi, Fatema. "About Fatema." Fatema Mernissi, n.d. https://fatemamernissi.com/about-us.

Mernissi, Fatima. *Scheherazade Goes West: Different Cultures, Different Harems.* New York: Washington Square Press, 2001.

Mernissi, Fatima. *The Veil and the Male Elite: A Feminist Interpretation of Women's Rights in Islam.* 1987. Reprint, New York: Basic Books, 1991.

Michael Collins. "Beirut Dreams in Colour." Video. *The Guardian,* 2022. https://www.theguardian.com/world/ng-interactive/2022/jun/22/one-good-song-can-do-more-than-5000-protests-the-queer-revolution-in-the-middle-east#:~:text=While%20this%20violent%20repression%20against.

Mikdashi, Maya. "How to Study Gender in the Middle East." CCAS, June 3, 2020. https://ccas.georgetown.edu/2020/06/03/how-to-study-gender-in-the-middle-east/.

Miller, Judith. "Libya's Women: Era of Change (Published 1986)." *The New York Times,* 2022. https://www.nytimes.com/1986/02/03/style/-libya-s-women-era-of-change.html.

Ministry of Foreign Affairs. "The Kingdom of Bahrain Has Acceded and Ratified to Core Human Rights Instruments." www.mofa.gov.bh. Accessed November 1, 2022. https://www.mofa.gov.bh/Default.aspx?tabid=9725&language=en-US.

Mir, Salam. "Palestinian Literature: Occupation and Exile." *Arab Studies Quarterly* 35, no. 2 (2013): 110–29. https://doi.org/10.13169/arabstudquar.35.2.0110.

Moctar, Hassan Ould. "Social Movements and Unrest in Mauritania since the Arab Uprisings." openDemocracy, June 2013. https://www.opendemocracy.net/en/social-movements-and-unrest-in-mauritania-since-arab-uprisings/.

Moghadam, Valentine M. "Algerian Women in Movement." In *Confronting Global Gender Justice: Women's Lives, Human Rights,* edited by Deborah Bergoffen, Paula Ruth Gilbert, Tamara Harvey, and Connie L. McNeely, 180–99. London & New York: Routledge, 2011.

Moghadam, Valentine M. "Gender Regimes in the Middle East and North Africa: The Power of Feminist Movements." *Social Politics: International Studies in Gender, State & Society* 27, no. 3 (2020): 467–85. https://doi.org/10.1093/sp/jxaa019.

Moghadam, Valentine M. "Organizing Women: The New Women's Movement in Algeria." *Cultural Dynamics* 13, no. 2 (July 2001): 131–54. https://doi.org/10.1177/092137400101300201.

Moghadam, Valentine M. "The State and the Women's Movement in Tunisia: Mobilization, Institutionalization, and Inclusion." New York: James A. Baker III Institute for Public Policy of Rice University, 2018.

Moghadam, Valentine M. "Women's Economic Participation in the Middle East: What Difference Has the Neoliberal Policy Turn Made?" *Journal of Middle East Women's Studies* 1, no. 1 (2005): 110–46. https://www.jstor.org/stable/40326851.

Mohamed, Deena. "Qahera—About." Tumblr, 2013. https://qaherathesuperhero.com/about.

Mohamed, Deena. "Qahera." qaherathesuperhero.com, June 13, 2013. https://qaherathesuperhero.com/post/64031330049.

Mohamed, Iman Abdulkadir. "Somali Women and the Socialist State." *Journal of Georgetown University-Qatar Middle Eastern Studies Student Association,* no. 1 (2015). https://doi.org/https://doi.org/10.5339/messa.2015.4.

Mohiedeen, Naba. "Sudanese Women Welcome Freedom to Travel Abroad with Children." VOA, July 14, 2020. https://www.voaafrica.com/a/africa_sudanese-women-welcome-freedom-travel-abroad-children/6192759.html.

Molina, Susana F. "Female Street Art Defies War in Yemen. No Peace without Women." *The Urban Activist,* January 12, 2021. https://theurbanactivist.com/idea/female-street-art-defies-war-in-yemen-no-peace-without-women/.

Moon, Terry. "Woman as Reason: Algerian Women at the Forefront." *News & Letters,* April 23, 2019. https://newsandletters.org/woman-reason-algerian-women-forefront/.

Mooro, Alya. *The Greater Freedom: Life as a Middle Eastern Woman Outside the Stereotypes.* New York: Little A, 2019.

Mordecai, Mara. "Protests in Lebanon Highlight Ubiquity of WhatsApp, Dissatisfaction with Government." *Pew Research Center,* November 19, 2019. https://www.pewresearch.org/fact-tank/2019/11/19/protests-in-lebanon-highlight-ubiquity-of-whatsapp-dissatisfaction-with-government/.

Mousavian, Seyed Hossein. "A Revolution and a War: How Iran Transformed Today's Middle East." *The Cairo Review of Global Affairs* 45 (June 7, 2022). https://www.thecairoreview.com/essays/a-revolution-and-a-war-how-iran-transformed-todays-middle-east/.

Moussa, Nedjib Sidi. "Algerian Feminism and

the Long Struggle for Women's Equality." *The Conversation*, October 4, 2016. https://theconversation.com/algerian-feminism-and-the-long-struggle-for-womens-equality-65130.

Muhanna-Matar, Aitemad. "New Trends of Women's Activism after the Arab Uprisings: Redefining Women's Leadership." *LSE Middle East Centre Paper Series* 5 (2014). http://www.lse.ac.uk/middleEastCentre/home.aspx.

Müller, Quentin, and Sebastian Castelier. "Omani Elections: Women Making Small Leaps in Politics." Middle East Eye, 2016. https://www.middleeasteye.net/features/omani-elections-women-making-small-leaps-politics.

Murphy, Kim. "Kuwait Women Resist Iraq, Seek Recognition of Role: Gulf Crisis: Chants, Posters and Peaceful Marches Are Their Arms against Invaders. Three Have Died so Far." *Los Angeles Times,* October 16, 1990. https://www.latimes.com/archives/la-xpm-1990-10-16-mn-2519-story.html.

Musawah. "About." Musawah. Accessed November 9, 2022. https://www.musawah.org/about/.

Musawah. "Mauritania: Overview of Family Laws and Practices." Musawah, 2017. https://www.musawah.org/wp-content/uploads/2019/03/-Mauritania-Overview-Table.pdf.

Naber, Nadine. "Women and the Arab Spring: Human Rights from the Ground Up." *International Institute Journal at University of Michigan* 1, no. 1 (2011): 11–13. https://www.peacewomen.org/assets/file/women_in_the_arab_spring-human_rights_from_the_ground_up.pdf.

An-Na'im, Abdullahi Ahmed. "Human Rights in the Arab World: A Regional Perspective." *Human Rights Quarterly* 23, no. 3 (2001): 701–32. https://doi.org/10.1353/hrq.2001.0026.

Najjar, Maria. "Reviving Pan-Arabism in Feminist Activism in the Middle East." *Kohl: A Journal for Body and Gender Research* 6, no. 1 (2020): 119–32. https://kohljournal.press/reviving-pan-arabism-feminist.

Nasrawin, Laith K. "Protection against Domestic Violence in Jordanian Law and International Conventions." *Arab Law Quarterly* 31, no. 4 (2017): 363–87. https://www.jstor.org/stable/26567164.

Nassar, Alaa. "Keeping Hope, but Still Waiting: Syrian Feminism and a Decade of Revolution." Syria Direct, March 4, 2021. https://syriadirect.org/in-a-decade-of-hopes-and-hopes-dashed-the-syrian-feminist-movement-mirrors-the-trajectory-of-the-revolution/.

Nassif, Gabriella. "Resistance, Gender, and Identity Politics: A Conversation with Rasha Younes." *Civil Society Review,* 2021. https://doi.org/10.28943/csr.005.005.

National legislative Bodies/National Authorities. "Yemen: Republican Decree, by Law No. 12 for 1994, Concerning Crimes and Penalties." Refworld, 1994. https://www.refworld.org/docid/3fec62f17.html.

The National Portal of the Kingdom of Bahrain. "Women in Bahrain." Bahrain.bh, 2011. https://www.bahrain.bh/new/en/equality-women_en.html.

NCLW. "Mission and Vision." NCLW. Accessed October 4, 2022. https://nclw.gov.lb/en/mission-and-vision-2/.

Neuman, Scott. "Tunisia's New Prime Minister Is the 1st Woman to Lead a Government in the Arab World." *NPR,* September 29, 2021, sec. Middle East. https://www.npr.org/2021/09/29/1041431089/tunisias-new-prime-minister-is-the-first-woman-to-lead-an-arab-world-government.

The New Arab. "In Conservative Kuwait, Women Launch Their Own #MeToo Movement." *The New Arab,* February 9, 2021. https://english.alaraby.co.uk/news/conservative-kuwait-women-launch-their-own-metoo-movement.

The New Arab. "Mesh Basita (It's Not Ok): Lebanese Women Stand up to Sexual Harassment." *The New Arab,* August 3, 2017. https://english.alaraby.co.uk/features/mesh-basita-lebanese-women-stand-sexual-harassment.

Nicholasen, Michelle. "Nonviolent Resistance Proves Potent Weapon." *Blog.* Harvard Gazette. February 4, 2019. https://news.harvard.edu/gazette/story/2019/02/why-nonviolent-resistance-beats-violent-force-in-effecting-social-political-change/.

Nilsson, Desirée. "Anchoring the Peace: Civil Society Actors in Peace Accords and Durable Peace." *International Interactions* 38, no. 2 (April 2012): 243–66. https://doi.org/10.1080/03050629.2012.659139.

Nonoo, Houda. "Bahrain's Women Pioneers: Dr. Nada Haffadh." Ambassador Houda Nonoo, March 11, 2012. https://houdanonoo.wordpress.com/2012/03/11/bahrains-women-pioneers-dr-nada-haffadh/.

NPR. "Tunisian Poet's Verses Inspire Arab Protesters." NPR, January 30, 2011. https://www.npr.org/2011/01/30/133354601/Tunisian-Poets-Verses-Inspire-Arab-Protesters.

OCHA. "Yemen | Global Humanitarian Overview." OCHA, 2022. https://gho.unocha.org/yemen.

OCHR Oman. "(25th of February) Ten Years On: Remembering the Omani Spring." The Omani Centre for Human Rights, February 19, 2021. https://ochroman.org/eng/2021/02/omani-spring/.

OECD. "Women's Political Participation in Jordan." MENA OECD, 2018. https://www.oecd.org/mena/governance/womens-political-participation-in-jordan.pdf.

Official Portal of the UAE Government. "Family Protection Policy." u.ae, n.d. https://u.ae/en/about-the-uae/strategies-initiatives-and-awards/federal-governments-strategies-and-plans/family-protection-policy.

OHCHR. "Arab Charter on Human Rights (Unofficial Translation)." *Https://Www.ohchr.org/Sites/Default/Files/Documents/*

Issues/IJudiciary/Arab-Charter-On-Human-Rights-2005.Pdf. OHCHR, 2005.

OHCHR. "Experts of the Committee on the Elimination of Discrimination against Women Praise Morocco for Legislation Prohibiting Discrimination, Ask about High Maternal Mortality and Female Illiteracy Rates in Rural Areas." OHCHR, 2022. https://www.ohchr.org/en/press-releases/2022/06/experts-committee-elimination-discrimination-against-women-praise-morocco.

OHCHR. "Girls' and Young Women's Activism—Report of the Working Group on Discrimination against Women and Girls." United Nations, May 9, 2022. https://www.ohchr.org/en/documents/-thematic-reports/ahrc5025-girls-and-young-womens-activism-report-working-group.

OHCHR. "Human Rights Council Debates Situation of Human Rights in Syrian Arab Republic in Special Session." OHCHR, August 22, 2011. https://www.ohchr.org/en/press-releases/2011/08/human-rights-council-debates-situation-human-rights-syrian-arab-republic.

OHCHR. "Israel/Palestine: UN Experts Call on Governments to Resume Funding for Six Palestinian CSOs Designated by Israel as 'Terrorist Organisations.'" OHCHR, April 25, 2022. https://www.ohchr.org/en/press-releases/2022/04/-israelpalestine-un-experts-call-governments-resume-funding-six-palestinian.

OHCHR. "UN Treaty Body Database: Mauritania." Ohchr.org. Accessed November 7, 2022. https://tbinternet.ohchr.org/_layouts/15/TreatyBodyExternal/Treaty.aspx?CountryID=110&Lang=EN.

OHCHR. "UN Treaty Body Database." Ohchr.org. Accessed October 1, 2022. https://tbinternet.ohchr.org/_layouts/15/TreatyBodyExternal/Treaty.aspx?CountryID=88&Lang=EN.

OHCHR. "Women in the United Arab Emirates: A Portrait of Progress." OHCHR, 2008. https://www.ohchr.org/sites/default/files/lib-docs/HRBodies/UPR/Documents/Session3/AE/UPR_UAE_ANNEX3_E.pdf.

O'Keefe, Abby. "A Patriarchal Peace in Syria." Carnegie Endowment for International Peace, November 6, 2020. https://carnegieendowment.org/sada/83158.

O'Keeffe, Rebecca, and Karma Ekmekji. "Women at the Table: Insights from Lebanese Women in Politics." Beirut: UN Women and ESCWA, December 2022.

Open Societies Foundations. "Casualties of War: Iraqi Women's Rights and Reality Then and Now." Opensocietyfoundations.org, 2003. https://www.opensocietyfoundations.org/events/casualties-war-iraqi-womens-rights-and-reality-then-and-now.

Osman, Hibaaq. "Hibaaq Osman Twitter Profile." Twitter, December 8, 2021. https://twitter.com/hibaaq/status/1468654469554610180.

Osman, Hibaaq. "Special Statement from Hibaaq Osman: Democracy IS Women's Rights."

Karama, March 8, 2011. https://www.elkara.ma/news/content/special-statement-from-hibaaq-osman-democracy-is-womens-rights.

Osman, Nadda. "Egypt Orders Arrest of Hotel Rape Suspects Following Investigation." *Middle East Eye,* August 25, 2020. https://www.middleeasteye.net/news/egypt-metoo-cairo-hotel-rape-arrest-suspects.

Ottaway, Marina. "Women's Rights and Democracy in the Arab World." Carnegie Endowment for International Peace, 2004. https://carnegieendowment.org/2004/02/07/women-s-rights-and-democracy-in-arab-world-pub-1453.

Overmeyer, Lara. "The Uprising of Women in the Arab World: Fighting Patriarchal Tyranny." Qantara.de—Dialogue with the Islamic World, 2013. https://en.qantara.de/content/the-uprising-of-women-in-the-arab-world-fighting-patriarchal-tyranny.

Oweidat, Nadia, Cheryl Benard, Dale Stahl, Walid Kildani, Edward O'Connell, and Audra K. Grant. "The Kefaya Movement: A Case Study of a Grassroots Reform Initiative." Rand, October 26, 2008. https://www.rand.org/pubs/monographs/MG778.html.

Owen, Roger. "The Arab Economies in the 1970s." *MERIP Reports* XI, no. 8–9 (1981). https://merip.org/1981/11/the-arab-economies-in-the-1970s/.

Parline: the IPU's Open Data Platform. "IPU Comparative Data On." Accessed October 26, 2022. https://data.ipu.org/compare?field=country%3Afield_suffrage%3Afield_right_to_vote*ion=middle_east_and_north_africa#map.

Parvez, Zarqa. "Is 'Feminism' Really Helping Women's Rights in the Middle East?" *Middle East Monitor,* January 31, 2019. https://www.middleeastmonitor.com/20190131-is-feminism-really-helping-womens-rights-in-the-middle-east/.

Pepicelli, Renata. "Rethinking Gender in Arab Nationalism: Women and the Politics of Modernity in the Making of Nation-States. Cases from Egypt, Tunisia and Algeria." *Oriente Moderno* 97, no. 1 (2017): 201–19. https://doi.org/10.1163/22138617-12340145.

Permanent Mission of the State of Qatar to the United Nations. "Word from the Permanent Representative." Mission.qa. Accessed November 8, 2022. https://ny.mission.qa/en/the-embassy/the-permanent-representative.

Petkar, Sofia. "Woman Who Campaigned for Female Literacy Shot Dead in Broad Daylight." Metro, January 7, 2017. https://metro.co.uk/2017/01/07/woman-who-campaigned-for-female-literacy-shot-dead-in-broad-daylight-6366535/#:~:text=A%20female%20charity%20worker%20who.

Phillips, Susan A. "Op-Ed: 'Say Their Names': How Graffiti Is Cutting to the Heart of the Protests." *Los Angeles Times,* June 14, 2020. https://www.latimes.com/opinion/story/2020-06-14/graffiti-protests-los-angeles.

Podgers, James. "Arab Spring Brings No Thaw for Women's Rights." *ABA Journal*, April 1, 2013. https://www.abajournal.com/magazine/article/arab_spring_brings_no_thaw_for_womens_rights.

Porras-Gómez, Antonio-Martín. "Constitutional Transformation and Gender Equality: The Case of the Post-Arab Uprisings North African Constitutions." *Oxford Journal of Legal Studies* 42, no. 1 (September 29, 2021). https://doi.org/10.1093/ojls/gqab028.

Prager, Laila. "Emirati Women Leaders in the Cultural Sector from 'State Feminism' to Empowerment?" *Hawwa* 18, no. 1 (2020): 51–74. https://doi.org/10.1163/15692086-12341370.

Pratt, Nicola. *Embodying Geopolitics: Generations of Women's Activism in Egypt, Jordan, and Lebanon.* Berkeley: University of California Press, 2020.

Press TV. "Police Arrest 12 Female Protesters in Comoros." PressTV, March 28, 2019. https://www.presstv.ir/Detail/2019/03/28/592068/-Comoros-Police-Protestors.

Pringle, Rosemary, and S. Watson. 1992. "Women's interests and the post structuralist state." In M. Barrett and A. Phillips, eds., *Destabilizing Theory: Contemporary feminist debates.* Cambridge, UK: Polity Press, 53–73.

PWC. "MENA Women in Work Survey 2022: Young Women, Powerful Ambitions." PWC, 2022 https://www.pwc.com/m1/en/publications/-images-new/woman-in-work/mena-women-in-work-survey-2022.pdf.

Qatar National Day Committee. "History of Qatar." SNDCOC—The State National Day Celebration Organizing Committee. Accessed October 20, 2022. https://www.qatar.qa/en/qatar/history-of-qatar-qatar-national-day-committee/.

Quawas, Rula. "'A Sea Captain in Her Own Right': Navigating the Feminist Thought of Huda Shaarawi." *Journal of International Women's Studies* 8, no. 1 (January 11, 2013): 219–35. https://vc.bridgew.edu/jiws/vol8/iss1/17.

Rachidi, Soukaina. "Huda Shaarawi: A Remarkable Egyptian Feminist Pioneer." *Inside Arabia*, July 6, 2019 https://insidearabia.com/huda-sharawi-a-remarkable-egyptian-feminist-pioneer/.

Radi, Abdelaziz. "Protest Movements and Social Media: Morocco's February 20 Movement." *Africa Development / Afrique et Développement* 42, no. 2 (2017): 31–55. https://www.jstor.org/stable/90018190.

Randle, Michael. *Civil Resistance.* London: Fontana Press, 1994.

Ranganathan, Deepa. "'Girls Know What's Best for Them': A Conversation about the Power and Agency of Girl-Led Activism on International Day of the Girl, 2021." FRIDA | Young Feminist Fund, October 11, 2021. https://youngfeministfund.org/girls-know-whats-best-for-them-a-conversation-about-the-power-and-agency-of-girl-led-activism-on-international-day-of-the-girl-2021/.

Refaat, Taarek. "Syria's 1st Parliament Speaker 'Hadiya Abbas' Dies of Heart Attack." see.news, November 14, 2021. https://see.news/syrias-1st-parliament-speaker-hadiya-abbas-dies-of-heart-attack.

Regilme, Salvador Santino, Jr. Fulo, and Elisabetta Spoldi. "Children in Armed Conflict: A Human Rights Crisis in Somalia." *Global Jurist* 0, no. 0 (March 16, 2021). https://doi.org/10.1515/gj-2020-0083.

Remaoun, Malika. "Les Associations Féminines Pour Les Droits Des Femmes." *Insaniyat* no. 8 (August 31, 1999): 129–43. https://doi.org/10.4000/insaniyat.8331.

Rennick, Sarah Anne. "Introduction: What Is New About Post-2011 MENA Diasporas?" *Arab Reform Initiative,* July 26, 2021. https://www.arab-reform.net/publication/introduction-what-is-new-about-post-2011-mena-diasporas/.

Represent Women. "Country Brief: Arab States Brief." representwomen.app.box.com, 2021. https://representwomen.app.box.com/s/2rt8ot8qo32nbv3k7bbembqwuslu5kr9.

Reuters. "Moroccan Single Mother Burns Herself in Protest." *Reuters,* February 23, 2011, sec. Top News. https://www.reuters.com/article/cnews-us-morocco-protest-idCATRE71M4ZF20110223.

Reuters. "Timeline: Anti-Government Protests in Bahrain." *Reuters,* March 16, 2011, sec. Editor's Picks. https://www.reuters.com/article/us-bahrain-protests-events/timeline-anti-government-protests-in-bahrain-idUSTRE72F4RR20110316.

Rice, Xan, Katherine Marsh, Tom Finn, Harriet Sherwood, Angelique Chrisafis, and Robert Booth. "Women Have Emerged as Key Players in the Arab Spring." *The Guardian.* April 22, 2011. https://www.theguardian.com/world/2011/apr/22/women-arab-spring.

Richter-Devroe, Sophie. "Gender Equality and Women's Rights in Palestinian Territories." Policy Department Citizens' Rights and Constitutional Affairs, 2011. https://www.europarl.europa.eu/document/activities/cont/201110/20111027ATT30536/20111027ATT30536EN.pdf.

Right Livelihood. "Asha Hagi Elmi—Right Livelihood," August 10, 2021. https://rightlivelihood.org/the-change-makers/find-a-laureate/asha-hagi-elmi/.

Robinson, Kali. "What Is the Kafala System?" Council on Foreign Relations, March 23, 2021. https://www.cfr.org/backgrounder/what-kafala-system.

Rose, Aaron T. "Protesters Demand Women's Rights in the Constitution." dailynewsegypt.com, November 13, 2013. https://dailynewsegypt.com/2013/11/13/protesters-demand-womens-rights-in-the-constitution/.

Ross, Michael. *The Oil Curse: How Petroleum Wealth Shapes the Development of Nations.* Princeton, NJ: Princeton University Press, 2013.

Rouhshahbaz, Shadi. "Youth Agency in Peacebuilding in Post-Jasmine Revolution Tunisia." *Journal of Youth, Peace and Security* 1, no. 1 (2021): 22–26. https://unoy.org/ypsrn/shadirouhshahbaz/.

Sadik, Noreen. "The Uprising of Women in the Arab World." *New Internationalist,* March 8, 2013. https://newint.org/blog/2013/03/08/-womens-rights-campaign-arab-world.

Sadiqi, Fatima. "New Feminists in Morocco Are Innovating Cultural Change." *The Wilson Center Middle East Women's Initiative* (blog), March 8, 2020. https://www.wilsoncenter.org/blog-post/new-feminists-morocco-are-innovating-cultural-change.

Safa, Oussama. "Social Development Report 2—Inequality, Autonomy and Change in the Arab Region." UNESCWA, 2018. https://archive.unescwa.org/sites/www.unescwa.org/files/publications/files/social-development-report-2-english.pdf.

Safi, Michael. "Life Has Got Worse since Arab Spring, Say People across Middle East." *The Guardian,* December 17, 2020. https://www.theguardian.com/global-development/2020/dec/17/arab-spring-people-middle-east-poll.

Said, Edward. *Orientalism.* New York: Pantheon Books, 1978.

Sakr, Naomi. "Seen and Starting to Be Heard: Women and the Arab Media in a Decade of Change." *Social Research: An International Quarterly* 69, no. 3 (September 2002): 821–50. https://doi.org/10.1353/sor.2002.0033.

Salame, Ghassan. *The Foundations of the Arab State.* London: Routledge, 2013.

Saleh, Heba. "Nawal El Saadawi, Feminist Author and Political Activist, 1931–2021." *Financial Times,* March 26, 2021. https://www.ft.com/content/44db1483-4a0f-4e0e-a611-aad6a132adfb.

Salem, Elise. "Shaking Things up in Lebanon: Women, Revolution, and the University." *Al Raida* 44, no. 1 (2020): 93–98. https://doi.org/10.32380/alrj.v44i1.1826.

Salhi, Zahia Smail. "Algerian Women, Citizenship, and the 'Family Code.'" *Gender and Development* 11, no. 3 (2003): 27–35. http://www.jstor.org/stable/4030558.

Saliba, Therese. "Arab Feminism at the Millennium." *Signs* 25, no. 4 (2000): 1087–92. https://www.jstor.org/stable/3175492.

Salih, Zeinab Mohammed. "'I Was Raised to Love Our Home': Sudan's Singing Protester Speaks Out." *The Guardian,* April 10, 2019. https://www.theguardian.com/global-development/2019/apr/10/alaa-salah-sudanese-woman-talks-about-protest-photo-that-went-viral.

Saudi Vision 2030. "رؤية المملكة العربية السعودية 2030." Vision 2030, 2022. https://www.vision2030.gov.sa/.

Sawer, Marian. 1990. *Sisters in Suits: Women and Public Policy in Australia.* Sydney: Allen & Unwin.

Sayigh, Rosemary. "Current Challenges Facing the Arab Women's Movements." *Al-Raida Journal* 20, no. 100 (2003): 49–92. https://doi.org/10.32380/alrj.v0i0.444.

Sayigh, Yezid. "The Crisis of the Arab Nation-State." Carnegie Middle East Center, November 19, 2015. https://carnegie-mec.org/2015/11/19/crisis-of-arab-nation-state-pub-62002.

Scene Arabia. "A Girl Is Born: The Podcast Dialing up the Voices of Arab Women." *Scene Arabia,* March 8, 2021. https://scenearabia.com/Life/A-Girl-Is-Born-The-Podcast-Dialling-Up-The-Voices-Of-Arab-Women.

Schaer, Cathrin. "Murdered because of Snapchat? Social Media Uptick in Honor Crime." *DW.com,* January 29, 2021.

Schmitz, Charles. "Yemen's National Dialogue." Middle East Institute, March 10, 2014. https://www.mei.edu/publications/yemens-national-dialogue.

Schock, Kurt. "The Practice and Study of Civil Resistance." *Journal of Peace Research* 50, no. 3 (May 2013): 277–90. https://doi.org/10.1177/0022343313476530.

Scott, Joan W. "Feminism's Difference Problem." In *Arab Feminisms Gender and Equality in the Middle East,* edited by Jean Said Makdisi, Noha Bayoumi, and Rafif Rida Sidawi, 157–63. London & New York: I.B. Tauris, 2014.

Search for Common Ground, and UN Women. "Across Divides to Advance Women's Rights through Dialogue: Experiences from the Ground." UN Women, 2017. https://www.sfcg.org/inclusive-dialogue-womens-rights-mena/.

Seikaly, May. "Women and Social Change in Bahrain." *International Journal of Middle East Studies* 26, no. 3 (1994): 415–26. http://www.jstor.org/stable/163696.

Semerene, Gabriel. "The Words to Say It." *Language.* Mashallah News, 2016. https://www.mashallahnews.com/language/words-to-say.html..

Senthilingam, Meera. "Sexual Harassment: How It Stands around the Globe." CNN, 2017. https://www.cnn.com/2017/11/25/health/sexual-harassment-violence-abuse-global-levels/index.html.

Sha'arawi, Huda. "Huda Sha'arawi, Speech at the Arab Feminist Conference, 1944." Speech. *TBR Reading.* Presented at the Arab Feminist Conference, March 20, 2019. https://www.tbr.fun/huda-shaarawi-speech-at-the-arab-feminist-conference-1944/.

Shahwan, Najla M. "The Ongoing Struggle of Palestinian Women | Opinion." *Daily Sabah,* March 20, 2020. https://www.dailysabah.com/opinion/-op-ed/the-ongoing-struggle-of-palestinian-women.

Shakirat, Ganiyu O., Muhammad A. Alshibshoubi, Eldia Delia, Anam Hamayon, and Ian H. Rutkofsky. "An Overview of Female Genital Mutilation in Africa: Are the Women Beneficiaries or Victims?" *Cureus* 12, no. 9 (September 4, 2020). https://doi.org/10.7759/cureus.10250.

Shalaby, Marwa, and Ariana Marnicio. "Women's Political Participation in Bahrain." In *Women Rising: In and beyond the Arab Spring,* edited by Rita Stephan and Mounira M. Charrad, 321–29. New York: New York University Press, 2020. https://doi.org/10.18574/nyu/9781479846641.003.0036.

Shalhoub-Kevorkian, Nadera. "Indigenizing Feminist Knowledge: Palestinian Feminist Thought between the Physics of International Power and the Theology of Racist 'Security.'" In *Arab Feminisms: Gender and Equality in the Middle East,* edited by Jean Said Makdisi, Noha Bayoumi, and Rafif Rida Sidawi, 205–16. London; New York: I.B. Tauris, 2014.

Sharifi, Maedeh. "#MeToo in MENA: The Women Shake Region out of Its Silence on Sexual Harassment." *The New Arab,* March 9, 2021. https://english.alaraby.co.uk/features/mena-women-shake-region-out-sexual-harassment-silence.

Sharma, Shalendra D. "The Arab World amidst the Global Financial Crisis of 2008–2009." *Contemporary Arab Affairs* 3, no. 1 (2010): 38–52. https://www.jstor.org/stable/48599700.

Sharp, Gene. *Politics of Nonviolent Action: Power and Struggle (Vol 1).* Boston: Porter Sargent, 1973.

Shehab, Bahia. "Adhan (Call to Prayer)." Fine Acts, 2014. https://fineacts.co/bahia-shehab.

Shehab, Bahia. "Mokhak Awra." Bahia Shehab. Accessed November 10, 2022. https://www.bahiashehab.com/graffiti/mokhak-awra.

SIDA. "Multidimensional Poverty Analysis for the Middle East and North Africa." Swedish International Development Cooperation Agency, 2019. https://cdn.sida.se/app/uploads/2021/08/24151349/MDPA-For-MENA-2019.pdf.

SIGI. "Social Institutions and Gender Index." Genderindex.org, 2019. https://www.genderindex.org/.

Siim, Birte. "Helga Maria Hernes: Welfare State and Woman Power. Essays in State Feminism, Norwegian University Press, Oslo 1987, 176 Pp." *Scandinavian Political Studies,* no. 3 (January 1, 1988). https://tidsskrift.dk/scandinavian_political_studies/article/view/32609/30667.

Singh, Yvonne. "What Does It Take to Be an Arab Feminist in 2019?" *Middle East Eye,* July 5, 2019. https://www.middleeasteye.net/discover/what-does-it-take-be-arab-feminist-2019.

Soliman, Nagwan. "Sudan Spring: Lessons from Sudanese Women Revolutionaries." GIWPS, April 11, 2020. https://giwps.georgetown.edu/sudan-spring-lessons-from-sudanese-women-revolutionaries/.

Srouji, Mayada. "'Bayneh W Baynek': A Place Where Arab Women Can Speak about Their Struggles without Any Judgement!" *MVSLIM,* February 27, 2019. https://mvslim.com/bayneh-w-baynek-a-place-where-arab-women-can-speak-about-their-struggles-without-any-judgement/.

Stephan, Rita. "Four Waves of Lebanese Feminism." E-International Relations, 2014. https://www.e-ir.info/2014/11/07/four-waves-of-lebanese-feminism/.

Stephan, Rita. "Lebanese Women's Rights beyond the Cedar Revolution." In *Arab Women's Activism and Socio-Political Transformation: Unfinished Gendered Revolutions,* edited by Sahar Khamis and Amel Mili, 73–88. New York: Palgrave Macmillan, 2018. https://doi.org/10.1007/978-3-319-60735-1_4.

Stephan, Rita, and Mounira M Charrad. *Women Rising: In and beyond the Arab Spring.* New York: New York University Press, 2020.

Stephen, Chris, Irina Kalashnikova, and David Smith. "Libyan Women: It's Our Revolution Too." *The Guardian,* September 16, 2011. https://www.theguardian.com/world/2011/sep/16/libyan-women-our-revolution-too.

Supreme Council for Women. "National Strategy to Protect Women from Domestic Violence." www.scw.bh, 2015. https://www.scw.bh/en/InformationCenter/Pages/nsdv.aspx.

SWANA Alliance. "What Is SWANA?" SWANA Alliance, n.d. https://swanaalliance.com/about.

SWPM. "About Us." The Syrian Women's Political Movement. Accessed November 9, 2022. https://syrianwomenpm.org/abous-us/.

The Syrian Women's Political Movement. "SWPM: Mariam Jalabi." SWPM, 2020. https://syrianwomenpm.org/members/mariam-jalabi/.

TAS News Service. "After Nearly 17 Years, Oman's First Woman Minister Dr Rawya al Busaidi Steps Down." The Arabian Stories News, August 25, 2020. https://www.thearabianstories.com/2020/08/25/after-nearly-17-years-omans-first-woman-minister-dr-rawya-al-busaidi-steps-down/.

Tawfik, Fatima. "Rising in the Rankings, Arab Women Dream of Gender Equality—Ms. Magazine." msmagazine.com, February 18, 2022. https://msmagazine.com/2022/02/18/arab-women-politics-gender-equality/.

Tazi, Maha. "The Arab Spring and Women's (Cyber)Activism: 'Fourth Wave Democracy in the Making?' Case Study of Egypt, Tunisia, and Morocco." *Journal of International Women's Studies* 22, no. 9 (September 17, 2021): 298–315. https://vc.bridgew.edu/jiws/vol22/iss9/20.

Tazi, Maha, and Kenza Oumlil. "The Rise of Fourth-Wave Feminism in the Arab Region? Cyberfeminism and Women's Activism at the Crossroads of the Arab Spring." *CyberOrient* 14, no. 1 (January 2020): 44–71. https://doi.org/10.1002/j.cyo2.20201401.0002.

Team Qatar. "Programmes and Initiatives | Team Qatar." www.olympic.qa. Accessed August 28, 2022. https://www.olympic.qa/programmes-and-initiatives#:~:text=The%20Qatar%20Women.

TED. "Bahia Shehab: A Thousand Times No." Video. *YouTube,* September 28, 2012. https://www.youtube.com/watch?v=R_U9GUlSOC4.

TEDx Talks. "Because I'm a Fighter! | Lina

Khalifeh | TEDxPragueWomen." www.youtube. com, January 18, 2017. https://www.youtube. com/watch?v=tIDwTmYR1Cs.

Temlali, Yassine. "The 'Arab Spring' Rebirth or Final Throes of Pan-Arabism?" *Perspectives, Political Analysis and Commentary from the Middle East,* 2011, 46–49.

Tétreault, Mary Ann, Helen Rizzo, and Doron Shultziner. "Fashioning the Future: The Women's Movement in Kuwait." In *Mapping Arab Women's Movements: A Century of Transformations from Within,* edited by Pernille Arenfeldt and Nawar Al-Hassan Golley, 253–80. Cairo: American University in Cairo Press, 2012

Thompson, Elizabeth. *Colonial Citizens: Republican Rights, Paternal Privilege, and Gender in French Syria and Lebanon.* New York: Columbia University Press, 1999.

Timmons, Debra M. "The Sixth Clan—Women Organize for Peace in Somalia: A Review of Published Literature." Edited by Mary E. King. Geneva: University for Peace, 2004. http://maryking.info/wp-content/TheSixthClanWomenOrganizeforPeaceinSomalia.pd.

Tnani, Najet. "Tunisian Women at the Crossroad: Between a Feminist Spring and an Islamist Winter." *Al-Raida Journal,* no. 151 (July 17, 2020): 35–44. https://doi.org/10.32380/alrj.vi.1768.

Tønnessen, Liv. "Sudanese Women's Revolution for Freedom, Dignity and Justice Continues." *Chr. Michelsen Institute* (blog), 2020. https://www.cmi.no/publications/7355-sudanese-womens-revolution-for-freedom-dignity-and-justice-continues.

Touaf, Larbi. "Touaf on Charrad, 'States and Women's Rights: The Making of Postcolonial Tunisia, Algeria, and Morocco.'" *H-Gender-MidEast.* H-net Reviews, 2003. https://networks.h-net.org/node/6386/reviews/6614/touaf-charrad-states-and-womens-rights-making-postcolonial-tunisia.

Toumi, Habib. "Women Candidates to Test Their Luck in Qatar Polls." gulfnews.com, April 10, 2011. https://gulfnews.com/world/gulf/qatar/-women-candidates-to-test-their-luck-in-qatar-polls-1.789916.

Tran, Mark. "First Women Elected to Kuwait Parliament." *The Guardian,* May 17, 2009. https://www.theguardian.com/world/2009/may/17/kuwait-women-elected-parliament.

Tripp, Aili Mari. "Beyond Islamist Extremism: Women and the Algerian Uprisings of 2019." *CMI Brief* 2019:09, no. 9 (2019). https://www.cmi.no/publications/6983-beyond-islamist-extremism-women-and-the-algerian-uprisings-of-2019.

Tripp, Aili Mari. "The Fight for Democracy & Women's Rights in Algeria: A Long Legacy of Struggle." *Transatlantic Policy Quarterly* (TPQ), June 26, 2019. http://turkishpolicy.com/article/957/the-fight-for-democracy-womens-rights-in-algeria-a-long-legacy-of-struggle.

Tripp, Aili Mari. "Women Are Deeply Involved in the Algerian Protests—on International Women's Day, and All the Time." *The Washington Post,* March 8, 2019. https://www.washingtonpost.com/politics/2019/03/08/-women-are-deeply-involved-algerian-protests-international-womens-day-all-time/.

Tunisia Office Center for Middle Eastern Studies Harvard University. "#EnaZeda,the Birth of a Movement against Sexual Harassment in Tunisia." cmestunisia.fas.harvard.edu, January 8, 2020. https://cmestunisia.fas.harvard.edu/event/enazedathe-birth-movement-against-sexual-harassment-tunisia.

UAE MFNCA. "Women in the United Arab Emirates: A Portrait of Progress." OHCHR, 2008. https://www.google.com/url?q=https://www.ohchr.org/sites/default/files/lib-docs/HRBodies/UPR/Documents/Session3/AE/UPR_UAE_ANNEX3_E.pdf&sa=D&source=docs&ust=1668532711517486&usg=-AOvVaw09U6f0nWy0-XMYfaczkG5f.

UC Press. "Author Spotlight: Nicola Pratt on Women's Activism in the Middle East." UC Press Blog, October 13, 2020. https://www.ucpress.edu/blog/52517/author-spotlight-nicola-pratt-on-womens-activism-in-the-middle-east/.

UC Press Blog. "Author Spotlight: Nicola Pratt on Women's Activism in the Middle East." UC Press Blog, 2020. https://www.ucpress.edu/blog/52517/author-spotlight-nicola-pratt-on-womens-activism-in-the-middle-east/.

UCA. "Comoros (1975-Present)." uca.edu. Accessed November 4, 2022. https://uca.edu/politicalscience/dadm-project/sub-saharan-africa-region/comoros-1975-present/.

UIA. "Collectif 95 Maghreb Égalité | UIA Yearbook Profile | Union of International Associations." uia.org, 2004. https://uia.org/s/or/en/1100003794.

UN Women. "Arab League Presents Regional Action Plan for Women, Peace and Security." UN Women—Arab States, October 13, 2015. https://www.google.com/url?q=https://arabstates.unwomen.org/en/news/stories/2015/10/arab-league-presents-regional-action-plan&sa=D&source=docs&ust=1667930886822053&usg=AOvVaw3j74I-t_iGKPFlfvjjQ2Ik.

UN Women. "A Group of Women Has Bridged Differences towards Peace in Syria." UN Women—Arab States, November 1, 2022. https://arabstates.unwomen.org/en/stories/feature-story/2022/11/a-group-of-women-has-bridged-differences-towards-peace-in-syria.

UN Women. "Historic Day for Women in Lebanon as Parliament Repeals Rape Law." UN Women, August 18, 2017. https://www.unwomen.org/en/news/stories/2017/8/news-lebanon-parliament-repeals-rape-law.

UN Women. "The Impact of COVID-19 on Gender Equality in the Arab Region." UN Women Arab States, April 2020. https://arabstates.unwomen.org/sites/default/files/Field%20Office%20Arab%20States/Attachments/

Publications/2020/04/Impact%20of%20 COVID%20on%20gender%20equality%20-%20 Policy%20Brief.pdf.

UN Women. "#Ismaani—a Hashtag for Women from the Arab States." UN Women Arab States, February 13, 2019. https://arabstates.unwomen. org/en/news/stories/2019/2/a-hashtag-for-women-from-the-arab-states.

UN Women. "Working with Men and Boys for Gender Equality: State of Play and Future Directions." New York: UN Women, 2021.

UN Women Arab States. "Facts and Figures: Ending Violence against Women and Girls." UN Women—Arab States. Accessed October 29, 2022. https://arabstates.unwomen.org/en/-what-we-do/ending-violence-against-women/-facts-and-figures-0#:~:text=37%25%20of%20 Arab%20women%20have.

UNDP. "Documentation and Downloads." hdr. undp.org. UNDP, 2022. https://hdr.undp.org/-data-center/documentation-and-downloads.

UNDP. "Gender Justice and the Law: Djibouti." *UNDP.org.* UNDP, 2019. https://www.undp. org/sites/g/files/zskgke326/files/migration/ arabstates/Djibouti.Summary.19.Eng.pdf.

UNDP. "Latest Human Development Composite Indices Tables." hdr.undp.org. UNDP, 2022. https://hdr.undp.org/data-center/-documentation-and-downloads.

UNDP. "Making Globalization Work for All." UNDP, 2007. https://www.undp.org/ publications/undp-annual-report-2007.

UNESCWA, and ILO. "Towards a Productive and Inclusive Path: Job Creation in the Arab Region." UNESCWA and ILO, August 2021.

UNESCWA and UN Women. "The Impact of COVID-19 on Gender Equality in the Arab Region." ESCWA and UN Women, 2020.

UNESCWA, UNFPA, UN Women, and UNDP. "Gender Justice & Equality before the Law," 2019. https://www.undp.org/arab-states/ publications/gender-justice-equality-law.

UNESCWA. "The Arab Gender Gap Report 2020." UNESCWA, 2020. https://publications.unescwa. org/projects/aggr/index.html#%5C31.

UNESCWA. "ESCWA Marks International Women's Day with Call to Action: The Time Is Now." ESCWA, March 5, 2019. https://www. unescwa.org/news/escwa-marks-international-women%E2%80%99s-day-call-action-time-now.

UNESCWA. "Operationalizing Intersectionality in the Arab Region: Challenges and Ways Forward." Beirut: UNESCWA, 2019.

UNESCWA. "Social and Economic Situation of Palestinian Women and Girls: July 2012—June 2014." New York: United Nations, 2015.

UNFPA, and UNICEF. "Child Marriage in the Context of COVID-19: MENA Regional Analysis." UNFPA, June 2021.

UNFPA. "Closing of the 16 Days of Activism against Gender-Based Violence Including FGM." UNFPA Djibouti, September 4, 2020. https://djibouti.unfpa.org/en/news/

closing-16-days-activism-against-gender-based-violence-including-fgm.

UNFPA. "Female Genital Mutilation." UNFPA Egypt, April 11, 2016. https://egypt.unfpa.org/ en/node/22544#:~:text=However%2C%20 the%20recent%20history%20of.

UNFPA. "Navigating Comprehensive Sexuality Education in the Arab Region," 2020. https:// arabstates.unfpa.org/sites/default/files/pub-pdf/ situational_analysis_final_for_web.pdf.

UNFPA. "State of the World Population 2021." UNFPA, 2021. https://www.unfpa.org/sowp-2021.

UNFPA. "Yemen: One of the World's Largest Humanitarian Crises." United Nations Population Fund, October 11, 2022. https:// www.unfpa.org/yemen#:~:text=largest%20 humanitarian%20crises-.

UNFPA. "Youth Participation & Leadership." UNFPA Arab States, 2022. https://arabstates. unfpa.org/en/topics/youth-participation-leadership.UNHCR. "Preventing and Reducing Statelessness: Good Practices in Promoting and Adopting Gender Equality in Nationality Laws." UNHCR, 2014. http://www.unhcr.org/531a001c9. pdf.

UNHCR. "Refworld | Sudan: The Sudanese Women's Union (SWU) Including Activities, Roles, Organization and Problems Faced in Sudan." Refworld, 2002. https://www.refworld.org/ docid/3df4bea84.html.

UNHCR. "Regional Summaries: The Middle East and North Africa." UNHCR, 2020.

UNICEF. "Arab Girls' Summit: A Space for Girls and Young Women to Make Their Voices Heard." www.unicef.org, October 11, 2022. https://www.unicef.org/mena/press-releases/-arab-girls-summit-space-girls-and-young-women-make-their-voices-heard.

UNICEF. "Situational Analysis of Women and Girls in the MENA and Arab States Region: Pillar 1 Health and Wellbeing." UNICEF Middle East and North Africa, October 2022.

UNICEF. "Situational Analysis of Women and Girls in the MENA and Arab States Region." UNICEF Middle East and North Africa, October 2022.

UNICEF. "Sudan Enters New Era for Girl Rights with Criminalization of FGM." www.unicef. org, 2020. https://www.unicef.org/mena/press-releases/sudan-enters-new-era-girl-rights-criminalization-fgm.

UNICEF. "Universal Periodic Review—Human Rights Council Oman." OHCHR. Accessed September 21, 2022. https://www.ohchr. org/sites/default/files/lib-docs/HRBodies/ UPR/Documents/Session10/OM/UNICEF_ UnitedNationsChildren%27sFund_eng.pdf.

UNICEF. "Yemen Crisis." Unicef.org. UNICEF, 2022. https://www.unicef.org/emergencies/ yemen-crisis.

UNICEF MENA. "Facts and Figures: Female Genital Mutilation in the Middle East and North

Africa." www.unicef.org, February 2020. https://www.unicef.org/mena/reports/facts-and-figures-female-genital-mutilation-middle-east-and-north-africa.

UNICEF MENA. "UNICEF Middle East and North Africa." Unicef.org. Accessed October 20, 2022. https://www.unicef.org/mena/.

UNICEF Sudan. "Gender Annual Report." Khartoum: UNICEF Sudan, 2021. Union of International Associations. "The Yearbook of International Organizations | Union of International Associations." uia.org. Brill, 2021. https://uia.org/yearbook?qt-yb_intl_orgs=3.

UNICEF Sudan. "Sudan Gender Report." Khartoum: UNICEF Sudan, 2021. https://www.unicef.org/sudan/media/8516/file/UNICEF%20Sudan-%20Gender-%20Report%20(2021).pdf.

United Nations. "$4.3 Billion Needed to Help over 17 Million People across Yemen." *UN News,* March 16, 2022. https://news.un.org/en/story/2022/03/1114032.

United Nations. "Ministry for the Promotion of Women, Family Well-Being, and Social Affairs National Ten-Year Evaluation Report on Implementation of the Beijing Platform for Action." *Republic of Djibouti Office of the Prime Minister.* UN, 2004. https://www.un.org/womenwatch/daw/Review/responses/DJIBOUTI-English.pdf.

United Nations. "The Paris Agreement." United Nations, n.d. https://www.un.org/en/climatechange/paris-agreement#:~:text=The%20Agreement%20is%20a%20legally.

United Nations. "Policy Brief: The Impact of COVID-19 on the Arab Region an Opportunity to Build Back Better." New York: United Nations, July 2020. https://unsdg.un.org/resources/policy-brief-impact-covid-19-arab-region-opportunity-build-back-better.

United Nations. "Report of the World Conference of the International Women's Year." In *The World Conference of the International Women's Year,* 1–199. New York: United Nations, 1976.

United Nations. "Special Focus: Gaza Strip—Is the Closure of the Tunnels from Egypt Further Suffocating the Gaza Economy?—WFP Food Security Analysis." *Question of Palestine,* February 2014. https://www.un.org/unispal/document/auto-insert-196041/.

United Nations. "United Nations Treaty Collection." treaties.un.org. Accessed October 29, 2022. https://treaties.un.org/pages/ViewDetails.aspx?src=IND&mtdsg_no=IV-8&chapter=4&clang=_en#EndDec.

United Nations. "Women and the Arab Spring." *UN Chronicle* 53, no. 4 (December 2016). https://www.un.org/en/chronicle/article/women-and-arab-spring.

United Nations. "The World's Women 1970–1990 Trends and Statistics." New York: United Nations, 1991.

United States Department of State. "U.S. Department of State Country Report on Human Rights Practices 2004—Comoros." Refworld, 2005.

https://www.refworld.org/docid/4226d9698.html.

UNOY. "Policy Brief: Beyond Dividing Lines in Libya." UNOY, 2018. https://unoy.org/downloads/policy-brief-beyond-dividing-lines-in-libya/.

UNSC. "Resolution 1325." New York: UNSC, 2000. http://unscr.com/en/resolutions/doc/1325.

UNSC. "United Nations Support Mission in Libya: Report of the Secretary General." UNSC, January 7, 2019.

UNSMIL. "Martin Kobler: Establishment of Women's Empowerment Unit a Key Step to Include Women in Politics." UNSMIL, September 9, 2016. https://unsmil.unmissions.org/martin-kobler-establishment-women%E2%80%99s-empowerment-unit-key-step-include-women-politics.

UPWC. "UPWC about Us." UPWC—© Official website. Accessed October 14, 2022. http://upwc.org.ps/.

Ventura, Luca. "Global Finance Magazine—Richest Countries in the World 2019." *Global Finance Magazine,* July 25, 2019. https://www.gfmag.com/global-data/economic-data/richest-countries-in-the-world.

Verso. "Memorialising Complexity: The Many Lives of Nawal El Saadawi." *Verso,* April 2021. https://www.versobooks.com/blogs/5052-memorialising-complexity-the-many-lives-of-nawal-el-saadawi.

Voorhoeve, Maaike. "The Tunisian Law on Violence against Women." *Cahiers D'Études Africaines,* no. 242 (2021): 377–94. https://doi.org/https://doi.org/10.4000/etudesafricaines.34304.

Webster, Kaitlyn, Chong Chen, and Kyle Beardsley. "Conflict, Peace, and the Evolution of Women's Empowerment." *International Organization* 73, no. 02 (2019): 255–89. https://doi.org/10.1017/s0020818319000055.

WEF. "Global Gender Gap Report 2022." Geneva: World Economic Forum, 2022. https://www.weforum.org/reports/global-gender-gap-report-2022/.

WHO. "Devastatingly Pervasive: 1 in 3 Women Globally Experience Violence." www.who.int. World Health Organization, March 9, 2021. https://www.who.int/news/item/09-03-2021-devastatingly-pervasive-1-in-3-women-globally-experience-violence.

WHO. "Review of the Birth Spacing Programme." World Health Organization—Regional Office for the Eastern Mediterranean. Accessed October 28, 2022. https://www.emro.who.int/omn/oman-news/review-of-the-birthspacing-programme.html.

Wiley, Katherine Ann. "Women in Mauritania." *Oxford Research Encyclopedia of African History,* July 30, 2020. https://doi.org/10.1093/acrefore/9780190277734.013.529.

Williams, Ella. "#Masaktach: Social Media and Sexual Violence against Women in Morocco." *Oxford Middle East Review (OMER),* July 3,

2020. https://omerjournal.com/2020/07/03/-masaktach-social-media-and-sexual-violence-against-women-in-morocco/.

WILPF. "In Lebanon, the Revolution Is a Woman." *WILPF,* December 11, 2019. https://www.wilpf.org/in-lebanon-the-revolution-is-a-woman/.

WILPF. "Iraq—1325 National Action Plans." 1325 NAPS, n.d. http://1325naps.peacewomen.org/index.php/iraq/.

WILPF. "1325 National Action Plans—an Initiative of the Women's International League for Peace and Freedom." 1325 NAPS, n.d. https://1325naps.peacewomen.org/.

Wilson Center. "Book Talk: 'Women Rising: In and beyond the Arab Spring.'" Wilson Center, 2020. https://www.wilsoncenter.org/event/book-talk-women-rising-and-beyond-arab-spring.

Wilson Center. "The Global Impact of 9/11: Twenty Years on | Wilson Center." Video. Wilson Center, September 9, 2021. https://www.wilsoncenter.org/event/global-impact-911-twenty-years.

Wilson Center. "Timeline: The Rise, Spread and Fall of the Islamic State." Wilson Center, October 28, 2019. https://www.wilsoncenter.org/article/timeline-the-rise-spread-and-fall-the-islamic-state.

Woman This Month. "Sisters Doing It for Themselves." womanthismonth.com, May 1, 2018. https://www.google.com/url?sa=t&rct=j&q=&esrc=s&source=web&cd=&cad=rja&uact=8&ved=2ahUKEwiepsns7Iv7AhXwEEQIHZyiAgEQFnoECAoQAQ&url=https%3A%2F%2Fwomanthismonth.com%2Fsisters-doing-it-for-themselves%2F&usg=AOvVaw1C8RcxKpAnuRAGy30EA2XY.

The Women to Drive Movement. "The Women to Drive Movement." Oct26driving.com, 2010. https://oct26driving.com/.

Women's Learning Partnership. "Aminetou Ely (Mint El-Moctar) Oral History Audio Files | Women's Learning Partnership." learningpartnership.org, 2015. https://learningpartnership.org/resource/aminetou-ely-mint-el-moctar-oral-history-audio-files.

Women's Learning Partnership. "Equality: It's All in the Family (Video, English)." learningpartnership.org, 2017. https://learningpartnership.org/resource/equality-its-all-family-video-english.

Women's World Conference, *1975 World Conference on Women,* Mexico City, 19th June—2nd July 1975.

Wood, Johnny. "104 Countries Have Laws That Prevent Women from Working in Some Jobs." World Economic Forum, August 13, 2018. https://www.weforum.org/agenda/2018/08/104-countries-have-laws-that-prevent-women-from-working-in-some-jobs/.

World Bank. "Labor Force Participation Rate, Female (% of Female Population Ages 15+) (Modeled ILO Estimate)—Middle East & North Africa | Data." Worldbank.org, 2019. https://data.worldbank.org/indicator/SL.TLF.CACT.FE.ZS?locations=ZQ.

World Bank. "Labor Force Participation Rate, Female (% of Female Population Ages 15+) (Modeled ILO Estimate) | Data." data.worldbank.org, 2022. https://data.worldbank.org/indicator/SL.TLF.CACT.FE.ZS?name_desc=false.

World Bank. "Literacy Rate, Adult Total (% of People Ages 15 and Above)—Arab World | Data." data.worldbank.org, 2022. https://data.worldbank.org/indicator/SE.ADT.LITR.ZS?locations=1A.

World Bank. "Nearly 2.4 Billion Women Globally Don't Have Same Economic Rights as Men." World Bank, March 1, 2022. https://www.worldbank.org/en/news/press-release/2022/03/01/nearly-2-4-billion-women-globally-don-t-have-same-economic-rights-as-men.

World Bank. "Republic of Yemen the Status of Yemeni Women: From Aspiration to Opportunity Poverty Reduction and Economic Management Department Middle East and North Africa Region." World Bank, 2014. http://documents1.worldbank.org/curated/en/640151468334820965/pdf/878200REVISED00Box0385200B00PUBLIC0.pdf.

World Bank. "Tunisia: Breaking the Barriers to Youth Inclusion." Washington, D.C.: World Bank, 2014. https://www.worldbank.org/content/dam/Worldbank/document/MNA/tunisia/breaking_the_barriers_to_youth_inclusion_eng.pdf.

World Bank. "Unemployment, Total (% of Total Labor Force) (Modeled ILO Estimate)—Tunisia | Data." data.worldbank.org. Accessed June 9, 2022. https://data.worldbank.org/indicator/SL.UEM.TOTL.ZS?locations=TN&fbclid=-IwAR1V4GLsL2T0Y7ivmUckfMZAJZ9OU7-WFrtaVo83G2drlu6-f-js5S1PdzY.

World Bank. "Women, Business and the Law 2022." Washington, D.C.: World Bank, 2022. doi:10.1596/978-1-4648-1817-2.

WUNRN. "First Arab Woman President of UN General Assembly—Shaikha Haya of Bahrain." WUNRN, September 12, 2006. https://wunrn.com/2006/09/first-arab-woman-president-of-un-general-assembly-shaikha-haya-of-bahrain/.

WUNRN. "Tunisia—Lifting of CEDAW Reservations Is Landmark Step for Gender Equality." Wunrn.com, 2014. https://wunrn.com/2014/05/-tunisia-lifting-of-cedaw-reservations-is-landmark-step-for-gender-equality/.

Yacoubi, Imen. "Sovereignty from Below: State Feminism and Politics of Women against Women in Tunisia." *The Arab Studies Journal* 24, no. 1 (2016): 254–74.

Yadav, Punam. "Can Women Benefit from War? Women's Agency in Conflict and Post-Conflict Societies." *Journal of Peace Research* 58, no. 3 (June 19, 2020): 449–61. https://doi.org/10.1177/0022343320905619.

Yahya, Maha, and Marwan Muasher. "Refugee Crises in the Arab World." Carnegie Endowment for International Peace, 2018. https://carnegieendowment.org/2018/10/18/refugee-crises-in-arab-world-pub-77522.

Yassine, Hussein. "What Is Civil Marriage and Does It Work in Lebanon?" *The 961,* January 5, 2021. https://www.the961.com/civil-marriage-in-lebanon-explained/.

Yemen News Agency (Saba). "Yemeni Women Call for Their 15 Percent Quota." www.saba.ye, August 21, 2008. https://www.saba.ye/en/news162183.htm.

Young, Sydney. "The Women's Revolution: Female Activism in Sudan." Harvard International Review, May 25, 2020. https://hir.harvard.edu/-the-womens-revolution-female-activism-in-sudan/.

Zaanoun, Abderrafie. "The Impact of the Quota System on Women Parliamentary Representation in Morocco: A Series of Reforms or a Regressive Path?" *Arab Reform Initiative,* April 14, 2022. https://www.arab-reform.net/publication/the-impact-of-the-quota-system-on-women-parliamentary-representation-in-morocco-a-series-of-reforms-or-a-regressive-path/.

Zaatari, Zeina. "From Women's Rights to Feminism: The Urgent Need for an Arab Feminist Renaissance—Zeina Zaatari." In *Arab Feminisms: Gender and Equality in the Middle East,* edited by Jean Said Makdisi, Noha Bayoumi, and Rafif Rida Sidawi, 54–65. London & New York: I.B. Tauris, 2014.

Zatat, Narjas. "10 Events That Drastically Changed the Middle East." *Https://English.alaraby.co.uk/,* December 23, 2019. https://english.alaraby.co.uk/news/10-events-drastically-changed-middle-east.

Zayat, Iman. "Tunisia Marks Long Struggle for Women's Rights | Iman Zayat." The Arab Weekly, August 15, 2020. https://thearabweekly.com/tunisia-marks-long-struggle-womens-rights.

Zeffane, Rachid, and Linzi Kemp. "Emiratization: Benefits and Challenges of Strategic and Radical Change in the United Arab Emirates." In *Case Studies in Work, Employment and Human Resource Management,* edited by Tony Dundon and Adrian Wilkinson, 245–53. Australia: Tilde University Press, 2019. https://doi.org/10.4337/9781788975599.00049.

Zeidan, Tarek. "Gender and Sexuality Library." Facebook, October 23, 2022. https://www.facebook.com/Tarek.Zeidan/posts/pfbid02A422nMZz5rjCQLLX6iDqJkA5iytJshgGAZD1b68diPJqYcEvLkBwunGPQRfXU4v4l.

Ziad, Melissa. "@Melziad Instagram Post." Instagram, March 4, 2019. https://www.instagram.com/p/BulgCDUnn97/.

Zinsser, Judith P. "From Mexico to Copenhagen to Nairobi: The United Nations Decade for Women, 1975–1985." *Journal of World History* 13, no. 1 (2002): 139–68. https://www.jstor.org/stable/20078945.

Zoepf, Katherine. "Shopgirls in the Kingdom." The New Yorker. Condé Nast, December 15, 2013. https://www.newyorker.com/magazine/2013/12/23/shopgirls.

Zoepf, Katherine. "Talk of Women's Rights Divides Saudi Arabia (Published 2010)." *The New York Times,* May 31, 2010, https://www.nytimes.com/2010/06/01/world/middleeast/01iht-saudi.html.

Zughair, Reham. "Fiction as a Tool of Resistance against the Reality of Womanhood: Arab Women Writers' Approach to Truth." *Honi Soit,* August 17, 2021. https://honisoit.com/2021/08/fiction-as-a-tool-of-resistance-against-the-reality-of-womanhood-arab-women-writers-approach-to-truth/.

Zuhur, Sherifa. "Women and Empowerment in the Arab World." *Arab Studies Quarterly* 25, no. 4 (2003): 17–38. https://doi.org/https://www.jstor.org/stable/41858460.

مؤلف. "Michelle & Noel Keserwany: 3al Jamal Bi Wasat Beirut (عالجمل بوسط بيروت)." Lebanese Arabic Institute, February 12, 2018. https://www.lebanesearabicinstitute.com/3al-jamal-bi-wasat-beirut/.

Index

ABAAD 71, 83, 140, 146, 161, 164, 188, 191
Abboud, Hosn 140
Abou-Habib, Lina 84, 111, 212
abuse 2, 31–35, 63, 71, 73, 76, 78, 89, 97, 100–101, 103, 110, 125, 162, 168, 214, 218
Abu Zain Eddin, Banan 140
Adhan (Muslim call to prayer) 122, 128, 221
aftermath 33, 50, 52, 70–71, 73–74, 77, 82, 86, 90, 129, 195
agency 14, 30, 39, 43, 66, 71, 73, 86–87, 91, 111, 148, 156, 164, 174–175, 180, 201, 213
Ahmed, Yazz 118
Akasha, Yosra 98–100, 145, 147, 150–151, 155–156, 164, 166, 168
Alamuddin, Rana 109, 194, 196, 214
al-bu'd al-junūsi (the gender dimension) 38
Al Fassi, Hatoon 19, 140, 152, 158, 188, 196–197
Algeria 11–13, 22, 27, 30–31, 33–34, 41–42, 55–56, 58–59, 62, 65, 68, 72, 79, 87, 104, 191, 200, 221
Al Mokaddem, Fatima 142, 145, 205
Al Obeidli, Noura 141, 144, 147, 154, 165, 167, 182, 192
Al Raida 221
al-tashakkul al-thaqāfi wa'l-ijtimā'i li'l-jins (the cultural and social construction of sex) 38
Al Taher, Aya 158
Al-Thawra untha 91, 221
American University of Beirut 108, 111, 183, 212
Amro, Xena 108, 207–208
Anani, Ghida 83, 140, 144, 188
Arab Barometer 33
Arab Institute for Women (AiW) 9–10, 39, 54, 91, 123–124, 146, 157, 170, 174, 179, 183, 190, 201, 221
Arab Spring 18, 39, 49, 68, 70–73, 75, 78, 86–90, 96, 107, 111, 116, 131, 133, 175–176, 211–212, 217
Arab Women Development Society (AWDS) 53

assault 29, 33, 78, 90, 107–110, 193
Association for Middle East Women's Studies (AMEWS) 183
Association Tunisienne des Femmes Démocrates (ATFD) 63, 71
authoritarian regime 49, 71, 82
autonomy 14, 31, 34, 126, 144, 186, 189, 193–195
Ayb 221

Ba'athist 54, 221
Badran, Hoda 20, 43, 73
Badran, Margot 73, 87, 90, 213
Badran, Rym 141, 146, 166, 168–169, 177–178, 199
Bahrain 12–13, 22–23, 27, 30–31, 52–53, 57, 61, 65, 68–69, 76, 85–86, 89, 106, 110, 114, 118, 122, 129, 136, 157, 160, 179, 186, 193, 197, 200, 214
Bayne W Baynek (Between Me and You) 109
Beghalat (Cinderella) 123
Beirut 20, 110, 213; 3al Jamal Bi Wasat Beirut (A Camel in Downtown Beirut) 119; Beirut Call for Action 201; Port blast 77, 91, 102, 152, 203; *see also* Lebanon
Bel Haj Hmida, Bocha 139, 165
Bi'Ideh (in my hand) 123
Boladian, Sossi 140, 142

care work 24, 26, 100
casualties 94, 111
CAWTAR 183
Chebaro, Abir 144, 147–148, 150, 163, 184
Chebbi, Aya 18, 218–219
civic 45, 61, 74, 135
civil disobedience 105
civil society 49–50, 52, 55, 68, 71, 74, 76–77, 79, 81, 93, 95, 97–99, 111, 115, 128, 150, 161, 174, 191, 197, 200–202, 204–205, 212
Comoros 11–13, 22–23, 27, 55, 57, 63, 79
conflict 18, 20–21, 23–24, 33–35, 37, 48–49, 52, 54, 58, 60, 64, 68, 73, 75, 77–78, 80–81, 83–86,

89–94, 98–99, 101, 131, 135, 148, 155–156, 206, 212, 216; zones 44
contraception 23; in Oman 60; in Yemen 76
Convention on the Elimination of Discrimination Against Women (CEDAW) 29, 49, 57, 59, 61–65, 69, 71–72, 75, 77, 205
corruption 49, 62, 70, 77, 87, 88, 101, 105, 118–119, 135, 150
Covid-19 20, 77, 80, 91, 102, 110, 145, 162; effects on women 24, 26–27, 32, 49, 75, 88
culture 3, 7, 13, 20–21, 29, 32, 40, 42–43, 49, 52, 59, 64, 100, 108, 114, 132, 141–142, 146, 149–150, 156, 159–160, 174, 179, 193, 205
cyberactivism 74, 107
cyberfeminism 83, 97, 106–107, 110

Darwazeh, Nada 140, 152–154, 158, 163–164, 166
decolonize 12, 138, 190, 195
democratization 74, 85
depression 25, 109, 130
Diab, Assil 115–116, 119–120, 123, 125, 127, 131–132, 143
diaspora 8, 11, 18, 45, 59, 94, 135, 167–168, 170, 179, 191, 198, 202–204, 208, 217
dirāsat al-nau' (studies of kind) 38
disability 14, 26
discrimination 2, 8, 14, 18, 21–24, 26, 29, 31, 33, 44–45, 49, 56–57, 60–62, 64, 70–71, 76, 89–90, 98, 108, 117, 123–124, 137, 139, 142, 146, 161, 175, 177, 182, 187–188, 202, 204, 212
displacement 20, 23–25, 63, 73, 75, 80, 83, 95
diversity 5–6, 12–13, 15, 19, 38–39, 47–48, 51, 55, 68, 82, 87, 94, 112, 155–156, 159, 165–166, 181, 185, 189, 199, 201–202, 204–205, 210–211
Diwan, Kristin 145
diya 61, 221
Djibouti 11–13, 22–23, 27, 33, 55, 57, 63, 65, 72, 79, 81
domestic violence 24, 31, 63, 70–

71, 75–76, 79, 81, 100, 108, 130,
    143, 159, 168, 185, 198, 208
domestic workers 26, 34, 75–76,
    151, 154
donors 44, 99, 155, 159, 164, 201

economic crisis 64, 79, 102
economic growth 66
economic opportunities 177,
    181, 203
economies 51, 80, 162
education 2, 7, 15, 17–18, 22–26,
    31, 34, 45, 50, 52–57, 60, 64–66,
    69–70, 72, 77–78, 82, 88, 130–
    131, 141, 150, 156, 167, 170, 176,
    181–187, 189, 195, 203, 205, 208,
    211, 218; sex 24, 186; women's
    25, 53, 186
Egypt 4, 12–13, 22–23, 27, 29–33,
    38–44, 46, 50, 52, 55, 57–59,
    64–65, 68, 73, 77–78, 80, 82,
    86, 88–90, 107, 110, 114, 116–117,
    120–122, 125, 128–129, 132,
    136–137, 146, 148, 161, 166, 181,
    184, 187, 191–192, 194, 198, 202,
    208, 221
Ekmekji, Karma 206
El Awady, Mehrinaz 83, 140, 152
El Rahi, Nay 212
Eltahawy, Mona 5, 35, 108, 112,
    147, 191, 208
employment 26, 31, 45, 50, 54,
    56–57, 60, 64, 70, 88, 179
empower 1, 4, 14, 19, 23, 26–27,
    38, 49, 53, 55, 61, 67, 70, 72, 75,
    78, 81, 85, 87, 91–92, 94, 100, 102,
    109, 126, 135, 137–138, 143, 154,
    156, 165, 180–181, 185–187, 191,
    203, 205, 219
equity 14, 21, 74, 137–138, 165,
    190–191, 207
ESCWA 35, 83, 140
ethnic 12–13, 34, 53, 66, 171, 204
Ezzahraa El Fattah, Fatima 47

family planning 23, 76
Fatwa 221
female candidates 28
Female Genital Mutilation (FGM)
    33; in Djibouti 63, 79; in Egypt
    55; in Kuwait 69; in Somalia 63;
    in Sudan 55, 79, 98
Fragile States Index (FSI) 22

Geha, Carmen 101–103, 134, 150–
    152, 163–164, 184, 194, 212
gender and development 63
Gender-Based Violence (GBV)
    71, 77, 79, 98–99, 138, 145, 194
Gender Development Index 22
Gender Inequality Index 21–22
gender roles 84, 90, 100, 116, 118,
    138, 192
Ghanem, Yara 142, 144, 156, 162,
    173, 177, 184, 194, 198–199
girl 4, 8, 22, 25, 29–30, 32–34, 37,
    57, 70, 86, 97, 103, 112, 123, 140–
    142, 148, 151, 156, 157, 159, 166,

173, 180, 182, 184–186, 192–194,
    199, 201, 221; education 24–26,
    186
girl-child marriage 34, 98, 186,
    193
Global Peace Index 81
Gross Domestic Product (GDP)
    27
Gulf 11, 13, 23, 27, 31, 34, 52, 57,
    60, 62, 68, 75, 80, 92, 110, 144–
    145, 199–200
Gulf Cooperation Council (GCC)
    73, 147

Haddad, Joumana 1, 3–4, 17, 36
Hadi, Haneen 143, 153, 155–157,
    159, 169, 171, 185
hajj 108, 221
haram 127, 147, 199, 221
harassment 4, 21, 26, 29, 32,
    34, 68, 71, 77, 78, 81, 97, 100,
    102–103, 106, 108, 110, 117, 127,
    182, 193–194, 197, 218
Harb, Tala 158, 167, 199, 203
Hijab 58, 98, 121, 221
honor killings 33, 61–62, 70, 77,
    194
Hzaineh, Laila 108, 185

identity 10–11, 13, 15, 38–39, 46,
    50, 53, 58, 102, 109, 111, 141–
    142, 145–146, 155, 159, 163, 167,
    189, 192, 197, 202, 204–205,
    214, 217
ideology 14, 37, 58, 80, 136, 221
inclusive 6, 12–14, 38, 43, 53, 81,
    83, 86, 89, 94, 102, 133, 136, 140,
    146, 156, 159, 170, 180, 190, 200,
    208, 216
income 26, 57, 103, 187
independence 39, 41, 42, 50,
    52–53, 56, 90–91, 180–181, 185
inequality 8, 14, 15, 20–23, 25,
    29–30, 33, 35–36, 41, 51, 59, 64,
    66, 68, 91–93, 100, 106, 108, 117,
    134–135, 137, 141–142, 145, 155,
    167, 176, 178, 180, 182–183, 188,
    201, 207
inequity 190
injustice 2, 7–8, 14–15, 35, 40, 93,
    100, 106, 109, 117, 119–120, 124–
    125, 140–142, 176, 205, 214–216
Internally displaced persons
    (IDPs) 23, 99
International Conference on
    Population and Development
    60
International Monetary Fund
    (IMF) 64
International Women's Day 35,
    69, 71, 79, 104, 109
intersectionality 10, 14–15, 146,
    174, 190, 207, 210
Intifada (uprising) 91–92, 108,
    210, 221; first 62; second 70
Iraq 12–13, 20, 22–23, 25–26, 28,
    30–31, 33–34, 54, 60–62, 65,
    68, 70, 73, 75, 77, 81, 84, 87, 105,

110, 135, 143, 153, 156, 159, 161,
    168–169, 171, 179, 185, 191, 200
Islamic 12, 34, 42–43, 53, 56, 58,
    68, 71, 75, 77, 89, 108, 116, 153,
    161; feminism 49, 51, 58, 56, 81,
    161–162; law 29, 51, 56, 205, 221
Islamic State of Iraq and Syria
    (ISIS) 71, 77, 98
Islamic State of Iraq and the
    Levant (ISIL) 34, 71

Jalabi, Mariam 93–96
Jordan 12–13, 23, 31, 33, 40, 42,
    50, 54, 59, 62, 64–65, 70, 77, 81,
    86, 90, 100–101, 108, 136–17,
    139–140, 148, 150, 159, 161,
    181–185, 190, 194, 200–201
justice 3, 9, 14, 20–22, 29, 32,
    44, 46, 50, 68, 79, 83, 87–88,
    94, 99, 102, 122–123, 136–137,
    140, 142–143, 145, 161, 163–164,
    174–176, 180, 182, 189–190, 202,
    210, 214, 218

kafala system 34, 76, 221
Karam, Charlotte 37, 91, 111, 144,
    211, 213
Keedi, Anthony 92, 146, 164,
    191–193, 207
Kefaya (enough) 73, 88, 221
Kellon Yaani Kellon (all of them
    means all of them) 101
Keserwany, Michelle 118
Keserwany, Noel 118
Keserwani sisters 119, 123–124, 213
Khalaf, Salma 157, 159, 161–162,
    192, 198
Khalifeh, Lina 100–101, 148
Khilqit Binit (A Girl is Born) 109
Kurdi, Chérine 141
Kuwait 12–13, 22, 27, 31, 33, 52–
    53, 61–62, 64–65, 68–69, 75, 110,
    112, 137, 167, 180, 185, 200, 207

labor 34, 70, 88, 151, 193; force
    25–27, 82; law 70, 72, 75; market
    186, 205
leadership 26–27, 50, 62, 74, 84,
    86, 88, 102, 141, 165–166, 181,
    207–208, 218–219
Lebanon 4, 8–9, 11–14, 23, 25, 27–
    28, 30–34, 37–38, 40, 44, 50, 54,
    57–59, 62, 64–65, 68, 71, 77, 81,
    87, 90, 101–103, 105, 108–110, 112,
    118–120, 123–124, 130, 135–142,
    144–146, 151–152, 154, 156, 159,
    161–164, 166–167, 169–170, 177,
    179–181, 183–187, 189, 191–192,
    194, 199–205, 208, 212, 214
legislation 17, 24–25, 29, 31, 34,
    62, 66, 68, 70–71, 75, 79, 82, 108,
    159, 174, 211
Lesbian, Gay, Bisexual,
    Transgender, Queer, and
    Others (LGBTQ+) 15, 38,
    44, 102, 112, 145–146, 151, 162,
    176–177, 185, 190–191, 196; *see
    also* queer

Levant 13, 34, 54, 61, 70, 76, 92, 199
liberation 4, 41, 43, 47, 49, 52,
  58–59, 67, 85, 112, 114, 126, 137,
  175, 186, 190, 210, 215, 218–219
Libya 12–13, 22–23, 27–28, 31,
  33–34, 55, 59, 63, 65, 68, 72, 78,
  80–81, 85, 90, 110, 135–136, 138,
  178–180, 191, 200

mahr (dowry) 55, 221
mahram 31, 221
marginalized 12, 15, 34, 40, 42,
  56, 62, 72, 77, 78–79, 84–85,
  94, 98, 135, 138, 141, 144, 146,
  155–156, 175, 190, 203, 207;
  healthcare 23
marriage 26, 30–31, 34, 54–55, 61,
  63, 72, 75, 98, 103, 118, 148, 154,
  166, 170, 186, 194
masculinities 43–44, 84, 101–111,
  149, 191–193
Member of Parliament 29
Mernissi, Fatima 12, 56, 58
Mirshad, Hayat 101–103, 139,
  142, 184
mobilization 16, 18, 45, 49, 56,
  62–63, 66–68, 74, 80–81, 105–
  107, 109, 112, 126, 135, 162–163,
  196, 199, 203, 206, 216, 219
Mooro, Alya 117–118, 126, 129,
  143, 148–149, 158, 178, 182–183,
  192, 202
morality police 88; *see also* rape
Morocco 12–13, 22–23, 27, 30, 31,
  33, 41, 44, 47, 50, 55–56, 59, 63,
  65, 68, 71–73, 79, 81, 90, 108–109,
  117–118, 127, 131–132, 137, 142,
  148, 156, 165–166, 180, 185–186,
  201, 221
mosque 127, 221; #MosqueMeToo
  108; *see also* Islam; *hajj*
Moudawana (Morocco's family
  code) 31, 63, 221
Moukalled, Diana 140, 151–154,
  162–163, 169, 204, 214
Muna, Maha 170
Musawah (Equality) 50, 161, 221

Nassar, Muna 92
Nassif, Gabriella 36, 92, 146, 151,
  155, 161–163, 175, 180, 190, 197,
  207–208
National Action Plan (NAP) 72,
  81
National Commission of
  Lebanese Women (NCLW) 62,
  140, 152
Nehme, Alexander 205
network 11, 16, 51, 55, 57, 59, 60,
  62, 74, 77, 91, 99–100, 129, 155,
  164, 185, 188–190, 196
NGO 11, 62, 71, 145, 190, 198
NGOization 212
niqab 121, 221
nonviolent 70–71, 92, 112, 215

Oman 11–13, 22, 30, 52–53, 58, 60,
  65, 69, 76

online 10, 11, 18, 74, 78–79, 88,
  106–107, 109–110, 121, 133, 190,
  196–199, 214, 218; activism 106,
  109–110, 199; learning 26
opposition 40, 58, 69, 71, 93–95,
  147, 171, 179
oppression 35, 40, 42–43, 54–55,
  66–67, 74, 76, 82, 100, 105–106,
  111, 114, 118, 123, 126, 131, 140,
  142–143, 146, 148, 150, 174, 182,
  189–190, 210, 214, 219
orientalist 40, 51

Palestine 8–9, 12–13, 20, 22–23,
  25–26, 32–33, 36, 38, 41–42, 44,
  54–55, 57, 61–62, 64–65, 68, 70
Palestinian Liberation
  Organization (PLO) 54, 62
pandemic 24, 27, 32, 35, 49, 74, 77,
  80, 88, 91, 110, 145, 162, 218; *see
  also* Covid-19
patriarchy 2–4, 13–14, 16–22,
  26–30, 32, 35, 37, 39–43, 46–47,
  51, 56, 58, 60, 62, 66–67, 74, 83–
  85, 87, 90, 92, 94, 96, 100–102,
  106, 111–113, 116–117, 122, 129,
  134, 137–140, 142, 146–151, 154,
  157–158, 160, 165, 168, 171, 174,
  179–183, 185–187, 189–193, 203,
  208, 210–211, 216, 218
Post-Traumatic Stress Disorder
  25, 195
poverty 24–25, 64, 66, 68, 77–78,
  81, 88, 95, 100, 103, 116, 162–163,
  170, 176
power imbalance 17, 57
progressive 54, 56, 68, 76, 150,
  154, 157, 169
protection 20, 26, 32, 56–57, 67,
  69, 72, 75, 99–100, 127, 131, 140,
  145, 170, 188, 190, 194; from
  domestic violence 70, 76, 81

Qatar 12–13, 22, 27–28, 30–31, 34,
  52–53, 61, 64, 68–69, 76, 182, 210
queer 15, 138, 145, 185, 190, 191; *see
  also* LGBTQ+
quotas 27–28, 70–72, 78–79, 81,
  88, 151, 153–154, 174

race 3, 12, 14, 139, 141, 153, 190
rape 21, 31, 33–34, 62, 76, 78–79,
  88, 90, 98–99, 102, 109, 119, 125,
  130, 159, 166; marital 31, 61,
  63, 174
refugee 20, 23–24, 34, 80, 95, 99,
  102, 144, 156, 163
Regional Action Plan 81

Sadiqi, Fatima 156
Saudi Arabia 4, 7, 12–13, 22, 24,
  27, 31, 33–34, 37, 52–53, 57,
  60, 65, 68–69, 75, 90, 96–98,
  108, 110, 121–122, 124, 132, 137,
  139–140, 157–158, 169, 181, 184,
  188, 191–192, 197, 200, 206,
  221–222
school 1–2, 7, 24–26, 36, 53, 58,

  98, 104, 108, 141, 182, 184–186,
  189, 192, 206
sexual and reproductive health
  177, 194
sexuality 4, 33, 117, 185, 190; *see
  also* LGBTQ+; queer
Sfeir, Myriam 39, 91, 124, 134,
  146, 150, 157, 170, 174, 201, 205
Sharia 221
Shehab, Bahia 114, 116–117, 120–
  122, 125–126, 128–129, 132, 184,
  188, 198, 208
Shi'a 23, 52, 89, 221; *see also* Islam
Shisha 156, 221
Siniora, Randa 145, 160, 166, 205
social media 33, 74, 78–79, 87,
  91, 96, 98–99, 106–110, 120, 126,
  129, 159, 196–201, 219; *see also*
  cyberactivism; cyberfeminism
solidarity 4, 8, 43–44, 48, 50, 55,
  57, 82, 87–88, 97, 106–110, 127,
  139–140, 145–147, 153, 158, 163,
  165–166, 196, 199–200, 208, 210,
  215, 219
Somalia 11–13, 22, 25, 27, 34,
  55–56, 63–64, 72, 191
Soultana 117–118, 127–129, 131–
  132, 142, 147–148, 185–186
state feminism; 16–17, 48, 50,
  53–57, 59, 66–67, 73, 81, 151–152,
  211–212; co-opted feminism
  16–17, 42, 45, 48, 52, 60, 65, 121,
  151–152, 212
Stephan, Rita 87, 134, 171, 203–
  204, 207
Subay, Haifa 116, 128, 130–131, 195
Sudan 12–13, 22, 27, 33, 41, 45, 55,
  63–64, 72, 79, 81, 87, 98–99, 104,
  109, 115–116, 119, 123, 125, 127,
  131–132, 143, 145, 147, 150, 155–
  156, 164, 166, 168, 170–171, 198
Sudanese Dream 98–99
Sunni 23, 52, 69, 89, 221–222; *see
  also* Islam
Supreme Council for Women 69
survey 6, 10–11, 27, 32–33, 44,
  135–136, 139, 142, 146, 170, 176,
  178, 192, 194, 200
Sustainable Development Goals
  21–22
Syria 12–13, 20, 22–23, 25, 27, 30–
  31, 34, 41, 46, 55, 57, 71, 75–77,
  93–95, 142, 144, 170, 177

Takatoat 139–140, 148, 150, 158–
  159, 182, 184
Tamtam 121–122, 124, 132, 139,
  192, 206
Tasfih 218, 221
terrorism 73, 79, 93, 105; *see also*
  war on terror
transitional 54, 68, 71–72, 74, 79,
  86, 88, 91, 99, 111
transnational 40, 50, 60, 64, 106,
  110, 145, 161, 163, 171
trauma 4, 8, 25, 190, 195–196
Tunisia 12–13, 23, 27–29, 31, 33,
  34, 41, 44, 50, 55–56, 58–59,

63–65, 68, 71–72, 78, 80–82, 86, 88, 90, 107, 114, 135, 138–139, 165, 178, 183, 188, 190–192, 194, 200–201, 205, 218–219, 221

UNICEF 23, 26
United Arab Emirates (UAE) 12–13, 22, 27, 52–53, 61, 64–65, 68, 70, 75, 81, 110, 137, 141, 144, 147, 154, 165, 167, 179, 182–183, 189, 192
United Kingdom (UK) 52–53, 80, 148
United Nations (UN) 16, 22, 59, 76, 78, 83, 94, 140–141, 158, 160, 198, 201; Arab Human Development report 45; Conference on Women 57; General Assembly 57, 69

United Nations Security Council Resolution 52, 81

veil 43, 169, 197, 22; *see also hijab*; *niqab*
violence against women 7–8, 17, 24, 31–34, 49, 63, 67, 70, 72, 75, 78–79, 81, 100–101, 110, 137, 148, 161, 169, 177, 194–195, 200; domestic 24, 31, 70–71, 75–76, 79, 81, 143, 159, 168, 185, 208; intimate partner 31–33, 108, 110, 187; sexual 26, 33, 56, 63, 78, 100, 107–108, 125, 151

Wahhabism 53, 222
wali (male guardian) 30, 222
war on terror 73; *see also* terrorism

Women, Peace and Security (WPS) 22, 81, 201; Index 21–22
Women's Cultural and Social Society 53

Yemen 12–13, 20, 22–23, 25, 30, 33–34, 41–42, 52, 54, 59, 61, 64–65, 68, 70, 73, 75–76, 81, 84–85, 89, 90, 107, 116, 128, 130–131, 138, 170, 191, 194–195
young people 18–19, 24, 46–47, 87–88, 123, 135–136, 170, 173–178, 182, 186, 201, 216
Youssef, Elie 119, 125–126, 130–131, 192, 207

Zeidan, Tarek 145, 185, 190, 195–196